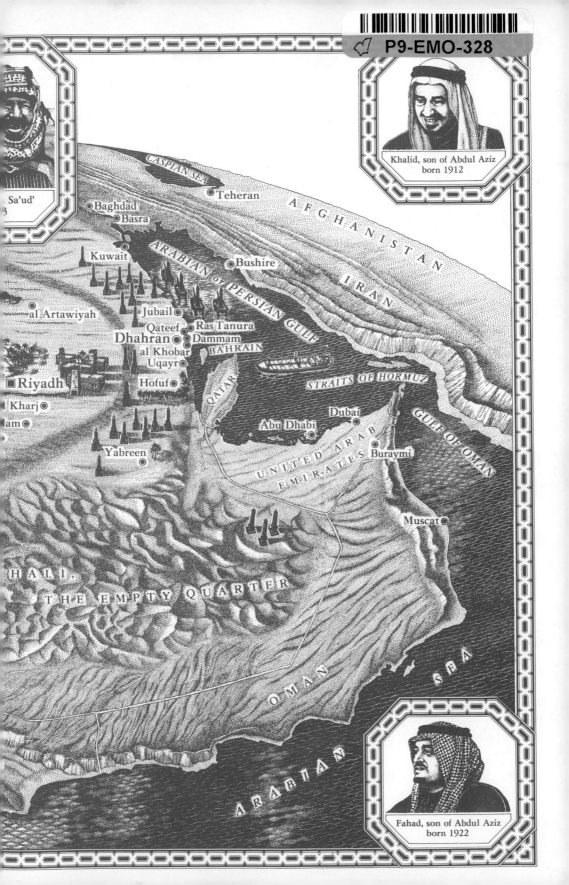

Sa'ud'

Khalid, son of Abdul Aziz
born 1912

CASPIAN SEA

AFGHANISTAN

Teheran

Baghdad
Basra

IRAN

Kuwait

ARABIAN or PERSIAN GULF

Bushire

al Artawiyah

Jubail

Qateef   Ras Tanura
Dhahran   Dammam
al Khobar   BAHRAIN
Uqayr

Riyadh

Hofuf   QATAR

STRAITS OF HORMUZ

Kharj
am

Dubai

GULF OF OMAN

Abu Dhabi   Buraymi

Yabreen

UNITED ARAB
EMIRATES

Muscat

HALI,

THE EMPTY QUARTER

OMAN

SEA

ARABIAN

Fahad, son of Abdul Aziz
born 1922

The
KINGDOM

Robert Lacey

Harcourt Brace Jovanovich, Publishers

New York and London

Requests for permission to make copies of any part of the
work should be mailed to: Permissions, Harcourt Brace
Jovanovich, Publishers, 757 Third Avenue, New York,
N.Y. 10017

Library of Congress Cataloging in Publication Data

Lacey, Robert.
    The Kingdom
    Bibliography: p.
    Includes index.
    1. Saudi Arabia—History.   I. Title.
DS244.52.L29   1982   953'.805   81-83741
ISBN 0-15-147260-2   AACR2

Printed in the United States of America

To Sandi

Contents

Illustrations

Egyptian pilgrims troop the Mahmal, the litter carrying ornamental hangings for the Ka'aba in Mecca (The Searight Collection)

A portfolio of photographs by Snouck Hurgronje, the Dutch Arabist who lived in Mecca at the end of the nineteenth century (Snouck Hurgronje, courtesy of David Loman)

Pilgrims circle the Ka'aba in the central courtyard of the Grand Mosque in Mecca today (Keystone)

A Jeddah merchant smokes a hubble-bubble in the *majlis* of his home (Royal Geographical Society)

Between pages 126 and 127

The first known portrait of Abdul Aziz, photographed by Captain William Shakespear in Kuwait, March 1910 (Royal Geographical Society)

The Al Sa'ud photographed in Kuwait by Captain Shakespear (Royal Geographical Society)

Abdul Aziz's army on the march, photographed by Captain Shakespear near Thaj in eastern Arabia, March 1911 (Royal Geographical Society)

Captain Shakespear on leave in England in 1907 (Mrs Joan Wright)

A desert execution (Royal Geographical Society)

Abdul Aziz with his brothers and sons photographed in March 1911 by Captain Shakespear (Royal Geographical Society)

Between pages 158 and 159

Harry St John Philby in 1918 (Imperial War Museum)

Lawrence of Arabia, drawn by Augustus John (National Portrait Gallery)

Abdul Aziz meets Sir Percy Cox and Miss Gertrude Bell in 1916 (Mansell Collection)

Abdul Aziz with captured Turkish cannon in Riyadh (Popperfoto)

Abdul Aziz and his family photographed by Philby in 1918 (H. St J. Philby)

Prince Faisal ibn Abdul Aziz travels to London, 1919 (Humphrey Bowman)

Prince Faisal has his portrait sketched on board the *Kigoma* en route to London, 1919 (Humphrey Bowman)

Ahmad Thunayan (Gerald de Gaury)

Prince Faisal ibn Abdul Aziz visits Kim Philby at Kim's prep school in Eastbourne (H. St J. Philby)

Abdullah Suleiman (Marie Hansen, *Life*)
Abdul Aziz and sons at Taif, 1934 (Lechenperg, Black Star)
Abdul Aziz leads his sons in the *ardha*, the sword dance (Popperfoto)
Abdul Aziz's harem car (AP Wide World)
Abdul Aziz with Amin Rihani and Hafiz Wahba (Norman Mayers)
Prince Talal ibn Abdul Aziz with his *akhiwiya*, 'little brother' (Gerald de Gaury)
Jeddah architecture: Philby's house, the Beit Baghdadi (Andrew Ryan)
Jeddah pleasures: staff of the British Legation relaxing (Andrew Ryan)

Between pages 318 and 319
Abdul Aziz meets President Roosevelt on board USS *Quincy* in the Great Bitter Lake, Egypt, February 1945 (Fox Photos)
Abdul Aziz with Winston Churchill at the Auberge Hotel on Lake Karoun, near Cairo, February 1945 (Imperial War Museum)
Abdul Aziz receives American envoys, December 1943 (AP Wide World)
Winston Churchill's Rolls-Royce leaves Jeddah, 1946 (courtesy David Parker)
A prisoner of the Sa'udi police, photographed in Asir in 1946 (Wilfred Thesiger)
A slave in the Asir, 1946 (Wilfred Thesiger)
Abdul Aziz feasts with the Sheikh of Bahrain and US Minister J. Rives Childs, Ras Tanura, 1947 (AP Wide World)
Cyril Ousman, British pro-vice-consul, murdered by Prince Mishari ibn Abdul Aziz, November 1951 (Andrew Ryan)
Abdul Aziz in old age (Bob Landry, *Life*)

Between pages 350 and 351
Sa'ud ibn Abdul Aziz as Crown Prince (Muhammad Asad)
A present from King Sa'ud ibn Abdul Aziz (Ralph Morse, *Life*)
King Sa'ud dances the *ardha* (Black Star)
The tanker deal: King Sa'ud with Aristotle Onassis, July 1955 (AP Wide World)
King Sa'ud on board SS *Constitution*, travelling to America, January 1957 (Popperfoto)
The Shah meets King Sa'ud, with his crippled son Mashour ibn Sa'ud (Popperfoto)
Talal ibn Abdul Aziz gives a press conference in Cairo, September 1962 (Popperfoto)

Ex-King Sa'ud arrives in London with his sons, October 1968
  (Popperfoto)
President Nasser welcomes ex-King Sa'ud to Cairo, January 1967
  (AP Wide World)

Between pages 414 and 415
King Faisal at prayer, 1968 (Frank Spooner)
King Faisal dances the *ardha*
Yemen: peace agreed between King Faisal and President Nasser,
  Khartoum, August 1967 (AP Wide World)
Faisal as Foreign Minister after a meeting with President
  Eisenhower, March 1953 (AP Wide World)
King Faisal on pilgrimage, Mecca 1964 (Press Association)
King Faisal, 1967 (Camera Press)
Time, March 1979 (Time Inc.)
Faisal ibn Musa'id, assassin of King Faisal, with American friend
  (John Hillelson)
Sheikh Ahmad Zaki Yamani (Camera Press)

Between pages 446 and 447
Dancing the *ardha*: Khalid, Faisal, Fahad and Abdullah ibn Abdul
  Aziz (Azad Photo)
Muhammad ibn Abdul Aziz, elder brother of King Khalid (Azad)
Sa'ud al Faisal, Foreign Minister of the Kingdom since 1975 (Azad)
Sultan ibn Abdul Aziz, Sa'udi Minister of Defence and Aviation since
  1962 (UPI Popperfoto)
Salman ibn Abdul Aziz, Governor of Riyadh, receives petitions in his
  majlis (David Holden, Camera Press)
Adnan Khashoggi in Arab and Western dress (Triad)
Fahad and Abdullah ibn Abdul Aziz on pilgrimage (Ahlan
  Wasahlan)
A judicial caning (Camera Press)
Mecca, November 1979; smoke rising from the battle in the Grand
  Mosque (UPI Popperfoto)
Juhayman, leader of the Mecca revolt (Visnews)
King Khalid ibn Abdul Aziz and Crown Prince Fahad, February 1977
  (Frank Spooner)

Photographs from the collections of Humphrey Bowman, Norman
Mayers, H. St J. Philby and Andrew Ryan are reproduced by
permission of St Antony's College, Oxford, Middle East Centre

Maps and Charts

Endpapers, charts and maps by Iain Stuart. The first five maps are based upon the *Historical Atlas of Saudi Arabia*, compiled by Dr Ibrahim Jam'a, Riyadh: King Abdul Aziz Research Centre, 1392 AH (AD 1972)

Welcome
to the Kingdom

Oh love of the people,
Oh Khalid, our king,
Oh lion of the desert,
Your praises we sing . . .

It is scarcely classic poetry, but King Khalid seems to be listening to it quite seriously. He has to spend a lot of time listening to poetry. His subjects come to declaim it to him as he sits every day to hear their greetings and grievances, and now an old man with an amber-tinged beard and a white muslin halo circling his headdress is standing before him, bare feet planted firmly on the carpet, shouting out loudly the verses he has composed in his sovereign's honour.

It is a long poem, every verse built round the cry *'Ya Khalid!'* ('Oh Khalid!'), and each time the king hears this exclamation he looks up to smile his thanks for the offering – only to see the old man drawing breath for yet another stanza.

King Khalid is a tall man, upright and firm-featured. His weathered face and hands are blotched with patches which could be freckles, or could be age spots. By his chair lies a rough wooden stick with a heavy black rubber pad on the end, for the king needs to lean on this when he walks.

He is out in the desert hunting, and the tribesmen are driving in to greet him.

'Welcome,' says the king as he rises to embrace them.

'Welcome to you, Khalid,' they reply, for 'Majesty' is not a word you use when talking to the King of Sa'udi Arabia – not, at least, if you are a Sa'udi. 'Khalid' is good enough.

They nuzzle up to their monarch's shoulder, hugging him and kissing him just below the collar bone, then go and sit, cross-legged, in one of the lush velvet armchairs around three sides of the white marquee. On the ground is cast a patchwork of rugs, flung one on top of the other in a lurid jigsaw, and the old poet is still planted there, shouting out his verses unheeded by his fellow tribesmen, who are now sipping little cups of coffee and chattering quietly among themselves.

Outside the marquee perch the falcons, sleek, hooded and murderous on their tasselled pommels driven into the sand like so many huge leather golf tees. The scouts are out already beyond the horizon, scouring the wilderness for game, and, when their reports come in, the coffee drinking stops and so do the poems.

King Khalid has a Range Rover with the top sawn off. His brothers who are hunting with him are in a GM Suburban which has been similarly decapitated, and into the gutted shells of each vehicle have been inserted huge, plush sofas on which the royal party bounce off towards the hills.

When they see the game, a button is pushed and King Khalid's armchair rises into the air above the level of the windscreen. He pulls the leather hood from the falcon's head, looses the jesses that secure the creature's yellow-scaled gaiters, and the bird flies off down the wind in pursuit of the flash of black and white feathers which indicate its prey. The seat descends, the Range Rover bumps across the desert, and in its wake the other cars take up the pursuit, fanning out to avoid the dust clouds each throws up.

When the hunt is over, the cars drive back to camp in the same formation, and if the hunting has been good King Khalid picks up the microphone of the walkie-talkie in his dashboard. Into it he sings the verse of a victory chant sung from time immemorial by bedouin returning from a successful raid, and in their cars the other princes pick up their microphones to join with him in the chorus and to make up new verses of their own as they drive home across the desert.

If it were not for a freak of geology, few people in the western world would give a fig about King Khalid and his falcons. The inhabitants of the Kingdom of Sa'udi Arabia would be welcome to enjoy their desert and their poets and their very particular way of running their lives undisturbed, and we would read about them every so often in the pages of the *National Geographic Magazine*.

But 500 million years ago, when life was just a soup of tiny plants and animals, the warm seas swept across the land that we now call Arabia, and as the waters retreated they left their life behind them. The millions of dying amoebae decayed in the mud of the ebbing seas, a honeycomb of fatty debris in the sand, and the wrinkling of the planet's surface hardened and thrust this oil-bearing rocky sponge thousands of feet below the ground.

Geologists call this porous limestone Arab-D, and it is unique to the eastern coast of Sa'udi Arabia. No one bothers much about Arabs-A, -B or -C, but the limestone labelled Arab-D is one of the richest oil-bearing rocks ever discovered, and 200 years ago the house of Sa'ud first conquered the sands which lie above it. They did not do it for the sake of the buried limestone, and few of them, even today, could tell you what Arab-D stands for. But geology's whim has made the rulers of the Kingdom one of the richest families that the world has ever seen; and in 1981 it is difficult to think of another single family that wields more international power.

It is a power of astonishing fragility. The USSR could invade the Sa'udi oilfields tomorrow. So, of course, could the USA – and contingency planners on both sides of the Iron Curtain regularly update their scenarios for doing precisely that. But each superpower holds back from the grab through fear of how the other would retaliate, and it is in the shelter of this massive mutual blackmail that the Kingdom of Sa'udi Arabia is free to do a little business of its own. They have got the oil, and we have got to pay for it.

The sums are quite easy to do. The Kingdom of Sa'udi Arabia today produces and sells to the world some 10 million barrels of oil per day, sometimes a little less, sometimes rather more. At the time of writing, that oil is selling for an average of roughly $32 per barrel – which makes an income of three hundred and twenty million dollars a day. The oil costs at the most 50 cents per barrel to extract, process and market – $5 million in all. So that leaves the Kingdom with a daily balance in its favour of $315 million.

This constitutes impressive purchasing power. At its current rate of income the Kingdom could acquire all the stocks listed on US stock exchanges in 12 years 7 months and 8 days; it could buy General Motors in 1 month 12 days 4 hours and 48 minutes, Bankamerica in 12 days 7 hours 36 minutes, all the professional football teams in the USA in 2 days 14 hours and 24 minutes – and Tiffany's in just 7 hours 55 minutes. In the unlikely event of the White House finding its way

5

on to the market at mid-Washington redevelopment values, King Khalid could acquire a nice little palace by the Potomac for less than 18 hours' oil pumping* – and these fantastic riches are shared amongst 4–5 million men, women and children who live by a simple and severe moral code that has scarcely changed in centuries.

Noon, Taif, Sa'udi Arabia. The sun is beating down from directly overhead, and the tribesmen wrinkle their eyes, clustering together in the narrow shadows cast by their pick-up trucks. They have been bumping in from the desert and hills all morning, and now, just before midday, they are gathered round the sides of this dusty square.

Taif is a hill town. Ramshackle and untidy, it straggles along the top of the escarpment 5000 feet above the holy city of Mecca. The grandees of the holy city have been retreating up to Taif's cool heights for hundreds of summers. The turbaned viziers of the Turkish empire built their palaces on Taif's hills when they controlled Arabia's Red Sea coast, and today it is the house of Sa'ud that uproots its government every summer to rule the Kingdom for a month or so from here.

There are no women in the square. Their menfolk have dropped them off to do their shopping round the corner, and in the souq† the black-veiled shapes are drifting between the bright saucepan shops and spice stalls and ovens from which the bakers pull the rounds of thin flat bread. In the square the men pour themselves sweet tea in small cupfuls from their silver, jug-shaped vacuum flasks, and they rub their teeth with the bristly pith of twigs whose bark they strip off from time to time in neat circlets with their daggers. Every man is wearing a dagger. Many have revolvers on their hip, and over their robed chests are criss-crossed bandoleers.

A throat is cleared in one corner of the square, a gravelly, much-amplified throat, and suddenly a fierce bellowing stirs everyone to life. From the cone-shaped speakers of a minaret comes the call to prayer – 'Allahu akbar!' ('God is most great!') – and the men rise to their feet, kick on their leather-thonged sandals and start shuffling

---

* 17 hours 48 minutes to be precise. This hypothetical value for the White House has been arrived at by multiplying its area, 18 acres, by $300 per square foot, a land valuation figure provided by the District of Columbia Real Estate Tax Auditors, February 1981. For the other figures given, see source list on page 562.

† Souq: market. See glossary on pages 16–19 for this and other Arabic terms.

through the sand across the square towards two marble-framed double doors which soldiers are pushing open for them: the Taif office of the Ministry of the Interior.

Inside all is marble and coolness. At the end of the hall a little fountain is tinkling softly into its mosaic basin, and just above it is a curved-topped niche, an alcove without a statue. The men are slipping off their footwear. They start forming lines, and from a lift door emerges a short plumpish figure with solemn features and a trimmed moustache – Prince Naif, brother of the king, and Interior Minister of the Kingdom. He takes a spare place in the front line, between a wild-bearded bedouin and a cross-eyed youth, and, looking down at the marble floor like the hundred or so men around him, he begins to murmur his prayers.

At this moment in Taif, Mecca and Jeddah, tens of thousands of other men are doing the same. Offices close, shops pull down the shutters, and life goes still, as it does five times a day in Sa'udi Arabia while the Kingdom says its prayers. 500 miles to the east in Riyadh, they are already halfway through their devotions, and 250 miles yet further eastwards, in the towns of the coastal oilfields, the shops are rolling open their shutters again, for the Kingdom times its worship by the progress of the sun as it moves overhead nearly a thousand miles from east to west.

When the bedouin have finished praying with their prince in Taif, they will sit with him and sip coffee, and he will listen to their problems as he does for an hour or so every day at this time. But first they pray.

Talking about it afterwards, Prince Naif does not find it at all odd for a whole country to stop everything to kneel down and worship for twenty minutes, five times a day.

'This Kingdom', he says, 'was created in the name of God.'

'In the name of God.' The phrase is printed across the top of every sheet of official notepaper in the Kingdom. They are the opening words of the Five-Year Plan. It is the motto scrawled across television test patterns. Pilots welcome you on board their airliners with it. Computers are programmed to throw it up at the beginning of every print-out. 'In the name of God.'

In the name of God, thieves have their hands chopped off in Sa'udi Arabia. Murderers and rapists are executed in the street – and so are proven adulterers, even princesses.

*　　*　　*

Sheikh Ahmad Zaki Yamani is sitting behind his desk in Riyadh. From the outside, the Sa'udi Ministry of Petroleum is a drab, mud-coloured building. But inside you see that the walls are studded with little triangles of coloured glass, and these glow brightly as the sun shines in.

Sheikh Yamani looks older than you would expect from his photographs. He is fifty-one now, but his face has been with us for nineteen years as Sa'udi Oil Minister, for it was quite a young man who first shocked the world with news of the price it would have to pay thenceforward for its energy.

Sheikh Yamani is not a member of the house of Sa'ud. He is one of the dozen and a half non-royal ministers who work alongside the princes in the cabinet, but, if any single face says 'Arab oil' to the western world, it must be his.

'People recognize me in the street, and in many of the poorer, simpler countries people come up to greet me. They recognize me because I am the Oil Minister and they have probably seen my face on the television. But that is not usually why they greet me, and it is not oil that they usually want to talk about.'

Sheikh Yamani is dressed in a white cotton *thobe*, the same long plain shirt-to-the-ankles worn by all Arabians, and on his head is the standard red and white cotton headdress, chequered like a duster, woven in Taiwan or Manchester, £5 in the Riyadh souq, and worn by Sa'udis rich and poor in the winter months. In the summer they usually switch to plain white, lighter cotton headgear.

'In the West you see us as just an oil state, the country that exists to keep your gas tanks filled. But that is a very modern way of looking at Arabia. It is not how we see ourselves, and it is not how our country is seen by the millions of people who share our religion.

'If you want to understand the Kingdom you must understand that 1400 years ago God revealed his word to the Prophet Muhammad in the Holy Cities of Mecca and Medina. They are on the other side of Arabia from the oilfields, but they are part of the same country and in our eyes they matter more than anything else.'

A servant pads into the room in open sandals, bearing a curvaceous brass pot, to pour sharp jets of cardamom coffee into little cups, each no bigger than an eyebath, and Sheikh Yamani looks thoughtfully at the thin greenish liquid.

'That is why the people in poor Muslim countries greet me – because they know I come from Mecca. It is Mecca and Islam that

8

they talk about, so if I have to say one thing that this Kingdom stands for, above all others, it is not oil. It is Islam. One day even we will run out of oil. But we will never run out of Mecca and Medina.'

On 20 October 1973, in the name of God, and in the cause of the religion revealed to Muhammad 1400 years ago in Mecca and Medina, King Faisal of Sa'udi Arabia declared jihad (holy war) on Israel and on all the countries who supported her, and as part of that holy war he imposed a total embargo on the Kingdom's oil shipments to the United States. The world has not been the same since.

All through the 1960s the Western economies and Japan paid less than $2 per barrel for the oil they received from Sa'udi Arabia and the other Middle-Eastern oil producers: $1.80 for 42 American gallons, not much more than 4 cents per gallon. A decade later we are paying $32 for the same 42 gallons which make up the barrel—an increase of 1500 per cent in less than a decade. No wonder the Kingdom is getting so rich. No wonder we are feeling so poor.

It now looks as if King Faisal's holy war marked one of the major turning points in twentieth-century history. The Arab oil embargo which Faisal headed, and the energy price explosion which that embargo provoked, initiated a transfer of the world's wealth the like of which has never been seen.

The Empress Club, up the road from the Ritz and just south of Berkeley Square, was where London's high society used to enjoy itself. It was named after Queen Victoria, and founded to celebrate her Diamond Jubilee in 1897. After the Second World War the clientele at the Empress tended to be American, enjoying the purchasing power of the mighty dollar in cut-price Europe.

Today the Empress is an Arab nightclub, and inside it is the kasbah – smoke, noise, chattering, while strange lutes and pipes wail out off-rhythm melodies. A belly dancer is reaching the climax of her performance, seesawing a sequinned walking stick across the top of her melon-like breasts, and men are leaping up to dance with her, snaking their hips and swaying their arms above their heads.

It is not cheap to enjoy yourself at the Empress – £70 for a bottle of Scotch and £100 for a bottle of champagne. Even the good Sa'udis present have to pay £10 for their jug of orange juice. And now the

9

men are stuffing £20 notes into the spangled bra and pants of the belly dancer, quivering herself into a jelly of delight, while at one of the tables a creative young fellow produces a plastic Scotch tape dispenser to tape together a lei of notes with which he can garland the girl.

The inhabitants of the Kingdom are reserved and private people on the whole; but there are enough fun-loving Sa'udis to fill at least one table at the Empress every night. Right against the stage sit a group of them, laughing and stamping, and they have brought some guests along who are conspicuously non-Arab – two ladies from an escort agency and the managing director of a container construction company.

'Any excuse for a celebration,' he sighs. 'I'll be lucky if I get home in time for breakfast.'

He does not. It is half past eight before the party reel out into the grey morning, stumbling happily into taxis while Londoners plod past them to their work – those who are left in work, that is, with unemployment heading towards the 3 million mark.

Lengthening dole queues, recession, growing balance-of-payments deficits, the sudden stagger which has unbalanced even the economies of West Germany and Japan in the years since 1973, these are some of the penalties the developed world has suffered through paying too little for energy before King Faisal's oil embargo, and too much for it ever since.

10, 12, perhaps even 15 per cent of the world's cash flow has been diverted in the last eight years from America, Europe and Japan to Sa'udi Arabia and the oil producers of the Middle East, and this book tells the story of the part which Sa'udi Arabia played in that. Well, some of the story.

'I have lived in this Kingdom for over thirty years,' said a Georgetown-educated member of the house of Sa'ud to this writer. 'Yet if I were to try to put down on paper how my family and this country work, I would be lucky if I got a B+ mark.

'You have spent four years with us. The best that you can hope for is C.'

The Kingdom is an enigmatic place, and it unveils its mysteries only grudgingly. Someone who takes up the challenge, who goes to live among its people, who visits its palaces and oil wells and bedouin tents, and who is lucky enough to be invited inside the homes of Sa'udi Arabians, humble and mighty, encounters true warmth and

10

hospitality, much that is banal, a few things that are scarcely believable – and a great deal of reserve and paradox.

This book is a mixture of all those things. It is an amalgam of history, first-hand observation, bazaar gossip, visions of the future – and the memories of old men going back decades to a world so different from our own they could be talking of centuries past.

That is where the story starts. One hundred years ago Arabia was a poverty-stricken desert peninsula ruled by petty sheikhs and sultans. No one dreamt seriously of combining the scattered sheikhdoms from Red Sea to Persian Gulf into one coherent state. No one dreamt of the fabulous dividends that would reward anyone who succeeded in doing that.

But then was born, just over a century ago, in the mud-walled desert settlement of Riyadh, a boy called Abdul Aziz. He became known to the west as 'Ibn Sa'ud'. He was the father of King Faisal and also of King Khalid; and the story of the Kingdom's creation is his story.

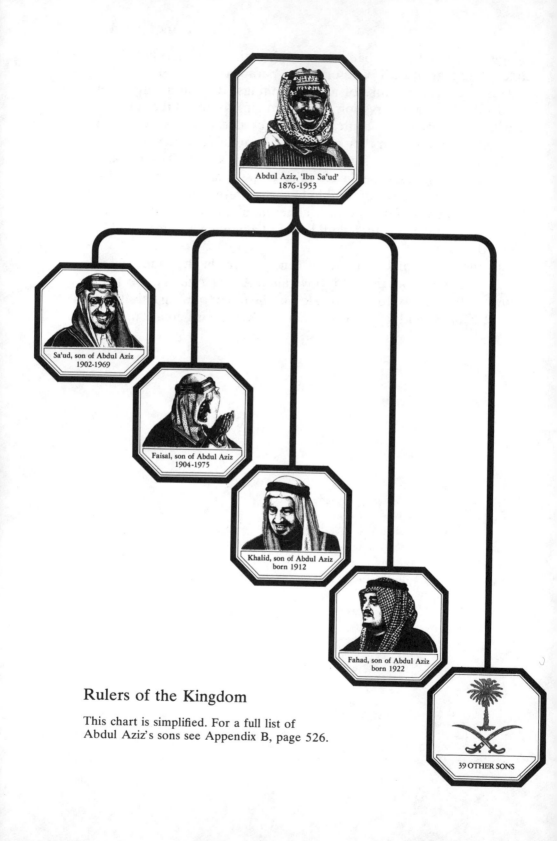

Abdul Aziz, 'Ibn Sa'ud'
1876-1953

Sa'ud, son of Abdul Aziz
1902-1969

Faisal, son of Abdul Aziz
1904-1975

Khalid, son of Abdul Aziz
born 1912

Fahad, son of Abdul Aziz
born 1922

39 OTHER SONS

Rulers of the Kingdom

This chart is simplified. For a full list of
Abdul Aziz's sons see Appendix B, page 526.

Notes

Names

In the early years of this century the house of Sa'ud emerged from the desert to conquer the greater part of the Arabian peninsula, and they called the empire they created after themselves: Sa'udi Arabia. They control the Kingdom to this day.

Yet understanding any family business involves knowing who is who, and it comes as something of a shock to discover that the house of Sa'ud included, at the last count, no fewer than forty Prince Faisals and forty-three Prince Khalids, not to mention twenty-eight Prince Muhammads and twenty-seven Princess Nuras in the central line alone.

Like many Arab families, the house of Sa'ud names its children to commemorate the brave deeds and virtues of distinguished forebears. So, by tradition, there are only some twenty names that each sex uses with any frequency, and these have to be shared out among a clan numbering 4000 by official estimate – almost a tribe in its own right.

This makes for difficulties large and small. There are two especially prominent Prince Turkis, for example, whom outside commentators have confused more than once, while Westerners at the Riyadh camel races find it difficult to follow precisely what is going on when they are told that the leading beast is owned by Prince Sa'ud ibn Muhammad and the runner-up belongs to Prince Muhammad ibn Sa'ud – all the Sa'uds and Muhammads involved being completely different people.

It is best not to get too worried about it – members of the family happily admit they cannot trace all the relationships of their countless cousins – but it does help to know who a man's father is or was, and this is indicated by the word 'ibn', 'son of' (sometimes written as 'bin'). Thus the present King of Sa'udi Arabia, Khalid ibn Abdul Aziz, is Khalid, son of Abdul Aziz.

Spelling

Arabic words appear in this book, wherever possible, in the spelling with which English readers are most familiar – 'Koran' and 'bedouin' rather than 'Quran' and 'badawin' or 'badu' – and the names of towns and

13

countries are as they appear in *The Times Atlas*. Less common words have been transliterated from the Arabic according to the table on page 538.

The name of the house of Sa'ud itself has been spelt with an apostrophe in an attempt to render its pronunciation, which is not 'sword' or 'pseud' but 'Sa-ow-d' – or thereabouts.

Uncles and aunts

In the early years of this century it was quite common for senior members of Arabian families to take a number of wives over an extended period of time. This meant that a man of twenty could well have a father of forty who was still taking teenage brides, and that the young man probably had half-brothers and half-sisters who were younger than his own children.

His children therefore had baby 'uncles' and 'aunts', and for this reason the 'uncles' in these pages may not be much older than their nephews – though, if they are actually younger, this will be pointed out.

Dates and ages

All dates and ages in this book have been standardized and converted into Christian years AD, but the Kingdom follows the Muslim calendar which dates from a turning point in the birth of Islam – the migration of the Prophet Muhammad from Mecca to Medina in the Christian year AD 622. From this migration, the *hijrah*, all Muslim history is dated, and it is reckoned in *hijrah* years, AH (Anno Hegirae), which are based upon the cycles of the moon.

Each month in Mecca people scan the sky for the appearance of the new moon, and only when it has been seen and attested is the month deemed by the Islamic authorities to have started. Astronomical calculations of when the new moon *should* be visible are not accepted. Only when the moon has actually been sighted, and the sighting corroborated, does the new month begin.

This means that the beginning of each Islamic month can only ever be predicted to within one or two days, and also that the full Islamic year totals only some 354 days – eleven or so days short of the modern Western Gregorian year. So Muslims who reach the Western age of thirty-three are already thirty-four by Islamic years, while Muslim centenarians are three Gregorian years short of the Western century.

This shorter year also means that Ramadhan and other Islamic feasts 'move' through the Western calendar, getting roughly eleven days earlier every year, and a comparative table of the AH and AD calendars is given in Appendix E.

While this book was being written, the Islamic world moved into the fifteenth century, the year 1401 AH beginning on 8 November AD 1980.

14

Arabs, Arabians and the Persian Gulf

President Nasser used to define an Arab as 'anyone whose mother tongue is Arabic', a good working definition.

Most Arabs are Muslims. and they inhabit that great swath of countries which run along the northern edge of Africa from Morocco to Egypt into the area commonly known as the Middle East.

The inhabitants of the Arabian peninsula are Arabs. But they can also be described more precisely as Arabians, and they will be called Arabians in these pages when it is wished to distinguish them from other Arabs.

Iranians – or Persians – are not Arabs, and they speak a different language. Until the 1950s the waterway separating Iran from the Arabian peninsula was known as the Persian Gulf. Then the Arabs proclaimed it Arabian. Persian Gulf is the name used in these pages when referring to those years before which the name was disputed. Thereafter it is called the Gulf.

Ibn Sa'ud and the Al Sa'ud

The founder of the Kingdom, Abdul Aziz, was often known to his people, and was usually known to Westerners during his lifetime, as 'Ibn Sa'ud', 'Son of Sa'ud'. This was more a title than a name, and it might be compared to the titles borne by Scottish clan chieftains who are known as 'the MacTavish' or 'the MacDuff'. The title had previously referred to Abdul Aziz's father and to his grandfather before that, but wherever employed in the pages that follow it refers to Abdul Aziz himself.

The house of Sa'ud themselves will usually be referred to as the Al Sa'ud – 'Al' with a capital 'A', meaning family, clan or tribe. This word, pronounced 'Aal' in Arabic, is different from 'al' with a small 'a', the Arabic definite article, which is pronounced as in 'alley'.

Currency

During the period covered by this book the British pound has varied, in terms of the American dollar, from a little below $5 to a little below $2.

These fluctuations have often been so intense that any attempt to equate pounds, wherever they appear, with dollars would be misleading in giving a sense of definitive value to the reader. Accordingly, pounds have been allowed to stand in the text without conversion.

Glossary

The meaning of these Arabic words and expressions is usually explained when they first occur in the text.

Abu Father. Fathers in Arabia are traditionally referred to by the name of their eldest son. Thus Abdul Aziz was known in the early years of this century as 'Abu Turki', 'Father of Turki', his eldest son who died in 1919.

Aghal The double headcord worn on top of the Arabian cloth headdress.

Akhiwiya 'Little brother'. The name given to the slave children who grew up as companions of their master's children in Araia before the abolition of slavery in 1962.

Araif A bedouin word for camels lost in a raid and recovered in a counter-raid. It was coined by Abdul Aziz to describe a group of his cousins who split from his branch of the family in the early years of this century.

Ardha The traditional sword dance of central Arabia.

Baksheesh A gratuity or tip.

Bay'ah The oath of allegiance sworn to those in authority.

Bhisht The Kuwait term for the traditional Arabian outer robe or cloak, usually known in Sa'udi Arabia as the *mishlah*.

Bin (sometimes written 'ibn'). Son of. Faisal bin Abdul Aziz was Faisal, son of Abdul Aziz.

Bint A girl, or daughter. In a name it means 'daughter of'. Nura bint Abdul Rahman was Nura, the daughter of Abdul Rahman.

Caliph Literally 'successor' (to the Prophet Muhammad). This title was adopted by leaders of the Muslim community after the Prophet's death. It was appropriated by the Ottoman Turks in the sixteenth century and became the title used by the Ottoman sultan until 1924.

Dishdasha The Kuwaiti name for the full-length, shirt-like garment known in Sa'udi Arabia as the *thobe*.

16

Eed al Adha The feast celebrating the end of the Pilgrimage and marking the day on which the pilgrims offer sacrifices in Mecca.

Eed al Fitr The feast celebrating the end of the fast of Ramadhan. The two eeds make up the two principal holidays in Sa'udi Arabia.

Emir, or **Ameer** Literally 'commander'. The word can designate the governor of a town or province. Male members of the house of Sa'ud are known as 'emirs', and this is usually translated as 'prince'. The English word admiral comes from the Arabic 'Emir al Bahr', 'Commander of the Sea'.

Ghazzu The raid.

Ghutra The Arabian cloth headdress. Traditionally Sa'udis wear a red and white headdress, sometimes changing to a plain white headdress of finer material in hot weather.

Hadhdh The bedouin word for luck. A person with *hadhdh* is someone 'born under a lucky star'.

Hadhar The Arabian word for settled folk, as opposed to nomads. *Hadhar* derive their livelihoods from farming and trading.

Hadith The Traditions – the personal acts and sayings of the Prophet Muhammad and of his Companions. There are several collections of Hadith, all gathered after the Prophet's death.

Hajj The Pilgrimage, one of the five pillars of Islam. All Muslims are required to make their *hajj* to the Holy City of Mecca at least once in their lives, if they can afford it. The *hajj* must be made in the pilgrimage month which culminates in the Eed al Adha, the Feast of the Sacrifice.

Hajji Pilgrim.

Houris The spiritual companions the good Muslim expects in paradise. These have frequently been interpreted as luscious and shapely nymphs, but the Koran does not specify this.

Ibn (sometimes written 'bin'). Son of.

Ikhwan Brothers. The name adopted by the fanatical Muslim warriors who formed the core of Sa'udi armies from 1919 to 1928.

Imam Literally 'he who goes before' to lead his fellow Muslims in prayer. This title was once borne by Sa'udi leaders, reflecting their leadership of the religious community. Today it is the title of those who lead prayers in Sa'udi mosques.

Insh'allah 'As God wills'.

Jihad Holy war. This has a more than military meaning, reflecting the total effort of the Muslim community to achieve a religiously sanctified objective. Thus, today, it embraces boycotts, embargoes and economic sanctions.

17

Ka'aba The 50-foot-high cube-like monument which is the focal point of the Grand Mosque in Mecca, and towards which all Muslims pray. Muslims revere the Ka'aba as the House of God built by Abraham, and they believe that its black cornerstone – today cased in silver – was cast down by God to Adam as a sign of his reconciliation with mankind after the expulsion from the Garden of Eden. The Ka'aba is traditionally draped in rich black and gold hangings which are renewed every year.

Koran The Muslim Holy Book. God's revelation to the Prophet Muhammad containing 114 *suras* or chapters.

Majlis Reception or sitting room, from the Arabic *yajlis*, 'he sits down'.

Majlis al Shura Consultative Council.

Mishlah The traditional Arabian outer robe or cloak, usually black, brown or cream and trimmed with gold thread.

Nasrani A Christian, literally a follower of the man from Nazareth.

Qadi A judge.

Quran An alternative transliteration of Koran.

Ramadhan The Islamic month of fasting in which Muslims celebrate God's gift to man of the Koran.

Riyal The unit of currency in modern Sa'udi Arabia. Exchange value in April 1981: $ = SR 3.3; £ = SR 7.8.

Rub al Khali The traditional transliteration of the name given by bedouin to the great desert occupying the south-east corner of Arabia (see endpapers). In English it is usually called 'The Empty Quarter', but this is a mistranslation of *al rabba al khali*, 'the barren lands'.

Salaam *(As salaam alaykum)* 'Peace be upon you.' The traditional Arabian greeting to which the reply is '*wa alaykum as salaam*', 'and upon you be peace'.

Shareef Descendant of the Prophet Muhammad. Shareefs of the Hashimite family ruled Mecca for many centuries until expelled by the house of Sa'ud in 1924.

Shariah The law of God – Islamic law.

Sheikh Literally 'elder', since the primary meaning of the Arabic root is 'age'. The style or title of 'sheikh', which is earned and not inherited, is an acknowledgement of respect with many connotations. It applies traditionally to the leader of a tribe, but today in Sa'udi Arabia employees will use the title for their boss, and any public figure can earn the title – Sheikh Yamani being a well-known example of a non-tribal sheikh. The title is also given to leaders of the religious community in the Kingdom.

18

Souq Market.

Tawilah A tweezer-like copper coin used in eastern Arabia until the early years of this century.

Thobe The long shirt-like garment worn by Arabian men. In the summer it is usually white and made of thin material. In winter heavier material is used, and the *thobe* may well be dark or striped.

Ulema Religious scholars. Today the word is used for the grouping of holy men who regulate religious life in Sa'udi Arabia. They meet weekly with the king. When the Grand Mosque in Mecca was seized by terrorists in November 1979, King Khalid asked the *ulema* to issue a *fatwa* (religious ruling) giving permission for Sa'udi troops to invade and fight in the holy place.

Umm Mother. Wives in Arabia are traditionally referred to by the name of their eldest son. Thus two of Abdul Aziz's favourite wives were Umm Mansour and Umm Talal, the mothers of Mansour and of Talal.

Wadi Rocky watercourse, dry except in the rainy season.

Wallahi! 'By God!', a common Arabian exclamation.

Zakat Religious tax.

For the location of the tribes mentioned, see the map on page 95.

Part One

The Desert

1 Bedouin

We had ridden far out over the rolling plains of North Syria to a ruin of the Roman period which the Arabs believed was made by a prince of the border as a desert-palace for his queen. The clay of its building was said to have been kneaded for greater richness, not with water, but with the precious essential oils of flowers. My guides, sniffing the air like dogs, led me from crumbling room to room saying 'This is jessamine, this violet, this rose.'

But at last Dahoum drew me: 'Come and smell the very sweetest scent of all' – and we went into the main lodging, to the gaping window sockets of its eastern face, and there drank with open mouths of the effortless, empty, eddyless wind of the desert. . . .

'This', they told me 'is the best. . . .'

T. E. Lawrence, *Seven Pillars of Wisdom*, p. 38

IT is sunrise in the desert. The sky is grey, the wind is cold. The camels cough and gurgle, irked by the thongs that hobble their forelegs. And on the carpet in front of one of the black goat-hair tents a boy is making coffee.

As he puts wood on the fire he calls for water and for coffee beans, and over the embroidered hanging that shuts off the women's section of the tent a hand passes them to him silently. He puts the water in a blackened brass coffee pot to boil. The beans, dry and greenish, he roasts in a shallow open pan.

Their aroma has barely started to rise when he tosses them, pale brown, into a heavy brass mortar, and, as they cool, he pounds them hard, striking the side of the mortar with alternate blows to make a bell-like sound. The ringing echoes round the camp, and robed men start sauntering to the fire. They sit cross-legged, feet bare. The elders lean on the sheepskin of a camel saddle, watching the sun slowly warm and colour the landscape.

Now the boy is calling for cardamom seeds, and another hand – or is it the same one? – passes the grey pods to him over the divider. He pounds the spice hard into the mortar, tipping its fibrous dust into the pot, and, when coffee and cardamom have boiled together three times, he puts a twist of date palm coir into the spout. This strains the liquid and he samples it, dashing a few drops into a small handle-less cup.

23

He takes up a stack of these little cups, balancing them one inside the other on his right hand, while he grasps the pot in his left, and then he walks around the circle, pouring out thimblefuls of the cloudy green-brown liquor.

When the men want more they hold out their cup. When they have had enough, they hold out their cup again, but this time they waggle it from side to side. Then the boy takes the cup back into the bottom of his stack and stays standing until the last man has finished.

It could be dawn any morning in the deserts of modern Sa'udi Arabia – pick-up trucks parked beside the black goat-hair tents, a plastic and chrome cassette radio wailing out music on the rich woven carpet. But it is nearly a century ago, somewhere in eastern Arabia, and the boy making coffee is Abdul Aziz ibn Sa'ud, the founder of the Kingdom.

The Al Sa'ud are refugees. Rulers of Riyadh for decades, they have been evicted from their town by the rival dynasty of Rasheed, and now they possess no more than they can strap on the backs of their camels, itinerants like the wandering tribesman or dung beetle, pushing their worldly wealth across the blistered face of the wilderness. It is the spring of 1891.

The modern history of the Kingdom begins somewhere in these sands on the fringe of Arabia's dead southern waste. It is a desert within deserts so bleak and lunar that even the bedouin know it as the Rub al Khali – the Empty Quarter – and when the Al Sa'ud were chased from Riyadh in 1891 it was towards the Empty Quarter that they fled. They had connections with the Murrah tribe who ranged its desolation, and that was how young Abdul Aziz ibn Sa'ud, fifteen years old in 1891*, came to be pounding coffee outside the Murrah's black hair tents.

Bedouin hospitality usually lasts for three days. Any traveller can stop near your tent, adjust his camel harness slowly, and then you must go out to welcome him. Even your wife, if she is alone, must go out with a bowl of camel milk. She must invite him to the man's side of the tent divider, and he can rest there till you return. Then you must give him of your best, slaughter a sheep, feast him. And he can stay with you three nights, after which you may inquire of him politely

* The precise birthdate of Abdul Aziz is not known, but this author sets it at 1876 for the reasons set out in the source note on pages 561–2.

24

where he is going and whether you can help him on the way, and that is his signal to be moving on.

But Abdul Aziz's father, Abdul Rahman ibn Faisal, was more than just a passing stranger, for, in earlier days, when the Al Sa'ud were ruling Riyadh, Abdul Rahman had persuaded the Murrah to go raiding with him. Together the townsmen of Riyadh and the Murrah bedouin had attacked the Beni Khalid who held eastern Arabia for the Turks in the 1870s, sharing out good booty. So when in 1891 Abdul Rahman sought sanctuary from the conquering Rasheeds, the Murrah's tents were the obvious place to go, and the Al Sa'ud stopped running somewhere south of the oasis called Yabreen.

Tradition has it that the Prophet Muhammad spent his boyhood in the desert. It was held to be one root of his wisdom, his common sense. His descendants, the Shareefs who ruled Mecca, used to send their sons out to the bedouin to be hardened – it was a common way for oasis families to round off the education of their young men – and, after he became ruler of Arabia, Abdul Aziz liked to talk up his youth as a barefoot bedouin, his long hair parted in the middle and plaited, wearing rough ragged clothes, riding, hunting, surviving on a handful of dates and a bowl of camel's milk. His adult vocabulary was studded with Murrah phraseology, simple desert expressions that he used to the end of his life, and he loved to tell stories of the tracking prowess that the Murrah taught him – how to tell from a camel's traces where it had come from, where it was heading, what sex it might be, and even its colour.

The depth of the hoofprint shows whether the beast was ridden or a pack animal – riding camels are females, pack animals bulls; if the footprints are soft, brushed by the tatters of loose skin strips, then the creature has come from the sands, not the gravel plains that polish hooves hard and smooth – and that helps locate the tribe of the camel's owner, and hence its colour, since different tribes breed different shades of brown or black or beige.

Camel droppings, broken open, betray the vegetation that the beast has cropped; the moisture or dryness of the droppings indicates how long it was since the creature passed that way; raiders hurrying home with a stolen herd make one complex of tracks, a heavily laden merchant caravan another.

The Murrah could read all these signs, and in the 1930s and 1940s Abdul Aziz was to employ them as trackers in the desert police posts of his kingdom. He liked to claim that the Murrah could even tell from a woman's footsteps whether she was a virgin or not, and he would appear deadly serious as he expounded the mechanical effect that intercourse has upon the way a maiden holds her legs.

The territory that the Murrah claimed as theirs was vast. Including the Empty Quarter it stretched across an area the size of France or Texas, and within this each family would travel at least 1000, perhaps as many as 3000, miles every year in the wake of their camel herds.

The Western image of the camel is of a camel train moving deliberately nose to tail – and that is indeed how pack animals travel. But most camels in Arabia were, and still are, females* tended for their milk in dairy herds. They drift like sheep grazing from one patch of scrub to the next, for the Arabian desert is not one barren expanse of rolling sand dunes. There are some areas like that, notably the Empty Quarter. But the very name of that desert shows how different it is from the rest of Arabia; bedouin call it 'the emptiness'.

North and west of the wilderness, most of the peninsula is stone or gravel land, sparsely covered with vegetation and scenically resembling the cowboy country of Western movies – the brush and tumbleweed of Colorado or Arizona. It may not be lush enough to support settled cultivation year-round, except in oases, but it is sufficient to maintain nomads like the Murrah comfortably in their mobile dairy farms – fifty, sixty, perhaps as many as ninety or a hundred milch camels drifting with the three or four tents of a father, his sons and their womenfolk.

It was in such units that Abdul Aziz learnt the rhythm of the nomad life. In summer with the midday temperatures ferocious – 120° F (45–50° C) – the Murrah would drift south-west to their permanent wells where they could be sure of water. Then with the cooler days of October and November they would start travelling quite fast and purposefully, 30 or 40 miles a day, northwards towards the winter grasses. After the rains in December and January, vast expanses of central Arabia can, for a month or so, look astonishingly like Alpine meadows – vivid green grass sprinkled with brightly coloured flowers – and the camel flocks graze this like so many cows.

This is the season when the nomadic life is at its best – warm days, cool nights, contented flocks, milk in abundance, time to relax, time to raid – and it was through raiding with the Murrah tribe that the

---

* Bull camels are usually killed for meat when young, the more so nowadays when they are not needed as pack animals.

26

founder of the Kingdom acquired his mastery of the desert, for raiding in Arabia before the motor car was not a criminal or a minority activity like, say, cattle rustling in America at the time. The *ghazzu*, the raid, was the full-time preoccupation of the bedouin male.

To ride out through the night with your companions, to camp stealthily by day behind dunes, to strike far away from the caravan trails till you were crawling on your belly to a wadi's edge – Abdul Aziz learned the thrill of all this: how to unhobble camels silently and then to drive them home, half triumphant, half fearful, riding fast over rocks and stony outcrops where pursuers would lose your trail.

And if someone did catch you, then you did not shoot them – and nor, God willing, did they shoot you. For to raid and to be raided was the way of the desert, and raiding was governed by serious etiquette, as befitted any serious sport.

The traditional bedouin raid was 'a cross between Arthurian chivalry and County Cricket'. This is the comparison made by Sir John Glubb ('Glubb Pasha'), who, as Captain John Glubb, was one of the last Europeans to live among the bedouin when the *ghazzu* was still a way of life. On one occasion in the 1920s Glubb came across the captured leader of a raiding party being entertained to a sheep by the emir of the tribe that he had just tried to attack, while later Glubb happened to be in an encampment at the very moment it was raided. Those of the visiting team who were captured were promptly welcomed into the tents of their intended victims and packed off home after a meal with water and supplies – though their camels and weapons were confiscated, and they were allowed only one rifle between all of them, since trudging back to camp after an unsuccessful raid was, apparently, part of the game.

The *ghazzu*, or raid, was quite distinct in bedouin convention from *harb*, war – or from the highway robbery that tribes would practise on any caravan caught passing through their territory without prior payment. You raided to take camels, not merchandise, land or life, and the protocol was precise: no raiding between midnight and dawn, no stealing of sheep or goats – and no molesting of women. Even if you raided a camp in serious war, the women were inviolable. To touch or harm them would be *haram*, a shameful thing, and, should you destroy other tents, you should always leave at least one for the women, with provisions, cooking things and coffee pots; for though you might be the victor today, tomorrow it might be your own mother or sisters at the mercy of someone else's *ghazzu*.

27

God gives and God takes away. The only constant treasure in life is life itself – and that is won too hard to be jeopardized lightly. Which is why, Abdul Aziz learned, the bedouin make poor allies in adversity. When a battle goes against a chief, it is his bedouin followers who turn first on his tents, for why should the enemy, they ask, enjoy all the spoils? Have we not served you longer? Have we not earned the first share?

Bedouin youths were 'blooded' in the *ghazzu*. It was the mechanism by which the tribal hierarchies recruited spirited new blood and sloughed off the less agile; and the end, means and basis of the entire social system was that unique beast, the camel. Abdul Aziz used to refer to the creature by its bedouin name, *ata Allah*, 'God's gift' – and, indeed, without the camel, even God could scarcely have created the bedouin. They are its parasites.

Camel's milk is the staple of the bedouin diet – warm, frothy, salty, straight from the udder, or kept for a little and lightly curdled. On feast days it is camel flesh that the tribesmen eat – tough but tasty, like gamy beef. The delicacy they fight for in horseplay round the cooking pots is raw camel liver, rubbed in salt, dripping in blood. Even the hoofs of the beast are consumed, ground into powder, baked into cakes in the embers of the fire. Nothing goes to waste. Women of the Murrah tribe saved camel urine to wash their hair. The men used it to bathe sand-scratched eyes or to wash wounds clean. The whole tribe consumed it as a purgative.

The camel's importance derives from its legendary capacity to go without drinking – as long as six weeks if the vegetation is lush. But more significant is its ability to convert vegetation and undrinkable, brackish water into milk, top-quality human nutrition, for almost twelve months of the year. In the 1930s Colonel H. R. P. Dickson estimated that fully a quarter of the bedouin living in the deserts round Kuwait were living on nothing but camel's milk, another quarter on camel's milk and dates, and the remaining half on camel's milk, dates and unleavened bread.

Coupled with the ability to transport the entire social unit – men, women, children, tents, supplies – 20 miles a day at leisure, 40 in emergency, this life source makes the camel precious enough. But not reproducing until the age of five, and then taking a whole year to gestate, and a further year to nurse one single offspring, each camel comes to be a very valuable piece of property.

To keep the numbers up today, the Kingdom imports camels. They

28

arrive every week or so in the port of Jeddah, peering curiously over the rails of the steamers from Somalia. They are a relatively scarce commodity with a solid value of their own; and, even in the age of the pick-up truck and riyal note, they are still the basic unit by which a bedouin assesses his wealth.

A nomad has no reason to value land, no means of transporting treasure in any quantity. The wealth that he prizes is the wealth that has four legs to transport itself – and it is this that gives bedouin life its unique flexibility and equality, for it is impossible to hoard. Sons may inherit their father's camels, but if they lack the vigour that built up the herds they will soon forfeit them. In the raiding environment of Arabia a hundred years ago, the idle and cowardly lost their wealth, the brave and energetic prospered. There was no mechanism by which unearned privilege could be maintained.

Here is the source of bedouin self-confidence, the assurance which you see today as the men from the desert stalk proudly into the presence of the Kingdom's rulers. An emir* for them is only the first among equals, and the Al Sa'ud welcome this pride.

But the house of Sa'ud cultivates the noble savage as much because he is savage as for the sake of his nobility, since the bedouin has mastered his cruel environment only through a certain cruelty of his own. He has conquered the desert by his ability to go without the comforts of life – little water, rare meat, no permanent home, the stony ground to lie on at night. His pleasure is to suffer, his satisfaction is to abstain, and this has left his soul bare and primitive: he has no sense of aesthetics, no refined sensibilities, no philosophy, literature, art, no complex mythology even, for all these adornments of the human spirit have been stripped off and cast aside by the bedouin as useless encumbrances in the battle to survive. The desert burns him by day and chills him by night, kills many of his children, tortures him with drought, dresses him in rags, gives him scraps to eat – and he stands uncrushed.

But his victory is at a price. His sensations blunted, his intellect fallow and incurious, the bedouin is primal, instinctual, contemptuous of nuance. Why did Lawrence's Arab friends prefer the air of the desert to all the perfumes they could sniff in that ruined palace on the north Syrian plain?

Because, they told him, 'it has no taste.'

* Emir: commander, governor or prince; see page 17.

29

The fifteen-year-old boy who pounded coffee outside the Murrah's tents did not spend more than two years living in the desert. By 1893 or 1894 Abdul Aziz and his family had moved on towards the coast of the Persian Gulf and the relative comforts of the seaport of Kuwait.

But in later life 'Ibn Sa'ud' always cited his apprenticeship among the Murrah as the time when he acquired the skills with which the Kingdom was constructed. Every night he had wrapped himself up in his coarse wool camel-blanket and slept out in the open beneath the stars. In winter he had to roll up tight, for in December and Janaury frost comes to the desert, and the night cold pierces to the bone. In summer he needed only his *thobe* – his long day-shirt and night-shirt – and he could lie down to sleep with nothing but that single layer of cotton between himself and the high dome of darkness and stars.

It falls very quiet in the desert at night. Every sound carries: the rasp of a camel clearing its throat, the growl and whimper of a dog. Abdul Aziz dreamed in the silence of many things, by his own account, as he slept beside the tents of the Murrah bedouin in the early 1890s – dreams of recapturing Riyadh, of avenging family honour, of sweeping across the whole of Arabia to re-create the empire of his forefathers.

But one thing the Kingdom's founder could not have dreamt as he slumbered upon the bluish night sands of eastern Arabia was that beneath his gritty pillow lay the largest oilfield on earth.

Previous page
Sand dunes in the Empty Quarter

These pages
Landscape picture Desert wells
Below Hunting falcons on their blocks
Left Watering the camels

Top A boum sailing from Kuwait to Zanzibar
Above Unloading cargoes in Kuwait

2 Exile

WHEN you ask the inhabitants of the Kingdom today to tell you something about the remarkable man who forged their country, they may well recount a story:

Abdul Aziz and the Virgin Bride

Abdul Aziz was fighting the Ajman. Of all tribes, they were ever the most troublesome and rebellious, and the campaign was going badly for the Al Sa'ud. There seemed no hope of victory, and the men were losing heart. At night the bedouin began to steal away, for there would be no booty to take home. Abdul Aziz had lost his flair.

Then one morning in a skirmish Abdul Aziz was wounded. A bullet struck him in the belly just above the groin, and, though Abdul Aziz told his companions to keep it secret, the news soon spread all round the camp. It was the final omen.

So Abdul Aziz summoned the emir of the village where they were camped, and questioned him. He wanted to know about the emir's daughters. Were they of marriageable age? And, if so, were they honourable women? Were they virgins?

The emir assured him that they were.

'In that case,' replied Abdul Aziz, 'kill the sheep for a feast. For I shall marry the fairest of your daughters – and this very night.'

So sheep were slaughtered and camels as well, the whole army feasted abundantly, and when the time came Abdul Aziz went in to his bride.

Now it was in those days the bedouin custom for a new bride to defend her modesty on the first night of marriage. She would fight off her husband as a token of her chastity, and the women of the tribe would listen outside the bridal tent. The sounds of struggle proved her honour, and the struggle might last for quite a while.

But on this night the struggle was brief indeed, and in no time the women of the village were running out with the bloodstained wedding sheet. They displayed it, as was their custom, to prove that the bride had been a virgin.

But the soldiers of Abdul Aziz saw another proof in the blood of maidenhood so rapidly taken. Even wounded, their leader was potent as ever. And so the next day they set upon the Ajman and defeated them utterly.

Abdul Aziz took his first wife when he was sixteen or seventeen, and every good Muslim knows that the purpose of marriage is procreation. But no man begets forty-three sons and twenty daughters (a conservative estimate) in less than half a century solely in the cause of duty, nor did Abdul Aziz ever claim not to enjoy the process involved most heartily.

There was no earthly pleasure like it, he told Sheikh Abdullah al Salim Al Sabah, 'to put his lips to the woman's lips, his body on her body and his feet on her feet' – although this is not, on the best available evidence, the style of coupling favoured by Abdul Aziz's Murrah mentors. Professor Donald Cole, who lived among the Murrah as an anthropologist in the 1960s, tells us that intercourse is performed by the Murrah hurriedly from the rear, and that this face-to-face posture described by Abdul Aziz is considered by them to be somewhat licentious.*

Abdul Aziz's potency was to become a core element in the identity that inspired his followers' loyalty – a master of the desert, a servant of God, and a Caesar of the bedchamber.

'Women are your fields,' says the Koran – the word means almost tillage, crops. 'Go then into your fields when and how you will.'

The famous verse in the Koran which allows the Muslim man to 'marry the women of your choice, two or three or four', has an important proviso attached to it: 'If ye fear that ye shall not be able to deal justly with them, then take only one'; and later in that chapter

---

* 'Because of close quarters and lack of privacy, married couples perform intercourse at night with the minimum of precoital love play, without undressing and with practically no sound. A man ejaculates quickly, sometimes within a minute of insertion. He occasionally continues coitus until he has ejaculated a second or even a third time. The proper sexual position, according to the men, is for the man to enter the woman from behind as she faces away from him: face-to-face coitus is considered risqué.'

God tells His people: 'Ye are never able to be fair and just between women, even if it is your ardent desire.'

Modern young Sa'udis sometimes cite these verses as divine advice that they should, in practice, take only one wife at a time since they will find it impossible to be fair and just to more than one.

But Abdul Aziz never had any doubt that he could deal evenly and impartially with all his wives as God commanded him. He married up to his full limit of wives as soon as he could afford to, and he also bought himself slave girls in large numbers – though he did privately admit to friends in later life that, despite this abundance of female companionship, he did not usually indulge his passion more than once in any night.

Allowing Muslims to take four wives was the Koran's solution to the large number of widows and orphaned daughters created by the battles that Islam fought in its early years; and, since these battles also yielded up large numbers of female captives, Muslim men were told that they could also take, as slaves, 'those that your right hands possess'.

Nowhere does the Koran endorse concubinage in so many words, but, since it does not specifically condemn the practice either, it became the historical custom of many Islamic princes and rulers to enjoy a female entourage of varied shapes and colours – and Abdul Aziz fell in happily with this tradition as soon as he acquired the means to do so.

When he married for the first time, however, Abdul Aziz barely had the wherewithal to acquire one wife, let alone a harem. The Al Sa'ud were so poor, we are told, when they moved from the desert to the port of Kuwait in the mid-1890s, that there was no money for a wedding. Abdul Aziz's marriage had to be postponed until a merchant took pity on the family and put up the cash.

Such humiliation became a way of life during the family's long sojourn in Kuwait. From their arrival around 1894 or 1895 until the early years of the twentieth century, the Al Sa'ud had to survive in a lowly three-roomed mud house in a warren of seaside alleys where the prevailing odour, wrote a visitor in 1904, was of shark oil and human excreta. Kuwait's sewage was deposited in 'large open public cesspools', and though the wealthy had their private water closets along the seafront – little wooden shacks connected to the shore by rickety bridges – ordinary citizens simply squatted on the beach and let the ebb and flow of the tides do its work.* The Al Sa'ud's cramped quarters were not salubrious, and less than six months after her marriage Abdul Aziz's first wife died.

Abdul Aziz never liked to reminisce about his half dozen years in Kuwait as he later revelled in the tales of his much shorter stay among the Murrah bedouin. But he did not lose touch with the desert, for most of Kuwait, even today, is barren gravelly wasteland. Where the town stops, open desert stretches as far as the eye can see, and until quite recently black hair tents were dotted among the camel scrub and salt brush. Large bedouin communities sustained an existence there, and at the turn of the century the town itself looked like part of the desert.

'Low houses the colour of sand' barely broke the skyline when Mrs Elizabeth Taylor Calverley arrived to start work for the American Arabian Mission in 1912. 'In the whole picture was scarcely a tree or a patch of green.'

This unpromising driblet of sand in the armpit of the Persian Gulf is today, *per capita*, by far the wealthiest country on earth.† But in 1904 the British government surveyor attached no special importance to the 'bitumen which exudes from the ground in a hollow near the Burqan hill', while the requirements of the townspeople's lamps and winter stoves brought a special steamer once a year from the Standard Oil Company of New Jersey. It sold kerosene oil.

The wealth of Kuwait when Abdul Aziz was living there derived from its harbour. *Kut* means 'fort' in Arabic. 'Kuwait' is a diminutive of that, and the importance of the 'little fort' was that it guarded the entrance to the largest and most sheltered natural harbour on the Persian Gulf – or anywhere on the 4000-mile coastline of the Arabian peninsula.

Kuwait was the principal port through which goods from the outside world reached central Arabia. Long caravans from the inner plateaux arrived every fortnight to pick up rice, tobacco, coffee and firearms from the ships anchored in the crescent-shaped bay, and the wide mouth of the bay was unimpeded by the sand bars that stunted

---

* This spectacle provided, as Violet Dickson discovered when she arrived in 1929 as wife of the British Political Agent, the principal sight from the verandah of the house that had become the British Agency in 1904.

† Kuwait's Gross National Product per head of the population according to the *1980 World Bank Atlas* was $15,970 in 1978 – compared to $12,990 for Switzerland, $9,770 for the USA, $5,720 for Britain, and less than $200 for countries like India, Burma and Ethiopia.

the development of the Shatt al Arab, the 'River of the Arabs', some 60 miles up the coast. That combined channel of the Tigris and Euphrates rivers had been the starting point for Sinbad the Sailor's legendary voyages, but by the 1890s Kuwait had become a more thriving centre of the Arab seafaring tradition.

Every autumn the huge wooden *boums* would set off along one of the ancient routes Arab navigators discovered a thousand years earlier, either south-east along the Indian coast to Ceylon, using the seasonal monsoon winds to blow them first down, then back, or else south-west to Aden and then on to Zanzibar, selling their cargoes of dates, pearls and Arab horses for salt, spices, timber, ivory and ghee (clarified butter).

'Seest thou not that the ships glide on the sea by Allah's grace?'

Just below the quarter where the Al Sa'ud were packed together, Kuwait's shipbuilders plied their trade. There were hundreds of yards of beached sailing craft being rubbed brown and shiny with aromatic shark-oil, and every so often along the seafront could be seen the bare white ribs of a boat being constructed to that design unchanged since the days of Noah's Ark.

Dhow, not an Arab word though it looks like it, is the name that outsiders apply indiscriminately to all Arab vessels. *Boum* is what the Kuwaitis call the sharp-prowed craft that they have developed, some of them up to 200 feet long, bigger than a frigate of Nelson's day.

The *boums* would glide out of Kuwait harbour, fifteen to twenty oars on each side swinging in unison, 'with a stateliness I have never seen surpassed,' wrote Dr Paul Harrison, another of the American missionaries who arrived about this time, 'the men chanting as they worked. . . . There was a splendid silk flag flying at the stern.'

Dr Harrison was describing a departure for the Persian Gulf pearl banks, 100 miles south of Kuwait, the richest in the world, and a principal source of the town's wealth. There the oars would be lashed out horizontally from the ship, stones or lead weights on ropes tied to each, and the divers, with wooden stoppers in their noses, would stand on the weights to sink rapidly to the bottom. 40 feet below the surface they would move rapidly, cutting and pulling oysters into a basket until, after two minutes, perhaps longer, their breath gave out. Then they would be pulled back to the deck and the shells piled up to be searched next day under the captain's careful eye.

More than 400 captains of these *boums* emptied their little red flannel bags on to the counting desks of Kuwait's pearl merchants

35

every summer. At the height of the season they were employing almost 10,000 divers, Arabs from all round the Gulf, and, with the crews of the ocean-going merchantmen, it made up a cosmopolitan environment: the bedouin selling their camel dung for fuel, or beating Maria Theresa dollars into stubby, pitted jewellery in their black hair suburb of tents beside the walls; Persians with their blue coats and high felt hats; Jews with their own synagogue, and several thousand blacks, whose clubs throbbed to their special kind of music and were marked by boards painted with mysterious sky signs.

Abdul Aziz watched it all carefully and took many things away with him: an open mind, a realization that the world did not end but was only just beginning at the fringes of Arabia, and a gastronomic predilection unusual in an Arab from the inner deserts – a taste for fresh fish.

The Al Sa'ud's host in Kuwait was the town's ruler, Sheikh Mubarak Al Sabah, a Machiavellian character blessed with that iceberg ruthlessness which inspires such respect in Arabia. Mubarak seized power one night in May 1896 by murdering his two half-brothers as they lay sleeping on the roof of the Al Sabah's palace, and the shelter and support which Mubarak gave the house of Sa'ud did not stem from charity.

Kuwait was strongest, in Mubarak's eyes, when central Arabia was divided against itself. The capture of Riyadh and the flight of the Al Sa'ud had given too much power to the Rasheeds. Mubarak wanted to see the Rasheeds confined to the northern deserts around their capital of Hail, and to that end he lent his backing to the plans the Al Sa'ud were nursing to recapture Riyadh.

Abdul Aziz could not wait to be off. One day, the story goes, he rallied some young friends and headed his camel south-west into the heat haze. He planned to gather up bedouin along the way and recapture Riyadh just like that.

Captain Armstrong, one of Abdul Aziz's earliest biographers who picked up this tale in Jeddah in 1933, says that it was Sheikh Mubarak who took Abdul Aziz under his wing and showed him more realistic ways of achieving his ambitions – and this part of the story, at least, is true. Eye-witnesses of later meetings between Abdul Aziz and Mubarak remark on the extraordinary respect which Abdul Aziz paid to the older man.

Mubarak's eyes, said one observer who met him in old age, were those of Richelieu and, even in his final years, there was 'something of Richelieu's ambition as yet unquenched within him'. Mubarak was a born politician, wise in the wiles of his own Arab world and also, as events soon proved, in those of the wider world beyond, where the great powers were coming to eye Kuwait and its strategic position at the head of the Persian Gulf. Abdul Aziz could not have found a shrewder statist in all Arabia under whom to serve his political apprenticeship.

By the beginning of the twentieth century the founder of modern Sa'udi Arabia was reaching manhood. We have to wait another ten years for the earliest first-hand description of him (and also for the first photograph), but already we can picture a large, square-built young man with an open face, long firm nose and direct gaze. He clearly had great charm, he was soon to demonstrate his ability to win the trust of others, and he was consumed by one overwhelming ambition.

In 1927 Abdul Aziz told Muhammad Asad* of a dream that he had while he was in Kuwait. Dreams were something that he took very seriously. He was, as king, to employ a soothsayer whose full-time job it was to interpret his dreams. But this dream in Kuwait did not need much interpreting. He was riding alone in the desert on horseback when in front of him he saw Ibn Rasheed, Riyadh's new ruler, who was also on horseback.

We were both unarmed, but Ibn Rasheed held aloft in his hand a great, shining lantern. When he saw me approach, he recognized the enemy in me and turned and spurred his horse to flight; but I raced after him, got hold of a corner of his cloak, and then of his arm, and then of the lantern – and blew out the lantern. When I awoke, I knew . . .

Did Abdul Aziz never once despair, one wonders, had his faith not even faltered, as he idled his time away, month after month in Kuwait? The question holds no meaning, for despair is alien to the fatalistic world where destiny lies in Allah's hands. But we are told that the young man's strength of purpose did waver on at least one

---

* Muhammad Asad began life as a Polish Jew, the grandson of a rabbi in Lvov. As a journalist in the Middle East he became friendly with figures like Abdul Aziz, converted to Islam, and described his conversion in an original and complex book, *The Road to Mecca*. This Jewish Muslim climaxed his career by being chosen by the new Islamic state of Pakistan to be its representative at the United Nations. At the time of writing he is living in Tangiers.

occasion – and we have two different versions of the episode to choose from.

The first, related by one of Abdul Aziz's younger sons, describes his father inquiring of his slaves and companions where it was they went at night. It seemed most exciting. They would slip off into the port's backstreets and not return till dawn, bragging of music, carousing, women. He wanted to join them. Would they not take him with them one night?

'Never,' said his slave without hesitation. 'You are Abdul Aziz. You are different from us, and you must never forget that. You must stay different, for we must look up to you always, ready for the day when you will lead us from here.'

And so Abdul Aziz stayed at home.

But another tale, told by Abdul Aziz in his old age to one of his advisers, Jamal Bey Husaini, suggests that the young man did venture out at least once into the backstreets, for somehow he met up with a lady of the town and suggested that they might, perhaps, retire together somewhere more private.

'Who are you?' shouted the whore* for all to hear. 'Abdul Aziz ibn Sa'ud? You should be ashamed of yourself. Stop hanging around here wasting your strength and spirit! Come back when you've achieved something you can truly boast about. We'll know what measure of man you are when you have conquered Riyadh!'

---

* Saved by a whore. The Arab attitude to prostitution at this time was ambivalent. In Kuwait in the early twentieth century, brothels were confined to the south and south-west of the town, and the girls who worked them were flotsam, with no known male relatives – for these would certainly have killed them for dishonouring the family name. On the other hand, troupes of women who worked as prostitutes were invited to sing and dance at respectable family occasions like weddings and circumcision feasts where men and women celebrated separately. On these occasions they mixed, talked and laughed freely with the women.

3 The Great Adventure

How often have the few conquered the many through the will of God!

Koran, II, 249

IN the late summer of 1901, His Majesty's Ship *Perseus* was bobbing in Kuwait Bay, her commander a bored and unhappy man. Captain E. R. Pears had spent four sweltering months lying at anchor off the low strip of sand and huddle of flat-roofed dwellings which it was his duty to protect because the British government suspected Turkey and the Germans of making a play for Kuwait.

The gunboat commander could not see what all the fuss was about. 'A more dreary and uninteresting spot', wrote Captain Pears, 'could hardly be imagined.'

He took the *Perseus* off down the Gulf for a few days' target practice to relieve the monotony.

But on his return to Kuwait Bay in September 1901, Captain Pears was astonished to spy through his binoculars 'enormous numbers of flocks, camels, horses and Bedouin tents' filling the desert around the town. There had been no trace of them when he left a week earlier. 'Something', he decided, 'was in the wind.'

The captain was correct, for he was witnessing the defence mechanism of Kuwait's tribesmen. When they sensed danger, they would come out of the desert to cluster round the walls of the town, and in September 1901 the danger came from the raiding parties of Ibn Rasheed.

Earlier that year Mubarak of Kuwait had led a bedouin horde – the Al Sa'ud among them – 400 miles across northern Arabia to threaten the Rasheed heartland around Hail. He had been defeated, and now the Rasheed were bringing the war back into Mubarak's territory. They were only three days' march away from Kuwait.

Captain Pears took his officers ashore to investigate. Their launch was met, as usual, by horses up to their bellies in water – the Sheikh's device to prevent visitors dirtying their boots on the mudflats – and the British lit up cheroots as usual (their own device for combating the particular aroma of the foreshore). They found Mubarak waiting for them – and in fine fettle.

39

'Full of the expectation of fighting,' wrote Captain Pears, 'the old chief was in the highest spirits. I had never seen him unbend and talk so much before.'

There seemed every possibility of a pitched battle here at the gates of Kuwait between the Al Rasheed on the one side, and Mubarak with his Sa'udi allies on the other, and the British naval party were invited to inspect the Kuwait–Sa'udi forces.

'The Sheikh rode a splendid white horse, with gorgeous trappings, and headed the cavalcade, which was preceded by a large escort of Arabs armed with rifles,' recorded Captain Pears. This escort cleared the way through the town, marching the full width of the street 'singing loud sonorous war-songs', and everyone had put on their finest robes – red, orange, light brown. 'The people drew back into doorways and corners shouting cheers to the Sheikh; the veiled women waved their hands and cried in a continuous shrill squeak, "La-La-La-La-La!" Every man we saw, except the blind or helpless, even old grey-beards, carried a rifle.'

As Mubarak led the British officers down the seething lines of warriors, 'all the men, wild with excitement, danced, waved their rifles, and yelled, making a terrific din to which drums loudly added. Most of the men looked wild and barbarous, with long hair streaming in the wind, but many of the older ones were fine-looking old patriarchs, reminding one of pictures from the Bible.'

They were dancing with 'the motions of a man compelled to stand on hot bricks – i.e. alternate feet raising rapidly', and in front of the inspecting party, 'as we moved along, a pair of mounted bedouins would wildly gallop, meeting each other half-way and firing their rifles in the air as they passed.'

'It was', wrote Captain Pears, 'a wonderful and rare spectacle. There must have been at least 10,000 people scattered over the plain.' And among them were the forces of the Al Sa'ud, raring for their chance to strike a blow at the house of Rasheed.

The Sa'udi banner was green, the traditional colour of the cloak the Prophet wore, and it bore a fine tracery of Arabic inscription: 'There is no god but God. Muhammad is the messenger of God.' That is the Islamic creed. It is all you need to say to become a Muslim; and today that war banner is the flag of modern Sa'udi Arabia, with the addition of just a sword below the motto as a reminder of the pennant's battlefield origins.

Ibn Rasheed was evidently deterred by the size and ferocity of

40

Mubarak's rally – and he must have been still more disturbed by the news of the *Nasrani*, Christians,* in their strange blue and gold costumes riding down the lines beside the old sheikh. Britain was apprehensive of German plans to run a railway from Berlin to Baghdad, finishing on the Gulf coast at Kuwait. If the port now fell into the hands of the Rasheeds, these tribesmen might, through their Turkish allies, prove amenable to Germany's ambitions. So in September and October 1901 the crew of the *Perseus* and several more British warships landed guns to protect Sheikh Mubarak's town from the landward side, and they anchored with their own batteries trained on the desert.

Ibn Rasheed was foiled. He had to content himself with seizing a few hundred sheep to keep his bedouin happy, and then he withdrew northwards to ponder – and also to confer with the Turkish authorities in Baghdad.

This was Abdul Aziz's moment. The bulk of Ibn Rasheed's forces were as far as they were ever likely to be from Riyadh; their principal preoccupation was Mubarak and the formidable foreign technology he had inveigled into the traditional techniques of Arab warfare; and the small Rasheed garrison in Riyadh, unaware of this novel difficulty, would be lulled into a false sense of security.

The young man asked his father and Mubarak for permission to try his luck, and permission was granted – though less in confidence of victory, probably, than in the knowledge that at another time the dangers could be much worse.

Forty is the number which the bedouin often pick upon when they want to describe a smallish body of men, and forty is the number of companions which Abdul Aziz is said to have had with him when he left Kuwait in late September 1901. Some of them were members of the Al Sa'ud household – relatives, servants, slaves; some were friends or plain adventurers. Abdul Aziz was their leader, and his second-in-command was his half-brother Muhammad.†

---

* *Nasrani*: literally, followers of the man from Nazareth.

† Half-brother, meaning usually a son by the same father but a different mother, is not a word favoured by Sa'udis. 'We are all brothers,' they say, dismissing outsiders' attempts to distinguish between full brothers and half-brothers. But inside Sa'udi families, and particularly inside the Sa'udi royal family, 'brothers' are fully aware of which mother gave birth to them and brought them up, and since this basic blood tie determines internal family politics, the term 'half-' and 'full brother' will be employed here whenever it is wished to make this distinction clearer.

Muhammad was about the same age as Abdul Aziz, born to another of Abdul Rahman's wives in the days before exile. He might have been older, but is generally said to have been younger than Abdul Aziz. Tough, stocky and beetle-browed, Muhammad had a thicker, blacker beard than his half-brother, but his features, to judge from later photographs, were less intelligent. He looks better at carrying out orders than initiating them.

Closer in spirit to Abdul Aziz were his lieutenants for the sortie, a group of cousins whose branch of the family stemmed from a previous period which the Al Sa'ud had spent in the wilderness. They were called bin Jaluwi, a name derived from *jaluwa*, exile, and the fiercest of them, Abdullah bin Jaluwi, was to make a decisive contribution to the fortunes of the little group that left Kuwait in the autumn of 1901.

They rode south and west, the Persian Gulf coast to their left, looking for supporters among the tribes which today supply the workers for the Kingdom's oilfields. They were like any other raiding party drumming up support – and they received it. The bedouin of the Beni Khalid and the Ajman joined them, and by mid-October 1901 Kuwait was agog with reports of Abdul Aziz's success raiding near Majma'a north of Riyadh. Abdul Aziz and his men rode on.

At night they slept in desert hollows, careful to make no silhouette on the skyline. The camels were hobbled and couched in a circle round the sleeping men. Rifles and saddles lay at the ready. The men survived on water from their goatskins, butter carried in lizardskins, dates hung from the pommels of their saddles – and whatever food they could raid as they came swooping down on a caravan or encampment.

As they raided, the original force of forty swelled to over 200 men, and Abdul Aziz's strategy was to lead his little army up towards Riyadh from the south. He would attack the town by the route of least resistance, for he judged the south to be more loyal to the memory of the Al Sa'ud.

But the grand strategy misfired. Abdul Aziz's raiding did not generate sufficient booty to satisfy the bedouin. Ibn Rasheed had got wind of his activities and alerted his men in Riyadh. It was wintry, still hottish by day, but painfully cold at night; and the holy month of Ramadhan was approaching.

Ramadhan is well known to non-Muslims as the Islamic month of fasting, and the Christian connotations of fasting are of abstinence

42

and penance. But Ramadhan is not like Lent. It is the Islamic month of celebration, when Muslims give thanks for God's greatest gift to them, the Koran, through which he disclosed his message to mankind. Muslims fast totally all day, abstaining from food and drink and sex, and from refreshment of any kind, including cigarettes. They usually sleep. But every sunset they break fast and feast through the night in convivial gatherings which grow more and more epicurean, building up to a climax at the Eed al Fitr, the feast celebrating the breaking of the fast. Elaborate food and special Ramadhan sweets are prepared. Presents are exchanged. The atmosphere is something like Christmas.

Abdul Aziz's bedouin were not forgoing that for the discomforts and dangers of raiding after uncertain rewards. His army melted away, back to their families, flocks and tents, and by November 1901 Abdul Aziz was left with only a score more men than the forty he had started out with – sixty or seventy at the most. He withdrew to Haradh, north of the Empty Quarter, and it was there that a messenger from Kuwait reached him. He brought Abdul Aziz a letter from Mubarak and from Abdul Rahman warning that Ibn Rasheed was reported to be enlisting Turkish help. The obvious course for Abdul Aziz was to return to the safety of Kuwait, and in expectation of that the British News Agent in the town reported on 11 November 1901 that the Sa'udi raiders were awaited back on the 15th.

Abdul Aziz drew his remaining followers around him and he read them the letter, emphasizing the dangers which they now faced. Cut off out here at Haradh with just their camels and rifles, these few score men amounted to little beside the forces that Ibn Rasheed could muster. There no longer seemed much prospect of raising the tribes.

But Abdul Aziz himself would not surrender. He could not stomach the ignominy of a retreat to Kuwait. He would rather die, he said, on the battlements of Riyadh, and he invited those who wished to die with him to come and stand on his right hand. Those who preferred to go home should stand on his left.

It was, Abdul Aziz later remembered, the point of no return. He had a trick, when emphasizing a dramatic moment, of dropping his voice to little more than a whisper, and his listeners would go still, holding their breath in with him. Though Abdul Aziz might sit before them four square, very obviously the conquerer of Riyadh and of almost all Arabia, he could transport them back to the Haradh oasis, to that moment in the winter of 1901 when he, and the hopes of the house of Sa'ud, faced a callow and undistinguished end in the sands of the Empty Quarter. Would his men now respond to his appeal?

They did not hesitate. Sixty of them moved to the right. 'To the death!' they shouted.

Some accounts maintain that not a single man went to the left, others that a few took the safe option. But something around sixty is the generally agreed figure for the striking force who pledged themselves to Abdul Aziz at Haradh in November AD 1901 – and the young Sa'udi leader turned dramatically to the messenger:

'Go back to my father and let him know what you have seen. Ask him to pray for us. Tell him we shall meet again, God willing, in Riyadh.'

Then Abdul Aziz rounded up his sixty diehards and led them southwards towards the Empty Quarter, turning his back on Riyadh. He was about to gamble his life on one throw, but not without lessening the odds with a little strategy. The Rasheed garrison in Riyadh would hear of the bedouin deserting his standard and of this withdrawal over the south-eastern horizon – and, if they heard no more, they would relax.

Into the Empty Quarter went Abdul Aziz to vanish from the world somewhere near the oasis of Yabreen – Murrah country. By day he rested, his whole party lying low and out of sight. By night his men would creep to tribal wells, uncover them, fill their goatskins and then steal away, brushing over their tracks. No one must know they were still alive. For nearly fifty days they survived, resting, snoozing, half-comatose in the fashion that bedouin lull away months of their lives between bouts of frantic activity, their bodies out of gear, idling at less than idling speed.

Their camels grazed similarly, humps swelling for the hard ride ahead. It is not true that camels store water in their hump – all their body tissues are highly absorbent* – but the hump does store fat, building, as every mammal does, an energy reservoir in times of ease that exertion will deplete. So beast and man hibernated together near Yabreen as Ramadhan began in the middle of December 1901.

Every morning the sun bleached the sands, blackening the few pools of thornbush shade where Abdul Aziz and his companions

---

* The camel's ability to go long periods without water derives from the flexibility of its blood temperature which can rise as much as 6° F before the animal starts to perspire, combined with kidneys that eliminate body waste with very little loss of liquid. The camel urinates very short and very strong.

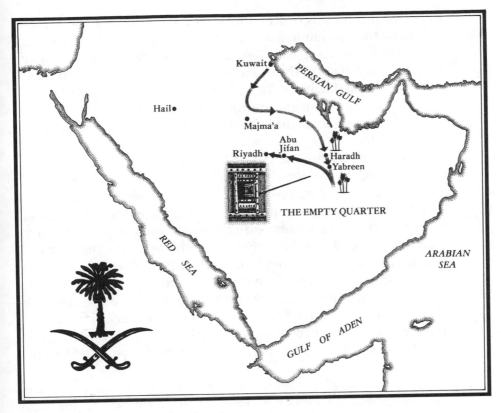

Abdul Aziz's route to Riyadh, 1901–2

huddled dozing. Then with darkness they would light a fire in a hollow, make coffee, chew dates, toast a little meat if someone had been lucky enough to snare a bird or a lizard, and nibble at the hot gritty carapace of bread baked in the embers of the fire.

This bread is the staple foodstuff of the bedouin on the move, cooked from small sackfuls of flour as they travel. Little buns and scones are kneaded and thrust into the ashes around the coffee pot, and when prised free they are tossed around the *majlis* circle with 'ohs' and 'ows' and shouts and chuckles, as calloused fingers try to crack open the scorching grey grenades to the moist salty dough inside. It is one more game in the meandering stream of campfire diversion, swapping stories, playing jokes, launching fantasies of luscious women, great feasts and gorgings – or dreaming aloud of clear cool springwater, untainted by the goatiness of waterskins.

Each evening the Ramadhan moon grew fuller, until at night the

45

sand shimmered silver, and the scouts lying behind their camel saddles on the surrounding hillocks could survey the bright desert for miles. Then one week after it had begun to wane, early in January 1902, Abdul Aziz gave the order to mount. There were seven nights' riding to Riyadh. Each one would be blacker than the one before, and they should arrive beneath just the slimmest crescent, when the Eed al Fitr, the end-of-Ramadhan feast, would conspire with the darkness to aid his plan.

A slow camel travels at 3 m.p.h. A good one can maintain a 4 m.p.h. average over several days' riding. To touch 5 m.p.h. is really speedy, and Abdul Aziz's party had to cover 30 miles a night to make Riyadh in a week – not impossible by day, more difficult after dark while scouting to make sure no one caught sight of them passing.

By the end of Ramadhan they were still 40 miles short of their target. They had reached the wells of Abu Jifan, due east of Riyadh, and it was there that they made their own Eed al Fitr celebration. But the feasting was short. They saddled up and rode hard through the night, so that dawn found them on the plateau overlooking Riyadh and the plain to its north-east, where Abdul Aziz's sons and grandsons today recline in over-stuffed armchairs to watch their camels racing.

The raiders lay all day up in the hollows of the plateau, undetected as farmers and townspeople slept off the festivities of the night before, and Abdul Aziz selected his force for the assault – forty men. The remaining twenty or so were to stay up on the plateau with all the camels, blankets, provisions and baggage. If they heard nothing in the next twenty-four hours, they must make their escape back to Kuwait as fast as they could, for Abdul Aziz would either be dead, or else a prisoner of the Rasheeds.

The tale of the famous odyssey exists in many versions, all recounted later by Abdul Aziz at different times to different people, for he loved to relive the saga. It took him back into a younger, simpler world, and he would sweep his listeners along into the adventure with his musical voice and eloquent hands, his thumbs bending strangely backwards as he gestured.

Princess Alice, Countess of Athlone, could speak no Arabic. But when she met Abdul Aziz in 1938, his wealth of drama and gesticulation was such that she needed only a few words of translation to catch the gist of his narrative. It was Abdul Aziz's standard preamble to any conversation with visitors, from the British colonial servants he courted in the early years, to the New World representatives drawn by oil; and as late as March 1950 America's first Ambassador to Sa'udi Arabia was told the tale, duly dispatching the details back to Washington 'as being of historical interest'.

Each of Abdul Aziz's sons heard the story so often they knew it off by heart; Abdul Aziz's early biographers all received the epic in detail from his own lips; and among Abdul Aziz's friends – who had to listen to countless variations on the theme over coffee for more than a quarter of a century – Harry St John Philby grew so weary of it that, when commissioned to write the definitive history of Sa'udi Arabia in the mid-1950s, he noted shortly that 'the details of that dramatic tale have been told too often to need repetition here'.

Every Sa'udi schoolchild knows the tale of Abdul Aziz setting off with his little band of companions into the desert. He is their twentieth-century Robin Hood – courageous, foolhardy, desperate, wreathed in all the glamour of the few who pit themselves against the many – and his great raid on Riyadh has become Arabia's Storming of the Bastille.

But the myth is clouded, for, although all the many renderings are derived from Abdul Aziz's own lips, each one varies so much it is impossible to work out one definitive version in the Western historical sense – and you certainly will not be reading it in the pages that follow.

The difficulty is partly that Abdul Aziz, when excited – and he grew very excited in the retelling of this tale – would intensify his colloquialisms so that the best foreign Arabists could not follow properly. But deeper lies the difference between the Western and the Arabian concepts of historical truth. Mistranslation is only a part of the story, since most of Abdul Aziz's hearers understood him perfectly – and they also understood that he was creating something much more precious than a bare recital of dates and facts. He was spinning history in the way that the Old Testament scribes spun their legends or the creator of the *Chanson de Roland* wove his epic, for even today it remains the pleasant obstinacy of the Arab to be less captivated by the distinctions between fact and fiction than by mystery, romance, poetry, imagination – and even by downright caprice.

'Tell him the story of your journey to Riyadh,' said Philby, introducing a young American oilman to Abdul Aziz in the late 1940s, and the old king duly obliged.

'I never heard you tell it that way before,' said Philby afterwards.

'You're right,' said Abdul Aziz. 'I never have. I felt like a change.'

Myths, it seems, even provoke a certain weariness in those who make them.

At sunset, around six in the evening on 15 January 1902, the forty men moved forward. They carried just their weapons – daggers, swords, a few rifles – and they walked about an hour and a half till they were on the north-east fringe of Riyadh in al Oud, somewhere south of the modern railway station and the tomato ketchup factory.

In January 1902 it was the spot where the palm groves ended, and Abdul Aziz picked out a small scouting party of half a dozen, leaving the remainder of his striking force beneath the trees. His half-brother Muhammad was to bring them forward when the advance guard had discovered how the land lay.

Abdul Aziz moved forward with his handful of scouts into the darkness. Between the palm groves and the town itself lay Riyadh's vegetable gardens, a maze of paths, irrigation channels, water wheels, storage huts and palm-thatched shelters, and the scouts picked their way through them till they were beside the town wall. Using an old palm trunk as a ladder they were soon inside the dark and sleeping streets, and no watchman saw them.

Abdul Aziz's objective was the Mismak fortress, the stronghold of the Rasheed garrison in the middle of the town. Today it is still standing, and by night its thick mud walls slope up into the darkness from thickets of glowing Sanyo and National Panasonic signs, the neon heraldry of Riyadh's transistor radio and quartz watch souq.

In January 1902 the Mismak stood proud in its own square of beaten mud, a cleared area into which the fortress's garrison could direct fire from the walls. Around this square stood Riyadh's brown-walled mud mansions, and Abdul Aziz was heading for one of these, directly opposite the fort's main gates, for he had been told it was the residence of the Rasheed governor, Ajlan.

Near by was the home of a farmer known to be loyal to the Al Sa'ud, and it was on his door that Abdul Aziz knocked first, some time around midnight. A woman answered, but she would not open up.

'I am from the governor,' said Abdul Aziz, and spun a story about buying livestock on the governor's behalf.

The woman was not convinced. It was no hour for a stranger to come knocking on the door of a house where women were present.

So Abdul Aziz blustered with his borrowed authority. If she did not let him in, he said, the governor would get to hear of it and her master would suffer.

The woman went away, and after a while a man opened the door gingerly. Abdul Aziz and his companions were ready. They rushed inside. The man was indeed an old friend of the Al Sa'ud.

Now Abdul Aziz heard how the land lay. The Rasheed governor, Ajlan, a sheikh of Jabal Shammar, had a house just two doors away, facing the main gates of the fortress. But only his wife slept there. Ajlan himself usually spent the night inside the fortress walls for safety's sake, only emerging about half an hour after sunrise, when he would cross the square to take breakfast with his wife, or perhaps go riding on one of the horses that grooms would line up and tether for him at dawn. He was always attended by several guards, and there was a strong garrison of Rasheed soldiers inside the castle, with sentries on the gates. But there were no sentries on Ajlan's house.

Abdul Aziz and his companions crept up on to the flat roof and over into the house immediately next door. They found a man and his wife sleeping there, gagged them with their blankets, tied them up and moved on. Ajlan's house was a storey taller than its neighbour, and the intruders had to climb on each other's shoulders to reach the roof. Inside they found two figures lying side by side in the main bedroom. Had they stumbled by good fortune on Ajlan, risking a night outside the fortress walls? Abdul Aziz and Abdullah bin Jaluwi stole across the bedroom, weapons at the ready.

This was another of the climaxes to which Abdul Aziz built up with zest in later years, miming his stealthy progress across the room with a cartridge in his rifle, while his cousin crept beside him, shielding a lighted candle with one hand.

But it was a false climax, for though one of the sleepers was indeed Ajlan's wife, a Riyadh girl he had married, the other figure was her sister. Abdul Aziz and bin Jaluwi tied and gagged the two women, and then broke an opening through the mud wall into the house from which they had come. They needed a route by which Muhammad and his back-up force could get inside the governor's house without attracting attention, and one of the scouts was sent back to the palm groves to bring the reinforcements along.

Soon all forty men were gathered together looking out through the

49

wood lattice windows across the square at the fortress they must storm when the sun rose. There were several long hours to wait until dawn.

They killed the time in the best desert tradition, sipping coffee, reciting the Koran and dozing. Before sunrise, at that prescribed moment when a black thread can be distinguished from a white thread laid beside it on the back of your hand, they washed and lined up to say the morning prayer, facing away from the fortress in the direction of Mecca, and Abdul Aziz led his companions through their kneelings, prostrations and soft murmurings to Allah.

They heard the sound of the horses being brought out and tethered for Ajlan's morning ride, and they looked across the square for the governor to appear.

Today any passer-by can go and stand in the very gateway of the Mismak fortress on which Abdul Aziz and his companions looked out as their great adventure reached its climax. You can touch it and prod it unhindered, for there are no curators or turnstiles – little sign of any special attention at all, in fact, except for one bare neon tube tacked crookedly in the mud wall above its lintel.

Little boys lean their bicycles against the Mismak's dusty nail-studded door, unprettied by 'restoration' in the last three-quarters of a century, and in the centre of the door is set a little gate-within-a-gate, barely 2 feet wide and 3 feet high. In Western medieval castles it would be called a postern, a small door allowing the passage of a few people, one at a time, without the need to swing back the main gate.

But here in Riyadh it is more a hatchway than a door, for it is cut into the wood of the main gate a full 3 feet above the ground, and you can clamber through it only with the greatest difficulty – which is the intention, since it is so designed that you have to insert a single leg or arm or head over the waist-high sill, at the mercy of any guard standing inside with his sword.

It is not an aperture one can pass through with any ease or dignity – which was why, when Ajlan, Governor of Riyadh, eventually emerged for his breakfast and morning exercise in January 1902, the main gate itself was opened for him, and then closed again behind him. He strode across the square in the sunshine heading for his wife and horses.

Accounts differ as to what precise plans Abdul Aziz had laid in advance against this moment. There is a tale that he had dressed the smallest of his party in the clothes of the serving-woman who usually opened the door to the governor, intending to trick Ajlan inside and then murder him. That would have been neat. Another narrator insists that Abdul Aziz stationed men in the upper room to give covering fire while he duelled with Ajlan in front of the house, while a third version suggests no set plan at all, asserting that Abdul Aziz, tense and over-anxious, panicked and rushed out at Ajlan before the moment was ripe.

But one of the Sa'udis who actually took part in the skirmish later described Abdul Aziz as being totally composed in the moments before the confrontation. 'How cool and calm he was!' he told Harold Dickson. 'He had discarded his *aghal* [his double headcord] and tied his *kaffiyah* [his cloth headdress] over his head and around his neck, and had followed it by carefully tying the long sleeves of his *dishdasha* [his full-length shirt or smock] round the back of his neck.'

Thus stripped down for battle, Abdul Aziz rushed out into the open towards Ajlan and the fortress with an enormous shout, and he took the governor completely by surprise. Ajlan had only a few guards with him. But he was still relatively close to the fortress gate, and as Abdul Aziz's men streamed out into the square with their weapons the Rasheed guards turned to take refuge through the postern opening. One by one they dived through the hatchway, and from the walls the sentries began to fire down upon the mêlée.

Abdul Aziz grappled with Ajlan. The governor was retreating, so that Abdul Aziz had to bring him down from behind with a flying tackle, and the adversaries slugged it out, face to face, Abdul Aziz parrying the blows of Ajlan's sword with his rifle butt. Hafiz Wahba asserts that the governor turned and might have got clean away, had he not been winged by a shot from Abdul Aziz's rifle – in the arm, says Wahba, in the leg, says one of Abdul Aziz's sons.

All agree that Abdullah bin Jaluwi's role was crucial, for he killed one of the Rasheed guards who was about to strike down Abdul Aziz. Then bin Jaluwi turned to Ajlan, narrowly missing him with a ferocious javelin thrust, and he buried his weapon so deep in the woodwork beside the postern door that it could not subsequently be removed without breaking off the spearhead and leaving it embedded there.

By this time a tug-of-war was going on through the narrow opening. The Rasheed garrison had Ajlan's head and shoulders inside the fort, while the Sa'udis on the outside were tugging desperately upon his flailing legs. Suddenly Ajlan, struggling furiously, managed to direct a heavy kick into Abdul Aziz's groin, and the Sa'udi leader went down, badly winded. He released his grip on Ajlan's feet, and the governor was dragged inside. If Abdullah bin Jaluwi had not flung himself heedlessly through the opening at this moment after Ajlan, all might have been lost.

Did bin Jaluwi now catch Ajlan again 'by the leg . . . just inside the gate' and kill him, thus bringing about the surrender of the garrison? Did he 'cut him down' (Armstrong) or 'shoot him' (al Zirikly), 'running up the steps of the mosque' (van der Meulen), or inside the mosque doorway after Ajlan had taken refuge there and had been dragged outside again (Ahmad bin Abdul Aziz)?

Or was it, perhaps, Abdul Aziz himself who managed, somehow, somewhere, 'to draw his dagger and kill the Governor' as the British minister, Reader Bullard, believed after hearing the tale from the great man's own lips in 1937?

Abdul Aziz himself usually gave the credit to his cousin, but it hardly mattered, for the result was the same. The Rasheed garrison laid down their arms. Riyadh belonged to Abdul Aziz, and at noon that day several thousand citizens gathered to swear their *bay'ah* of allegiance to the young hero and to pray behind him in ranks in the main mosque. The Al Sa'ud were masters in their own home again – and they have remained the masters ever since.

Riyadh today, consumed by its love affair with pre-cast concrete and by the orgies of demolition that accompany it, shows little awareness of the scuffle that determined its twentieth-century destiny. No signposts point you to the Mismak fort.

Yet, if you fumble in the fortress woodwork just to the right of that door-within-a-door where history was made, your finger will stop on the rough edge of some metal buried deep inside the timber. It is embedded so far that it has defied eight decades of local indifference and one decade of foreign souvenir hunters, and you cannot see the pointed end to which it tapers.

But just by touching this fragment of grey and twisted metal you can gauge something of the force behind the spear which Abdullah bin Jaluwi flung one morning in January 1902 – and venture with your fingertip some small communion with that ragged scrimmage in the fortress gate less than eighty years ago.

Part Two

The House of Sa'ud

4 No god but God

Lost and Found
Call Housekeeper, extension 5.
Luggage Check Room
Contact the Concierge, extension 2.
Manner of Dressing
Islamic customs require that women wear long loose dresses with long sleeves and that they cover their hair with a scarf. Men are not to wear tight trousers, open shirts or chains.
Messages
Dial either no. 1 or 3 when red light is lit on your phone.

From the *Guest A–Z Directory*, Intercontinental Hotel, Riyadh, May 1981

THE little mud-walled settlement that Abdul Aziz recaptured for his family in January 1902 was remote from the twentieth century in almost every sense. Western map-makers could not even put a latitude and longitude on the place; Riyadh was a dot placed capriciously somewhere in the central wilderness. In 1865 one Englishman had ventured across the 250 miles of desert that separated the town from the Persian Gulf. But Lieutenant-Colonel Lewis Pelly was only the fifth European known to have visited Riyadh in the entire course of its recorded history, and the next Westerner did not arrive until 1912.

In 1902 the Arabian peninsula was a patchwork of rival sheikhdoms and sultanates, and the area surrounding Riyadh was known as Nejd. Nejd had never been especially wealthy, but it did have a character all its own. The men of Nejd were Muslims, and they pursued an austere and purist version of Islam whose most obvious characteristic to outsiders was the denial of worldly pleasure. When Lewis Pelly arrived in the palm groves around the Sa'udi capital in 1865 he was requested to conduct his smoking activities *outside* the town walls, since tobacco was strictly banned within them.

Smoking was only one of several indulgences which Riyadh's inhabitants frowned upon. 'Dour men, lean in body and outlook,' wrote a traveller some years later, '. . . they refused all the pleasant things: wine, fine food, tobacco, soft clothes' – even minarets on their mosques or prayer mats to kneel on. The men of Nejd interpreted the

55

Koran puritanically and literally. Isolated in the central deserts, this little community of the godly were the Plymouth Brethren of Islam.

The world called them Wahhabis,* after the teacher and reformer Muhammad ibn Abdul Wahhab, the Luther, Calvin and Brigham Young of Islam in Arabia, who had formulated their austere interpretation of the Koran in the middle of the eighteenth century; and one of the first stories told to every young inhabitant of the Kingdom today is the tale of Ibn Abdul Wahhab and of how the bleak simplicities of his creed came to be linked so closely with their destiny.

The Tale of the Teacher

Muhammad ibn Abdul Wahhab was born in 1703, and he chose to dedicate his life to God, studying the Koran and interpreting its words in the strictest and most literal way he could.

By 1740 the Teacher was ministering in Nejd and organizing purges of the idolatrous objects that stood between man and the true God. Working as a *qadi*, a judge, he used his position to have holy shrines demolished and to destroy the tombs to which pilgrimages were made, for in the years before his coming the Muslims of Arabia had fallen prey to superstitions. They revered fertility trees and even monuments raised to the dead.

'Mud cannot save you,' taught Ibn Abdul Wahhab. 'Pray to God and God alone.'

The Teacher interpreted the law in all its strictness – the law of God, the Shariah, which had been dictated by God to the Prophet Muhammad at the beginning of Islam but was now being practised only laxly – and when the Teacher came upon a woman guilty of adultery, he organized her punishment in the fashion prescribed in the Shariah. He had her stoned to death.†

---

* The Wahhabis have always disliked the name customarily given to them. They have preferred to be known as 'Unitarians' (*Muwahhidun*), for to call themselves Wahhabi would be to fall into one of the great errors they have always condemned – the glorification of men, saints or prophets so as to dilute contemplation and worship of the one supreme God. But 'Unitarian' has, of course, Christian connotations to outsiders, while other suggested titles like 'the Religion of Unity' (*Din al Tawhid*) have failed to stick. So, like it or not, the Wahhabis have, along with the Quakers, remained known by the name first assigned to them by their detractors.

† To establish adultery, the Shariah requires a minimum of four witnesses to the act of intercourse itself, or a thrice-repeated confession, and it is usually said that the woman put to death by Ibn Abdul Wahhab confessed her guilt of her own free will.

Many men resented the changes wrought by Ibn Abdul Wahhab, and with this stoning those who sheltered him would no longer have him as their *qadi*. So it was fortunate for the holy man that his message had been heard by Muhammad ibn Sa'ud, the ruler of Dar'iyah, which stands among the palm trees in the Wadi Hanifah a few miles north of Riyadh (Riyadh was not then ruled by the Al Sa'ud).

'Welcome to a country that is better than your own country,' said Muhammad ibn Sa'ud; and the Teacher became the *qadi* of Dar'iyah.

Thus was forged, around the year 1744, the great alliance between the house of Sa'ud and the faith of Muhammad ibn Abdul Wahhab. The Teacher reformed Dar'iyah: smoking, dancing and music were banned lest they might detract from contemplation of the true God. Shrines and luxury were all swept away.

But the Wahhabi call demanded more than just reform. The Teacher preached conversion too. It was the duty of the good Muslim to put his own life in order, then to purify those around him – and, if his fellow Muslims would not respond to friendly persuasion, then stronger methods were called for. The ruler must proclaim jihad – holy war.

The Al Sa'ud started moving outwards soon after the coming of Muhammad ibn Abdul Wahhab. They attacked the nearby town of Riyadh, then rode out into Nejd to subdue Arabia's heartland. They conquered to the very shores of the Persian Gulf.

It was not done easily. It took many years. The first Ibn Sa'ud passed away, and so did Muhammad ibn Abdul Wahhab. But their sons continued in Nejd the partnership that their fathers had forged. Inspired by Wahhabi teachings and under the leadership of the house of Sa'ud, the armies of Nejd were ferocious – indifferent to death and fired only by the wish to do God's will.

In 1802 they turned west towards the Holy Cities of Islam. Taif on the edge of the escarpment above Mecca resisted, and it suffered a ghastly fate. Every male inhabitant who could not escape was massacred.

Mecca opened its gates in terror to the Wahhabis. So did Medina. The men of Nejd smashed every shrine and image, and, when the pilgrim caravans arrived from Egypt and Syria, the Wahhabis turned these pilgrims away as idolaters.

The Holy Cities were cleansed, and for the first time since Islam's early days most of Arabia was united under a single authority. By the

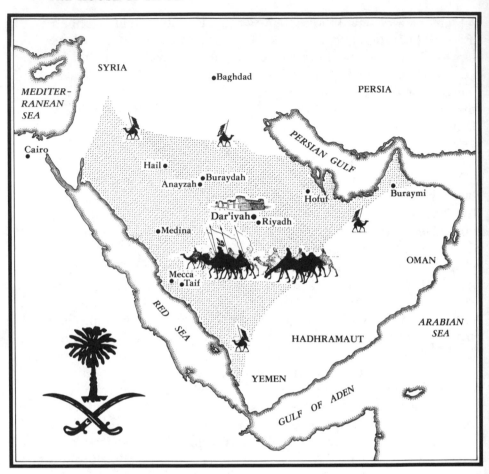

The first Sa'udi empire, *c.* 1804

beginning of the nineteenth century the house of Sa'ud controlled from Nejd an empire that covered nearly one million square miles – and they had done it all in the name of God as revealed to them through the teachings of Muhammad ibn Abdul Wahhab.

In 1981 you can detect the influence of the Teacher even before you set foot in the Kingdom. As you fasten your seat-belt and switch to Channel 1 on the headsets in your Saudia Tri-Star, it is the chanting of the Koran which speeds you on your way. No alcohol is served on the plane. You eat your flight-tray lunch – which will not include ham or pork – with apple juice or Mecca water. And when you arrive in the

58

Kingdom, you will have to open all your trunks and suitcases to be fumbled through by diligent searchers after alcohol, bacon or 'indecent material' – which comprises virtually every 'adult' publication sold in the bookstalls at the airport of your departure.

Christians are prohibited from holding religious services in Sa'udi Arabia (foreign embassies and companies organize discreet weekly 'lectures' for their nationals); supermarkets that have tried to import Christmas trees have had their consignments burned as infidel totems; in August 1979 the sale of even non-alcoholic 'beers', 'wines' and 'champagnes' was banned in the Kingdom lest people might *imagine* the taste and effect of alcohol while they were sipping the innocuous beverages – and all these, and many more, manifestations of the Wahhabi spirit in the age of the computer and of the silicon chip are maintained by 'Committees for the Propagation of Virtue and the Prevention of Vice' whose bearded representatives patrol the streets with canes. As twilight descends over Riyadh and the robed old men shuffle round the dusty alleys of the souq, beating on the windows and calling out *'Salaat!'* ('Prayer!'), the shutters come rattling down and you may well wonder just what century you are living in.

Abdul Aziz's Western friend Harry St John Philby used to describe Muhammad ibn Abdul Wahhab as the 'co-founder' of Sa'udi Arabia. Until his coming the Al Sa'ud had been a minor sheikhly clan like many others in Nejd, townsmen and farmers, making a comfortable living from trade, dates and perhaps a little horse-breeding, combining with the desert tribes to raid outwards when they felt strong, prudently retrenching in times of weakness. Modestly independent, they were in no way empire builders, and it is not likely that the wider world would ever have heard of them without their alliance with the Teacher.

But Muhammad ibn Abdul Wahhab switched the house of Sa'ud in a new direction, and the family name reflected this. Chroniclers have traced the clan's origins back to AD 1446, when a father and son, thought to be descended from the Anazah tribe, came out of the desert to farm lands around the settlement of Dar'iyah. Ten generations later a descendant whose first name was Sa'ud produced the son, Muhammad, who offered refuge to Ibn Abdul Wahhab in 1744.

We know little of this Sa'ud. We are not even certain of the name by which he and his forebears chose to be known. But Sa'ud's son Muhammad, who established the family's partnership with Wahhabism, was known as Ibn Sa'ud, 'Son of Sa'ud' – so this became the family name of his descendants ever afterwards, since it was in the reign of the son of Sa'ud that the family began to count for something.*

Abdul Aziz's recapture of Riyadh in January 1902 was inspired by the memory of his family's proud achievements as bearers of the Wahhabi banner. With the seizure of Mecca and Medina a century earlier, the Al Sa'ud had become lords of the largest Arabian polity to be created since the heyday of Islam. In 1804 they took tribute from more territory – and more people – than the fledging United States of America could lay claim to at that time. From Nejd the Sa'udi writ ran from the Red Sea to the Persian Gulf, from Yemen to the deserts of Syria, and the family felt strong enough to defy the sultan-caliph in Constantinople, turning away the pilgrims who came to the Holy Places under his safe-conduct and authority.

But Sa'udi power at its height lasted little more than a dozen years, for the Tale of the Teacher had an unhappy sequel.

The Tale of the Apple and the Carpet

When the sultan-caliph in Constantinople heard that Mecca and Medina had been sacked by the men of Nejd and that they had turned away the pilgrims, he was much displeased. He claimed to be the guardian of the Holy Places. So he commanded Muhammad Ali, his viceroy in Egypt, to punish them for their arrogance, and in 1813 Muhammad Ali sent armies down the Red Sea. They recaptured Mecca and Medina, but whenever they attempted to march inland towards the central deserts they were defeated, until Muhammad Ali despaired of ever capturing Nejd or of punishing the house of Sa'ud.

One day he was sitting in his palace in Cairo when he took an apple and placed it in the middle of a large carpet. All his generals were sitting around, boasting that, if only he would entrust the care of his armies to them, then they would conquer Nejd without difficulty.

'It is not that easy,' replied Muhammad Ali. 'The task of conquering Nejd resembles this apple in the middle of that carpet, for it is a

---

* Arab names are very flexible in this respect. Out of the house of Sa'ud have sprung two other families, the al Thunayans and the bin Jaluwis, each of whom has fixed on the first name of a distinguished Sa'udi prince – Thunayan in one case, Jaluwi in the other – and has chosen to be known especially as their descendants. In the last few years, the sons of the late King Faisal (d. 1975) have come to be known as al Faisal, and the brothers and sons of Crown Prince Fahad are called the al Fahad – though there are no hard-and-fast rules in all this.

large carpet, and only he who can seize the apple without setting foot on the carpet is capable of seizing Nejd.'

So the generals looked at the apple and racked their brains for a way they might pick it up without treading on the carpet. But none could devise a method until Muhammad Ali's second son, Ibrahim Pasha, asked if he might try his hand at the test.

'Certainly,' said his father.

So young Ibrahim walked to one side of the carpet, knelt down and then began to roll up the carpet until he could reach out and seize the apple with ease.

He was the man his father had been looking for. So Ibrahim Pasha was given command of the Turkish armies, and he sailed down the Red Sea to recapture the Holy Cities. Then he headed inland and started to roll up Nejd's carpet – the patchwork of tribes whose loyalties he could seduce with guns and money.

The Otayba joined him. So did the Harb and the Mutair. One by one the tribes deserted the house of Sa'ud, for the bedouin are fickle friends. Ibrahim Pasha moved slowly, and he moved steadily, and after months of bribery and conquest his army stood before the walls of Dar'iyah.

But though Ibrahim Pasha had rolled up the carpet of Nejd, he now found it difficult to seize the apple. He had brought guns, howitzers and a French engineer to attack the mud walls. But the inhabitants resisted bravely. The fighting grew bitter. The Turks cut down all the palm trees in the wadi – thirty years' livelihood. If Ibrahim Pasha captured any Nejdi, he had the captive's head cut off to be sent to Cairo, and, when the basketloads of heads grew too heavy, ears were dispatched instead. Muhammad Ali paid 5 thalers for each pair that he received. They were cruel and bloody days.

Finally, after six months of slaughter, the chief of the Al Sa'ud, Abdullah, decided to spare his people more suffering. He surrendered to Ibrahim Pasha and was sent in chains to Cairo. There Muhammad Ali sent him on to the sultan-caliph, and in Constantinople the Turkish imams and sheikhs sought to persuade him out of his beliefs. But Abdullah ibn Sa'ud stood firm by his own principles, and when the Turks saw this they had him executed. His head was cut off and crushed in a mortar, and his body was hung up for all to see, the death warrant impaled by a dagger that pierced through his heart.

Nor was he alone in his martyrdom. Back in Nejd, Ibrahim Pasha devised the devilish torture of playing music to one especially pious elder, a grandson of Ibn Abdul Wahhab, before sending him to the cemetery to be shot. He pulled out all the teeth of another condemned sheikh.* He murdered without compassion, and he gave orders that Dar'iyah was to be destroyed. Every door, stick and beam of the town must be burnt, every remaining palm tree cut down.

So the soldiers of Ibrahim Pasha made sure his orders were obeyed, his gunners bombarded the walls once again for good measure, and then the Turks marched back to Egypt.

The modern visitor to Dar'iyah cannot help but be awed by the efficiency of Ibrahim Pasha's 1819 razzia, for the shattered walls and gutted homes of the original Sa'udi capital remain today almost as the Turks left them a century and a half ago.

The palm trees grew again after Ibrahim Pasha had departed, but their leaves shade a ghost town. There is the palace where the Al Sa'ud entertained in their glory 400 or 500 bedouin every day. Near by is the stud where, it is said, 300 of Arabia's finest horses were stabled. There are mosques, shops, watchtowers, homes, the busy structure of an entire metropolis, all open to the sky and eerily vacated like a sand-blown Pompeii.

For the first time in recorded history the heartland of Arabia had been invaded and conquered by a foreign army, and the howitzers of Ibrahim Pasha taught a harsh lesson to the house of Sa'ud: what happened to a primitive society that provoked the wrath of a superior technology.

The Al Sa'ud never attempted to rebuild Dar'iyah. As they patched and pieced their power in Nejd after the Turks' departure, they left the shell of their old capital behind them, an enduring reminder of the frontiers of the possible. They moved the dozen miles down the Wadi Hanifah to Riyadh, and it was from Riyadh that they built up through the nineteenth century a second Sa'udi state, more modest than the first – only to lose that in 1891 to the Rasheed dynasty when it came marching down from Hail.

---

* The style or title of 'sheikh' is an acknowledgement of respect with many connotations. It applies traditionally to the leader of a tribe, but today employees in Sa'udi Arabia will use the term of their boss, and any public figure can earn the title, which is not hereditary. The title is also accorded to leaders of the religious community – and this is the sense in which it is used here. The word is well translated as 'elder', since the primary meaning of the Arabic root is 'age'.

The rooftops of old Riyadh

Left The postern door of the
Mismak fortress in Riyadh. The
guard points to bin Jaluwi's
imbedded spearhead (below)

Right Riyadh market place,
photographed in 1935

Below Muhammad, brother of
Abdul Aziz

Bottom The palace of the Al Sa'ud
in Riyadh, in the late thirties,
showing the covered bridge to the
mosque

Top right Abdullah ibn Sa'ud before his execution
by the Turks after the fall of Dar'iyah, 1818

Above Abdullah bin Jaluwi with his attendants

Left Sa'ad, brother of Abdul Aziz

Abdul Aziz ibn Rasheed, killed by Sa'udi
forces at Rawdhat al Muhanna in 1906

Sa'ud al Kabeer in old age

British officers being carried ashore at Kuwait,
November 1903

Abdul Aziz's recapture of Riyadh marked the beginning of a third attempt at Sa'udi empire building, and he started out by getting married. His new wife was Tarfah, the daughter of Sheikh Abdullah ibn Abdul Lateef, *qadi* of the town. This Sheikh Abdullah was chief among Riyadh's religious leaders, the *ulema*, those with the knowledge of God's word – and he was also a direct blood descendant of Muhammad ibn Abdul Wahhab.*

* The descendants of Muhammad ibn Abdul Wahhab became known after his death as 'Al alSheikh' – 'of the family of the Sheikh' – and they preserve their separate identity in the Kingdom to this day. They remain one of the four families with whom the Al Sa'ud intermarry; they are prominent in the *ulema*; they are second only to the Al Sa'ud in the Council of Ministers (the ministries of Higher Education, Justice and Agriculture were all headed by members of the Al alSheikh in June 1981); and they also hold important commands in the police and armed forces.

5 Fusillade

THE Cadillacs shine darkly in the courtyard, reflecting the moonlight that filters through the leaves of the fan palms. It is a still, warm night, and as the limousines roll to a halt beside the palace steps their tyres squeak softly on the marble. The cars' occupants adjust their headdresses as they get out, kick off their sandals as they reach the doorway, and then stride barefoot across the rugs inside. It is almost any night in modern Riyadh, and a group of princes of the house of Sa'ud are gathering for dinner.

The food is being stewed in huge meat kettles, cauldrons which each hold one whole sheep, and the mingled scents of boiled fat and woodsmoke waft across the courtyard. Inside the *majlis* the guests sip their coffee, and when a new guest arrives they leap to their feet to embrace him, hugging him gently, kissing him on the forehead and, sometimes, rubbing noses with him slowly, smilingly, eyes open.'

When the food is ready they leave the *majlis* to squat down cross-legged on the floor around the huge dishes, a full 4 feet across, which it takes two men to carry in, staggering a little. A crater of white rice fortifies the rim a foot thick, and rising inside is a pyramid of steaming limbs, ribs, haunches, crowned by the boiled heads of the sheep, their tongues curling between glistening white teeth and bared gums.

The host seizes on the hard pink crescents, yanking them from their gaping jaws to present them to his honoured guests; and over the meat mountain a servant pours more delicacies – liver, kidneys, salted little knots of yellowed intestine for chewing like gum, and the thick white tail-pad of fat that is the sign of a well-fed sheep.

These morsels tumble around the pyramid in an avalanche of grease and juice and melted butter, and as the glossy liquids form a moat that starts to seep out over the rice ramparts, it is time to start eating. Sleeves are rolled back and fingers get to work as a dozen men nudge in a circle round the tray. The technique is to mould and knead your rice into a small soggy ball which you flip into your mouth, packing it with strips that you pull off the carcass, or pieces of liver and kidney that your host may present to you, for it is his duty to make sure that his guests are content.

He fusses round the circle, wielding his knife to hack off titbits that may entice the less voracious. But after a while even the heartiest appetite flags, and, as the first eaters withdraw, they are replaced at the breach by a second wave of attackers, the household retainers, who tuck in heartily before the tray is borne away.

Now the men sit back replete, washing their fingers in the bowls of water that the servants bring and holding out their hands for the perfume that is sprinkled round. There is another cup of tea, then coffee, some jokes, some stories, much conversation – and then a boy appears, walking round the *majlis* with a small silver brazier. The incense blows out in clouds which the princes sniff and fan into their beards, and then they leave, for the arrival of the incense is the signal to rise and to be gone.

Abdul Aziz gave many feasts in the weeks after he took Riyadh in January 1902. To squat round a carcass tearing off strips of mutton is the time-honoured Nejdi mechanism to fête friends, heal feuds and celebrate great events, and Abdul Aziz had much to settle.

Riyadh belonged to the Al Sa'ud, but it did not, in these first weeks of conquest, belong to Abdul Aziz. Its capture was generally seen as an exploit he had carried out on behalf of his father, Abdul Rahman. It was now assumed that the plump fifty-year-old head of the family would return from Kuwait to resume the authority that the Rasheeds had appropriated twelve years earlier, and outside Riyadh the clan chieftain's title of Ibn Sa'ud continued to refer to Abdul Rahman. Abdul Aziz, only twenty-six, was viewed simply as his father's chief of staff.

Yet the inner workings of the Al Sa'ud have never been precisely what they appear to the outside world. By some inner family osmosis, authority flows, and is usually allowed to flow, to him who is most capable of exercising it at any one time. The family tree shows rulers dotted all over the different lines of descent drawn by Western genealogists, for there is no single bloodline which preordains, Debrett-style, who succeeds whom – nor any protocol which determines even that the family head at any given moment is necessarily the man who is in full charge of affairs: in 1981 King Khalid is the ruler of Sa'udi Arabia; but his younger brother Fahad, the crown prince, effectively supervises the day-to-day running of the Kingdom; while senior to both men is their elder brother Muhammad, who renounced the succession and has lived largely out of public view since 1964.

It makes perfect sense if you look at Sa'udi Arabia as a tribal hierarchy and not as a monarchy in the Western sense, for the tribal tradition is that the fittest should rule. It is the way bedouin clans and the Nejdi merchant classes have learnt to survive: the elders retain the ultimate vested family sovereignty, but running the family business from day to day has to be delegated to the best man for the job.

So when, in the summer of 1902, Abdul Rahman arrived in Riyadh from Kuwait with his wives and younger children, and his victorious son dutifully handed the town over to him, the father refused the offer firmly.

'You captured it,' he said. 'You keep it.'

The father passed to his son an ancient engraved sword – the symbol of the day-to-day rule and command of the family forces that he was now handing over to him. From that day forward Abdul Aziz was Emir of Riyadh.

But Abdul Rahman remained the ultimate head of the family. When Daan van der Meulen, Dutch Consul in Jeddah, witnessed Abdul Aziz welcome his father to the newly captured town in 1926, he was amazed to see the conqueror of Arabia bow down and kneel publicly in the dust beside Abdul Rahman's horse. Then the old man eased himself out of the stirrups and stepped down on to his son's shoulder in order to reach the ground.

Abdul Aziz quickly earned respect in Riyadh as his rule grew established in 1902. Merchants lent him money. Promissory notes survive from an early date, and the ordinary people turned out to repair the town walls so efficiently that when, a year later, the testing time came, the fortifications were high and breachless.

The *ulema* took longer to convince. The religious sheikhs scarcely knew Abdul Aziz when he arrived in January 1902. He had left Riyadh just a boy, and they were mistrustful of his upbringing amid the fleshpots of Kuwait. They refused at first to accept the family's delegation of power to him, and, at a formal gathering of the religious elders in the Grand Mosque of Riyadh, Adbul Rahman had to argue on his son's behalf. The sheikhs would only accept Abdul Aziz's *de facto* authority provided that Abdul Rahman retained the title 'imam',* head of the Muslim community, and the new young ruler had to work hard to prove his piety. To emphasize his commitment to the historic alliance between the Al Sa'ud and Wahhabism he gave full authority for law and morality in the town to the *ulema*, he received the chief *qadi*, Sheikh Abdullah ibn Abdul Lateef, every day in his *majlis* – and he married the *qadi*'s daughter, Tarfah.

Abdul Aziz was already a family man. He was known as 'Abu Turki', 'father of Turki', after the little boy that had been born to him some time in 1900. Turki's mother was of the Uray'ir clan, chiefs of the Beni Khalid who raided with Abdul Aziz in the eastern Arabian campaigns he fought to keep Ibn Rasheed out of Kuwait, and she had borne him a second son while he was away conquering Riyadh. Abdul Aziz decided Turki's brother must have come into the world on the very day that Riyadh became his – 5 Shawwal 1319 AH, 16 January AD 1902 – and he called the child Sa'ud.

Abdul Aziz loved little children. After his siesta and the afternoon prayer, he liked to ride out to the desert or down into the shade of the Wadi Hanifah's palm trees, and he would clap one of his little boys up into the saddle in front of him, running the heavy reins through the baby's fingers and cantering to and fro. His sons still remember it – the rhythm of the horse and the chuckling of the belly against which they were clamped by a sunburnt hand.

Abdul Aziz installed his new wife Tarfah in his mud palace beside the grand mosque, and within a year or so she bore him a third son, a frail little fellow with large staring eyes whom his father called Faisal, 'the Sword'.

'Abu Turki' had little time for domestic pleasures in 1902. He had to prepare for battle.

Half a century earlier the house of Rasheed had been an ally of the Al Sa'ud, for in the years after 1819, when Abdul Aziz's grandfather and great-grandfather were attempting to retrieve Sa'udi power from the nemesis of Dar'iyah, the two clans had worked in partnership – the Al Sa'ud based in Riyadh, the Rasheeds centred upon Hail.

---

* 'Imam' means literally 'he who goes in front' of his fellow Muslims to lead them in prayer. Thus the men who lead prayers in Sa'udi mosques today are called imams, though the practice of calling the head of the whole Sa'udi commonwealth 'imam' has faded out.

But around the time of Abdul Aziz's birth Sa'udi authority in Nejd was weakened by family quarrels, and the Rasheeds had taken advantage of this to occupy Riyadh. Abdul Aziz's father Abdul Rahman had organized a rebellion, his allies had been defeated in January 1891, and it was to flee Rasheed retaliation that Abdul Rahman had taken his family to shelter in the Murrah's black hair tents.

Now in 1902 the new young leader of the Al Sa'ud had to brace himself for the onslaught that would be led by the redoubtable and warlike leader of Hail, another Abdul Aziz, usually known by his clan chieftain's title, Ibn Rasheed – and the onslaught, fortunately, took its time a-coming.

'The rabbit is in the hole,' laughed Ibn Rasheed when he heard of the impudent Sa'udi capture of Riyadh, 'and the caravan is waiting round it.'

Ibn Rasheed felt confident he could pick off the Al Sa'ud at his leisure, so he let the cool months pass, and then the hot months, and with every month's delay the new regime in Riyadh grew stronger. The ruler of Hail granted his young Sa'udi adversary more than ten months' grace, and Abdul Aziz put the time to good use.

Friends and relatives had rallied to him from the start, for the return of the Al Sa'ud meant more power and importance for almost everyone in Nejd. The Rasheeds were not harsh or tyrannical rulers, but they ruled Riyadh and its neighbouring settlements for the benefit of Hail several hundred miles away. Many prominent Nejd families had longstanding links with the Al Sa'ud, and foremost among these were the Sudairis, a clan of warriors from the north of Riyadh.

Abdul Aziz's mother was a Sudairi. Sara, the daughter of Ahmad Sudairi, was a tall, big-boned woman with the frame of all her clan, and she is usually credited as the source of her son's massive stature. At six foot four, Abdul Aziz towered literally a head taller than most of his contemporaries. His younger brother Sa'ad, Sara's last child, was not so tall, but he had the aggression and ambition which distinguish the Sudairis to this day and which were to make this family a principal ally of the Al Sa'ud in the building of the Kingdom.

Sa'ad returned from Kuwait with Abdul Rahman in May 1902 and he joined the Round Table of young campaigners fighting to build a new Sa'udi empire – Muhammad ibn Abdul Rahman and the bin Jaluwi cousins, headed by Abdullah. They made up an impressive group – committed, determined, most of them already seasoned in battle – as they rode out of Riyadh to the neighbouring settlements on whose support the reborn Sa'udi dynasty must depend. They sat on the *majlis* cushions around Abdul Aziz while he drank coffee. When prayer time came they washed and prayed with their hosts. They would feast in the evening, sleep beneath their camel blankets and then, next morning, saddle up to ride on to the next encampment or village.

It was grassroots politics, Arabian style. At each settlement, at each group of tents, Abdul Aziz would smile and talk and gesticulate, shaking hands, canvassing support for the challenge ahead. Men were curious to meet the hero of the already legendary capture of Riyadh – and Abdul Aziz had one special asset to offer. He had used the money he had borrowed from Riyadh's merchants to buy large stocks of ammunition and to recruit a band of marksmen from Kuwait.

Ibn Rasheed bypassed Riyadh as he moved south in November 1902. The town with its newly repaired walls would require a major siege to reduce it. In any case Abdul Aziz was not there. He was rallying his forces in the south round al Kharj, al Dilam and al Hawtah. These were all major settlements to the south of Riyadh, prosperous mud-walled towns with their own date gardens, farms and wells. They had little in common with the North Arabians based in Hail. So as Ibn Rasheed pursued Abdul Aziz southwards, he found himself in increasingly hostile territory.

The confrontation came outside the mud-walled farms and wells of al Dilam, then the principal settlement of the al Kharj area, where Abdul Aziz had stationed his men in the dusty palm groves around the town. They lay behind their camel saddles, their rifles trained on the open ground.

As Ibn Rasheed's forces advanced unsuspecting towards the settlement – bedouin armies did not expect to find their adversaries in fixed positions – Abdul Aziz ordered his men to lie silent. Not until the enemy were almost upon them did the Sa'udi and Kuwaiti riflemen open fire, and then it was with a devastasting fusillade that turned the Rasheed forces right round. They retreated to attack the palm grove with more strategy. But every onslaught in the course of a long and hard day's fighting was checked by a barrage of rifle fire. Darkness fell.

When the sun rose next morning the enemy could be seen packing up their blankets and withdrawing. Abdul Aziz had met the Rasheed army in face-to-face confrontation, and the Rasheeds had retreated.

69

The capture of Riyadh had not been a fluke, and the news of the Sa'udi victory was soon broadcast round the desert.

But Abdul Aziz kept the price of his victory to himself. His day of non-stop rifle fire had cost him all the stocks of ammunition for which he had borrowed so heavily. As he used to admit when later discussing his decisive first encounter, he could not possibly have kept the fire-storm blazing for another day. It was not for another ten years that the Sa'udi army could afford to fight by fusillade.

Abdul Aziz was as poor as a mosque mouse. His treasury was literally the gold he carried in his camel-bags – his Kuwaiti riflemen were probably paid no more than one small piece each – and the territory he was conquering did not represent a strong economic power base. The palm groves, gardens, flocks and camel herds of central Arabia produced scarcely enough for the inhabitants to survive on – let alone wage a sustained military campaign.

It was subsistence skirmishing: levies of swordsmen sitting atop their largest capital investment, their horse or camel, and highly cautious of risking it except for the best of reasons. Desert 'campaigns' involved long months of shadow boxing by irregular bands who wore no uniforms and rode with none of the formation or discipline that could justify the use of the word 'army' in the Western sense. They would manoeuvre for months out of sight of each other, and would usually hope to stay out of sight until events presented an advantage that could be seized without too great a risk, since neither side possessed the wherewithal for a sustained confrontation.

This was why the British guns and firepower in Kuwait Bay had been such a trump card for Sheikh Mubarak Al Sabah; and it was why Abdul Aziz's novel tactics at al Dilam, actually standing his ground and fighting, perplexed Ibn Rasheed probably as much as it hurt him. A more thoughtful adversary might have calculated the cost of the Sa'udi strategy and waited it out. But Ibn Rasheed was fighting in the way that desert campaigners had always fought, while it was Abdul Aziz's shrewdness to comprehend the Western wealth and technology that were just beginning to break in on Arabia's immemorial way of doing things.

In the months after al Dilam, Rasheed–Sa'udi campaigning reverted to a more traditional form. Abdul Aziz could not afford anything else. Twenty years later, describing the tension of these early months,

70

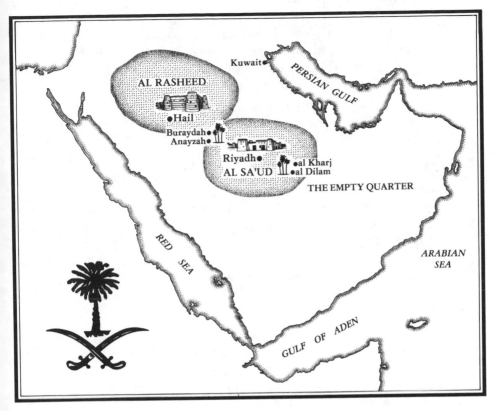

Abdul Aziz's early conquests, 1902–5

he held up his hand and swept it slowly, undulating, across in front of him as he evoked the excitement of a forced march, racing for hour after hour to catch the enemy unawares or just to get to the wells before he did. 'A thousand camels on the march – a brisk, even pace – the murmur and buzz of the motion – the squeak of the saddles – a concrete body, moving, moving like a stream of water down a slope, without a single pause.'

There were no more battles after al Dilam, but Abdul Aziz proved more proficient than Ibn Rasheed at the game of desert manoeuvring, so that, as campaigning petered out in the heat of midsummer 1903, the Al Sa'ud found themselves in control of the principal settled areas to the north of Riyadh. With the allegiance of the towns around al Dilam as well, Abdul Aziz could count on settlements for a hundred miles north and south of his new capital – less than eighteen months after he had conquered it.

71

The following winter he headed north again, aiming for Qaseem, the prosperous no-man's-land between Riyadh and Hail and the traditional skirmishing ground between the Rasheeds and the Al Sa'ud. The ownership of this middle ground was a fair indicator of which of the two dynasties was predominant at any given moment, and the area was dominated by the twin towns of Anayzah and Buraydah, prosperous, fortified trading posts on the great caravan route across Arabia from Kuwait to Medina. Ibn Rasheed had entrusted the two settlements to a couple of his cousins, Majid and Ubayd ibn Hamoud, and these brothers had thoroughly purged the area of Sa'udi sympathizers, chasing them to Kuwait.

Now the exiles returned to fight alongside Abdul Aziz, and the exultant letter that the young general sent to Mubarak of Kuwait in the spring of 1904 tells its own story:

'May God preserve you,' he wrote in Old Testament terms which owe something, but not everything, to the English translation in which the letter survives today in the archives of the India Office in London.

We sent word to Your Highness before this by the hand of your servant Madi that it was our intention to set forth on an expedition. So we proceeded against Majid, and he was in his tents in the region of Hamlan of Anayzah, and by the help of God and with your assistance, we halted our camels over above Uthaithiya at the break of day. . . .

And when it was the fourth hour of the night we bestirred ourselves and came to Anayzah. . . . And after we had said the morning prayer, we sent against them Abdullah ibn Jaluwi, with him 100 men of the people of Riyadh to assist. And we marched against Majid, and when we saw the horsemen, God lifted his hand from off them and helped us against them. And we broke them and slaughtered of them 370 men. . . . And, by Almighty God, but two Bedouins on our side were slain. . . .

Majid ibn Hamoud Al Rasheed made good his escape, but his brother Ubayd had the misfortune to be captured and to find himself on the swordpoint of Abdul Aziz. Whether Ubayd had some killing in his past that called for blood vengeance, or whether Abdul Aziz was just riding on the blood-lust of Anayzah's capture is now uncertain.

'I struck him first on the leg,' he later recalled, 'and disabled him; quickly after that I struck at the neck; the head fell to one side, the blood spurted up like a fountain: the third blow at the heart, I saw the heart, which was cut in two, palpitate like that. . . . It was a joyous moment. I kissed the sword.'

6 Britons and Turks

March. Halt. Dismount. Surrender. Lay down your arms.
Do not be afraid, we are English soldiers.
Where is the headman of the village? Bring him here.
How many horses have you? I will pay you cash for everything.
If you do not collect everything in two hours, I will send my soldiers.
Speak the truth, tell no lies, and do not hide anything
or it will be the worse for you.
I will take everything and give you a receipt.

Useful Arabic phrases for British officers,
from De Lacy O'Leary, *Colloquial Arabic*, first published in 1926

NOWADAYS the representatives of Great Britain tread with a certain wariness in the Kingdom of Sa'udi Arabia. In April 1980 Her Britannic Majesty's Ambassador was summarily ordered out of the Kingdom when a British television film about the death of a Sa'udi princess caused displeasure to King Khalid ibn Abdul Aziz – and this was not the first occasion on which British diplomats have been instructed by their Sa'udi hosts to pack their bags and leave. Britain's ambassadors have spent seven of the last twenty-five years banished from the Kingdom.

Things were rather different in November 1903 when George Nathaniel, Viscount Curzon, Viceroy of India, sailed into the Persian Gulf with a flotilla of eight British warships.

'We were here before any other power,' declared Lord Curzon to the assembled sheikhs of the coastal states, '. . . and the British Government must remain supreme.'

Lord Curzon and his officers were carried from their boats on the backs of local Arabs, and more Arabs did their homage to the gold and silver viceroy's throne that had been brought along for the journey.

'We found strife and we have created order,' declared his lordship in ringing tones. 'We saved you from extinction at the hands of your neighbours. . . .' Britain's efforts in the Persian Gulf, he informed his Arab audience, made up a 'century of costly and triumphant enterprise . . . the most unselfish page in history.'

Lord Curzon's claims to selflessness were somewhat undermined by his position as Viceroy of India, since it was clearly for India's sake, and not for Arabia's, that Britain had appointed herself nanny of the Middle East. In 1882 she had occupied Egypt and the Suez Canal in order to safeguard her connections to India and to British Australasia, and long before that it had become an axiom of British policy that the security of Britain's empire in India was best assured when the Persian Gulf enjoyed the effective status of a 'British lake'.

This 'lake' was administered from Bushire on the Persian coast by 'His Britannic Majesty's Political Resident in the Persian Gulf' ('really', confided Curzon in a private letter, 'the uncrowned King of the Gulf'), and, though this Resident had certain responsibilities for the Persian coast on which he was stationed, he looked out primarily towards the creeks and jagged headlands that ran along Arabia's eastern shoreline – the 'Pirate Coast'.

This maze of islands and shallow-mouthed inlets provided the lairs that had earned the coastline its name, for it was eighteenth-century pirate attacks that had first provoked British intervention in the area. Abu Dhabi and Dubai were the principal Pirate Coast sheikhdoms, and a series of punitive expeditions against them from Bombay had led to the Truce of 1839 which gave the Pirate Coast a new name. The sheikhs of the Trucial Coast surrendered control over their foreign policy in return for British protection, and this protection was embodied in Muscat, Bahrain and later in Kuwait by a British colonial servant, a local babysitter for the Pax Britannica whose functions were so discreet as to appear nonexistent – until Britain's interests were threatened. Then, as Dr Paul Harrison of the American Mission noted, the local British Political Agent became 'an absolute czar'.

Dr Harrison's scientific eye scrutinized every category of *homo sapiens* which had made the Gulf its habitat, the Desert Arab, the Merchant Arab, the Pearling Captain, the Date Farmer – and the British Government Servant occupied an anthropological niche of his own. 'The majority are the products of the best secondary schools in England,' explained the doctor, 'the so-called "public schools".' This tended to make them hardworking, efficient, 'of clean life and of incorruptible uprightness.' But marching to Kipling's rhythm towards their two-column *Times* obituaries, Britain's Persian Gulf representatives could also be patronizing and inflexible. Imbued with a 'blind confidence in the divine perfection of the system [they] followed,'

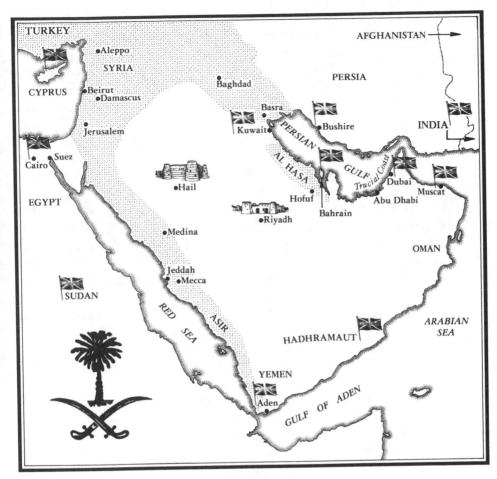

Britons and Turks, 1900–14 (Turkish sphere shaded)

wrote Harrison, they tended to react with a 'surprised impatience at the least question of its fundamental correctness.'

'To me the message is carved in granite,' declared Lord Curzon, 'it is hewn out of the rock of doom – that our work is righteous and that it shall endure.'

The embrace of such empire builders was not, on the face of it, the obvious first resort of a proud desert sheikhdom fighting for its independence. But within months of Abdul Aziz's capture of Riyadh in 1902, the Al Sa'ud were petitioning the British Gulf Resident to consider their new regime as 'one of those having relations with the British government', and, after the victory of al Dilam later that year,

75

Abdul Aziz actually tried to join the British Trucial system. The Al Sa'ud were willing to welcome a British Agent to Riyadh, he said, and even to sacrifice their independence like any other of the Trucial sheikhs; for in the eyes of Abdul Aziz and his family it was not the British who were feared as imperialists. It was the Turks.

It takes a certain stretching of the 1980s world-view to appreciate how, at the opening of our own century, the two great dinosaurs lowering over eastern Europe and the eastern Mediterranean were the empires of Austria and of Turkey. In 1900 both were counted weighty combatants in the power play leading up to the First World War, and they were attributed far more tonnage at that date than the distant and juvenile USA – for in 1900 the Ottoman empire* still controlled much of the Middle East: the Turks ruled Palestine and the area made up today by Syria, Iraq, Lebanon and Jordan, and they also dominated the eastern and western coastlines of modern Sa'udi Arabia; they had held effective control of Mecca and Medina ever since Ibrahim Pasha had ousted the Wahhabis from the Holy Places, and in 1871 they had profited from the squabblings that broke out between Abdul Aziz's uncles to invade and occupy the Al Sa'ud's richest territory, the eastern area of al Hasa.

Today this north-eastern sector of Arabia is where the Kingdom's oilfields lie. A century ago it was trade in dates and pearls that made al Hasa rich, and Turkey's conquest had precipitated the downfall of the Al Sa'ud in the 1870s and 1890s, since Riyadh relied on the revenues of al Hasa to purchase the loyalty of the central Arabian tribes.

Resistance to the power and ambitions of the Ottoman Turks was an obvious direction for Sa'udi foreign policy to take as Abdul Aziz became established in Riyadh in the years after 1902. But if the young Sa'udi leader had learnt one thing from his years in Kuwait it was that no one could cut much of a dash around the Persian Gulf without the assistance – or at least the tolerance – of the British government. Abdul Aziz was to become adept at playing off foreign powers against each other as he built up the Kingdom, and in 1902 he wanted to pull off the trick that Sheikh Mubarak had managed in

---

* The Turkish empire bore the name of its founder, Othman I (d. 1326), whose successors, the Ottomans, expanded its borders to include, at its peak in the sixteenth century, Hungary, the Crimea, the Black Sea coast and the Balkans (most of modern Yugoslavia, Czechoslovakia, Albania, Romania and Bulgaria), Greece, Crete, Cyprus, Algeria, Tunisia, Tripoli and Egypt, in addition to the Middle-Eastern possessions that it still held in 1900. Turkey remained nominally sovereign over Egypt after Britain's occupation of 1882.

Kuwait – to win effective independence of Turkey by cultivating the friendship of Britain.

But Mubarak had something of value to offer His Majesty's Government: the best natural harbour on the Gulf. The Al Sa'ud offered Britain nothing but the prospect of conflict with the Turks, who claimed central Arabia for themselves. The Ottomans were in a position to make trouble for Britain elsewhere in the Middle East and in Europe, and His Majesty's Government was quite content to let the Turks lord it over Arabia's inner emptiness, if that was what they wanted.

'Turkey', declared Lord Palmerston in 1833, 'is as good an occupier of the road to India as an active Arab sovereign would be': and that remained British policy in Arabia at the beginning of the twentieth century.

So the Gulf Resident did not even condescend to reply to the approach that the Al Sa'ud made to him in 1902. The letter was filed, deliberately unanswered, and the same fate met overtures that the family made in 1903, for, if the British thought about the Al Sa'ud at all, it was in terms of the Wahhabi conquests a century earlier and of the havoc that they had wreaked in Mecca. His Majesty's Government knew little about Abdul Aziz, but his family history suggested he must be a fanatic – an 'Ayatollah' figure, in 1980s parlance. Britain had no wish to get involved in the tribal rivalries that a Wahhabi leader seemed likely to promote – nor to offend Turkey, who already laid claim to Nejd.

Early in 1904 the Turks decided to make good their claim. In May of that year six battalions of Turkish troops, 2400 men, and artillery – six field-guns slung between mules – were ordered to march from the Euphrates into central Arabia to rendezvous with the forces of Hail, for the Ottomans had decided that they must bring Nejd firmly under their control; and they intended to accomplish that in alliance with the armies of Ibn Rasheed.

The Turks brought two unpleasant novelties to twentieth-century warfare in central Arabia – artillery and discipline – and Abdul Aziz does not appear to have appreciated the dangers of either as he camped casually in the palm groves east of Anayzah, close to the combined Turkish–Rasheed forces in July 1904. He had chosen a position that a bedouin army would not have attacked.

But the Turks charged the Sa'udis head-on in Western style, bombarding Abdul Aziz's defences in advance with their field-guns. Many bedouin had never heard or seen such a cannonade; Abdul Aziz was wounded unpleasantly as the shrapnel flew, and it was all he could do to prevent his army's retreat becoming a rout. He had to forsake his camp to the Turks, and if a friendly contingent from Anayzah, unaware of the setback that their leader had suffered, had not stumbled at sunset upon the looting Turks and routed them in turn, the day would have been counted as a severe defeat for the Sa'udis.

Abdul Aziz was no Napoleon. The military campaigns that built the Kingdom are sometimes depicted as a series of clean and striking tactical victories. But Abdul Aziz's battlefield record was, in reality, a muddied one. In combat he was a brave but poor strategist; indeed, he was never once victorious in conventional face-to-face confrontations. His coups were surprise attacks like the seizure of Riyadh.

But when the stalemates occurred – and these drawn contests were the norm in desert campaigning – Abdul Aziz had the nerve and courage to stand his ground and to keep his forces fighting. He had charisma, he could draw men to give of their best for his smile, for his handshake and embrace – and these personal qualities told in the long hot summer weeks after July 1904, as the two irregular camel armies withdrew to lick their wounds in the dusty palm groves near Anayzah. Abdul Aziz himself was painfully wounded in one hand and in one leg, so that he limped. Both he and Ibn Rasheed faced the task of holding together their cobweb alliances of bedouin and townsmen, and as the days dragged by the contest became essentially one of will and leadership.

It was Ibn Rasheed who cracked first. Late in September 1904 his bedouin decided to head for home, and their leader had little choice but to retreat with them. Abdul Aziz's scouts caught the Rasheed army trying to creep away under cover of darkness and they proved easy prey, while the Turks, deprived of cavalry support, fell victim to Abdul Aziz's swordsmen. By the end of the fighting on 27 September 1904 there were only 700 survivors of the 2400 Turkish soldiers who had marched so confidently into Nejd. The Turkish pay chest was captured, and also the Turkish field-guns. The Al Sa'ud had artillery for the first time in their history.*

It was time for a truce. The Turks decided to abandon Ibn Rasheed, at least as far as his claims on Nejd were concerned, and Abdul Aziz

---

* Ancient cannon from this era are still wheeled out in Sa'udi towns at Ramadhan to sound the sunrise and sunset guns that mark the beginning and end of each day's fast.

decided to make his peace with the Ottomans, sending his father to talk on his behalf with the Turkish authorities in Basra. In February 1905 the Turks agreed to recognize Sa'udi possession of Nejd, and Abdul Aziz agreed in return to accept the Turkish title of *qaimaqam* (district commissioner), thus accepting Ottoman overlordship in a total reversal of his hitherto anti-Ottoman policy.

'Kiss your enemy,' say the bedouin, 'if you cannot kill him.'

As news of Riyadh's agreement with the Turks became known, the British officials in the Gulf were pleased, for it seemed to give them more or less what they had wanted – Turkish blessing on Mubarak's Sa'udi allies – without any troublesome British involvement. But when it was learnt that Abdul Rahman might be visiting the town of Kuwait early in 1905, Captain Knox, the British Agent there, was firmly ordered to avoid meeting the Sa'udi elder if he possibly could. Direct Sa'udi–British contact of any sort was considered unnecessary and undesirable.

In the summer months of 1905, the young Emir of Riyadh set off for the Pirate Coast to display his victory trophies.

'By God! Oh Zayeed!' wrote Amr bin Shaban, a local notable, in some alarm to the Sheikh of Abu Dhabi, a senior ruler of the coast. 'My eyes did not fail to see the trays, tents, house furniture, coffee pots of Constantinople make, belonging to bin Rasheed. . . . Your turn has come now!'

Abdul Aziz was marching south-eastwards, welcoming local emirs to his *majlis* and showing off the panoply of his conquests over the Rasheeds – and, as the reports started reaching the British Gulf Resident, it sounded ominously as though the Sa'udi chieftain was reviving his Wahhabi ancestors' claim to eastern Arabia and the Pirate Coast.

'I will explore the country belonging to my father and grandfather,' declared Abdul Aziz to Amr bin Shaban. Britain's worst fears seemed realized.

'I will, if God please, visit these parts without fail [again] when the spring comes,' wrote Abdul Aziz to the Sheikh of Dubai as he turned to march home in August 1905. 'My object in doing so is to look into certain affairs.'

Mubarak of Kuwait laughed off this ominous vagueness when he first heard of it: 'a mere attempt to extort money from the various coastal sheikhs', he told Captain Knox, and he may have been right. But a few days later the old sheikh actually called at the house of the British Agent to discuss the matter further, and he grew heated on the subject of his former protégé, whom he now described as 'an ignorant savage'. On reflection he evidently took seriously the possibility that the Al Sa'ud might be planning to seize a piece of the Gulf coast for themselves.

It was a clear test for the British undertakings to protect the Trucial sheikhs, and the challenge was met by the spry forty-year-old officer recently promoted to the Gulf Residency on Lord Curzon's personal initiative, Major Percy Zachariah Cox.*

'Cockus', as Abdul Aziz came to call him, exemplified the finest strain in the breed of British government servant anthropologized by Dr Harrison. 'Tall and spare, blond and blue-eyed, with an almost Wellingtonian nose that was none the less commanding for being somewhat out of line', Cox was taciturn, diplomatic,† lacking in panache and restrained in all things except his appetite for work. Harry St John Philby recalled him in his office of a hot afternoon, struggling against the prevailing torpor with a blue pencil and a pile of draft dispatches: 'I would see his head nodding drowsily, his writing grow unsteady and then a bold blue streak right across the paper as nature conquered and his head went down. . . . I used to stand my ground in dead silence till he woke with a start to continue his work as if nothing had happened.' Anyone who could make Harry St John Philby stand his ground in dead silence must have had presence indeed, even while dozing.

Percy Cox was an excellent Arabist.‡ It was his habit to draft all his local communications first in Arabic to make sure that their meaning

---

* Major Cox (1864–1937) retired from his post as High Commissioner of Iraq in 1923 as Major-General Sir Percy Cox, GCMG (Knight of the Grand Cross of the Order of St Michael and St George), GCIE (Knight Grand Commander of the Indian Empire), KCSI (Knight Commander of the Order of the Star of India) and was elected President of the Royal Geographical Society in 1933. His death of a heart attack out hunting in Bedfordshire on 20 February 1937 was marked not simply by an obituary in *The Times* but also by a leading article, 'The Man on the Spot'. It is said that, when Cox left the Gulf in 1923, new-born Iraqi babies were having his name bestowed on them, but the author has been unable to ascertain whether any Iraqi 'Cockus's' are still living.

† Cox was let down in this respect on one occasion by some relatives of his wife who visited him in the Gulf, and insisted on referring to the sheikhs with whom he was dealing as 'romantic old dears with dusters on their heads'.

‡ Arabic linguist.

was plain, and to translate them into English thereafter only for the record.

'When travelling in your parts in Novr. last,' he wrote in letters he dispatched to all the principal Trucial sheikhs in April 1906, 'I heard it discussed among Arabs whom I met that Abdul Rahman bin Saood or his son Abdul Aziz . . . was entering into communication with the Trucial Chiefs.' Cox was the ultimate in unflappability, and he managed to float out some of his magisterial calm to his panicky charges. 'In writing to the Great Govt. I mentioned this report, but said that I thought that Ibn Saood had quite enough to employ him in his own place. . . . The Great Govt. are also of this opinion.'

Yet here, in the suavest tones, came the threat:

So that there may be no misapprehension . . . they think it advisable to warn the Trucial Sheikhs that the display of any inclination on the part of any of them to give encouragement to, or to intrigue with ibn Saood or his Agents will not be regarded by Govt. with complacency.

You, my friend, will of your own accord refrain from anything of the sort, but it is incumbent on me to communicate to you the views of the Government. May you be preserved and salaams.

signed P. Z. Cox

Cox sent this final paragraph in identical form to each of the Trucial sheikhs to whom he wrote, but his duplicated courtesy was never put to the test, for in the spring of 1906 Abdul Aziz had started fighting again with Ibn Rasheed.

The Turks had stationed garrisons at Anayzah and Buraydah to police and separate the warring chieftains of Hail and Riyadh. But raiding the caravans that carried supplies to the Turks had become a profitable business for both sides, and early in April 1906 Ibn Rasheed was engaged in this very sport 20 miles north of Buraydah. He was camped in the oasis of Rawdhat al Muhanna, sharing out the spoils of a looted camel train, confident that the nearest Sa'udi forces were several days' march away.

His scouts had failed him. Abdul Aziz was at that very moment near by, soothing the feelings of the looted caravan master. It is said that a sandstorm was blowing as the Sa'udis advanced stealthily through the night towards the palm groves of Rawdhat al Muhanna in April 1906 and caught the Rasheed forces before they had time to organize. Ibn Rasheed himself could have turned and fled, but, like the warrior he was, he chose to stand and fight, shouting his warcries loudly to rally his fleeing men until he fell, battling almost alone, riddled with bullets beneath the palm trees in the first light of dawn.

The victors stuck his head on a pole and paraded it round the local settlements, while his relatives raced back to Hail to compete for his succession in a tawdry, bloody and long-drawn-out imbroglio which heralded the end of the Rasheeds as a major force in North Arabian politics for a decade.

Nor did the Turks survive much longer in Anayzah and Buraydah. Abdul Aziz had acknowledged their overlordship only as the price of protection against Ibn Rasheed; and after the decisive ambush in the palm groves of Rawdhat al Muhanna he had no further need to kiss his Turkish enemy.

So the Sa'udi leader proved less than zealous in his responsibilities as the Ottomans' *qaimaqam*. He made no attempt to discipline tribes who chose to attack the Turkish caravans and supply lines, and the Ottoman troops, miserable in their hard and thankless assignment, began deserting in droves. One day in 1906 the British Agent in Kuwait spied a pitiful line of soldiers struggling homewards through the desert – and that was the end of the Turkish presence in central Arabia.

7 The House of Hashim

I N a villa beneath the pine trees on the banks of the Bosphorus
there was living in the early years of this century a very short, very
grand little man with long bushy eyebrows and a thick white beard,
whose great pleasure it was to recite his family pedigree back to
Adam and Eve. This process took several hours, and it was an
exercise of doubtful historical validity once he had passed the thirty-
eighth generation backwards.

But up to the thirty-eighth generation, the family tree of Husain
ibn Ali of the clan of Hashim fully justified his claim to be a direct
descendant of the Prophet Muhammad: Hashim was the fore-
father from whom the Prophet's family name was derived,* and for
centuries the house of Hashim had enjoyed a special status in Islam's
Holy Places; by virtue of being a shareef, or descendant, of the
Prophet, one Hashimite or another had ruled as Emir of Mecca since
AD 1073 – and the Hashimites had traditionally controlled not only
the cities of Mecca and Medina but often the entire Red Sea coastal
area of the Hijaz as well.

Shareef† Husain ibn Ali was some twenty-five years older than the
young Abdul Aziz whose principal adversary he was destined to
become in the struggle to control twentieth-century Arabia, and no
one who met him ever failed to be struck by the force of his character
and purpose.

'A small neat old gentlemen of great dignity and, when he liked,
great charm,' noted one British diplomat, 'he smiled rarely and his
smile had no warmth. His eyes were grey, lustrous and cold.'

Husain liked to wear the traditional white turban of a Meccan
notable, he had pronounced and unbending views on every subject,

* The Prophet's full name was Muhammad ibn Abdullah ibn Abdul Muttalib ibn Hashim.
† Every direct descendant of the Prophet is entitled to the style of 'Sayyid' or 'shareef'. The
shareef ruling over Mecca was known as the Grand Shareef, or Emir of Mecca.

he worked ferociously whenever his own personal ambition was at stake, and, when he entered the lists against the house of Sa'ud in the early years of this century, his name, connections and family history gave him many advantages.

As an Arabian, however, Husain's credentials were less impressive. He had been born in Constantinople and, thanks to Hashimite family in-fighting, he had spent nearly half his life in exile there intriguing among the viziers, spies and eunuchs that clustered round the Turkish sultan-caliph. He spoke Arabic, but whenever roused he lapsed readily into Turkish, and his literary Arabic as it survives in the convoluted diatribes which he dictated in later years to the official Mecca newspaper *al Qibla* is a byzantine farrago of subjunctive and gerundial clauses in the style favoured by functionaries of the Ottoman court.

The position of Grand Shareef, or Emir of Mecca, had lain in the gift of the Ottoman Turks since 1840, when they had incorporated the Hijaz into their empire as a *vilayet*, or province. To secure the post, the various Hashimite contenders had to jockey for the favour of the sultan-caliph in Constantinople; and the entire adult life of Shareef Husain ibn Ali had been consecrated to triumphing in these convoluted family rivalries that were as dangerous as they were bitter and devious. Since his birth in 1853 two emirs had been deposed and one had been assassinated, and the triumph of a rival branch of the family had consigned Husain to exile in 1893. In 1905 he came within a whisker of success, only to be foiled by a cousin whose judicious disposal of some 70,000 lire and a gem-studded gold dinner service was said to have secured him the emirate. But Husain kept up his intrigues undismayed, and his perseverance was finally rewarded when in 1908, after years of strain, the centuries-old Ottoman empire began to crack apart.

Since 1876, Sultan-Caliph Abdul Hamid II had been retreating deeper and deeper into his private labyrinth of paranoia in Constantinople. He banned from his empire the works of playwrights from Sophocles to Shakespeare who dealt with the deposition of rulers, he refused electric light in his palaces until he was persuaded conclusively that there was no similarity between dynamos and dynamite; he carried firearms all the time, more than once shooting down innocent servants clumsy enough to startle him, and he employed, in addition to several hundred cherubic young concubines, male and female, a 20,000-strong army of food-tasters, bodyguards and spies who combed his empire for dissent – and who totally failed to forestall the group of young army officers who, in July 1908, seized power in the name of the Committee for Union and Progress and lost little time in dispatching Abdul Hamid into exile with 213 concubines and his favourite cat.

The advent of the Young Turks was to have immense repercussions throughout the Balkans and the entire Middle East, for their destruction of the Ottoman system paved the way for the creation of a dozen independent countries from Albania to Iraq, and Shareef Husain ibn Ali was among the earliest to benefit from their upheaval. In the brief battle between the sultan and the Young Turks, Abdul Hamid had nominated Husain as the Hashimite most likely to uphold his interests in the distant but prestigious Holy Places, and Husain was appointed to the Emirate of Mecca on 1 November 1908. But the sultan vanished within months,* and from then onwards, thanks to the convulsions in Turkey, Husain was able to exercise his authority from Mecca with more effective independence than many of his recent predecessors had enjoyed. So even as the Al Sa'ud were disposing of the Rasheeds and Turkish garrisons in central Arabia in the years 1906–8, a new and more dangerous rival was establishing a power base to the west of them on the Red Sea coast of the Hijaz.

The land of the Hijaz where Shareef Husain arrived as emir on 3 December 1908 was scarcely a rich one. The town that served as gateway and port for Mecca was Jeddah, on the rotting coral shore of the Red Sea coast. A Frenchman who arrived there just a few years before Husain conveyed his first impressions vividly: 'Legions of mosquitoes assail you night and day, the water is bad, the heat damp and oppressive, and not the least trace of greenery enlivens the sad and mournful countryside . . .' T. E. Lawrence, who was to arrive a few years later, was equally dismayed. 'The heat of Arabia came like a drawn sword and struck us speechless,' he wrote, '. . . the atmosphere was like a bath.'

This did scant justice to Jeddah's sweaty charms – the lattice-work balconies and screens that still tumble across the façades of old Jeddah houses in cascades of cock-eyed beauty. But the prospect that greeted Shareef Husain ibn Ali as he looked out in 1908 across the

* Abdul Hamid was replaced as Sultan-Caliph by Mehmed V who ruled from 1908 to 1918, but power from 1909 onwards was effectively in the hands of the Young Turks and the army.

shimmering Red Sea reefs cannot, on the face of it, have been an impressive one. The Hijaz produced no valuable minerals or raw materials; its fishermen barely satisfied their own needs; and its farmers survived at subsistence level. It boasted no local art, little culture, no permanent foreign community, and for those career diplomats compelled briefly to sojourn there it was rated among the hardest of all hardship posts. The Hijaz was an impoverished and backward land by any standard. But its squalor and seediness were redeemed by a unique invisible export – holiness.

In Muslim eyes this particular corner of the earth had been blessed from the moment that Adam and Eve, expelled from the Garden of Eden,* were reunited with each other and with God on the Mount of Mercy beside the Plain of Arafat in the bowl of rocky hills around Mecca. There in Mecca, at the very beginning of human history, God cast down from heaven a sacred black stone – a meteorite, suggest some Western interpreters – and this was his sign to the grandfather and grandmother of mankind that he had forgiven them for their misconduct in the Garden (no Muslim feels plagued by the guilt of original sin). Soon after this Eve died, to be buried near the sea, and her grave can be seen to this day in modern Jeddah. It lies in the cemetery behind the barracks beside the Foreign Ministry, the site concealed by high walls in deference to Wahhabi distaste at such antique superstition. But Eve's name is proclaimed none the less proudly, for *jeddah* in Arabic means grandmother, and that is thought to be the most likely origin of the town's name.

Centuries after the Creation, Hagar, the mother of Abraham's first-born son, Ishmael, came to Mecca. The Old Testament relates (Genesis 16: 1–16 and 21: 8–21) how Abraham's childless wife Sarah gave her maid Hagar to her husband, how Hagar bore Abraham a son, Ishmael, and how Sarah, in her jealousy, drove Hagar into the wilderness, where mother and baby were only saved when God guided Hagar to a spring of fresh water miraculously welling up from the sand. Muslims believe this story, as they accept much of the Old Testament, and they locate the life-saving spring† only a few yards away from Adam's sacred black stone in Mecca – to which, they say, Abraham himself came at a later date, when Ishmael was grown up.

* Some Muslim tradition places the Garden of Eden in the green and pleasant hills of Yemen, citing the name of the port of Aden as substantiation of this.

† The spring is known as the well of Zamzam. According to tradition Hagar cried out 'Zam! Zam!' (meaning 'Stop! Stop!') when the waters started flowing.

'Take now thy son, thine only son . . . whom thou lovest,' God ordered Abraham in Genesis 22: 2, 'and get thee into the land of Moriah and offer him there for a burnt offering.'

And so Abraham took his son to Moriah, and went up into the mountain there, ready to sacrifice his child in obedience to God's will – only to be spared this ultimate test by God's last-minute intervention.

This famous tale of the absolute obedience which God demands of his faithful servants is central to the message of the Koran as it is to the Old Testament. But whereas Genesis identifies the boy led for sacrifice as Abraham's second-born son Isaac (father of the Jews), the Koran insists it was his first-born, Ishmael (father of the Arabs), who was taken to the mountain top.* Muslims also believe that 'the land of Moriah' was near Mecca and that, after God had spared Ishmael, father and son came down rejoicing into the valley to build in Mecca a high, square house, the Ka'aba, to show their gratitude to God, using Adam's sacred black rock conveniently standing there as a cornerstone.

So, with this Ka'aba rising some 50 feet in the centre of the town, Mecca was already a holy spot when, in the seventh century A D, the Prophet Muhammad began receiving God's final spiritual revelation to mankind. It built on his previous revelations in the Old and New Testaments (Muslims revere almost all the biblical heroes and prophets – Joseph, Moses, Aaron, David, Solomon – and Jesus above all, who is ranked second only to Muhammad as a prophet, though Islam believes it blasphemous to describe him as the son of God), and there in Mecca, concentrated within a few yards of each other, were Adam's sacred black stone, Abraham's cube-like house to God, and Hagar's life-saving spring.

These shrines were already venerated by pilgrims and by Meccans for their links with Allah, the supreme divinity recognized in the town, but they were only a few shrines among many. Mecca was a centre for worship of gods of all sorts – Hubal, for example, an idol of red cornelian, was the local god of Mecca itself – and it was Muhammad's revelation that these totems must all be swept away. Allah was

---

* Muslims cite the Old Testament itself in justification of this, for the text in Genesis refers to 'thine only son'. Ishmael was born when Abraham was eighty-six (Genesis 15: 16), but Isaac was not born till his father was 100 (Genesis 21: 5), so Isaac was never an only son, while Ishmael was, for fourteen years. Isaac's name appears in the Old Testament account, argue Muslim scholars, only as a result of subsequent, but inefficient, 'doctoring' of history.

not the chief god. He was the *only* god, and the essence of his faith was to believe simply that 'there is no god but God'. Muhammad was his Prophet.

To say this at least once out loud with belief and understanding became the first pillar of Islam (Islam means 'submission' to God's will; a Muslim is one who submits). The second pillar is to pray five times a day, the third to give the community a share of your wealth, the fourth to fast during the holy month of Ramadhan, and the fifth to go on at least one pilgrimage to the Holy Places in the course of your life if you can afford it. Every single member of the vast community of Muslims throughout the world has to try his or her utmost to travel at least once to the Hijaz, and there do homage at the Holy Places, and it was this fifth and final pillar of Islam, the *hajj*, which provided the emirs of Mecca with their international significance, and also with the principal source of their wealth.

Every year in Dhul Hijja, the final month in the Muslim calendar, the pilgrims started gathering in Jeddah, the men clad in nothing but two seamless white towels – the pilgrim garb that the Prophet had prescribed. A report on the 1907 pilgrimage set the numbers at some 120,000 – Russians, Indians, Indonesians and Africans as well as Arabs – who had all endured months of arduous travelling to reach the Holy Land. Nigerians often took several years to wend their way on foot across the southern Sahara and the Sudan to the Red Sea ferries. Syrians traditionally set out in a huge caravan from Damascus surrounded by armed guards to protect them from the bedouin whose annual sport was to raid the pilgrims on their forty-day desert trek – and, once in the Hijaz, the pilgrims fell among thieves of another colour.

Every *hajji* was required to register with a local *mutawwaf*, a sanctified tourist guide who would shepherd him to kiss the holy black stone, walk seven times around the Ka'aba, drink water from the holy well, stand praying at Arafat and help him carry out the other rituals of the pilgrimage. For this guidance the pilgrim paid a fee. He also paid a fee for a camel or donkey to transport him the three days' journey from Jeddah to Mecca, a fee for his food and lodging once he reached the Holy City, a fee for the sheep or goat which had to be sacrificed in order to complete his pilgrimage – and, should the pilgrim choose, in addition, to visit Medina where the Prophet was buried, then that cost him still more money.

The *hajj* was indeed 'the bread of the Hijaz', and in theory the shareefs of Mecca were responsible for restraining the inevitable greed with which the local inhabitants fell upon the pious and defenceless worshippers, intent only on reaching their sacred goal and not too concerned, at this supreme spiritual moment in their lives, with what happened to them physically in the meantime. To die on the pilgrimage, indeed, was a blessed thing, and pilgrims who died went straight to heaven, washed of their sins.

But the only check on the fees the shareef set for the hire of a camel, the purchase of a sacrifice, and so on, was the corps of foreign consuls who supervised the interests of their own nationals in the Hijaz (over half the pilgrims, coming from India and Africa, were British subjects; another major contingent, from Indonesia, were Dutch), and these consuls had to wrestle vainly with the reality that the Grand Shareef himself depended on the pilgrim revenues as parasitically as his subjects did. So the price of piety was never cheap.

Shareefian wealth had always relied on the ignoble trade of fleecing pilgrims – and it was not a totally firm basis either. Famine, epidemic or war in one of the populous Muslim countries could sharply reduce the flow of visitors to Mecca in any year, with resultant hardship in the Holy Land. So the need for other revenues turned the eyes of the new shareef inland towards the farming and commercial areas of central Arabia. Husain's ambition was monumental, seldom influenced by morality, and never by practicality. From 1909 onwards he started striving to push his authority into inner Arabia, and the fact that the house of Sa'ud also laid claim to the same area did not bother him in the slightest.

8 The Jewel

SOME time in the years before 1910, Abdul Aziz found himself a new wife, and he fell very much in love with her. She was the sister of Ibn Musa'id, a young member of the bin Jaluwis who had helped him capture Riyadh, and her name was Jauhara – 'the jewel'.

Jauhara was to add two more healthy sons to Abdul Aziz's growing brood, Muhammad and Khalid (the present king), a couple of little boys so attached to each other they would cry if they were separated; and Abdul Aziz's attachment to their mother was so intense that he also was to cry, and bitterly too, when illness took Jauhara from him.

Abdul Aziz seldom allowed himself to get sentimental about women – at least, not in front of other men. He discussed the bodies of his slave girls freely. Siesta time was when he liked to dally with them, and when he had finished with a girl he might pass her over to his friends. Bawdy jokes, lingering sexual reminiscence and erotic discussion which was so earnest and technical it bordered on the academic, these were staples of conversation among Abdul Aziz's male intimates – and, as is the way with stag talk, it tended to be bragging.

'I have no use for women older than thirty,' boasted Abdul Aziz on one occasion. 'I divorce them automatically when they reach that age.'

But that was untrue. Several of Abdul Aziz's wives lasted long past thirty, remaining with him to the end of his life, in fact; for the private Abdul Aziz was a more gentle and affectionate character than he sometimes liked to pretend.

'How have you stayed so long with such a lion?' his elder sons once dared to ask Umm Talal, the favourite of his later years, thinking of their father's rages and the readiness with which he would lash out and beat men – including his own sons – when he was offended with them.

90

'You do not know your own father,' laughed Umm Talal. 'He is a different man with us from the man that you see.'

One of his grandsons once surprised Abdul Aziz in his private quarters just after nine o'clock at night. This was the witching hour, something of a joke at court, when Abdul Aziz would start to fidget, look at his watch and then, promptly on the hour, get up and head for his harem. Men smiled and winked discreetly at each other, doubtless imagining the lion of Nejd tearing ferociously to the boudoir of the wife he had selected for his evening's pleasure.

But this grandson was astonished to discover Abdul Aziz still sitting calmly in his own apartment. One of his slaves was shaving him and sprinkling him with perfume. He had bathed and groomed and was just stepping into a clean-pressed white *thobe* as if starting a new day.

'My wife is preparing herself for me,' he said. 'Should not I prepare myself for her as well?' Then he strode off down one of the covered mud bridges that linked the main palace with the women's quarters and that private world where no other man could follow him.

'We are promised forty houris in paradise,' Abdul Aziz would often say, referring to the Koran's description of heavenly companions – whom he confidently expected to be shapely damsels. 'But I am hoping, in view of my services to Islam, that I may be granted an extra ration.'

Abdul Aziz's craving for women's company was legendary, but it extended beyond sensuality. In his harem he liked to relax, sip coffee, play with his children, lead a different life and savour with his womenfolk the relationships of which we know virtually nothing, except that some of them mattered enough to last his life long. In 1981 four of Abdul Aziz's wives are still alive and every day or so, around 9 o'clock in the evening, Umm Talal starts preparing coffee to bring back the memories of the private man whom his sons did not know.

The clean *thobe*, the coffee sipping, the gentleness: can it be, for all the braggadoccio, that women were more than playthings for Abdul Aziz?

His best friend throughout his life was a woman – Nura, his sister, a year older than him, his closest playmate in the dusty courtyards of Riyadh in the early 1880s, and as the Al Sa'ud were chased from their town in January 1891, Abdul Aziz and Nura shared a camel.

In the 1930s, when the telephone came to Riyadh, the first line was run, not to the house of a brother or adviser, but to the house of Nura.

She was his confidante. It was Nura, Abdul Aziz used to say, who kept him resolute in the dark days in Kuwait – he could tell her things he could not admit to any man – and, in his marriage before 1910 to Jauhara bint Musa'id, Abdul Aziz's need for more than physical communion became similarly apparent.

He used to write love poems to Jauhara and once, in later years, he confided to Muhammad Asad: 'Whenever the world was dark around me and I could not see my way out of the dangers and difficulties that beset me, I would sit down and compose an ode to Jauhara; and when it was finished, the world was suddenly lighted and I knew what I had to do.'

Love, tenderness, vulnerability – we glimpse a different man. But it is a stolen glimpse.

9 Night Caravan

ABDULLAH ibn Hamoud al Tariki, the fiery and radical Sa'udi Oil Minister who preceded Sheikh Yamani in the job, and who did more than any other Arab to bring about the creation of OPEC, had an exciting time getting to school as a boy.

Tariki's father was a caravan owner living in Zilfi near Buraydah in the early decades of this century, and he made a comfortable living organizing the camel trains that carried goods between Kuwait and the central deserts. Riyadh was a full week's plod away – to reach Kuwait took even longer – and all these journeys had to be made across the grazing grounds of different bedouin tribes.

This meant that a caravan owner had to be more than just a merchant and camel expert; he had to be a politician as well. Each tribe required bribing or pacifying before it would let the caravan pass across its territories in peace; and, since the desert was in ferment at the moment when Abdullah Tariki's father decided to send his boy to school in Kuwait, the caravan had to travel for more than a week under cover of darkness. At dawn the little party sought out dunes where they could spend the daylight hours in hiding, taking it in turns to keep watch. At sunset they would set off again, and because little Abdullah, tired and scared in the darkness, kept slipping off or letting fall his camel-stick, he was popped into a camel-bag every night for safekeeping.

Subduing Arabia's anarchic nomads was to prove the most difficult of all the tasks that Abdul Aziz set himself in the creation of the Kingdom. When negotiating in later years with foreign diplomats, he would often shrug his shoulders when the arguments were getting tough.

'Of course,' he would say, 'I am just a simple bedouin.'

Usually this was the signal for some new, devastatingly subtle line of negotiation which he would advance with a self-deprecating smile, or else it meant that he was bored, and was handing the whole matter over to his advisers: it was all too difficult for a simple desert-dweller like him to handle.

But Abdul Aziz was not a bedouin and he knew that very well, since the Al Sa'ud had lived for centuries among the settled people of Arabia, not the nomads. The family is proud to claim a distant descent from the Anazah bedouin. This gives them pedigree, a certain nobility, but the roots of their power lie among the permanent inhabitants of Riyadh and the towns of central Nejd – townsmen, farmers, traders – and Sa'udi princes will point out today how the shiftless bedouin have never had the vision or staying power to found great dynasties.

Any townsman will tell you this more robustly:

'Why does it take thirteen bedouin to change a light bulb?'

'One to hang on to it. The other twelve to twirl him round.'

The bedouin fulfil the same function in Arabian humour as the Poles in America or the Irish in England, and this is the schizophrenia of Arabia, the tension between oasis and desert.

Coming into town a bedouin will sometimes roll a little plug of cloth and stuff it up his nose to exclude the evil odours of over-adjacent humanity. You will see him, the cloth dangling gracelessly from his nostrils. He will be touchy, gloomy, morose – and not until he can yank out the bandage and breathe freely in his open spaces will he relax and start gossiping again. The bedouin despise the *hadhar* (townsmen) as weak and crafty, paying too little and charging too much, while the townsmen fully reciprocate the mistrust.

Bedouin and *hadhar* depend upon each other to survive in the unhelpful environment of central Arabia. They both come originally from the same stock, and Abdul Aziz always made much of the Al Sa'ud's original relationship with the Anazah tribe; but that did not impress the tribes through whose territories Riyadh's caravans had to pass.

The grazing grounds of the Ajman, Otayba and Mutair tribes formed a horseshoe around the northern fringes of Nejd, and their sheikhs had rather enjoyed the rule of the Rasheeds from distant Hail. It left them free to exercise power in their lands as they wished, and they did not welcome the renaissance of Riyadh under Abdul Aziz. The house of Sa'ud had been busybodying its bedouin neighbours since the days of Ibn Abdul Wahhab, and the leaders of these three tribes had long histories of resistance to its ambitions.

94

Top Shareef Husain ibn Ali in 1916
Above Egyptian pilgrims troop the Mahmal, the litter carrying the
ornamental hangings for the Ka'aba in Mecca

A portfolio of photographs by Snouck Hurgronje, the Dutch Arabist who lived in Mecca at the end of the nineteenth century:

This page a doctor; a merchant with his white slave; a secretary to the Grand Shareef

Opposite A Mecca woman in bridal array; young members of the Shareef clan; a servant and eunuch with the child of their master

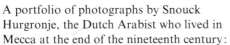

Top Pilgrims circle the Ka'aba in the
central courtyard of the Grand Mosque in Mecca today
Above A Jeddah merchant smokes a hubble bubble in the *majlis*
of his home. A 19th century engraving

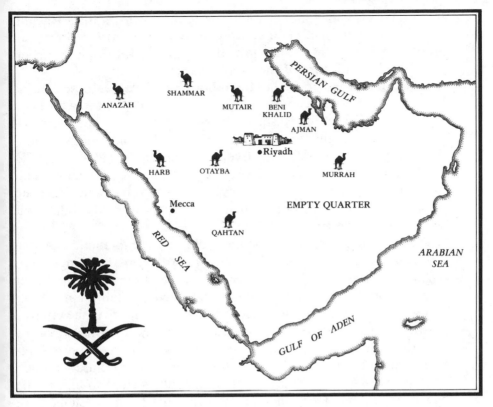

The principal tribes of Sa'udi Arabia

The sheikhs of the Mutair were of the Daweesh clan, and in 1819. one Faisal al Daweesh had enthusiastically linked his tribe with the army of Ibrahim Pasha that destroyed Dar'iyah. He had done his utmost thereafter to obstruct the nineteenth-century revival of the house of Sa'ud, and now, as Abdul Aziz attempted a similar resurrection ninety years on, the recalcitrant chieftain's great-great-grandson and namesake, another Faisal al Daweesh, took up the cudgels. By the spring of 1907 the Mutair were attacking Riyadh caravans and raiding other tribes in defiance of Sa'udi authority.

The Emir of Riyadh might have dealt more effectively with this challenge if he had not been assailed from other directions, but in 1910 the Al Sa'ud found themselves threatened by another old problem – friction in the family. The trouble went back to the rivalries which had brought ruin to the house of Sa'ud in the 1880s, for the quarrels between Abdul Aziz's uncles had not died with them. It was

95

these quarrels which had enabled the Rasheeds to capture Riyadh, and the vendetta had been continued by a dozen or so cousins of Abdul Aziz who had neither joined the exile in Kuwait nor partici- pated in the recapture of the family capital.

While others had flocked to the reborn Sa'udi cause, these cousins had remained conspicuously aloof. Some of them had even been living at the court of Ibn Rasheed under a loose form of house arrest – and it was as such that they had been captured in ambiguous circum- stances when the Sa'udi army overran Anayzah in 1904.

Had these cousins been actively helping the enemy against their own kin – hoping, perhaps, to be given Riyadh to rule as Rasheed protégés? Or had they been forced unwillingly to fight Abdul Aziz against their own true inclinations?

Their cousin plumped for the more charitable explanation. Abdul Aziz welcomed his long-lost relatives with open arms, laughingly dub- bing them the *araif* – a bedouin word for camels lost in a raid and later recovered in a counter-raid – and he instituted in celebration a flurry of intermarriages, always the best way to heal a rupture in the family.

Abdul Aziz bestowed three of his own sisters upon his wayward cousins,* and the supreme token of reconciliation was the presenta- tion to his eldest cousin, Sa'ud, of his favourite sister Nura – though since Nura was Abdul Aziz's confidante, still as close to him as she had been in childhood, there may well have been an element of precaution in the gesture.

His new brother-in-law became known henceforth to his relatives as Sa'ud al Kabeer ('Sa'ud the Great' or 'Sa'ud the Elder'), to distinguish him from Abdul Aziz's second son, Sa'ud – a welcome admission that even the family sometimes has difficulty finding its way through its labyrinthine genealogy – and Sa'ud al Kabeer's marriage to Nura was celebrated as visible proof that the *araif* were welcome back in the fold. So far as Abdul Aziz was concerned, whatever had happened in the past was forgiven and forgotten.

But other members of the Al Sa'ud did not share their leader's trust in the *araif*. Abdul Aziz's younger brother Sa'ad was particularly resentful of the welcome extended to them. The *araif* had been suspiciously happy, in Sa'ad's eyes, to live under the wing of Ibn Rasheed, and Sa'ad was soon at odds with the *araif*'s leader, Sa'ud al Kabeer. There was a row, and in 1910 the *araif* rode out of Riyadh to

* See Appendix D, page 533.

96

rouse up the Ajman bedouin to raiding and disorder.

We do not know the precise occasion for the rift. Family quarrels are not subjects which the Al Sa'ud are fond of discussing with outsiders. Sa'ud al Kabeer evidently wanted more real power for his own branch of the family – to be governor of a subordinate town, perhaps, or emir of a tribal area. He felt that Sa'ad was blocking this. Abdul Aziz could not resolve the rivalry, so Sa'ud al Kabeer rode off eastwards with his own brothers at the beginning of 1910 to stir the Ajman to the same sort of revolt that Faisal al Daweesh's Mutair were pursuing to the north – ambushing caravans and raiding those tribes that stayed loyal to Riyadh.

It was a perilous tactic to adopt, but Sa'ud al Kabeer liked to live dangerously. Some of his family tell a story of his passion for Nura. He could never have enough of her, apparently. His *mariage de convenance* had turned into a love match, and the great regret of his quarrel with her brother was that he had had to leave her with her family in al Kharj, the green farming oasis down the wadi from Riyadh where the Al Sa'ud had their summer palaces.

One day he was raiding in the area and being chased by the forces of Abdul Aziz, when Sa'ud al Kabeer decided to steal away to his beloved. He saddled his camel at sunset and rode as fast as he could to al Kharj. There he scaled the palace wall, tiptoed into the harem and spent the night in the arms of Nura, creeping stealthily away before dawn again unseen, like any lover on an illicit adventure.

Nine months later the royal family decided that the king's sister had indeed been engaged in illicit goings-on, and by the desert code this reflected more seriously on her brother's honour than on her husband's.* Many an eyebrow was raised in Riyadh. But not in the camp of Sa'ud al Kabeer, who laughed heartily at the news – as did Abdul Aziz, once he discovered that the joke had been on him. Nura, it seemed, had not shared this little secret with her favourite brother.

*   *   *

* The Islamic penalty for adultery is death, and it was not uncommon when cases of adultery arose in traditional Arabia for fathers or brothers to take the law into their own hands and to kill the woman who had stained the reputation of their family. But a wronged husband would never do this. It would be demeaning for him to admit that a woman's frailty could move him to any emotion warmer than contempt. The woman would be divorced with indifference. It was the honour of her father's family that she had besmirched, and it would be for her own menfolk to deal with her thereafter.

Sa'ud al Kabeer's night tryst with Nura showed that the trouble inside the Al Sa'ud was not as bitter as it might have been. Still, it was no way to run a country, and in the middle of 1910 came the proof of that, for Abdul Aziz was away in the east trying to deal with the Ajman and the *araif* when Shareef Husain ibn Ali launched his challenge for central Arabia from the west.

The shareef's claim was not an impressive one. The name 'Hijaz' means a barrier, and refers to the high barrier of rocky hills, a formidable escarpment in places, which run parallel to the Red Sea coastal plain and separate it from the inland desert plateau. It is a natural frontier, and the territory of the Hijaz had always lain to the western, sea-coast side of the barrier.

The areas claimed by Husain lay very distinctly on the *eastern* side of the barrier – parts of them were closer to the Persian Gulf than they were to the Red Sea – but that did not discourage the shareef. He went scouting for support in the territory of the Otayba, and he was more than 300 miles east of Mecca when he enjoyed an immense slice of good luck, for Abdul Aziz's controversial younger brother Sa'ad was in the same area. Sa'ad was raising taxes for Abdul Aziz's campaign against the rebellious *araif*, and somewhere among the Otayba occurred one of those shifts of allegiance which were the essence of wayward bedouin politics. Sa'ad's hosts took him prisoner and handed him over to the shareef.

The old man had his hands on the ideal hostage, the favourite brother of Abdul Aziz, and he lost no time exploiting his windfall gleefully. To ransom Sa'ad he demanded from Abdul Aziz an annual tribute amounting to some £4500, and Abdul Aziz had no choice but to agree. The revolt of Sa'ud al Kabeer and the *araif* made it impossible for him to move against the shareef, and he was prepared to pay any price to get his younger brother back.

Once Sa'ad was safely home in Riyadh, Abdul Aziz reneged immediately on his undertakings, saying they had no validity since they were made under compulsion, and he never, in fact, paid a penny in tribute to Shareef Husain.

But the episode had been an ignominious one. For the first time since the capture of Riyadh, Abdul Aziz had had to own himself publicly defeated. The shareef crowed delightedly over his coup, and news of it circulated all over Arabia. It was a major reverse to the Sa'udi story of success, and Abdul Aziz could only take consolation in disgruntled ridicule.

The Tale of the Shareef and the Historic Fart

There was once a young shareef who boasted of his desert knowledge. He understood the bedouin, he said. He knew how they hunted and tracked and how they sat down to eat their food with their fingers. He used to boast of his expertise, sitting with his family in Mecca, eating Turkish food with a Turkish fork and spoon.

But one day the tribes from the Asir came riding up from the south. They threatened the Hashim family's hill resort at Taif, and the Grand Shareef grew alarmed for the safety of his palaces. He must enlist the help of the local bedouin – and who better to go out and bribe them than the young shareef who talked so much about the desert?

So the young man was sent out to buy bedouin help, and when he came to the first encampment with his saddlebags overflowing with gold, he was received with great courtesy, for the tribesmen seldom saw a shareef, and they invited him to sit down and drink coffee with them.

But the young shareef was not accustomed to sitting down on his haunches to eat and drink, and as he tried to squat down beside the bedouin chief he farted. It was a long fart and a loud fart and everyone sitting round the *majlis* heard it very clearly indeed.

The young man was deeply embarrassed. But he pretended that nothing had happened, and out of courtesy to his rank and to his money the bedouin went along with the pretence. They took his gold, they rode against the men of Asir, they saved Taif – and never once did they betray by so much as a whisper or a hint of a smile that they had noticed the young shareef's fart.

But the young man himself was not so sure, and he was so mortified by what had happened that he henceforward gave up all pretence at being a desert expert. Indeed, plagued by the thought that he might one day encounter someone who had heard him fart, he forsook the Hijaz altogether and went to live in Constantinople – where the soft city ways are, of course, the ways that the house of Hashim love best of all – and he did not return to Arabia until the very end of his life when he decided he would like to die in Mecca, and when, he also presumed, the last man who heard him fart must be long dead himself.

Now it so happened that, on the road from Jeddah to Mecca, his camel needed watering, and while it drank at a well along the road he

99

fell into conversation with a young bedouin who was watering his camel there at the same time.

'Do you know', said the shareef, who was now old, grey and bent, 'that it is over forty years since I was last here – when the men of Asir attacked Taif?'

'*Wallahi!*' said the young bedouin. 'That must be many many years ago indeed, for my grandfather often told me about the year of the shareef's fart.'

It was a good story – and an old story. Its original is in the *Arabian Nights*. But it was poor comfort for the humiliation Abdul Aziz had had to suffer to ransom his brother Sa'ad, and he turned with some passion to deal with the rebellion of his cousins. 150 miles south of Riyadh on the edge of the Empty Quarter, the Hazzani family who ruled the town of Layla had joined in the revolt of the *araif*, and Abdul Aziz took the town by storm. He captured almost every leading member of the rebellious Hazzanis, and among his prisoners he also found Sa'ud ibn Abdullah, one of the leading members of the *araif*. Sa'ud was one of the cousins to whom Abdul Aziz had given a sister, Haiya, in marriage.

Abdul Aziz gave his captives twenty-four hours' grace and sent out messengers into the surrounding desert. A platform was erected swiftly outside the mud walls of the town, and next morning three sides of the square around it were packed with bedouin. One by one the Hazzani who had succoured the *araif* were led out to kneel down in front of Abdul Aziz, and at his signal a negro slave went through the ritual of public execution which is still seen today, every month or so in the main squares of Sa'udi Arabian towns.

With the sharp end of his sword the negro pricked the kneeling man hard in the back or side. The victim stiffened upwards, arching his back in pain and terror, and before the reflex was completed the executioner's sword had severed head from body in a fierce backhand blow. The negro's sword flashed eighteen times that morning outside Layla, and, as the nineteenth victim knelt before him, Abdul Aziz halted the slaughter. He rose and ordered the pardoned man and the watching crowd to go tell the desert what they had seen of his justice. This was the price of rebellion, he warned, and he would never hesitate to exact it.

There is a tale that Abdul Aziz's brother-in-law, Sa'ud bin Abdulah, was the nineteenth man pardoned even as the sword was ready to fall. But this seems unlikely. Abdul Aziz would not have inflicted such public degradation on any member of his own family. He spared his cousin, and this Sa'ud remained close ever afterwards to his brother-in-law.

But Sa'ud al Kabeer and the other rebellious cousins remained at large, tribes like the Ajman and Mutair continued to defy the central authority of Riyadh, and the appetites of Shareef Husain ibn Ali were keener than ever.

Abdul Aziz's grisly vaudeville outside the walls of Layla was a resort to traditional methods of tribal intimidation, and it dealt decisively enough with the Hazzani chiefs. But it was not the way to unify Arabia on a permanent basis.

10 Captain Shakespear

IN the spring of 1910, in his thirty-fifth year, Abdul Aziz had his photograph taken. It was the first time he had seen a camera, so far as we know. He told his photographer it was the first time he had ever seen a white man,* and the heavy glass negative of this earliest known portrait is today preserved in London at the Royal Geographical Society, filed with the other desert memorabilia of Captain William Shakespear, a distantly related descendant of his namesake, the playwright, and distinguished in his own right as one of the great Western explorers of the Arabian peninsula.

Captain Shakespear was Britain's Political Agent in Kuwait, and by 1910 His Majesty's Government was no longer filing letters from the Al Sa'ud unanswered. Even though the Turks still laid claim to Nejd, Abdul Aziz was clearly a presence in Arabia to be reckoned with, so when Captain Shakespear heard in February 1910 that the Emir of Riyadh and his brothers had arrived at the court of Sheikh Mubarak he lost no time inviting them to dinner.

Shakespear had a loathing of bedouin food. He liked his mutton roast with mint sauce. So he invited the princes of Riyadh to dine with him European style, and was happy to report that they 'appeared to appreciate a Western table and menu'.

Emboldened, Captain Shakespear asked his guests if they would consent to be photographed, and Abdul Aziz – himself emboldened, perhaps by his success with knife, fork and spoon – readily agreed.

The sheikhs and *ulema* in Riyadh would not have approved. The Koranic prohibition on depicting the human form had been strongly emphasized by Ibn Abdul Wahhab, for down this path lay the graven image and idolatry. But away from Wahhabi strictures Abdul Aziz was more relaxed, and there was in any case an Islamic rationalization

---

* This was certainly an exaggeration, for there is at least one documented instance of Abdul Aziz meeting Europeans in Kuwait before 1910.

102

of photography which even Riyadh's fundamentalists came later to accept, for the camera, suggested one ingenious theologian, does not so much engrave an image as preserve a reflection – just like a mirror, only more so. Since the Prophet never prohibited mirrors, cameras must also be acceptable.

So down sat Abdul Aziz with his brothers and Sheikh Mubarak to have their reflections preserved in March 1910, and Captain Shakespear vanished under his black cloth hood. It is clear from some of the less successful poses – surviving today among the long, glass, Cinemascope-like slides which Shakespear developed himself in an improvised desert darkroom – that the spectacle of the uniformed English dignitary stooped and fumbling beneath his veil-like headgear struck the Emir of Riyadh as somewhat comical. Abdul Aziz's face is blurred, and old Mubarak is looking down at the ground unimpressed. But eventually Shakespear got everyone to sit still and facing his bulky wood and brass plate camera, and now their eyes stare out at us levelly across seventy years of history, Abdul Aziz holding a string of oval beads between his long forefinger and thumb, Mubarak beside him, apparently clad in a brocade dressing-gown beneath traditional robes (see illustrations).

'Abdul Aziz is a fair, handsome man,' wrote Captain Shakespear, '. . . with a particularly frank and open face and, after the first shyness, genial and courteous manners. . . . His reputation among Arabs is that of a noble, generous and just man.'

Arabia's New Solomon

A woman came to Abdul Aziz one day demanding the death sentence on the killer of her husband.

'How did your husband die?' asked Abdul Aziz, who used to sit every day in his palace or tents to hear the cases that his people brought to him.

'This man was picking dates in a palm tree when he fell down on my husband below,' said the woman, 'and now I come before you a widow.'

'Did this man fall down with malice?' asked Abdul Aziz. 'Did he know your husband? Was it his intention, you believe, to break your husband's neck?'

'I know not who he is nor why he fell,' replied the widow. 'But I do know that thanks to him I am now alone in the world and my children are fatherless. I demand my blood price.'

This was, by law, the widow's right, and Abdul Aziz could not deny it her. So he asked her in what form she would like to take her compensation.

'His head,' she said at once. 'A life for a life. I will accept no less.'

Abdul Aziz remonstrated with the woman. What good was another man's death to her – or to her children? She needed money, and she would receive it, for even though the man clearly fell from the palm tree by accident, he was still bound to pay her husband's blood price.

But the woman would not be dissuaded from vengeance, and so Abdul Aziz spoke again.

'It is your right to take compensation, and it is your right to ask for this man's life.

'But it is my right, by God, to decide in what fashion he must die. And so now hear me well. You may take this man outside with you instantly and he shall be tied to the foot of a palm tree. Then you yourself shall climb to the top of that palm tree and drop down upon him from on high. Thus you may take his life as he took your husband's, and then you will have received what is rightfully yours.

'Or perhaps,' added the emir in the long pause that followed, 'you would prefer to take the blood money, after all . . .'

And so the widow took the blood money hurriedly, and all marvelled at the justice of Abdul Aziz.

'The ultimate source of power here, as in the whole course of Arab history,' wrote Gertrude Bell in 1917, 'is the personality of the commander.'

In Kuwait in 1910, Captain Shakespear was Britain's first representative to experience Abdul Aziz's personality at first hand – and it made a powerful impression. He promptly filed a report to his superior, Percy Cox, the Gulf Resident, recommending Abdul Aziz as a 'broadminded "straight" man who could probably be trusted further than most Arabs'; and Abdul Aziz responded with equal warmth to the uncompromising British functionary who offered sheikhs Edwardian dinner parties and always wore his uniform, puttees and solar topee in the desert. He invited Shakespear to come and see him on his own ground, and so next spring the British Agent rode to meet Abdul Aziz at Thaj, in eastern Arabia.

104

By now the arrival of Abdul Aziz in any part of the desert drew the tribesmen from miles around. Their chiefs did not always like it, but Abdul Aziz's reputation as a Solomon was difficult to resist, and men were also drawn by the largesse that he distributed, for the generosity of the young Emir of Riyadh was already as legendary as his justice.

He gave everything away. 'Nothing made him so genuinely unhappy', wrote Hafiz Wahba, one of his advisers in later years, 'as to find that his resources would not cover all the necessary grants and gifts.' Money had no value for him. Wahba and others would struggle to make savings. But 'he laughed at us, invariably replying, "Hoarded money never does anyone any good." '

Abdul Aziz's compulsive open-handedness was to wreak havoc in later years when the oil revenues started flowing. But it was the simple ethos of the nomad who has no means of hoarding, even if he wishes to, and it was an ethos to which the nomads of Arabia's deserts responded warmly.

One of Abdul Aziz's secretaries had a big leather-bound ledger, and, as bedouin came to meet the emir in Riyadh or on his travels, their names would be recorded in the book. They would live at Abdul Aziz's expense, eating at his table, sleeping round his tents or in his palace outbuildings for the prescribed three days, and, before they left, the Sa'udi leader would study the ledger and write against each name, in his own hand, the gift he considered appropriate – a dagger, a sack of rice, a rifle. No one left him empty-handed. His generosity was proverbial, and every sheikh to whom Captain Shakespear spoke bore witness to it.

Captain Shakespear was also struck on this second meeting by the absence in Abdul Aziz or his brothers of 'the fanatical spirit which might have been expected from the ruling Wahhabi family'. He found he could wander freely around the Sa'udi camp without provoking 'that suspicion which generally attaches to a foreigner among Arabs of the interior', and when he dared launch a religious discussion he found himself answered not with heat but 'with calm and intelligent reasoning'.

Abdul Aziz was a sincere Muslim, but he was no mad mullah. He had a wind-up gramophone with which he liked to relax in the privacy of his own tent – while Captain Shakespear relaxed with a bottle of Moselle in the privacy of his.

Yet on one subject the Wahhabi emir did grow very heated. The Al

105

Sa'ud, he told Captain Shakespear, 'cordially hated' the Turks. He wished to make it clear to his English guest 'that he did not consider himself a vassal of the Ottoman Sultan', and that his past professions of subservience were only gestures of convenience. As a Wahhabi, said Abdul Aziz, he could never accept the sultan's claim to the Islamic caliphate, for the Turkish perversions of the Koran were abominable, and he was now planning to recapture for his family the eastern Gulf coast province of al Hasa that the Turks had stolen from them in 1871.

Abdul Aziz clearly expected his British visitor to react to this attack upon the Turks with warmth, or with curiosity at the least. But Captain Shakespear represented a country whose official policy remained the endorsement of Ottoman authority in central Arabia. His Majesty's Government, said the captain, was on good terms with the Turkish government and 'would be averse from anything of the nature of an intrigue against it'. Just to be listening to the plans Abdul Aziz was hatching against Turkey was compromising for a British Agent, and 'I said at once that I had not come to discuss politics but to enjoy touring in the desert.'

So Abdul Aziz had to drop the subject. If Britain was not willing to help him, he said gloomily, then his plans were doomed to failure.

Two months after Abdul Aziz met Captain Shakespear in 1911, Italy invaded the Ottoman territory of Tripolitania (modern Libya); the next year Greece attacked Turkey to gain much of Macedonia, as well as Crete; Bulgaria, Bosnia and Herzegovina were already lost. The great Ottoman empire was crumbling, and in desperation the Young Turks started pulling back their soldiers from their Middle East garrisons.

It looked as if the Arabs could now gain their freedom as other former Ottoman subjects were doing, and when Abdul Aziz met up with Captain Shakespear in May 1913 near Majma'a, in the northern part of Nejd, he informed the British Agent that the moment had come 'for Nejd to rid itself of all shadow of Ottoman suzerainty and to drive their troops from Hasa'.

Captain Shakespear was appalled. This desert chieftain, whom he had come to know and rather like, was proposing to 'try conclusions with a world power which could, if it exerted itself, crush him utterly'. Abdul Aziz stood to lose all he now possessed. 'As his friend I could not let him labour under so serious a misapprehension of Turkish strength', and it was also the captain's duty, as the representative of His Majesty's Government, to make clear that Britain would give Abdul Aziz no support of any kind if he decided to attack the Turkish garrisons in al Hasa.

Abdul Aziz seemed cast down. He was 'manifestly disappointed', thought Captain Shakespear, 'that I could give him no encouragement or even the faintest hope that his ambitions would have approval, tacit, disguised or otherwise, of the British government', and on this discouraging note emir and agent said goodbye, Shakespear riding back on a fortnight-long journey to Kuwait, where he wrote up his report for Percy Cox.

The British Agent dispatched that report some time early on 15 May 1913. But later that same day messengers arrived in Kuwait with fresh news from al Hasa. Sa'udi troops had invaded the province, said the reports, and now the entire area and 300 miles of Gulf coast down to Qatar was in the hands of Abdul Aziz.

Al Hasa had an ancient and distinguished history. Arab legend has it as the original homeland of Abraham. Bedouin will show you to this day the cave where, they believe, the patriarch lived before he migrated to Ur of the Chaldees; and this Old Testament link was one reason why the early Zionists are said to have accepted al Hasa along with Uganda and Palestine on one shortlist of possible homelands drawn up in the late nineteenth century. They were not aware of al Hasa's rather special geology when they rejected it soon afterwards, and one of the twentieth century's more intriguing 'ifs' is what might have happened had Zionist fervour aimed at the land which proved to cover the Gulf's richest oilfields, rather than crusading for the Palestine coastal strip.

Before oil, al Hasa's wealth was based upon the date palm and the sea. The harbour of Uqayr had provided the first two Sa'udi empires with their own commercial seaport, and the oasis of Hofuf, the principal settlement of the area, generated much of the trade that passed through it. The rich dark amber *khalas* date of the al Hasa palm groves was famous throughout Arabia – small but sweet, translucent with a lusciousness that set it above other drier varieties. Starting in September the finest dates were picked by hand and packed in boxes in time for the Christmas market in Europe and

America. The medium-quality fruit was traded locally, and the very poorest was exported in bulk, usually to English distilleries.

The date's concentrated sugar content – up to 80 per cent, a most effective germ inhibitor – made it a dietary staple in a climate where most fresh fruit was liable to spread disease. It travelled easily. It outlasted the longest desert trek. It was ideal nutrition for the bedouin, the underpinning of his life structure – as the olive supported the Mediterranean way of life – and the farmers of al Hasa made sure that nothing went to waste.

'Take good care of your mother, the palm tree,' the Prophet told his followers – and she certainly took good care of them. Palm fronds provided baskets or shelters; the trunk was of serviceable soft wood; lucerne and vegetables were grown in the dappled blue-green shade beneath the branches; and the date stones were either fed to camels to aid their digestion or else ground up with other flours to make a nutty-tasting bread which can still be purchased in Hofuf.

The date palm had made al Hasa so prosperous that the area boasted its own coinage, the *tawilah*, a wishbone-shaped tweezer of copper which circulated alongside the Indián rupee and Maria Theresa thaler,* two foreign currencies established by trade patterns as the cash acceptable anywhere in the peninsula. When Colonel Pelly attempted to assess the wealth of the Wahhabi empire in 1865, he decided that fully half its revenues came from Hofuf and the al Hasa district, which also contained nearly a quarter of the peoples then owing allegiance to Riyadh. The loss of al Hasa to the Turks in 1871 had been a severe financial blow to the Al Sa'ud.

But the Turks had found the eastern province easier to capture than to hold. They were not welcomed by the bedouin and, not for the first time in Arabia, they found that their authority extended little further than the walls of their forts. The main road from Uqayr to Hofuf became especially notorious. Goods passing from the port to the capital were stopped six or seven times in less than 100 miles by Ajman bedouin extorting protection money.

So when Abdul Aziz arrived in al Hasa early in May 1913 he received a heartfelt welcome from the townsfolk. He had been

---

* Until Abdul Aziz's introduction of the Sa'udi riyal, Arabia had to rely on other people's currency – the Indian rupee, the British gold sovereign and the 'Maria Theresa' thaler or dollar. So named after the Empress of Austria (1740–80), whose ample bust it features, this silver coin was valued for its stable bullion content, and it can still be found on moneychangers' tables in the souqs of modern Arabia.

secretly in touch with several of Hofuf's leading merchants for some time, and one family, the prosperous mercantile dynasty of al Qosaibi, had been organizing support for him.

Abdul Aziz had moved rapidly after he said goodbye to Captain Shakespear, riding hard to Riyadh to raise a levy of townsmen, and then marching at once with these *hadhar* to within five hours of Hofuf. Here, on 4 May 1913, he selected just 300 men, and rode on eastwards with them to arrive after sunset in the palm groves near the town. Abdul Aziz was planning a repetition of his successful Riyadh coup. The camels were tethered, some palm trunks prepared as makeshift scaling ladders, and then Abdul Aziz led his men stealthily forward to the outer walls. Two hours after midnight the first Sa'udi raiders were on top of Hofuf's battlements lowering ropes to their comrades and, as soon as a good number were inside, they moved to open the western gate.

It was only now that the Turkish sentries were aroused. They blazed away at the shadows in the darkness and then withdrew to the 'Kut', the fort within a fort where their ammunition and treasure were stored. They were totally cut off, and the townspeople came out of their houses to welcome Abdul Aziz. Hofuf was his.

Next morning he sent a messenger to the Turkish commander. He and the garrison could have a safe conduct to the coast, take their arms, and would even be provided with transport and pocket money if they would surrender immediately. If not, he would detonate the explosive with which the mud walls of the Kut had been mined.

By noon the commander had surrendered, and sent messages to his outlying garrisons to do the same. Inside the Kut, Abdul Aziz found treasure worth 4000 dollars, twelve large guns, two machine guns and a large stock of rifles and ammunition. The Turks marched to Uqayr, embarked on boats for Bahrain and, after a soggy attempt to reland at Qateef, did not trouble the new masters of al Hasa again.

The daring coup which captured Riyadh is justly celebrated in the history of the Kingdom. But it was the night's work of 4 May 1913 which secured for the Al Sa'ud the land which is today the most valuable piece of real estate on earth.

11 Jarrab

THE news that Abdul Aziz had enlarged his central Arabian empire to the shores of the Persian Gulf was received in Whitehall with some dismay, for the officials of the Foreign Office were that very summer negotiating a protocol on the assumption that he did not exist. The Anglo-Turkish Convention of July 1913 carved up the Middle East between Britain and the Ottomans, and the second clause of the convention described the ten-year-old Sa'udi empire as 'le sandjak Ottoman de Nedjd'* – 'the Ottoman region of Nejd' – making no mention of the house of Sa'ud, and alluding to Nejd as if it were as firmly Turkish as the mainland of Asia Minor itself.

This agreement, remarked Sir Percy Cox drily, appeared 'somewhat irreconcilable' with the fact that Abdul Aziz had just expelled the last Turk from the entire extent of Nejd, but his observation was not kindly received. Cox and Captain Shakespear, in Whitehall's view, were showing too much sympathy for this Bin Sa'ud. Were they both going 'bush'?

Shakespear was rebuked by the Foreign Secretary himself for having met with Abdul Aziz – 'a course which does not seem to have been a necessary condition of any mission with which he has been charged' – and the captain's report on his meeting with the Emir of Riyadh was annotated 'a great pity' at one point and 'nonsense' at another. The memoranda flew, and the margin scribblers had a field-day.

This bureaucratic sniping reflected a fundamental division between two rival departments of Britain's civil service abroad. Captain Shakespear, Sir Percy Cox and the other British officials on the ground in the Gulf were employees of the British Government of

* A *sanjak* was an Ottoman district inside a larger *vilayet* (province).

110

India, and as such they looked at Arabia from the local viewpoint of Gulf security. They reported, in the first instance, to New Delhi, and for them Abdul Aziz was an important regional figure with great potential to strengthen – or to disturb – the status quo it was their duty to maintain to the north-west of India.

But, for the Foreign Office in London, Arabia was a minor distraction on the sidelines of the grand European power play. Whitehall was more concerned with Turkey than with the attitude of some distant desert chief, for Turkey controlled the Dardanelles, the crucial sea link between Russia and the Anglo-French entente, as well as the soft southern flank of Austria-Hungary, and, if the price of Turkish friendship was to describe the wastes of central Arabia as 'le sandjak Ottoman de Nedjd', then it seemed a very small price to pay.

This was the reason for the Sa'udi letters' being filed unanswered in Britain's diplomatic archives. Membership of the Trucial system, the Foreign Office told the India Office, must be restricted to sheikhs along the coast of the Gulf itself. The Al Sa'ud did not qualify.

Abdul Aziz himself, meanwhile, was scarcely behaving as someone whose existence depended on the permission of distant memorandum-writers. 'We, the Islamic and Muhammadan Arabs,' he wrote proudly to Sir Percy Cox on 13 June 1913, 'will rise to uphold our honour and will recover our rights with the last drop of our blood.' Abdul Aziz sought Britain's friendship, but he saw no need to grovel for it. He had a government of his own to establish.

He chose as Governor of al Hasa his cousin Abdullah bin Jaluwi, the hero of the Mismak doorway battle. The only way to organize a far-flung empire where messages took days, if not weeks, to arrive was to delegate outlying areas to relatives who could be trusted implicitly and Abdullah bin Jaluwi was one of these. Dr Paul Harrison saw him a few years later in a *majlis* sitting on the floor at the feet of Abdul Aziz. 'That cold pitiless face', wrote the doctor, 'was fairly transformed by the love and loyalty that shone out.'

Away from Abdul Aziz's presence, however, Abdullah bin Jaluwi's face was not noted for its shining love. It was rare that a smile broke through his shaggy black beard; he dressed untidily – 'his *aghal* was torn and his *abba* [cloak] old and shabby,' said Colonel Dickson – and the reputation that Abdullah bin Jaluwi soon established in al Hasa was fearsome, for he took on its raiders, footpads and highwaymen with ferocity. It was not long before his severity became a byword the entire length of the Gulf, since his remedy for any trouble was straightforward – to unsheathe the executioner's sword. Nor did Abdullah bin Jaluwi stop at heads and hands.

The Big Toe and the Sack of Coffee

A villager was walking one day down the road to Hofuf, when he saw a heavy sack lying beneath a palm tree. Curious as to what might be inside it, he got down from his donkey and nudged it with his toe. It felt like coffee. He wondered whether to pick it up and take it with him. But he did not know the owner and did not wish to be accused of theft, so he rode on into town and dismounted outside the *majlis* of Abdullah bin Jaluwi. There he told the emir what he had seen beside the road.

'How could you tell', asked the emir, 'that it was a sack of coffee?'

'Because I prodded it with my toe,' replied the villager honestly.

'Then take him outside and sever that big toe immediately,' said the emir. 'He knew the sack was not his, so he should not even have touched it.'

In February 1920 Harold Dickson met one of bin Jaluwi's execution-ers who 'had decapitated 22 men and cut off the hands of scores. The latter process, he grimly said, did not hurt, but what did make the men cry out was putting the severed stump into boiling fat.'*

In 1922 Amin Rihani was travelling from Hofuf to Riyadh when he saw a camel tethered at the wayside, obviously dying. Its owner had gone back to Hofuf to collect another beast, and that might take him as many as five days. But he had left all his merchandise beside the camel, for he knew that, even though, when he returned, the ravens might be picking at the poor beast's carcass, his goods would still be lying there, totally untouched. The tale of the big toe had evidently received wide circulation.

*　　　*　　　*

* The boiling fat was to sterilize the wound. Nowadays in Sa'udi Arabia medical attendants dress amputated limbs and also administer local anaesthetics – though it should be said that judicial amputations are today not as much part of the Arabian routine as Westerners often imagine. They are not imposed in cases of theft until after the third offence, and in the eighteen months that the author lived in Sa'udi Arabia from 1978 to 1980 fewer than ten such sentences, which are a matter of public record, were carried out.

In December 1913 Abdul Aziz met Captain Shakespear again, this time in the company of Major A. P. Trevor, the British Agent in Bahrain, and in homage to his British friend's culinary fastidiousness Ibn Sa'ud had one of Bahrain's best cooks brought over for the occasion.

But in other respects the Sa'udi leader was growing less and less willing to accommodate the British. After his conquest of al Hasa, which made him as much a Gulf coast power as any Trucial sheikh, he had requested the opening of formal relations with Britain in June 1913. But he had received no satisfactory answer to that request, nor to another approach made during the same month, and he was getting frustrated.

'If the situation is now altered,' he wrote, 'and Great Britain is not willing to preserve former friendship, which is his earnest desire, [he asks that] he may be definitely informed, so that he may look to his own interests.'

Sir Percy Cox passed the Sa'udi query onwards, requesting authorization to negotiate seriously with Abdul Aziz, since Cox did not see how he could credibly organize British power in the Persian Gulf around the fiction that the Turks were still controllers of the al Hasa coast.

But Whitehall's eyes were fixed on Europe and the Dardanelles. Nothing should be done in Arabia that might incur the displeasure of Constantinople. 'The cardinal factor of British policy', insisted the Foreign Office, '. . . is to uphold the integrity of the Turkish dominions in Asia.'

So when Shakespear and Trevor met Abdul Aziz at the end of 1913 they were not empowered to offer him official recognition, let alone a treaty of friendship or alliance – and the Sa'udi leader took the point. In the spring of 1914 he rode north to meet Turkish representatives near Kuwait, and in May he accepted from them the title of hereditary Ottoman *wali* (governor) and Commandant of Nejd, including al Hasa. In theory he renewed his 1905 acknowledgement of Turkish suzerainty, but in practice he remained very much his own master, and in clause 9 of his agreement he undertook 'not to grant concessions to foreigners' – in other words, the British.

Two years later, after British troops had captured Basra, this secret agreement was unearthed among the Ottoman archives, and Sir Percy Cox had a translation prepared for forwarding to the Foreign Office.

113

'This is the treaty', ran a note scribbled pointedly on the flyleaf, 'which Bin Saud was obliged in self-defence to make when we left him to his own devices in the early part of 1914.'

The bitterness was understandable, for by 1916 Britain was locked in a fierce and bloody struggle with Turkey for control of the Middle East, and the Foreign Office policy of appeasing Turkish pretensions was an acknowledged failure. It had not stopped the Young Turks lining up with the Kaiser in October 1914, and history was taking a momentous turn for that area of the world once called Ottoman.

Captain Shakespear was at Aldershot in September 1914. He had returned home from Kuwait earlier that year, travelling right across Arabia on an epic journey that had taken him to Riyadh for a time and even out with a Sa'udi raiding party. But he had reached London to discover little interest in all he had to tell about Abdul Aziz and his central Arabian possessions. He was brushed off with a file of old correspondence to read, and with the outbreak of war he turned his back on the Middle East. He volunteered for service in Europe, and was down in Aldershot training a squad of recruits when the Foreign Office finally appreciated that, if Turkey was going to join up with Germany, then Abdul Aziz would be a useful ally to have in central Arabia.

Instantly a frantic search was initiated for the Sa'udi leader's English acquaintance. Captain Shakespear was eventually intercepted making his preparations to depart for the trenches of northern France, and within days the captain was on a boat heading for the Persian Gulf with sealed letters from His Majesty's Government to the Emir of Riyadh.

Abdul Aziz, it appeared, did exist after all.

Captain Shakespear located Abdul Aziz on the last day of 1914 at Khufaisa on the edge of the bleak gravelly plains near al Artawiya, 200 miles north of Riyadh. It was windswept and cold. At night water froze in the waterskins. The Sa'udi army was on campaign, manoeuvring against a Shammar force sent out by the Rasheeds who, nearly a decade after the death of the great Ibn Rasheed, were making a comeback with Turkish help. The camp throbbed to the drumming and chanting with which bedouin work themselves up for battle, and the tribesmen hopped, danced and sang for days while Abdul Aziz and Shakespear negotiated.

The captain found the emir in a difficult mood. Abdul Aziz had always said this day would come, but now that Britain was the supplicant in search of a friend he gave a lesson of his own in aloofness. His position, reported Captain Shakespear, was 'one of complete political detachment from the British Government', for Abdul Aziz did not appreciate being 'now asked to commit himself in open war with his most powerful and bitter enemies [the Turks] . . . by the Power which six months earlier had informed him that it could not intervene on his behalf.' The emir was not impressed by the letters that Shakespear had brought. He wanted nothing less than 'a signed and sealed treaty with the British Government,' reported the captain. 'Nor will he move a step further towards making matters either easier for us or more difficult for the Turks . . . until he obtains in that treaty some very solid guarantee of his position with Great Britain.'

Captain Shakespear sympathized wholeheartedly with his friend, and sat down to draft a treaty that warmed the atmosphere considerably. But he had his private doubts about what his superiors would do with it. 'They will probably go on messing about', he wrote to his brother, 'until they make Bin Saud so utterly sick that he will chuck his present friendly attitude.'

Captain Shakespear turned from politics to the spectacle few other Westerners had ever witnessed – an Arabian army preparing for battle – and he described it to his brother:

Bin Saud has some 6000 of his men here in tents, and thousands of badawin all round. There is never any knowing what these badawin will do; they are quite capable of being firm friends up to the battle and then suddenly changing their minds and going over to the other side in the middle of it. Bin Saud wants me to clear out, but I want to see the show, and I don't think it will be very unsafe really.

They broke camp and moved westwards towards Zilfi, the Englishman riding on his camel beside Abdul Aziz. At the head of the army fluttered the huge green Sa'udi war banners with their white lettering, and behind them the motley throng of townsmen and tribesmen fanned out, raising the dust of the plain. Bedouin contingents tacked themselves on to the cavalcade as they rode, and they all camped that night on the edge of the sand dunes. They were now very close to the enemy, and Abdul Aziz came to Shakespear's tent to ask him for a second time to leave before battle was joined.

115

But Shakespear would not go. Abdul Aziz was fighting the Rasheeds for his own dynastic reasons, yet the battle for central Arabia could be crucial to Britain's Middle East strategy as well. A defeat for the Rasheeds would be a defeat for the Turks, and Captain Shakespear was already imagining himself riding at the head of Abdul Aziz's army on a grand campaign of Arabian conquest. 'I shouldn't be surprised', he wrote to Gertrude Bell, 'if I reached Hail in the course of the next month or so as Bin Saud's political adviser!'

Shakespear's cook Khalid later recalled the conversation. 'It was dishonourable to turn back,' said the captain. By one account Abdul Aziz begged his infidel friend to wear desert robes at least, and the Englishman said 'no' to that as well. He always had a scorn of fancy dress.

So Captain Shakespear was wearing the khaki uniform of the 17th Bengal Lancers when he rode out on the morning of 24 January 1915 to the battlefield he called Jarrab. It was a patch of mounds and dunes on the same open, featureless plain where Rawdhat al Muhanna had been fought, the traditional Sa'udi–Rasheed skirmishing ground, and Jarrab proved a traditional skirmish – except for the presence of the uniformed Englishman standing beside the Sa'udi guns.

At least one old man who fought at Jarrab still remembers the 'Inglayzi', tall and broad in his strange foreign helmet beside the big guns which had been captured from the Turks. Subsequent British accounts, by people who were not there, stress the role Captain Shakespear played as an observer, taking out his camera to photograph the skirmishing horsemen on the plain. But Walayd bin Shawiyya remembers the Englishman getting very much involved. He kept looking towards the enemy with his field-glasses and shouting orders to the novice Sa'udi gunners beside him on the ridge. He was directing their aim as the battle swirled closer, oblivious of danger – even after it became clear that something had gone very badly wrong.

Abdul Aziz's Ajman contingent was supposed to hold the Rasheeds' Shammar cavalry on the plain. But the Ajman wheeled, and the Shammar horsemen broke through to head for the guns. Had the Ajman switched sides deliberately, or just decided that things were getting too hot for them? The Sa'udi gunners and riflemen did not stay to find out. They made brief attempts to bury their field-guns, then turned and fled, leaving one uniformed British officer alone on the ridge with his revolver.

After the battle of Jarrab, one of Captain Shakespear's servants

116

passed by the battlefield and saw his master's bullet-marked body stripped of all but its ganji vest. But the captain had no burial place. The Rasheeds bore off his solar helmet in triumph and gave it to the Turks, who hung it up outside the gates of Medina, evidence of the Al Sa'ud's involvement with the infidels.

Abdul Aziz himself wrote in sorrow to Sir Percy Cox. 'We pressed him to leave us, but he refused . . .'; and when, in later years, the first ruler of Sa'udi Arabia was asked to name the most remarkable non-Muslim he knew of, his reply came with no hesitation at all: 'Shakespear.'

When he said this to Captain John Glubb in 1928, Glubb was at first surprised that an Arab chieftain should display such a command of English literature. But then Glubb realized that Abdul Aziz was referring to the first Englishman he had ever known as a friend, the sturdy and obstinate captain whose death represented for the Emir of Riyadh a personal loss – and more than that; for the battle of Jarrab in January 1915 marked the beginning – and the end – of active Sa'udi involvement in the First World War.

12 The Arab Revolt

ENTER Lawrence of Arabia, screen left. Captain Shakespear had been visualizing before he died a glorious campaign of trans-Arabian conquest, and, if Jarrab had proved a victory in January 1915, then he might have accomplished it. The Englishman and the emir had the makings of a fine team. They might together have secured central Arabia for the Al Sa'ud and for Britain – and, if that had happened, the pattern of the Great War in the Middle East, not to mention Hollywood's roster of desert epics, might have looked very different.

But, as it was, the battlefield defection of the Ajman, which cut short Shakespear's ambitions so tragically, also dealt Abdul Aziz a blow from which he did not easily recover. For nearly two years after Jarrab his energies were consumed by the rebellions of tribes who simply refused to accept the limitation of their freedom which Sa'udi occupation of the eastern province entailed.

The rebellion was led by the Ajman, but Abdul Aziz's old mentors, the Murrah, joined in as well, and the entire disaffection was aided enthusiastically by those members of the *araif* who were still at large. The revolt brought Abdul Aziz's authority to so low a pitch that it seemed doubtful at one stage whether his regime could even survive, and whatever hopes Britain had nurtured of serious Sa'udi help against the Turks were also brought low. In their First World War strategy the British had to look to the other side of the peninsula for Arab allies, and in October 1916 there disembarked in Jeddah from SS *Lama* a short, mousy-haired temporary captain on holiday from the British army's map-making department in Cairo, Captain T. E. Lawrence.

Lawrence of Arabia has generated controversy on the scale that only heroes can inspire. The heart-stopping vigour and nobility of his masterpiece, *Seven Pillars of Wisdom*, and his self-abasing appetite

118

for having his buttocks spanked, composed a paradoxical blend of knight-errantry and degradation susceptible to endless analysis, and the Lawrence myth remains one Western topic about which Arabs are perennially curious: cemeteries for dogs and the parole of murderers are two Western phenomena which can mildly excite the unwondering wonder of present-day Sa'udi's, but neither can stir conversation like the enigma of El 'Aurens – despite the fact that Lawrence, who never saw central Arabia nor met Abdul Aziz, firmly hitched his star not to the Sa'udi cause but to that of the Hashimite shareefs of Mecca.

Shareef Husain ibn Ali had proclaimed the Arab Revolt in June 1916. It was ostensibly a spontaneous call to his fellow Arabs to take control of their own destiny and rid the Middle East of foreigners – by which the shareef meant the Ottoman Turks and their infidel German allies. But Shareef Husain had infidel allies of his own – the British – and his movement was less an Arab revolt than an Anglo-Hashimite conspiracy. Husain saw the rebellion and the British military assistance that went with it as the ideal vehicle for his own dynastic ambition, while Britain nurtured imperial schemes, for her part, which were very different from the anti-imperialistic rhetoric that she was sponsoring.

Sir Henry McMahon,* the British High Commissioner in Egypt who made the promises that induced Husain to turn on the Turks, later explained how his fundamental aim had been to suborn the loyalties of the Arab soldiers fighting in the Ottoman armies: 'At that moment a large portion of the Turkish force at Gallipoli and nearly the whole of the force in Mesopotamia were Arabs. . . . Could we give them some guarantee of assistance in the future to justify their splitting with the Turks? I was told to do that at once . . .'

So McMahon embarked on the correspondence with Shareef Husain which, between July 1915 and January 1916, promised British aid during the war to a Hashimite attack on the Turks, and committed British support, after the war, to 'the independence of Arabia and its inhabitants' – a momentous and unpredictable change

---

* Lt-Col. Sir Arthur Henry McMahon (1862–1949) came to Egypt in 1914 from negotiating the McMahon Line frontier between India and Tibet. 'McMahon was slight, sunbaked and spectacled, always courteous, but . . . rather lightweight,' according to Laurence Grafftey-Smith, who worked under him in Cairo. 'His only visible enthusiasm was locusts. He had had some success with locust control in India, and would discuss his methods with all and sundry. Hence a nickname, "Loki", which also became the combination of the Chancery safe.'

in Britain's attitude towards the Middle East, if the promise meant what it said.

'It was', admitted McMahon later, 'the most unfortunate date in my life.'

The High Commissioner's regret stemmed from the peacetime chaos which Britain's wartime promises provoked. Under the strain of the campaigns in Gallipoli, Mesopotamia and on the Western Front, Britain's representatives went shopping for help with a series of conflicting Middle-Eastern pledges which came to be seen, after the war, as impossibly contradictory, not to say devious in the eyes of some, and McMahon's undertakings to Shareef Husain were the first of these deals.

'Nothing to do with me,' said the High Commissioner when confronted with the mess after the war, '. . . purely military business.'

It was this military business which Captain T. E. Lawrence turned into such a thrilling and historic adventure. Before Lawrence landed in the Hijaz in 1916 the Arab Revolt had been foundering, for Shareef Husain ibn Ali's military performance had been unimpressive. The shareef's June proclamation of revolt had taken the Turks by surprise, but they had soon rallied and had made good use of the Hijaz railway which ran down from Damascus to rush supplies and reinforcements into Medina.

The Hashimite forces, a motley collection of mercenaries, Turkish deserters, impressed townsmen and bedouin, were no match for the regular Turkish army. It looked as if the shareef's revolt might collapse within months and yield to the Turks the entire Red Sea coast, the flank of the route by which Britain's Indian Army, half of all her disposable forces, were being ferried, via Suez, to the Western Front.

Some voices in Cairo and Whitehall began calling for the dispatch of a full-scale British Expeditionary Force to save the Hijaz, but young Captain Lawrence returned to Cairo from his Hijaz excursion of October 1916 with a better idea. He had travelled north from Jeddah, inspected the Hashimite forces at first hand, and had been most impressed by their leader, Shareef Husain's third son, Feisal.*

---

* Some Western writers have adopted the convention of spelling the name of Husain's third son as Feisal and that of Abdul Aziz's second surviving son as Faisal. This convention has no basis whatsoever, since both men bore exactly the same name in Arabic, but it will be adopted here to help distinguish one from the other. The spelling of Shareef Husain's name is similarly distinguished in this book from that of his great-grandson, the present King Hussein of Jordan.

The Arabs did not need British reinforcements, reported Captain Lawrence. A British army entrenching itself in Islam's Holy Land could provoke immeasurable complications. What the Hashimites needed was gold, guns, ammunition and a few advisers – himself among them – who could teach the bedouin tricks like blowing up the railway which was proving to be the Turks' lifeline. Cairo and Whitehall seized on Lawrence's advice with alacrity, and thus was born the irregular guerrilla campaign subsequently to win immortality for itself and its inspirer.

In the summer of 1917 Lawrence set off with just thirty or so camelmen across the fierce and arid mountains of the northern Hijaz. The plan was daring and risky – to bypass the Turkish army in Medina and capture the town of Aqaba at the head of the Red Sea, gateway to Palestine and Syria – and the plan succeeded brilliantly. Aqaba fell, constant mining attacks on the Hijaz railway kept the Turks bottled uselessly in Medina, and the road was open for the victorious Arab entry into Damascus of the armies headed by Feisal bin Husain. It was an arduous and dramatic adventure, and Lawrence's account of it in *Seven Pillars of Wisdom* did full credit to its miseries and glories, a triumphant coup for the Hashimites and a unique and immortal achievement for the little Englishman himself.

Modern detractors have been as eager to demythologize Lawrence's war in the desert as his contemporaries were happy to glorify the clean action and individual daring which made the Arab Revolt such a refreshing contrast to the impersonal carnage and stalemate of the Western Front. But Arabs are not jealous of their heroes – nor of other people's.

'Lawrence a great man?' said one venerable sheikh to this author. 'I do not know. We never saw him in Medina. But we all feared him greatly. We knew that he was out there with the bedouin. We knew that he could lead them, that he could make them fight, that he could get them gold and guns and dynamite. He could organize them better than the Hashimites could. He succeeded where the shareef had failed.

'Perhaps what we heard was all Turkish propaganda. They wanted to discredit the shareef for accepting infidel aid. But anyone could see that before Lawrence came the Ottomans were winning, and that after he came they lost.'

13 Sir Abdul Aziz bin Sa'ud

Abdul Aziz and the Leather Bucket

Abdul Aziz dreamed one night that he was drawing water from a well. It was a deep well. He could hardly see the bottom, and it was a struggle for him to haul the heavy leather bag, filled with water, to the top. But he pulled and pulled until the bucket came into view and then, just as he was about to stretch out and seize it, the cord broke. Bucket and water went crashing down to the bottom.

Abdul Aziz awoke in some distress, for he knew that this dream could not augur well, and he asked Sheikh Abdul Aziz al Nimr to interpret it for him.

'Your long weary hauling of the water', said the sheikh, 'signifies your struggle to conquer and subdue the warring Arabs of Nejd. And the breaking of the cord at the last minute signifies a catastrophe that is just about to befall you.'

And so it came to pass. Within months of his dream, Abdul Aziz was defeated at the battle of Jarrab and, for two years after that, he had to struggle to exhaustion point with the rebellion of the most powerful and troublesome of his tribes.

The rebellion was led by the Ajman. Their sheikhs of the Hithlain clan had been friendly to the Al Sa'ud so long as they concentrated their empire building around Riyadh. But Abdul Aziz's capture of Hofuf had changed all that, for Abdullah bin Jaluwi's forceful assumption of leadership in al Hasa meant that the Hithlain were no longer lords of the east. Their tribesmen grew restive at bin Jaluwi's ban on raiding, and when he began to levy tax in the name of Abdul Aziz their discontent became uncontrollable.

The transfer of local wealth to be spent in Riyadh has always been an eastern grievance against the Al Sa'ud. It was one reason for the riots which caused havoc in Qateef in December 1979; and in 1915 the Ajman boiled over. They rode reluctantly with Abdul Aziz when he ordered them to Jarrab, their support in the battle was halfhearted at best – and it was deliberately treacherous at worst. Abdul Aziz certainly believed he had been betrayed, and he determined to teach the tribe a lesson they would not forget.

Abdul Aziz's anger had been played upon by his brother Sa'ad. He was still pursuing the quarrel that had led the *araif* to take refuge with the Ajman in 1910, and the two brothers, furious at the check to their ambitions administered by these eastern tribesmen, stirred up each other's emotions at the expense of their better judgement. Six months after Jarrab they had pursued the Ajman to Kinzan, 20 miles west of Hofuf, and there they attacked the rebels in a palm grove one night in the summer of 1915 – to be defeated disastrously.

After the catastrophe, it was Sa'ad who got the blame. Abdul Aziz was negotiating with the Ajman, it was said, when his younger brother persuaded him to launch a treacherous surprise attack. There was to be peace next day, but Sa'ad wanted blood, and the betrayal he inspired received the punishment it deserved. Taken by surprise, the Ajman rallied against the Sa'udis in righteous fury and slaughtered them with no quarter given. Kinzan was the most severe defeat Abdul Aziz ever suffered.

Sa'ad's excuse for the disaster will never be known, for as the bullets flew in the darkness he was wounded mortally, while Abdul Aziz beside him was also hit. The Sa'udis had to fly for safety to Hofuf with barely enough troops to hold the town, leaving the Ajman with 'the run of al Hasa', according to a British intelligence report. The rebellious tribesmen controlled all the roads, so that Abdul Aziz was 'practically a prisoner in Hofuf', and he was lucky to escape with the help of rescue forces under his brother Muhammad and Salim, Sheikh Mubarak's son. Sa'udi authority had not sunk to so low a state since 1902.

Ten years later, when the Middle East was still riven by the consequences of the First World War, and when Shareef Husain ibn Ali, puffed up by the success of the Arab Revolt, had proved to be infinitely more troublesome to his British mentors than the stabler and more reasonable Abdul Aziz, it was to be suggested by some that Britain had 'backed the wrong horse' in Arabia. The money and arms channelled through Lawrence into the Hijaz, it was argued, would have been better directed towards Nejd.

But no one could have argued this during the First World War itself.

The disaster of Kinzan compounded the Sa'udi defeat at Jarrab, and, with most of eastern Arabia in revolt against him in 1916, Abdul Aziz could scarcely help himself, let alone the British.

In December 1915 Abdul Aziz met Sir Percy Cox for the first time. The Sa'udi leader still had an Ajman bullet in his arm, and most of al Hasa was still in revolt against him. But Cox had confidence in the Al Sa'ud's long-term ability to subdue the bedouin, and he met with Abdul Aziz at Qateef when the emir came to the Gulf coast to conclude the negotiations that Shakespear had initiated before Jarrab.

The Anglo-Sa'udi friendship treaty as finally agreed between Cox and Abdul Aziz in December 1915 represented a triumph for both men. It gave the Al Sa'ud virtually everything they had been asking for since they first wrote their unanswered letters to the British in 1902, and it represented for the Gulf Resident the expansion into Arabia of his Trucial sphere of influence which the Foreign Office had so steadfastly blocked until the outbreak of war with Turkey.

Abdul Aziz gave Britain trading privileges and superintendence of his foreign policy in return for British protection against his enemies at home and abroad, and, while the relationship sounded colonial on paper, in practice it was a major step forward in the creation of an independent Sa'udi state. The guarantee of British military protection ended Turkish claims to central Arabia in any practical sense, and the concessions that Abdul Aziz granted in return for international recognition only represented the reality of living on the coast of a waterway controlled and patrolled by the British navy. Inside his own territories Abdul Aziz was free to act as he wished – and now he had solid great-power support to strengthen his internal authority: in 1915 the British sent him 300 captured Turkish rifles and 10,000 rupees; in 1916 he received 1000 more guns, 200,000 rounds of ammunition plus a further £20,000 in cash, and with this help he was able to subdue the Ajman and restore order in al Hasa.

Twelve months after concluding his friendship treaty with Britain, Abdul Aziz was firmly in control of Nejd once more, and the India Office had work for him to do. Sir Percy Cox wanted Abdul Aziz to attack the Rasheeds again, for there was a British army fighting a desperate campaign against the Turks north of Basra, and Rasheed forces had been harassing the British flank. There had been mutterings in Whitehall that the India Office's decades of nurturing Arabian tribal chiefs were yielding few practical benefits now that it really mattered, so at the end of November 1916 Cox summoned all his Persian Gulf protégés to a 'Great Durbar' to co-ordinate policy; and Abdul Aziz was invited as the newest member of the club.

The Sa'udi leader made an immediate impression on his hosts: 'tall, dignified and observant,' noted Cox's deputy, Captain A. T. Wilson,* approvingly, 'he looked as big a man as he was.' This was the first opportunity Abdul Aziz had had to meet British representatives *en masse*, and from the Kuwait durbar of November 1916 came one of the classic Western assessments of the Sultan of Nejd.

'Ibn Saud is now barely forty, though he looks some years older,' wrote Gertrude Bell, Cox's Oriental Secretary and assistant at the durbar (by late November 1916, Abdul Aziz was, in fact forty Western years old and forty-one by the Muslim reckoning).

He is a man of splendid physique, standing well over six feet, and carrying himself with the air of one accustomed to command. Though he is more massively built than the typical nomad Sheikh he has the characteristics of the well-bred Arab, the strong marked aquiline profile, full-fleshed nostrils, prominent lips and long narrow chin accentuated by a pointed beard. His hands are fine, with slender fingers, a trait almost universal among the tribes of pure Arab blood, and in spite of his great height and breadth of shoulder he conveys the impression, common enough in the desert, of an indefinable lassitude, not individual but racial, the secular weariness of an ancient and self-contained people, which has made heavy drafts on its vital forces and borrowed little from beyond its own forbidding frontiers.

His deliberate movements, his slow sweet smile and the contemplative glance of his heavy-lidded eyes, though they add to his dignity and charm, do not accord with the Western conception of a vigorous personality. Nevertheless report credits him with powers of physical endurance rare even in hard-bitten Arabia. Among men bred in the camel saddle he is said to have few rivals as a tireless rider, as a leader of irregular forces he is of proved daring, and he combines with his qualities as a soldier that grasp of statecraft which is yet more highly prized by the tribesmen. To be 'a statesman' is perhaps their final word of commendation. Politician, ruler and raider, Ibn Saud illustrates a historic type.

* Captain Wilson, who was killed in action in 1940 as Lt.-Col. Sir Arnold Talbot Wilson, KCIE, CSI, CMG, DSO, MP, JP, was an energetic imperial servant in the Percy Cox tradition. Known to his colleagues as 'A.T.', he left the Indian civil service after the First World War to work for the Anglo-Persian Oil Company, on whose behalf he was to make a bid for Sa'udi oil-exploration rights (see page 170). Wilson's brave and romantic death as a volunteer gunner, at the age of 55, was the basis for the character of Sir George Corbett played by Godfrey Tearle in the film *One of Our Aircraft is Missing*.

Miss Gertrude Bell was much impressed by the Emir of Riyadh, and her eloquent assessment of his qualities was circulated to British officials throughout the Middle East. But Abdul Aziz was less impressed by her. It was the first time in his life that he had seen a woman outside the restraints of the harem, and the culture shock of being delivered into the charge of an unveiled female, and to be shepherded by her from place to place, was compounded by his dismay at Miss Bell's notoriously forceful manner.

'Ya Abdul Aziz, ya Abdul Aziz!' she cried as she sought to get his attention.

Abdul Aziz had his Riyadh cronies in stitches when he returned home to mimic his escort's shrill voice and gestures – though it was a tribute to his courtesy, if not to his frankness, that Miss Bell never realized how her efforts to entertain succeeded in a fashion that she had not quite intended.

Abdul Aziz had enormous fun at the Kuwait durbar. For the first time in his life he travelled in a train, was driven in a car, saw an aeroplane fly, and looked at the bones in his own hand under a Röntgen ray. He also attended his first – and only – Christian service of divine worship, when the British took their guests on from Kuwait to Basra for a military display. They travelled by warship, and since it was a Sunday the emir asked if he might attend the morning service on board. By chance, the naval chaplain could not take the service, so the warship's commander, Rear-Admiral Sir D. St A. Wake, took his place, and Abdul Aziz was most impressed. The reverence of the congregation pleased him, he said afterwards, but the fact that the Admiral of the Fleet himself conducted the service was most remarkable.

It is quite possible that this unrehearsed display of religious conviction on the part of an infidel warrior and his followers impressed Abdul Aziz more than all the technological wonders that the British staged for the amazement of their desert guests. Whenever explaining his preference for the British over the Turks, Abdul Aziz always talked in terms of honesty and piety, and certainly something more than military might moved him in Kuwait to an outburst of loyalty and affection which his hosts had not expected. Condemning the Turks for their attacks on other Muslims and their attempts to weaken the Arabs by exploiting their differences, he praised the way in which the British government was encouraging Arab unity. This even led him to make an unprecedented public declaration of support

126

The first known portrait of Abdul Aziz,
photographed by Captain William Shakespear in Kuwait,
March 1910

The Al Sa'ud photographed in Kuwait by Captain Shakespear. Front row, sitting from left to right: Abdul Aziz, his first son Turki, Sheikh Mubarak of Kuwait (in brocaded jacket), Abdullah ibn Abdul Rahman and Muhammad ibn Abdul Rahman; Sa'ad ibn Abdul Rahman stands behind Turki ibn Abdul Aziz and Sheikh Mubarak; Sa'ud ibn Abdul Rahman stands behind Abdullah ibn Abdul Rahman and Muhammad ibn Abdul Rahman

Below
Abdul Aziz's army on the march, photographed by Captain Shakespear near Thaj in eastern Arabia, March 1911

Captain Shakespear on leave in England in 1907, sitting between Winifred and Dorothea Baird

Top A desert execution. It is not known whether this was a
genuine execution or whether it was enacted for Shakespear's benefit

Above Abdul Aziz with his brothers and sons photographed in March 1911
by Captain Shakespear. Sa'ad ibn Abdul Rahman, with plaits, stands to the right
of Abdul Aziz; Muhammad ibn Abdul Rahman sits to Abdul Aziz's left

for the Shareef of Mecca, urging his listeners to unite behind Husain and to support the Arab Revolt – a generous gesture for him to make at any time towards a man he mistrusted so much, but especially gracious in the face of the shareef's recent conduct, for only a few weeks previously Husain had had himself proclaimed in Mecca as 'King of the Arabs'.

This had been affront enough to Abdul Aziz, but the shareef had compounded it by sending back to the Sa'udi leader a letter in which Abdul Aziz had reminded him of Riyadh's own independence and sovereignty. Abdul Aziz should look over the letter again, said the shareef, and 'reflect on what you wrote', since it could only have been composed by a 'man bereft of his reason'.

Such provocations were swept aside in a warm pro-British atmosphere in which Abdul Aziz's speech 'struck the key-note'. Sir Percy Cox had opened the proceedings by presenting Abdul Aziz with a knighthood, and as Knight Commander of the Most Eminent Order of the Indian Empire, the Emir of Riyadh could be styled 'Sir Abdul Aziz Bin Saud'. British documents referred to him as such for several years afterwards.

But Abdul Aziz himself never used the title. He wore the bright sash and jewelled star for one day so that the British could take photographs of him. Then he put the insignia away, and he never wore them again.

14 Philby

IN the autumn of 1917 a British mission arrived in Riyadh which almost doubled, in one month, the number of Europeans known to have entered the town in the entire course of recorded history.* Sir Percy Cox was anxious to integrate the forces of the Al Sa'ud into the big push which Britain was planning against the Ottomans that winter (Lawrence had set off northwards a few months earlier). Abdul Aziz's role in the campaign would be to launch an attack upon the Rasheeds, and Cox chose as the co-ordinator of this effort a bright young member of his office staff, Harry St John Philby.

Conceited, irascible and thoroughly perverse, Harry St John Philby was the father of Kim Philby, the British double-agent who defected to Russia in 1963, and it is a pity that no one has yet addressed systematically the fascinating question as to what impelled both father and son to turn on their native country with such enthusiasm. After similarly promising beginnings at Westminster and Trinity College, Cambridge, both St John and Kim Philby after him joined Britain's government service abroad, only to renounce king and country with an ardour that became a life's passion for both – though St John Philby's rejection of Britain and her works was not clandestine like his son's, since the father took positive pride in the contrariness which landed him in prison during the Second World War for his anti-British sentiments.

He was 'one of those men', wrote A. T. Wilson, 'who are apt to assume that everything they come across from a government to a fountain-pen is constructed on wrong principles and is capable of amendment' – to which Philby delightedly replied that he had 'never yet had the good fortune to encounter either a perfect government or a perfect fountain-pen'.

* The British Mission to Riyadh of 1917 consisted of Harry St John Philby, Col. R. E. A. Hamilton, Col. F. Cunliffe-Owen, military attaché, and Cunliffe-Owen's batman, Schofield.

In Abdul Aziz ibn Sa'ud, however, Philby met in 1917 a man as close to perfection as any he would ever encounter. He was as captivated by his first meeting with Abdul Aziz as Gertrude Bell had been, and in this case the respect was returned – even though Philby's delegation had arrived outside Riyadh on 30 November 1917 looking more like a troop of baboons than the representatives of a great international power. Their curious appearance derived from the high-domed solar topees which they decided to wear with the rims cut off beneath chequered Arab headdresses, since they could not believe that the cloth headdresses alone would protect them from the sun.

No one appears, however, to have commented on the extraordinary shape of their skulls, and they were taken inside the walls of the town to be introduced to a 'little old man somewhat inclined to stoutness, sharp-featured and bright eyed,' who plied them with coffee, questions and courtesy – and who then retired.

Only at that point did Philby realize that 'another person had been in the room all the time . . . a very giant of a man.' It was Abdul Aziz himself, waiting respectfully upon his father Abdul Rahman before greeting his British visitors, and thus began a friendship between the emir and the prickly English eccentric that lasted more than thirty years. It amounted to hero worship on Philby's side and a wary affection on the part of Abdul Aziz, for right at the outset of their relationship he was presented with evidence of what a contrary character Harry St John Philby could be. Within a week, Philby had quarrelled so bitterly with his principal companion, Colonel R. E. A. Hamilton, British Agent in Kuwait, that Hamilton had left Riyadh in disgust and had returned to the coast.

But being left to his own devices thoroughly suited Harry St John Philby. It gave him the chance, when he had finished his discussions with Abdul Aziz, to ride off to the Red Sea, partly to annoy the Shareef of Mecca, who had declared the Riyadh–Hijaz road too dangerous for foreigners to use (a dig at Ibn Sa'ud's authority), and partly to join the select handful of Westerners who had succeeded in crossing the peninsula – his account of his adventures providing the first in a veritable bookshelf of brilliant, verbose and cliché-ridden narratives about his adventures in Arabia.

There was much that was noble, little that was gracious about Harry St John Philby. That was probably why he got on so well with the Arabs. His books are awash with self-importance, but from them can be plucked gem-like vignettes of Abdul Aziz, particularly when Philby drew the emir into arguments.

'Do you know', he once asked him, intent on teasing Abdul Aziz about the Koran's elementary geography, 'that you can reach America both by travelling westward and travelling eastward?'

Abdul Aziz was puzzled, even when someone reminded him of *kurrawiyat*, the 'roundness' of the earth to which the Koran refers, and when Philby asserted that he could, by setting off eastwards or westwards, travel round the world and return again to his starting-place without retracing his steps, Abdul Aziz decided the Englishman must be mad.

What language did people speak in America? he inquired. And Philby surprised him again.

'Are they of English stock?' asked the astonished emir. 'I thought they were of Indian origin.'

So Philby explained to him Red Indians and the West Indies, and, still intent on making mischief, he asked Abdul Aziz whether America was mentioned in the Koran.

'Yes,' came the answer flatly.

But America had not been discovered in the days of Muhammad, argued the infidel.

'God knows everything,' responded Abdul Aziz, 'and the Koran is His word.'

Philby was one of the few people prepared to stand up and argue with Abdul Aziz. At times the two men had blazing rows, for both were short-tempered, Philby stomping out of the royal *majlis* in high dudgeon, not to reappear for several weeks. But in these early days at the end of the First World War the Englishman trod diplomatically.

Several times he was invited out for picnics with Abdul Aziz and his family. Abdul Aziz loved to sit in the shade of the palm groves in the wadis around Riyadh, and one day Philby found him there playing with little Muhammad and Khalid, the sons of the beloved Jauhara.

Abdul Aziz's eldest son Turki was by now grown up and married, old enough to be commanding a detachment of Sa'udi troops in Qaseem on the fringes of Rasheed country. But Muhammad and Khalid were still little boys, making dams and playing in the mud of the irrigation channels that flowed through the garden, while their father flicked water at them every so often with his fan and sent them off screaming into the peach trees.

Playing with them were the orphan sons of the dead Sa'ad – Faisal,

Fahad and Sa'ud bin Sa'ad – whom Abdul Aziz had taken under his care by marrying their mother and whom he was bringing up as his own children. Marrying your brother's widow was traditional in Arabia, and Abdul Aziz took the tradition a stage further when he married Sa'ad's widow, another Jauhara, Jauhara al Sudairi, for she bore him two sons – Sa'ad (named in honour of the dead warrior) and Musa'id bin Abdul Aziz – and when she died giving birth to a third, Abdul Mohsin, Abdul Aziz then married her sister Haiya so that she could look after the collected offspring – *and* bear him more sons of her own (Badr, Abdulillah and Abdul Majeed bin Abdul Aziz).*

Philby had an appetite for such genealogical complexities. He loved to pathfind his way through the thickets of Sa'udi family relationships, sitting for hours listening to the conversation flowing round him, then going home to jot down the details; and this was what he was doing this morning beneath the fruit trees of the Wadi Hanifah, where the First World War seemed very far away. Abdul Aziz's orchards were luxuriant. Pomegranate and fig trees shaded the picnickers, and grapes hung down from the trellises 'like stalactites', wrote the Englishman.

An old poet declaimed some verses as Abdul Aziz sipped his coffee, and then the conversation turned political, the Emir of Riyadh having to argue quite fiercely with his brother-in-law Sa'ud al Kabeer. The leader of the *araif* had been reconciled with Abdul Aziz soon after the death of Sa'ad at Kinzan, and now he was a prominent figure in the family's inner circle, arguing his views persuasively, but apparently without rancour. The quarrels of the recent past were forgotten, and the little sons of the dead Sa'ad played around the feet of al Kabeer.

Another day there was a shooting match when Abdul Aziz took on his talkative younger brother Abdullah, one of Abdul Rahman's later sons, who was actually younger than Abdul Aziz's own first-born Turki. The old imam had celebrated the restoration of the family fortunes with a succession of new wives and children, and he was to go on into the 1920s siring sons enthusiastically until a few years before his death. Abdullah was the brightest of these, a sharp, argumentative young man, but he was not a good shot. The mark was at 50 yards'

---

* It is often assumed today that Crown Prince Fahad and his six influential brothers, all sons of Hassa bint Ahmad al Sudairi, are the only sons Abdul Aziz had by a Sudairi wife. But his sons by the sisters Jauhara and Haiya bint Sa'ad al Sudairi bring the total of 'Sudairi' sons up to fourteen – with, probably, ten daughters as well.

distance, a stone about 18 inches high and 6 inches wide, and Abdullah did not hit it once in ten shots – though his elder brother scarcely did much better. Abdul Aziz only managed to hit the mark once, and that was just a graze on the tip.

All present thought this great fun. There was much goodnatured bantering at the atrocious marksmanship, and then it was time for the sunset prayer, everyone kneeling down together side by side and bowing in unison towards the Tuwaiq hills to the south-west.

Religion seemed to run naturally into every capillary of Abdul Aziz's life. He recalled his youth on the edge of the Empty Quarter, when he had eaten *dhab* (lizard) among the Al Murrah. Had that been unclean food, he wondered, as his father thought? What about the *jerboa*, the desert rat? The Prophet never pronounced on the subject. Everybody knew that the ass was *haram* (forbidden): good Muslims could neither eat its flesh nor drink its milk. So what about the horse? Muhammad never ate horseflesh, someone thought; but he had refused actually to declare the meat of the horse unlawful.

Such was the stuff of everyday conversation at the court of Abdul Aziz: simple chit-chat much concerned with life's practicalities and curiosities, with the Koran and Hadith as the points of reference – and conversation is much the same today now that Khalid bin Abdul Aziz is King of Sa'udi Arabia, not a little boy being flicked with water by his father's fan.

'When did you first go on your Pilgrimage?' the king asks, and then everyone around chips in their memories of their first experience, how many times they have been since, how Mecca has changed, what is the best age to do your first *hajj*, what the Koran and Hadith have to say on the subject.

Discussion is seldom as political as outsiders imagine, anything but intense, much lubricated with jokes and the pleasure of shared memories and the same basic, Islamic, assumptions.

At the end of the First World War Harry Philby found that passions were roused bitterly only by the subject of the shareef in Mecca, and the help that the British were giving to the Hashimites.

'The real enemy of Nejd high and low', said Abdul Aziz with feeling, 'is the shareef. . . . Some day you will bitterly regret your mistaken policy.'

Abdul Aziz's basic problem was that he really did not want the shareef's Arab Revolt to succeed, for he could see that, the more victories Lawrence and the Hashimite forces won, the less important

132

Riyadh would become to British policy-makers – and so it came to pass. As the First World War in the Middle East rose towards the climax of the Arab entry to Damascus, Britain came to identify more and more closely with the Hashimite cause, and backtracked sharply away from that of the Al Sa'ud. Philby's mission to Riyadh of 1917 proved to be a last attempt at Sa'udi–British collaboration – and a failed attempt.

In the early months of 1918 Sir Percy Cox was recalled sharply to London for a briefing on the new situation. Major military assistance to the Al Sa'ud was now considered unnecessary, he was told, since the Arab Revolt was advancing northwards very nicely without it. The 10,000 rifles judged requisite by Philby's mission only a few weeks earlier could be reduced to 1000, for the Foreign Office were starting to worry that the Al Sa'ud might use their British arms against the shareef.

Nor was Ibn Rasheed to be considered an enemy any more. 'His total elimination from Arab politics might prove an embarrassment to us,' minuted the Viceroy of India. 'His retention will assist us in the maintenance of balance of power between Ibn Saud and Shareef.' So Cox's new orders were to keep Abdul Aziz in play with 'little doles', but not to supply him with arms or arms instructors, 'except very sparingly'.

When Philby learnt of this switch of policy he was furious. He tried, on his own initiative, to generate a Sa'udi expedition against Hail with some spare funds at his disposal. But Abdul Aziz understood the policy of His Majesty's Government better than did that government's own representative. The Emir of Riyadh had watched battalions of British soldiers march past him in Basra and squadrons of aeroplanes fly up into the sky, and he could see the gap between what had been available then and what he was being offered now.

'Who after this', he asked contemptuously, 'will put their trust in you?'

15 Britons and Arabs

AS the First World War drew to a close, His Majesty's Government began to sidestep smartly, for Britain's confusing promises to her allies were coming home to roost – and two of them came to light in the same fateful month of November 1917.

The first was discovered by accident, for, rifling through the tsarist archives after their October revolution, the Bolsheviks had stumbled upon an extraordinary document that laid bare the great powers' plan for the Middle East after the war, and they lost no time in publishing it. Britain, France, Italy and tsarist Russia had agreed on a four-way carve-up of the Ottoman empire which gave northern Turkey to Russia, southern Turkey and the Dodecanese Islands to Italy, greater Syria to France (modern Syria and Lebanon), and just about everything else in the Middle East, except Arabia, to Britain. Outside the peninsula, the Arabs would not be allowed to keep the countries they had helped to liberate.

The Anglo-French details had been worked out in February 1916 by Sir Mark Sykes and a French diplomat, Georges Picot, and the Sykes–Picot agreement made a nonsense of the promises that had inspired the Arab Revolt. It was just possible, on paper, to reconcile the letter of its terms with what McMahon had actually promised in his correspondence with Shareef Husain, and modern scholars have managed to demonstrate this in great detail. But the Sykes–Picot agreement clearly contradicted the spirit of the Arab Revolt – why else had it been kept a secret? – and T. E. Lawrence, at least, never made any attempt to deny the deception in which he knowingly participated:

'I risked the fraud', he wrote, 'on my conviction that Arab help was necessary to our cheap and speedy victory in the East, and that better we win and break our word than lose.' Lawrence knew from the beginning that 'the promises to the Arabs were dead paper:

134

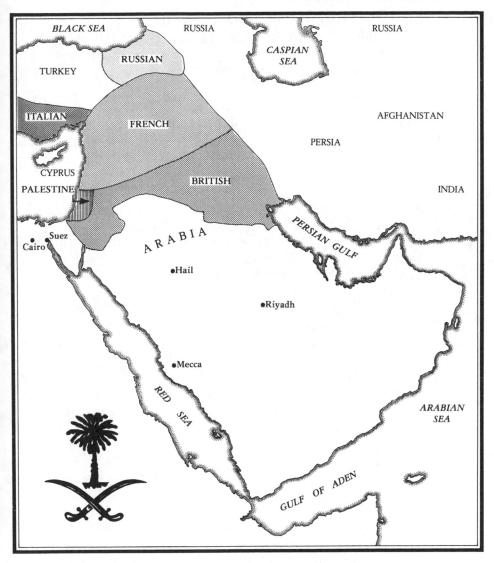

The Great Powers' partition of the Middle East, as proposed by the Sykes–Picot Agreement and by the Balfour Declaration, November 1917

. . . Had I been an honourable adviser [he wrote] I would have sent my men home, and not let them risk their lives for such stuff. Yet the Arab inspiration was our main tool for winning the Eastern war. So I assured them that England kept her word in letter and spirit. In this comfort they performed their fine things: but, of course, instead of being proud of what we did together, I was continually and bitterly ashamed.

135

The Sykes–Picot agreement delivered the most developed and educated areas of the Middle East, those most ready and thirsty for independence, into the hands of the colonial powers, and sowed there a hatred and mistrust of Western 'friendship' that sour the area to this day.

But still more bitter have been the consequences of another British war bargain revealed in that same November of 1917, when a letter from Arthur Balfour, the British Foreign Secretary, to Lord Rothschild, President of the British Zionist Federation, was published in London:

His Majesty's Government view with favour the establishment in Palestine of a national home for the Jewish people and will use their best endeavours to facilitate the achievement of this object, it being clearly understood that nothing shall be done which may prejudice the civil and religious rights of existing non-Jewish communities in Palestine.

Balfour wanted to enlist Jewish support in Britain and America – as well as behind the lines in Germany – for a last push of the Allied war effort; he saw a need to direct the 'undoubted, but mischievous' Jewish genius towards the rebuilding of Zion and not the subversion of the existing European imperial system after the war; and he also saw protection for the Suez Canal in a pro-British Jewish presence in Palestine – a policy objective realized by Sir Anthony Eden's Suez adventure of 1956. The wishes of Palestine's Arab inhabitants themselves in all this counted for little, as the dwarfing phrase 'existing non-Jewish communities' made clear, for it made the Arabs sound like a minority in Palestine – not 92 per cent of the population.

Two years later Balfour put the position more clearly:

In Palestine, we do not propose even to go through the form of consulting the wishes of the present inhabitants of the country. . . . The Four Great Powers are committed to Zionism. And Zionism, be it right or wrong, good or bad, is rooted in agelong tradition, in present needs, in future hopes, of far profounder import than the prejudices of the 700,000 Arabs who now inhabit that ancient land.

There could have been no clearer statement of Britain's indifference to Arab aspirations should these clash with her own imperial interests, and, though the Balfour Declaration did not affect the territory of Nejd, and the Sykes–Picot agreement left Arabia as an 'indepen-

dent' area, Britain had her own ideas as to what form that independence should take.

'What we want', Lord Crewe had written several years earlier, 'is
not a United Arabia, but a weak and disunited Arabia, split into little
principalities as far as possible under our suzerainty – but incapable of
co-ordinated action against us.'

As chief of one of those 'little principalities' that Britain wanted to
keep little, Abdul Aziz nursed few illusions about the reality of
great-power politics. He spoke kind words at durbars, he truly
respected upright characters like Percy Cox; but he wasted no sentiment over the 'friendship' that Britain offered him – any more than
his sons today overvalue the 'special relationship' extended them by
the new English-speaking superpower of the post-1945 world.

Abdul Aziz was Britain's friend, in the last analysis, because he
reckoned he could not survive as Britain's enemy, and he knew where
his bottom-line interests lay. When the coffee was poured and Arab
talked to Arab, the truth emerged.

'They spin and spin – spin nets for me,' said Abdul Aziz talking of
the British to Amin Rihani in 1922. 'When the Inglaiz want something, they get it. When we want something we have to fight for it . . .'

He made an eloquent spinning gesture with his hands to illustrate
the devices that the infidels were weaving around him for their own
purposes.

'What I cede of my rights under force,' he declared, 'I will get back
when I have sufficient force, *Inshallah*.'

Part Three

The Brethren

16 Al Artawiya

Cling one and all to the rope of God's faith
And do not separate.
Remember God's blessings,
For you were enemies
And He joined your hearts together
And now you are brothers . . .

Let there arise from you
A band of people
Attractive to all that is good,
Urging what is right,
And forbidding what is wrong.
Such men shall surely triumph.

The Koran, III, 103, 104

TODAY the drive from Riyadh to Kuwait is very long and
very dull, and 160 miles into it you could easily sweep past the
village of al Artawiya quite unnoticing. Two black and grease-stained
petrol stations flank the tarmac. The smoke of hubble-bubbles blends
with diesel fumes above the stretched-string sofas of an open café,
and halfway up the hill some green and white police Pontiacs list
crookedly amidst discarded Pepsi cans. Languid, bleak and rubbish-
strewn, al Artawiya today resembles any other of the townships
dotted over the windswept gravel plains of northern Arabia, and its
name means little to most young Sa'udis.

But the eyes of their fathers and grandfathers light up strangely at
the mention of al Artawiya, for this village was once famous all over
Arabia. It was notorious, indeed. The mere mention of its name could
strike terror into men's hearts; and on the rise and fall of this austere
and uninviting little settlement rode for a time all the fortunes of the
house of Sa'ud.

Seventy years ago there was no settlement there at all, just some
wells where the Kuwait-bound caravans from Nejd and Qaseem
joined trails. *Al artawi* means pasture in Arabic, and, since al
Artawiya lay in the territory of the Mutair tribe, it was where the
Mutair's chief, Faisal al Daweesh, would sometimes graze his camel
herds. Then around the Muslim year 1330 (1912 in the Christian

141

calendar) some religious enthusiasts, Arabian Pilgrim Fathers seeking a location where they could shape a community according to their
own beliefs, arrived at the wells of al Artawiya and decided to raise up
around them a citadel of the godly. The water and pasture provided
an excellent location to site their mosque and houses of mud, and very
soon the fame of al Artawiya's zealots spread. They became known,
and were proud to be known, as al Ikhwan, the brotherhood.*

We do not know precisely when Abdul Aziz first heard of the
Ikhwan. The earliest reference to the brotherhood is in the diary of
Captain Shakespear who passed near al Artawiya on his way from
Kuwait to Riyadh in February 1914 – 'Conversation regarding Akh-
wan al-Artawiya,' he noted briefly.

But at this date the Ikhwan were not the fighting force they were
later to become. Abdul Aziz had captured Hofuf in 1913 without
their help, and they did not make a major contribution to the Sa'udi
effort at Jarrab in 1915. Had they been present in force, they would
not have tolerated the presence of the infidel, Captain Shakespear,
and the result of the fight would almost certainly have been different –
for in their twenty-year history the Ikhwan never wavered in battle as
the Ajman had done at Jarrab. The brethren were God's soldiers,
heedless of death and thirsty for glory, and it was as well-nigh invincible warriors that they were to loom so large in the history of the
house of Sa'ud.

The Ikhwan movement was a twentieth-century revival of the
religious reform preached by Muhammad ibn Abdul Wahhab, puri-
fication according to the literal word of God, and the Ikhwan found in
the Hadith (the collected doings and sayings of the Prophet and of his
Companions) a treasure chest of advice and instruction to regulate
every detail of their existence in a holy fashion. They followed it
slavishly. The Prophet, it seemed, never wore the black rope-ring
aghal round his headdress, so the Ikhwan imitated him, adopting in its
place a halo-like circlet of white muslin. The Prophet condemned
personal ostentation, so the Ikhwan shunned silk, gold, jewellery and
ornaments, including the gold thread traditionally woven round the

* The Ikhwan of Nejd sent missionaries to the Syrian desert in the 1920s, and these played some
small role in the development of the Muslim Brotherhood in Syria. But the Sa'udi Ikhwan never
developed links, and should not be confused with the Muslim Brotherhood founded in Egypt in
the 1930s and still active there. The Muslim Brotherhood is today active in some Sa'udi
universities, but its connections are with the Egyptian movement, not the Ikhwan – whose aged
survivors can still be recognized occasionally in Riyadh and desert settlements.

dark *bhisht* or *mishlah*, the outer robe – and they also cut their *thobes* short above the ankles. This was because the Prophet had declared clothes that brushed the ground to be an affectation, and the same went for luxuriant moustaches. So the Ikhwan clipped the hair on their upper lip to a mere shadow of stubbliness – while adopting a different rule for hair on the chin. In this case, they argued, it would be affectation to trim and shape, so beards must be left to grow as long and to straggle as far as God might will them.

The Ikhwan's distinctive appearance proclaimed their holy rejection of the world and its ways, but their interpretation of the Islamic scriptures was not always obvious for its consistency. The brotherhood fiercely banned smoking on the grounds that tobacco was not known to Muhammad, who had therefore not sanctioned it, and this was the basis for their rejection of a whole range of post-Koranic innovations, from the wireless to the telephone.

But the Ikhwan had no hesitation in blessing the rifle and its use, which was certainly not known to the Prophet, for logic and reason were not priorities in a movement whose dynamic was blind faith. The brethren were zealots whose mainspring was personal conviction; they were soldiers of God whose mission was to cleanse and purify, as Muhammad ibn Abdul Wahhab had cleansed and purified 150 years earlier; and singing, dancing, even children's games, were banned from al Artawiya in a fashion of which the first Wahhabi would certainly have approved.

There was one important difference between the Ikhwan movement of the early twentieth century and the original Wahhabi crusade. Muhammad ibn Abdul Wahhab had been a townsman. He had grown up among caravan trains and merchants, and his message had been preached to, and adopted primarily by, townsfolk.

But the Ikhwan of al Artawiya were bedouin, and their mission was aimed at bedouin. Out alone in the desert where no one could reach, teach or preach to him, the camel herder remained a creature of superstition, touching rocks and murmuring spells to ward off evil spirits, never entering a mosque or seeing a Koran, and saying his prayers but twice a day, if that often. The aim of the al Artawiya brotherhood was to bring the nomad out of the wilds where superstition flourished and to settle him by a mosque where the imam could instruct him and his children in the true way – and the Ikhwan's distinctive headdress symbolized this. The black *aghal* was originally a double loop of rope used for hobbling camels. When not in use, the bedouin stored it on his head – a visible sign of his vocation. So in forsaking the camel rope for the Prophet's white muslin turban the ex-nomad was proclaiming a transformation in his life that was both material and spiritual.

We do not know whether the first brethren came to Abdul Aziz of their own accord or whether, hearing of the zealots digging in at al Artawiya, the young Emir of Riyadh investigated their activities and found that they were good. But it is certain that the Ikhwan movement could not have flourished and spread as it did without his active encouragement and material assistance: he gave them land; he sent more missionaries out to the desert to bring back fresh recruits for their settlements; when tribal chiefs stood in the way of the good work, he summoned them to Riyadh to win them over with threats and blandishments; and some time around 1917 Abdul Aziz ordered at his own expense from India a large new printing of Ibn Abdul Wahhab's primary manual of faith, *The Three Fundamentals and Their Proofs*, so that the thoughts of the Teacher could be propagated more thoroughly than ever in the deserts.

Abdul Aziz set himself firmly at the head of the movement that sprang from the first settlement of brothers at al Artawiya in 1912, and, as a token of his own personal commitment to the austerity that the Ikhwan preached, he had his pride and joy, the wind-up gramophone from Kuwait with which he liked to relax in his tent at night, publicly destroyed. The news of his sacrifice was spread around the coffee hearths of Nejd, and the brethren nodded and waggled their long beards in approval. Abdul Aziz was clearly one of their brothers.

One broken gramophone was a small price to pay for the solution the Ikhwan offered to the problems facing Abdul Aziz in the years after 1912, for he clearly had to find some new way to discipline the wandering tribes – and he also faced a potent threat from Mecca. The Arab Revolt was lending the Hashimite armies some impressive weaponry and experience and, once the revolt was over, Shareef Husain ibn Ali would certainly start looking inland in pursuit of his claim to be 'King of the Arabs'.

These were major challenges to the continuing authority of the house of Sa'ud, and the sudden explosion of the Ikhwan movement in the years after 1912 must have seemed truly providential, for the brethren offered the Emir of Riyadh a solution to both his domestic and his foreign dilemmas: a religious revival among the bedouin would tame the tribes – in 1914, for example, Faisal al Daweesh voluntarily forsook his rebellion to come in from his tents and settle among the mud huts of al Artawiya – while the Ikhwan also offered Abdul Aziz a military potential of unique power and scope.

There were two types of desert warfare, Abdul Aziz's grandfather Faisal had told Colonel Pelly in 1865: religious war and political war. Political warfare involved compromise. But 'when the question is one of religion,' the old man had explained, 'we kill everybody.'

It was the religious dimension that had made the armies of the first Sa'udi–Wahhabi empire so feared, and now the Ikhwan revived in the twentieth century the same fanatical spirit in which human life counted for nothing. Each brother believed it a blessing to die in battle, for death in the cause of jihad, holy war, took the warrior straight to the gates of heaven – while anyone who opposed the jihad forfeited his life by definition. God's warriors took no prisoners. 'All who are taken with arms are unmercifully put to death,' wrote Burck- hardt of the Sa'udi armies of the early nineteenth century. 'This savage custom has inspired the Wahabys with a ferocious fanaticism that makes them dreadful to their adversaries.'

This was the spirit that the brothers of al Artawiya regenerated in the years after 1912, and it was the cutting edge of their religious revival. Since they preached the true way, it must follow that all other ways were false, for tolerance was a concept quite alien to their simple faith, and they sought converts with all the ardour of those who are converts themselves. They sent out their missionaries to preach God's word, but the Prophet's teaching of jihad showed them how they might convert with force where persuasion failed, and the Ikh- wan settlements that sprang up between 1912 and 1918 along the lines of al Artawiya were as much military cantonments as pastoral communities: there were stables and fodder bins in the main square where the soldiers could be marshalled from the mosque roof, and central magazines where ammunition was distributed; one of the first actions of al Artawiya settlers was to build watchtowers on the plateau to the north of the town, and the population lived on constant military alert.

The bedouin tradition of raid and counter-raid was institutional- ized by the Ikhwan into constant readiness for holy war, and from the beginning Abdul Aziz seized on the military potential of the move- ment. As the brethren came asking him for land, he sited them in strategic locations like Ghot Ghot, near Riyadh, a colony whose fame

145

soon came to rival that of al Artawiya. Ghot Ghot was 50 miles south-west of the capital on the road to Mecca, its inhabitants drawn from another once rebellious tribe, the Otayba, and under its emir, Sultan ibn Bijad, the settlement became the principal bastion of Sa'udi defence against attack from the Hijaz.

By 1917 there were over 200 such settlements dotted all over Nejd, none of them more than a day's march from another, an extraordinary military network. There were probably some 60,000 men of fighting age available to Abdul Aziz in the Ikhwan settlements at the height of the movement, which meant that, within a matter of years, something like a quarter of a million men, women and children had shifted from their moving black hair tents to permanent mud settlements. It was a momentous transformation of the Nejdi way of life – and the outside world knew virtually nothing about it.

This was partly because the Ikhwan were ferociously hostile to all outsiders, and particularly to Western infidels intent on chronicling their doings. Even Philby, nosy and keen to prove that he could venture anywhere in Arabia, kept his distance. In 1918 he surveyed al Artawiya cautiously through binoculars from 3 miles away, for the Ikhwan were becoming notorious at this time for their practice of forced conversion: jihad on a one-to-one basis. They simply killed anyone who declined their invitation to join the movement. Pious Muslims unfortunate enough to halt in al Artawiya on their way from Kuwait found themselves imprisoned in a sort of quarantine until the brethren were satisfied they had not been contaminated by the wicked ways of the seaport, and foreigners would have fared no better.

Thus few people were aware of the military machine that Abdul Aziz was building in Nejd during the years after 1912. It was his deliberate policy to veil the Ikhwan in secrecy, and when Harold Dickson was charged in 1920, on his first mission to Arabia, with discovering more about the movement, he found himself up against a wall of silence: 'It was obvious to me that people had been given the hint, by someone or other in authority, to give away as little as possible,' he wrote, and 'one could not help but come to the conclusion that Bin Saud himself was at the bottom of the matter.'

If questioned directly about the Ikhwan, at the time or even later, Abdul Aziz would become blandly disingenuous, at least when he was talking to foreigners. He had encouraged the movement, he later told the American philanthropist Charles R. Crane, 'to develop stable qualities of character among the Bedouin, by giving them a fixed home, and to train them to become useful citizens.'

But down in Mecca the shareef and his sons were not deceived. Abdul Aziz, complained Feisal bin Husain, was not building up the Ikhwan for religious or social reasons, but to advance his own personal ambition. 'When his time comes he will direct the force of the Bedu . . . against the settled peoples of Arabia,' prophesied Feisal, while Shareef Husain himself denounced the Ikhwan as a 'political society in the cloak of religion', and called upon the British government to be firm with Abdul Aziz and compel him to disperse the brethren.

It was September 1918, the First World War was drawing to a close, and the old shareef, riding triumphantly on the crest of the Arab Revolt's victories, believed that his sons' armies were invincible and that the British would sustain his ambitions in peace as they had supported them during the war. But the Ikhwan were to disillusion Husain sharply and rapidly on both counts.

The confrontation came at Khurmah, a collection of oases on the black volcanic plains beyond Taif, a no-man's-land lost in the deserts that separated Riyadh from Mecca. Traditionally these hundreds of square miles of waste land between Hijaz and Nejd were abandoned to the Otayba bedouin. But when the rulers of either Mecca or Riyadh felt like extending their authority, then emissaries would be sent to Khurmah to woo or to subdue the emir of the dusty little oases. Shareef Husain ibn Ali had been fishing for support in this area when he had happened to set hands upon Abdul Aziz's brother Sa'ad in 1910, and in the years after 1912 it was the Ikhwan missionaries who took the initiative. By 1916 they were firmly established not only in Khurmah but even further west at Turabah, a settlement on the plateau little more than 100 miles from Mecca itself, and down in the Holy City the shareef began to get alarmed.

Husain himself had chosen and appointed Khurmah's emir, Khalid ibn Mansour ibn Lu'ay, a shareef from another branch of the Hashimite clan. But bad blood had developed between the two men when Khalid, an austere and puritanical Wahhabi, like most of Khurmah's inhabitants, welcomed the Ikhwan preachers from Nejd; and when, in 1917, the shareef tried some missionary work of his own, sending to Khurmah a preacher that he hoped might turn the people away from Wahhabism, Khalid drove the holy man away.

The dispute escalated. In 1918 Husain sent troops to Khurmah to discipline Ibn Lu'ay, but they too were driven away on at least three occasions. Ikhwan fervour inspired Khurmah's villagers to band together in a display of arms which sent the shareef's soldiers home discomfited.

But Husain had sent only a token force to Khurmah. The bulk of his armies lay elsewhere, half with Feisal and Lawrence on the road to Damascus, the rest with his second son, Abdullah, besieging the obstinate Turkish garrison of Medina, and, once the war had ended, it was clear that the shareef and his sons would waste no time bringing Khurmah to heel.

To the Ikhwan of Nejd the issue was simple. Their brothers in Khurmah were being persecuted, and force must be met with force. Abdul Aziz must lead them to confront the armies of the 'old grey devil' in Mecca, or, at the least, unleash Sultan ibn Bijad and the Otayba Ikhwan of Ghot Ghot, many of whom came from the Khurmah area. And why stop at Khurmah? This was the chance to purify Mecca, Medina and the entire Red Sea coast.

Abdul Aziz told the British he would accept arbitration over the boundaries of Nejd and Hijaz in the Khurmah area, but he knew better than most that holy wars are not settled by arbitration. War fever was sweeping the brethren and, if Abdul Aziz did not set himself at the head of their righteous indignation, then it would not be long before someone else did – probably a tribal leader like Faisal al Daweesh. Abdul Aziz had conjured up for himself in the Ikhwan a genie that he could not subdue.

In Whitehall Foreign Office officials might have chosen the metaphor of the Sorcerer's Apprentice – and applied it to themselves, for, as one India Office man noted, the net result of all their wartime activities seemed to be the 'establishment of two powers in Arabia mutually hostile, but to both of whom we have given pledges of support'; and they had two mutually hostile sets of officials to go with them.

Foreign Office men argued for what became known as the 'suzerainty policy' by which Britain would reward Husain for his Arab Revolt by supporting his bid to gain supremacy over all the chiefs of Arabia, including Ibn Sa'ud. But, from the Gulf, India Office officials pointed out the impossibility of Abdul Aziz's ever accepting Hashimite overlordship, Sir Percy Cox characterizing the suzerainty policy as 'impractical', and Philby dismissing it as 'entirely Utopian'.

'The advice of local officers is so conflicting', stated one perplexed memorandum writer, 'as to make it impossible for His Majesty's Government to form an equitable judgment on the merits of the case.'

Lord Curzon had no doubt that, if it came to war between Mecca and Riyadh, then 'we should support King Hussein'. But everyone hoped devoutly that the Khurmah dispute would never escalate that far – and even if it did, wrote one official consolingly, 'the consequences may not be so formidable as is sometimes apprehended. Past experience of inter-Arab warfare tends to show that the results are not always very striking or decisive.'

His complacency was misplaced, for the Ikhwan were about to transform the face of inter-Arab warfare as recognized by Britain's colonial officials – or by Abdullah bin Husain, who started marching south towards Taif, Turabah and Khurmah the moment that the Turks surrendered Medina to him. Abdul Aziz responded by ordering Sultan ibn Bijad to take 1100 Ikhwan down from Ghot Ghot to defend the oases, and he wrote to the British pointing out that he had agreed to submit the dispute to arbitration. 'I shall not be responsible if he [Husain] commits aggression,' he warned.

Abdullah, meanwhile, had captured Turabah. He had over 5000 men, ten field-guns and twenty machine-guns, and he felt confident that he could roll on from Khurmah to Riyadh and capture the whole of Nejd, even to the Gulf coast in the east. He would be at Bahrain, he informed his father, in a fortnight, and he addressed Abdul Aziz's messengers in similarly boastful terms. Pilgrimage time was approaching, and Abdullah told them that he was planning to celebrate the Feast of the Sacrifice at the conclusion of the pilgrimage season in the heart of Nejd itself. 'We did not come to Turabah for the sake of Turabah and Khurmah only,' he bragged.

If all this was intended to intimidate, it produced exactly the opposite effect. Howls of rage arose in the camp of the Ikhwan when they heard of Abdullah's threats, and before the sunset prayer the brethren started marching on Turabah. They had already demonstrated one of the several innovations which they brought to Arabian warfare – the ability to move fast in large numbers, like a massive raiding party, over very large distances: the Ikhwan had ridden more than 300 miles from Ghot Ghot in a matter of days; each man carried just a small bag of flour, some dates and a waterskin; many rode two to a camel; in these early days many of the Ikhwan lacked rifles,

149

counting on picking one up in battle; and each brother rode into battle confident that he was a soldier of God, destined for immediate entry, if killed, to Allah's garden of streams, greenery and luscious houris.

Arriving at Turabah before dawn, the Ikhwan demonstrated the other qualities that were to make them 'the white terror of Arabia'. Abdullah's camp was sleeping when the brethren fell upon it in a wild mixture of horses, camels and white-haloed men slashing about them with their daggers and screaming their warcry: 'The winds of paradise are blowing!' Heedless of death, welcoming it indeed, the Ikhwan slaughtered every man they could lay hands on.

'I saw the blood at Turabah running like a river between the palms,' said a youth lucky enough to have escaped from the massacre. 'I saw the dead piled up in the citadel before I jumped out of the window. But the strangest thing I saw . . . was the sight of the Ikhwan during the battle stopping long enough to enter the mosque to pray, then returning to the fray!'

It was 26 May 1919. The battle was over before sunrise and Abdullah bin Husain was lucky to escape from the disaster in his nightshirt. With him fled just sixty or seventy other survivors, most of them officers in night attire, and when they reached Taif the news of the catastrophe provoked panic, for, with Abdullah's army destroyed, the Hijaz was defenceless. There was nothing to stop the Ikhwan now marching on to capture Mecca within days, and, if they did, the slaughter would be terrible.

But Abdul Aziz knew that his moment had not come. If he wished to capture and to hold the Holy Places permanently, he knew that he had to be welcomed to them. It was still too early for a Sa'udi conquest of the Hijaz to be tolerated by Britain or by the Muslim world as a whole. So telling the Ikhwan that he needed them to meet the Rasheed challenge from Hail, Abdul Aziz coaxed the brethren back home. He had proved what his holy warriors could accomplish.

17 Death of the Jewel

IN 1919 the great Spanish influenza epidemic claimed more lives around the world than the First World War had taken in four years, and Riyadh was not immune. Somehow the infection reached the town through a traveller from Kuwait, and the havoc it wrought was terrible.

'They had a very bad time of it here,' reported Dr Harrison, who was called urgently to Riyadh from Bahrain. 'The death rate was up toward a 100 a day for a few days and the whole town was sick, so much so that the bodies were carried out on donkeys and camels – 2 to a donkey and 4 to a camel.'

Dr Harrison conservatively estimated the dead at a thousand – roughly one in ten of the population – and the Al Sa'ud suffered with everyone else. Arabian parents hardened themselves to the death of young children. It was God's will to draw them early away. Still, the death in the epidemic of a small five-year-old son, Sa'ad, and of young Faisal's favourite brother, Fahad, was a bitter blow, and the death of Abdul Aziz's eldest son Turki, tall, handsome, dashing, already a leader of men and father himself, with a son and three daughters to his credit by the age of nineteen, was the cruellest loss of all.

Turki was already his father's trusted lieutenant and companion, part of his father's own identity, since it was as 'Abu Turki' ('Father of Turki') that Abdul Aziz was most usually addressed. The British sent the Emir of Riyadh a note of official condolence, and this moved the sorrowing father to respond with a letter that fairly breathed his distress: 'You have been affected by my loss, and have participated with me in my sorrow ... the sorrowful sudden happening ... it being the loss of my son, in the glory of his youth, who has gained the hearts of all friends.'

Public mourning for a lost son and warrior was acceptable. But it

151

was in private that Abdul Aziz had to grieve for the loss of his most dearly loved wife, Jauhara, the mother of his sons Muhammad and Khalid – the woman to whom he wrote love poems when the world seemed black around him. We can only guess at the sorrow that he felt. Muhammad Asad later speculated that the libertine and sensual side to his nature that Abdul Aziz indulged more and more in later years reflected the death of Jauhara and 'a dim, insatiable desire to recapture the ghost of a lost love'.

The Ikhwan did not favour displays of sorrow in the face of phenomena that were manifestly God's will. They called 1337 AH (AD 1918–19) 'the Year of Mercy', because it was the year when God looked kindly on his people and drew them in thousands to his presence. But for Abdul Aziz the sorrow never went away. Thirteen years later, by the account of one witness (thirty years later by the account of another), he still could not speak Jauhara's name without a catch in his throat and tears starting to well up in his eyes.

18 A Trip to London

IN July 1919 the British government invited Abdul Aziz to visit London. Britain was organizing goodwill visits for her wartime allies, and she also wanted to discuss the trouble at Khurmah with the Emir of Riyadh. But with the Ikhwan aroused, Abdul Aziz could not afford to leave Nejd, nor could he send his second son, Sa'ud, who, since Turki's death, had to be established around the coffee hearths as his father's new lieutenant and successor.

So Abdul Aziz's next son, Faisal, went instead. He was only a little boy, delicate, grave and quiet, but he had learnt his Koran – and that was how the future King Faisal of Sa'udi Arabia became, at the age of fourteen, the first member of the house of Sa'ud ever to visit western Europe.

Nowadays they do it in two hops of a private plane, coming down into Rhodes or Heraklion to refuel. In 1919 young Prince Faisal and his party had to embark at Bahrain on an aged paddle steamer, the RIMS *Lawrence*,* which took ten days to transport them to Bombay, and there he had a further ten days to kill until a liner could take him via Suez to England.

'Bring your Arabs to Poona Races,' cried Bombay's governor to Humphrey Bowman, Faisal's British escort, 'and we will show them what we can produce in horseflesh!'

So the Arabs took tea at Poona, stayed in the Taj Mahal Hotel and travelled first class on the train. They also enjoyed diversions appropriate to a fourteen-year-old guest of honour.

'Visit to Elephant,' say the accounts for 18 September 1919. 'Tip, 5 rupees.'

Abdul Aziz sent two guardians to accompany his son. The elder, Abdullah al Qosaibi,† was a member of the al Hasa merchant family

---

* Royal Indian Marine Ship *Lawrence*.
† Great-grandfather of Ghazi al Qosaibi, poet and Sa'udi Minister of Electricity and Industry since 1975.

who had helped the Al Sa'ud capture Hofuf. He was now acting as Abdul Aziz's commercial agent in the east, and one reason for his travelling with Faisal was to make purchases in Europe for his master. Some time after his return, Nejd's first motor car, a Model 'T' Ford, arrived in Riyadh, courtesy of Abdullah al Qosaibi and a caravan of camels which dragged it on ropes across the red Dahna sands.

Faisal's other companion was younger, a distant cousin, Ahmad Thunayan, whose task was to say to the Foreign Office what Abdul Aziz felt about the Khurmah dispute, and also to convey to Lord Curzon a pledge which the emir had decided to make over the Hijaz – that the Al Sa'ud would not make war there for three years at least.

The original Thunayan had been a brother of the very first Ibn Sa'ud in the middle of the eighteenth century, but Thunayan had stood back from his elder brother's endorsement of Muhammad ibn Abdul Wahhab. The Thunayans were more liberal than the main line of the Al Sa'ud – cosmopolitan even – and Ahmad Thunayan had spent his childhood in Turkey until the Al Sa'ud's recapture of Riyadh. This had kindled Ahmad's enthusiasm for his Nejdi roots, and he returned to take part in the family's military campaigns, limping proudly from a wound received in one of them. He wore his hair in long plaited bedouin ringlets, he was fiercely boastful of the new Sa'udi–Wahhabi empire that Abdul Aziz was creating, and he alarmed Humphrey Bowman during the voyage down the Persian Gulf by hinting darkly at a 'much vaster kingdom' which, he said, the Al Sa'ud would be building in the future.

Al Thunayan also pestered Bowman continually with complaints that his young charge Faisal was not being accorded equal dignity with the other Arab guest travelling to England in the same party, Ahmad ibn Jabir, grandson of the late Mubarak and shortly himself to become Sheikh of Kuwait. Stout and hearty, Ahmad was a good-tempered fellow, but he did not see why, as a grown man of thirty, he should defer to a fourteen-year-old boy.

Little Faisal himself caused no trouble. Serious, reserved and rather sickly – there are several bills for doctors and medicine in the accounts – the boy worked unassumingly at the mission which initiated his career as the twentieth-century's longest-serving Foreign Minister. He learnt off the names of the five great world powers* in English.

But Ahmad Thunayan had been charged by Abdul Aziz with

---

* Britain, France, Germany, Russia and the United States of America.

upholding his son's dignity, and relations between Kuwait and Nejd had been deteriorating ever since the Sa'udi conquest of al Hasa. The Al Sa'ud were now challenging the pre-eminence of Kuwait in north-eastern Arabia, and, on board the RIMS *Lawrence* paddling down the Persian Gulf, feelings were exacerbated by religious differences: the Nedjis stuck strictly to their prayer times, but the Kuwaitis were much less conscientious – *and* they smoked the occasional cigarette.

Still, both delegations worked manfully together at their 'knife and fork' drill, lessons which Major Bowman organized in the deployment of the Western table implements that Faisal had never seen before, and both shared the sense of betrayal with which, at the Poona Hotel, they saw their British mentors cheerfully abandon knife and fork to pick up the asparagus in their fingers. After a moment of pained surprise, the Arabs resumed their cutting and jabbing doggedly.

There were surprises to come in London. The Government Hospitality Fund was only told a few days before the Kuwaiti–Sa'udi delegation disembarked at Plymouth on 13 October 1919 that the party consisted, with chaperones and coffee servers, of eleven persons, and not the two sheikhs which were all they had been led to expect. Frantic telephoning eventually located a hotel in Upper Norwood willing and able to accommodate the party for a week or so. But after the call to prayer had rung out down the hotel corridors at 5.15 in the morning, the management decided that their rooms were available for only one night, and requested that their oriental guests should leave that day.

The trouble was that no other hotel would take them. The Government Hospitality Fund had been forced down to the South London suburbs by the refusal of 'some scores of hotels' to accommodate Arab guests. It was partly the calls to prayer five times a day. It was partly the readiness of the coffee servers to kindle open fires almost anywhere, and their insistence on sleeping on the floor outside their masters' doors. It was partly the profusion of water that Arab ablutions required to be splashed around bathrooms. Every major London hotel from the Savoy downwards declined the Hospitality Fund's request for rooms, and Philby, who had assumed charge of the Arab visitors at Plymouth, had to take them to a hostel for Indian Army orderly officers in St George's Road, Victoria.

This proved a cosy enough niche, but, since the lodging-house keeper could not provide meals for her guests, they had to walk to the Grosvenor Hotel in nearby Victoria Station to eat. The sight of the

155

Arabs in their oriental robes trudging to and from the railway terminus in the rain must have attracted attention, and soon the newspapers were on to the story of what the *Daily Graphic* denounced as 'a government bungle'. Even *The Times* felt constrained to regret 'a lapse of government hospitality'.

It was the habit of King George V to scrutinize every inch of *The Times* from personal column to letters page, and from Sandringham next day a letter winged its way to Whitehall. The King was concerned to have read about 'the important Chiefs from Central Arabia' and their treatment, for while he was sure the press was guilty, as usual, of exaggeration, the whole affair made for 'an unfortunate effect'; and an official inquiry was instituted. Prince Faisal was invited to meet the King at Buckingham Palace on Thursday, 30 October, at 11.45, and the boy took with him to present to the King an ornamental sword inlaid with pearls with hilt and sheath of solid gold. George V presented Faisal in return with two signed photographs, one of himself and one of his wife.

Abdul Aziz's second son was still a little boy in many respects. During the voyage over he had gone to Major Bowman weeping piteously because Ahman Thunayan was forcing him to take his medicine every day, and when, at London Zoo, a sealion charged towards a fish that had been dropped at the prince's feet, he picked up his robes and fled. But he was grown up enough to know when he was being patronized, and he did not appreciate Lord Curzon's offering him boiled sweets at the Foreign Office. Faisal had gone with Ahmad Thunayan for a meeting to discuss Khurmah and the Hijaz dispute, the solid meat of their mission, and the couple left, according to Major Bray, who was their escort in Paris, 'enraged' to have been treated 'like children'.

The Nejdis were sent to Paris to visit the recently abandoned battlefields of northern France. It was a sobering reminder to overseas visitors of Britain's appalling sacrifice in the First World War, and, after his tour of the mud, debris, barbed wire and desolation of Flanders, Faisal was always reticent to discuss his own war experiences in Arabia, which he would dismiss as 'nothing much'.

But another reason for sending the Sa'udis to Paris was the hope that they might there be induced to talk to Feisal bin Husain. The shareef's son was at the Versailles Peace Conference seeking some reality for his father's claim to be King of the Arabs, and for this reason Ahmad Thunayan at first refused to meet him.

'He has constantly insulted my master,' Thunayan told Major Bray, and he only agreed finally to a meeting on the condition that his own charge, Faisal ibn Abdul Aziz, did not attend. He could not expose the boy to the slights he expected – and duly received.

'Who are these Ikhwan?' asked the shareef's son jeeringly after some inconclusive conversation. 'I am told they are not allowed to cut their beards.'

The Hashimite prince and al Thunayan were sitting side by side on a large sofa, and, at the insult to the Ikhwan, Thunayan's hand reached to his sword hilt. Bray was sitting with Feisal's ADC, Ja'afer Askari, and they rose as one to separate their principals. The interview ended at that point.

The Sa'udis' itinerary was ambitious. In Europe they travelled to Cologne, Strasbourg and Marseilles. In Britain they visited the steelworks of South Wales and the Phoenix Park racecourse near Dublin. Prince Faisal enjoyed the stuffed gorilla at the Natural History Museum, South Kensington. It reminded him, he said, of one of his negro slaves at home. And he also enjoyed a visit to the Houses of Parliament where, to the dismay of his hosts at a time of rationing, he poured the entire contents of the sugar bowl into his tea.

What, asked his escort on this occasion, would the young prince choose of all the things he had seen and done in England as being the most enjoyable?

Faisal had seen a lot. He had inspected the Bank of England and a captured German submarine; he had been filmed by Pathé News and had seen the stars by day at the Greenwich Observatory; he had visited Philby's old college at Cambridge and Kim Philby's prep school at Eastbourne; he had walked up Snowdon in the snow; he had been to the *Mikado*, and he had seen his first typewriter, telephone and aeroplane.

But of all these new experiences, Prince Faisal knew at once the one that he had liked best. 'Going up and down the moving staircase at Piccadilly Circus,' he said.

It turned out that the fourteen-year-old boy had been so impressed with the escalators of the London Underground Railway Company that he had spent the better part of one whole morning riding them from top to bottom and back again.

19 Sultan

It was announced here Friday that six South Koreans working in the country had converted to Islam. . . . They were given Muslim names and are now called Abdullah Ahmad Jon Yong, Ali Kwah Shek, Mustapha Back Hong, Abdul Mannan Lee Jong, Sa'ud Hong and Othman Lee Hong. . . . The ceremony was attended by representatives of the Society for the Encouragement of Virtue and Elimination of Vice.

Arab News, 20 October 1979

IT was the time when the camels migrated. Young Harold Dickson, newly appointed British Agent in Bahrain and on his way to meet Abdul Aziz in January 1920, saw thousands of them on the move, grazing slowly as they went. One day near Hofuf he reckoned he saw 20,000 altogether chewing on the coarse grass they found between sand dunes, their Murrah masters shepherding them northwards on the four-month trek that would take them up to Kuwait and back again.

Hofuf, when he saw it, reminded Dickson of Damascus – 'an emerald in a setting of yellow sand'. He walked through the gardens, criss-crossing the network of open streams on stout little masonry bridges, revelling in the fruit trees, the rice fields, the brilliant green of wheat plots sprouting. Some Ikhwan in the street refused to speak to him. When Dickson greeted them, they put up their hands to shield their faces from his infidel gaze, and even in the emir's *majlis* two Ikhwan sheikhs got up and left the room, mumbling audible curses at the intrusion of the fresh-faced *Nasrani*.

'Perhaps you English don't know what the Ikhwan are,' said Abdul Aziz to his guest, and he launched into a long discourse on the wonderfully civilizing influence that the movement was having in Nejd.

'I am the Ikhwan!' he shouted at one point, banging his chest, quite carried away by the flow of his oratory. 'I am the slave of God the most merciful!'

The emir talked of the Koran, he talked of the caliphs, he talked of the Turks, and he talked of Nejd. Abdul Aziz in full spate was

158

Top Harry St John Philby in 1918
Above Lawrence of Arabia, drawn by Augustus John

Top Abdul Aziz (left) meets Sir Percy Cox (centre) and Miss Gertrude Bell
in 1916. Abdul Aziz wears the insignia presented to him as Knight Commander
of the Most Eminent Order of the Indian Empire

Above Abdul Aziz with captured Turkish cannon in Riyadh

Below Abdul Aziz and his family photographed by Philby in 1918. The present King Khalid
ibn Abdul Aziz believes he may be one of the children standing in the foreground

Above Prince Faisal ibn Abdul
Aziz travels to London, 1919.
He sits beside Major Humphrey
Bowman (far left); on the far right
sits Ahmad Thunayan; between
them sits the future Sheikh
Ahmad ibn Jabir of Kuwait with
the captain and officers of
RIMS *Lawrence*

Left Prince Faisal has his portrait
sketched on board the *Kigoma* en
route to London, 1919. To his
right sits Major Bowman, to his
left, with teacup, Abdullah al
Qosaibi

Top Ahmad Thunayan
Above Prince Faisal ibn Abdul Aziz visits Kim Philby (standing behind his
left shoulder in Eton collar) at Kim's prep school in Eastbourne

unstoppable. 'He is the type of man', wrote Dickson in his diary, 'that makes simple men go mad.'

In proclaiming his religious commitment, Abdul Aziz had been especially fervent in his denunciation of tobacco smoking – *haram*, he said, a deadly sin which he deplored and which he had strictly outlawed everywhere in Nejd. But later that evening, after the sun had set, there was a knock on Dickson's door and one of Abdul Aziz's advisers slipped inside with two tins of Egyptian cigarettes. The obligations of religion did not, apparently, obliterate those of hospitality – though the British visitor was requested to enjoy his gift only in the privacy of his own room.

Abdul Aziz had come to Hofuf to welcome his son Faisal home from London, and on 12 February 1920 the boy arrived, freshly disembarked from Bahrain with his entourage. His father was elated by his son's healthy appearance, and pleased too by a personal letter which George V had taken the trouble to write to him. The emir made Dickson translate and read out the King's letter several times in succession, and he rejoiced, as he always did when the family got together. Sheep were killed in regiments for a large homecoming feast.

But when Ahmad Thunayan produced the notes of his meeting with Lord Curzon at the Foreign Office, the emir's mood changed. Abdul Aziz sent for Dickson, and the Englishman discovered him suddenly despondent. It was a Friday, and Abdul Aziz felt so depressed, he told Dickson, that he had not been able to say his prayers that morning, nor even pay proper attention to the sermon in the mosque.

It was the preference which Britain was constantly showing to the Shareef of Mecca that had made the emir so melancholy. The Hijaz received a much larger British subsidy than Nejd, complained the emir bitterly, and his little Faisal had not been received in London, from what he heard, with the flourish accorded to the shareef's son.

'Why won't you English . . . realize facts?' he asked Dickson with bitterness. 'Don't you know that [the] Shareef is an absolute traitor? . . . You are supporting a broken pillar. . . . As sure as I hold this stick' – and at this point Abdul Aziz waggled the bamboo camel cane that he always carried – 'so surely do I know the Shareef's days are numbered.'

Meanwhile, on the other side of the peninsula, Britain's representatives were dealing with equally emotional outbursts on the part of the Shareef of Mecca.

159

Laurence Grafftey-Smith, drafted to Jeddah by the Levant Consular Service, spent over five hours one day, *tête à tête* with Shareef Husain, trying to persuade him to appoint a delegate who could negotiate a settlement of the Khurmah dispute under Britain's arbitration. But he got absolutely nowhere, and finally the old man took a sheet of paper torn from a notebook and drew on it with a quill pen, in spluttering strokes, a rough outline map of the Arabian peninsula, finishing it off with a little stab at Kuwait in the distant north-east corner.

'Let him go back there where he belongs!' the shareef cried. 'When he is in Kuwait again, I will consider arbitration!'

The defeat of the Hashimite forces at Turabah had not deflected Shareef Husain ibn Ali one whit from his ambition to subdue the Emir of Riyadh, and by the spring of 1920 the British press was on to the escalating conflict between the two Arabian clients who were both claiming British subsidies to finance battles against each other – and had apparently recruited rival British civil servants to their purpose. In May 1920 a group of MPs wrote to the *Daily Express* calling for the establishment of one single ministry to assume unified direction of Middle-Eastern affairs, for, though the war had ended two years earlier, the Arab world remained a jumble of military administrations and local rulers swirling in the vacuum left by the defeated Turks; and into this formless ether stepped Mr Winston Churchill, charged early in 1921 as His Britannic Majesty's Secretary of State for the Colonies, with the task of bringing order out of chaos.

Churchill's solution was to convene in one spot a brains trust of 'practically all the experts and authorities in the Middle East' – by which he meant some thirty-five or so Englishmen, one Englishwoman (Gertrude Bell) and two Arabs.* These 'Forty Thieves', as Churchill called them, met in Cairo in the middle of March 1921 to parcel out this particular corner of the world among the various interest groups they represented, and, between sessions, the conference chairman escaped to the Pyramids for some sketching, sitting before the Sphinx with his paints and easel in the shadow of an armoured car.

The bold brushstrokes that Churchill's conference painted on the canvas of the Middle East remain its political outline to this day: Syria and Lebanon were left to the French; Palestine was made a mandate

* These were Ja'afer Askari and Sasun Pasha, aides to Feisal bin Husain.

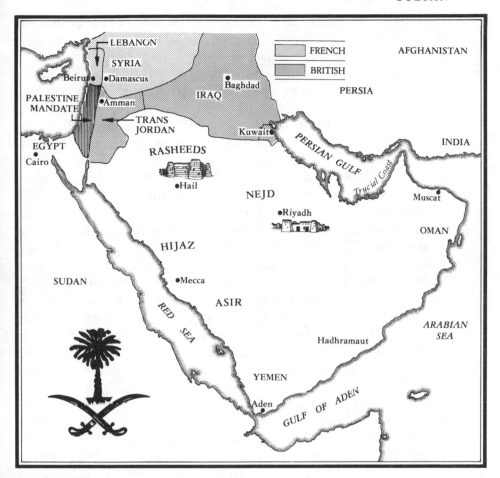

The Middle East after the First World War

where the British set themselves the task of reconciling native Arab with immigrant Jewish aspirations; Mesopotamia was renamed Iraq, and given to Husain's son Feisal under British tutelage; the 'vacant lot' between Palestine, Syria and Iraq was christened the Amirate of 'Trans-Jordan' and given to Feisal's brother Abdullah; their father, the shareef, was acknowledged as King of the Hijaz, and Abdul Aziz was left to his own devices in Nejd – though Sir Percy Cox did suggest that the emir's pension might be raised to the same level as King Husain's, to provide some consolation for his having been almost totally surrounded by a hostile crescent of Hashimite powers.

Outwardly, Abdul Aziz was contemptuous of Churchill's Cairo king-making. 'We have arrived at a state', he wrote to one tribal chief,

161

'where feet have assumed the position of heads', and he scorned the shareef's sons – 'silly little fools aping English wisdom'. But privately he was worried. 'They have surrounded me with enemies,' he confided to Amin Rihani, '. . . the grey-haired one in Mecca . . . his son Abdullah in Transjordania, his other son Feisal in al Iraq.'

Not for the first – or last – time Abdul Aziz decided on a pre-emptive strike. The Rasheed realm of Hail and Jabal Shammar covered an enormous expanse, the vast empty heartland of the Middle East, and it now lay between Abdul Aziz and his enemies, a protective buffer – or a means by which the Hashimites could infiltrate to the very borders of Nejd. So within weeks of the Cairo Conference, and before the shareef's sons could become established in their new fiefdoms, let alone think of looking outside them, Abdul Aziz was mobilizing to secure Hail and Jabal Shammar for himself.

He was helped by the self-mutilating impulse that had always bedevilled the Rasheeds, Arabia's Borgias, for in the spring of 1920 Sa'ud ibn Rasheed, who had ruled Hail well enough for a decade, was so careless during an impromptu family shooting contest as to josh one of his cousins on his erratic marksmanship. The insulted cousin promptly turned, levelled his gun at the centre of Sa'ud's forehead, and proved conclusively that his aim could be very good indeed when he tried.

Sa'ud's slaves cut the assassin down at once, and the succession passed to a thirteen-year-old nephew who proved a poor hand at rallying Hail's forces when Abdul Aziz decided to advance. As the Sa'udi armies invaded Jabal Shammar in the summer of 1921, the boy fled, and though his successor, Muhammad ibn Talal (brother of the touchy marksman), was a brave warrior, it was too late. The merchants of Hail had had enough of the dynasty which had switched leaders fourteen times in ninety years* – and they did not wish to provoke the fury of the Ikhwan contingents whom Abdul Aziz had brought from al Artawiya under Faisal al Daweesh. They opened the gates of Hail to the Al Sa'ud, and a few weeks later, in the first days of November 1921, Muhammad ibn Talal also surrendered.

Abdul Aziz had doubled his empire at a stroke, and he gave himself a new title. The Emir of Riyadh became the Sultan of Nejd.

* In the course of these fourteen changes, only two Rasheeds had died of natural causes.

The Tale of Abdul Aziz and the Captured Rasheeds

When Abdul Aziz captured Hail, he straightaway gave out food among the citizens to relieve their hunger. He forbade all looting or killing.

But Muhammad ibn Talal ibn Rasheed expected no such kindness, for he had refused to surrender with the citizens. He had withdrawn to Hail's fort to keep on fighting, and he knew the tales of Ibn Sa'ud's vengeance if he were crossed.

So when, after Muhammad's capture, servants came telling him to wash and bathe for a great occasion, the last Rasheed ruler feared this occasion must be his own execution, and, when Abdul Aziz himself came to sprinkle him with perfume, he became convinced he was to die. His enemy must be toying with him out of spite.

But when he put on his best robes to meet death with some dignity, he found himself being led into Ibn Sa'ud's *majlis* and being set in the place of honour.

'Sit here beside me,' said Abdul Aziz, rising to embrace and to kiss Muhammad ibn Talal. 'The time for death and for killing is finished. We are all brothers now, and you and yours will come to Riyadh to live with me as part of my own family.'

And so it came to pass. The Rasheed princes went to Riyadh as guests of Abdul Aziz and lived honoured in his palace for many years.

'When they punished us it stirred us to revenge,' Abdul Aziz used to say. 'So let us not punish them.' And he took special care of the Rasheed women. Three widows had been left by the fighting, and so the sultan gave one to his younger brother Sa'ud bin Abdul Rahman; the second he bestowed on his own eldest son, Sa'ud bin Abdul Aziz; and the third widow, Fahada bint Asi al Shuraim, he took as a wife for himself.

The product of Abdul Aziz's marriage to the Rasheed widow was his eighth son Abdullah, born within two years of Hail's conquest, and today Abdullah, head of the Sa'udi National Guard, is Second Deputy Premier after King Khalid and Crown Prince Fahad – a living reminder that, for Abdul Aziz, family building was empire building.

20 Boundaries in Men's Hearts

I N the summer of 1922 Harry St John Philby was inspecting a Roman ruin near Amman, the chief town in the newly created Emirate of Transjordan, when he was alarmed to see an unusual sign scrawled on the wall. A less practised eye would have ignored the graffito, but Philby, now British Representative in Transjordan, recognized it as the fresh *wasm*, or brand-mark, of Nejd's Anazah bedouin, the sign that the tribe branded on camels and scratched on wells to indicate their ownership. It was sometimes used by scouts to guide a raiding party to its quarry, and Philby grew worried. Could Ikhwan spies possibly have infiltrated this close to Amman?

Philby got his answer a few weeks later when his breakfast was interrupted one morning by the news that the Ikhwan were only 10 miles away. They had ridden up the Wadi Sirhan to fall on two Beni Sakhr villages, and had been surprised in their slaughter by a plane flying overhead on a routine mission. The Ikhwan had turned and fled, a column of 1500 men, riding back south as fast as they could go. But it was a long way to the Wadi Sirhan, and British armoured cars and planes caught up with them at Umm al Ahmad.

'I saw the long line of their flight,' wrote Philby, who drove out next day to the desert, 'dotted with the bodies of dead Wahhabis, swollen to balloons by the sun.'

When the survivors of the raid arrived home, Abdul Aziz had the ringleaders flung into prison. He expressed extreme displeasure with the Ikhwan for their lawlessness, and he apologized to the British authorities for their raid. But in his heart the Sultan of Nejd sympathized with the Ikhwan's wish to ride and raid wherever they cared to. It fitted neatly with his own ambition to re-create the empire of his forefathers, and, as his warriors of Islam expanded into the void left by the defeated Turks in the years after the First World War, Abdul Aziz acknowledged their conquests whenever he felt he safely could.

These tactics worked well in Asir, part of Arabia's south-western corner, where the Ikhwan went riding after their victory at Turabah. Sandwiched on the Red Sea coast between the Hijaz and Yemen, Asir was, before the Ikhwan's arrival, an independent enclave, a mini-statelet carved out by the Idrisi family in the nineteenth century, and its green mountains and sheer escarpments gave it a character closer to that of Ethiopia, across the Red Sea, than to the northern deserts and lava plains from which the Ikhwan came riding.

'The garden of Eden must be very like this,' wrote Philby when he came to map the southern borders of Asir for Abdul Aziz in the 1930s, '. . . and the human being one meets from time to time might have stepped straight out of Genesis, naked except for a loin cloth and sometimes a rifle, and with very fuzzy greased hair.'

Philby heard shepherds piping thin tunes that reminded him of Greece, and to this day the woven beehive straw hats, juniper forests and unveiled women tilling the terraced Asir hillsides in their pointed coolie hats give the damp, misty highlands a most un-Arabian air.

Asir was ruled by the Idrisi family, and in 1920 Muhammad Idrisi was trying to stave off the challenge of Shareef Husain ibn Ali who was as alert as Abdul Aziz to the opportunities that the departure of the Turks created. The shareef started annexing Asir's coastal plain, so Muhammad Idrisi almost welcomed the Ikhwan's riding south after Turabah. In the summer of 1920 he signed an agreement with Abdul Aziz acknowledging Sa'udi protection of Asir's mountains, and he regarded this as a friendship treaty. But when, after Muhammad's death two years later, his son sought to assert control over the territory his family had ruled for nearly a century, Abdul Aziz treated him as a rebel and sent the Ikhwan, under his son Faisal, to suppress his insubordination. The brotherhood had 'persuaded' settlements down to the very borders of Yemen to adopt their reformed faith, and some 4000 square miles had thus passed effectively under the control of Abdul Aziz.

Kuwait did not succumb so easily to these tactics. Ikhwan missionaries from al Artawiya infiltrated to the walls of the town. But Mubarak's son Salim declined to be intimidated. His father's writ had run at least 100 miles out into the desert. If he acquiesced in the Ikhwan's creeping annexation, he would be left with little more than the town of Kuwait itself, so he decided to define his idea of where his territories ended by building a fort near Manifa, a spot some 150 miles down the Persian Gulf coast.

165

Manifa would one day become the starting point of a major off-shore Gulf oilfield, and though Salim was staking a claim to land, not oil, his attitude foreshadowed a world where such natural resources would compel the definition of precise national boundaries.

This was not a world that the bedouin knew in the 1920s, nor one they were prepared to accept. There had never been a precise territorial frontier between Nejd and Kuwait – nor, indeed, between Nejd and anywhere else. That had been half the trouble at Khurmah, for the only boundaries that Arabia's nomads acknowledged were written in men's hearts. They were not lines scratched in the sand, but matters of allegiance, leadership, human authority.

The fact that a great sheikh like Mubarak had been able to command allegiance more than 100 miles away from Kuwait did not automatically entitle his humourless, inflexible and rather unpopular son Salim to claim the same territory as his of right. In the eyes of the Mutair Ikhwan, Mubarak's empire followed him to the grave; and this was the rationale which Abdul Aziz employed to settle the dispute, for Salim himself died fortuitously early in 1921, just as Faisal al Daweesh was rounding up his forces for an attack upon Kuwait.

Salim's successor was his nephew, Ahmad ibn Jabir, the steamship companion of young Faisal ibn Abdul Aziz on the 1919 expedition to London, a popular and accommodating character. He met with Abdul Aziz in April 1921, and the two leaders embraced, announcing that since they were friends there could be no quarrel between their peoples – and that there was no further need to define a frontier between Kuwait and Nejd.

This was a traditional desert reconciliation on the face of it. But the reality was that Britain had sent warships to protect Kuwait against the Ikhwan in the winter of 1921–2. Abdul Aziz could not have conquered the town if he had wanted to. His Majesty's Government cared little who controlled Asir. But Kuwait was a different matter – and so was Iraq immediately to the north. When an Ikhwan column 2000 strong set off under Faisal al Daweesh for the Iraqi deserts in March 1922, they were confronted by a contingent of Iraqi Desert Police with RAF warplanes flying overhead. The brethren decided, on this occasion, that discretion was the better part of valour.

This was how the great bulk of the Kingdom was shaped in the early 1920s. Abdul Aziz's warriors of Islam went out riding with their Korans and rifles, pushing forwards as far as they could and re-creating the great Wahhabi conquests of the eighteenth century in a style that had changed remarkably little in 150 years.

But there was one difference. British planes and armoured cars now defended Transjordan and Iraq in the north, while British ships protected Kuwait and the Trucial sheikhdoms nibbled out of the peninsula along the Gulf. So, whatever the importance of the boundaries in men's hearts, it was His Majesty's Government who determined for Abdul Aziz the frontiers of the possible.

21 False Start

IN November 1922 a curious figure waded ashore at the village of Uqayr in eastern Arabia. From a small Bahraini fishing boat stepped a burly and perspiring Westerner clad in suit, shirt and tie, an Arabian gold-trimmed outer robe, and a pith helmet draped with a chequered headdress and black headropes. This original apparition introduced himself as Major Frank Holmes, a New Zealand businessman and prospector, and with Major Holmes's landing in Arabia the history of the Kingdom was touched, for the first time, by oil – or, at least, by the possibility of its existence.

Frank Holmes was a bluff and engaging fellow who had claimed, while visiting Colonel Dickson in Bahrain, to be a butterfly hunter. He was after a rare black variety in the Qateef oasis, he told the British Agent. He had already named it the Black Admiral of Qateef.

But this was too transparent a camouflage for an oil prospector to employ. Violet Dickson guessed at once what Major Holmes was after: the black petroleum seepages of the Qateef region, in search of which Harold Dickson had himself mounted several expeditions. The Turks were said to have discovered these oily scum leakages when they controlled al Hasa, but moving dunes had since covered them, and Abdul Aziz himself gave little credence to their potential. Noah had smeared his ark with pitch, and Mesopotamia's Eternal Fires had burned for many years, but in 1922 no oil had been discovered on the Arab side of the Persian Gulf.

Abdul Aziz was at Uqayr in November 1922 talking to Sir Percy Cox. The British had decided that the disturbances along the Sa'udi frontiers with Kuwait and Iraq must be settled with a conference – the first international conference ever held on Sa'udi soil – and since Uqayr itself was scarcely a town, just a fort, a customs post and a few tumbledown shacks, Abdul Aziz had staged the meeting in a grand and Arabian fashion. He had had a vast tented settlement built around two high canvas pavilions, with an encampment of low black hair tents on one side for his Sa'udi retinue. On the other side was a cluster of high white marquees for his foreign guests, complete with upholstered chairs and camp beds.

Abdul Aziz had instructed his agent in the east, Abdullah al Qosaibi, to make sure his visitors felt at home, so the foreign tents were stocked with fruit from India, Perrier water, Johnnie Walker whisky and big black cigars, and al Qosaibi had also arranged separate kitchens and cooks, so every night for a week the British visitors were able to sit down in their own mess tent wearing their dinner jackets – and, in the case of Sir Percy Cox, also wearing polished black boots and spats.

We know of these intriguing details thanks to the presence at the Uqayr conference of Amin Rihani, a portly and inquisitive Arab-American whose disarming self-importance won the affection of Abdul Aziz. Rihani came from New York; he was proud of knowing Brooklyn-slang; but he had spent much of his childhood in Lebanon, and he made it his life's mission to try to kindle among his fellow Arabs the ambition, idealism and cohesion that he so admired in the USA. Travelling round the Middle East and writing about the personalities that he met, Amin Rihani came to Uqayr in November 1922, and there he chronicled the meeting between Abdul Aziz and Major Frank Holmes.

Abdul Aziz was always asking the British for doctors. He had the healthy hypochondria of the traditional Eastern potentate, according medical men a respect that extended beyond their purely medical abilities. The man trusted to prescribe pills was trusted when he prescribed in other areas, and to this day the senior policy adviser at the royal Sa'udi court is Dr Rashad Pharaon, the Syrian who came to Riyadh as a physician to Abdul Aziz in 1936, subsequently to become political adviser to King Faisal and now, since 1975, to King Khalid as well.

When the tragic epidemic of 1919 broke out in Riyadh, Abdul Aziz had invited to Nejd the doctors of the American Mission in Bahrain; but Sir Percy Cox suspected these missionaries of fomenting anti-British sentiments, and when Abdul Aziz asked in 1921 for yet another medical attendant, Sir Percy suggested Dr Alex Mann, a Jewish physician on his own staff.

Dr Mann's religion proved no obstacle to Abdul Aziz, who accorded him all the confidence he habitually placed in medical men, and in 1922 he appointed Mann his representative in London. He made the doctor an allowance of £1000 a year, and in London Dr Mann made contact with the Eastern and General Syndicate, a small group of speculators who specialized in buying oil concessions and selling them on to larger companies. Major Frank Holmes, ex-engineer, ex-Royal Marines, was the syndicate's man in the Gulf – and that was how Holmes came to be wading ashore at Uqayr in November 1922.

Sir Percy Cox was not amused. He had not come to Uqayr to haggle with merchant speculators. He had international borders to adjudicate, and he had devised an ingenious solution to the problems raised by 'boundaries in men's hearts' – a couple of 'Neutral Zones' in which the bedouin could wander freely and where Abdul Aziz would share sovereignty over the land and its assets with Iraq in one case and with Kuwait in the other. These were complicated questions.

So Holmes had to pitch his tent at a distance from the British encampment, and he sat there, pointedly ignored for most of the week, while the British unrolled their maps in the main pavilion.

Amin Rihani gave the major a more friendly reception. He had had brushes of his own with Sir Percy, and, when Holmes showed the Lebanese the clumsy letter of application he had framed to Abdul Aziz, Rihani set to work to reword its clogged Arabic. The New Zealander was asking for an oil concession – a licence to prospect and, if successful, to exploit the mineral resources of the Al Sa'ud's domains – and he was prepared to pay an annual rent in gold.

Sir Percy Cox was not encouraging. Having grudgingly agreed to a formal meeting with Holmes on the final day of the conference, he made clear his personal distaste for the major and poured cold water on his plans. 'The time is not yet ripe,' he told Holmes. 'Go slow about the concession . . . the British government cannot afford your company any protection.'

But Cox was being less than candid, for some time previously he had cabled his friend and former deputy, Captain (by now Sir) Arnold Wilson, a representative of the Anglo-Persian Oil Company in which the British government had a major shareholding,* and Wilson had responded by writing directly to Abdul Aziz. Wilson suggested that Abdul Aziz and Anglo-Persian might 'strike a deal about oil', and one of Abdul Aziz's advisers showed Amin Rihani this

* BP, British Petroleum, is the modern descendant of the Anglo-Persian Oil Company.

letter which explained why Percy Cox felt the time was not 'ripe' for Major Holmes's independent initiative.

'Evidently it is not untimely', wrote the Lebanese sardonically, 'for the APO to negotiate for a concession.'

Cox was doing his best to squeeze out the New Zealander, and he asked Abdul Aziz to inform Holmes that no concession could be granted until the matter had been discussed with the British government. Cox went so far as to draft in lead pencil the letter that he wished Abdul Aziz to write. 'Will the Sultan', he asked, 'please write letter in above terms to Major Holmes and send me a copy of it?'

Abdul Aziz was furious. It was not the first time at Uqayr that Cox had sent him pencilled scribbles he was expected to endorse. Three times the sultan refused to sign it, and three times Cox insisted, until the High Commissioner eventually got his way.

Amin Rihani was bitterly disappointed. Abdul Aziz 'says that he fears only Allah,' he wrote sourly. 'I'm afraid that he also fears losing his annuity.'

This had been the underlying reality of the Uqayr conference, for the British were the paymasters, and also the military quartermasters, of Iraq, Kuwait and Nejd. Abdul Aziz had come to depend heavily on the £60,000 gold he received every year from the British government, and he had come to Uqayr hoping he might get his subsidy increased, since the conquest of the Rasheeds and of the Asir mountains had doubled the number of chiefs whose loyalty he had to purchase. Holmes was talking in terms of only a few thousand pounds a year for his Arabian oil concession, and this counted for little when compared to the price of Sir Percy Cox's goodwill.

Holmes got the message. He packed his bags and left Uqayr. But before he left he presented Abdul Aziz with an extraordinary array of gifts: more than fifty cases, leather bags, boxes and guns, a parting example of the business style of which Sir Percy so obviously disapproved. Palm-greasing was not cricket – though arm-twisting apparently was.

The following spring Amin Rihani ran into Holmes again. The major was going through the motions of departing from Baghdad, paying his farewell respects and going to take tea with Lady Cox – good news for Sir Percy, since Holmes's departure should leave the way clear for Anglo-Persian to secure its position in Arabia.

But the major disembarked from his steamer, without warning, halfway down the Gulf, and headed rapidly inland before any more

171

lead-pencil notes could beat him to Abdul Aziz. Britain had announced she was ending her pensions to Arabian rulers, so the Sultan of Nejd felt less beholden to Sir Percy Cox – and he needed money.

In August 1923 Amin Rihani received a letter from Abdul Aziz saying that the sultan had granted the oil concession in his territories to Major Holmes and his syndicate, the Eastern and General. Anglo-Persian and the British government were foiled.

In one sense the whole adventure then petered out ignominiously. Cox had cautioned Abdul Aziz that Holmes's syndicate was not a proper oil company, only an agency which would seek to sell their contract onwards to another buyer, and his warning proved justified. The Eastern and General grew interested in Bahrain. They never found a buyer for their Sa'udi oil concession, they invested little effort or money in serious exploration, and finally they gave up their annual payments to Abdul Aziz – and hence their prospecting rights – in 1927. Frank Holmes, later to be known as 'Abu Naft', 'Father of Oil', for his work in paving the way to Bahrain's first oil strike in 1932, missed the infinitely larger treasure on the Arabian mainland.

Yet Holmes's successful thwarting of the Anglo-Persian Oil Company did have one important consequence. Anglo-Persian had the resources to prospect much more thoroughly than Eastern and General, and with British government backing they would have clung on to their concession more tenaciously than did Holmes's syndicate, whose failure gave American oilmen the chance to locate and unlock the kingdom's hidden treasure chest in the 1930s.

Modern Sa'udi Arabia's 'special relationship' with the USA derives from the fact that it was the Americans who first discovered and exploited Sa'udi oil – and it was the hunter of Qateef's 'black butterfly' who indirectly made this possible.

22 At Home with Abdul Aziz

A S Amin Rihani rode his camel into the walled town of Riyadh at the end of 1922, he saw several hundred people sitting on the clay benches moulded into the walls of Abdul Aziz's palace. After the conference at Uqayr the Sultan of Nejd had invited Rihani to come and visit him in his capital, and the Lebanese imagined that all these bystanders must have come out to witness his own arrival.

But then Rihani saw that beneath their robes many of the men were carrying enamel bowls and wooden platters. They were not waiting for him. They were waiting for lunch at the palace. Some 500 men came to eat as guests of Abdul Aziz every day, lunchtime and evening.

Abdul Aziz's quartermaster, Shalhoub, showed Rihani the central stores: dusty rooms full of camel saddlery, rifles, rugs, piles of flour, dates, sugar, metal vats full of clarified butter for cooking. Some of these provisions had been purchased with Britain's wartime subsidies, some were tribute from subjected tribes, some were battle trophies – and Abdul Aziz gave everything away. One Eed time Shalhoub distributed, he said, some 3000 gold-trimmed outer robes, bought in bulk from Syria. Ikhwan chieftains turned up at the stores with long shopping lists sanctioned by the sultan. And then, when the war banners were hoisted, Abdul Aziz collected the dividend on his generosity.

Amin Rihani stayed as Abdul Aziz's guest for several months through the winter of 1922–3, and his journal gives us a unique picture of Riyadh as it was sixty years ago. It was 'a city of bridges,' he said. The Al Sa'ud's palace was linked to the main mosque by such a covered way, a mud corridor raised on pillars so that Abdul Aziz could walk directly from his *majlis* to his prayers, and similar bridges took the sultan to his private quarters.

One day Abdul Aziz invited his guest to join him there, over three roofs, across two bridges and down several corridors.

173

'That is the harem,' said the sultan, pointing to four columned and crenellated buildings near by. 'Each one has a house of her own.'

Rihani looked round the sultan's own little rooms – his bathroom, with a huge water-boiler, tub and metal pans, and another room set aside for prayers. There was a cosy little *majlis*, rich with carpets and cushions, and a simple bedroom in which Abdul Aziz kept the 7-foot-long spear he had carried on the night he captured Riyadh.

Then the two men went on to inspect the harem, and Rihani was struck by the brightness and beauty of the decoration achieved inside buildings which presented such a drab exterior to the world. The doors, he wrote, were 'arabesqued in blue and green and yellow', while the walls, fretted with elaborate white plaster designs on top of a fawn-coloured background, looked 'as if they were covered with Valenciennes lace'.

One of Abdul Aziz's wives in 1922 was Fahada, the Rasheed widow whom Abdul Aziz had married after the fall of Hail. Another was Hassa, the daughter of Ahmad Sudairi.

The Tale of Abdul Aziz and Hassa

Hassa bint Ahmad al Sudairi was a beautiful little girl, a mere child when Abdul Aziz saw her first. Her father, Ahmad, was one of the Sudairis who had rallied to the Sa'udi cause at the very outset, and he had served the Al Sa'ud loyally ever since. Abdul Aziz gave Ahmad provinces to govern as he conquered them, and then one day he set eyes on his old friend's little daughter Hassa, running and playing and jumping with her friends.

Hassa had not yet reached the age to be veiled. She could not yet bear children. But Abdul Aziz was overwhelmed by her charm. He said that he would wait for her to grow up, and he did.

When Hassa reached the age of thirteen she married Abdul Aziz, and soon she bore him a son, Sa'ad, who lived for five years until he died in the epidemic which claimed Fahad and Turki.

Abdul Aziz divorced Hassa. Perhaps he thought she could bear no more children. We do not know what led to the divorce. So Hassa married her ex-husband's brother Muhammad bin Abdul Rahman, and to Muhammad she bore a fine son who lived for many years.*

* This son was Abdullah ibn Muhammad ibn Abdul Rahman. For details of Hassa's eight sons by Abdul Aziz, see Appendix B.

174

Yet Abdul Aziz came to regret divorcing the wife he had first seen as a little child. He found that he was missing Hassa. He brooded on her loss and he wanted her back. So he went to his brother Muhammad and persuaded him to divorce Hassa so that he might marry her himself again.

And this time the marriage lasted. Hassa bint Ahmad al Sudairi stayed with Abdul Aziz until the very end of his life, and she gave him in the course of their two marriages more children than any other of his wives – a total of eight sons, including Sa'ad, and five daughters. His first son by Hassa after their remarriage was born in 1921, and Abdul Aziz called him Fahad, 'the leopard'.

Rihani was being treated to a glimpse of the intimate Abdul Aziz. He saw the storeroom full of Dr Mann's drugs; the sultan brought out in his bedroom a leather case full of perfume which he insisted on sprinkling over his visitor's head, beard and chest; and then one afternoon Rihani was invited out for a picnic with the family.

He drove in the back of Abdul Aziz's motor car – the first car in Riyadh, the Model 'T' Ford sent from the east by Abdullah al Qosaibi, and dragged by camels half the way. With Rihani and the sultan was one of the Rasheed princes, living in Riyadh as 'an honoured guest'; there was another car filled with children, and accompanying the motorcade were 100 or so men on horseback whom the sultan's Indian chauffeur took great pleasure in outdistancing wherever the desert permitted him to speed up to 55 m.p.h.

The site selected for the picnic was a massive rock, weathered by blown sand into an arch and standing on a hillock several miles out of the town, the starting and finishing post for family horse races. Sitting in its shade, Abdul Aziz would watch the riders amble off towards the horizon. Then, 15 or 20 minutes later, they would reappear, still ambling to conserve their horses' stamina, and suddenly break into a furious gallop for the finish, onlookers leaping up and down, shouting out encouragement wildly.

It was a Rasheed prince who won on the afternoon that Rihani was there, beating Abdul Aziz's own son Sa'ud. But the sultan did not seem to mind. He ordered Shalhoub to give out prizes on the spot, fifteen gold sovereigns to the winner, ten to the runner-up. Whenever he went on motoring excursions, Abdul Aziz took a sack of gold coins with him.

175

The sultan dropped one into a bowl of water to start off the next entertainment. He had a little hand-cranked generator, and putting one terminal into the water he invited anyone to hold the other and retrieve the coin from the bowl while he cranked furiously. Competitor after competitor dropped the terminal with giggles of pain, until one determined soul first refused to let go – and then discovered he could not let go as the current took hold, and he fell to the ground, writhing in agonized laughter, and dragging bowl, water, coin and generator with him. He was the winner.

Throughout the afternoon children were playing around the sultan's feet, and every so often he would pick one up, hugging it close to his face for a whisper and a kiss. Some of them were Rasheeds, and Abdul Aziz pointed them out to Rihani.

'They are all ours,' he said, 'there is no distinction.'

There was still no formally organized school in Riyadh in 1922. Abdul Aziz's sons and nephews learnt their Koran together in a simple mud room where they read and recited under the supervision of a venerable member of the *ulema*. Their grandfather, Abdul Rahman, was still alive, plump, bright-eyed and active, and he took a close interest in his grandsons' spiritual progress. He would check on their attendance and obedience in lessons. Backsliders were consigned for the morning to a little cupboard like a prison cell.

Memorizing is a major element of traditional Arabian education. There is not the modern Western emphasis on personal probing and debate, and in the Kingdom's schools today children are encouraged less to criticize than to respect and learn the wisdom that their elders impart to them. This wisdom itself was learnt by heart from a previous generation, and this, in practice, means that the Koran and its related teachings form the basis of everything. Whole sections of the syllabus are blocked off for Koranic repetition, the child's creative instincts being focused on the clarity and power with which he (or, today, she) can learn by heart and repeat what has been read.

The Kingdom's equivalent of Saturday morning children's television (which happens on a Friday, the Muslim sabbath) consists of Yogi Bear cartoons interspersed with star pupils, nine- and ten-year-olds, reciting extracts of the Koran that they have learnt, to be evaluated by a jury of bearded, dark-glassed sheikhs.

The medium is different, but the message is unchanged from the years when the sons of Abdul Aziz, the present rulers of the Kingdom, were committing to memory those rambling strands of language knitted out like an endless scarf with just one recurring pattern – *'Bismillah al rahman al raheem'*, 'In the name of God, the Compassionate, the Merciful' – in one little mud room in Riyadh.

Today the education of King Khalid, Crown Prince Fahad and their brothers is officially described as a 'court education in religion, chivalry and politics', and this meant learning the Koran and then passing on, around the age of eleven or twelve, to a special finishing school devised by their father. Each young prince would be assigned his own bedouin tutor who would take him out in the desert to live for a period in the black hair tents. One bedouin would teach him how to ride and care for a horse. Another would give him lessons in rifles and marksmanship. A third would teach him tracking and desert lore. And when the young man's sojourn in the desert was completed he would return to Riyadh to sit in his father's *majlis* and listen there to the daily discussions of politics in Arabia and in the wider world.

It was not a conventional preparation for the conduct of late twentieth-century international relations, but it was not the only unusual aspect to the upbringing enjoyed by princes of the Al Sa'ud in the 1920s; each was accompanied through his education by an *akhiwiya*, or 'little brother' – his own personal slave.

Slavery was a flourishing institution in Arabia in the 1920s, and for several decades thereafter. It was not formally abolished in the Kingdom until 1962. The pilgrimage was the main source. Nigerians and Sudanese would sell their children in Mecca to help pay for their journey home, and the slave trade was one traditional source of the shareefs' wealth.

In Nejd every emir and sheikh had at least one black family living in his household, and their children were assigned as playmates to the children in the household of their age and sex, growing up with them and often becoming their close companions in adult life.

When Prince Faisal ibn Abdul Aziz visited New York in 1944, the management of the Waldorf Astoria were shocked that he brought his slave Merzouk with him. But they were still more horrified when the prince insisted that his companion should eat, as he always did, at the same table as his master – for this involved admitting Merzouk to the Wedgwood Room, and no black had ever been allowed in there before.

In December 1922 it was the austerity of Riyadh which struck Amin Rihani most forcibly. This partly reflected, he thought, the natural temperament of these desert dwellers, cut off from the twentieth-century world and having little choice but to discipline themselves if they wished to subdue their harsh environment. But there was also their religion. 'All that redounds to the glory of man is banned,' he wrote.

Singing and musical instruments were taboo. There was not a single plant or flowerpot in Riyadh's terraces and courtyards, and there were quarters of the town where you could not laugh inside your own home without risking a knock on the door and a reprimand for levity from a passing zealot.

These enforcers of the Wahhabi way are known today in the Kingdom as the 'religious police'. But they are better described as vigilantes – and Rihani's description of Riyadh sixty years ago makes clear why. The righteous of every neighbourhood banded themselves together into societies for 'The Propagation of Virtue and the Prevention of Vice', and it is their descendants who patrol the streets of Sa'udi towns today. In the 1980s they receive government subsidies, but they are still essentially volunteers engaged in their own variety of social work.

Abdul Aziz tolerated their severity, but there were occasions, he told Amin Rihani, when he felt that he was a stranger in his own town. Confronted with the most extreme manifestations of Wahhabi fervour, he could feel 'no contact of mind or heart – not even of soul'.

Sitting in the *majlis* one day reminiscing about past adventures, the sultan turned to one of the long-bearded members of the *ulema* who came to sit with him every afternoon. 'Do you remember the date of that battle, oh Sheikh?' he asked.

The sheikh shook his head and said nothing. Later the discussion turned to religious subjects, and again the sultan turned to the obvious man to give him help.

'You do not know?' enquired Abdul Aziz, pushing for the answer which the silent sheikh clearly did know – and yet again not one word was forthcoming.

'The *ulema*', Abdul Aziz confided ironically to Rihani as the two men left the *majlis*, 'do not condescend to speak to us.'

It was an open secret in Riyadh that the Sultan of Nejd was not happy with all the severities which were imposed upon his community in the name of religion. The moment he was out of sight and earshot of Riyadh, it was whispered, he would order his followers with the lustiest voices to break out into song.

178

Yet Abdul Aziz could afford his discreet impieties, for no one, in the last resort, could question the depth and sincerity of his personal faith. He was meticulous in his observance of the five prayer times, and he was famous for the thoroughness with which he had absorbed his own Koranic lessons as a boy.

'In the name of God, the Compassionate, the Merciful.' Between that leitmotiv at the beginning and end of every *sura*, the Koran twists and soars into a complexity of language and thought which can be compared in texture, if not in content, to the intricacies of James Joyce. Once inside the brain it must make an absorbing companion through life, and we know that Abdul Aziz thoroughly enjoyed its company.

He had cantors around his palace, and he would always take one with him on his journeys to recite away the tedious hours on camel-back. He sat every afternoon listening intently to some reading from the Hadith,* and when the reader stopped Abdul Aziz liked to take over, reciting the rest of the passage from memory, word perfect.

Even at night members of the sultan's family would hear his voice through the door of his private quarters. He was murmuring the Koranic verses at that moment of the night when the especially pious Muslim says private prayers and talks to God with his hands before his face. At those moments, said Abdul Aziz's relatives, they could hear the great voice crack, and Abdul Aziz would start sobbing.

The volatile emotions of Abdul Aziz struck Amin Rihani as remarkable. When the sultan lost his temper it was with ferocity and violence. He would fall upon anyone who incurred his wrath, lashing out with his camel stick – 'I could hardly believe I was in the presence of the same man.'

'But his anger', wrote Rihani, 'subsides as it blazes – quickly. No sooner does he strike the ground with his staff than he touches your heart.'

Rihani fell ill, and Abdul Aziz came to visit him every day he was in bed, bringing him a small get-well present on each occasion: fruit salts, biscuits and an ancient chronicle of the Al Sa'ud's history because he knew his guest was curious about that.

---

* Hadith: 'traditions', the personal acts and sayings of the prophet and of his Companions. To make a comparison with the New Testament, it is as if the pure words and message of Christ were gathered into one book (the Koran) while the anecdotes of his life, along with the applied laws and lessons to be derived from it, a combination of the Epistles with the folktales from the gospels, were gathered into another (the Hadith). Together the two books, the Koran and the Hadith, provide the basis for the Shariah – Islamic law.

Abdul Aziz, concluded Rihani, was a unique and extraordinary mixture. Blessed with charm and sensitivity to which a Westerner found it easy to respond, he could also be despotic and opaque in a fashion that could only be described as oriental. Animated by deep Islamic conviction and believing in his mission to lead the Wahhabi crusade in the twentieth century, he was also fiercely ambitious for his own family – and he was a consummate politician.

'I have now met all the Kings of Arabia,' wrote the Lebanese, 'and I find no one among them bigger than this man. . . . He is big in word and gesture and mind. He knows what he wants and – what is best – he knows how much he can get of it at a given time.'

23 Taif

IN Jeddah, as in Riyadh in the days before air-conditioning, night life took place on the roof, and one evening in 1920 Shareef Husain ibn Ali, King of the Hijaz, invited Britain's newly arrived Vice-Consul in Jeddah, Laurence Grafftey-Smith, to dine with him on the roof of the barracks beside Eve's Tomb. The shareef had a habit of force-feeding his guests. He liked to pluck out morsels from the main platter and push them into his neighbours' mouths, refusing all protests 'as if', wrote Grafftey-Smith, 'he was stuffing a turkey.' It was the old man's idea of hospitality. And his concept of after-dinner entertainment was equally droll. A black slave appeared on the roof leading a huge ape on a chain, which the shareef promptly set on to one of his guests who had a reputation for cowardice. The miserable victim more than confirmed this, for he rushed screaming round the roof, stumbling over chairs and people, and was about to cast himself in despair over the parapet, several storeys high, when the beast was called off.

'I was watching the King during this painful scene,' wrote Grafftey-Smith, 'and I saw how his eyes shone, and the thin drool of saliva at the corners of his mouth.'

The shareef, absolute ruler of the Hijaz since the expulsion of the Turks, was taking on all the arrogance of absolutism. Talking with him one day on a badly crossed telephone line, Ronald Storrs was surprised to hear Husain suddenly expostulate to the exchange 'in stronger language than I had expected from so holy a man, ordering them to cut off everybody's instrument in the Hijaz excepting his own and mine for the next half hour. This was instantly done, and we conversed henceforth in a silence of death.'

King George V was envious when he heard this tale. 'I couldn't do that in London,' he told Storrs wistfully.

But His Britannic Majesty's representatives in the Middle East were becoming less and less impressed with the imperious ways of Shareef Husain ibn Ali, for he was extending them into his foreign policy. Husain was declining to accept Britain's pattern of state making in the post-war Middle East, rejecting any suggestion of compromise, and London was losing patience.

It was the battle of Turabah that made the difference. Until May 1919 the British had considered the Hashimite armies they had financed, trained and equipped to be the dominant local force in the Middle East, and they tolerated Shareef Husain's obstinacy and megalomania because they assumed that they had no choice. But the overwhelming victory of the Ikhwan at Turabah and the rout of the Hashimite forces suddenly cast a new light on the power balance in Arabia.

'If the Sherif is not strong enough to maintain himself against the Wahhabis,' declared John Shuckburgh, of the India Office, a few weeks after the battle, '. . . he will have to go under, and the sooner we make up our minds to it the better.' His Majesty's Government began to distance itself from the King of the Hijaz.

'Imagine', wrote Reader Bullard, the British Consul who arrived in Jeddah in 1922, 'a cunning, lying, credulous, suspicious, obstinate, vain, conceited, ignorant, greedy, cruel Arab sheikh suddenly thrust into a position where he has to deal with all sorts of questions he doesn't understand and where there is no power to restrain him, and you have a picture of King Husain.'

Husain's trouble was that, for a man of sixty-nine, he possessed an energy and appetite for work which acknowledged no limits. The most minor administrative problems of the Hijaz were all sent to him for his personal attention, and his civil servants had good reason to avoid taking any action without his express authorization, for Husain would consign the objects of his displeasure to a prison below his palace in Mecca, the *qabu*, to which he would descend with a large club when the feeling took him, to vent his fury on the wretches he kept in darkness there.

Most outsiders reacted to such viciousness with disgust and scorn. The consequences of elevating Husain to his despotic eminence moved Sir Arthur Hirtzel to quote a Kurdish proverb: 'Do not encourage an Arab, or he will come and commit a nastiness on the skirt of your coat.'

But the sad truth was that Shareef Husain ibn Ali was losing his reason. The ape on the chain, the club in the cellar, the long serpentine monologues which were his idea of 'conversation', all betokened a dark side to the old man's character that was taking over his entire personality.*

Age, the conceit of power and the frustration of its limits were overbalancing the amiability that had once struck all who met him, and one morning in February 1921 the two sides of the old man's schizophrenia were dramatically revealed as Major Batten, the British Consul, was taking his leave after an apparently charming interview. The Englishman was just reflecting that Husain appeared to have recaptured his old self, when he turned back unexpectedly to discover that 'the mask had fallen, and it was a very different man, brooding and sullen, who stood in the place of the kindly patriarch of a moment before'.

Shareef Husain's brooding was not unjustified, for the post-war reality of his life was cruelly different from all the hope that the Arab Revolt had raised. The Turks had gone and he was undisputed King of the Hijaz, but he had precious little else to show for his wartime efforts on Britain's behalf, since he did not regard the gift of Iraq and Transjordan to his sons as adequate recompense for the risks that he personally had taken.

He was particularly bitter at the surrender of Palestine to the Jews, and it is seldom recognized by the Arabs who malign this deranged old man to this day that Shareef Husain ibn Ali was the first Arab leader clearly to perceive and to fight against the threat that the Balfour Declaration held for Palestine's Arab inhabitants. He absolutely refused to sign the Hijaz–British friendship treaty which Lawrence himself brought to Jeddah in July 1921 because it required acceptance of the British Mandate in Palestine, and thus of the creation of a Jewish homeland there.

'Palestine does not want you,' said Lawrence bluntly, believing the shareef's interest in the issue to be purely personal or dynastic.

'This does not affect us,' replied Husain. 'I am not asking this for myself or for my sons: all we are asking is that Britain keep her plighted word to the Arabs.'

Shareef Husain badly needed the treaty that Lawrence was offering, for it promised him money as well as military support. During the Arab Revolt, Britain had paid him £25,000 a month, but now the

* In 1952 Shareef Husain's grandson Talal was deposed as King of Jordan in favour of his son, the present King Hussein, following difficulties stemming from his unpredictable and schizoid nature.

subsidy was gone and Husain could not keep the tribes in order without British gold. The Harb bedouin of the coast became particularly unruly. Merchants who ventured out of Jeddah without escorts risked having to return home, stripped of everything down to their underdrawers.

The shareef imposed a desperate series of levies on the Hijazis in order to raise revenue – an income tax, an exchange tax, a stamp tax, a water tax, a burial tax even – and his exactions at the expense of the visitors on their pilgrimage were still more severe. His tolls doubled the price of the Jeddah–Mecca round trip in six years, and, since the pilgrimage camels were a royal monopoly, more modern forms of transport were prohibited.

'As the Prophet had found the country,' declared Husain, 'so it should remain for every good Muslim', and he personally demolished with an iron bar a motor car that he one day discovered in Mecca – his crazed impulse to control everything extending even to the sale of dried lizards, a tonic much prized at that time by both Meccans and pilgrims. All around the Holy City signs directed visitors to the royal stalls where the only officially authorized dried lizards could be purchased.

King Husain, observed Sir Ronald Storrs, was becoming 'less and less a practicable member of the comity of kings'. Looking from Iraq, Sir Percy Cox opined that the shareef appeared 'practically demented', while by May 1922 even the shareef's own son Feisal was acknowledging 'the mad obstinacy of his father which has alienated his subjects as well as hostilized his neighbours.'

How would Feisal react, asked Cox, gingerly sounding out an option which almost every British official in Jeddah had felt driven to propose, if his father the shareef were to be deposed?

'In principle,' came the reply, 'that would be a salutary measure which he would welcome at heart' – though Feisal ibn Husain did not, of course, contemplate the solution now beginning to form in a number of British minds.

'The feeling is growing', wrote Sir Arthur Hirtzel in June 1922, 'that it would be a good thing if Ibn Saud *did* establish himself in Mecca.'

Abdul Aziz had never doubted his military capacity to capture the Holy Cities.

'Oh, if you English would only allow me to carve out my fortune by the sword,' he had exclaimed to Harold Dickson in 1920, 'I would have Hejaz inside a week' – and Gertrude Bell thought this boast justified. 'I.S. [Ibn Sa'ud] is much the stronger of the two,' she wrote in that same year, comparing the relative strengths of Abdul Aziz and Shareef Husain. 'It is only the fact that he has acted in accordance with our wishes which has prevented him gobbling up the Hijaz.'

Yet Abdul Aziz's moderation towards Husain had always depended considerably upon the £60,000 a year that the British government had been paying him since the end of the First World War, and when Britain decided in 1923 to end her Middle-Eastern subsidies, this removed a major restraint upon the Sultan of Nejd's ambitions. As from March 1924, the date set by Britain for the final payment of her pensions to Arabia, Abdul Aziz had little to lose if he incurred the displeasure of Whitehall; and it was in March 1924 that Shareef Husain ibn Ali chose to put the Sultan of Nejd's new independence to the test.

The shareef was visiting his son Abdullah in Amman that month. He had travelled up the Red Sea from Jeddah on one of the wheezing steam yachts that constituted the Hijaz's attempt to winkle Red Sea pilgrim traffic out of British hands, to be greeted at Aqaba by a procession of motor cars, whose use he disdained in Transjordan as scornfully as he did in the Hijaz. So the seventy-one-year-old ruler of Mecca had mounted a mule to trot briskly for two days across the 75 miles of desert to Ma'an railway station.

'He never seemed to wilt,' reported Philby, who witnessed this performance admiringly, 'and whenever I saw him on the way he was riding upright, stiff as a ramrod.'

Shareef Husain ibn Ali had too much energy for his own good. On 3 March 1924 he heard that Kamal Ataturk, in his programme to modernize post-Ottoman Turkey, had formally jettisoned the title of caliph and thus the leadership of Islam claimed by the Ottomans for 400 years, and, while Ataturk viewed the caliphate as abolished, Shareef Husain saw the office as miraculously vacated. Who better to assume its dignity than himself?

On 5 March 1924, in Amman, Husain proclaimed himself caliph, Successor of the Prophet, Guardian of Islam, and leader of Muslims throughout the world – dignities that impressed his Hijazi subjects, when the news reached Jeddah, as much as the idea 'that relativity or bimetallism should become the state religion', reported Reader Bullard.

'The announcement was listened to without enthusiasm,' wrote the British Consul, 'and a speech from a young Syrian ending with "Long live the Caliph Husain!" was received in dead silence.'

The news was received more coldly still in the rest of the Muslim world. The Javanese prophesied that the shareef would be struck down by God for his effrontery. In India the Islamic nationalists were convinced the manoeuvre was British inspired. The British themselves expressed shock, refusing to recognize Husain's new title – and in Nejd the reaction was one of profound and unappeasable anger.

The Assembly of Notables which met in Riyadh on 5 June 1924 was not the first such gathering that Abdul Aziz had called. Five years earlier he had organized at least one similar convocation when Ikhwan practices like forcible conversion were causing concern and when he wanted the *ulema* to discipline the brethren.

But Western words like 'assembly' and 'conference' probably over-ritualize what was, in essence, the routine seasonal gathering of sheikhs and emirs for the Eed al Adha – the pilgrimage feast – when relatives and clients of the Al Sa'ud all came to Riyadh to pay their respects. It was the time when the half-yearly gifts were distributed, and in June 1924 Abdul Aziz formally called in the allegiance he was purchasing by inviting comment on Shareef Husain ibn Ali's assumption of the caliphate.

The Ikhwan leaders present waxed predictably indignant, and Sultan ibn Bijad, the leader of the Ghot Ghot Ikhwan, led the attack, reciting the litany of shareefian misdoings that had culminated in the assumption of the caliphate. He focused particularly on the ban that Husain had recently imposed on Nejdis carrying out the *hajj*, for the shareef had been understandably reluctant to open Mecca to throngs of Ikhwan 'pilgrims'. Ibn Bijad called on the brethren to march to Mecca and to force the old grey devil to let them do their pilgrimage.

But Abdul Aziz's immediate reaction to the Ikhwan's complaints was to take the shareef's side – and he himself prohibited any Nejdis from going on pilgrimage in the forthcoming year. Husain's assumption of the caliphate was sacrilegious, said Abdul Aziz, but he had to warn his followers that marching armed into the Holy Land was a still greater sacrilege, 'except as mandatories of the Islamic World, since the Holy Cities were a common possession of all Muslims.' The international Muslim community did not have happy memories of the last Wahhabi entry into Mecca and Medina, and Abdul Aziz knew that he would have to live with that.

The sultan was fortunate that Shareef Husain ibn Ali had contrived to alienate so many of his fellow Muslims, and this was particularly the case in India, where nationalist paranoia had interpreted Husain's assumption of the caliphate as a devious British plot. The Indian Khilafat Committee had always denounced British support for Shareef Husain as an unwarranted interference in Islamic affairs. Now, in the summer of 1924, it called on the Sultan of Nejd 'to render possible the establishment of concord among the Arabs of the Peninsula' – and Abdul Aziz needed no encouragement. He had decided on attack in any case. The Sultan of Nejd waited three months for the pilgrims to get clear of Mecca, and then in August 1924 he ordered Khalid ibn Lu'ay and Sultan ibn Bijad to lead their warriors, some 3000 Ikhwan, westwards from Turabah across the plains to Taif.

The shareef had been preparing for this day for some time. He had Taif's city wall rebuilt and a ring of watchtowers constructed round it. But when the Ikhwan presented themselves outside one of these towers on 1 September 1924, its little garrison surrendered promptly, and the occupants of the other outlying strongpoints all retreated to the safety of the city walls.

The Hashimite army, larger than the Ikhwan forces and equipped with superior weapons, was commanded by Shareef Husain's thin-faced and consumptive eldest son Ali. The British had passed Ali by in their organization of the Arab Revolt, correctly sensing the more warlike qualities they sought in his younger brothers, Abdullah and Feisal.

'I divine a weak chin under his small Charles I beard,' wrote Ronald Storrs of Ali, and the Arab Bureau's personality report on the shareef's heir described him as 'a very conscientious, careful, pleasant gentleman, without force of character' – an assessment which Ali fully justified by his handling of the Sa'udi siege of Taif. The Ikhwan had not even started seriously to invest the town when, on the night of 4 September 1924, King Husain's eldest son led his father's forces stealthily away under cover of darkness, abandoning Taif's inhabitants to the tender mercies of the warriors of Islam.

Precisely what happened next is disputed. A deputation of Taif

187

citizens, it is said, negotiated a surrender with Khalid ibn Lu'ay and Sultan ibn Bijad. Perhaps the gates were simply opened without formalities by local Ikhwan sympathizers. But certainly the towns- people were not considering any forcible resistance when the breth- ren's takeover of Taif suddenly turned into a dreadful massacre.

Afterwards it was said that the Sa'udis had been fired on from a police post, but whatever the provocation, real or supposed, the slaughter was merciless: the town's *qadi* and sheikhs retreated to a mosque, to be dragged out and cut to pieces; houses were destroyed, shops and market stalls looted; throats were cut and bodies were flung down the open wells of the town in a rampage that left more than 300 dead in a matter of hours.

The massacre of Taif threw the Hijaz into a panic, and King Husain appealed desperately to Britain for help. But he received no response, for, on hearing the news of the Sa'udi invasion, His Majesty's Government decided to let events follow their natural course. Abdul Aziz was sent a cable warning him not to jeopardize the safety of British pilgrims or the freedom of access to the Islamic shrines. But the message pointedly failed to mention King Husain or any rights that he possessed in the Hijaz – and from this Abdul Aziz concluded, correctly, that Britain was now abandoning her former ally.

The inhabitants of Jeddah rapidly came to the same conclusion and on 3 October 1924, 140 of Jeddah's leading citizens met under the presidency of Hajji Abdullah Alireza, the *qaimaqam* or governor of the town.

Hajji Abdullah was a much respected figure. The Alirezas were among the richest merchants in the Hijaz, with a reputation for good works – the *Falah** schools, the first modern schools in Arabia, were founded and financed by Muhammad Ali Zainal Alireza – and Hajji Abdullah proposed reform. Shareef Husain must abdicate and a new 'constitutional' government should be formed under the leadership of the inoffensive Ali. The general hope in Jeddah was that the departure of Husain – and with him the troublesome claim to the

---

* *Falah* means 'success' in Arabic. Muhammad Ali Zainal Alireza, 'the King of Pearls', who sold his wares to western jewellers like Cartier and Harry Winston, founded his first school in Jeddah in 1901 in defiance of the Ottomans, who disliked their subject peoples educating themselves. He devoted much of his personal fortune to these schools, which were free and from which many of the Kingdom's modern ministers and administrators were to graduate. Until the 1940s the *Falah* schools provided the only secondary education in Arabia.

188

caliphate – might induce Abdul Aziz to negotiate, and poor Ali, whose position as his father's hitherto favourite son had rested on his inability ever to contradict him in anything, had the unenviable task of travelling to Mecca to urge the merits of this policy upon Husain.

To everyone's surprise the old man listened to his son, and at 9 o'clock on the evening of the same day, 3 October 1924, in his deserted and darkened palace, King Husain took up his favourite quill pen and assented to his abdication. The Al Sa'ud's most tenacious Arabian adversary had surrendered with scarcely a struggle.

There now followed a brief hiatus in which ex-King Husain seemed unwilling to leave his ex-kingdom. But the days were spent packing personal belongings whose nature became clear when Husain finally took ship from Jeddah on 16 October 1924. The slaves carrying a succession of tight-clamped kerosene cans on board the Red Sea steamer *Two Mercies* were seen to stagger under their weight, for the cans contained gold – some £800,000 in gold sovereigns, sixteen years' profits from the pilgrimage plus the cream off Britain's wartime subsidies to the Arab Revolt.

So Shareef Husain ibn Ali had not done so badly out of the British, who now escorted him to Aqaba, and onwards later to exile on the island of Cyprus, and his farewell to Arabian history took the form of two brief telegrams dispatched on the same day from a coral reef somewhere in the Red Sea.

'Your steamer has run aground,' he cabled angrily to the British Agency in Jeddah. And then a few hours later came better news: 'Our steamer has floated off again.'

24 Mecca

The Holy Cities of Mecca and Medina are on the
other side of Arabia from the oilfields. But they
are part of the same country – and in our eyes
they matter more than anything else.

Sheikh Ahmad Zaki Yamani, January 1981

O N the same day that Shareef Husain ibn Ali set sail from
Jeddah, four Ikhwan warriors clad only in white towels rode
gingerly across the stony plains that led up towards the walls of
Mecca. The gates of the Holy City were swinging open, unguarded,
and through them the four pilgrims rode to find themselves in a ghost
town. The dusty carved wooden doors were closed, the shutters
barred, scarcely a soul was on the streets, and at the main gathering
points of the city the four men read out proclamations to the empty
air.

It was 16 October 1924 and Abdul Aziz, still in Riyadh, had sent
the strictest orders to his commanders that they should not approach
the Holy City. But news had reached Khalid ibn Lu'ay of a mass
exodus in the wake of Shareef Husain, for Mecca's citizens, terrified
that they would suffer the fate of Taif's inhabitants, had fled into the
desert or down the road to Jeddah, abandoning their shops and
homes to be pillaged by the local bedouin. So Sultan ibn Bijad had
ordered four of his Ghot Ghot Ikhwan to dress themselves as pilgrims
and to enter the town, clad just in their towels and without weapons,
to proclaim its annexation.

Next day Ibn Lu'ay and Ibn Bijad led their main force, also in
pilgrim garb, ceremonially into the city. Some of the more fanatical
brethren broke up a few street cafés, burning the cigarettes and
hubble-bubble pipes that they found there. A few domed tombs were
smashed or defaced. But no lives were lost and Ibn Lu'ay kept good
order in the Holy City until his master should arrive.

Abdul Aziz took his time a-coming. He did not arrive in the Hijaz
until 3 December 1924, more than three months after the Ikhwan
had taken Taif, and when he did reach Mecca he declined to take up
residence in King Husain's luxurious palace. He remained outside the
walls in a simple tented encampment in the hills, took off his sword,

190

Top Faisal al Daweesh, Sheikh of the Mutair and leader of the Ikhwan after his surrender in Iraq, 1929, sketched by Squadron Leader Stewart
Above Modern survivors of the Ikhwan at Abha, Asir Province, June 1979

Above Shareef Husain ibn Ali lays claim to all Arabia;
a postcard issued in the Hijaz in his reign
Left Ali, the shareef's eldest son and successor; King of the Hijaz, 1924–5
Right Abdullah, Shareef Husain's second son, defeated at
Turabah and later ruler of Transjordan

Winston Churchill at the Cairo Conference, 1921. To his left Sir Percy Cox;
behind Cox, T. E. Lawrence in the same row as Gertrude Bell

Above A village in the Asir, conquered by the Ikhwan in 1920
Below The fort at Busaiyah Wells, 1927
Inset Glubb Pasha

Above False start. Major Frank Holmes stands between Abdul Aziz and Sir Percy Cox at Uqayr, November 1922

Left Reconciliation. Abdul Aziz meets King Feisal of Iraq, son of Shareef Husain ibn Ali, on board the British warship HMS *Lupin*, February 1930

gold headropes and robes and, dressed like any other pilgrim in two seamless lengths of white cloth, he entered the Holy City through the Gate of Peace (Baab al Salaam), to walk bareheaded with the crowds to the Great Mosque.

'Here am I, O God, at Thy command,' he said, repeating the declaration made by every pilgrim as he enters the Holy City. 'Thou art One and Alone. Here am I.'

As suitors clustered round him, Abdul Aziz refused all attempts to kiss his hand or to kneel before him, as had been the custom with the shareef. 'Our Arab custom,' he said, 'is to shake hands only.'

Abdul Aziz was moving very cautiously. He could not forget that the last Sa'udi capture of Mecca had provoked the downfall of his family – the foreign intervention that had destroyed Dar'iyah – and the news of the Taif massacre had not been a good start on the road to international acceptance. Muslim reactions around the world to the news that the Wahhabis were moving on Mecca ranged from outright hostility to caution at best. The prospect of the unlettered zealots of the desert occupying Islam's Holy Land appealed to sophisticated Levantines and Egyptian intellectuals no more than it did to most Hijazis. So Abdul Aziz was at pains not to appear a conqueror, and his first public statement on entering Mecca in December 1924 was to invite representatives of Muslim countries around the world to come and confer with him on the future status of the Holy Places.

In January 1981 King Khalid ibn Abdul Aziz invited the leaders of the Islamic world to meet with him in Mecca and Taif, and they almost all accepted. A specially constructed meeting hall, roads, guest palaces, new hotels and communications equipment, together costing hundreds of millions of dollars, made the 1981 Taif Summit the most expensive conference ever staged anywhere in the world, and over forty Islamic heads of state flew to the Kingdom to pay tribute to the pre-eminence of Sa'udi Arabia in international Islam.

In December 1924 the world's Muslims responded less warmly to King Khalid's father. Abdul Aziz's invitation to confer with him on the future status of the Holy Places was almost totally ignored, and his only takers proved to be the Indian Khilafat Committee who turned up eagerly in Jeddah – only to become embroiled in vain attempts to mediate between Shareef Ali and Abdul Aziz and to depart in February 1925, having come to the conclusion that constructive decisions would have to wait on the departure from the Hijaz of the last Hashimite.

Nothing could have suited Abdul Aziz's purpose better, for, no matter what he said for international consumption, his settled intention in invading the Hijaz was to oust the Hashimite family and to take permanent and personal control of the Holy Places. The Al Sa'ud espoused, in his eyes, the purest practice of Islam, and his invitations to foreign Muslims had been based on the assumption that various forms of theoretical guardianship would be proposed that would develop, in practice over the years, into absolute control.

If foreign Muslims now declined even to offer him their suggestions, Abdul Aziz could scarcely be blamed for taking matters into his own hands; and, as hostilities dragged on with Shareef Ali through 1925, the Sa'udis proved to be peaceful and efficient administrators of the Holy City. This made it increasingly difficult for their critics to argue that the twentieth-century Wahhabis were anarchists or wreckers – and their critics included some of the most prominent local inhabitants of the Hijaz.

Jeddah's merchants boast today of the welcome to the Hijaz that they extended to the Al Sa'ud in 1925. But they forget that their great-grandfathers' first instinct after Shareef Husain's departure in October 1924 was not to surrender to the Wahhabis but to create an independent local regime to keep the uncouth invaders at bay. The 'Constitutional Democratic Government of the Hijaz' proclaimed after Husain's abdication, under the nominal leadership of his son Ali, was a bid for independence by the local mercantile community. Its aims were to acquire foreign arms, to fight Abdul Aziz until he could be forced into withdrawal, and to obtain recognition of the Hijaz as an independent entity. Its moving spirit came to be a 'Hijaz National Party' founded by Muhammad al Taweel, Shareef Husain's Director of Customs. The merchants of Jeddah did not see their future involving incorporation into the Nejdi empire of the Al Sa'ud.

Britain made its attitude towards the Constitutional Democratic Government of the Hijaz crystal clear when her consul, Reader Bullard, visited Shareef Ali soon after his accession. The visit, Bullard explained, was purely a courtesy call. It implied no British recognition, and to emphasize the point Bullard dressed in a lounge suit, not his ceremonial court dress.

Shareef Ali's brothers proved more helpful. From Transjordan Abdullah sent down 300 'volunteers', and these formed the nucleus of the Hijaz Victory Brigade whose commander-in-chief, a former physical training instructor in the Turkish navy, organized a morale-boosting march past headed by a military band playing 'Three Cheers for the red, white and blue' – an inappropriate theme song in the circumstances. Trenches were dug, barbed-wire coils were strung out a mile distant from the town walls, and a squad of armoured cars was marshalled to resist the Wahhabi onslaught. Similar vehicles had wreaked havoc among the Ikhwan on their 1922 raid towards Amman, and now the same results were anticipated on the plains of Jeddah. Abdul Aziz and his bedouin would be driven back into Nejd.

Yet Shareef Ali's armoured cars were not, unfortunately, all that they appeared. It was rapidly discovered that they were simply lorries on to which iron sheeting that was far from bullet-proof had been tacked – bargain items of Italian war scrap purchased by an outlandish Hashimite agent, Habeeb Lutfullah. This Lebanese had paid £100,000 for the post of Hijazi Ambassador to Rome, the right to design his own chocolate-soldier uniform, the title of 'Brins' (Prince) of the Hijaz and the task of creating an Hijazi air force. For this project Lutfullah had commissioned the same scrapyards that supplied his 'armoured cars', and he recruited as pilots some White Russian refugees who were offered the contradictory incentive of a bottle of whisky per day and £5 bonus every time they brought their aircraft back in reflying condition.

The alcohol proved stronger than the cash inducement. The Royal Hijazi Air Force succeeded in crashing and immobilizing its craft faster than the Wahhabis could shoot them down, and even its reconnaissance bulletins proved worse than useless since, reported Reader Bullard, 'Shirikoff [the chief pilot] refuses to fly over enemy territory at less than 9000 feet. . . . His observer is a one-eyed officer who always wears dark glasses.'

The Royal Hijazi Air Force provided one of the few sources of amusement for the dwindling number of foreigners left in Jeddah, where the determination of the Constitutional Democratic Government to rally round Shareef Ali depressed all the foreign consuls – and a good number of the local citizens as well. Abdul Aziz was clearly destined to capture Jeddah, and the resistance that the Hijaz National Party was organizing in Ali's name threatened only to increase the final retribution when it came. Several hundred Hijazis decided to put the Red Sea between themselves and the Wahhabis, Port Sudan becoming colonized in a matter of weeks by the evacuated families of Jeddah merchants, and inside the beleaguered citadel a group of dissidents, headed by Qasim Zainal Alireza, nephew of the

193

town's governor, tried unsuccessfully to negotiate a secret armistice with Abdul Aziz – only to be caught and arrested by Shareef Ali. Ali released the dissidents on payment of heavy fines, but he went on defending Jeddah as doggedly as ever.

Abdul Aziz's attitude to this continuing resistance was one of disdain. He moved his forces forward to besiege Jeddah and sent detachments of Ikhwan to surround Medina and its port at Yanbu, but he ordered them all to avoid bloodshed, for he knew that time was on his side. He had no need to risk all-out assaults, and while his forces sat around Jeddah, Yanbu and Medina, lobbing shells over the walls in a desultory fashion, he concentrated on establishing himself in Mecca.

On 8 January 1925 the Wahhabi *ulema* from Nejd had met with the religious sheikhs of the Holy City and had settled their differences with remarkable speed and lack of rancour. Mecca's *ulema* had been no more enamoured of Shareef Husain than anyone else; Abdul Aziz had proved on personal contact to be the opposite of fanatical, while he offered the religious authorities a chance to occupy the same sort of pre-eminence in their own community that the *ulema* possessed in Nejd.

The only point of difference was Abdul Aziz's invitation to foreign Muslims to regulate the status of the Holy Places, for Mecca's religious leaders did not want divines from Egypt or India telling them how to do their job, and the local population shared this feeling. When Abdul Aziz repeated yet again his pledge that an Islamic Conference should decide the future government of the Hijaz, there were complaints. So on 21 January 1925 Abdul Aziz summoned the leaders of the town to his presence.

'We have a popular saying,' he declared: ' "The people of Mecca know best about Mecca's mountain passes" ', and he proposed the formation of a Majlis al Shura, a local consultative committee that would rule in conjunction with him.

The Majlis al Shura was formed immediately, and it provided the mechanism by which Abdul Aziz administered Mecca for the rest of 1925. The heads of the principal Meccan families, the chief religious sheikhs and the more successful merchants joined together in a body which met occasionally for formal sessions but did its most useful business conferring directly with Abdul Aziz as individuals or groups in the royal *majlis*. Could property abandoned by Hashimite partisans be confiscated? How much could bedouin charge for sheep at the next sacrifice? How could pilgrim transportation be reorganized and who should own the rights in it? Such questions mingled private profit and public interest, and Abdul Aziz resolved them all in the same fashion that he worked in Nejd, arriving at decisions which were usually arbitrary but which both participants and spectators came to perceive as largely balanced, consistent and fair.

The Sa'udi master-stroke proved their organization of the pilgrimage in the summer of 1925. The Hashimite forces at Jeddah and Yanbu controlled the traditional landing spots, but in February 1925 Abdul Aziz announced that *hajj* terminals would be established in the fishing villages of Rabigh, Lith and Qunfudhah, and, though only a few thousand hardy souls, mainly Indians, took up the invitation, they found themselves shepherded about their devotions rapidly, courteously – and with a singular lack of extortion.

They took home glowing reports of the new Wahhabi administration, and attempts by the 'Royal Hijazi Navy', one ageing steam launch armed with one small gun, to create a blockade by firing across the bows of an Indian *hajj* ship only generated scorn in the outside world and a comparison between the Hashimites and the Al Sa'ud that was more favourable than ever to the newcomers.

By September 1925 Shareef Ali's cause in Jeddah was clearly hopeless. The Wahhabi bombardment of the town with old field-guns was a lazy affair that caused little damage – the very first shell of all had bounced on to Reader Bullard's bed when he was, fortunately, out of the room – but it lowered morale in the town. People huddled in their cellars when the shells started falling; the price of the tobacco-coloured 'drinking' water oozing out of the seawater condenser rose to prohibitive levels as coal stocks dwindled; and the Hashimite 'volunteers' from Transjordan became mutinous as their pay fell further and further in arrears.

When old Shareef Husain sent a telegram exhorting his former subjects to greater efforts, Ali drafted a reply pointing out that their efforts would have been more considerable if they had had the benefit of the £800,000 in gold sovereigns that Husain had taken off in his kerosene cans. But, meek and mild to the last, the dutiful son decided not to send it, and the British Agency discovered just how bad things were getting for him when they heard that one of his secretaries had tried to raise a loan of £10 for the royal household from a Jeddah merchant – and had been refused.

'Poor, kind, gentle Ali is at his wits' end,' reported Sir Gilbert

Clayton, the British emissary who arrived in Jeddah in October 1925. Clayton's arrival signalled that the writing, in Great Britain's eyes, was very clearly on the wall, for Clayton was sent not to talk to Ali– he spared him only a few minutes' smalltalk on his way through Jeddah – but to negotiate with Abdul Aziz in the desert beyond. The Sa'udis had made their camp near Bahra on the road to Mecca, and here Clayton and his Palestinian secretary, George Antonius, arrived on 10 October 1925, having walked the last half-mile after their car gave up the ghost in a rocky wadi on the way.

Clayton had come to talk frontiers – did Britain's emissaries ever talk anything else? – for the British had taken advantage of the Nejd–Hijaz war to seize control of Aqaba at the head of the Red Sea. This town had traditionally been administered by the Hijaz. Shareef Husain certainly considered it as his own, but the British eyed it as a most useful bulwark for their Middle-Eastern sphere of influence, and within a week of Husain's abdication they had started laying plans for Abdullah of Transjordan to annex Aqaba and its hinterland of 5000 or 6000 square miles from the beleagured Ali – a brotherly gesture which Abdullah executed in midsummer 1925 while the siege of Jeddah was proceeding. Ali remarked acidly that he was too concerned with what his enemies were taking from him to worry at what his friends might steal, and the issue was, in reality, an academic one for him, for Abdullah's annexation of Aqaba was effectively at the expense of the Al Sa'ud, who could expect shortly to take over the Hijaz and all its territorial claims.

Abdul Aziz certainly interpreted it as such, and he protested bitterly at the theft of Aqaba. Clayton's mission of October 1925 was to soothe his feelings and to attempt a deal: Clayton should seek Abdul Aziz's agreement on the new line of his northern frontier, and the unspoken *quid pro quo* would be British acquiescence in the Sa'udi conquest of the Hijaz – for, though Britain had proclaimed her strict neutrality in this 'purely religious dispute', neutrality had its price.

In the diary which Gilbert Clayton kept of his trip to meet Abdul Aziz in 1925, the British diplomat paints a portrait of the forty-nine-year-old Sa'udi leader on the eve of his supreme conquest, 'a fine looking man – very tall and strongly built', who impressed Clayton greatly. 'He has a clean-cut handsome face . . . a striking and commanding figure. His expression in repose is rather sad, even at times slightly sulky, but his face lights up very attractively when he smiles.'

Clayton, who found the sultan's rapidly spoken Nejdi Arabic

196

difficult to understand, warmed to Abdul Aziz. But he was less impressed by his aides. Since the end of the First World War a number of clever and ambitious Arab nationalists, forced out of their own countries by British or French domination, had found refuge in Nejd, and Abdul Aziz had taken them on to his staff. Hafiz Wahba, a former Egyptian journalist and political activist, was actually a fugitive from British justice, and Yussuf Yassin was a sharp and argumentative Syrian refugee from Palestine. 'They are the familiar type of "pinch-beck" oriental politician whose methods consist in arguing every small point,' wrote Clayton, 'employing a certain amount of low cunning and resorting at all times to a policy of consistent obstruction.'

In the years to come successive Western negotiators were to echo Gilbert Clayton's complaints at Wahba, Yassin and the other non-Arabian Arabs whom Abdul Aziz employed as his front-men. They would nag and haggle endlessly, going back on their word, never taking no for an answer and driving their adversaries to distraction with their uniquely Levantine cocktail of slipperiness, cunning and apparent stupidity.

But they got results. One of the points at issue between Britain and Nejd was control of the Wadi Sirhan which ran up from the deserts north of Hail into Transjordan, and Clayton had been instructed to yield it to the Sa'udis only as a last resort. But after hours with the 'vultures,' as he nicknamed Wahba and Yassin, Clayton succumbed with relief to the charm and directness of Abdul Aziz. In agreements named after Bahra and Hadda, the nearest villages to the Sa'udi camp, the British recognized Sa'udi possession of the conquests the Ikhwan had been making up the Wadi Sirhan, while Abdul Aziz gave only vague verbal undertakings about Aqaba in return. 'Ibn Saud', wrote Clayton, '. . . is a fine type of the true desert Arab and possesses all his good points.'

An incident one evening outside the Sa'udi camp provided the British diplomat with an example of how direct and forceful Abdul Aziz's ways could be.

Clayton and Antonius had been taking their daily sunset promenade prior to retiring to their tent for a surreptitious whisky and soda ('an important ceremony,' confided Clayton in his diary), when they were accosted by two 'fanatical looking Arabs'. These Ikhwan knew nothing of the foreigners' secret drinking, but they cursed them roundly as 'dogs of Christians' for having ventured near their camp

197

site, and when Clayton arrived back at the royal camp he felt he should apologize to Abdul Aziz for having trespassed.

Abdul Aziz promptly summoned the two brethren to him.

'God greet you with prosperity,' the couple saluted him in the usual way.

'God greet you with shit on your faces,' responded the furious sultan, and he had both men caned thirty times in his presence and then dispatched to prison in Mecca to reflect on the wisdom of insulting the sultan's guests, infidel or otherwise.

'Such are the drastic measures by which Ibn Saud maintains his personal prestige and authority,' reflected Clayton. 'But on the other hand, he is the father of his people and some 2000 persons feed at his table daily.' The Sa'udi soup kitchen had followed Abdul Aziz to the Hijaz.

On 5 December 1925 Medina surrendered. The city had only been holding out through the last few weeks of its Ikhwan siege thanks to food supplies which Abdul Aziz had smuggled in to the inhabitants, for the besieging Ikhwan were headed by Faisal al Daweesh, and Abdul Aziz did not want the second of the Holy Cities to fall into the hands of this fanatic.

Medina, the site of the Prophet's tomb and the shrines of other Islamic heroes, had always been somewhat suspect in Wahhabi eyes. Medina was a particular resort of the idolatrous Shia Muslims, and its treasures might well provoke an Ikhwan rampage. So Abdul Aziz arranged for the smuggling of secret supplies to keep the inhabitants' resistance alive, and ordered his son Muhammad to march there immediately. Muhammad was Abdul Aziz's third surviving son after Sa'ud and Faisal, and he was now a broad, upstanding lad in his late teens, already renowned for his warlike ways. On 6 December 1925 Muhammad bin Abdul Aziz entered Medina at the head of the Sa'udi forces and walked to the green-domed Prophet's Mosque to say his prayers. The Al Sa'ud controlled the Holy Places.

The news of Medina's fall threw Jeddah into final distress. The Prime Minister and Foreign Minister of the Constitutional Democratic Government packed their bags for Egypt, ostensibly 'to secure assistance' there, and the Victory Brigade locked itself into a mosque, petulant at a year's unpaid wages. Poor Ali phoned for advice to his brother Feisal in Baghdad and gladly accepted an invitation to come and take refuge with him. He told his remaining ministers of his decision to abdicate, and on 17 December 1925 a party of Jeddah notables headed by Hajji Abdullah Alireza rode 10 kilometres out of Jeddah to negotiate surrender with Abdul Aziz at Ragamah, today a neon-lit wedding garden, 'Kilo Ten', where television sets flicker beside the arches of a mammoth traffic interchange on the modern pilgrim highway to Mecca.

In 1925 Ragamah was a simple farm, and there was concluded, in a series of meetings, the agreement that unified Arabia: an amnesty for all Hijaz government supporters, job security for civil servants still at their posts, fares and pocket money to get the foreign soldiers home, and the retention by the Hashimite family of all the lands they had held prior to the accession of Shareef Husain – an act of generosity on Abdul Aziz's part thanks to which the shareef's great-grandson and namesake, the present King of Jordan, today enjoys landholdings in some of the most valuable development areas of modern Sa'udi Arabia.

Shareef Ali left Jeddah shyly on Sunday 20 December 1925 on the British ship HMS *Cornflower*, and his former subjects prepared to meet their new master. A tented pavilion was built outside the city walls in the gardens of the Kandara Villa, today the site of the Kandara Palace Hotel. The villa had been built by the Saqqaf family, traders in the Far East. But they had fled the Hijaz with the Hashimites, and their exotically named villa now became the spot where the citizens of Jeddah, on 23 December 1925, first did homage to Abdul Aziz ibn Sa'ud.

Hajji Abdullah Alireza formally handed to the Sultan the keys of the city, along with his own resignation as *qaimaqam*.

'My mission is over,' he said to the sultan.

'Your mission has just begun,' replied Abdul Aziz, reinstating to his governorship the old man who had helped organize resistance to him for more than a year.

Such a gesture of reconciliation was taken as propitious. Next day the victorious Sa'udis entered the city peacefully through the Medina Gate, and Abdul Aziz rode on horseback to the home of Muhammad Nasseef where he was to spend his first night in Jeddah. The Nasseef house, with its heavy brown casements, still soars high above the jumbled alleys of the Jeddah souq, its tree in the little square outside the front door once the only, and now the oldest, tree in the town. Inside the house the curious central stairway with sloping shallow treads was designed for the camels that padded their way up every day to unload water into the tanks on the roof, five storeys high.

In a *majlis* in one of these upper storeys Abdul Aziz met with Hajji Abdullah and other Jeddah notables who had a proposition to put to him. They had sent a delegation to Mecca which had been most favourably impressed by the security, good government and respect for local feelings embodied in the Majlis al Shura there. Still, they remained unwilling to be incorporated wholesale into Nejd – which might create problems with the local community, apart from inflaming international feeling – so they proposed a novel solution: the creation of a dual polity, Hijaz and Nejd, which Abdul Aziz would rule in tandem, and they invited him to become King of the Hijaz immediately.

Ten days later this proposition was put forward publicly by the Majlis al Shura in Mecca. Abdul Aziz summoned the *ulema* to discuss it formally, and on 7 January 1926 he issued a statement regretting the indifference of foreign Muslims to his several previous requests for advice about the Holy Places.

'As I find that the Islamic World is not concerned about this important matter,' he declared, 'I have granted them [the people of the Hijaz] the freedom to decide what they will.'

After noon prayers next day, on 8 January 1926, Abdul Aziz strode out into the crowds clustering outside the Holy Mosque. Beside him was the mosque's imam, who made a brief declaration announcing the name of the Hijaz's new king. Then guns boomed a salute from Shareef Husain's old fortress, crowds of citizens shuffled forward to greet their new sovereign, and one by one the people of the Hijaz shook hands and swore their *bay'ah*, as the people of Riyadh had welcomed the unknown young warrior from the desert twenty-four years earlier.

25 Sabillah

Heavy firing is reported from Mecca, Sa'udi Arabia, where government troops are still fighting to regain control of the Grand Mosque which was seized by religious fanatics a week ago. The rebels are said to be protesting at the westernization of the Kingdom, and their grievances include the unchecked use of video machines and the spread of other Western pleasures and pastimes – including football.

BBC World Service, 27 November 1979

WHEN the Ikhwan reached Jeddah in 1925, they started cutting down the telephone lines. There were not many to sever, but they aroused the anger of the brethren. Telephones were a modern innovation, like the car and wireless set, mysteries in which sorcery, and therefore Satan, must be involved. God had not authorized them in the Koran – and God's soldiers took special pleasure in destroying the lines leading to the residences of Abdul Aziz. They had grown disenchanted with their leader.

In 1924 the Sultan of Nejd had left Riyadh on the back of a camel to conquer Mecca. In 1926 the King of the Hijaz returned to Riyadh sitting in the front of a motor car – and the Ikhwan took this as symbolic. Celebrating the first Eed al Fitr in the Holy City, the Ikhwan chieftains took advantage of their courtesy calls to issue a warning.

Now that the Holy Land had been conquered, good Muslims should beware of being seduced by foreign influences, cautioned Faisal al Daweesh. They should watch for any departure from the true path of Islam, and they should punish it 'not only in the case of the Shareef, but in the case of all who follow in his footsteps and commit the misdeeds which he committed'.

Hafiz Wahba, who was sitting in the *majlis* and who, as an educated Egyptian, represented one of the new foreign influences that the Ikhwan mistrusted, was struck by the enthusiasm with which the other Ikhwan generals endorsed Faisal al Daweesh's barbed remarks. Wahba found their attitude 'ominous', and Abdul Aziz's young brother Abdullah agreed with him. Abdullah bin Abdul Rahman had been appointed commander of the Sa'udi armies in the Hijaz. He had had to deal, from day to day, with the prickliness of the brethren, humouring them and cajoling them to obey orders, and he found their arrogance both offensive and dangerous. He was one of a group in the Al Sa'ud – Abdullah bin Jaluwi was another – who deplored the free rein that Abdul Aziz allowed his holy warriors. He should stamp on insubordination before it became something more sinister.

But Abdul Aziz laughed at such fears. 'The Ikhwan are my children,' he would say. So, if one of the brethren criticized his moustache as too long, he would send for a barber to have it publicly clipped shorter, and would treat the whole matter as a great joke.

Yet in the first pilgrimage after Jeddah's conquest, in the spring of 1926, Ikhwan arrogance became more than a joke. The trouble revolved around the rich black and gold hangings which draped the Ka'aba, Abraham's house to God, and the focal point of Mecca's Grand Mosque. This huge cloth covering had traditionally been sewn by craftsmen in Egypt and, as Egypt's annual present to the Hijaz, it was dispatched every year from Cairo with great ceremony in an ornate litter, the Mahmal. Every *hajj*, Egypt's pilgrim procession crossed the Red Sea and marched south to Mecca behind the Mahmal in a veritable army thousands strong, disciplined and protected by its own little corps of armed pilgrim masters who passed their orders up and down the train by an elaborate system of bugles and trumpeting.

The arrival of the Mahmal and its followers in Mecca was one of the great events of every pilgrim season – and one at which the Ikhwan took instant offence. The glorious shoulder-borne litter smacked to them of idolatry, its retinue of armed guards piqued their pride, and an outburst of 'music' (bugling), as the Egyptians rallied for one of the pilgrimage ceremonies, was taken as the final sacrilege. A group of Ikhwan began to stone the musicians, the Egyptians fired back in self-defence, and the brethren were just rallying to exterminate the foreign idolaters when Abdul Aziz appeared on the scene, to shout them down and beat them back. Some forty pilgrims were killed in the mêlée, and the Mahmal was never trooped again in glory through the streets of Mecca.

Yet the Ikhwan counted this a small triumph, for, judged by almost everything they held dear, the conquest of the Hijaz had proved a bitter and frustrating anticlimax. Only for a few glorious hours at Taif had they been able to satisfy their holy indignation. Thereafter Abdul

Aziz had held in check the expectations that he himself had cultivated – no 'purifications', no plunder and no real power, even. He had handed back authority in Mecca and Jeddah to the merchant families who had controlled them for centuries. He had actually connived with the inhabitants of Medina to keep Faisal al Daweesh away from their shrines – and he had even forbidden raids upon the Hijaz bedouin.

The brethren were foiled on every front. Abdul Aziz was so anxious to conciliate his new Hijazi subjects and the watchful foreign consuls in Jeddah that he acted as if his own stormtroopers, and not the infidels, were the real enemy. So after hanging around the Hijaz for the best part of a year, the brethren rode home to their settlements in Nejd with little booty, little sense of triumph or of honour satisfied, and the growing realization that they had worked themselves out of a job.

This was the heart of the matter. The brethren's fanaticism had given Abdul Aziz Asir, a half stake in each of the 'Neutral Zones' with Iraq and Kuwait, the entire Rasheed realm and now the Hijaz as well. But if Abdul Aziz wished to extend his desert territories further, it would have to be at the expense of the British or of their protégés – and that, as Abdul Aziz well realized, simply was not possible. Britain would not allow another of her Hashimite clients to fall.

When he returned to Riyadh in 1926 Abdul Aziz had himself proclaimed King of Nejd to round off his 'Dual Kingdom of Hijaz and Nejd', and he could take pride in being the ruler of the largest independent Muslim state in the world. But he knew that was the end of his conquests. There was nowhere else for him to go. The empire built by the Ikhwan must now abandon their methods.

In September 1927 the British authorities in Iraq began constructing a police post at Busaiya Wells, a group of watering holes some 80 miles inside Iraqi territory. The police post was built largely on the recommendation of Captain John Bagot Glubb. His job since 1924 had been to patrol this section of the Nejd–Iraq frontier, and he had been having increasing trouble with Nejdi raiders since the Ikhwan returned to their settlements from the Hijaz.

Young Captain Glubb had served in the trenches of the First World War, where part of his jaw was shot away – hence his bedouin nickname 'Abu Huneik', 'Little Jaw'. He identified fiercely with the nomads and semi-nomads that it was his duty to protect, and especially with the local sheep-herding tribes whom the camel-herding bedouin despised and attacked with particular ferocity.

'The terror of the women in their flight, the anguish depicted on the faces of the children, the miserable donkeys laden with the few pathetic possessions of the shepherd families' – these real-life consequences of the romantic-sounding Ikhwan raids had stirred Glubb deeply when he first encountered them in 1924, and, after a couple of years of relative tranquillity while the brethren were away in the Hijaz, the trouble had started up again in 1926 and 1927.

Frustrated and hungry for the plunder denied them in the Hijaz, the Ikhwan began turning their eyes north-east towards the traditional victims of Wahhabi fervour, the shrine-worshipping Shia Muslims of the Iraqi borderlands; through the early months of 1927 the raids into Iraqi territory grew more and more frequent – and they were vicious as well, for these were not the traditional, relatively chivalrous bedouin raids that young John Glubb understood and quite admired.

The lowly shepherd status of the victims, and their religion, injected real venom into the Ikhwan attacks: men and boys were slaughtered mercilessly; women were killed too, according to some sources, though never raped; al Artawiya was the headquarters of the campaign and Faisal al Daweesh was its mastermind.

The construction of the police post at Busaiya Wells brought matters to a head. Incensed that infidels should presume to obstruct their right to wander anywhere, a party of al Daweesh's Mutair fell upon the police post on the night of 5 November 1927 and massacred all twelve of the workmen there, with the exception of one whom they left for dead. The following weeks saw more raiding and bloodshed than ever; Faisal al Daweesh himself rode out to demonstrate his people's right to ride and raid where they wished; the British retaliated by ordering the RAF first to bomb, and later to pursue the raiders far into Nejdi territory; Britain lodged formal protests at Nejd's incursions into Iraq, and by the end of December 1928 a full-scale international incident was bubbling fiercely.

Abdul Aziz's first reaction was to take his subjects' side. The construction of the police post at Busaiya Wells, argued Abdul Aziz, violated nomadic custom.

But Iraq – or rather the British who ran Iraq's defences – stood firm. Oil had just been discovered in Kirkuk. His Majesty's Government was committed to keeping Feisal in Baghdad as it had never been committed to his father Husain in Mecca. The British rebuilt their fort at Busaiya Wells, manned it more strongly than before, instituted regular armoured car and RAF patrols and started building more forts. If Abdul Aziz could not, or would not, prevent his subjects from violating international frontiers, then both he and they would suffer.

The King of Nejd and Hijaz found himself impaled upon the horns of a most uncomfortable dilemma. His warriors of Islam knew no more about twentieth-century international relations than they did about how a telephone worked. They neither understood nor cared for their leader's attempts to adjust to the realities of the wider world, and they were ready to throw off his authority if he declined to lead them in jihad against the infidel police posts.

Abdul Aziz tried to explain his dilemma to the British delegation which came to Jeddah in May 1928 to discuss the frontier trouble with him. But this was not the first occasion on which Britain's representatives had had to meet with the ruler of Nejd to try to sort out the difficulties of his northern borders. Abdul Aziz had given solemn undertakings on every occasion, and still, in 1928, the disorder and bloodshed were as bad as ever.

It was not as if the Ikhwan were ordinary tribesmen going about their everyday business: they were a paramilitary organization with avowedly expansionist aims, nurtured and armed by the ruler of Nejd, who was forever claiming helplessly that they were acting outside his control – and then promptly capitalizing on whatever gains they made for him. It was difficult for the British not to believe that Abdul Aziz really wished in his heart that his holy warriors should sweep towards the Euphrates as the ancient Wahhabis had done, and in a moment of frankness Abdul Aziz admitted as much to John Glubb, who was a junior member of the British delegation:

'Why do you people in Iraq want to control bedouin tribes?' he asked. 'Town Arabs do not understand anything about them. Ibn Sa'ud is the king of all nomads.'

Abdul Aziz seemed to Glubb to see the desert as a vast ocean which he should rule as Britain had once ruled the waves. Bedouin navigated this ocean from the Empty Quarter up through Nejd to the deserts of Iraq, Transjordan and Syria, and, since Abdul Aziz understood the mentality of these wandering folk so well, it seemed only natural to him that he should be their guide and mentor; the best way of organizing the desert was the traditional one, where great chiefs

205

expanded to the natural limits of their authority, enforced law and order within bedouin concepts of what was acceptable – and where police posts were unnecessary.

Glubb found Abdul Aziz a persuasive and inspiring figure. The Englishman had difficulty reminding himself that this was the man who encouraged and effectively licensed the Ikhwan brutalities he had seen inflicted on the shepherd tribes, for Abdul Aziz 'seemed to radiate benevolence. There was something very paternal and reassuring in his manner. I fell under his spell as everyone else had done'.

Abdul Aziz would come on his own to visit the British at their quarters every evening and, sitting cross-legged, tailor-wise, with his feet tucked up beneath him on a sofa, he talked freely to Glubb and his colleagues, 'passing lightly over religion and lingering fondly over the beauty of women'.

The King of Nejd and Hijaz gave his views on everything – on the best way to rule, for example:

'A despotic government may appear to hold its subjects in a band of iron, but, in a crisis or in war, if the iron were to snap, the whole structure falls to pieces. Government by consent is like a thread. A thread is sometimes stronger than iron.'

On the British:

'I have nothing in common with the English; they are strangers to us and Christians. But I need the help of a Great Power, and the British are better than the other Powers.'

The British found themselves entertained in lavish style. The Kandara Villa, where they stayed, was well stocked with whisky, cigars and cigarettes freely dispensed by an efficient staff of Egyptian waiters. But the bottles were put away when the king drove out through the town gates across the desert to visit them every evening:

The royal procession consisted of several saloon cars, packed with negro slaves in scarlet and gold. The King travelled in a large limousine, with slaves standing on the running-boards at each side, so that they completely blocked the windows. Handgrips had been fixed to the body of the car to enable them to hold on. As soon as the convoy stopped before the front door of our villa, a horde of gorgeously-clad negroes carrying silver-mounted swords jumped out of the cars and raced round the house. Some entered by the front door, and some by the back, others stationed themselves beneath the windows or scattered over the garden, while one or two apparently especially confidential retainers enquired where the King would sit and carried out a hasty examination of the room.

206

This Arabian Nights retinue was an innovation. The Emir of Riyadh and Sultan of Nejd had never travelled with liveried flunkeys, for these were foreign fripperies, an example of the new royal style which the puritans of Nejd found offensive in Abdul Aziz.

Nor did these theatrical trappings cut much ice with the British visitors of May 1928, for, though Abdul Aziz worked hard to please and impress Sir Gilbert Clayton's delegation in every way, he could get nowhere at all on the issue that really mattered: the removal of the police post at Busaiya Wells. The British would not budge an inch and the Jeddah conference of 1928 ended in deadlock.

Abdul Aziz had to go back to the brethren and confess failure, and it was difficult to see how their reaction could be anything less than a call for holy war, with him or without him. The King of Nejd and Hijaz was cornered – and he was cornered by the logic of his own deliberate policy for the last dozen years.

Having planted and fostered fanaticism in these simple folk, encouraging them to fear no earthly power and to welcome death as the gateway to paradise, Abdul Aziz could not now argue the futility of charging against Britain's planes and armoured cars. Having incited them to suspect and hate every non-Wahhabi as an agent of the devil, he could not now plead the merits of compromise with the infidel British – and, since he had elevated these murderous innocents to be the principal element in his armed forces, he could now pursue his disagreements with them only at the risk of his own destruction.

Abdul Aziz had sought to have the best of both worlds, to secure twentieth-century power with seventh-century means, and the contradiction had caught up with him.

By the summer of 1928 Abdul Aziz was one or two years past the age of fifty, nearer fifty-five by the Muslim reckoning, and in describing the Sa'udi leader's conduct and appearance at the Jeddah meetings of May that year John Glubb always referred to Ibn Sa'ud as 'the old King': Abdul Aziz's eyesight was poor, he wore spectacles all the time, and he picked his way up the steps of the Kandara Villa with some difficulty as his velvet-jacketed myrmidons scampered ahead to their places inside.

Somewhere in the ten-year campaign to conquer the Rasheeds, capture the Hijaz, pacify the wider world and now to subdue the ultimate defiance of the Ikhwan, the lithe young warrior chieftain had vanished. It was as if Abdul Aziz, in rising to meet all the complex challenges confronting him, had made some great draught on his reserves that had exhausted him: the suave buffeting of British diplomats, the rough obstinacy of the Ikhwan, the cupboard love of Hijaz businessmen, and the constant swirls and counter-currents among his own sons, brothers and cousins, all this made up a vortex of pressures that Abdul Aziz had mastered only at the cost of draining himself of something precious. He had faced them all virtually single-handed and had triumphed essentially through his own efforts. But now he had to confront the supreme crisis of his career in a state of peculiar isolation – for in June 1928, in his palace at Riyadh, his father Abdul Rahman had died.

'I shall never forget', wrote Muhammad Asad, who was with Abdul Aziz in Mecca at the time, 'the uncomprehending stare with which he looked for several seconds at the messenger and the despair that slowly and visibly engulfed the features that were normally so serene.'

It was not manly for an Arab to show grief, nor godly for a Muslim to question the will of Allah, but Abdul Aziz's desperation was understandable, for, while your father is living, the signs of your own mortality seem less threatening; Abdul Rahman had always been a solid and unquestioningly loyal supporter of his son – and the old man's position as imam and senior member of the family had also represented a certain sharing of the political load.

Abdul Rahman would certainly have been a helpful presence in the great confrontation looming for Abdul Aziz with the Ikhwan in the autumn of 1928, and it may well have been his father's death that now triggered the dramatic tactic which Abdul Aziz adopted in his last-ditch attempt to wrestle off disaster. When the notables of Nejd gathered in Riyadh at his invitation in November 1928 to discuss the Iraqi forts and other grievances of the Ikhwan, Abdul Aziz stood up in front of them and solemnly offered them his abdication.

The King of Nejd and Hijaz had staged the meeting carefully. A large balcony in his mud palace had been set aside for the assembly, and the seating plan carefully arranged in advance. Ulema, hadhar and Ikhwan sat in separate sections. The routine of seating took a quarter of an hour, and in connecting rooms off the balcony were set rugs and cushions and armrests for listeners. The entire common-wealth of Nejd was represented at this Estates General of 5 November 1928, some 800 souls, and, when coffee had been served to all, Abdul Aziz rose and made his offer to abdicate.

208

His gesture had the stunning effect he must have planned. The delegates had been streaming into Riyadh for weeks, the bedouin camping in vast black hair townships that stretched for miles, the *hadhar* lodging inside the town, mounting guard and firing off rifles on the walls at night. The atmosphere was tense. Everyone knew that the three principal Ikhwan potentates, Faisal al Daweesh (Mutair), Sultan ibn Bijad (Otayba), and Dhaidhan ibn Hithlain (Ajman) had rejected Abdul Aziz's invitations to come to Riyadh and that he was fuming at their insubordination.

Furious retaliation was expected, and Abdul Aziz's offer of resignation took everyone by surprise. He had no desire, he said, to rule a people who did not want him as their ruler; he wished to avoid the sin of arrogance; and he was happy, he said, to give up his authority and to retire forthwith to a life contemplating God's mysteries.

'Choose any member of my family to rule you,' he declared, pointing histrionically at his assembled brothers and cousins, 'and I will bow the knee to him with you.'

The uproar was immediate and unanimous.

'We'll have none but you to rule us,' cried the delegates, and Abdul Aziz had the whole assembly behind him from that point onwards. The different interest groups sitting together mistrusted each other more fiercely than anyone mistrusted him, and Abdul Aziz knew that, since the death of his father, there was no other figure in his family around whom all loyalties could group. He issued his dramatic offer to abdicate in the full knowledge that it would not be taken up.

But the bravura was more than just political manipulation. Abdul Aziz's offer of November 1928 was also a reminder to his audience – and to the world – of the ultimate legitimacy on which Sa'udi rule rested. Abdul Aziz had unified Arabia with the sword and with ferocious religious discipline; he maintained his power with force, and he delegated it to lieutenants like Abdullah bin Jaluwi who exercised far more force than he did. But the bedrock of Abdul Aziz's authority was the consent of the peoples that he governed; they offered him their *bay'ah* voluntarily, and in now offering to release them of their oath Abdul Aziz showed he had not forgotten what underpinned the structure of his newly adopted royal panoply. To hold a community together in a crisis, as he had told Captain Glubb, the strongest bands of iron could not compare to the thread of consent.

Abdul Aziz came away from the Riyadh Assembly with his authority greatly strengthened. Invited to pronounce on modern innovations like the telephone and the wireless, the *ulema* had declared that they could discover no Islamic precedent for condemning them and that their use could therefore be tolerated. The Ikhwan's representatives had all renewed their oaths of loyalty to Abdul Aziz, and after a full day ventilating their grievances the brethren had also agreed to side with Abdul Aziz against any trouble that Faisal al Daweesh, Ibn Bijad or Ibn Hithlain might cause – though this support was conditional upon the removal of the Iraqi forts from the desert, which Abdul Aziz said that he could accomplish in a couple of months. If the forts were demolished, it seemed, the Ikhwan would be Abdul Aziz's men once more.

It was a big 'if'. Abdul Aziz himself was probably carried away by the emotion and goodwill generated as men opened up their hearts on the mud balcony in Riyadh and at the evening feast that followed. In cold reality the King of Nejd must have known that it was simply impossible to cajole the British to remove their forts from Iraq in two months, if at all, and, if Faisal al Daweesh and his fellow malcontents had only had the patience to hold their hands for those two months, they might well have turned all the fervour generated in Riyadh to their own advantage.

But the Ikhwan rebels were not calm and rational men. It was their zealous irrationality that had set them at odds with Abdul Aziz in the first place, and within weeks of the Riyadh Assembly they launched a series of furied raids which put paid to peace – and which also deprived them of much of the sympathy they had hitherto been able to count on. In December 1928 a detachment of Ghot Ghot raiders set upon a group of defenceless Nejd camel traders at Jumaymah on the Iraq frontier, massacred every one, and made off with their beasts.

This was neither raiding nor holy war. It was plain murder and theft at the expense of fellow citizens, and when, soon afterwards, a group of Anazah bedouin in the north were massacred by an Ikhwan war party, it became clear that the Al Sa'ud and Nejd as a whole were facing something much more serious than religious dissension: the Ikhwan were mounting an attack on the very nature of Abdul Aziz's new state; they were rejecting law and order, the obligations of a centralized society, the discipline imposed by a sedentary govern-

210

ment, and, for all their religious terminology, they were also rejecting the settled priorities of the Ikhwan townships. They wanted to go back to being bedouin again.

Muhammad Asad, who lived with Abdul Aziz through these difficult years, never spoke in terms of the 'Ikhwan rebellion'. He always preferred to talk of the 'bedouin revolt', seeing the brethren's insurrection as the final hopeless fling of the nomads against the constraints of twentieth-century reality – and the Ikhwan themselves spoke in these terms too.

'You have also prevented me from raiding the Bedouins,' complained Faisal al Daweesh in a moving letter he wrote to Abdul Aziz's son Sa'ud in 1929, 'so we are neither Moslems fighting the unbelievers, nor are we Arabs and Bedouins raiding each other and living on what we get from each other. You have kept us away from both our religious and our worldly concerns.'

Raiding was the essence of bedouin life which Abdul Aziz had not suppressed but had skilfully diverted when he herded the tribesmen into their townships. He had provided for their material needs – and offered holy war to satisfy their sense of honour. Now that he was proclaiming the end of holy war as well, he was offering the brethren nothing better than the reservations with which the white man sought to buy off the Red Indian in North America.

'*Pax Saudica*', wrote Harold Dickson, 'means boredom and deprivation of the opportunity for men to distinguish and enrich themselves by raiding.' And in his Bahrain missionary hospital Dr Paul Harrison saw two ungodly bedouin leap into the air with joy at an (unfounded) rumour that Abdul Aziz was dead.

'Since that man has ruled,' they explained, 'no one has raided an enemy and no one has stolen so much as a chicken! Nothing to do but stay at home like women.'

The rebellious Ikhwan chieftains were fighting to preserve the centuries-old source of their bedouin identities in a world that had no place for them, and, if their struggles took on a demented and despairing quality, then that is often the way with doomed species.

The cavalcade of motor cars in which Abdul Aziz set out to discipline his desert bandits in March 1929 symbolized the underlying realities of the struggle. In the long term the camel-riding Ikhwan could not hope to triumph against such a mechanized armada and all the weaponry with which it was equipped. The cars were marshalled by one of the secretaries to whom Abdul Aziz dictated his letters,

Abdullah Suleiman al Hamdan, a scribe from Qaseem, and this young man organized the complicated logistics of fuel, spare parts and ammunition with an industry and skill that were shortly to earn him the position of Abdul Aziz's principal and, for many years, only minister.

The motorcade drove first to Anayzah and Buraydah to call up levies of the townsfolk there, and Abdul Aziz elicited a warm response. Just as the *hadhar* had manned the walls of Riyadh against the bedouin the previous November, so now in March 1929 men saw the forthcoming battle with the Ikhwan as a fight for their own futures. It was like the old days when the Al Sa'ud had not pandered to the erratic zealots of the desert – though a fair number of bedouin had also rallied to the Sa'udi standards.

Abdul Aziz was using all his money and influence in the tribes, and as each tribal chief brought his followers in he received six gold pounds from Abdul Aziz's treasury; each common tribesman or townsman received three pounds for turning up, with the promise of more when he had completed his service, and by the end of March 1929, when Abdul Aziz finally came face to face with Faisal al Daweesh and Ibn Bijad on the plain of Sabillah near al Artawiya, his army outnumbered the combined rebel forces by at least three to one.

Al Daweesh and Ibn Bijad would not normally have allowed themselves to be cornered against such unfavourable odds. But they did not expect to have to fight at Sabillah, for they believed that Abdul Aziz had gone soft. The Sa'udi leader had not done battle personally for more than a dozen years, since the disaster at Kinzan in 1916, and the brethren were confident he was no longer good for anything but talking. They had been fighting his battles for him since 1919, and this had become for al Daweesh and Ibn Bijad both a grievance and a source of contempt. Abdul Aziz's humouring of Ikhwan insults to his face and his unwillingness to confront the British in battle had been widely interpreted as laziness, cowardice or both.

But Abdul Aziz proved aggressive enough, as the succession of mediators passing between the Sa'udi and Ikhwan camps failed to find any common ground. He was stung to the quick when a sheikh sent by Ibn Bijad ostentatiously refused to return his *salaam alaykum*, in keeping with the Ikhwan practice of not greeting those they did not consider true Muslims, and, by the time Faisal al Daweesh himself came in to talk, Abdul Aziz had lost all taste for compromise. The king warned the rebel imperiously that if he did not submit at once 'the full force of punishment would fall on him', while al Daweesh went back to the Ikhwan camp, for his part, with the news that the Sa'udi forces were nothing but an army of flabby cooks and soft men used to sleeping on mattresses. 'They are about as much use', he said to Ibn Bijad, 'as camel-bags without handles.'

Bedouin contempt for the *hadhar* could not, in the last analysis, be talked away – and it roused the old rough-rider in King Abdul Aziz.

Next day he rose and strapped on his bandoleers before dawn. After morning prayers, orders were given for all waterskins to be filled – a traditional desert precaution in case the drift of battle carried the army away from its watering holes – and messengers were sent to the Sa'udi advance guards stationed between the rival armies telling them to hold their ground and not to come back into camp for their morning meal until the main force had reached them.

Abdul Aziz rode out on his warhorse in front of his troops, dismounted to pick up some handfuls of sand, and flung them in the direction of the enemy. This was the gesture that the Prophet Muhammad had made before battle, his invocation to Allah to confound and confuse the foe, and soon the shooting began.

The Ikhwan riflemen had stationed themselves on the higher side of a wadi and had built themselves a wall of loose stones from which they could fire down with some advantage – until they caught sight of the Sa'udi advance guard returning to camp for their belated breakfast. Interpreting this as a general retreat, the Ikhwan broke cover in pursuit, to be caught in the deadly crossfire of a dozen machine-guns whose existence Abdul Aziz had carefully concealed till that point. Several hundred men went down immediately, the surviving Ikhwan turned in flight, and Abdul Aziz launched his cavalry upon them. The battle of Sabillah was over in half an hour.

It was the first battle the Ikhwan had ever lost; Faisal al Daweesh's womenfolk came to seek shelter in the Sa'udi camp – a traditional desert gesture of submission – and al Daweesh himself had been laid low by a wound that was bizarre retribution for one who had taunted his enemy with flabbiness. A bullet had entered one side of his not inconsiderable paunch and passed clean out on the other. The rebel leader was weak, losing blood, flat out on a stretcher, and it seemed to many that he must die.

Abdul Aziz was feeling merciful. He spared the life of the warrior who had helped him in more battles than he had opposed him, and the news of his leniency tempted the chieftain of Ghot Ghot, Ibn Bijad to offer his surrender too. But the Sa'udi leader was not letting the Ikhwan off scot-free to sneer at his softness once again. He had Ibn Bijad arrested and Ghot Ghot demolished. Then Abdul Aziz paid rewards to his loyal troops, compensated them for their losses, sent them back to their homes, and set off himself to Mecca to make his pilgrimage, for the Ikhwan rebellion, in his judgement, was now at an end.

26 The Kingdom

THE shattered walls and crumbling mud fragments of the once proud settlement of Ghot Ghot can be seen to this day in the desert south-west of Riyadh. A new village has sprung up beside the old one, and bright green vegetable plots have sprouted amidst the ruins. But in 1929 the devastation of Ghot Ghot was a grim affair, and it struck at the spiritual heart of the Ikhwan movement, for, of the three rebel chieftains who had been opposing Abdul Aziz, Ghot Ghot's leader, Sultan Ibn Bijad, was the most religiously fanatical. His opposition to the King of Hijaz and Nejd had stemmed from genuine revulsion at infidel influences, and with his surrender and confinement to prison the purely religious component of the Ikhwan had been crushed.

But Faisal al Daweesh was more complicated. He retained the political ambitions which had always animated the leaders of the Mutair bedouin against the Al Sa'ud, while Dhaidhan ibn Hithlain, the leader of the Ajman, was the heir of a similarly independent tradition.

Sabillah had been such a striking victory that the Mutair and the Ajman might both have kept their heads down for a season. Dhaidhan ibn Hithlain had been in the east at the time of the battle, and the news of his allies' defeat prompted him to sue for peace. But in May 1929 he went to discuss peace terms with Abdullah bin Jaluwi's son Fahad under the flag of truce, and he was done to death in a fashion that blew all Nejd into rebellion once again.

The Ikhwan naturally maintained that Fahad had intended treachery from the start: Dhaidhan had been lured to Fahad's tent with false promises, they alleged, only to be betrayed in a shameful fashion. The bin Jaluwis said it was a misunderstanding, and that when, after an evening of peace talks, Ibn Hithlain declined Fahad's invitation to stay the night in his camp on the grounds that 'my people

215

will come for me if I do not return', Fahad took this as a threat. Fahad ordered Ibn Hithlain and his eleven companions to be tied up, and instructed his executioner to slit the throats of all twelve if the Ajman did come for their chief.

The Ajman came, the throats were slit, Fahad bin Jaluwi was shot point blank between the eyes, and in the breast pocket of Ibn Hithlain, stained with the blood that had trickled down from his lacerated throat, were discovered letters promising him safe conduct and signed personally by Abdul Aziz, Abdullah bin Jaluwi and also by Fahad.

The entire Ajman federation exploded in outrage; Faisal al Daweesh was sufficiently recovered to raise the war banners in al Artawiya; and the Otayba turned the desert between Mecca and Riyadh into a ferment of raiding and disorder. The situation was suddenly more perilous than it had ever been before Sabillah; and Abdul Aziz was cut off by the revolt while completing his pilgrimage down in Mecca. He would have to fight his way back to Riyadh.

But now, finally, Abdul Aziz's willingness to traffic with the infidels paid off, for Britain had altered her imperial policy of divide and rule – in Arabia at least. The complications and expense of dealing with local feelings elsewhere in the Middle East had thoroughly spoilt Britain's appetite for Arab politics. She wanted stability in the peninsula; and stability, in the eyes of His Majesty's Government, had come to mean Ibn Sa'ud. He was 'the one big Arab in Arabia', wrote a British official in December 1928; the call he made on Arab national and religious feelings was unique. So behind Abdul Aziz were rallied in the summer of 1929 the diverse resources of His Majesty's Government. In Iraq and Kuwait, Britain's representatives stamped firmly on the local rulers' plans to take advantage of the trouble in Nejd; arms were sent from India, and, secure in this reinforcement, Abdul Aziz set out to cross Arabia in another of his armoured cavalcades.

Muhammad al Mana, who travelled in Abdul Aziz's entourage on this journey from Jeddah to Riyadh, has left a colourful account of its adventures – wells and waterholes polluted by the rebellious Otayba, the fear of ambushes in craggy mountain passes, and then confrontation with the Otayba sheikhs themselves at the oasis of Dawadimi, where Abdul Aziz's oratory won temporary neutrality from the tribesmen. Seen from the bumping and primitive cars, axles breaking, wheels sticking, guards mounted every night, food and water running low, the journey must have seemed a tense and perilous undertaking.

But half a dozen vehicle-mounted machine-guns constituted most formidable weaponry against rifle-carrying camelmen, and, even as Abdul Aziz's armoured motorcade was advancing towards the north-east, British firepower was being marshalled to prevent the Ikhwan escaping in that direction. Britain's agents were telegraphing to Riyadh their intelligence reports on rebel movements. Abdul Aziz was using his own wireless network to co-ordinate his campaign, and, for all the uncertainty and tension of the drama, it is difficult not to see something inexorable in the grip of Western technology gathering round the reckless and doomed nomads, isolated in the desert with their rifles, bandoleers and camels.

Faisal al Daweesh decided to rouse up courage in the traditional way – an intrepid and glorious raid across the breadth of northern Arabia to illustrate the helplessness of the Al Sa'ud – and he picked out 600 of his finest Mutair camelmen under the command of his beloved eldest son Azaiyiz.* The raid was joined by some Ajman, and also by some senior Mutair campaigners, Ibn Shiblan and Ibn Ashwan, and in August 1929 they tore northern Arabia apart, rallying friends and pillaging enemies. They blazed a trail far north of Hail, capturing hundreds of camels from the Shammar and Amarat tribes, and raiding a caravan which contained – sweetest booty of all – 10,000 riyals of Sa'udi taxes on its way to Ibn Musa'id bin Jaluwi, the Governor of Hail.

Azaiyiz and his raiders turned for home in triumph, driving before them across the desert the vast herds of camels which proclaimed their successful defiance of Abdul Aziz. They had many hundreds more beasts than they knew what to do with. It was the raid to cap all raids. But August was not a traditional month for the *ghazzu*, and with good reason, for raiders had to return to base following routes between permanent wells that were easy to predict. From Hail, Ibn Musa'id bin Jaluwi sent out riflemen to dig in and wait for Azaiyiz's band at each successive watering hole. In searing daytime temperatures reaching 120° F, and driven away from each well by its entrenched defenders, the great raid soon faltered, and Azaiyiz al Daweesh called a council of war.

His lieutenants Ibn Shiblan and Ibn Ashwan argued for steering

* The boy was named Abdul Aziz. Azaiyiz was his nickname.

clear of the enemy and for making a dash towards the north-east around the Sa'udi flank in order to get home safely. But Azaiyiz rejected this course as dishonourable. 'God is on the side of the Ikhwan, his Elect,' he said. 'It would be a shameful thing to avoid battle!'

Azaiyiz al Daweesh wanted a head-on confrontation with Ibn Musa'id, and, when scouts brought news that the Sa'udi commander was personally fortifying the oasis of Umm Urdhumah, that decided him. It also decided Ibn Shiblan and Ibn Ashwan to get home safely while they could, so they headed north-east with their followers, leaving Azaiyiz to push forward with just 500 men.

By the time Azaiyiz reached Umm Urdhumah six days later, his riding camels had not drunk for four days, and the captured camel herds were long abandoned. All the Ikhwan waterskins were empty, and as they rode up towards the fortified wells none of Azaiyiz al Daweesh's men had drunk anything for eight hours. They were short of food, parched and desperate. They knew that they had to capture the wells or die, and so they knelt in the sand to say their prayers in the sight of the Sa'udi guns.

'Are we not of the Brotherhood and the Elect of God?' cried Azaiyiz al Daweesh before he led the charge. 'We must on and win the water, the Almighty will help his followers!'

It was midday. A heavy heat haze hung over the Sa'udi riflemen, and it lent the Ikhwan a certain cover as they charged in their desperate bid for water. Soon terrible, confused and ruthless hand-to-hand fighting was in progress around the wells with no quarter given or asked for, the thirst-maddened Ikhwan screaming their battle cries, the Sa'udis remorselessly bringing up fresh reserves, and, as the afternoon wore on, the numbers told. The Ikhwan slaughtered defenders in their hundreds, but they could not reach the water, and from the shambles of his desperate sally the exhausted and still-parched Azaiyiz was led away by five of his slaves to take refuge in the sand dunes. Two months later their dead bodies were discovered in the desert on the track for home, desiccated and paper-like where they had collapsed of thirst, the sad remnants of the last of the great bedouin camel raids.

It was said that Faisal al Daweesh never recovered from the death of his son Azaiyiz. Lieutenants like Ibn Shiblan and Ibn Ashwan – who both got home safely from the great raid – led Mutair war parties on sporadic offensives through the late winter months of 1929, but the heart had gone out of the hunchbacked rebel leader. He grew reclusive and morose. He even lost the hearty appetite that had sustained his high-profile paunch, and he began bitterly to advise those close to him to make their peace with Abdul Aziz. He could not expect his life to be spared again, but they might be able to save theirs.

The end was already in sight when Faisal al Daweesh made a formal approach to Captain Dickson in Kuwait at the end of October 1929. If he should go off with his warriors towards Riyadh, al Daweesh asked the British Agent, and had to leave his women, children and camel herds defenceless in north-east Nejd, would the British government protect them from vengeful Iraqi tribes or give them shelter in Kuwait?

Dickson referred the questions upwards, and the answers that came back might have been dictated by Ibn Sa'ud himself, for His Majesty's Government would neither protect the Mutair women nor allow them sanctuary. The rebels' only hope had been an aggressive and mobile guerrilla campaign against Abdul Aziz in central Nejd. Now they would have to stay in the north-east to protect their women and flocks, backing up against the wall of British defences as Abdul Aziz advanced upon them with his motor cars and machine-guns.

It was a hopeless situation, and Faisal al Daweesh was correct in his assumption that Abdul Aziz was no longer in a merciful mood. The tone of the fighting in this last stage of the Ikhwan revolt had been set at Umm Urdhumah, where, after the flight of Azaiyiz, Ibn Musa'id bin Jaluwi had beheaded all the Mutair captives that he took, some 250 men – and then, when he heard of forty more hiding out in the dunes, unarmed and still desperate for water, he had sent out riflemen to shoot them all down in cold blood.

As the circle closed towards the end of December 1929, Ibn Ashwan and a group of Mutair tried to wriggle round the flank of the advancing Sa'udis, to be caught by Abdul Aziz's sons Muhammad and Khalid, inseparable as ever and now commanding, in their late teens, a detachment of the Sa'udi motorized battle fleet. Ibn Ashwan and his followers dismounted and took up positions behind their couched camels, they were surrounded by the Sa'udi cars, trucks and machine-guns, and they were slaughtered to a man. No prisoners were taken.

A few score miles away, Captain John Glubb was driving towards the Iraq–Nejd frontier when he came across 'a small group of men sitting disconsolately on the ground round a small brushwood fire.

One of them we recognized as Hazza al Duweesh' (Faisal's second son whom Glubb had met earlier) 'who . . . rose and advanced towards our car to salute me. Behind him followed a thickset figure with an ungainly walk, a long brown beard, projecting teeth and cunning little eyes – the very face of the wicked ogre in a fairy story.'

Faisal al Daweesh had been surprised by a night attack of Harb bedouin loyal to Abdul Aziz, and now he was on the run, a fugitive whose only choices were whether to give himself up to Abdul Aziz, to the British in Iraq, or to the British in Kuwait.

Al Daweesh chose Kuwait on 10 January 1930, handing over his sword in a poignant little ceremony which saved his life, since the British declined to hand him back to Abdul Aziz without securing assurances that he would not be executed. The Ikhwan rebellion was finally over.

On 28 January 1930 the RAF flew Faisal al Daweesh and two other rebel chieftains to Abdul Aziz's camp near the Kuwait border. The Sa'udi leader had arranged an elaborate *majlis* with all his family, and he was weeping copiously as he invited al Daweesh to kiss him on the nose in bedouin fashion – keeping his promise to the British and allowing the rebel to live in prison until his death, eighteen months later, from a growth in his throat that haemorrhaged.

A few weeks later Abdul Aziz met for the first time with Feisal bin Husain, the ruler of Iraq, and this meeting of the two Arab kings on board the British ship HMS *Lupin* marked the end of an era in Sa'udi history. Being willing to smile, outwardly at least, and to embrace the most powerful of the hated Hashimites marked Abdul Aziz's public renunciation of the Al Sa'ud's traditional enmity towards that family, and also the abandonment of the ancient Sa'udi ambitions towards the northern territories that the Hashimites now controlled. Abdul Aziz's destruction of his holy warriors had been the token that his great era of expansion was drawing to a close, and it also acknowledged that his rule and power in the future would not be based on bedouin fanaticism, but would return once again to the priorities of the settled *hadhar* from whom the Al Sa'ud had sprung.

Two years later, in September 1932, King Abdul Aziz announced the unification of his dual kingdoms of Nejd and Hijaz into a single sovereign state that would be known as the Kingdom of Sa'udi Arabia. The Al Sa'ud felt entitled to call Arabia their own, and the lower half of the emblem that they gave to their new nation explained frankly how they had won the power to do it: a pair of crossed swords.

But above the crossed swords Abdul Aziz did not round off the national heraldry with the camel of the wandering bedouin whose holy armies had built the kingdom – for the bedouin had also come close to destroying it. He chose the palm tree of the settled oasis dweller.

So the Kingdom was created: a single country the size of western Europe. Add together the surface areas of Portugal, Spain, France, Great Britain, Ireland, Belgium, the Netherlands, West Germany, Switzerland and Italy and you reach 815,700 square miles. The surface area of Sa'udi Arabia, according to the UN Statistical Office, is 830,000 square miles. The Kingdom is today the twelfth largest country in the world – and it was created from nothing, in our own century, by one extraordinary man.

It is not fashionable today to construct history around heroes. The anthropology, sociology and economics of Arabia in the early years of this century should, in theory, explain how the disparate sheikhdoms, towns and tribes of the peninsula came together to form this massive and extraordinary state. But they do not. The only satisfactory answer resides in the unique vision and skills of Abdul Aziz himself.

He was inspired by family honour and ambition – the drive to re-create the empire his forefathers had controlled a century before his birth – and he was guided by the lessons of family disgrace, the memory of Dar'iyah's destruction which persuaded him of the need to avoid provoking foreign intervention in Arabia ever again.

But Abdul Aziz was motivated principally by the sincere and powerful belief that worship across the peninsula, and in the Holy Places in particular, should be regulated by the disciplines of his own Wahhabi faith. This rigorous obedience to God was part of his family's very identity, and it was this that gave shape and meaning to his own inner life.

For most people in the West today, Sa'udi Arabia only began to exist in 1973 – or, at the earliest, in the late 1930s when oil was discovered. But for the Kingdom and those who rule it now, the important part of the story had been completed by 1932. What came afterwards was only God's footnote, His reward for the brave achievement that had gone before.

Part Four

Oil

27 A Man and a Horse

M R Charles R. Crane owed his millions to the manufacture of ingenious and efficient bathroom and sanitary fittings, and the Crane Bathroom Equipment Company of Chicago, today incorporated into the $1.5 billion Crane Company of New York, is a memorial to his family's role in the history of twentieth-century plumbing. But Charles R. Crane, who served briefly as president of the family company from 1912 to 1914, never felt greatly drawn to the world of sprinkling and flushing, and his more significant contribution proved to be to the history of modern Sa'udi Arabia – for Charles Crane was the catalyst by which the Kingdom found its oil.

Mr Crane was first sent to the Arab world by President Woodrow Wilson in 1919. The president was concerned that the Balfour Declaration and the private arrangements that Britain and France had made for the share-out of the Middle East flouted Article XXII of the League of Nations Covenant, which stipulated that the wishes of the local communities should be 'a principal consideration' in any new arrangements arrived at. He proposed that the Allies send a Commission of Investigation to the Middle East to examine this problem, and he may not have been entirely surprised when France and Britain declined to co-operate.

But the American commissioners went just the same, and President Wilson gave the job to Dr Henry Churchill King, a professor at Oberlin College, and to Mr Charles R. Crane, who had been a principal supporter of Wilson's election campaign and who had decided to dedicate the wealth and leisure that his sanitary-fittings empire gave him to the betterment of his fellow men.

The King–Crane Commission carried out their inquiries, and found that they could not approve the scheme Britain and France had devised for the future of the Middle East – least of all in Palestine. Their brief was to measure the situation against the principle of

self-determination, and, 'if that principle is to rule', they wrote, so
that 'the wishes of Palestine's population are to be decisive as to what
is to be done with Palestine, then it is to be remembered that the
non-Jewish population of Palestine – nine tenths of the whole – are
emphatically against the entire Zionist program.'

Dr King and Mr Crane interviewed Arab opinion at every level,
and 'there was no one thing upon which the population of Palestine
were more agreed than upon this. To subject a people so minded to
unlimited Jewish immigration, and to steady financial and social
pressure to surrender the land, would be a gross violation . . . of the
people's rights. . . .'

The recommendations of the King–Crane Commission were dropped
into the maelstrom of the Versailles Peace Conference to vanish
without trace. But from the experience Charles R. Crane, at least,
took something positive away: a fascination and affection for the
Arab people and their way of life, and a wish to help them improve it.

Crane had helped the Imam Yahya, ruler of the Yemen, to organize surveys for artesian water, and he hoped to make a similar
contribution to agriculture further north in Arabia. He visited the
Hijaz twice in the 1920s to this end, but, in the long-drawn-out
breakdown of Hashimite authority and the Sa'udi takeover, he was
able to make little impact, except to leave behind him in Jeddah a
sample of his sanitary company's workmanship – a four-legged pink
enamel bath complete with the latest chromium accoutrements
which, totally devoid of connection to any water system or drainage
facilities, occupied a place of honour on the roof of Shareef Husain
ibn Ali's Red Sea palace.

But Charles R. Crane was a persistent man – and a brave one.
Motoring near the Kuwait border in 1928 with an American missionary, Henry Bilkert, he approached a group of camelmen in strange
white turbans, to discover they were members of the notorious Ikhwan – and to find himself being fired upon as an infidel. Poor Bilkert
was killed, but Crane escaped, fortunately for Arabia, keener than
ever to bring help to its primitive and hostile peoples. He started a
date farm on his ranch in California, researching to improve Arabian
strains and breeding techniques, achieving some success and proudly
selling his products through local San Francisco grocers at a dollar a
box; he started to breed camels and horses to the same end, and it was
in pursuit of fine Arabian horses that Charles R. Crane came, towards
the end of 1930, to the *majlis* of Sheikh Fawzan al Sabik in Cairo.

226

Sheikh Fawzan al Sabik was King Abdul Aziz's representative in Egypt. Like the Qosaibis in Bahrain and the Nafisis in Kuwait, Sheikh Fawzan was an expatriate Arabian who made the clerical staff of his successful merchant business available for the paperwork of Sa'udi visas and consulate formalities, taking his reward from the dividends of acting as the conduit for commercial initiatives to and from Arabia. So when Charles R. Crane first walked into Fawzan al Sabik's *majlis* in 1930 and introduced himself, the sheikh presumed that the elderly American was about to offer him a special deal in sanitary fittings.

But Charles Crane wanted a horse. He had heard of Sheikh Fawzan's famous stud of pedigree Arabians, and he wanted to purchase a mare and a stallion for breeding.

'When can you go to the stables?' asked al Sabik through the American's interpreter – since, for all his Arabophilia, Charles Crane could not speak much Arabic – and a convenient time was arranged.

Next day Crane was back at Fawzan al Sabik's *majlis* again, and by now the sheikh had done some research into his unusual American visitor.

'Which horses did you like?' he asked, and Crane named two which demonstrated a sound grasp of what makes a good Arabian.

'They're for you,' said al Sabik promptly.

'How much will that be?' inquired the American.

'Nothing,' replied the sheikh. 'They are a gift. You like us, I hear, and so we like you.'

Charles Crane was speechless. He had, apparently, never been treated to the generosity which Arabs can exercise, on occasions, with such bravura, and it took some persuasion from the Egyptians present to convince him that this was the Arabian way, and that to refuse the gift, or even to offer too effusive thanks for it, would be taken as an insult.

But Charles R. Crane was undaunted. 'Your country is a poor one,' he said. 'But beneath the ground there must be mineral riches of some sort, if only water. Please let me offer you the services of an engineer who can carry out surveys in Arabia to discover what may be there.'

Now it was Sheikh Fawzan's turn to be speechless, for it was Abdul Aziz's settled policy not to admit foreign prospectors to Arabia. The view from the walls of Jeddah was the most that infidels were permitted to see of the Holy Land, and straight after the Ikhwan revolt was an especially bad moment to send foreign survey teams out into the desert. Crane's tragic experience on the Kuwait border had shown what could go wrong.

But al Sabik said that he would telegraph Mecca just the same – and, to his surprise, the answer came back immediately. Abdul Aziz had heard of Crane. The king hoped the American could come to Jeddah between Ramadhan and the pilgrimage; and thus began the process by which, within a matter of years, the Kingdom started to enjoy the benefits of its fabulous mineral riches.

Abdul Aziz was desperately in need of mineral riches – or riches of any sort – at the beginning of the 1930s. The tale of 'A Man and a Horse' might suggest that Charles R. Crane came to Jeddah in February 1931 only as a consequence of Sheikh Fawzan al Sabik's truly Arabian generosity. But the cold truth is that by that date Abdul Aziz was so desperate for money he would have found Charles Crane anywhere – and, if Crane had not existed, then he would have found someone else to provide what the American offered.

The root of the trouble was the Depression which had been wreaking havoc with the world's economy since 1929, and which had drastically cut the number of pilgrims who could afford to travel to Mecca. With annual pilgrim arrivals sometimes totalling 130,000 by the end of the 1920s, the Nejd–Hijaz authorities had come to regard 100,000 pilgrims as the minimum upon whose dues they could count in any year. But in 1930 this figure halved, falling to less than 40,000 in 1931, and this downturn was mirrored by a fall in demand for Nejd's few exports, such as dates.

It was the pilgrimage that mattered most. During the First World War Britain had reckoned Abdul Aziz's total annual revenues in central Nejd at less than £3000 a week, while at the same period they calculated that bullion exports from the Hijaz – profits from the pilgrimage which were being invested or exchanged overseas – were running in excess of £1 million per year.

The figures are not strictly comparable, but they do convey the difference in scale between the economies of Nejd and the Hijaz – and also the transformation that the conquest of the Hijaz initially made to the finances of Abdul Aziz. Suddenly he had many times more money than he had ever had before – literally millions of pounds – and his new wealth had been a major factor in his defeat of the Ikhwan rebels. Abdul Aziz had used pilgrim dues to buy support

228

in the tribes, and it was one reason why the Sa'udi leader went straight down to Mecca after his victory at Sabillah in March 1929. He had wanted to make sure that his annual income was being gathered in correctly, for the *hajj* had become the bread of all Arabia.

With the collapse of pilgrim revenues, Abdul Aziz's finances collapsed too. From over £5 million his annual disposable income slumped to less than £2 million; he suddenly found himself more than £300,000 in debt; his proud new riyal currency disintegrated – and the merchants of Jeddah began buying up gold bullion and exporting it to their banks in Cairo for safekeeping as they had done in the bad old days of the shareef. Abdul Aziz had to declare a moratorium on his debts, and the overall effect of the financial crisis was to depress him in the extreme. He felt lost and bewildered by the unfathomable phenomena afflicting him, and his customary vitality and optimism deserted him entirely. He felt it beneath his dignity to resort to commerce like the sheikhs of Oman and Qatar but, facing bankruptcy, he was prepared to forget the reservations he had once held about selling off mineral concessions in his territories.

'If anyone would offer me a million pounds now,' he confided wearily one day to Philby while driving in his car to Taif, 'he would be welcome to all the concessions he wants in my country.'

Charles Crane did not come to Jeddah bearing a million pounds, but his offer of a free geological survey promised to be a step in that direction, and so Abdul Aziz welcomed him warmly when he arrived in Jeddah on 25 February 1931.

Crane was the first American Abdul Aziz had ever met, and in his honour the king ordered the dancing of the *ardha*, a ceremonial version of the war dance Captain Shakespear had witnessed on the eve of Jarrab, the bedouin hopping and chanting, loosing off rifles into the sky as their passions mounted and brandishing their swords ever more extravagantly in the air. The Hijazis present found this Nejdi ritual rather a bore, but Abdul Aziz delighted in it. He dressed up in robes and bandoleers and led some of his sons in a display of mock sword-jousting that greatly impressed his American guest. This was exactly what Charles Crane had come to Arabia to see.

Crane delighted in the blind cantors who sang Koranic chapters for him in the high dark chambers of the Nasseef house where he stayed in the heart of the souq, but his greatest pleasure was finally to meet Abdul Aziz himself – 'an essentially shy person,' noted his diary, 'especially when it comes to the softer duties of life.' As Crane said his

229

hellos, the king kept hold of his visitor's hand, mumbling almost inaudible words of welcome with his head turned downwards.

Abdul Aziz's downcast eyes and suppressed mumbling may have had something to do with the gift that Crane brought him – a dollar box of dates. Coming from his home-made oasis in California, these meant a lot to Crane, but to offer a sample of Arabia's basic foodstuff to its king was, as David Howarth has remarked, rather like presenting the Queen of England with a packet of fish and chips.

Still, from that beginning matters could only improve, and Crane was deeply impressed by King Abdul Aziz. 'When at rest his face is immobile and usually overcast, as though with some permanent sadness,' noted his diary. 'But all of a sudden the subject moves him, or a secretary glides in with some whispered message, and his features light up with excitement or curiosity.'

Crane had several ideas for the advancement of the Sa'udi kingdom. Perhaps, he suggested, he might take one of the king's many sons and give him an education in the West.

Abdul Aziz thought this a bad idea. What was required in Arabia, he explained, 'and more especially for members of the ruling house was an education which should fit them to be leaders of men. . . .

'In order to be a leader of men, a man has to receive an education in his own country, among his own people, and to grow up in surroundings steeped with the traditions and psychology of his countrymen. Not only did Western education not fulfil that condition, but it tended also to wean a young man from the customs and traditions of his country. . . .'

Undismayed to have this particular offer rejected, Mr Crane responded that the king's views corresponded precisely with those of his friends Mr Henry Ford and Mr Thomas Alva Edison, and His Majesty might also be interested by the tale of his friend Mr Westinghouse, who was actually advised by his teacher to leave school at an early age, and who had done very well for himself as a consequence.

The last days of Crane's week-long visit were hampered by stomach upsets provoked, in his belief, by a stuffed tomato to whose temptations he injudiciously succumbed at the civic banquet which the Jeddah Municipality offered in his honour. But this did not mar the cordiality with which his mission was concluded, nor the accomplishment of its basic objective.

A few weeks later Sheikh Fawzan al Sabik received in Cairo a list of the twenty or so engineers, with their qualifications, whom Charles Crane was offering to survey the mineral potential of Arabia.

'Which one shall I choose?' asked Sheikh Fawzan, holding the list upside down because he could not understand a word of English. Then, having stared fixedly at the paper for several minutes, he stabbed at a name in the middle.

'Which one is this?' he asked.

When the list was turned the right way up, it appeared that the sheikh had picked on the name of Mr Karl S. Twitchell, an American engineer who had carried out surveys for Charles Crane in Abyssinia and in the Yemen, and who had already been proposed by Crane to survey the prospects for artesian water around Jeddah.

So Karl Twitchell, a bustling and enthusiastic character, arrived in the Hijaz in April 1931. His first surveys were for water in the Wadi Fatima off the road to Mecca. He went on a trip further north to investigate disused gold workings reputed to be the legendary King Solomon's Mines, and in the winter of 1931–2 he set off eastwards towards al Hasa.

The staff of Jeddah's British Legation watched him go. 'It seems fairly clear that nothing of much importance will result from Mr Twitchell's investigations,' minuted one of them. 'He appears to be something of a busybody.'

The preliminary results of Karl S. Twitchell's journey across eastern Arabia in the winter months of 1931 appeared to justify the hopeful pessimism of the British Foreign Office. Twitchell did not see the Qateef oil seeps for which Major Frank Holmes had gone searching eight years earlier with his butterfly net, and, on the strength of his researches alone, he did not feel he could report very encouragingly on the prospects for oil.

But while he was on the Persian Gulf coast, Karl Twitchell did discover that oil was being prospected just a few miles across the water on the island of Bahrain, and as a geologist he could work out what that might mean.

'There is little difference in the geology between Bahrain and the mainland,' Twitchell explained to Abdul Aziz when he got back to Riyadh. So, if the Bahrain prospectors found oil, 'you would probably have it in your country.'

The geologists on Bahrain had come to the same conclusion. They were prospecting there for Standard Oil of California (Socal), and since 1930 they had been gazing thoughtfully across the Gulf's green shallows. Every evening the sunset silhouetted a promising-looking hill structure on the mainland, but Socal's efforts to investigate the Dammam Dome had come to nothing – for the company had chosen to make their approaches to Abdul Aziz through the agency of the man who had secured the last Arabian oil concession from the Sa'udi king, Major Frank Holmes.

Major Holmes was truly one of those hapless souls awakened in the night by the striking of history's clock, only to count the strokes wrong. His Eastern and General Syndicate had allowed the Arabian concession they won after Uqayr in 1922 to lapse, largely because they had become caught up in the complexities of selling on a similar concession in Bahrain. These serpentine convolutions – which are peculiar to the wheeler-dealering of oil, and are made the more incomprehensible to outsiders by the proliferation of capital letter acronyms – left Holmes, after several years of tortuous negotiations, with a Bahrain deal incorporating the one acronym we shall bother with, Socal, and the disfavour of Arabia's king.

Abdul Aziz had taken pains after Uqayr to resist the pressures of Sir Percy Cox and to award the al Hasa concession to the New Zealander in 1923 – only for Holmes to turn his attentions to Bahrain and to default on the deal. So Abdul Aziz considered that the Eastern and General Syndicate owed him at least two years' rental, £5000, and this debt was the reason why Socal's attempts to reach the Sa'udi mainland through Major Frank Holmes from 1930 onwards had come to nothing.

We do not know if the major actually made the advances to 'his old friend Abdul Aziz' that he claimed to his Socal partners, or whether he knew better than to try. But by the summer of 1932 the light was slowly beginning to dawn on the Americans, and they were just casting round for new ways of getting to Ibn Sa'ud when they struck upon Karl S. Twitchell, who had actually crossed to Bahrain in the course of his researches for Abdul Aziz – to be rebuffed by Socal's prospectors, who were suspicious of his Arab dress. The men on the ground were convinced that this inquisitive American must be a spy.

Back at headquarters, however, the value of an American geologist who had dealt personally with Ibn Sa'ud was grasped immediately, and Socal found out why Twitchell mattered through Harry St John

Philby – who can now finally enter the tale which he has been itching to join from the start.

If you read his own accounts – and there are several – Philby was in there from the very beginning. It was he who, in the autumn of 1930, started off the whole story of Sa'udi oil by telling Abdul Aziz in his car at Taif that he was 'like a man sleeping on top of buried treasure'; it was he who told the king about Charles Crane; it was he who arranged for Crane to come down to Jeddah from Egypt – and later Philby even published his displeasure that 'Mr Crane never so much as sent me a postcard of thanks for the part I had played'.

But Charles R. Crane was certainly unaware of the pivotal role in his life being played by Harry St John Philby, and we only have Philby's word that he was the master puppeteer pulling every string in the discovery of Sa'udi oil, until May 1932 when Philby was visiting England and received a letter from Mr Albert Halstead, the American Consul General in London.

'Please permit me', wrote Halstead, 'to introduce you to the Honorable Francis B. Loomis, formerly Under Secretary of State of the United States, and a gentleman whom I have known most favorably for many years. Mr Loomis has been impressed with your work in the desert in Arabia, and would like to meet you.'

It was the measure of Philby's conceit – and also of the fact that he was not so hot on the trail of oil as he later claimed to have been – that he assumed Francis Loomis, a principal executive of Standard Oil of California, to be keen for a chat about desert exploration. Philby had just crossed the Empty Quarter and, back in London to boast about it to various learned societies, he presumed that the American oilman desired nothing more than to listen to his traveller's tales.

But once Philby realized the true reason for the American's curiosity, he picked up the ball and ran with it hard; and from this point onwards, it must be said, the role that Harry St John Philby played in establishing the Kingdom's great oil concession was a central one.

Philby had become a Muslim two years earlier, being welcomed to Islam by Abdul Aziz in August 1930 and given the new name of Abdullah, 'Slave of God'. Jeddah's merchants grumbled that it should have been Abdulqirsh, 'Slave of Sixpence', since they assumed that the Englishman's motive for converting was to advance the interests of the various commercial agencies he had acquired, from Ford cars to Marconi wireless sets.

This was unfair. No one ever tried to suggest, least of all Abdullah

Philby himself, that he became a Muslim for spiritual reasons: he had been a freethinker and atheist all his adult life, and no soul-shattering conversion inspired him suddenly to thirst for that religion which glorifies above all things God's control of man's every action. But Philby had come to admire Islam and to appreciate that he could never become fully part of Arabia until he adopted the rhythms and rituals that permeate its existence. It was a way of life, not a religion, that Abdullah Philby thirsted for. He wanted to kneel down with his companions at sunset in the desert, to wander freely beyond Jeddah's walls, and, most important of all perhaps, he wanted to get closer to his friend and idol Abdul Aziz.

From the moment of his conversion, Abdullah Philby became able to participate fully in the cameraderie of the Sa'udi court, to lounge with Abdul Aziz in his house at Mecca looking down from its balcony into the courtyard of the Grand Mosque below, to share the long Ramadhan nights of feasting and gossip, to test out the slave girls – Abdul Aziz gave him one, Mariam, in 1931 – and to become a fully fledged member of that knot of boon companions, half Privy Council, half gang of chums, who went everywhere with Abdul Aziz, chatting, laughing and arguing, discussing politics one minute, playing practical jokes the next.

It was as a member of this *cercle intime* that Philby was approached by Francis Loomis in the summer of 1932 in London, and as such he was able to tell the American, over lunch at Simpson's in the Strand on 11 July 1932, that what Abdul Aziz wanted for his oil concession was cash on the nail; the king would be less interested by the small print of any agreement offered him than by how much money was paid up front, preferably in gold sovereigns.

Having lodged that point firmly with Standard Oil of California, Philby promptly passed on to old friends in the British oil business the news that the Americans had their eyes on an Arabian oil concession. So in Jeddah, six months later, the representatives of Socal deputed to purchase the rights in Sa'udi oil found themselves up against the British representatives of IPC, the Iraq Petroleum Company – formerly the Anglo-Persian Oil Company who had tried to keep out Major Holmes in 1922. The stage was set for an auction to the highest bidder, and it does look as though the scenery had been arranged by Harry St John Philby.

The rival protagonists were, for Socal, a stocky, smooth-faced lawyer of forty, Lloyd N. Hamilton, the company's land-lease expert.

He was accompanied by Karl Twitchell, temporarily hired by Socal as the one geologist who had actually covered the ground in question, while the representative of IPC was Stephen Hemsley Longrigg, a sauve and gifted Arabist who later became the historian of oil ventures in the Middle East.

The Americans brought their wives – which considerably brightened Jeddah's male-dominated gin-and-bridge set – staying in the top floor of the newly completed Egyptian hotel; while Longrigg lodged at the British Legation, which boasted, after decades of consuls, the first fully fledged Minister Plenipotentiary accredited to Arabia, Sir Andrew Ryan, an upright, mildly stuffy British diplomat whom Philby had baited from the moment of his arrival, rowing out drunk to HMS *Clematis* to recite to the minister a poem of welcome whose every line rhymed with 'Ryan'.

Between this cast of characters Philby himself scurried about with delighted self-importance. He later confessed that he was offered, and accepted from Lloyd Hamilton, a secret $1000 a month retainer to facilitate the American cause, but this did not prevent him from accepting confidences from the British, nor from fixing with Abdul Aziz and Abdullah Suleiman a Sa'udi asking price of £100,000 gold, towards which he worked very hard to push his American paymasters.

With the unique facility of being able to go to Mecca, Philby would drive off for conferences with Abdul Aziz and al Suleiman, returning to the expatriates trapped in Jeddah to drop mysterious hints, coax out higher bids and generally impart to the proceedings an atmosphere of tension which the facts did not justify; for the British bid was not, at heart, a serious one, and the Iraq Petroleum Company never came close to catching Socal in the race, since they did not basically believe that there was any oil in eastern Saudi Arabia.

Offered their second opportunity to secure a grip on Sa'udi Arabia's oil rights, the British were adopting the same tactics they had employed against Major Holmes at Uqayr ten years earlier – happy to obstruct, but unwilling seriously to commit themselves. The IPC's surveyors told them that there was no oil in Arabia (they had said the same in Bahrain, which was how Socal came to be established there); even if there was oil below the Dammam Dome, IPC already had more oil than they knew how to handle in Iraq; the world market was characterized by massive over-production and falling prices – oil did not have the glamour and scarcity value it acquired in the 1970s –

235

and IPC's main reason for sending Stephen Longrigg to Jeddah in the spring of 1933, as Longrigg himself later admitted, was simply to try to keep the Americans out.

This rapidly became apparent as the bids went on the table, Longrigg talking grudgingly in terms of £200 a month, while the Americans were prepared to go at least halfway towards the daunting Sa'udi demand for £100,000.

As it became clear that the sums added up in favour of the Americans, 'everybody in the Court was glad,' remembers Muhammad al Mana, '. . . for we all felt that the British were still tainted by colonialism. If they came for our oil, we could never be sure to what extent they would come to influence our government as well. The Americans on the other hand would simply be after the money, a motive which the Arabs as born traders could readily appreciate and approve.'

Al Mana is careful not to include Abdul Aziz in this political assessment of the merits of dealing with the USA *vis-à-vis* Great Britain – and he is correct. By 1933 Abdul Aziz knew more about the United States than he had when he asked Philby if all the inhabitants were Red Indians, and he had always appreciated the wisdom by which the bedouin, if they could choose between a distant ally or a neighbouring one, would usually favour the distant one on the grounds that it was less likely to interfere in their own local affairs.

But the favour Abdul Aziz eventually showed to Standard Oil of California in the negotiations for his oil concession cannot be interpreted as a farsighted bid to break out of the imperialistic British orbit that had confined him since 1902. He was as sceptical of oil's existence as the British were. He did not believe that the concession would come to anything. No one at the time foresaw the way in which the confused haggling on the Red Sea coast over the value to be set on a hypothetical mineral resource would one day link Sa'udi Arabia so closely with the power which did not, in 1933, even have a diplomatic representative in Jeddah. Abdul Aziz tried right to the very end to push the deal Britain's way.

He gave up trying only when Britain's minister Andrew Ryan quietly told him to accept the American offer – it was money for nothing – and the figures spoke for themselves: the best that IPC could come up with was £10,000, while the American bid totalled over £50,000 – in gold.

On 8 and 9 May 1933 Abdul Aziz gathered his advisers round him in Mecca to hear the final agreement as negotiated between Abdullah Suleiman and Socal: £35,000 down, £20,000 after eighteen months, £5000 rental per year, £50,000 more if oil were discovered and a further £50,000 a year later, all advance payments to be set against royalties of 4 shillings gold per ton.

It was hot weather, and Abdullah Suleiman droned on through the small print of the contract – preferential rights in the neutral zones, fieldwork to start in four months, a local refinery to be erected, exemptions from tax and customs duties – and, as the recital burbled onwards, Abdul Aziz dozed off, not to waken until the expectant silence at the end of the lullaby.

'Ah, must have been sleeping!' he said with a start. 'Well, everyone, what do you think of it?'

All present gave the nod of assent that they knew was expected, and the king turned to al Suleiman.

'Very well,' he said. 'Put your trust in God and sign.'

So concluded the chapter of happy accidents that had begun with the bath magnate's search for a horse. It may well be that, knowing the spectacular outcome of the saga, some of the participants subsequently made the incidents along the way sound happier and more accidental than reality at the time strictly justified. But Abdul Aziz himself certainly saw the whole thing as fortuitous, for he found it difficult to believe that there really was any oil beneath his territories. He tended to agree with the British minister that he was getting £50,000 in gold for nothing.

28 Well No.7

He asked water, and she gave him milk.

Song of Deborah. Judges 5:25

IT is said that when Abdul Aziz's Finance Minister took delivery of the first payment for the rights in Sa'udi Arabia's oil – £35,000 in gold sovereigns – he promptly stashed it under his bed. Abdullah Suleiman's sons today deny that tale. They remember the chests of treasure being dragged into the family home in Jeddah in the summer of 1933, but the boxes were far too heavy, they say, to be taken upstairs to the sleeping quarters.

The point remains: the appearance of £35,000 was a big event in the Sa'udi Arabia of 1933; the Kingdom lacked an administrative infrastructure – merchants abroad handing out visas, the Finance Minister keeping the exchequer in his own home and, as might be expected in a country named as if it were the personal property of one family, the distinction between what was public and what was private was blurred to the point of nonexistence. Abdul Aziz saw the money paid by Standard Oil of California as belonging to him personally, not to the state, a concept which had no meaning for him.

Today public and private are strictly separated in the Kingdom – on the surface. National revenues are meticulously divided so that the pensions paid to the royal family are separate from the government budget. But much of that budget is spent on development projects carried out by companies in which princes have a financial stake. The stipend is only the beginning of princely wealth.

Ordinary Sa'udis operate in a similar diverse fashion. When the present writer took up residence in Sa'udi Arabia in 1978 and went to the bank to open an account, he was told by the manager (a) that he was just off on a holiday paid for by a client to whom he had made a large loan, and (b) that he would not be coming to the office much after the holiday, since he had business of his own to attend to.

Civil servants driving taxis, soldiers rearing flocks of sheep, commission payments so integral to business that their level is set by law: Arabian business ethics are not Western ones.

238

But the good-humoured continuance of such a system – if it can be described as such – relies on a comparative absence of greed and upon ample supplies of money, and if money gets tight then greed, which is a relative thing, tends to appear more oppressive. At this point good humour vanishes, and Western words like 'corruption' start being bandied about. This is what happened to Abdul Aziz at the beginning of the 1930s, for though Socal's gold sovereigns were a welcome windfall, there was still not enough money to go round.

'I swear by God as a Muslim', Abdul Aziz told Colonel Biscoe, the Persian Gulf Resident whom he met early in 1932, 'that I have no money for my children, for my family, and I know not if they will have money for food and clothing.'

The effects of the international Depression were still biting. The numbers of pilgrims coming to Mecca continued to drop, and his debts had reached such a size, the Sa'udi king told Biscoe, that he had had to tell his tribal chiefs that he could, in future, receive them only on stated occasions, and that they were not to visit him at other times – a sad and dangerous lapse from his rule by largesse. Philby, appointed by Abdul Aziz to investigate why the royal cars were always running out of petrol, discovered that the chauffeurs were pilfering the petrol to stay alive: their pay, like that of all government servants, was five or six months in arrears.

Abdullah Suleiman did his best. His idea of being a Finance Minister was to gather the money in quickly and let it out slowly – never a bad rule. He sent Muhammad al Taweel, the old Hijazi collector of customs, to apply his shareefian extraction techniques to the east, and a little customs post was set up in the fishing village of Jubail through which, it was ordered, must henceforward pass all Nejdi commerce that formerly went through Kuwait. Taxes were levied on the tribes, and Abdullah Suleiman went personally, and without shame, from door to door of the merchant establishments in Nejd and in the Hijaz, soliciting for his master 'loans' that all concerned knew would never be repaid.

Foreign businessmen coming to the Kingdom nowadays marvel and curse at the mutual enrichment society that operates behind the appearance of competition between merchants, bureaucrats, bankers and royal family. But the Sa'udi freemasonry was formed in the days of mutual impoverishment. The Alirezas, Kakis, al Rajhis and countless other Sa'udi business dynasties laid the foundation of their modern prosperity in the 1930s by managing a smile as they handed to

239

Abdullah Suleiman money they could ill afford, and by not being too ungracious in their attempts to get some of it back.

But cash from outside the country was what was really needed, and if the pilgrims could not bring it, and if international commerce was too depressed for it to be earned, Sa'udi Arabia would have to get a loan. This was what Abdul Aziz had been after when he was pleading poverty to Colonel Biscoe in February 1932, and, as the oil concession showed, Britain was no longer the only source of ready cash abroad. So, with a willingness that his present-day successors prefer to forget, Abdul Aziz turned for help in 1932 to the Soviet Union.

The Russians had been the first country to recognize Abdul Aziz as King of the Hijaz in 1926, and they were also the first to accredit a fully fledged minister to Jeddah, Comrade Kerim Hakimoff, a former miner who entered into his duties with spirit, donning Arab costume and wearing the headdress at all times. The first attempt at Sa'udi–Soviet trade had foundered when a cargo of Russian goods was dumped in Jeddah in 1927 at low prices that incensed the local merchants. But in 1932 the Soviets tried again, and Prince Faisal bin Abdul Aziz, by this time Foreign Minister and also his father's viceroy in the Hijaz (since that was where he had to live to deal with the foreign diplomats), was invited to include Moscow in the itinerary of a long fund-raising tour of Europe which he was planning for that summer.

Faisal was learning the ways of diplomacy. When questioned in London about a streaming nose and red eyes he had developed, he said it was definitely a *French* cold he had caught before his arrival, and he charmed his way across Europe. He did not raise much money, but in Warsaw he did manage to order some Polish rifles which were delivered to Jeddah – and, so far as is known, were never paid for. Then from Warsaw the prince travelled on by train to Moscow, where he was received with the dignity usually provided 'for State guests considered to belong to the second category of importance'.

Brass bands played the *Internationale* and the Russian idea of 'Arabian airs', Moscow station was decked out with bunting, and in the course of his visit Faisal met with Comrades Kalinin and Molotov, travelling to Leningrad and then down to the Caucasus to demonstrate to the Muslim population there the friendliness that the Arab guardians of the Holy Places evidently felt towards the Soviet regime.

'We are charmed with the natural beauties of the Transcaucasian Republics,' Prince Faisal radiogrammed as he left Baku on the steamer *Pravda*, heading for the Persian shore of the Caspian Sea. 'We were specially impressed by the oil derricks and the technique of getting oil.'

The Bolsheviks, decided the British diplomats who were monitoring the prince's progress anxiously, were evidently seeking to purchase themselves a position in the Muslim world. Russian petrol worth £30,000 was delivered to Jeddah, and talk of a million-pound Soviet loan started floating round the diplomatic community.

But the Russian price for their loan was a long-term trade and friendship agreement, and the most to which Abdul Aziz would tie himself was a three-year commitment. So the great Sa'udi–Soviet flirtation petered out, and in 1938 the Russian ambassador was ordered to pack up his embassy and return to base, where he vanished in Stalin's purges, as did all his staff with the exception of the legation doctor, who had the sense to slip out of the porthole of the Russians' steamer before it left the Jeddah roads.

Sa'udi–Soviet relations have never been resumed since then, and the USSR is today one of the ritual devils that Sa'udi foreign policy statements love to stone: the Soviets are atheistic, they attack free enterprise, and Prince Faisal, as king, developed the settled conviction that communism secretly operated in alliance with Zionism and the State of Israel to disrupt Arab solidarity and Islam.

So there is no Russian embassy in Jeddah today, nor any official contact between the two countries. But the Soviets could, if they wished to, call in one quite unique debt of gratitude, for the £30,000-worth of petrol they delivered to Jeddah at the height of their courtship in the early 1930s was never paid for. So the USSR can claim the distinction of being the only foreign government ever to have given oil to Sa'udi Arabia.

Prince Faisal's sally to the republics of godlessness yielded little, but he did bring back with him a new wife, a woman whose impact on Sa'udi Arabia was to prove, in its way, more revolutionary than anything that a Soviet friendship treaty was likely to have achieved.

Iffat al Thunayan, intelligent, articulate and forceful, was to bring about major changes in the male-dominated destiny of her sisters in Sa'udi Arabia. Among the several dozen wives of Arabia's four modern kings (Faisal was to reign from 1964 to 1975) Iffat was, and is, the only one ever to be popularly known as 'queen', though that title does not officially exist in the Kingdom, for she had remarkable personal qualities, which, Faisal used to say, he recognized the moment he set eyes on her in Constantinople in the summer of 1932.

Because Faisal found her in Constantinople, Iffat al Thunayan was often known as his 'Turkish' wife, but she was, in fact, as Sa'udi as he was. The Thunayans were like the bin Jaluwis, fully fledged members of the Al Sa'ud, and Iffat came from that branch of the family transplanted to Turkey by the Ottomans. She was the niece of Ahmad Thunayan, who had accompanied Faisal as a boy to London in 1919, but her father had died before Faisal came to Constantinople, leaving some dispute about lands he had claimed in Taif. So Iffat and her mother called on Abdul Aziz's second son to enlist his help in this dispute, and Faisal, who had an eye for attractive young ladies, suggested that mother and daughter should come to Jeddah where he could arrange everything to their advantage.

Faisal bin Abdul Aziz was to die a pious and austere old king, renowned throughout the Arab world for his asceticism. But he led a wild youth. Foreign diplomats in the 1920s and early 1930s never thought he would amount to much, he was so tied up by his women. Iffat al Thunayan changed all that, and Faisal settled down with her to a marriage remarkable, in its time, for the comparative equality between the partners – and also for the strictness with which their children were brought up.

Many Arabian children are shamefully spoilt. It is a legacy of the desert ethic, when a little indulgence did no harm to children playing in the dust all day. Transplanted to the twentieth century, it has resulted in such immoderation as Sa'ud, Abdul Aziz's eldest son, providing a car plus chauffeur for each of his children to be driven to school – inside the palace grounds – and, as in so many things, Sa'ud was only extending to extremes the tendencies of his father.

But the sons and daughters of Faisal and Iffat were not spoilt, and they were also educated. Their parents provided their girls with an English nanny, Mrs Mellor. Faisal quietly abandoned the paraphernalia of bedouin coaches in chivalry and desert-craft, sending his sons to a mud-wall school near Taif where they endured conditions of Spartan simplicity, and then he dispatched them onwards to the Hun School at Princeton and to various Western colleges.

Faisal and Iffat also had their daughters educated privately, but in this they were not quite alone. Abdullah, Abdul Aziz's disputatious younger brother, was already having his daughters taught the same curriculum as his sons, so that they are today a rarity in Sa'udi Arabia, sixty-year-old ladies who can read and write – for in the 1930s schools for girls were quite unthinkable. That was not to come for another twenty years, largely under the aegis of Iffat, for, in the decade after the Ikhwan revolt, educational innovations of any sort had to run the gauntlet of the Wahhabi *ulema*. When the zealots got to hear, for example, of some variations in the routine of Koranic recitation in Mecca schools, they became most upset: drawing would encourage children to create representations of the human face and form; foreign languages would enable them to learn the religions and sciences of ungodly people; while geography taught them to believe that the world was round, not flat.

Hafiz Wahba tried to reason with the sheikhs: drawing, he pointed out, was indispensable in the creation of maps; the Prophet's companions spoke the languages of surrounding countries and used that ability to subdue them; while geography dealt in proven facts.

Abdul Aziz worked out a compromise – a little more English, the geography of Islamic lands, and no drawing. He was skilled at dealing with the *ulema*. When they complained about anniversary celebrations he had instituted to commemorate the Hijaz's conquest, he gave way.

'Oh Lord, I have added to my sins,' he declared publicly, and that was the end of non-religious celebrations.

But when Abdul Aziz really wanted to win the argument, then he did.

The Tale of Abdul Aziz and the Wireless

Sheikh Abdullah ibn Hassan Alalsheikh, a descendant of the great Ibn Abdul Wahhab and himself, later, chief *qadi* of the Hijaz, could not reconcile himself to the radio stations that Abdul Aziz was building all over Arabia. He was convinced that they were the work of the devil, and he complained to Abdul Aziz so frequently that the king grew exasperated.

'How do you imagine, by God,' he asked the sheikh, 'that the devil gets these machines to work?'

'By God, I do not know,' replied the sheikh. 'But verily Satan must visit your stations at special times each day so that the men there can make sacrifices to him.'

So Abdul Aziz rose straight up from his *majlis* – he was in Mecca at the time – and took the sheikh by the hand to lead him to the wireless station in his palace.

'There, you see!' said the king. 'Not a trace of sacrifice!'

And, truly, there was in the room not a sign of blood or horns or wool.

But Sheikh Abdullah believed he had been tricked by the king. He took to visiting the radio station unannounced, hoping to catch the staff offering sacrifices, and eventually he offered baksheesh to the operator to tell him the hours when the devil called. He had decided that Satan must carry the wireless messages through the air himself.

The sheikh's visits and cross-questionings became so troublesome to the radio operators that they complained to Abdul Aziz, and so the king called the sheikh to him again.

'How far, do you imagine,' he asked, 'would the devil be willing to carry the word of God?'

The sheikh looked at the king bewildered, not understanding what he meant. So Abdul Aziz asked again. 'Would Satan carry God's word from here to Riyadh? Or from Riyadh back to here again?'

At that the sheikh grew angry. 'Verily, ya Abdul Aziz,' he cried, 'you joke with me. For you know and I know that Satan would never carry the word of God one inch, let alone from Mecca to Riyadh or from Riyadh back to Mecca again!'

'I do not joke with you, oh long of life,' replied the king gravely, and then he led Sheikh Abdullah once again to the radio station.

'I have asked the imam of the Great Mosque in Riyadh', he explained, 'to go to my radio station in the palace there, and I want you to listen.'

So Sheikh Abdullah listened, and within minutes he heard the first verses of the Koran come crackling through the receiver of the radio set.

'Is that you?' he called in surprise to his friend in Riyadh, and the imam of the Great Mosque there replied that indeed it was.

So then Sheikh Abdullah chanted some verses from the Koran himself, and 800 miles away in the middle of Nejd his listener told him that he could hear the word of God coming straight from Mecca.

So finally Sheikh Abdullah was convinced. From that day forth he blessed the radio as God's own miracle – and so did all the *ulema*.

*　　　*　　　*

This tale is multi-purpose, for it is also recounted, with variations, to explain how Abdul Aziz persuaded the *ulema* to accept the telephone and the transmission of radio programmes as well. Giving way on small things like national-day celebrations, Abdul Aziz got his way with the bigger ones that enabled him to give his disparate empire some genuine cohesion: it was thanks to his wireless network that he was able in 1932 rapidly to suppress the revolt of Ibn Rifada, a chieftain of the northern Hijaz who led a foray southwards at the instigation of Abdullah of Transjordan; a southern uprising in Asir was similarly suppressed.

As the *ulema* yielded ground on the things that mattered, a few frivolities crept in too. In 1935 Colonel Dickson reported that Abdul Aziz's servants were to be seen smoking openly in the Riyadh palace courtyards; after an initial blockage, tobacco imports resumed in the Hijaz, Abdullah Suleiman being careful that they were properly taxed; and even alcohol was allowed into Jeddah to sustain the infidel community.

Life for the few dozen foreigners in Sa'udi Arabia became in many ways quite tolerable, if never riotous, as the 1930s progressed. They were allowed their gramophones, provided they did not play them too loudly; they could motor a mile or so north of Jeddah to play nine holes of rough golf or shoot duck and gazelle in the desert that stretched from the lagoon to the Obhor creek; and the growing community of foreign ladies enjoyed one facility that their present-day successors are denied: during a stay with her father in the later 1930s, Philby's daughter Diane took some of Abdul Aziz's womenfolk for a motoring excursion into the desert, and she did all the driving.

Meanwhile, on the other side of Arabia, the geologists of Standard Oil of California had got to work. Socal had created a new company and, confusingly, a new acronym, Casoc (California Arabian Standard Oil Company), to exploit their concession from Abdul Aziz, and by the winter of 1933 the Socal/Casoc prospectors had made their base at Jubail.

Their priority was to examine the promising-looking structure of the Dammam Dome, and within eighteen months they had got their first rig erected, breaking up the rock of the collar the hard way, alternately getting it hot with a wood fire, then drenching it in cold water.

245

Well No. 1 produced 100 barrels of oil a day, good enough for a well in Pennsylvania, but hardly a commercial quantity on its own in distant Arabia, so the drilling went on. Well No. 2 produced 3840 barrels, then 'went wet', gushing up little else but water, and Wells 3, 4, 5 and 6 produced still less, two of them proving 'dusters' – 2000 feet each of total dryness.

By the time drilling started on Well No. 7 it was the end of 1936, and spirits were beginning to flag. The strike on Bahrain and the erratic results on Wells 1 and 2 showed there should be oil somewhere around. But where?

The Americans started to fan out into the desert around Dhahran. They got permission for a light plane, and the surveying parties would guide the pilot over their routes by digging out huge arrow shapes from the earth with shovels, sprinkling them with gasoline and firing them to leave black markers in the sand. They travelled in trucks with low-pressure balloon-like tyres, allegedly modelled on the foot of the camel, and everywhere they went they were accompanied, on Abdul Aziz's instructions, by Sa'udi guards and guides.

One such guide was Muhammad ibn Khursan, deputed by the Emir of Jubail to look after Casoc's chief field geologist, Tom Barger, and Muhammad's account of an expedition towards Riyadh conveys some idea of the friendly mystification with which the Sa'udis – and their king – stumbled into contact with the technology that was to transform their lives.

The Emir [of Jubail] sent for me and said: 'These men want to explore in the kingdom. They are dear to us. . . . We want you to serve them well and to tell them the truth.'

So I said: 'All right, it will be a blessed hour when I am able to be of service to one and all. . . .'

We explored caves everywhere. There was one detestable long cavity which was so deep that we could not find an end to it. We went right down, Tom Barger and I, with a pressure lamp. We went into it with the lamp, crawling and creeping on our bellies for four hours without reaching its far end. He picked up rocks and shells, seashells, something like oyster shells. We did the same thing in many caves. . . .

The geologists were searching for fossils that would enable them to date the rock formations they were exploring, and Tom Barger, who was to spend over thirty years working in Arabia's oilfields, well remembers his caving days with Muhammad ibn Khursan – though he suspects that his guide's memory must have condensed several later incidents to produce the description of what happened next.

Then the King, His Majesty Abdul Aziz, came from Riyadh and encamped to the west of us. We went to visit him, and by God we found him sitting there.... Coffee was brought, and the King ordered coffee to be served. ...

When we finished, Tom Barger said: 'We wish to make you some coffee' – using the English word coffee.

The King replied: 'What are you saying? What is he saying?'

I said: 'Yes, Your Majesty, may God prolong your life. This boss of mine Tom Barger wishes to invite you to coffee at the time you choose, any hour you like.'

The King said to me, for Tom Barger spoke no more: 'It is a blessed hour. This night you'll have dinner at my place, you and all your companions. The day after tomorrow, Monday (I think it was Monday), in the morning we shall be with you, God willing.'

And the King said to me: 'This companion of yours will not be here more than a couple of years more before becoming a real boss, because he is a first-rate man. It is evident that he is one of those excellent men who undertake to do things properly. . . .'

The presence of this paragraph in the tale may not be unrelated to the fact that, by the time Muhammad ibn Khursan committed his memories to paper, Tom Barger had risen to become the local president of the oil company.

When evening came, we were served two large trays with four sheep on each. Tom Barger and I dined with the King. The King spoke to Tom Barger saying: 'We would like to dig here a well of sweet water, if you can find it.'

Tom Barger replied: 'It is a blessed hour. Whatever you wish, I'll arrange to do.'

After dinner we went back to our companions and our camp. Then Tom Barger and I took shotguns and went hunting in the hollows. We hunted birds – bustard and sand-grouse. We brought these back with us, and they were prepared for the King's breakfast. The King came as he had promised . . . and Tom Barger spoke through an interpreter about many things which I cannot recall.

The King then asked me: 'What are they searching for here? What is their work? What places seem to interest them most?'

I said: 'By God, may God prolong your life, the thing they mostly pick up, the thing they look for most, is anything that shows the mark of the sea. . . . I, by God, do not know the reason for their aim at all. Some of what they do I have no knowledge of.'

247

The Americans had not told Abdul Aziz about the driblets of oil their drillings had extracted from the Dammam Dome, and the king was not surprised that their scavenging for seashells in desert caves was proving unproductive. What interested him, as his talk with Tom Barger made clear, was the possibility of sweet water beneath the sands, and he got Casoc's engineers to drill him several water wells. Abdul Aziz still found it difficult to believe in the existence of petroleum, and the Americans seemed unable to prove him wrong.

Abdul Aziz's final foreign war was the attack that he launched on Yemen in the spring of 1934. Two large Sa'udi armies of Ikhwan veterans and town levies under the princes Sa'ud and Faisal bin Abdul Aziz advanced southwards in a pincer movement designed to capture the isolated and sparsely populated kingdom that stretched from Asir down to the borders of Britain's Aden Protectorate.

Various justifications were advanced for the Sa'udi invasion of Yemen at the time – disputes over frontier towns, Yemeni trouble-making in Asir, a personal vendetta with the Yemen's ruler, the Imam Yahya – but they all boiled down to the geography of the matter. Yemen was the one remaining portion of Arabia where the Al Sa'ud could expand without coming into conflict with the British: the Imam Yahya had no powerful foreign or local allies to come to his rescue, and the Sa'udi empire would be the neater for including the south-western corner of the peninsula.

The Imam of Yemen's hill guerrillas, however, gave a geography lesson of their own to the Al Sa'ud. Prince Faisal's army advanced smoothly enough along the flat Tihama Plain of the Red Sea coast; but the main Sa'udi push under Faisal's elder brother Sa'ud got hopelessly stuck in the mountains, well short of Sana'a. The wiry riflemen of the Yemen hill tribes could make their rocky cliffs and passes virtually impregnable against invading armies – and especially against Sa'udi forces used to war on the desert plains.

Because the pride of his two eldest sons was involved, and because his third son, Muhammad, was no diplomat, Abdul Aziz sent his fourth son Khalid, a gentler soul, to negotiate peace terms with the Yemeni imam's representative at Taif in May 1934. Not for the first or last time in the Middle East, the two countries dusted themselves off from their altercation swearing each other 'perpetual peace and firm and everlasting Muslim Arab brotherhood'.

Western countries conclude wars with armistices of grudging coolness, but Arabs, like eternally feuding spouses, patch up their
disagreements with bouts of passion which seek to obliterate the
memory of their quarrel.

'The parties,' read clause 17 of the 1934 Sa'udi–Yemeni Treaty,
'who are bound by the ties of Islamic brotherhood and Arab origin,
declare that their nations are one nation, that they wish no one evil,
and that they will endeavour to promote the interests of the nation in
tranquillity' – which did not quite mean what it appeared to.

Sa'udi Arabia and the Yemen were not declaring a union in May
1934, any more than the modern Arab countries who have quarrelled
and made up with similarly grandiose statements of reconciliation in
recent times, for the Arab is capable of both hating his brother Arab
and feeling part of him with a rare intensity – and his remorse adopts
extravagant language when he realizes how his anger has overcome
his love.

Early on the morning of 15 May 1935, Abdul Aziz was performing
hajj at Mecca with his son Sa'ud, and was in the process of walking
bareheaded round the Ka'aba amid thousands of other white-
towelled pilgrims, when three men suddenly detached themselves
from the throng.

The attackers were brandishing daggers they had hidden in their
clothes and, making straight for the king, they would have killed him
if Sa'ud had not thrust his burly bulk in their way. Sa'ud took a nasty
wound in the shoulder, and Abdul Aziz himself was wounded on the
shin as the bullets of his guards threw up marble splinters from the
courtyard tiles.

When the fusillade had ended, three Yemenis were lying dead on
the floor of the mosque, and subsequent investigation showed them
to have been soldiers in the Yemeni army which had fought the
Sa'udis the previous year.

What precise motive inspired this trio in their assassination attempt
could not be established. Sa'udi and Yemeni investigators never got
to the bottom of the matter, but Abdul Aziz's escape from death was
taken as a propitious sign. He had had a presentiment, he later explained, the previous day while waiting among the crowds at Arafat:
he had wondered what he would do if an assailant should come
at him while he stood there unarmed in his towels among the multitude, and he had started to devise schemes for his own protection.

Then he had put the idea out of his mind, realizing that he lived under the protection of God – and events had proved that he did.

The hero of the hour was Sa'ud, and the tale of his valour was elaborated in ever more extravagant forms to the furthermost corners of Arabia. By the, time it reached the pages of the *Daily Telegraph* in London that June, his spontaneous lunge to shield his father had turned into a lithe running battle fought single-handed against three leaping assailants, and those who met the Sa'udi crown prince on the couple of trips he made to Europe in the mid-1930s must have been rather surprised by the mild, lumbering form who beamed at them dimly from behind pebble spectacles.

Big, soft and generous, Sa'ud bin Abdul Aziz was never quite the warrior that his adulators claimed in his youth – nor quite the degenerate in later years that his detractors made him out to be. He had become his father's heir when Abdul Aziz, after the death of his first-born, Turki, in 1919, had fixed on his only other son anywhere near manhood. But it was not realistic to expect any one man to be able to straddle the consensus that Abdul Aziz had spent a lifetime building up. Sa'ud was tall like his father, but not quite so tall; charming, but not quite so charming; imperious, but never able to command allegiance as his father could – and over the years Abdul Aziz came to acknowledge this and to moderate his succession plans.

Since family loyalty would focus more readily around a partnership than around a single figure, it was decided by the mid-1930s that Sa'ud would not rule alone after his father's death but in tandem with his brother Faisal as crown prince. Faisal was making a name for himself as Viceroy of the Hijaz. Sa'ud, holding the same position in Nejd, was proving rather less dynamic, and it was also agreed that the succession would, after Sa'ud, pass from brother to brother rather than descend, father to son, in any single line that might inflame family conflict. Brotherly rivalry was proving to be a problem as Abdul Aziz's sons grew up, and one of the chief troublemakers was the king's third son Muhammad, the next eldest prince in line after Faisal and Sa'ud.

Muhammad ibn Abdul Aziz was already known throughout Arabia as 'Abu Sharrain', 'the father of twin evils'. He had a fierce temper and a fiercer tongue, and though the tribes loved and feared him it was because he took on his enemies with ruthlessness in the bin Jaluwi tradition: Muhammad's machine-gunning of the Ikhwan rebels in 1929 had been merciless.

250

Muhammad tended to hone his fractiousness at the expense of his brothers, and he quarrelled especially with Sa'ud. So, when in 1936 Abdul Aziz was invited to London to attend the coronation of King George VI the following summer, he decided that Muhammad and Sa'ud should travel together as his representatives. It would teach them to get along together better, and it should also broaden their outlooks a little.

The two Sa'udi princes' trip to London certainly achieved the latter aim, but it was not quite in the way that their father had intended, for, while fulfilling their public mission with dignity, Sa'ud and Muhammad bin Abdul Aziz privately sampled in plenty the delights of London's night life. Arabs feel little guilt if they infringe their strict Islamic moral code, only shame if they are caught out doing so – and not too much of that either. They can see all too clearly the gap between the pure ethic of their austere home environment and the degeneracies offered by a Western city like London, and their reaction is that of many a British businessman finding himself in Pigalle or on the Reeperbahn: dismay at the naughtiness of which foreigners are capable, and a determination to make the most of it while released from the *mores* of home. So in 1937 Princes Sa'ud and Muhammad bin Abdul Aziz enjoyed London's pleasures to the full, and no one thought the worse of them. They were very discreet about it.

Several outsiders travelled to the heart of Arabia in the late 1930s, and they all paint a picture of a world on its own, still embalmed against the twentieth century by religious conviction and a social conservatism whose strength rested ultimately on the sheer physical isolation of Riyadh.

There were modern touches, like the truck which brought foreign mail from Kuwait every three or four weeks and dumped it in a pile by the corner of the main mosque – but the townsfolk dealt with that as medieval villagers might have done. They dived into the pile looking for anything addressed to them, and if they came across a letter or package for a friend or neighbour they would tuck it under their arm and deliver it on their way home.

'Everything got distributed within half an hour,' remembers Dr Rashad Pharaon, who came to Riyadh from Syria in 1936.

Dr Pharaon had the only refrigerator in town. As a colleague of Abdul Aziz's personal physician, Dr Midhat Sheikh al Ardh, he ran

251

the palace X-ray machine, and he needed the fridge to store the chemicals to develop his X-ray plates. When the bedouin came in to pay their respects and pick up their subsidies on the Eeds, the use of the royal doctors was one of the hospitalities that Abdul Aziz extended to them, and then Dr Pharaon was hard at work from the dawn prayer onwards – though the 30,000 or so inhabitants of Riyadh itself, he remembers, were pretty healthy on the whole: there were no mosquitoes then, nor any of the insects and infections that aeroplanes later brought, since travellers to Riyadh with diseases either gave up before they started, got better, or died on the way. It was over a week's hard drive from Jeddah and little less from the Persian Gulf coast, with no roads, signs, hotels or guest houses along the way. Visitors had to navigate their own route across the desert, carry their own food and water, and camp out every night.

Sir Andrew Ryan made this trek at the end of 1935, bearing with him the plum-coloured plumed hat, garlanded plum robes and other insignia of the Royal Order of the Bath, which His Majesty's Government had decided to bestow on King Abdul Aziz. Ryan, drawing to the end of his stay in Sa'udi Arabia, had never been overawed by the Sa'udi monarch, with whom he had had one or two stiff quarrels. He used to refer disparagingly to the king's 'famous magnetic smile' which, in the British minister's opinion, was switched on and off far too mechanically. But Ryan was impressed by Abdul Aziz in his native setting, and so was Ryan's companion, Captain Gerald de Gaury, MC, the new British Agent in Kuwait.

Unlike Ryan, de Gaury was an Arabist and a romantic. He wrote a memorable book about his journey called *Arabia Phoenix*. Like Charles Crane in Jeddah's Nasseef house, he was entranced by the blind Koranic chanters who sang in the corridors, bridges and galleries of Abdul Aziz's mud palace in the dusk before dinner:

'They sit concealed in the shadows of archways,' he wrote, 'a little distant from the king's own sitting place, so that their voices come softly to him like sustained notes on a distant organ.'

After dinner,

. . . the king took from the inner pocket of his gown a phial of scent and drew its long, tapered glass stopper, on which glistened essence of sandal-wood, across the palms of our hands. Then the incense burners came to waft the smoke from censers . . . going backward and forward between us, returning to each of us three times, and boys came to sprinkle us with rose water from long-necked silver flasks.

Perfume, confided Abdul Aziz, was one of his principal worldly delights. The other two were prayer and women, and in this the king felt he bore a certain resemblance to the Prophet Muhammad, who also drew great contentment from these three special joys.

Abdul Aziz imparted exactly the same confidence to Sir Reader Bullard when Bullard visited Riyadh the following year. The king evidently did not appreciate how prone British diplomats are to publishing their memoirs. Bullard was Ryan's replacement as British minister, getting his first view of Arabia since his spell as a vice-consul to the Hashimite Kingdom of the Hijaz in the early 1920s, and the change that struck him most was the law and order that now prevailed everywhere. In the days of the shareef it simply had not been safe to go out of sight of Jeddah's walls, and Bullard was impressed by what Abdul Aziz had done for Arabia.

He was also impressed by the system of scribes and translators who, every afternoon, took down the news bulletins broadcast by Europe's radio stations, and then read them out to the king after the sunset prayer. Bullard judged Abdul Aziz to be 'better informed on international affairs than many educated Europeans'.

Still, the sardonic young vice-consul who had reported on the inanities of the 'Royal Hijazi Air Force' had not been entirely swallowed up in the dignity of his full ministerial rank. Shown round the endless mud corridors of the new Murabba Palace that Abdul Aziz was building outside the city walls, Bullard remarked that the king had proved 'less successful as an architect than as a statesman'.

The minister was disturbed by signs of luxury among the younger princes, but he felt that no one could convict Abdul Aziz of personal extravagance: 'One of the features of a royal dinner was a large violet and white enamel mug, chipped with long use, which an armed retainer held ready, filled with camel's milk, for the king to drink from.'

Part of Bullard's mission to Riyadh was to survey the ground for an unprecedented expedition planned for the spring of 1938, a trip across Arabia by Princess Alice, Countess of Athlone, the granddaughter of Queen Victoria and cousin of the recently crowned King George VI. It would be the first time European royalty had ever visited Arabia, and the first occasion on which Abdul Aziz had publicly received a woman.

'I wore a black dress,' wrote Princess Alice after the great event, 'as I felt the king would be less disgusted with me in that attire . . .

253

although I thought afterwards that, as he must have heard lurid tales from his son of nude English ladies, he may have been disappointed after all.'

Princess Alice wrote home to her family a lively series of letters describing her experiences, which included a meeting with two of Abdul Aziz's wives, Umm Mansour ('Mother of Mansour') and Umm Talal ('Mother of Talal'):

The oldest [Umm Mansour] is the favourite, very ill. . . . Poor thing, she looked pathetic, but very fine in a gold embroidered magenta gown with a spangled veil arrangement like the lady-in-waiting. The other [Umm Talal] . . . was younger and very good-looking and covered in jewels, modern bracelets and rings on thumbs and all fingers which were painted brown to the first joint. . . .

Three charming little boys came in, sons of each, and one so obviously the king's son. . . . Several babies arrived this year to add to the number of 29 boys and 30 girls. . . . It appears the king adores his small children and takes them everywhere and even nurses them to sleep.

Like all Western visitors, the princess was charmed by the little palm-shaded Badiah guest palace in the Wadi Hanifah outside Riyadh, 'too absolutely romantic and frightfully simple and whitewashed'. But she found it difficult to enthuse over the reproduction French–Egyptian furniture that Sa'ud had brought back from his trips: 'clocks and glasses and horrid English wardrobes and lodging-house dressing-tables and always high, hard divans or chairs set right around the walls.'

The princess concluded her tour in the east of Arabia on the Gulf coast, where yet another style of architecture was taking shape – the compact, electric-lit bungalows, neat, tarred roads and embryo gardens of the Main Street America that the oil company were building at Dhahran.

' 'We British were awful juggins's,' wrote the princess home, 'as we were offered the concession for this remarkably rich oilfield and turned it down as being no good; the Americans came along, used the same drills and found the oil – and we can't even have any of the share.'

The princess was woolly on her details, but she had grasped the main point. It was 20 March 1938, and only a few days earlier Casoc's prospectors had finally struck the oil they had spent nearly five years looking for. They had drilled seven wells into the Dammam Dome,

Top The oil concession. Abdullah Suleiman and
Lloyd Hamilton of Socal sign, 29 May 1933
Above Charles R. Crane

Above Max Steineke, Chief Field Geologist, prospecting near the Dammam Dome

Right Abdul Aziz inspects Well No. 7, May 1939

Below The *D. G. Schofield* leaves Ras Tanura with the first tanker load of Sa'udi oil, May 1939

Well No. 1

Top Well No. 7: the first camp, the first mosque
Above Prince Faisal ibn Abdul Aziz inspects rock specimens
with Aramco geologists

and none yielded anything significant. But the decision was taken to deepen Well No. 7, and eventually, more than a year after they had started drilling, and nearly a mile below the surface, they struck oil that flowed and went on flowing: 16 March, 2130 barrels; 17 March, 2209; 18 March, 2128; 19 March, 2117; 20 March, 2149; 21 March, 3372.

Queen Victoria's granddaughter had arrived in Dhahran at the very moment the oilmen were celebrating their strike, which heralded the transformation of almost everything she had seen on her way across Arabia.

29 The Second World War

O N 1 May 1939 Abdul Aziz went to inspect his oil wells. The king looked over his first drilling rig, his first pipeline, his first tanker – an 8000-tonner called the *D. G. Schofield*, which carried the Sa'udi crude away from the little terminal that the oil company had constructed on the sand spit of Ras Tanura – and then he travelled back to Riyadh in high spirits. He was in a cavalcade of cars with his brothers and some of his elder sons, and, as they bounced back through the desert tinged green by the spring rains, the Al Sa'ud sang the victory songs of returning raiders, chanting in unison and capping each other with alternate couplets which they pulled exultantly out of the air.

Abdul Aziz was bringing back the ultimate booty. Casoc had paid him over £200,000 in gold to mark their oil strike, and, in the months after Well No. 7 started flowing, the company's prospectors discovered firm signs that this was just a small beginning. Sa'udi Arabia's eastern province clearly covered one of the largest pools of oil in the Middle East, and the royalties to which the Al Sa'ud could look forward in the future were phenomenal.

But then on 1 September 1939 Hitler invaded Poland, and the outbreak of the Second World War brought the growth of Arabian oil production to a sudden halt. International oil markets were disrupted, and tankers could not be spared for the long and hazardous journey round to the Persian Gulf. Well No. 7 and its new companions were squeezed down to the production of a few thousand barrels of oil a day, most of the oilmen went home, and for the next six years Abdul Aziz and his Arabia lived in limbo.

Towards the end of the Second World War, Winston Churchill was to praise Abdul Aziz for 'his steadfast, unswerving and unflinching loyalty' to Great Britain and to her allies throughout the course of the struggle against Hitler. But the Prime Minister was over-generous, or ill informed, for, though by 1945 it was possible to look back on Abdul Aziz's war record as one of neutrality that had proved, in the event, to be benevolent towards the victorious side, the Sa'udi king had not, at the opening of hostilities, been acting in a fashion that was conspicuously loyal to his oldest infidel friends.

In January 1939 Sa'udi Arabia had opened diplomatic relations with Nazi Germany, and in February that year Abdul Aziz sent a messenger to Berchtesgarten with a personal letter assuring Hitler 'that it is our foremost aim to see the friendly and intimate relations with the German Reich developed to the utmost limits.'

German archives captured after Hitler's defeat were to make clear just how energetically Abdul Aziz had courted the Third Reich in the build-up to the Second World War. In long personal interviews in January and February 1939 the Sa'udi king told Dr Fritz Grobba, head of German operations in the Middle East that, at heart, he 'hated the English', and Grobba reported back to Berlin that strong anti-British feeling animated the king's immediate entourage: there was Philby, of course, gleefully predicting the imminent collapse of his homeland; while the king's private secretary, Yussuf Yassin, and the royal doctor, Midhat Sheikh al Ardh, were both so emotionally pro-German that, when the war broke out, they would cheer like football fans as news of German victories came over the radio in the royal *majlis*.

The Sa'udi king had already concluded an arms agreement with Mussolini. Now in July 1939 he did a deal with Hitler for 4000 German rifles, ammunition and the construction of an arms factory near Riyadh, while he also ratified a treaty of friendship and trade with the Axis's eastern component, Japan, who had sniffed out the significance of Casoc's spectacular strike before any other foreign power and had made a bid for a Sa'udi oil concession of its own.

Yet throughout these flirtations the Sa'udi king took care to remain on the best of terms with Britain's representatives in Jeddah, swearing undying loyalty to His Majesty's Government. The British did not realise how warmly Abdul Aziz was dealing with the Germans, and the American diplomats who started coming to the Kingdom in the war years were unaware of any strong pro-Axis sentiments. As one historian was later to remark after comparing the captured Nazi archives with what British and American documents of the same date had to say, 'Abdul-Aziz ibn Saud was clearly adept at being all things to all men'.

257

As the war progressed, Abdul Aziz was to inch himself gently down from the fence on to the winning side with a number of modest, not to say prudent, gestures on which Churchill was to base his extravagant praise in 1945. Strapped for cash, the Sa'udi king never made a down payment on his German arms, so he never took delivery of them. Squeezing more money out of Casoc, he courteously declined Japanese interest in his oil. Hearing that Philby was planning a defeatist and anti-war lecture tour of America, he tipped off the British so that they were able to detain Philby in Bombay in August 1940; and the Sa'udi king declined any open support for Rashid Ali al Kilani's anti-British rebellion in Iraq in April 1941.

But Abdul Aziz did later give refuge in Riyadh to Rashid Ali, defying British attempts to extradite him. He kept his options open between 1939 and 1945 as skilfully as he had switched between Britons and Turks in the early years of the century, and it is not difficult to see how Hitler, if he had won the Second World War, would surely have been talking of Abdul Aziz in the same glowing terms that Churchill was to employ. The Sa'udi–German diplomatic contacts of 1939 could easily have become the foundations of a 'steadfast, unswerving and unflinching' friendship between Abdul Aziz and the German peoples, especially since one of the purposes of the abortive Sa'udi–Nazi arms agreement of July 1939 was to increase the flow of weapons which Abdul Aziz had secretly been sending to the Arabs fighting in Palestine.

These Arab guerrillas had been harassing the British authorities in the mandate since 1936. Militant Palestinians had come to feel that only violence could check the Zionist influx that had followed the Balfour Declaration, and when these terrorists asked Abdul Aziz for help he supplied them with weapons. The Sa'udi king might exaggerate his dislike of Britain when he was talking to the Germans, but his feelings about the Jews could scarcely be overstated.

Abdul Aziz never countenanced the Nazi 'final solution'. He was horrified by Hitler's extermination of the Jews, and he said so flatly to Lord Belhaven, the British Agent in Bahrain, when he visited the island in 1939. But his abhorrence was relative. There was no need for Hitler to have killed them, he said, just 'to have shorn them of their possessions'; for the Jews were, in his eyes, 'a race accursed by God, according to His Holy Book, and destined to final destruction and eternal damnation'.

Islam has a love–hate relationship with Judaism. The Koran

enjoins respect for the Jews as 'people of the Book'. Like Christians, Jews share many of Islam's prophets. Islam and Judaism have similar dietary rules: meat must be slaughtered in a specified fashion, pork is forbidden. Jewish and Muslim males are circumcised. Jews and Arabs are both Semites; and, at the beginning of Islam, Muhammad and his followers prayed towards Jerusalem.

But soon after he moved to Medina in 622 AD, the Prophet came into conflict with the Jewish community in the area. Islamic teachings about Judaism became more aggressive. The *qibla*, the direction of prayer, was switched from Jerusalem to Mecca, and the flames of this ancient hostility were fanned in the twentieth century by the Zionist revival.

'Our hatred for the Jews', Abdul Aziz told Harold Dickson in 1937, 'dates from God's condemnation of them for their persecution and rejection of 'Isa [Jesus Christ] and their subsequent rejection later of His chosen Prophet [Muhammad]. . . .

'Verily the word of God teaches us – and we implicitly believe this O Dickson – that for a Muslim to kill a Jew [in war], or for him to be killed by a Jew, ensures him an immediate entry in Heaven and into the august presence of God Almighty.'

Abdul Aziz made this statement to Dickson as part of his protest at the Peel Report, Britain's 1937 plan to partition Palestine into separate Jewish and Arab areas, thereby granting the Zionists the basis for the independent state that they dreamed of:

How, O Dickson, would the people of Scotland like it if the English suddenly gave their country to the Jews? . . . It is beyond our understanding how your Government, representing the first Christian power in the world today, can wish to assist and reward those very same Jews who mistreated your 'Isa . . . an accursed and stiff-necked race that, since the world began, has persecuted and rejected its prophets and has always bitten the hand of everyone who has helped it.

Britain's collaboration with the Zionists – whose ambitions extended, in Abdul Aziz's belief, to the creation of a Jewish-dominated state stretching down to Medina and across to the Persian Gulf – grieved the Sa'udi king intensely. Reader Bullard, invited to what should have been a joyful occasion, the reception of the BBC's first Arabic broadcast in 1938, found that the atmosphere round the heavy battery set suddenly went sour when the newsreader announced the hanging by the British authorities in Palestine of an

Arab caught with arms in his possession.

The party broke up in silence, and next day Abdul Aziz had tears in his eyes as he reproached the British Minister Plenipotentiary. 'If it had not been for the Zionist policy of the British government,' he wept, 'that Arab would be alive today.'

Bullard did not know what to say, for twenty years after the Balfour Declaration Britain was finding herself ambushed in Palestine between the same deadly crossfire of righteous causes that was to catch her in India–Pakistan and later in Northern Ireland. As details of Hitler's atrocities seeped out of Germany, it seemed obvious to Zionists, and to an increasing proportion of British and Western opinion, that Jewish refugees should be offered unlimited sanctuary in Palestine.

But the Arab inhabitants of that country were equally outraged that European barbarity should be expiated at their expense. The Arabs had done nothing to harm the Jews of Poland and Germany, and if Britain and America felt so sorry for those Jews they could welcome them into their own communities.

'But no,' said Abdul Aziz bitterly, 'it is easier to give away other peoples' countries and not so dangerous.'

Reader Bullard and George Rendel, head of the Foreign Office Eastern Department for most of the 1930s, were always convinced that the help Britain gave to Zionism from 1917 onwards was the reason why Abdul Aziz moved away from Britain towards the end of the 1930s and had, by the conclusion of the Second World War, effectively ended the special friendship with London which had been a cornerstone of his foreign policy for so many years.

This assumption was based on the same touching – or patronizing – disregard for Sa'udi *Realpolitik* which had so often taken for granted Sa'udi allegiance to the 'great government'. Abdul Aziz's championing of the Palestinian Arabs was deeply felt, but it also represented the continuation of a long-running feud. The Sa'udi king was suspicious of his old enemy, Abdullah of Transjordan, who had plans to incorporate Arab Palestine into his own Hashimite kingdom – and Abdul Aziz's secret arms shipments to the Palestinian freedom fighters were intended as much to frustrate Hashimite ambitions as to help the Palestinians fight the British or the Jews.

The takeover of Arab lands by Jewish expertise, industry and wealth was a blow to Abdul Aziz's ethnic pride that hurt him as bitterly as it has rankled with Arabs ever since. But loyalties beyond his frontiers, however worthy, never had too much sway with the Sa'udi king. Charity began for him at home. So, while the Second World War was indeed to mark the ending of Sa'udi Arabia's special ties with Great Britain, Sa'udi Arabia emerged from the hostilities entwined more closely than she had ever been linked to London with the infidel power that was soon to prove the State of Israel's most fervent sustainer and friend: the United States of America.

In the summer of 1941 the US State Department requested President Franklin Delano Roosevelt to offer Lend–Lease assistance to the Kingdom of Sa'udi Arabia. The department felt that official government aid to the Arabian king would help safeguard the Sa'udi oil concession for America until the war was over. But there were many requests for aid on the president's desk in the dark days of 1941, and on 18 July Roosevelt scribbled a quick note to his Federal Loan Administrator, Jesse Jones:

Jess –
Will you tell the British I hope they can take care of the King of Saudi Arabia. This is a little far afield for us! F.D.R.

The special relationship between Sa'udi Arabia and the United States which has, by the 1980s, become one of the dominant international facts of life – if not always to the obvious pleasure of either partner – took its time a-growing. The USA did not formally recognize the existence of the Sa'udi state until May 1931 – five years after Britain and the Soviet Union – and throughout the 1930s the State Department resisted suggestions that America should actually send any representative to the Kingdom.

In June 1939, Japan's fleeting interest in Sa'udi oil aroused Washington to the major commitment of American capital that Casoc's Dhahran concession represented, and America's Cairo minister was instructed to include Arabia in his bailiwick. But Roosevelt's cheerful shrug of the shoulders in July 1941 remained typical of official America's attitude towards the Arab world. At the outbreak of the Second World War the State Department's Division of Near-Eastern Affairs had just a chief, an assistant chief, seven desk officers and four clerks – a total staff of thirteen, of whom only three could speak local languages. Dealing with an area that stretched from the Atlantic Ocean to the borders of India, the division's slender and amateur talents were inevitably spread thin: J. Rives Childs, later American Ambassador in Jeddah, recalled how he had borne at one stage in his career 'primary responsibility' for Palestine, Jordan, Egypt, Sa'udi Arabia, Yemen, Ethiopia, Libya and Tunisia all at the same time, without an assistant or even a secretary to help him.

America regarded the Middle East as Britain's sphere of interest, and Casoc's spectacular 1938 oil strike was almost five years past before Washington started to think hard about the fact that an American company controlled one of the largest reservoirs of oil in the world.

The impetus that was to transform America's blithe apathy towards Arabia into smothering concern in a matter of months was one of the 'energy crises' whose traumas regularly disturb the self-satisfaction of the developed world. In 1943 the panic was called a 'strategic shortage', and it derived from the realization that America, as the petrol tank of the Allies' war effort, was pumping out 63 per cent of the entire world's oil consumption every day from her own reserves. The terrifying statistic was 3.8 million barrels per day (little more than a third of Sa'udi Arabia's 10.3 million b.p.d. in 1981), and at this rate, the experts calculated, the national reservoir was dropping at the rate of 3 per cent per year.

The problem had already been noted by the State Department, who foresaw perceptively in 1941 how America's future search for oil abroad would compel her post-war foreign policy to become more aggressive and even imperialistic in the British mould, but the diplomats' discreet forward planning was pre-empted by the politicians: 'Before another generation comes on stage,' thundered Senator Owen Brewster (Republican, Maine), 'America will be a mendicant for petroleum at the council tables of the world.' With such language America's oil supplies became, for a season, 'the question of the moment'.

The answer was supplied by Roosevelt's flamboyant Secretary of the Interior, Harold L. Ickes, Petroleum Co-ordinator for National Defence since May 1941 and confident he knew just how to save American oil: burn foreign oil instead. In the western hemisphere lay the reserves of Venezuela which could be shipped conveniently northwards; in the eastern hemisphere American companies had rights in the Middle East; the Dammam Dome seemed to promise supplies which could stave off the evil day for America's own reserves for may years to come.

262

'It is our strong belief', recorded a US memorandum of December 1942, 'that the development of Saudi Arabian petroleum resources should be viewed in the light of the broad national interest.'

These were historic words. Under the stresses of war and the need to relieve political pressures built up by the 'strategic shortage' scare, America's national concerns had become linked for the first time with the shores of the Persian Gulf 10,000 miles away: in just nineteen months Sa'udi Arabia had moved from being 'far afield' to become 'vital to the defence of the United States'. This was the formula President Roosevelt employed when on 18 February 1943 he reversed his earlier decision and formally declared the desert kingdom eligible for Lend–Lease assistance under Executive Order no. 8926; and out in the desert Abdul Aziz rapidly discovered how comforting it could be to have America playing the rich uncle.

In the three and a half years since the start of the Second World War the Sa'udi king had received annually from Great Britain some £3 million in goods and silver coins, plus some £750,000 which Casoc advanced in 1941 and again in 1942 against royalties anticipated from post-war oil sales. But in the two years after the signing of the February 1943 Lend–Lease order some $33 million (nearly £8 million) in cash, goods and bullion flooded into Sa'udi Arabia from the USA on top of oil revenues, and Abdul Aziz was at least £1 million a year better off – for, in their eagerness to make up for lost time in Arabia, the Americans gave with both hands.

Abdul Aziz was never reluctant to accept delivery of hard cash, and the early years of the war had been a difficult time for him in some ways. Pilgrim arrivals in Jeddah had fallen to still lower levels than in the early 1930s – only 32,000 pilgrims arrived in 1940 – while drought and famine in Nejd had caused the tribes to make heavier demands than usual upon the royal purse. But the three or four million pounds a year which the British and Casoc paid between them in the early 1940s was not a bad income for a country which had, a dozen years earlier, made do on less than two, and, by the standards of combatant countries suffering from rationing and shortages, Sa'udi Arabia did very nicely out of its neutrality.

The Al Sa'ud themselves could scarcely be said to have tightened their belts, for, despite frequent pleas of poverty, Abdul Aziz managed to start on the construction of a huge bow-windowed palace of prestressed concrete in the gardens of al Kharj near Riyadh, while he was more than generous to the growing number of his sons who were entering adulthood. By 1943 over a dozen of them had reached the age to marry and have children, and their father provided the funds to set them up in a line of new mud palaces down the road from Riyadh towards Dar'iyah. Impressive motor cars drove in and out of the gates, and, when visiting America in the autumn of 1943 to celebrate the new friendship between Sa'udi Arabia and the USA, Prince Faisal and his brother Khalid requested fourteen more to be sent home for family use. The princes were quite surprised when they were told that wartime restrictions permitted the release of only two, and they showed themselves distinctly upset.

In Whitehall not a little resentment developed at the Sa'udis' spendthrift ways: 'It is apparent that the Saudi Arabian Government', minuted the Foreign Office tartly in February 1944, '. . . will spend as much money as His Majesty's Government are prepared to give them.'

The Sa'udis, complained Whitehall, were making 'no effort to cut their coat according to their cloth', for British representatives had been making a careful tally of the little treats that the Al Sa'ud had been giving themselves. 'The continued demands for more currency to meet necessary governmental expenditure, when apparently un-limited rials can be found for such luxuries as palaces at El Kharj, make a bad impression,' wrote Whitehall, while 'the extravagance of the royal princes can only be regarded as an abuse of His Majesty's Government's generosity.'

An additional problem was the high proportion of the British subsidy that appeared to be sticking to the fingers of corrupt officials, and in sombre moods Abdul Aziz would acknowledge this. 'It is like date wood,' said the king to the British minister in March 1944, admitting 'the rottenness of the financial administration of the country'.

Yet such confessions were usually a prelude to requests for still more aid, and the root of the problem was that revenues reckoned in tens of millions of dollars were simply too much for Abdullah Sulei-man's elementary housekeeping to cope with. The minister's first rule had always been that the king should have whatever he asked for, and Abdul Aziz had never been a greedy man. But the tastes of his growing family were less restrained, and the old king, now into his sixties, was a doting father and grandfather. His natural generosity could not withstand the appetites of his ever-expanding clan, who already numbered hundreds approaching the thousand mark, while the king kept up his subsidies to the tribes via their chiefs, as well as maintaining the prodigal hospitality that still fed several thousand visitors every day in the courtyards of his Riyadh palace.

'Saudi financial controls and accounting', stated one gloomy American report in 1944, could only be described as 'chaotic'; the taxation system was 'inadequate', book-keeping was 'backward and very inefficient' – and this did not augur well for the day when oil started to bring in really major revenues.

The British Minister at Jeddah thought that things should be put right before it was too late. Stanley Jordan was a breezy Australian who had served as vice-consul in Jeddah in the final days of Hashimite rule in the Hijaz, and, arriving back in Jeddah in August 1943, he felt qualified, as an old Arabian hand, to speak his mind.

Abdullah Suleiman, in Jordan's opinion, had got to go. The job had simply become too big for him – and the British minister made his criticisms to Abdul Aziz's face, offering the king the services of a native Indian government adviser who, as a Muslim, would be able to work in Mecca on the reform of the Finance Ministry from the inside. Abdul Aziz showed interest in the idea and early in 1944, as an apparent first step towards reform, he sacked one of Abdullah Suleiman's aides, Nejib Salha, an official who had developed a certain reputation for venality.

It is scarcely likely that Abdul Aziz sacked Nejib Salha solely on the say-so of the British minister. The viziers around the Sa'udi king swam in a constant maelstrom of intrigue, and one of them probably seized on Jordan's criticisms as a good moment to push Nejib's head below the water for a while.

But rumour had it that Abdul Aziz had acted in deference to the British minister. When the American chargé d'affaires in Jeddah, James Moose, heard the gossip, he was outraged. It seemed to him to confirm two of Washington's darkest suspicions about their British allies in Arabia: that Britain had been stealing all the credit for providing the Sa'udis with aid which would never have been possible without America's generous Lend–Lease assistance to London; and, worse still, that the British were planning to use the leverage this aid gave them to demand a *quid pro quo* from the Sa'udis and to 'horn in', as Roosevelt put it, 'on Saudi Arabian oil reserves'.

James Moose was only a second-rank diplomat who spoke little Arabic. He had opened up America's first legation in Jeddah in May 1942, and when the State Department decided to upgrade the mission, they passed over Moose for minister in favour of his assistant, Colonel William Eddy.

But Moose was a faithful interpreter of State Department policy. Washington was determined that Britain should not exploit American war aid to re-establish her empire once hostilities had ended. President Roosevelt viewed British imperialism as outmoded and a source of international instability in the long term, and his feeling was shared with particular fervour in the State Department's Division of Near-Eastern Affairs. Sa'udi Arabia was already being identified by Near East's Arabists as a primary US interest in the post-war Middle East – so Stanley Jordan's one-man campaign to reform the Sa'udi finances aroused Washington's worst fears, particularly since Jordan was openly critical of America's lavish financial aid which was, he complained, quite spoiling Abdul Aziz's appetite to balance the books.

James Moose and the Near East division became convinced that Stanley Jordan was actively working to undermine the American position in Sa'udi Arabia, and in the summer of 1944 Washington lodged a formal protest with Whitehall at the behaviour of His Majesty's Minister in Jeddah.

The Foreign Office declined to be alarmed. 'American impulsiveness and inexperience in dealing with the Arabs may sometimes lead them to act injudiciously,' read a minute for August 1944, 'but we must endeavour to persuade and guide them on the right lines and be patient with their mistakes.'

At least the British understood the possibility (which the release of the British and American documents for 1944 has since confirmed) that the Sa'udis were playing off Jordan and Moose against each other in Jeddah in order to provoke an auction between rival benefactors. Jordan himself was for Britain getting out of the bidding: 'The Americans wish to sink millions of dollars in the desert sands of Saudi Arabia,' he wrote in September 1944, because 'they will be taking billions out of the same sands in the form of oil. But I see no reason why we should be drawn into this vortex.'

In London officials sniffed at America's 'squandermania', for it hurt to watch the mighty dollar buying influence in preserves that Britain had considered hers for a century. But by the end of 1944 President Roosevelt had come to identify Sa'udi Arabia as the perfect example of a country where he could develop the vision he had for the post-war era: generous US aid would help the poorer peoples of the world increase their purchasing power to their own advantage – and also to the advantage of America, who would be providing them with things to purchase. The president was not going to let London stand in his way.

So a grandiose $57 million post-war Sa'udi aid package that the British could not possibly match was worked out, old-fashioned imperialism yielded sway to new-fashioned neo-colonialism, and Roosevelt discreetly laid plans to meet up with Abdul Aziz personally after the Yalta Conference of February 1945. The president had William Eddy, by now American Minister in Jeddah, make the arrangements secretly with Abdul Aziz so that no one in Sa'udi Arabia should find out, and then, on the night the Yalta Conference was ending, Roosevelt casually let Winston Churchill know that he was meeting the King of Arabia in a few days' time.

The British Prime Minister was thunderstruck and 'burned up the wires to all his diplomats', according to Eddy, trying to arrange a meeting of his own with Abdul Aziz. But Churchill had to make do with an appointment after the American president, for by February 1945 the United States' relationship with the Kingdom of Sa'udi Arabia had already become a special one.

The first outsider to get wind of Abdul Aziz's secret arrangement to meet with Franklin Delano Roosevelt was probably the Dutch Minister at Jeddah, Daan van der Meulen, who had been invited up to Riyadh for an audience with the king, and had set out early in December 1944.

It had been raining, van der Meulen's old station wagon had got stuck in the mud, and nine days out of Jeddah the Dutchman was still 80 miles short of his objective, sheltering in the ruined mud fort of the Marat oasis. Damp, cold and lonely, van der Meulen was looking out over the sodden desert disconsolately, when he was amazed to see a long convoy of heavily laden lorries come into view from the direction of Riyadh – 200 or more, virtually every truck in Sa'udi Arabia.

It could only mean that Abdul Aziz was on the move, and, sure enough, by nightfall, the red machine-gun-mounted lorries of the royal bodyguard had appeared, a long *majlis* tent had been erected, and two wireless units had their aerials up and working. Cooking fires were started, the cries of sheep and goats filled the air, and finally a posse of limousines with dark-glass windows and black curtains bumped through the camp.

It was the king's harem – wives, daughters, relatives and serving-girls – and these seventy or so ladies were accommodated out of sight of the men's encampment, a few hundred yards away behind a hillock.

Next morning van der Meulen attended the royal *majlis*, sitting by invitation in the place of honour beside the king – to the evident disapproval of the local sheikhs and tribesmen, who had come in their best robes and with black-kohled eyes to drink coffee with Abdul Aziz – and the Dutchman was embarrassed to hear the king launch into one of his diatribes against the Jews.

Van der Meulen was still more embarrassed when Abdul Aziz turned to ask him what he thought about the accursed race, and the Dutch minister, representing a country whose people were more notable than most for the heroism with which they were shielding Jews from Nazi barbarity, did not know what to say. Mortified by his own mumblings, he left the *majlis* soon afterwards and tried to sort out his thoughts by walking up a nearby hill – to be checked by furious shouts. In his distraction van der Meulen had committed the ultimate delinquency, for he had climbed up the nearby hillock to a point from which he could look down into the women's camp.

Soon Jeddah was surprised by the arrival of the royal entourage, and no one connected it with the appearance, shortly afterwards, of USS *Murphy*, a destroyer making the first ever visit by a US naval vessel to Jeddah.

12 February 1945 was the day fixed for Abdul Aziz's departure. But the king's planned rendezvous with the American president – the Great Bitter Lake in the Suez Canal – was still within range of German bombers, and, requested by the Americans to preserve security as long as possible, Abdul Aziz imbued his getaway with all the secrecy of a pre-dawn raid.

At 3 o'clock on the afternoon of 12 February, Abdul Aziz ordered his entourage to get ready for a move to Mecca, and not until they were in their cars did he tell the drivers to head instead for the harbour pier. There he embarked on waiting launches, and by 4.30 p.m. the Sa'udi king was steaming away from Jeddah on the *Murphy*, leaving the town behind him in a frenzy of rumours from abdication to kidnapping. Abdul Aziz's womenfolk were almost the last to hear the truth when, wailing, they went to Faisal who, with Sa'ud in Nejd, had been entrusted by his father with interim authority.

Out in the harbour, the decampment did not go quite as smoothly as had been planned, for Abdullah Suleiman had preceded his master to the *Murphy* with a hundred live sheep for the voyage: Abdul Aziz had presumed that the American officers and crew would be eating as his guests for the two-day trip, and the *Murphy*'s commander was still explaining US naval regulations with regard to livestock on board warships when Abdul Aziz arrived with the American minister.

Colonel Eddy, a competent Arabist whose contribution to Arab–American understanding included framing the Arabic rules of basketball, managed to persuade the king that the entire crew of the *Murphy* would be clapped in irons if they ate his sheep and failed to observe the official diet prescribed for them by the authorities. But Abdul Aziz was horrified at the idea that he and his entourage should be expected to consume the old meat that the Americans kept in their cold boxes. Good Muslims should eat flesh fresh-slaughtered every day. So a compromise was arrived at, ninety-three sheep earned a brief reprieve, and, of the seven allowed reluctantly on board by the *Murphy*'s commander, one was already being slaughtered and skinned on the fantail of the destroyer as it steamed out of Jeddah roads.

The next few days provided a foretaste of the revelations and misunderstandings awaiting American and Arabians in the many years of collaboration upon which they were embarking. Instructed by Washington that the Sa'udi party must be limited strictly to twelve people, Eddy told his superiors they must expect twice that number, and he thought he had done rather well when only forty-eight came on board.

There were no cabins for most of them, but that did not worry the cooks, bodyguards, coffee servers and slaves who made themselves at home in nooks and crannies around the destroyer's open deck. They cheerfully started fires and brewed their coffee in the gun turrets and beside live-ammunition racks, and they all slept out in the open on the deck – where Abdul Aziz joined them, spurning the captain's cabin that had been specially prepared for his use.

The Sa'udi king preferred to sleep out on rugs beneath the canvas awning stretched across the fo'c'sle, and inside this 'tent' he held his *majlis* all day long. Five times a day the ship's navigator brought the king the exact compass bearing of Mecca, and having verified it with his own astrologer, Majid ibn Khataila, Abdul Aziz would then turn with his entire company towards the Holy City and lead them in their prayers.

269

The American sailors were much more surprised and impressed by their Arabian guests than most of the Arabs were by life on board a metal warship – or perhaps the Americans just showed their wonder more openly. Eddy felt that the ability of the Arab to get off a camel and entrust himself to a mysterious machine like a destroyer without any special display of excitement or apprehension showed the strength of Islam and the submission by its adherents to a God who can accomplish any miracle.

But Arab fatalism is a racial as well as a religious characteristic. It contains a strong element of incuriosity – plain intellectual idleness – and it also involves a certain amount of arrogance and 'face'. An Arab may well be excited or scared by some infidel mechanical marvel, but he is not going to let the infidel know that.

Abdul Aziz was untypical in this respect. Perhaps his achievements as the greatest Arab of his generation, now going to meet, as an equal, with the President of the United States, gave him the confidence openly to show how intrigued he was by the various devices of destruction which the destroyer deployed. He inspected all the armaments with keen interest, and was delighted by displays of anti-aircraft fire at smoke-shells, and when depth-charges were discharged at targets towed behind the ship.

His sons were intrigued by less military matters. A film projector was wheeled up on deck after sunset to treat the royal party to a screening of *The Fighting Lady*, a stirring documentary about an American aircraft carrier in the Pacific war. But Prince Muhammad bin Abdul Aziz discovered that the projector was to be used later in the evening for screening more frivolous fare in the crew's quarters.

The prince called the American minister aside. Would Eddy prefer, he inquired, to be killed on the spot or to be chopped up in small pieces bit by bit?

This was Prince Muhammad's idea of a joke. He wanted to see the Hollywood films with the crew, and he got his way. That evening he and his younger brother Mansour, Abdul Aziz's bright eighth son who had just been named the first Sa'udi Minister of Defence, occupied the front row in the crew's mess to enjoy the antics of Miss Lucille Ball cavorting in various states of undress around the dormitory of a men's college.

An encore was rapidly organized at which fully half the Sa'udi party were present, and fortunately Abdul Aziz never got to hear of the escapade. He had been disapproving enough about the documentary. It was a wonderful film, he said, but 'I doubt whether my people should have moving pictures like this. . . . It would give them an appetite for entertainment which might distract them from their religious duties.'

When East met West at the Great Bitter Lake on 14 February 1945, cultures clashed at a more substantial level. President Roosevelt, welcoming Ibn Sa'ud on board the USS *Quincy*, wanted to enlist the Sa'udi king's help with the problem of Palestine. Roosevelt believed that the British were mishandling the question, and Jewish lobbies in the USA were elevating the need for a Jewish homeland into a major political issue.

The Jews of central Europe had suffered most terribly at Hitler's hands, the president told Abdul Aziz – eviction, torture, mass murder. Roosevelt felt a personal responsibility to help these poor people now – indeed he had committed himself to finding a solution to their problems. Did the King of Arabia have any suggestions to make?

The king did. 'Give them and their descendants', said Abdul Aziz, 'the choicest lands and homes of the Germans who oppressed them.'

This was not what the president had had in mind at all. The Jewish survivors of the holocaust, he explained, had an understandable dread of remaining in Germany where they might suffer again, and they also had 'a sentimental desire' to settle in Palestine.

Abdul Aziz ignored this last point, for surely, he said, Britain and America were planning to defeat Nazi power in a total fashion. He could not see what the Jews had to fear if the Allies were fighting a serious war, for he, Ibn Sa'ud, could not conceive of leaving an enemy in any position to cause trouble after his defeat.

This was an exaggeration, for Abdul Aziz had got himself into trouble several times in his military career through showing leniency to defeated opponents – notably to Faisal al Daweesh after the battle of Sabillah. But his firmness disconcerted Roosevelt, who seems to have believed that a few hours' personal chitchat and some lavish Lend–Lease assistance would win the King of Arabia to his purposes.

The president tried another tack. He was counting on the legendary hospitality of the Arab, he said, to help solve the problem of Zionism. But Abdul Aziz did not see why the Arabs of Palestine should feel especially hospitable towards the Jews.

'Make the enemy and the oppressor pay,' he said; 'that is how we Arabs wage war.'

It was not the Arabs of Palestine who had massacred the Jews. It was the Germans and, as 'a simple bedouin', the Sa'udi king could not understand why the president seemed so eager to save Germany from the consequences of its crimes. The bedouin saved kindness for their friends, not their enemies – though he did have one final suggestion to make.

It was the bedouin custom in war, Abdul Aziz explained, to distribute the innocent survivors and victims of battle among the victorious tribes, to be cared for according to their number and supplies of food and water. This might, perhaps, now be done with the Jews among the fifty or so members of the Allied camp. But Palestine, said Abdul Aziz, was among the very least of these, and it had already taken more than its fair share of refugees from Europe.

Roosevelt moved on to generalities, but, when the memorandum of the five-hour conversation between the two leaders was subsequently put on record, it turned out that the president had made some notable accommodations to the point of view which Abdul Aziz had argued so stolidly.

Roosevelt promised the Sa'udi king that 'he would do nothing to assist the Jews against the Arabs and would make no move hostile to the Arab people', and he encouraged a plan which Ibn Sa'ud had been nursing, to send a mission to the West to explain the Arab viewpoint on Palestine.

'The President stated that he thought this a very good idea because he thought many people in America and England are misinformed', and, speaking to Congress on his return, Roosevelt declared that 'from Ibn Saud, of Arabia, I learned more of the whole problem of the Moslems and more about the Jewish problem in 5 minutes than I could have learned by the exchange of a dozen letters.'

Abdul Aziz said his farewells to the American president well pleased. Roosevelt was the first infidel head of state he had met in all his sixty-nine years, and now, within three days, he was due to meet another, Winston Churchill, who would be calling on him at the Auberge Hotel on Lake Karoun south-west of Cairo. Abdul Aziz's very first question to Roosevelt after greeting him on the *Quincy* had been whether the president minded his meeting the British Prime Minister at this time, and FDR, having stolen a march on his British ally, was magnanimity itself.

'Why not?' he said 'I always enjoy seeing Mr Churchill and I am sure you will like him too.'

Abdul Aziz did not like Winston Churchill very much as it turned out – at least he did not warm to him as he had to FDR – and this was partly because the American president had gone to considerable pains not to offend the king's Wahhabi sensibilities. As the two men were descending to luncheon in separate lifts on board the *Quincy*, Roosevelt had reached out and pressed the red emergency button and, suspended in the liftshaft, had smoked two cigarettes in rapid time before continuing his journey to rejoin Abdul Aziz at the luncheon table, where no alcohol was being served.

Winston Churchill, however, made a little speech to the effect that, while he realized 'it was the religion of His Majesty to deprive himself of smoking and alcohol, I must point out that my rule of life prescribes as an absolutely sacred rite smoking cigars and also the drinking of alcohol before, after and if need be during all meals and in the intervals between them', and the Prime Minister proceeded to sip whisky and puff his pungent cigars through much of his three-hour discussion with the Sa'udi king – which sounded very funny in his memoirs.

Abdul Aziz was less amused. Churchill's smoking and drinking might not have mattered if the British Prime Minister had shown himself as receptive to Abdul Aziz's view on Palestine as the American president appeared to be. But Churchill had considerably more experience than Roosevelt in Middle-Eastern politics – indeed his activities at the Cairo Conference of 1921 had contributed not a little to their complexity – and he knew better than to make undertakings as bold as those Roosevelt had given to the Sa'udi king. The President's Great Bitter Lake promise to consult with the Arabs was soon to cause the US government some embarrassment, and the British Prime Minister adopted a different approach.

'Mr Churchill opened the subject confidently wielding the big stick,' Abdul Aziz later reported to Colonel Eddy in Jeddah. 'Great Britain had subsidized me for twenty years, and had made possible the stability of my reign.' So, argued the Prime Minister, 'since Britain had seen me through difficult days, she is entitled now to request my assistance in the problem of Palestine where a strong Arab leader can restrain fanatical Arab elements, insist on moderation in Arab councils, and effect a realistic compromise with Zionism.'

This approach did not go down at all well. Abdul Aziz was nettled by Mr Churchill's 'big stick', and he later described himself to Eddy as giving a fierce answer to the 'preposterous' idea that he should

273

compromise with Zionism. The king probably embellished his description somewhat for the benefit of the American minister, but Laurence Grafftey-Smith, who was present at the Sa'udi–British discussions on the verandah of the Auberge Hotel, also remembers impasse over Palestine and a certain atmosphere of strain.

'You'd think they'd be grateful,' grumbled Churchill later, 'after all we did for Feisal and Abdullah.'

Grafftey-Smith was too shy to point out that his Prime Minister had got his dynasties muddled up, and that Abdul Aziz could hardly be expected to feel gratitude for what Britain had done for the Hashimites. But Churchill did feel some twinges of remorse that evening, as he tried on the magnificent robes, jewelled sword, dagger and diamond rings which Abdul Aziz had given him – and which the Prime Minister valued at £3500.

Churchill had only had a £100 case of scent to hand over in exchange and, disconcerted to hear that Roosevelt had given the Sa'udi king his own wheelchair and a DC3 aircraft as a present, the Prime Minister had made Abdul Aziz a grandiose off-the-cuff promise: the scent was only a token, he said, for he had made plans to have the very first Rolls-Royce off the Derby production line after the war shipped out to Arabia for the Sa'udi king's use – 'the finest motor car in the world, with every comfort for peace and every security against hostile action.'

Abdul Aziz went back home on a British cruiser – there were no gunnery demonstrations, no tents on the deck, and no fraternizing with the crew, he later complained – to be greeted by intense rejoicing in the streets of Jeddah. The *ulema* were angry with him for having left the country without consulting them, and they were suspicious of his secret discussions with infidel leaders. But the news that the king had secured for fellow Arabs in Palestine pledges from the American president of consultation and protection was counted a solid success, and on 5 April 1945 Roosevelt formally renewed his promises to Abdul Aziz in a letter which went to some lengths to make clear that the undertakings were not just personal, but were being issued deliberately 'in my capacity as Chief of the Executive Branch of this Government'.

One week later Franklin Delano Roosevelt was dead, and the new chief executive of the US government chose to disregard the commitments that his predecessor had given. Abdul Aziz was rather less dismayed by this than were the State Department diplomats who had to explain to the Sa'udi king the strong support which President Truman elected to lend to Zionist ambitions in Palestine, culminating in recognition and assistance to the new State of Israel. As an absolute monarch, Abdul Aziz quite understood how the promises that a ruler made died with him, and how a successor might well switch loyalties in deference to any constituency which strengthened his succession.

Just the same, the Sa'udi king would have been surprised if he could have heard quite how casually Harry Truman tore up the promises that Roosevelt had given to the Arabs at the Great Bitter Lake. In the autumn of 1945, less than six months after Roosevelt's death, President Truman summoned to Washington the US Chiefs of Mission in Sa'udi Arabia and the other countries principally concerned with the Palestine problem, to hear their report on the fear and anger being aroused in the Arab world by the favour that the new president was showing to Zionist ambitions.

When their report had been presented, Mr Truman asked some questions and listened some more. But nothing he heard appeared to change his mind.

'I'm sorry, gentlemen,' said the president, summing up his position with the utmost candour, 'but I have to answer to hundreds of thousands who are anxious for the success of Zionism; I do not have hundreds of thousands of Arabs among my constituents.'

30 Riches

The oil brings money. But in many ways it is a burden to me.
Abdul Aziz to G. Clinton Pelham, H.M. Ambassador to Saudi Arabia, 1951–55

THE British went to some trouble to get their Rolls-Royce just right for Abdul Aziz. It proved impossible to fulfil Winston Churchill's promise to the letter and to present the Sa'udi king with the very first car off the post-war production line. Rolls-Royce were still just producing aircraft engines. But an almost unused Phantom III 'All Weather' convertible was discovered and refitted by Hoopers the coach builders for conditions in central Arabia: the cocktail cabinet was removed and replaced by a large silver bowl in which Abdul Aziz could perform his ablutions before prayers; the silver cocktail shakers were exchanged for vacuum flasks to store the king's favourite Mecca drinking water; and the back seat, with room for three, was converted into one huge armchair, for the British had heard how the wheelchair given to the king by Roosevelt had proved unable to accommodate the generously proportioned royal stern, and they made sure their upholsterers took no chances. The cost of the remodelled automobile ex-works was £3281.17s.

When the limousine arrived in Jeddah in the summer of 1946, it appeared fit for a king in every respect, down to its green reflective paintwork, its gun rack, its wide running boards and the chrome grab-handles which had been screwed to the exterior for the convenience of the royal bodyguard.

All that remained was to deliver the vehicle to the king 900 miles away in Riyadh, and the British minister, Laurence Grafftey-Smith, Stanley Jordan's successor and, like Jordan, an old Jeddah hand who had known the town in Hashimite days, chose for the trip one of his junior officers, David Parker, and Britain's pro-vice-consul in Jeddah, Cyril Ousman:

Ousman had first come to Jeddah in 1929 as engineer in charge of the town's seawater condenser and, as a pillar of the expatriate community, he had got on quite close personal terms with Abdul Aziz and a number of the royal family. Now, in July 1946, Ousman tested the car and touched up its paintwork, and on 9 August he drove out of the town in style.

Enthroned in the back of the limousine was Ousman's companion David Parker, and the two Britons bumped across the desert for five days, camping out along the way, to be received with delight by Abdul Aziz in Riyadh.

It was Ramadhan, so the presentation of the car together with a letter from Britain's new Prime Minister, Mr Attlee, was made in the middle of the night. But as the old king, whose eyesight was deteriorating with every passing year, began to look around the vehicle, something appeared to be troubling him. He was not interested by the throne-like rear upholstery with its silver bowl and flasks, for only women sat in the back of cars. Men sat in the front beside the chauffeur – to this day the king and senior Sa'udi princes sit cooped up in the front seat of their long limousines – and, in all their modifications, the British made a crucial omission. They had failed to switch the car's steering from right- to left-hand drive. So King Abdul Aziz would have to sit on the left-hand side of his driver, the position of dishonour – and the moment the king realized this the Rolls-Royce lost all its charm.

'You can have it,' he told his brother Abdullah, who happened to be with him at the time, and that was the end of Winston Churchill's present to the King of Sa'udi Arabia.

Twenty years earlier a free Rolls-Royce, right- or left-hand drive, would not have been received in Riyadh in such an offhand fashion. But already, by 1946, Abdul Aziz was becoming a rich man. The American navy had begun to buy Sa'udi oil in bulk before the end of the Second World War. Annual crude production had vaulted from less than ½ million barrels in 1938, to 8 million in 1944 and some 60 million by 1946 (when oil revenues alone totalled $10 million), while, with peace, pilgrim receipts picked up sharply as a backlog of foreign Muslims hastened to perform their *hajj*. The American government continued to provide aid – in the Middle East only Turkey received more assistance than Sa'udi Arabia – and, most important of all, Abdullah Suleiman had discovered that, with all that oil in the ground, the world was suddenly eager to lend him money.

Sa'udi Arabia had been heavily in debt before oil was struck, but the effect of increasing oil revenues was not to reduce but spectacularly to enlarge her borrowing. Under the pressure of insatiable royal spending, the Sa'udi Finance Ministry took all the loans that foreign bankers had to offer in the 1940s, so that a dozen years after the Second World War the country was to find itself teetering on the brink of bankruptcy.

History has tended to blame Abdul Aziz's son and successor, Sa'ud, for the financial crisis that afflicted Sa'udi Arabia in the late 1950s. But by the time Sa'ud bin Abdul Aziz came to the throne in 1953 a formidable deficit had already been built up by his father.

The Tale of Abdul Aziz and the Gift Horse

When Abdul Aziz's knees and legs started to give him pain in his old age, he went to Hofuf to get relief by bathing in the hot springs there, and during his cure one of the Hofuf citizens presented the king with a fine grey horse.

Abdul Aziz now only rode in motor cars, but he was delighted with the gift, and called for his vizier to bring him the great leather-bound ledger in which he still wrote down personally the details of the presents to be bestowed upon each of his visitors.

'300 riyals,' he wrote against the name of the citizen who had given him the horse, and that was many riyals more than the horse was worth.

But as the king wrote the figure down in his ledger, the nib of the royal pen got stubbed into the paper, and a little shower of ink blobs flew out across the page, turning 300 riyals into 300,000 – for in Arabic the zero is not written as an open 'O' but as a closed dot like a full stop.

The vizier drew his master's attention to the row of little ink blots.

'This figure, oh long life, should read 300 riyals, I presume, and not 300,000,' he said.

The king studied the ledger carefully.

'I see,' he said, 'that my pen has clearly specified 300,000. So that is what you must pay – and immediately. My hand has written it, and I will have no one say that the hand of Abdul Aziz is more generous than his heart.'

The generosity that had once been the mainstay of the Sa'udi polity became its bane as oil revenues started expanding in the late 1940s. When Abdullah Suleiman tried in March 1946 to draw up some sort

278

of budget based on the first twelve months of oil royalties since the end of the war, he found that in the coming twelve months he would have to balance expenditures of £17.5 million against revenues of only £13.2 million – which meant that Abdul Aziz would have to borrow £1 in every £4 that he spent.

But this rate of indebtedness was less alarming than some of the heads of expenditure that made up the £17.5 million. Philby enumerated them: £2 million on existing debts that had to be repaid; £2 million for the expenses of the royal garages; £1 million for court hospitality and entertainment – and just £150,000 for new schools and national education.

Philby tried to rationalize the royal spending when he talked to foreign visitors: the mud palaces that were Riyadh's only signs of the new wealth flooding into the capital were, he explained, a sort of Arabian 'New Deal' project: the king was anxious to provide his subjects with work, and so he got them building palaces.

But this was plain humbug. Philby could plausibly have argued that Abdul Aziz was hoarding nothing for himself. The old king was never *nouveau riche*, and most of his wealth, apart from the cash that his sons spent on foreign luxuries, filtered down in one way or another to tribesmen and the bazaar, since the Arabian system of rake-offs at every level is a reasonably efficient wealth-distributor. Philby could even have argued, and probably did, that bedouin coming to Riyadh cared little for alien and impersonal ministries or school buildings and were much happier with endless palaces where they could visit each prince, chat, drink coffee, sleep and gorge themselves for days at no expense.

But to pretend that Abdul Aziz had Western notions of national development was ridiculous. In the eight years from the end of the Second World War until Abdul Aziz's death in 1953, the only major public works that he provided from some $400 million of personal revenues were a railway from Dhahran to Riyadh, a jetty in Jeddah, some tarmac roads and a network of water wells. The old man's imagination could not stretch any further than simple generosity. He just gave his money away, and when his son Talal came to him in 1949, requesting permission to build a public hospital in Riyadh, the ageing king stared at the youth in astonishment. He could not imagine what the boy was getting at.

Talal, then Abdul Aziz's seventeenth surviving son, just coming up to the age of twenty, explained to his father that he had discussed the

279

subject with his brothers, and he produced a letter signed by more than a dozen of them from Khalid down to Naif (the modern Interior Minister who was then sixteen). Several of them had visited Western countries, and they had also seen the health and welfare facilities that the oil company was providing for its employees and their families at Dhahran. The royal family should offer the same sort of service in Riyadh, said Talal.

The old king's eyes filled with tears as he listened. 'Do you really wish to do that, my son?' he asked, as though listening for the first time to some totally novel mode of behaviour. 'Is that how you want to spend your money? Then so be it. What could be more wonderful?'

But the hospital never got beyond the planning stage in Abdul Aziz's lifetime, for the infrastructure of a modern centralized welfare state was alien to a ruler who liked to show off his financial system by summoning sacks of gold up from the royal treasury.

'That's my financial system,' he would say triumphantly, pointing at the bags of bullion surrounding him. 'I ask for the money and it appears. What more do I need to know than that?'

As a young man Abdul Aziz's strength had lain in his openmindedness, his readiness to accept innovation. In old age, the very reverse seemed the case. The Sa'udi king even declined to recognize his own national anthem, a ditty knocked out on the spur of the moment by the bandmaster of King Farouk of Egypt when it was discovered, shortly before Abdul Aziz's arrival on a state visit in 1946, that Sa'udi Arabia had no anthem.

The old Wahhabi in Abdul Aziz rebelled at showing reverence to a piece of music – and to other new-fangled innovations. His state *was* a welfare state in his eyes. Anyone who came to his palace door for a meal received one, and until the day of his death in 1953 visitors to Riyadh remarked on the hordes of bedouin living on royal charity in their tents around the town that still depended on water hauled from the ground in leather buckets.

Riyadh was still very much the desert settlement in which Abdul Aziz had been born and in which he had grown up.

'One of the first things that strikes you in Riyadh', wrote R. S. F. Hennessy, one of the Anglo-American commissioners who visited Ibn Sa'ud in 1946 to ascertain his views on the escalating Palestine crisis, 'is a curious prolonged musical note, which appears to come from the country all round you, like the faint after-hum of a bell or the sound of wind through telephone wires.'

It was the sound of wooden water wheels, screeching and gurgling endlessly as blindfolded camels plodded round in circles, dragging leather buckets from their earthen wells. The perpetual creaking and sighing of their timber ratchets made up a lullaby that must have soothed the baby Abdul Aziz to sleep in the 1870s – and babies for centuries before that. From the air, Hennessy discovered, Riyadh was still 'a medieval walled city, surrounded by vivid greenery, and then stark desert'.

The airport was a cleared sand strip, with a windsock and a few old tents where visitors were offered sweet mint tea and coffee. Every plane had to receive the king's express permission to land or to take off. Passengers flying across the Kingdom from Dhahran to Jeddah had to disembark in Riyadh and wait in the tents there, sipping coffee, while a messenger drove into town to discover whether His Majesty required the plane to transport any of his family or possessions to Jeddah; if it was siesta time, then everyone waited until the royal slumbers ceased.

To the end Abdul Aziz fought to retain personal control over every aspect of a society that had, in truth, been too complex and wide-spread for one man to handle since the addition of the Hijaz in 1925. But his selectivity was bizarre. The king got to hear of lingering circumcision practices in a few south-western villages that were bar-barous indeed: the ceremony was delayed until adolescence, and then the skin of the victim was peeled back not just from the head of the penis but right along and up the lower belly.

The image of such pain inspired Abdul Aziz to put things right with a fury he could never muster for the inefficiency and peculation of those around him, and so it was that in the late 1940s the explorer Wilfred Thesiger, then making a locust-control survey, came across three boys in a Tihama village, each nursing 'a bundle of stained wrappings which concealed the suppurating stump of his right hand'.

The boys had suffered twice, first from the savage initiation cere-mony in which they were deemed to have been willing participants, and then from the savage remedy with which Abdul Aziz sought to stamp it out.

The royal world-view defied the complexities of the mid-twentieth century. Abdul Aziz could not understand why the USA did not take advantage of her nuclear superiority to drop the atom bomb on Russia before the communists could make one of their own. His conviction that communism was evil involved the settled opinion that

281

acts of incest could be witnessed frequently in the public parks of Moscow. And while the Sa'udi king allowed locust-control officers like Wilfred Thesiger to investigate the Empty Quarter, he was dubious of their efficacy. Bedouin tradition had it that locusts were spewed out of the mouths of fishes, and where could fishes be found among the sands?

It was not surprising that Marianne Likowski, a bright young American from Long Beach, California, who met and fell in love with an attractive Sa'udi in her class at Berkeley, should feel she had stumbled back into the Arabian Nights when she travelled to Jeddah in the mid-1940s as Mrs Ali Alireza. Her new sisters-in-law came on board the Khedivial steamer to envelop her in a thick black veil, and she was whisked back to the family harem where her fifteen years of tedium, laughter and sisterhood became the basis of the fascinating and deservedly successful book she later wrote.*

Thanks to Marianne Alireza, the outside world first gained some insight into the day-to-day reality of life behind the veil, and the American also charted a little of that vast unknown hidden half of the Al Sa'ud, the women of the family, dominated in the late 1940s by the king's sister Nura, then by his favourite wives, and after that by his daughters.

Abdul Aziz's daughters today occupy the same special niche on the distaff side of the family hierarchy as their brothers do in public. At weddings and family functions any bint† Abdul Aziz takes precedence, lesser cousins and sisters-in-law deferring and bowing to them. They are tall and heavily built, most of them, like their father, and when women gather with women unveiled, the splendour of their costume is nothing less than regal.

'Their billowy robes had gold embroidery and multi-coloured sequins,' wrote Marianne Alireza, describing a female *majlis* on one of the last pilgrimages that Abdul Aziz made to the Hijaz, 'which made every inch of the garments glitter under lacy black outer coverings. The sleeves were so tightly fitted from elbow to the wrist that I wondered how they got them on, until I was told that the sleeves are sewn onto the arm at each wearing and ripped each night when undressing.'

* Marianne Alireza, *At the Drop of a Veil* (Boston, Houghton Mifflin, 1971).
† Bint: daughter of.

The princesses had with them their teams of black slave girls, who straddled the mutton carcasses down the centre of the tent at dinner time, tearing off strips of flesh which they tossed unceremoniously on to the platters of their mistresses. Then the American was taken to be presented to the old king himself, who impressed her properly, even from behind two substantial thicknesses of black georgette. 'I thought he had the biggest hands I had ever seen.'

Abdul Aziz gestured continually as he spoke to his womenfolk, and to the black shape of the foreign wife that young Alireza had brought back with him, he had just one thing to say: 'We hope that you become a Muslim.'

The old man meant it deeply. He could conceive no other meaning to existence, no alternative route to earthly contentment, and long and earnest were his attempts to persuade J. Rives Childs, US minister from 1946 to 1951, to accept the superiority of the Muslim arrangements for soul and body. Childs was to write his own memoirs of his time in Arabia, curiously parallel to, but eerily remote from those of Marianne Likowski/Alireza, who lived in Jeddah throughout the same period but could not even attend functions at her own legation if men were present. Childs describes how Abdul Aziz, in his efforts to demonstrate Islam's superiority with regard to sexual matters, offered him a houri to enliven the lonely nights the American often had to spend in Riyadh.

Later Childs recounted the episode to his diplomatic colleagues in Jeddah, making it clear that he had refused the royal offer.

'Only an American would,' sniffed his French counterpart with disdain.*

J. Rives Childs was to spend more than five years in Sa'udi Arabia, and one of his principal duties as the old king's life drew towards its close was to assess the character and ability of Crown Prince Sa'ud, for the State Department was naturally apprehensive as to whether the son was the measure of the father.

But Childs found it difficult to give Washington any solid answer. The Department must be aware', he minuted in July 1947, 'that the

* The French Minister's scorn may have had something to do with the fact that Childs's principal leisure pastime was collecting and cataloguing eighteenth-century erotic literature. The minister's private library provided many happy hours for young officers bored by Jeddah's few distractions.

patriarchal discipline maintained by the King at Riyadh does not tend to the expression of individual personality.'

So although, on one occasion, Sa'ud unburdened himself to the American minister, spilling out all his unhappiness at the waste and lack of constructive development in the country and urging Childs to talk firmly to his father about it, the crown prince finished up by begging that these personal opinions should not be attributed to him. As late as 1950, after Sa'ud and his English-speaking younger brothers had one evening staged a well-rehearsed programme of speeches and skits for some American medical visitors, the crown prince asked the doctors anxiously not to mention the entertainment to the king when they were attending him next day.

In the royal presence all the princes would sit on the extreme edge of the *majlis* submissively. If invited to come and speak with their father, they would creep forward, head bowed, to seat themselves not in the chair beside him but on the carpet at his feet – and that went for Sa'ud and Faisal, men well into their forties, as well as for their younger brothers.

Abdul Aziz's strictness with his children was understandable, for one of the darker themes of his declining years was their inability to handle the bounty that he showered upon them. The upbringing and education of his sons simply had not prepared them for the sudden rush of wealth that permitted them to gratify almost any whim.

In June 1947 Prince Nasir bin Abdul Aziz held a party. Nasir twenty-seven, was the fifth of the king's surviving sons, he ranked immediately below Khalid in the line of seniority, and his father had made him Emir, or Governor, of Riyadh, an important post which involved supervising all aspects of the capital's life, including the police and the administration of justice. In this capacity Prince Nasir found it easier than most to stockpile whisky and also to have a secret still operated on his behalf. But the still was an inefficient one. The wood alcohol it produced was poisonously impure, and after drinking it at the party he held in June 1947 seven of Prince Nasir's guests – most of them women – died.

The fatalities would probably have been hushed up if they had not included one of the princes from the house of Rasheed. He had lived at the Sa'udi court since the fall of Hail, and his relatives presumed that the poisoning was deliberate (poisonings in the Rasheed family usually were). So two of his cousins stole away from Riyadh to take refuge in Iraq, and there the Hashimite authorities gleefully made much of the Al Sa'uds' saturnalia.

The moment Abdul Aziz heard of the affair, he flung Nasir into prison, depriving him of his Riyadh governorship, and summoning a gathering of all his elder sons to watch while he belaboured their errant brother with his walking stick. Nasir cringed on the carpet as his father rained down blows upon his back, and then Abdul Aziz harangued his sons, warning them against the dangers of departing from the principles of their forefathers.

'Have things come to this?' Philby reported the king as crying. 'I would have doomsday now!'

The pity of it was that Nasir had, in earlier years, been known for his piety and rigidly abstemious habits which had, apparently, crumbled totally in the course of just one brief visit to the United States. A more elastic and forgiving creed than Wahhabism might have stood the strain of the young man's American excursion and turned it into a gently broadening experience. But the rigid 'dos' and 'don'ts' of the desert catechism allowed no compromise, and, failing to resist the culture shock, they had been totally swept away.

J. Rives Childs treated the tragedy with some insouciance, explaining to Washington how Nasir had sought 'to telescope many lost weekends into one'. The prince's crime, thought the minister, was that of 'transplanting Western customs too suddenly to Sa'udi Arabia' – as if Wahhabism would, in time, adapt itself to the ways of the West, and whisky would one day be swilled openly in Riyadh bars.

But the sheikhs and *ulema* had, of course, no such vision of the future. The essence of their dogma lay in its refusal to compromise, and the case of Prince Nasir suggested a sterile future for contacts between Wahhabism and the West: either hostility and confrontation in the Ikhwan tradition, or moral chaos in which the old rules were cast aside and no new rules took their place.

Another tragedy occurred in November 1951. Cyril Ousman, British pro-vice-consul and more than twenty years in Jeddah, had made many friends among local Sa'udis, entertaining them in his home, and serving them the alcohol that non-Muslim foreigners were permitted to import in those days. Prince Mishari bin Abdul Aziz, aged nineteen and the eighteenth surviving son of the king, was at one such party, on the evening of 16 November 1951, when a row developed.

Mishari left, to reappear shortly afterwards carrying a gun with which he proceeded to spray bullets into the Ousmans' home. Mrs

Dorothy Ousman, secretary to successive British ministers, was shielded by her husband, but, as he pushed his wife to safety, Cyril Ousman was shot dead.

The pro-vice-consul was buried next day in Jeddah's high-walled non-Muslim cemetery, where his simple marble gravestone can still be seen, and, though few people visit it today or even know of its existence, Cyril Ousman does have a memorial of which every non-Muslim in Sa'udi Arabia is well aware. In 1952 Abdul Aziz revoked the import concessions hitherto allowed to foreigners, and banned all alcohol totally from his kingdom.

Dorothy Ousman left Jeddah quietly, accepting Sa'udi compensation, on which she lives, at the time of writing, in retirement in South Africa. Mishari was put in prison, saved from the death penalty by his royal status. There was nothing about the incident of which the Al Sa'ud could feel proud.

The oil bonanza churned up an ethical morass. Violence like Mishari's proved an exception, but that was not the essence of the problem. Laziness, hypocrisy, shallowness, tastelessness, these were the creeping vices which oil wealth brought to corrode old decencies in post-war Arabia, since those inhabitants of the Kingdom who scrambled for the pleasurable enticements of the West showed little interest in the traditions and disciplines that went with them.

America was a wonderful place, enthused one young man to Philby, and of all the things he had seen there the one that impressed him most was a glass-walled restaurant set below a swimming pool where you could eat your lunch while looking up at the naked legs of the ladies swimming past.

The Kingdom had survived adversity and impoverishment. Could it now survive prosperity?

Top Abdul Aziz with
two of his sons in the 1930s
Above Abdullah Suleiman

Above Abdul Aziz with Amin Rihani
(left) and Hafiz Wahba (right)

Right Prince Talal ibn Abdul Aziz with
his *akhiwiya*, 'little brother'

Opposite page
Above Abdul Aziz and sons at Taif, 1934

Below Leading his sons in the *ardha*, the
sword dance

Inset Abdul Aziz's harem car

Top Jeddah architecture: Philby's house, the Beit Baghdadi
Above Jeddah pleasures: staff of the British Legation relaxing

31 The Lion Dies

FOR someone in his seventies, Abdul Aziz was still *muy hombre* – 'very much a man' – thought Laurence Grafftey-Smith who, as British minister, had frequently to do business with the old king in the late 1940s. Tall and deep-chested, Abdul Aziz looked 'impressively square cut', in the minister's eyes. 'He still had more than the mere remains of great physical strength, and the gentle hands and charming smile that made many love him.'

So Grafftey-Smith was surprised one day to find the old king weeping. Abdul Aziz had just learned, he told the British minister, that 'there were as many as 5,000 Jews living in the city of New York'.

Grafftey-Smith had always suspected that Abdul Aziz was weak on figures over a thousand, and he had good reason to know the true proportions of New York's ethnic mix, since Great Britain had just delayed a policy initiative in Palestine in deference to President Truman's anxieties over the mayoral elections in that city.

But the minister guessed that adding more zeros to the old man's statistic would only increase his sorrow, and Abdul Aziz had grasped the point in any case: the Americans he had originally welcomed to Arabia as businessmen who would confine themselves to making money and who, in the 1930s, had been happy to leave local politics to the Arabs, had turned out, in the 1940s, to be committed to a disruption of the Arab world more drastic and permanent than any of the meddlings of the old imperial powers.

America's support for the Jewish struggle to establish the State of Israel in the years after the Second World War did not chime with President Roosevelt's Great Bitter Lake assurances to Abdul Aziz. But the dying president, under the spell that the Sa'udi king managed to weave around all who met him, had been too eager to please, since Roosevelt was as aware of American political realities as his successor Truman turned out to be. Roosevelt knew well that when it came to election time any American president had 'to answer to hundreds of thousands . . . anxious for the success of Zionism', and electioneering in 1944, he had publicly endorsed the Zionists' Biltmore Program. Roosevelt shared America's general sympathy for the holocaust's survivors' wish to plant themselves in the Middle East, and his hope for Palestine before his death seems to have been that he might somehow arrange a conference between the Jewish leadership and Arab figures like Ibn Sa'ud to hammer out a compromise.

It fell to Harry Truman to discover that compromise was impossible in the much-too-Promised Land. When Britain gave up on the whole peck of troubles and dumped Palestine into the lap of the United Nations in 1947, America supported the UN plan to partition the country into separate Jewish and Arab areas. But the Arab states rejected partition totally, holding out for an independent Arab Palestine in which the Jews would have to take their chances as a minority.

'If you want to be generous, then be generous out of what you possess,' declared Prince Faisal bin Abdul Aziz, head of the Sa'udi delegation to the United Nations General Assembly in 1947. Faisal expressed astonishment that members of the US Congress, who were at that moment resisting the entry of Jewish and other European refugees into their own country, should be urging 'uncontrolled and unconditional immigration into Palestine as if that country had no owners and as if her rightful inhabitants had no say in the matter'.

What would be the position of the United States Government and the American people at large, were the parliament of some foreign country to pass a law which urges opening the gates of immigration to Jewish and non-Jewish refugees . . simply because the United States is vast and can absorb millions of people?

Gentlemen, try and put yourself in our place today. . . .

Arab arms and guerrillas poured into Palestine. The Jews fought to defend and to extend the area granted them by the United Nations, and, as the last of Britain's troops withdrew, the situation degenerated into total war.

'The choice for our people, Mr President, is between statehood and extermination,' Dr Weizmann told Harry Truman in April 1948, and by that stage of the conflict he was right.

The State of Israel came into existence at 6.00 p.m. on 14 May 1948, and at 6.11 p.m. President Truman announced its *de facto* recognition by the United States of America.

Faisal bin Abdul Aziz was outraged. He had been booed and spat upon in New York by Jewish demonstrators – an experience he never forgave or forgot – and on the strength of private State Department assurances he had worked hard to persuade fellow Arab delegates to the UN that America would not, in the last resort, endorse partition or a sovereign Jewish state – only to be left looking like an American stooge, and a discarded stooge at that. The fact that President Truman had overruled his pro-Arab State Department advisers for personal and political reasons did little to salve Faisal's sense of betrayal, and he urged his father to break off links with America at once.

But Abdul Aziz ignored him. While mobs in other Arab countries stormed American legations in furied demonstrations, and their governments blustered of economic war against the USA, Sa'udi Arabia confined itself to expressions of 'shock', sent a token force to join the armies of the Arab League in Palestine, and declined to take up the unused portion of a $15 million loan from America's Export–Import Bank.

It was a slap on the wrist after decades of big talk, and, in this first serious testing of the US–Sa'udi relationship, State Department officials discovered, with some relief, that, when it came to events outside Arabia's frontiers, their Sa'udi partners had a very realistic 'sense of what they can and cannot do'.

David Niles, an aide to President Truman and to Roosevelt before that, put it more brutally: 'President Roosevelt said to some of us privately he could do anything that needed to be done with Ibn Saud with a few million dollars.'

If that sounded cynical, it almost paraphrased Abdul Aziz's response when Iraq called on him to cut off his oil sales and declare economic war on America over Israel. 'Give me $30 million', he said, 'and I'll join you.' Abdul Aziz had become the hostage of his oil revenues.

Prince Faisal and his militant younger brothers felt humiliated. But Sa'udi Arabia scarcely proved itself more self-interested in the first Arab–Israeli war than Egypt – who secured for itself the Gaza Strip – or than Abdullah of Transjordan – who exploited the efforts of the allied Arab armies to pocket Arab Palestine for himself, enlarging his territories on to the west bank of the Jordan River by over 2000 square miles. The first combined Arab assault on Israel provided in 1948–9 a model for all the others to come in its mutual mistrust and individual self-seeking; and Abdul Aziz's halfhearted commitment had much to do with his unwillingness to further the ambitions of his ancient Hashimite enemy.

The Sa'udi king, said Grafftey-Smith, was always susceptible to two sorts of gossip – rumours of new aphrodisiacs, and dirt about Abdullah of Transjordan – and Abdullah's annexation of Arab Palestine and half Jerusalem justified Abdul Aziz's worst suspicions. When Abdullah sought international recognition in 1950 for his combined Palestinian and Transjordanian territories, to be known henceforward as the Hashimite Kingdom of Jordan, his Arab brothers in Riyadh were conspicuous in their silence, and the news of Abdullah's assassination at the hands of an Arab nationalist in 1951 elicited little pretence at sorrow.

By that date the Al Sa'ud were engaged in some empire building of their own, for on 14 October 1949 Sa'udi Arabia had officially notified the British government of her claim to nearly 50,000 square miles of the deserts stretching eastwards from al Hasa – a vast extension of the Sa'udi frontier as hitherto recognized. The Kingdom claimed land which stretched out along the Trucial Coast towards the Strait of Hormuz in a bulge clipping large chunks off the territories which the rulers of Qatar, Abu Dhabi and Muscat had long regarded as their own, and, since the only significant settlements in these suddenly coveted wastelands were the threadbare gardens, huts and palm groves that made up the oases around Buraymi, it was by the name of Buraymi that the Sa'udi demand, and the twenty-five-year-old dispute to which it led, came to be known.

The Sa'udi claim to Buraymi was couched in ancient and historic terms: Abdul Aziz's Wahhabi ancestors had occupied the area for a time, some inhabitants of Buraymi had considered themselves Sa'udi subjects at certain periods in the last century and a half, and aged documents were dusted off to prove the venerable nature of ties alleged to link the oasis to the rulers of Riyadh.

But the dispute was not about history; it was about oil. Abdul Aziz's American oil partners had come to suspect that substantial energy reserves lay below the drab sand and gravel plains of the Trucial Coast, and with that suspicion the poverty-stricken inhabitants of Buraymi suddenly discovered that their welfare was a matter of intense concern not only to the Al Sa'ud but even to powers like Britain and the mighty USA.

It was a measure of the success of America's oilmen in Arabia that within a decade of their oil strike of March 1938 they were helping to

shape the foreign policy of the Al Sa'ud. Before the strike, Standard
Oil of California had sold a share in their Arabian concession to the
Texas Oil Company in return for Texaco deals elsewhere, and after
the Second World War the companies had decided to split more of
their competitors in on their joint Arabian franchise. They needed
extra capital and marketing outlets – and they also foresaw how much
easier it would be to muster State Department leverage on their
behalf if they represented a broader section of the American oil
industry.

So Standard Oil of New Jersey (then Esso, now Exxon) and
Socony-Vacuum (Mobil) were allowed to buy in on the Sa'udi venture, and the whole partnership, known as the Arabian American Oil
Company, Aramco, soon became the largest single American enterprise operating anywhere outside the US mainland.* It outstripped
even Firestone Rubber in Liberia and the United Fruit Company in
Latin America.

Aramco's profits were phenomenal from the start. It was a poor
year in which effective returns on capital invested fell below 200 per
cent, since the company was able to supply its owners with crude oil
significantly below the market price. Yet, for all its size and prosperity, the mighty conglomerate felt a certain vulnerability in its Arabian
fiefdom, for it soon discovered that the Al Sa'ud could be remarkably
exacting landlords – as landlords tend to be when they are running
themselves into debt.

Never quite able to catch up on himself, Abdullah Suleiman was for
ever securing larger and larger foreign loans against future oil
revenues. But the interest on these loans, and the improvidence of his
masters, outstripped the actual revenues when they finally came in,
and, since the Finance Minister found it impossible to be strict with
Abdul Aziz, it was Aramco that he squeezed. Al Suleiman set up an
aggressive inspection post at Dhahran to monitor Aramco's expenses
and production volume; the oil company was pressed to pay higher
royalties, it was threatened with 'income taxes' if it refused, and in
1949 it was asked to surrender those areas of its concession that it had
not explored so that they could be offered to other companies.

Almost anywhere else in the developing world, such arrogance on
the part of a native regime would have received short shrift. But the
size and mystery of Arabia, and the very real power that the Al Sa'ud

* Shares in Aramco were distributed to Socal, 30 per cent; to Texaco, 30 per cent; to
Esso/Exxon, 30 per cent; and to Mobil, 10 per cent.

exercised inside its boundaries, prevented Aramco from treating the country like a banana republic. The oilmen felt constrained to behave in the Kingdom with a deference to local feelings uncharacteristic in their industry, and Aramco's history was one of enlightened and political concession: all the water wells Ibn Sa'ud wanted; help with his Riyadh–Dhahran railway, which everyone but he wrongly considered a white elephant; generous education and social welfare facilities for local Sa'udi employees; the first 50:50 profit-sharing agreement in the Middle East; and, in 1949, the claim on the Trucial Coast and its hinterland.

Enlisting Abdul Aziz's help in the claim for Buraymi was a good way for Aramco to increase the king's sense of partnership in their affairs, and it was also a necessary geographical exercise. In order to define the areas its prospectors had not explored, Aramco had to establish what territory it had been entitled to in the first place – and it rapidly discovered that no one knew precisely where Sa'udi Arabia's eastern frontiers lay, least of all the Sa'udis themselves.

One answer was contained in the Anglo–Turkish Convention of 1913 which had fixed the boundary of 'le sandjak Ottoman de Nedjd' along a 'blue line' to the west of the Qatar peninsula; another possibility was the 'red line' which Abdul Aziz had himself proposed in 1935, while various 'violet', 'brown', 'green' and 'yellow' lines had also been discussed in the 1930s during some inconclusive negotiations with Britain – complicated, at one stage, by a British minister who was colour-blind. Yet all these boundaries, including Abdul Aziz's own proposal of 1935, signally failed to include inside their limits the oasis of Buraymi where the oil was thought to lie, and so Aramco organized a team of Arabist scholars and researchers to see if they could not come up with something better.

They did. Delving into two chronicles compiled by poets whom the Al Sa'ud patronized, Aramco scholars formulated a glowing version of early Sa'udi history – which, in the absence of any alternative sources and research, remains to this day the basis of our knowledge about Muhammad ibn Abdul Wahhab and the early conquest of the Al Sa'ud. Then the Americans compared these chronicles with the records of taxes that the Governor of al Hasa had levied from time to time in the Buraymi area – to produce, eventually, a bulky three-volume compilation which claimed not just Buraymi for Sa'udi Arabia but also some 200 miles of 'beaches, banks and islands' along the Trucial Coast itself.

Aramco's scholars seized avidly on the bedouin tradition of 'boundaries in men's hearts' to support their case, claiming the Trucial Coast, for example, on the grounds that certain clans of the Beni Yas tribe, who fished and dived for pearls there, had given their allegiance at times to the Al Sa'ud.

'The deserts of Arabia are not the plains of Picardy,' explained the Aramcons, excusing themselves, as sophisticated scholars, for haggling over frontiers in the style of the unlettered Ikhwan.

But at least the zealots who had wreaked such havoc along the borders of Kuwait, Iraq and Transjordan in the 1920s had been bedouin on the ground, with a genuine stake in traditional grazing routes and rights of passage. Aramco were a Western corporation anxious to secure a fixed asset, and concerned with nomadic traditions only in so far as they could use them to prove their own case. They ignored the intrinsic nature of the allegiance that lies in men's hearts – that it is a mobile thing – for in the course of 200 years the inhabitants of Buraymi had inevitably shifted their allegiance in several directions, following the local power balance as it swung between the sheikhs and sultans on either side of them.

Abu Dhabi and Muscat/Oman had perfectly respectable tribal precedents of their own for claiming the oasis – not much stronger, but certainly no weaker than the Sa'udi claim. Nor did Aramco care to make much of the reason why the Al Sa'ud had originally coveted Buraymi: to levy taxes on the revenues of the slave market there, which still flourished in 1949 and was still dispatching caravans of slaves for service in Riyadh.

Thirty-three months after the formal Sa'udi statement of claim, the oilmen acted. Steering his way by Aramco maps, riding in Aramco trucks and stocked with Aramco supplies, a Sa'udi functionary from al Hasa, Turki ibn Abdullah ibn Utaishan, bumped across the 500 miles of desert from Hofuf to Buraymi and there proclaimed himself emir of the oasis.

Ibn Utaishan was accompanied by a staff of thirty to forty bureaucrats and armed policemen, and, since 1 September was the Eed al Adha, the new emir invited the local inhabitants to a series of feasts for which sheep were slaughtered by the score. Word soon spread of Ibn Utaishan's extraordinary hospitality, bedouin travelled for miles to enjoy it, and as they made their farewells they were very happy to put their thumbprints on the sheets of paper that the emir's aides had set out considerately on a table beneath the palms. Few, if any, of the guests can have realized, as they trailed home fed and happy into the wastes, that their thumbprints and names would soon be on their way to Geneva as proof to an international tribunal that their lands and flocks and homes should be consigned irrevocably to the sovereignty of Sa'udi Arabia.

It is not certain how much Abdul Aziz realized or cared what Aramco was doing in his name. Abdullah Tariki, later Sa'udi Arabia's first Oil Minister, then a young official charged by Abdullah Suleiman with the monitoring of Aramco's pumping, sales and royalty accounts, remembers accompanying Aramco executives to an early 1950s meeting with the old king, now crippled and almost immobile with arthritis in his palace in Riyadh.

It was Tariki's job as interpreter to get across the details of the various tactical ploys for which the oilmen sought royal support, but it soon became clear that Abdul Aziz was taking in very little of what they said.

'You are my friends, you are my friends,' he kept repeating, beaming rather vacantly at the earnest Americans with all their complex proposals. 'You can count on me. Anything you want, anything you want. . . .'

It was a sad final scene for the Lion of Nejd. 'Anything you want' was his response to the oilmen, to the American ambassador, to all the brothers, sons, wives and advisers as they came to him with their insatiable demands – and all that Abdul Aziz asked in return was for some medical assistance that would stop the pain in his knees and which, more importantly, would also revive his sexual powers. The king's forty-third and final son, Hamoud, had been born in 1947, and that child was a solitary arrival after four long and blank years filled with the desperate efforts of the royal physicians to revive the potency that had expired with a clutch of births in 1942 and 1943.

After the commander of the USS *Murphy* thought he had seen the last of the Sa'udis and all their sheep at Suez in 1945, he received a desperate call from one of Abdul Aziz's doctors who had left the royal medicine chest on board, and, sneaking a look inside before returning it, one curious American officer discovered it to be filled with the most extraordinary array of aphrodisiacs.

'I have my responsibilities,' Abdul Aziz used to mutter, 'I have my responsibilities,' and he brooded as old age made it more and more difficult for him to fulfil them.

It had long been Yussuf Yassin's special skill – and one key to his

294

influence – to secure ever more luscious concubines for his master, and in the quest for rejuvenation the Syrian drove their ages lower and lower, on the ancient theory that some transfer of vitality can be sparked by contact with the flesh of barely nubile little girls.

But it was to no avail. There were occasional flickerings of the old lasciviousness. At one soirée towards the end, Philby remarked on the new medical use of frogs in the West to determine whether or not a woman was pregnant, and a hilarious and increasingly ribald conversation developed as to how precisely the frogs might discover this. Were they especially small and slippery frogs?

Abdul Aziz quite recovered his old gaiety, and soon afterwards one of the royal entourage quietly slipped a bottle of Orston tonic pills to Philby to secure his translation of the precise dosage required.

In 1947 Dr E. A. White of the American Legation in Jeddah had given Abdul Aziz a thorough medical examination, and had been able almost to chart the king's life history on his body:

There are two exit and entry bullet wounds, anterior and posterior to the left iliac crest [the upper flank] . . . a sabre scar on the medial plantar aspect of the right foot. . . . The eyes reveal blindness of the left eye due to corneal scarring of trachoma. . . . All teeth are intact and in excellent condition. . . . The heart is not enlarged, pulse 76, blood pressure 158/90, sounds of good quality with a soft apical systolic murmur. The abdomen is soft and rather obese. There is a small umbilical hernia which has been present all his life.

Abdul Aziz was then seventy and Dr White summed up his patient's condition as 'one of excellent health for a man of his age'. The king's only serious affliction was hypertrophic arthritis in his knees, and the doctor gave Abdul Aziz a life expectancy of 'at least 10 to 15 years'.

But less than three years later, in April 1950, a special US medical mission to the Kingdom was reporting Abdul Aziz as 'considerably aged and enfeebled', 'increasingly senile' and confined permanently to his wheelchair.

The royal arthritis, which Abdul Aziz attributed alternately to ancient battle wounds and to bathing in cold water when a child, had struck him down cruelly, and the disability appeared to have afflicted his entire state of health, mental and physical, for the king did not even gesture to rise, but remained slumped in his wheelchair when greeting the American doctors, who included President Truman's own personal physician, Brigadier Wallace H. Graham. 'The fire', wrote Philby, 'had gone out of him.'

The king spoke in a low, hoarse and dejected whisper, he mumbled his words, and he had no appetite for food of any sort, subsisting on warm, slightly curdled camel's milk, which he continued to drink from the same ancient chipped enamel mug he had always used.

Ramps were built in his Jeddah palace so that Abdul Aziz could be driven by motor car, if he wished, right up on to the roof to hold his *majlis* in the old style. But his attention wandered, he would fall asleep, and everyone would sit around in embarrassed silence, shy of continuing their conversation, and scared of waking the king from his slumbers.

One British diplomat, quite unaware of the problem and angry at delays he was encountering at some lower level in the hierarchy, voiced his annoyance to the chief of protocol. 'Someone's going to sleep round here,' he complained, and the outrage he provoked required an apology at ambassadorial level.

There was an attempt in July 1950 to celebrate the golden jubilee of Riyadh's capture with free mutton and camel feasts in every town, village and settlement in Sa'udi Arabia – an expense, wrote Rives Childs, 'completely out of proportion . . . to the already wretched state of the country's finances'. But the celebration was ruined for the old king by the death on its eve of his beloved sister Nura. Then in the following year his bright young son Mansour, the Minister of Defence, also died, still only in his twenties.

Nearly blind in his good eye, practically immobile below the waist and wearing thick woollen socks and Western slippers to try to maintain the circulation in his ankles, Abdul Aziz took to spending more and more time in his harem, in the quarters of his favourite, Umm Talal, sipping coffee, gossiping gently of the past and slipping off into long reveries as he fingered nostalgically the 7-foot spear he still kept beside his bed.

He had little interest in the world around him. When Daan van der Meulen saw the old king in March 1952, the royal beard and moustache dyed black, the gaze dead and lustreless, the Dutchman was struck most painfully by the royal voice: the music had quite gone out of it.

An American oilman at the meeting tried to make conversation, telling the king how he himself had just recovered from a serious illness and how he now saw how wonderful God's world was, how beautiful the fair sex could be, and that what really mattered in life was not money or success but religion. Religion ranked above all other things.

The old Wahhabi was not impressed. 'Tell him', said Abdul Aziz witheringly to his interpreter, 'that if he had been a Muslim he need not have fallen ill in order to understand what matters in life. We knew that long ago.'

Overawed by their father to the end, Abdul Aziz's sons did prevail upon him in the final months to delegate some of his powers to Crown Prince Sa'ud and to a Council of Ministers formed in March 1953. In the blazing summer heat of that year, the seventy-seven-year-old king was flown south to the cool heights of Taif, lying on the wide interior-sprung mattress with which President Roosevelt's DC3 had come supplied, and there, at the old Hashimite mountain resort, inside the palace of his second son Faisal, Abdul Aziz ibn Abdul Rahman Al Sa'ud died in the small hours of 9 November 1953.

It was not, in truth, before his time. Abdul Aziz had outlived himself in many senses. The old man's mouldering away only six years into the ten to fifteen years that the American doctor had so confidently predicted for him in 1947 was not a consequence of some new illness, but rather a recognition that life held little more for him to give or to receive. Depression at his physical afflictions, sorrow at the deaths of those he loved, fury and confusion at debt in the midst of plenty and delinquency at the heart of his own family: a multitude of disillusionments contributed to the erosion of a great man's will to live; Abdul Aziz preferred to join his Maker in that garden where fruit and camel's milk appeared without the need for ledgers and budgets, and where he would never again fail to satisfy, or be satisfied by, the luscious houris who would wait on him morning, noon and night.

Abdul Aziz had invented a country, but when he died that country's flag did not fly at half-mast, for the Sa'udi flag is inscribed with the word of God, and that word cannot be lowered to mark the passing of any man, even if he has done as much for his Creator as Abdul Aziz had. The Lion of the Desert would not have expected otherwise, for he wore his Master's leash and collar to the end without chafing.

Nor can you today easily identify the last resting-place of His Majesty King Abdul Aziz, for, though a few plain flat stones were placed upon the spot where he was laid to rest in his simple shroud, there is no tombstone or graven monument to the greatest modern Wahhabi. His remains lie somewhere in the sun-bleached dust of a communal cemetery, his memorial in the hearts of his family and of his people.

32 King Sa'ud

Though the Wahhabi movement had thus, at the summit of its
power, subdued the whole peninsula with blood and arms and filled
the courts of Stamboul and Teheran with terror, it already bore
within it the germ of decay.

The heaping up of countless treasures in the capital necessarily
induced a corruption of simple customs – luxury, favouritism and
pride were the order of the day.

As an example, Sa'ud was not ashamed to wear a
gold-embroidered mantle worth two hundred thousand piastres.

Professor Julius Euting, describing the first Wahhabi empire
at its zenith in the early nineteenth century

NASRIYAH Palace was a home that Sa'ud bin Abdul Aziz
had built for himself as crown prince in the desert outside
Riyadh. Within Nasriyah's gates an avenue of tamarisk trees led past
flower beds, bushes and vivid green lawns, all sprinkled with water
from wells drilled tens of thousands of feet below the ground, and any
visitor reclining beside Nasriyah's blue-tiled pool where water gurg-
led and caged birds sang could well understand why one Arabic word
for garden is 'little paradise'.

Crown Prince Sa'ud liked to invite Western dignitaries to his
Nasriyah Palace towards dusk, and when the daylight had almost
vanished he would make a quiet gesture to one of his aides. Moments
later the darkening garden sprang alive as hundreds of coloured light
bulbs burst into light. Noiselessly they multiplied down groves and
avenues to the main palace and mosque, the minaret shooting out of
the darkness floodlit blue, yellow, green and red, the Riviera-style
architecture of the palace walls glowing a bright orange. 25,000 light
bulbs made up this sparkling patchwork mantle, and the vast
compound shimmered magically in the darkened desert as though
dropped down by some passing genie. The entire complex of buildings and gardens, it was estimated conservatively, must have cost the
crown prince at least £4 million.

When Crown Prince Sa'ud became King of Sa'udi Arabia in
November 1953, he ordered the Nasriyah Palace to be torn down. It
was no longer grand enough for him, and on its site there soon arose a
£10 million replacement.

The new improved Nasriyah Palace was surrounded by a 7-mile blush-pink wall set with porticoed gates which rivalled the Arc de Triomphe in grandeur; amid the esplanades, swimming pools, boating pools, fountains and palm groves inside were several mosques, a little hospital, a barracks and traffic lights to regulate the flow of Cadillacs around the township; Lebanese architects, the Busby Berkeleys of prestressed concrete, were called in to replace the old Riviera villas with a new palace complex, half Granada–Moorish, half Beverly Hills Hotel; and the entire conurbation was lit by still more thousands of multicoloured bulbs whose electric mosaics focused at regular intervals around glowing neon inscriptions from the Koran. It was a town in its own right, and its lighting, air-conditioning and irrigation were said to consume more electricity and water than the whole of the rest of Riyadh.

The gaudy Disneyland of Nasriyah was later taken as symbolic of all that went wrong in the reign of King Sa'ud ibn Abdul Aziz: too much carnival, too much money. Sa'ud was to end his eleven-year rule barricaded inside Nasriyah's blush-pink walls against the fury of his family, who blamed him for the lack of restraint that brought their prestige and power to the very brink of ruin, and the late and disgraced king still ranks today as a non-person in the pantheon of Sa'udi Arabia's modern rulers.

The photo-icons that hang in every government office, hospital and school feature King Abdul Aziz and his sons King Faisal and King Khalid – with a number of King Khalid's younger brothers usually thrown in for good measure. But of the man who was Crown Prince of Sa'udi Arabia for twenty years and king for eleven, there is little sign. The reign of King Sa'ud ibn Abdul Aziz is a blank in Sa'udi history books, an embarrassing breaking of wind that is never mentioned in polite company, even though King Khalid did cause his Minister of Information to declare in October 1979 that 'the name of the late King Sa'ud should not be omitted from stories of the Kingdom's history: some people skip King Sa'ud when reciting the chronology of Sa'udi rulers, because they think to please His Majesty King Khalid. It is exactly the contrary.'

This exercise in historical revision was prompted by a religious ceremony in Mecca's Grand Mosque which reminded King Khalid, at least, that that massive building and its prestressed concrete sister around the Prophet's tomb at Medina were both largely the work of his elder brother Sa'ud, whose generosity to Islamic causes was

300

prodigious. Sa'ud abolished the taxes which pilgrims had paid in Mecca since time immemorial. 'Let the pilgrim come,' he declared, 'and I will pay the tax. God has given me the money from oil.'

Sa'ud allocated $3 million to the construction of modern *hajj* reception and medical facilities in Jeddah, he constructed complex road systems for the thousands who took advantage of the new giveaway price arrangements in the Holy Land – and he even gave away his own palace in Medina to serve as the campus for an Islamic seminary and university.

Nor was Sa'ud any less lavish in secular matters, for he rushed into the creation of all the welfare facilities and state infrastructure that his country had lacked for so long.

'My father's reign may be famous for all its conquests and its cohesion of the country,' declared the new king on the morning of his accession. 'My reign will be remembered for what I do for my people in the way of their welfare, their education and their health.' The proof of his promise can be seen today in the lumpy megaliths which squat along the lower end of Riyadh's Airport Street: Interior, Communications, Agriculture and Water, Education, Health, all these ministries still occupy the 1950s buildings that King Sa'ud erected for them in a grand palm-lined avenue of secretariats, neo-Stalinist in scale, Cecil B. de Mille in style – and this was just the bureaucracy: several dozen hospitals, several hundred schools, two new universities* and several thousand miles of new metalled highway marked King Sa'ud ibn Abdul Aziz's great leap forward; and the Kingdom nearly went bankrupt in the process.

The Sa'udi budget had weathered the extravagances of Abdul Aziz's later years largely because the old king created few serious long-term financial commitments, and Sa'ud, on his accession, actually made an attempt to restrain royal extravagance by imposing set pensions on every male member of the family: $32,000 a year plus expenses. 'Expenses' was a concept that was interpreted very liberally, but even then royal spending alone never outstripped the oil revenues.

It was the cost of building a modern state infrastructure on top of this that was to bring Sa'ud down, and had he stuck to being a prodigal son he might have survived. What ruined him were his good intentions.

* Riyadh University was founded in 1957 as a 'College of Arts' (though the art section of the library was marked 'restricted access'), and Medina University started life as a theological seminary in 1961.

People who met King Sa'ud ibn Abdul Aziz in his earlier years searched hard for reflections of his famous father, and they seldom allowed themselves to be disappointed. 'Sa'ud presents the picture of a large and powerfully built man, of robust health, abounding vitality, physically and mentally alert, of unusually attractive personality, equipped with a strong decisive will, and possessing considerable animation and charm as a conversationalist.' This American assessment in the early 1950s could have been written of Abdul Aziz in his prime, and whenever Sa'ud set out to please foreign visitors, they invariably pronounced him gentle, charming and exceedingly goodhearted.

The bedouin liked him too, for Sa'ud's openhandedness to the tribal chiefs outdistanced even his father's. Sa'ud loved to camp out in the desert in huge air-conditioned trailers from which he dispensed hard cash in sacks, and when he drove out of Riyadh to pray at sunset in the desert he followed his father's example and took with him on the floor of the car two bags, one containing gold, the other silver coins. But, whereas Abdul Aziz would hand his bounty out carefully through the window of the car, Sa'ud literally scattered his largesse to the winds, sprinkling gold and silver in showers and laughing happily as children dived for the treasure in the dust behind his speeding car.

Sa'ud tried to emulate his father in many things, and, just as he exceeded his father's compulsive generosity, so he outdistanced his father's other great compulsions: to possess beautiful women and to father countless children. The number of King Sa'ud's wives and concubines was never counted, but his tally of offspring comfortably exceeded the hundred mark – some fifty-three sons and fifty-four daughters. So if Abdul Aziz, as it was said, built up his kingdom with a sword of steel and a sword of flesh, there could be no doubt that his son and successor possessed the fleshly weaponry at least.

And yet, and yet, something was out of key. The gold teeth that flashed when King Sa'ud smiled were one touch of luxury too much. The amiability that pleased so many went with an almost total inability to say 'No' to anyone – and 'No' is something that even a wealthy king must say from time to time. The grape-like eyes behind their thick pebble lenses lacked a spark, a certain vital wattage; and the royal handshake was somehow a flaccid affair. Big, soft and friendly, Sa'ud ibn Abdul Aziz was fifty-one years old when he inherited control of Sa'udi Arabia in 1953, and he had waited many years for the responsibility. He never quite rose to it.

The strengths and weaknesses of the new king became apparent in the very first weeks of his reign, when plans for a remarkable Sa'udi tanker fleet were drawn up in Jeddah. Instead of Aramco carrying away Arabia's oil in their own ships – to their own markets, and at their own prices – Sa'udi oil would henceforward travel in ships owned and controlled by the Sa'udi-Arabian Maritime Tanker Company. A Sa'udi Marine Training School would teach young Arabians to become tanker navigators and captains, and over ten years more and more oil would be taken away from Aramco's ships until, by the mid-1960s, all the shipping of Sa'udi Arabia's principal resources would be in Sa'udi hands.

It sounded in theory a project that was both visionary and shrewd. Its reality was more muddied, however, for the Sa'udi-Arabian Maritime Tanker Company was to be a partnership existing for the private profit of Abdullah Suleiman, some Jeddah merchants – and the Greek shipping magnate Aristotle Onassis, who flew down the Red Sea in January 1954 to put his signature on the deal.

Onassis was fêted by King Sa'ud in his Jeddah palace and presented with two gold-sheathed swords and a pair of Arabian horses; the Greek's wife Tina was entertained to tea in the royal harem, and Aramco, whose 1933 concession gave them the exclusive right not only to prospect and extract but also to 'transport, deal with, carry away and export petroleum', were told not a word of the agreement that struck at the very root of their monopoly.

Word of the agreement soon leaked out, however, through Onassis's middle-man, Spiros Catapodis, a loud-mouthed Monte Carlo playboy who had set up the deal with Abdullah Suleiman the previous summer in Cannes. The old Finance Minister, who retained his eminence into the beginning of the new king's reign, had been staying at the Hotel Martinez with Muhammad and Ali Alireza,* sons of Hajji Abdullah Alireza, the *qaimaqam* who had surrendered Jeddah's keys to Abdul Aziz in 1925; and the Sa'udis had seen profit for themselves and advantage for their country in the plan which Catapodis proposed. Muhammad Alireza would become Onassis's Sa'udi agent, Abdullah Suleiman would advance the Greek's case to the king, and Catapodis himself would collect a handsome

---

* Ali Alireza was the romantic Berkeley student who had married Marianne Likowski and swept her off to his Jeddah harem. He was in the Sa'udi diplomatic service, and finished his career as Ambassador to Washington in 1978.

OIL

commission on the deal – as he soon made known around the casinos and bars of the Côte d'Azur.

When Aramco heard the news, they turned straight to the US State Department, and on 20 April 1954 US ambassador George Wadsworth delivered a written protest to King Sa'ud. The Onassis-backed tanker fleet offered a direct threat to American interests, complained the ambassador in a strongly worded letter, and Prince Faisal ibn Abdul Aziz had to read the official protest out aloud to his brother, since the king's weak eyesight did not allow him to read ordinary type.

King Sa'ud was not impressed. 'He spoke with some heat and, I thought, irritation,' reported Wadsworth, who saw how America's protests only served to increase the Sa'udis' appetite for the deal. 'To their shrewdly trader mind it follows that if the foreigner cries, he must be hurt financially and they gain in corresponding measure.'

Within a month King Sa'ud defiantly and publicly ratified the hitherto secret tanker agreement, and it looked as if his new reign was going to mark a radical change of direction for Sa'udi Arabia's foreign policy. Sa'ud, it seemed, was intending to swing his kingdom into the fiercely independent and radical path being beaten by Neguib and Nasser, the leaders of the recent revolution in Egypt, and by the fiery Dr Mossadeq in Iran.

But Mossadeq's attempt to nationalize the assets of British Petroleum in 1951 had been foiled by the international oil companies' worldwide boycott of Iranian oil, and Aramco's partners decided to play it equally tough with Sa'udi Arabia. They organized a similar boycott of all Onassis tankers wherever they might be in the world, and they informed King Sa'ud that, when the first vessel of his new Sa'udi–Onassis fleet turned up at Aramco's Ras Tanura terminal, the ship would be turned away.

The king seemed undeterred, and in the middle of 1954 a delegation of Riyadh dignitaries flew to Hamburg to witness the launching of the 46,000-ton tanker *Al Malik Sa'ud al Awal*, the *King Sa'ud the First*. It was a vessel which Onassis had had on the stocks for some time as *Baunummer 883*, and the enterprising magnate decided to proclaim it the flagship of the new Sa'udi tanker fleet.

But Sa'udi social customs could not be bent quite so conveniently for the occasion. The Riyadh delegation adamantly refused to supply a woman to smash a bottle against the new ship's bows, and they agreed to Onassis's candidate, Princess Anne-Marie von Bismarck,

304

only with reluctance. Then they insisted that the dedicatory bottle should not be alcoholic but must contain holy water from the Zamzam spring in Mecca, and, since this does not build up pressure when shaken, Princess Anne-Marie's first attempt at launching clunked dismally against the metal hull. Her second attempt lodged in the floral decorations around the prow, and only at her third essay did the bottle crack and the *Al Malik Sa'ud al Awal* finally start sliding down the slipway.

More serious were the obstacles to King Sa'ud's plans being prepared by John Foster Dulles in Washington. President Eisenhower's Secretary of State could see that the Sa'udi bid to control its own tanker fleet was a first step to Sa'udi Arabia's getting control of her own oilfields; and to block this unthinkable possibility Dulles declared himself willing to 'utilize every means'.

'Every means' in Iran had involved, on top of the almost leak-proof international boycott of Dr Mossadeq's nationalized oil industry, a CIA-assisted coup to oust Mossadeq in favour of the young Shah Muhammad Reza Pahlavi – and Dulles instructed Ambassador Wadsworth to bring home the Mossadeq parallel to King Sa'ud. 'King and advisers', he minuted, 'should ask themselves where they would stand after three years or even one year without the oil revenues.' The effect on the Kingdom would be 'disastrous'.

The warning came just as King Sa'ud himself was starting to have second thoughts about Aristotle Onassis's ambitious project. It did not trouble Sa'ud at all that Abdullah Suleiman was clearly receiving large personal commissions for advancing the interests of the tanker scheme: in the spring of 1954 the king appointed Muhammad Alireza to be his first Minister of Commerce in the full knowledge that Alireza was the Greek's agent in Sa'udi Arabia. But it did worry other members of the royal family, who were not cut in on the deal, and who resented seeing the profits of shipping Sa'udi Arabia's basic resource being handed over to a family of Jeddah merchants.

Abdul Aziz had always banned his family strictly from taking part in business. 'There are two things which do not mix,' he liked to say: 'running a government and making money.' A ruler should concern himself with spending money, not with the sordid business of accumulating it, and he despised the Persian Gulf sheikhs who dabbled in trade. 'Do not compete with the merchants', he would say, 'and they will not compete with you.'

So when, in 1950, his son Talal had applied for permission to set up a cement factory in the east of the kingdom near Hofuf, Abdul Aziz had dismissed the notion out of hand. Only when Abdullah Suleiman had pointed out how young princes could set a good example to businessmen by investing in development projects did the old king relent. He had issued two simultaneous decrees: one granting Talal the cement concession, the other handing over the concession that same day to a local syndicate in which his son was just one shareholder among several.

Abdul Aziz's death let commercially minded members of the Al Sa'ud off the leash, and the new king encouraged their ventures in a bonanza of business concessions which satisfied both Sa'ud's notion of national development and his anxiety to keep all his relatives happy.

Yet one glittering prize in this new business boom was the shipping rights in Sa'udi oil – a guaranteed percentage, for very little work, of the Kingdom's principal export in perpetuity – and when the Al Sa'ud got to thinking about it they decided they did not like the idea of this immense income falling into non-royal hands. Gossip in the palaces of Riyadh began to swing against the Greek shipowner and his Jeddah agents – and Onassis gave his opponents plenty to gossip about.

The root of the problem was Spiros Catapodis. As middle-man, he claimed $2.8 million as his first payment for fixing up the Sa'udi tanker deal, and, when Onassis refused to pay, the outraged fixer assaulted the shipowner in a Nice Airport departure lounge, wrestling his fellow countryman to the ground with the ultimate insult: 'You're not a Greek! You're a goddam Turk, that's what you are!'

Catapodis claimed to any Riviera croupier who cared to listen that Onassis had deliberately deceived him, signing their agency agreement in vanishing ink, and on 24 September 1954 he took Onassis to court, publishing an affidavit whose thirty-four exhibits (letters, cables and photographs) indicated the most disreputable business practice on the part of the Greek shipowner – and willingness, on the part of various Sa'udi ministers and palace officials, to accept over $1.25 million in gifts and commissions.

From the Sa'udi point of view, the deal was dead from the moment it hit the headlines, for certain subjects are considered very very private in Arabia, and business commissions rank second only to family scandals in that respect. In our own day, revelation of the percentage paid to Sa'udis for facilitating sales to the Italian oil company ENI resulted in the immediate cancellation of the contract;

New York Times inquiries into the business empire built up by Crown Prince Fahad's son Muhammad led to a stern paternal instruction to retrench immediately; while the gossip-column attention which Adnan Khashoggi has attracted around the world has blighted his business profile, inside the Kingdom at least.

In 1954 Stavros Niarchos, Onassis's arch-rival, appreciated this completely. He had no interest in the Sa'udi tanker deal except to make sure it collapsed, causing his brother-in-law as much damage as possible, and he dispatched an agent to Jeddah to make sure that King Sa'ud was fully acquainted with the public scandal that Spiros Catapodis was creating in Europe, a mission in which he received direct assistance from the American government. The CIA placed their codes and network in Jeddah at the disposal of Niarchos's trouble-stirrer, since the intelligence agency appreciated how setting Greek on Greek could probably accomplish their immediate purpose in Sa'udi Arabia more efficiently than trying to stir up local intrigue.

The CIA were right. First shocked by the commotion, then bored by all the complications attending something that had seemed a good idea at the time, King Sa'ud dropped the notion of a Sa'udi-owned tanker fleet, allowing Aramco to take the Onassis contract to international arbitration, which resulted, eventually, in a decision in the oil company's favour.

'My mistake', said Onassis ruefully when he came to look back on his Sa'udi misadventure, 'was that I woke up too early and disturbed those who were still asleep'; and the Greek always maintained that his Sa'udi tanker scheme foreshadowed the world of OPEC and the nationalized oil industries of the contemporary Middle East.

But feuding Greek shipowners, shady middle-men and the louche glamour of Riviera *salles privées* had made up an unsavoury cocktail by any standards; the secret Sa'udi commissions and princely jealousies smacked more of private greed than of national purpose, and, instead of indicating what was bright and visionary in the new young reign of King Sa'ud ibn Abdul Aziz, the Onassis tanker affair illustrated more obviously what was mercenary, weak and vacillating.

Developments at Buraymi seemed to point in the same direction. Confident in their possession of the oasis, and holding the three-volume brief prepared by Aramco's scholars, the Kingdom agreed to submit its dispute with the British to international arbitration in the autumn of 1955. But eyebrows were raised at Geneva when the arbitrator from Pakistan arrived a week late – having broken his journey in Riyadh for unspecified reasons – and, when the hearings did open, successive witnesses presented compelling evidence of the money handed out by the Sa'udi government at every level.

The arbitration tribunal was made up of delegates from several countries, including Britain and Sa'udi Arabia, whose representatives were supposed to try to act in an impartial fashion. But quite early in the proceedings one of the Sa'udi witnesses admitted that 'of course' he had taken advice, when preparing his evidence, from the Sa'udi judge, Yussuf Yassin, and soon afterwards Yassin openly passed scribbled instructions across the courtroom to brief a witness who, in Yassin's opinion, was not presenting the Sa'udi case in its most favourable light.

Britain's representative on the tribunal, Sir Reader Bullard, the former minister to Jeddah, was not a stuffy man, but, amazed at such flouting of legal conventions, he felt he had no choice but to resign from the arbitration, and he was followed soon afterwards by the delegate from Cuba and the Belgian president of the tribunal. Sa'udi Arabia's crude attempts to buy influence had made it an international laughing-stock, and there was little sympathy with King Sa'ud's complaints when, in October 1955, a party of British-led troops from Oman occupied Buraymi and expelled the Sa'udi garrison.

Two years into the reign of King Sa'ud ibn Abdul Aziz, it became clear that things were going badly wrong. Sa'ud had cleared out the old guard – Abdullah Suleiman resigned in 1954 – and the new king created a new Council of Ministers. But Sa'ud took little advice from the Council, preferring to rule in consultation with his own sons and entourage, among them his chauffeur and chief mechanic, Eed ibn Salim, whom Sa'ud elevated to be director of the royal garages and then controller of royal budgets.

The new king evidently found it easier to listen to the flattery of men like Eed ibn Salim than to deal with the criticism that his own family began to voice more and more openly, and in the spring of 1955 his younger brother, Talal, the Minister of Communications, resigned his post. This was a public split in the family, the first time that private disagreements had come out into the open since the days of Sa'ud al Kabeer, and it was an ominous sign.

Harry St John Philby, now over seventy, white-bearded, nostalgic, and rather lost without his old idol Abdul Aziz, began to feel that the

308

end was in sight. At the opening of the new reign he had written some hopeful articles about King Sa'ud and his ambitions, but Philby soon came to believe that the latest Wahhabi empire was collapsing as its predecessors had done. 'Appalling corruption', he complained, was corroding every level of the Sa'udi administration – 'as the King knows full well' – and he denounced the young princes who were picking up their morals 'in the gutters of the west'. 'It is surely quite inappropriate,' he wrote, 'that only Muslims should have any alcohol to consume.'

Philby thought he was being reasonably oblique in his criticisms – and perhaps, by his own standards, he was. But King Sa'ud did not agree. He summoned his father's old friend to his presence and publicly spat upon him. All his entourage joined in.

The king demanded an apology and that the old writer should submit all his future work for censorship, and, when Philby flatly refused, two trucks were sent round to the Riyadh home where the Englishman lived with his Muslim wife (another of Abdul Aziz's special presents). A couple of Syrian drivers started loading their vehicles with the books and possessions Philby had accumulated over more than thirty years in Arabia, and on 15 April 1955 Abdul Aziz's oldest and truest Western friend set off northwards towards Lebanon and exile.

As he crossed the Sa'udi border, Philby bade farewell to a couple of bedouin who had accompanied him over the last few miles, and he offered them a gift, which they refused. The old Arabia, he was touched to see, was not yet quite dead.

But, as he drove off into exile, Philby reflected that it was really too simple to cast all the blame for the new Arabia on wicked foreign influence. Extravagance and prodigality were core elements of the Arabian personality – the other face of puritanism.

'Accustomed for generations to living from hand to mouth at the mercy of the seasons,' he noted, 'the Arab has no compunction in dissipating his heritage on the bounteous windfalls which occasionally fall to his lot.' Desert austerity had conditioned the Arabian not to save, but to spend whenever he enjoyed good fortune. Offer a bedouin a sheep, and he will eat it all. Offer him treasure, and he will squander it.

The proud bedouin youths who refused an old man's baksheesh were one authentic face of Arabia. The luxury and wastage of King Sa'ud's Riyadh were another.

33 Colonel Nasser's New Way

COLONEL Gamal Abdul Nasser offered the Arab world a new vision of itself in the 1950s. His intoxicating blend of nationalism and radicalism set the Middle East alight with pride, ambition and an excitement the Arabs had not experienced for centuries. The eloquent Egyptian leader was compared to the legendary Salahuddin (Saladin), a saviour come to chastize the infidel and to deliver the Arab of his woes, and he preached an inspiring doctrine.

The Arabs, declared Nasser, were one nation. They had been subdued by the Ottoman Turks, then divided against each other by the Western imperialist powers. The American-supported creation of Israel was the latest example of this. The time had come for the Arabs to unite once more, and to cleanse their world of Western exploitation.

Nasser had extraordinary personal presence. He was a tall man, broad and beefy like a boxer, with flashing eyes and a prodigious smile, and when he first came to Sa'udi Arabia in 1954 King Sa'ud embraced him as a brother. The Egyptian monarchy, which Nasser and his fellow officers overthrew in 1952, had always adopted a faintly patronizing attitude towards the Al Sa'ud, and when Nasser came to Mecca to do his pilgrimage and to request Sa'udi partnership in his crusade to unite the Arab world the new King Sa'ud responded warmly.

Sa'ud found Nasser as engaging and inspiring as most other Arabs did. The king drank in the Egyptian's heady notions of Arab unity and power, and he was flattered that Nasser had turned to him and not to the hated Hashimites for help. The new king equated Nasser's struggle to eject the British from the Suez Canal zone with his own battle for Buraymi, and he eagerly pledged Sa'udi support for the aggressive and independent Arab stance of Egypt's new regime.

310

Over the months that followed, the incongruous linkage between medieval monarchy and revolutionary state took on solid form. In January 1955 a 200-strong Egyptian military mission arrived to train the Sa'udi army, and generous Sa'udi cheques started encouraging Arab newspapers in Amman, Baghdad and Damascus to trumpet the Nasser line. In several Arab capitals Sa'udi subsidies also funded groups of pro-Nasser agitators – who were willing to turn out, if requested, with pro-Buraymi, anti-British demonstrations as well – and in June 1954 both Sa'udi Arabia and Egypt announced that they would shun Britain's attempt to form a pro-Western military alliance in the Middle East, the Baghdad Pact. The two countries denounced this attempt by an old colonial power to maintain its dominance over the Arabs. Sa'udi Arabia and Egypt considered themselves, and wished to be considered, as a new category of country: 'non-aligned'.

Displaying the same muddled enthusiasm with which he had taken up Aristotle Onassis's tanker scheme, Sa'ud ibn Abdul Aziz seized on Nasser's ideas as a chance to prove the originality and independence of his new reign, and as a substitute for the philosophy of a specifically Arabian modernization that he could not work out for himself. Sa'ud introduced a female *majlis* once a week where women could bring their grievances to him. He developed a school for girls inside the walls of Nasriyah, and on one memorable occasion the king appeared without warning among the unveiled ladies celebrating a Jeddah wedding, to hand out gold watches by the carton full.

The watches did represent tradition of a sort. But surprising unveiled women served little purpose except to offend, and several conservative Jeddah families declined to let their womenfolk attend court functions from that date onwards.

King Sa'ud could sense the trend that Gamal Abdul Nasser represented, but he appeared to have little idea of how to adapt and apply that trend to his own Sa'udi monarchy. Egyptian advisers arrived to set up the bureaucratic procedures of the king's new civil service with express instructions to administer away inefficiency and corruption. But the labyrinthine mechanisms of signatures, counter-signatures and rubber-stampings which they instituted – effectively the old Turkish file system – stimulated exactly what they were instructed to avoid, and the Egyptians' cumbersome procedures bedevil Sa'udi administration to this day.

More sinister, in the long run, were the Egyptian teachers who arrived to staff King Sa'ud's new schools. They were not all disciples

311

of Nasser, but they knew little, and cared less, about the traditional values of Sa'udi society, and they tended to fill their pupils' heads with their own varieties of discontent.

Western observers began to get worried. America and Britain were not totally surprised to hear Sa'udi Arabia praise Nasser's purchases of communist armaments. But then intelligence reports started to suggest that these arms were being paid for, in part at least, by Sa'udi oil revenues from Aramco; and, when Sa'udi Arabia herself began courting Moscow, welcomed a Red Chinese delegation to Riyadh, and sent two princes to Prague to discuss the purchase of Czech arms in December 1955, Washington's alarm bells started ringing.

'Sa'udi Arabia: a disruptive force in Western–Arab relations' was the title of an intelligence report dated 8 February 1956 which surveyed King Sa'ud ibn Abdul Aziz's erratic activities in his first few years of power; and it made depressing reading for American policy makers. The Onassis tanker deal, the Buraymi claim and the Sa'udi-financed subversion on Nasser's behalf throughout the Arab world: all indicated to the State Department 'a tribal dynasty trying to play the role of a twentieth-century nation-state' – and playing it rather badly. The Sa'udi regime 'often resorts to the traditional methods of tribal Arabia,' noted the report, and 'the results are contradictory policies and growing instability.'

King Sa'ud's flirtation with revolutionary Egypt was aiming the Kingdom on an impossible course. Gamal Abdul Nasser courted the Sa'udi monarchy because he wished to get the benefit of its independent prestige and of its money. But a few evenings listening to Cairo Radio made the ultimate objective of his 'Arab socialism' clear to anyone. Egypt and Sa'udi Arabia were supposed to be friends, but somehow this did not prevent Egyptian broadcasters from seizing on the tales of Sa'udi extravagance and corruption that came their way.

There was superciliousness in the way that Egyptians did homage to Sa'ud, 'the bedouin king' – and Nasser himself, in his spellbinding three-hour flights of oratory which were broadcast in their entirety, occasionally allowed himself to be swept away. Then the Egyptian leader would reveal just what he really thought of kings and sheikhs and sultans, and the reactionary obstacles that such antiquated regimes cast in the path of the Arab people's progress.

The first danger sign came in the summer of 1955. A mutiny occurred among a group of Taif army officers. There was talk of a plot to assassinate members of the royal family and to depose King Sa'ud.

Few doubted that Egypt had had a hand in the affair, and, whether Nasser was involved or not, the conspirators were clearly acting in imitation of the Egyptian's own route to power.

King Sa'ud reacted vigorously. One officer was executed and the king set up the internal security system which remains, in essence, the system that protects the house of Sa'ud today. Around himself Sa'ud strengthened his personal *khuwiya*, or immediate bodyguard, the velvet-and-gold-clad retainers who had served his father before him. Beside the army, he built up one crack regiment, the Royal Guard, whose personal loyalties were focused on the figure of the king, and he resuscitated from the network of old Ikhwan settlements a countrywide force of bedouin, half reservists, half full-time regulars, which became known as the 'White Army' because its members wore their own *thobes*, not khaki uniforms.

Today the 'White Army' wears uniforms, not *thobes*, and it is known as the National Guard. But its 30,000 members still wear the red-chequered Arabian headdress instead of a military cap, and the National Guard remains a tribal organization whose basic function is to protect the house of Sa'ud against all comers – including, if necessary, the other Sa'udi armed services.

The National Guard has its own armoured cars, its own independent computers, communications and command structures, and its battalions and platoons are based upon the original tribal groupings in which Abdul Aziz's warriors of Islam were organized. In the mid-1950s Sa'ud ibn Abdul Aziz – who, for all his love of Nasriyah's luxuries, also loved to sit out in the desert with his bedouin – hit upon the idea of revivifying the Ikhwan as a traditional force to defend the Al Sa'ud, and he gave one of his elder sons, Khalid ibn Sa'ud, the job of building up the White Army as a loyal tribal network. As a rabble-rousing townsman, Gamal Abdul Nasser might know how to subvert conventional army officers. He would have less luck with the bedouin.

King Sa'ud travelled to Cairo in the spring of 1956 to confer with Nasser. By now the Sa'udi king was growing suspicious of the Egyptian, but Nasser had a scheme to bring together Egypt, Syria and Sa'udi Arabia in a grand three-cornered union to dominate the Middle East, and Sa'ud reckoned he was better off inside such a grouping than excluded from it. The role Nasser envisaged for the Kingdom was as paymaster to its two more radical partners. Nasser had an annoying habit of calling the produce of the Gulf 'Arab oil', as

313

though the wells of Sa'udi Arabia and the Gulf sheikhdoms were communal property for him to enjoy of right; and, though Sa'ud would not go as far as union with Egypt and Syria, he did agree to finance a tripartite alliance and to stand by both countries in peace and in war.

So the king was not pleased to have his dinner in Riyadh interrupted a few months later by the news that Cairo Radio was announcing the nationalization of the Suez Canal. It was July 1956, and Nasser's momentous step threatened the possibility of war with the West – and the certainty that 40 per cent of Aramco's oil shipments together with 75 per cent of Sa'udi sea supplies, which passed through the canal, would be cast in jeopardy.

Sa'udi Arabia's Egyptian ally had not condescended to give King Sa'ud advance warning, let alone to consult him about Egypt's plan, and when Nasser flew to Sa'udi Arabia two months later, only days before the retaliatory attack which Britain, France and Israel were to launch upon Egypt, King Sa'ud was given still more reason to feel displeased.

Nasser flew to Dhahran, and Sa'ud flew to meet him. There had been strikes among the oilfield workers earlier that year, so local left-wing sentiments could possibly explain the enthusiasm of the huge crowds that turned out to greet Nasser in the east.

But there could be no face-saving rationalizations of the hysteria that swamped the Egyptian leader when he arrived in Riyadh. Tens of thousands of spectators rushed forward, cheering wildly, breaking through the police barriers, desperate to touch the godlike figure. The army had to force a passage for Nasser's car along the road into the capital, and, whenever the Egyptian leader appeared in public in the course of his brief stay, pandemonium broke loose.

Riyadh had never seen anything like it. No member of the house of Sa'ud had ever inspired such spontaneous displays of passion. Public effusions of sentiment were not, of course, in the Sa'udi tradition, but the fact that one Egyptian demagogue, through newspapers and a radio network, could stir the stolid folk of Nejd so deeply gave King Sa'ud much on which to ponder.

When the British, French and Israeli troops attacked Egypt in October and November 1956, King Sa'ud did his duty as a good Arab. He offered Sa'udi airstrips to Nasser's warplanes, and he ordered Aramco to cease oil sales to Britain and France – a curt political instruction which the oil company obeyed without demur,

314

setting a precedent whose importance no one, in the heat of war, fully appreciated.

But, at heart, King Sa'ud ibn Abdul Aziz was furious with Colonel Nasser. The king had had to plead with the Egyptian leader for the safety of the pipeline which carried Sa'udi oil via Syria to the Mediterranean. Iraq had failed to grovel in time and saw her own pipeline blown up. The closure of the Suez Canal and the oil boycott of France and Britain meant that the Sa'udi king had to suffer a 40 per cent drop in revenues at a time when he was heavily in debt – and all this sacrifice was for the greater glory of Gamal Abdul Nasser, whose role as champion of the Arabs was guaranteed for a decade by his Suez 'victory' over the Israelis and Western imperialists.*

It was all too much for the very considerable pride of King Sa'ud ibn Abdul Aziz, and when, towards the end of 1956, the USA offered to forgive and forget recent differences, and to make King Sa'ud the champion of American interests inside the Arab world, the Sa'udi king seized the opportunity eagerly. John Foster Dulles and President Eisenhower had decided that the Middle East was drifting dangerously leftwards, they saw 'non-alignment' as another word for communism – and they believed that only dollars could stop the rot. America's new willingness to buy Arab support was called the 'Eisenhower Doctrine', and King Sa'ud ibn Abdul Aziz was invited to the head of the queue in January 1957.

The first ever official visit of an Arabian head of state to the USA got off to a bad start when Mayor Wagner of New York ostentatiously refused to stage a welcoming ceremony for the Sa'udi king and his party. Sa'ud stepped off the SS *Constitution* from Naples, bearing in his arms his crippled son Mashhur, whom he was bringing to America for treatment, while Mayor Wagner denounced his Sa'udi visitor in that morning's papers as anti-Jewish and anti-Catholic – the latter accusation deriving from the Sa'udi ban on Christian services in Arabia.

But President Eisenhower made up for the snub. When Sa'ud flew to Washington on 30 January 1957, the president was waiting for him on the tarmac, the first time Eisenhower had ever driven out to the airport to welcome a guest, and the Sa'udis were fêted royally for a week.

British and French troops evacuated Suez on 22 December 1956 and the Israelis in March 957, largely on the insistence of President Eisenhower.

They were not all impressed. 'President Eisenhower must be a very poor man,' said one of the king's coffee boys, surveying the tastefully restrained antique guest rooms of Blair House. 'You'd think he'd have a newer place to put his guests in.'

Eisenhower, for his part, also found himself disappointed, for King Sa'ud, somehow, was not quite the man he had expected. The king was only moderately charming – and rather dull. Sa'ud delivered a conventional litany of Arab complaints against the West, but he did not appear to understand why Soviet arms shipments to Egypt and Syria should worry America so much. He thought it quite possible to take all that Russia had to give and yet remain independent of Russian influence.

The president was already under congressional pressure over the support he was offering to the Sa'udi king. 'Here we are,' exclaimed Senator Wayne Morse (Democrat, Oregon) '. . . pouring by way of gifts to that completely totalitarian state, Sa'udi Arabia, millions of dollars of the taxpayers' money to maintain the military forces of a dictatorship. We ought to have our heads examined!'

Stories of Sa'ud's extravagant lifestyle in Riyadh had already made good copy in the American papers, and the lavishness of the entourage the king brought to Washington did not contribute to the image of the wise and progressive Arabian leader that Dulles and Eisenhower wished to cultivate.

Still, there was a basis for negotiation. Sa'ud wanted more money and arms. America wanted his support in the Middle East, and also a renewal of the agreement by which American planes were allowed to use Dhahran Airport. The US Air Force had used Dhahran as a staging post and, at times, as a base since the end of the Second World War, and the existing agreement which sanctioned this was running out.

So a deal was done. King Sa'ud agreed to let the Americans go on using Dhahran for another five years, and he received in return a $180 million increase in American economic and military aid – plus a new American-backed role for himself in the Middle East. Under the aegis of the 'Eisenhower Doctrine', Sa'ud would act as a force for moderation among his neighbours, generally elevating himself as an alternative influence to the troublemaking radicalism of Nasser. A few months later he put the doctrine into practice with some success when the young King Hussein was threatened by a coup attempt. The conspirators were Nasserite sympathizers, and in April 1957 Sa'ud rushed troops and money to Amman to frustrate them.

In later years the monarchies of Jordan and Sa'udi Arabia were to clasp hands firmly to maintain each other's balance amidst the swirling currents of the republican Middle East. But in 1957 Sa'ud was breaking new ground in sending Sa'udi troops to buttress the power of Shareef Husain ibn Ali's great-grandson in Jordan, and he did it out of rivalry with Gamal Abdul Nasser. The Sa'udi king's mistrust of the Egyptian leader had grown into active envy and dislike, and, when in May 1957 Sa'udi police uncovered arms, ammunition and evidence of a serious assassination attempt being plotted by the Egyptian military attaché in Jeddah, Sa'ud decided to retaliate.

Nasser dispatched to Mecca an Egyptian religious leader who swore dramatically that the Egyptian government had known nothing of the mischief that their military attaché was planning, but Sa'ud was not impressed. He dreamed up a plot of his own, a double-pronged attempt to subvert Syria and Egypt at the same time, by bribing Syria's Information Minister to sabotage the union planned between the two countries – and Sa'ud put £2 million into the attempt.

The scheme was as far-fetched as the grandiose sum involved, and Sa'ud did not let his brothers know anything about his plan. He appears to have derived his inspiration largely from a Syrian wife who had told him that all Syria secretly longed to become part of Sa'udi Arabia, and Sa'ud used her father and uncle as go-betweens. For months secret Sa'udi subsidies were channelled to Damascus in an attempt to buy up Syrian politicians, subvert Egyptian relations and perhaps even create a dramatic new Sa'udi–Syrian axis to dominate the Arab world.

But Syrian rivalries betrayed the bribery, and when it was uncovered in March 1958 it left Sa'udi Arabia looking as foolish as she had done at Geneva. The Syrians scornfully publicized Sa'ud's attempts to buy them up like so many tribesmen, producing cheques from Riyadh and even a letter signed by one of Sa'ud's private secretaries; they also maintained that Sa'ud's plotting had encompassed plans to assassinate the Syrian President Quwatli and Gamal Abdul Nasser as well.

Whether this charge was true or not, the Arab world believed it, and Nasser seized on his chance to launch an all-out propaganda assault. Every night Cairo Radio exhorted the Arabian people who had cheered Egypt's leader in Riyadh to rise up against the tyranny of the house of Sa'ud and to bring about the destruction of the Kingdom.

The gloves were off.

34 Enter the Crown Prince

BY the spring of 1958 Faisal ibn Abdul Aziz was watching the behaviour of his elder brother Sa'ud with mounting dismay. Abdul Aziz's second surviving son, Crown Prince of the Kingdom since November 1953, had weathered from a grave little boy to a grave elder statesman. The wrinkles etched deep into Faisal's hatchet-like countenance added a decade to his fifty-four years, and around his fiercely hooked nose his features seemed to hang in a permanent expression of disdain. Faisal did smile sometimes, but it was a wry, surprised smile as if, said one observer, he had been sucking on a lemon and discovered something sweet inside.

Before Abdul Aziz died, the old king had called his two elder sons to the bedroom in which he spent most of his final months. Sa'ud and Faisal had a long history of personal rivalry and disagreement, and the dying king was worried what that might mean when he had gone.

'Join hands across my body,' he told his sons, 'and swear that you will work together when I am gone. Swear too that, if you quarrel, you will argue in private. You must not let the world catch sight of your disagreements.'

So the brothers clasped hands across their father's bed and swore to operate the partnership that had been envisaged for some time before the old king's death – Sa'ud as king, Faisal as crown prince.

But it became apparent quite soon after the accession of King Sa'ud ibn Abdul Aziz that the partnership was not working. Faisal was named President of the Council of Ministers, but Sa'ud treated the Council as a largely ceremonial body. He preferred to make his decisions autocratically, and Faisal resented this slight to the special dignity he felt to be his due. The two brothers were quarrelling from the start of Sa'ud's reign.

Sa'ud tried to rule as his father had, through a secretariat of personal advisers, for he appeared to assume that the full authority

318

Top Abdul Aziz meets President Roosevelt
on board USS *Quincy* in the Great Bitter Lake, Egypt, February 1945
Above With Winston Churchill at the Auberge Hotel on Lake
Karoun, near Cairo, February 1945

Above Abdul Aziz receives American
envoys, December 1943
Left Winston Churchill's
Rolls-Royce leaves Jeddah, 1946

Opposite
Above left A prisoner of the Sa'udi
police, photographed in Asir in 1946
by Wilfred Thesiger
Above right A slave, photographed
by Wilfred Thesiger in the Asir, 1946
Below Abdul Aziz feasts with the
Sheikh of Bahrain (to his right) and
US Minister J. Rives Childs (to
his left); Ras Tanura, 1947

Cyril Ousman, British
pro-vice-consul,
murdered by Prince
Mishari ibn Abdul Aziz,
November 1951

Abdul Aziz in old age

and undivided powers of Abdul Aziz were his to inherit without question. But Abdul Aziz's gigantic authority had been based on a unique and personal lifetime's work. His death left a void which no single figure could occupy, and Sa'ud ibn Abdul Aziz was like any new chief taking over a tribe. He had to earn himself his own consensus.

Sa'ud did not appear to grasp or acknowledge this, and his choice of advisers reflected his insouciance. Yussuf Yassin and Jamal Bey Husaini, an able Palestinian who had joined Abdul Aziz's circle in 1950, had been close to his father. But these non-Arabian favourites had always been isolated figures, the objects of local jealousy and of family irritation, and people actively disliked the ambitious chauffeur-turned-budget director Eed ibn Salim.

By surrounding himself with men who existed solely through his own favour, Sa'ud diminished his power base needlessly, and he displayed the same political ineptitude within his own family. He did pay some attention to his senior uncle, Abdullah ibn Abdul Rahman, Abdul Aziz's intellectual brother who had taken over Churchill's Rolls-Royce, and also to Musa'id ibn Abdul Rahman, a short, stout and pious man, both sons of a woman of the Beni Khalid, the tribe from which his own mother came. But it was not in Sa'ud's nature to listen very hard to advice he did not like, nor to argue very long in defence of his own point of view. He was not, in the final analysis, intelligent enough to do this, and so he found his dealings with his own brighter grown-up brothers painful. He shunned confrontations, and this distaste for natural debate lay at the heart of his poor relations with his brother Faisal, whose long experience of foreign affairs and of government in the Hijaz made the crown prince a difficult and stimulating man to argue with.

Sa'ud did not want to be stimulated. He wanted people to agree with him and to feel fond of him. He tried to buy affection with lavish gifts and handouts, themselves substituted for the hard graft of listening and talking to people. But he could not buy respect and, as he sensed family unhappiness with him growing, he turned more and more to the compliant companionship of his own sons.

At the outset of his reign Sa'ud made his son Fahad chief of his private office, his son Muhammad was given command of his personal bodyguard, and his son Abdullah had supervision of the royal farms and gardens. By 1957 Fahad ibn Sa'ud was Minister of Defence, Musa'id ibn Sa'ud was in charge of the royal palace guards, Khalid ibn

319

Sa'ud was in command of the new National Guard, while Sa'ad ibn Sa'ud had been appointed to command the Private Guard.

The king's brothers did not like it, for leadership was, and is, the principal asset that the Al Sa'ud have to offer Arabia. It is the most valuable commodity in the family shop, and King Sa'ud was devaluing it gravely, in the eyes of his relatives, when he started distributing important jobs to untried youths in preference to elder and better-qualified members of the family.

It also seemed as if Sa'ud was trying to create a dynasty within a dynasty. Today it is clear that the Kingdom is ruled by a collection of brothers, the thirty-one surviving sons of Abdul Aziz, all incredibly wealthy men and operating together in a consensus that reflects their varying ages, abilities and different power bases. It now seems obvious that the family could only develop in this way after the death of Abdul Aziz. But in the 1950s King Sa'ud's favouring of his sons roused suspicions that he was planning to switch the succession away from his brothers and towards his own bloodline. He was also dissipating precious royal patronage, since he did not need to give his own sons so many jobs to win their support. Like his foreign favourites, they were his partisans in any case, and King Sa'ud found himself dangerously isolated when the crisis broke upon him in the spring of 1958.

Finance provided the backdrop, for Sa'ud's ambitious plans to develop the Kingdom had far outstripped his revenues. His $200 million shift of the ministries from the Hijaz to their new buildings along the road to Riyadh Airport had been financed by printing money. The riyal had fallen against the dollar from SR3.75 to SR6.4, the king was $92 million in debt to Chase Manhattan and to other New York banks, and pay for the civil service and the armed forces was months in arrears. Sa'ud ibn Abdul Aziz was simply incapable of distinguishing between having quite a lot of money and having unlimited funds.

But money was only half the trouble. It was Sa'ud's bungled Syrian conspiracy and the sudden isolation in which Sa'udi Arabia found herself in March 1958 that brought matters to a head. The Hashimite kingdoms of Jordan and Iraq had proclaimed a union of their own the previous month. In March the Yemen proclaimed its adherence to the United Arab Republic of Egypt and Syria, which thus gained a foothold on the Arabian peninsula – and in the souqs of Riyadh and Jeddah radical Nasserite pamphlets started circulating.

Merchants were fleeing the riyal, the young and disaffected were stirred up by the rhetoric of Cairo Radio, and the old and religious were alienated by the licence and extravagance that King Sa'ud had sanctioned.

The family felt embarrassed, humiliated and threatened. Their leader had scarcely involved them in his decision making, but now his recklessness had threatened them all. Sa'ud's financial policies had brought his country to the brink of bankruptcy, and his bungled Syrian conspiracy had produced the ultimate Arab catastrophe: loss of face.

Arabs can accept defeat with an equanimity known to few other races. Shame is quite another matter. Sa'ud ibn Abdul Aziz had brought disgrace upon the Al Sa'ud, and disgrace stirred the family into prompt and decisive action.

One evening in March 1958, nine* of King Sa'ud's brothers gathered at the Fakhriyah Palace, the home of Prince Talal ibn Abdul Aziz in Riyadh, for a crisis meeting. They had just heard Gamal Abdul Nasser on the radio, crowing exultantly over the failure of the Sa'udi conspiracy in Syria; they knew of the financial troubles threatening ruin, and they had gathered in Prince Talal's *majlis* to discuss what must be done.

The senior brother present was Abdullah, today head of the Sa'udi National Guard and No. 3, after King Khalid and Crown Prince Fahad, in the hierarchy of the Kingdom. With his thick wedge-shaped black beard and flashing eyes, Abdullah ibn Abdul Aziz looks a fierce man. But he is, in fact, gentle, almost delicate to meet, with a slight hesitation in his speech. The brothers agreed that they must now somehow intervene to shift government in a new direction, and Prince Talal, who had a new private plane, flew down to Medina where the King was staying.

Sa'ud blustered to Talal, denying all knowledge of the plot to subvert the Egyptian–Syrian union. There had been no assassination plan, he claimed. But his protests were unimpressive. His denials would not convince any independent outsider, thought Talal, and the prince flew back to Riyadh to talk to Crown Prince Faisal.

---

* The brothers were: Abdullah, Abdul Mohsin, Misha'al, Miteib, Talal, Mishari, Badr, Fawwaz and Nawwaf ibn Abdul Aziz.

321

Faisal had only just returned to the Kingdom. He had been in America for the best part of a year undergoing serious surgery – a non-malignant tumour and a substantial portion of his stomach had been removed at New York Central Hospital. But urged home by his brothers, he was now camping out in the desert with his hawks north of the capital, and when Talal reached the Crown Prince's encampment, he found his normally impassive elder brother sitting in tears.

'Your brothers are waiting for you,' said Talal.

Back in Riyadh Faisal came to Fakhriyah, and there he and the nine brothers who had met together a few days earlier debated their ideas for reform. It was Ramadhan, so the nine-hour meeting started around 7.30 at night and went on into the small hours of the morning.

Misha'al, Talal and Badr had specific proposals: a defined constitution; new powers to make the old Majlis al Shura a genuine consultative council rather than the largely ceremonial body it had become; a reorganization of government in the provinces – and Talal wanted some better mechanism for consultation inside the family, since all present agreed that this was where Sa'ud had gone wrong. He had excluded his brothers from power. More sons of Abdul Aziz must be brought into a new government of national reform headed by Faisal; and when this scheme was put to Sa'ud next day, the King accepted it almost without demur. The sudden eruption of Nasserite fury had evidently scared him as much as it had unnerved the rest of the family, and, after only an hour's discussion on the evening of 22 March 1958, the assembled brothers reached agreement.

Later that evening the religious readings on Mecca Radio were interrupted with the news that King Sa'ud had handed the government over to his brother Faisal. Sa'ud would remain as king, but Faisal would take charge of the day-to-day running of the Kingdom, and Sa'ud appeared in public at the end of Ramadhan festivities to make clear his support for the new administration that his younger brother was now organizing in his name.

Faisal had already decided that he would have to act as his own Finance Minister to establish some control over government spending. With the end of Ramadhan approaching, he was plunged straight into a financial emergency, for Ramadhan is the time of salary bonuses in Sa'udi Arabia – one month's extra pay – and all the wage arrears that Sa'ud had built up would have to be paid off too. For

Faisal to default on civil service pay would be like a Western employer sending his staff home on Christmas Eve without their Christmas box – and no pay since the summer holidays either.

Faisal later said that, if he had known how bad things truly were in Ramadhan 1958, then he would never have taken the job his family forced upon him, for when the crown prince went to find out how much ready cash was on hand to meet his current expenses, he discovered just 317 riyals – less than a hundred dollars.

This 317 riyals has become part of the folklore of modern Sa'udi Arabia. It is the figure that Faisal's partisans specify whenever they describe the parlous straits from which he rescued the country. Others scoff at such an oversimplication of an oil state's financial affairs. But nothing could have been simpler than the reaction of the first source to whom the new Finance Minister turned in hopes of a SR25 million bridging loan to tide him over the next few weeks. Salim bin Mahfouz, the owner of Sa'udi Arabia's largest private financial institution, the National Commercial Bank, turned Prince Faisal down flat.

Salim bin Mahfouz was an entrepreneur from the Hadhramaut who, like many merchants from that sultanate on the coast of southern Arabia, had come north to Jeddah and Mecca to seek his fortune. Many modern Sa'udi business dynasties – al Amoudi, Binladen, Binzagr, Baroum – are of Hadhrami origin, and Salim bin Mahfouz arrived in the 1930s to work as a tally clerk on the money-changing tables of some relatives in the Jeddah souq.

From these humble beginnings he had built up the National Commercial Bank, today in the world's top two hundred, and one element in his early success had been the many depositors who, in obedience to the Koran's strictures against usury, had refused to accept the interest to which their substantial balances entitled them. The royal family had benefited from bin Mahfouz's handsome reinvestment margins, since most of the Al Sa'ud banked with him, and he had been able to float them through their recent cash-flow problems.

But by the spring of 1958 bin Mahfouz had had enough. Sa'ud had defaulted on several massive loans from the National Commercial Bank, and another SR25 million was just too much. The bank was already over-extended on other commitments.

Faisal was furious. He withdrew his own personal deposits with the National Commercial Bank and told his family to do the same. He had foreign consulates inform travellers on the forthcoming pilgrimage that no cheques drawn on the NCB would be honoured by the Sa'udi government, and bin Mahfouz, fearing appropriation, told his principal customers to clear their money out of their accounts with him while they could.

But, as Faisal was to admit when he publicly handed his own monies back to bin Mahfouz a year later, giving the banker power of attorney to handle his personal affairs, the shock of rejection concentrated the mind wonderfully. Faisal was able to secure a short-term loan from the smaller, newly founded Riyadh Bank, to send the government servants home happy with their pay arrears and Eed bonuses; and he persuaded Aramco to guarantee and renew debts of $92 million owed to the New York banks. The Crown Prince had won his breathing space. Now he had to make the economies that would turn his financial position around.

Faisal started by placing a total ban on the import of private motor cars. Princes could learn to run their Cadillacs a little longer before junking them. Faisal restricted the export of capital from the country, and he forbade all government expenditure except the payment of salaries and unavoidable emergencies. He cancelled his brother's £5½ million subsidy to Jordan along with Sa'ud's other subventions across the Arab world – which saved Faisal cash and had the additional advantage of placating Gamal Abdul Nasser. And in January 1959 Sa'udi Arabia's first royal Finance Minister produced the first national budget that was worthy of the name.

Previous attempts to forecast Sa'udi revenues and spending had been pious hopes at best. But Faisal proclaimed targets that he stuck to, most notably in the distinction he drew between private and public spending. The Privy Purse was set at SR252 million out of a total of SR1400 million – at 18 per cent still a princely proportion of the national income. But now this allowance became more of a limit than a starting point for royal extravagance.

The Al Sa'ud had been paying themselves set pensions from the exchequer for some time, but it had always been possible, in practice, for princes to get themselves more money when they wanted it. Now Faisal insisted that his family stuck within their allocated revenues. King Sa'ud could go on throwing gold sovereigns from his car windows if he wanted to, but this bounty must come out of his own allowance, and when it was finished there would be no more.

The government's central accounting office, the Sa'udi Arabian Monetary Agency, SAMA, was given increased authority to say 'No' to spending requests, all banks had to deposit 15 per cent of their funds with the agency, and by November 1958 SAMA was able to report that the legendary SR317 cash in hand had swollen in less than nine months to over SR60 million paper currency in the vaults. An elaborate repurchasing of riyals dragged the exchange rate against the dollar down from SR6.4 to SR4.75, and Faisal enlisted as his principal aide in his economy drive his plump and pious little uncle Musa'id whom he made Comptroller General of State Accounts.

Sometimes it was just impossible for Faisal to say 'No' to a spending request. He could not depart too radically from the generous traditions of his father. He would say 'Go and get the money from my uncle' and, when the petitioner arrived to see Musa'id, the Comptroller General would smile affably and explain how there was a temporary shortage of funds, but that it would be all right in a week, or perhaps two weeks, if the petitioner could come back then.

Two weeks later the money certainly was there, waiting to be paid out promptly. But now, of course, Musa'id would need a proper letter with Prince Faisal's signature on it. When the petitioner had managed to secure the letter, the document would need to be ledgered, endorsed and authorized by all manner of departments, where many small cups of sweet tea were drunk in silent waiting rooms until, from one gentle obstruction to another, more and more cash stuck inside the government's accounts. By 1960 Sa'udi Arabia was on the road to balancing its budget for the first time in its history.

At the heart of the economy drive was Crown Prince Faisal himself, for, if Sa'ud's bounty represented one aspect of the Arabian tradition, Faisal's austerity reflected another. The contrast could be seen in the very frames of the two brothers, Faisal's face lean and drawn, his spare body an emaciated shadow beside Sa'ud's overflowing bulk; and this distinction permeated every aspect of their lifestyle.

No velvet-clad bodyguards dripped off Faisal's car as he travelled without fanfare around Riyadh, driving himself without a chauffeur on occasions. His homes were simple, his children unspoilt. He spent long hours in his office, working laboriously through his in-tray, welcoming his brothers there to discuss and argue policy, and generally beginning to infuse Sa'udi-Arabian government at its highest level with a restrained and painstaking ethic it had never known before.

Prince Faisal and the Greedy Poet

King Abdul Aziz had spent many hours in his *majlis* listening to the recitations that ancient bards had composed in his honour. The old king accepted it as one aspect of his duties and, if, on occasions, the monarch's head could be seen nodding downwards on to his chest, the poets did not mind too much, for often they would find that their verses were the more richly rewarded afterwards.

But King Sa'ud ibn Abdul Aziz found these recitations antiquated. He developed the habit of extending his hand for the manuscript that the bard was reading from, and then, smiling graciously, he would pack the poet off to the treasury for his reward. This pleased everyone concerned, for king and bard were both spared the pains of recitation, and if it meant that poets started to multiply in the royal *majlis*, handing over their compositions unread and then beating a path to the royal counting house, that was not the sort of problem to worry King Sa'ud.

But when Prince Faisal ibn Abdul Aziz took over his brother's government, and when his own *majlis* began to reflect the new power and influence that he had acquired, then the poets began thinking that they should, perhaps, try sipping at this new well of patronage. Prince Faisal was known as a connoisseur of poetry – he had even written some well-rounded verses of his own – and so one day one of the regular composers of odes in King Sa'ud's honour appeared in the presence of the newly important crown prince.

Confidently the poet held out his roll of manuscript to the prince, and Faisal surveyed him quizzically.

'What,' inquired the crown prince, 'might this piece of paper be?'

'It is a poem, oh long of life,' explained the poet, 'a poem that I have composed in your honour.'

'And do you not usually read out your poems?' asked Faisal sternly.

'Why, certainly, oh long of life,' replied the poet stutteringly, and he read out his poem – which was, in truth, a short one, for he had not anticipated that he would be required to read it out aloud.

In the silence that followed, Prince Faisal appeared to be waiting for more – and then he held out his hand.

'I feel', he said, 'that there must be more of value than one can see at first sight buried inside your verse, and I would like to dig for it. Give me your paper and come back to me tomorrow.'

326

So the poet went away happily, confident that he must be due for some great reward if Faisal, having heard his ode, had expressed the wish to read and study it, and next morning the versifier presented himself expectantly before the prince.

'Ah yes,' said Faisal, recognizing the petitioner, 'I found your poem of yesterday most interesting and I have studied it closely. If you will permit me, I would like to offer you something which I hope you may find of equal value.'

The prince held out to the poet an envelope, which looked as if it must contain a very large reward indeed. But when the poet opened it he did not find money. Inside was a poem of his own which Prince Faisal had composed.

35 OPEC

IN the summer of 1960 in New York's Rockefeller Center, Monroe Rathbone, newly appointed chief executive of the world's largest oil company, decided on the tactics of the bargain basement. There was a glut in world oil supplies, and Standard Oil of New Jersey, known to motorists in 1960 as Esso and today as Exxon, was suffering more than any other company. The international economy was not active enough to burn up all the energy available to it. The Russians were making things worse by dumping oil at cut rates, and major customers were starting to tell Esso that they could get their oil cheaper elsewhere.

Esso would have to slash its own prices, decided Rathbone, and to maintain its profits it would have to reduce what it paid to the producing countries as well. So on 8 August 1960 Rathbone announced that Esso would henceforth be paying 10 cents less for each barrel of crude oil it purchased from the Middle East, and in the next few days BP, Texaco, Socal, Gulf, Mobil and Shell – the other six companies making up the 'Seven Sisters' who then dominated the world oil market – brought their prices down in line with Esso. Instead of receiving nearly $2 per barrel for her oil, Sa'udi Arabia would now receive $1.80, and this meant that the national revenues she had been counting on for 1960–1 would be cut by $30 million.

In Riyadh, Crown Prince Faisal ibn Abdul Aziz was most displeased. He was the more angry because the price cut had been made inside the boardroom of a private Western company which had not offered even token consultation with the producer countries that would be affected.

But Faisal was not caught entirely unprepared. Inside his Finance Ministry he had a radical and original oil engineer who had been planning against the day of such a price cut, and, when Monroe Rathbone made his unilateral announcement, this Director General of Sa'udi Petroleum and Mineral Resources was forearmed with a sharp response.

Abdullah ibn Hamoud al Tariki – the boy from Zilfi whose journey to school in Kuwait had been so perilous – had been a forthright character from an early age. When still a teenager in the 1930s, he had taken it upon himself to propose in the *majlis* of Abdul Aziz that Mecca should not be treated as the property of the Al Sa'ud, but should be an independent city run by a commission representing Muslims from all over the world – a sort of Islamic Vatican inside the Sa'udi state.

'Who is that boy?' growled Abdul Aziz. 'He's too young to know what he's talking about.'

The young man's outspokenness did not discourage Abdullah Suleiman. The Finance Minister sent Tariki on a training grant to study in Cairo, and then Tariki went on to the University of Texas, where he took a degree in petroleum engineering.

Tariki was, and is, an engaging character. He is intelligent, eloquent, with a disarming smile that somehow purses his lips while he flashes his bright white teeth. But he operates on a short fuse, and studying in Houston, Texas, in the 1940s, where people scarcely knew what a Sa'udi-Arabian was, he was several times mistaken for a Mexican. The experience did not sweeten him towards America and all her works.

When he came back to Arabia to work in the Finance Ministry, Tariki was sent by Abdullah Suleiman to Dhahran to monitor Aramco's pumpings and payments to the Sa'udi government. But in the mid-1940s the oil company operated a form of apartheid in its living arrangements, and though Tariki eventually made it into the 'senior' – and hitherto all-American – enclosure, he was originally offered the grade 2 compound.

This was part of what Tariki came to see as Aramco's patronizing exploitation of Arabia in America's interests. The company's president and chairman lived and worked in America and seldom came to Dhahran; they sold Sa'udi oil at special discounts to Aramco's partners, enabling Esso, Texaco, Socal and Mobil to make exaggerated profits on their refining and marketing operations; they pumped the easiest, cheapest Sa'udi fields, with no long-term policy of balanced depletion, and from the beginning they had flared off as waste the natural gas which Tariki saw as a precious national resource to be husbanded.

The oil company pooh-poohed the angry young Arab's complaints about their gas-flaring, and derided his knowledge of petroleum engineering as 'superficial'. But when America's consul in Dhahran confidentially asked Aramco's James MacPherson if the awkward Sa'udi knew what he was talking about, 'Mr MacPherson privately admitted to me that there was something to be said for Tariki's argument in theory and from a very long-range standpoint'.

In 1951 Tariki went to Venezuela. He persuaded Abdullah Suleiman to finance the trip so he could find out how the world's most sophisticated oil exporter had won itself a fair deal from the companies. The Venezuelans had gone to some trouble in 1947 to prepare documentation and to send a mission to the Middle East to compare notes with their fellow producers. But Aramco had prevailed on Abdul Aziz to keep the South Americans out of Sa'udi Arabia. They were troublemakers. So now Abdullah Tariki went to Caracas to do his own research, and what he discovered was a revelation.

In theory, Aramco split its oil profits with Sa'udi Arabia 50:50. This arrangement had applied since 1950, and it suited the oil company much better than expanding the royalty system which it had originally agreed with Abdul Aziz, because the Sa'udi share of the profits was called a local 'income tax' and as such it was eligible under the IRS's rules of double taxation to be deducted in its entirety from the company's American tax bill. This greatly convenienced Aramco, which was able in 1951 to give Sa'udi Arabia the $50 million it would otherwise have paid as tax to the IRS. It also suited the State Department. They could never have got such generous allocations of foreign aid to an Arab country through Congress at a time when Israel was still struggling for survival – and not until hearings six years later was it revealed how long and how massively Sa'udi Arabia had been subsidized in this fashion by the US taxpayer.

But if US legislators felt baulked when they discovered the truth about 50:50, Sa'udi Arabia felt equally cheated. The profit split was after expenses, and the American oilmen conducted their operations in lavish style, with private planes and generous fringe benefits for their American employees.

More serious were the discounts of up to 18 per cent which Aramco gave to its parent companies, who paid only $1.43 for the $1.75 oil that they loaded at Ras Tanura, but who still charged the full market rate for their product when they sold it on. The downstream marketing divisions of Esso, Socal, Texaco and Mobil all made large profits based upon the artificially low prices they paid for Aramco crude – and the Sa'udi government was quite excluded. The Kingdom still received its agreed royalties in addition to its share of profits, but Abdullah Tariki calculated that the special discounts to Aramco's owners reduced his government's share of the true market profit from 50:50 to 68:32 in favour of the Americans.

As Director General of Petroleum in the Ministry of Finance, Abdullah Tariki devoted much of the 1950s to clawing back this advantage from Aramco and its foreign parents. His ambition was to secure Sa'udi participation in every phase of oil production and its marketing – 'from the well to the car' was his slogan – and he made slow progress, forcing Aramco to absorb its special cut rates into its own accounts and to give Sa'udi Arabia its profit on the full posted price, regardless of discounts.

The turning point came in February 1959. The oil companies had put prices up during the supply dislocations after the Suez crisis, and Sa'udi-Arabian Light, the 34° 'marker' crude on whose price all other crude prices are based, had risen to $2.12 per barrel.* Then in February 1959 the 'Seven Sisters' decided to bring their prices down again, knocking some $132 million a year off the incomes of the four major Middle-Eastern oil producers at a stroke. In retaliation, the first Arab Petroleum Congress was convened in Cairo.

This meeting of April 1959 provided Gamal Abdul Nasser with a chance to loose off some anti-imperialist rhetoric, and to pursue his own optimistic attempt to secure a share of Arab oil. But more significant were the plans that the delegates laid behind closed doors. The Iranians and Venezuelans had sent observers to the congress, Venezuela being represented by her ancient oil crusader Perez Alfonzo, and in a private meeting Venezuela and Iran resolved with Tariki and the other Arab delegates that, if the oil companies cut prices again without proper consultation, the producing countries would take action to protect themselves. Their resolution was set down in a secret memorandum to which all assented, and when in

* The price of crude oil is based upon its specific gravity, and thus upon the ease and expense of processing it. This is usually expressed in degrees API, the American Petroleum Institute scale by which light crudes yielding a high proportion of light products – gasoline and kerosene – are denoted by high API numbers. Thus Arabian Heavy is 27° API and Arabian Light is 34°, while many light North African crudes go as high as 40° in Libya and 44° in Algeria. Prices tend to follow specific gravity, since this indicates the workability of the product: the lighter the crude, the higher the price.

331

August 1960 Monroe Rathbone announced his momentous price cuts, Abdullah Tariki knew that his moment had come.

He cabled Perez Alfonzo instantly. Scared of Venezuelan reactions, Esso had confined its 10 cent price cut to the Middle East. But Perez knew that this was the thin end of the wedge. Venezuela would lose sales in the long run to cheap Arab oil, and he told Tariki that he now stood ready to implement the secret agreement made in Cairo.

Tariki went to Prince Faisal. Faisal was his boss, as Minister of Finance, and the prince was indignant at the cavalier wrecking of his carefully worked budget plans. He backed Tariki's scheme to form a cartel of producers to confront this cartel of companies who seemed able to manipulate the world oil markets at will, but he did not want this rebel organization formed in Riyadh. There were not the hotels or facilities for a major conference, he told Tariki, and the influx of foreign pressmen could cause all sorts of problems.

Tariki suspected that the prince's reservations stemmed from a fear that the bold plan might not work. Sa'udi Arabia was about to offend both Aramco and America, and might end up with nothing to show for it except some empty resolutions and yet another Third World organization that made a lot of noise and achieved very little. That was the style of Colonel Nasser, who would himself feel upstaged if Riyadh took such an initiative. Much better for the Kingdom to keep a low profile.

So Tariki flew to Iraq where General Abdul Kareem Qassem was now in power, having ousted the Hashimites in an orgy of bitter blood-letting in July 1958, and Qassem proved eager to host an oil producers' meeting for the very reasons that Faisal had been reluctant. Defying the West and irritating Nasser were two pillars of Qassem's revolutionary fervour, and Tariki flew on to round up delegates from Kuwait and Iran, where the Shah was smouldering over Esso's price cut.

'Even if the action was basically sound,' he later said, 'it could not be acceptable to us as long as it was taken without our consent.'

So on 9 September 1960, in the seedy municipal hall of Baghdad, there gathered together the representatives of the five countries who between them controlled 80 per cent of the world's oil exports: Sa'udi Arabia, Iran, Iraq, Kuwait and Venezuela. They wasted little time on discussions, and they announced almost immediately the creation of the Organization of Petroleum Exporting Countries, known today the world over as OPEC (except to the French and Spanish, who call it OPEP*):

Members can no longer remain indifferent to the attitude heretofore adopted by the oil companies. . . .
Members shall demand that oil companies maintain their prices steady and free from all unnecessary fluctuation. . . .
Members shall endeavour, by all means available to them, to restore present prices to the levels prevailing before the reductions . . .

OPEC had no means of enforcing its demands, and the oil companies haughtily disdained to acknowledge its existence. 'We don't recognize this so-called OPEC,' declared Bob Brougham, President of Aramco. 'Our dealings are with Sa'udi Arabia, not with outsiders.'

For two years the oil companies refused to deal with the first chairman and secretary of the organization, Fouad Rouhani, in his capacity as an OPEC official: he had to attend negotiations wearing all manner of different hats. But the members stuck to the basic principle of solidarity upon which they had agreed: no country would break ranks to accept special terms from an oil company if this jeopardized his OPEC comrades.

This was something new, an agreement on which real power could, in the end, be built, and Abdullah Tariki was hailed as a hero when he brought the compact home to Riyadh. Crown Prince Faisal was especially warm in his enthusiasm, and the Council of Ministers unanimously ratified Sa'udi adherence to the new organization. Suddenly oil became the fashion. Journalists from all over the Middle East started coming on pilgrimage to the Riyadh office of Abdullah Tariki, and he explained to them how the Western companies were short-changing the Arab. They paid artificially low prices for their oil, they hid their profits in the complex accounts of their tanker companies, refineries and marketing organizations, they insisted on sharing their losses by cutting prices in times of glut – but they scarcely shared the massive dividends that they reaped when prices soared in times of shortage.

* The Organization of Petroleum Exporting Countries (Organisation des Pays Exportateurs de Pétrole in French, Organización de Paises Exportadores de Petróleo in Spanish) was founded by Sa'udi Arabia, Iran, Iraq, Kuwait and Venezuela in Baghdad in September 1960. Qatar, who had had representatives at the founding meeting, joined soon afterwards, and today the other members of the organization are Algeria, Gabon, Libya, Nigeria, Ecuador, the United Arab Emirates and Indonesia.

The oil companies' returns on their investment were several hundred per cent per year, claimed Tariki. He came up with a figure of $11 billion, which was, he said, the true profit made by the companies over the past seven years, and he claimed that half of this was due and should be paid to the Arab producers.

Oil started shifting to the forefront of Arab consciousness. People had long known that it was there, but now they began to sense the tangible potential for international influence and respect that lay beneath the sands of the Middle East. Nasser's Cairo speeches continued to articulate the aspirations of the Arabs. But with the 1960 foundation of OPEC it became possible to see how the power to achieve those ambitions might one day lie in Riyadh.

36 'Candidates for Liquidation'

RATIFYING Sa'udi membership of OPEC in 1960 was virtually the last act that Prince Faisal's Council of Ministers took, for at the end of that year King Sa'ud ibn Abdul Aziz announced that he was becoming a proper king again. On 21 December 1960 Sa'ud took back the powers he had relinquished to Faisal two years earlier, and although Faisal nominally remained a member of his brother's Cabinet he took little effective part in his government. King Sa'ud was at the helm once more.

Prince Faisal had been too successful. Balancing the budget, restoring the currency, calming the hostility of other Arab nations in only two years, he had wounded the pride of his elder brother – and he had also given Sa'ud the mistaken impression that running Sa'udi Arabia was quite an easy matter.

Nor were the family and kingdom entirely unhappy at Sa'ud's resumption of his powers, for the price of Faisal's financial achievements had been a sharp economic recession. Since all new development projects except roads had been stopped, and payments on existing works were being made only slowly, in an economy where the government was the prime source of cash, Faisal's thrift had led to business stagnation and unemployment. Villa rents in Riyadh had fallen from SR7000 or 8000 a year to SR3000 or 4000. Banks, merchants and princes who had speculated in real estate around the towns got their fingers badly burned. When Faisal discovered he was actually building up financial surpluses, he did not direct the money into new development projects, but chose to deposit it instead with the World Bank and the International Monetary Fund ($83 million and $55 million respectively in 1960). Putting savings under the bed demonstrated prudent, old-fashioned thrift. But it slowed down economic growth inside the Kingdom.

Commercial and political discontent with Faisal's stringent

economies began to come together. As the memory of the 1958 crisis faded, merchants and reformers found themselves agreeing on the need for more government investment in projects to develop the country, and this was the mood on which King Sa'ud had seized. Inside the royal family the thirty-year-old Prince Talal ibn Abdul Aziz represented a group of discontented and ambitious young princes who felt that they could develop the Kingdom in exciting new directions using the expertise of technocrats like Tariki. Talal and the brothers who had helped bring Faisal to power in 1958 were angry that he had not implemented the constitutional reforms that they had advocated, and it was with the support of this radical group that King Sa'ud took back for himself the presidency of the Council of Ministers in December 1960.

Faisal was demoted to Vice-President of the Council, retaining his Foreign Ministry and dignity as crown prince. But his control over finance was given to Talal, while Badr ibn Abdul Aziz and Abdul Mohsin ibn Abdul Aziz became Ministers of Communications and the Interior respectively. These were new faces, and relatively junior faces at that. Talal ranked only sixteenth in seniority among his brothers; Abdul Mohsin was tenth, Badr fifteenth. The average age of King Sa'ud's new Cabinet was thirty-nine, and it included six commoners, an unprecedented number, headed by Abdullah Tariki, whose new importance was indicated by the upgrading of his Petroleum Department to the level of a full ministry.

King Sa'ud appeared to have moved sharply to the left in that grand style peculiar to reforming monarchs, and under Talal's inspiration there was heady talk of a general assembly, open government, and a fresh democratic way ahead for Sa'udi Arabia. But the contradiction inside the king's new administration rapidly became apparent. On 25 December 1960, four days after Sa'ud resumed power, Mecca Radio announced that the king was going to grant a constitution to the country. On 29 December Mecca Radio denied this categorically. Sa'ud had allied himself with Talal, Tariki and a group of reform-conscious young men outside the royal family who called themselves 'Nejd al Fatah' – Young Nejd. They wanted radical changes in government, but once the King had re-established his position, he took to ruling again in very much the same fashion that he had before the crisis of November 1958.

Sa'ud did try to maintain some of Faisal's financial economies. He made a manful attempt to cut down on the lavishness of his own

entourage, and he started in his kitchens, summoning his Swiss catering manager, José Arnold, to his gilded office in Nasriyah one day for
a brief and brutal budget meeting:

'How many waiters do we have now?' King Sa'ud asked me.
'Forty-four, Your Majesty,' I replied.
'Dismiss twenty,' he said abruptly after a momentary pause. 'How many
cooks are there?'
Again a pause, and again 'Dismiss twenty'. . . .
King Sa'ud posed another question.
'How much money do you spend for palace functions each year?'
'Twenty-five million riyals,' which is approximately five million dollars.
'You must reduce this spending by half,' he said.

Standing over the king throughout this memorably simple exercise
in cost reduction was the former chauffeur, Eed ibn Salim, now
elevated to the directorship of the royal finances. Hovering in his
black robes, Eed looked, in Arnold's eyes, 'like a benevolent vam-
pire', and as the Swiss left the royal presence Eed handed him a sheet
of paper: 'Here is a list of stores where you are to buy the palace
supplies from now on.'
Arnold was not entirely surprised to discover that all the stores on
the list were owned by relatives of Eed or of other royal advisers, but
he was shocked when he went to these shops to replace stocks of
caviare and *pâté de foie gras* that had run low, to discover on their
shelves the very same tins that had been sitting in the palace pantry a
week earlier.
While Arnold was off duty, it transpired, servants of Eed and his
cronies regularly came to the royal kitchens to demand supplies for
their masters. The quartermaster did not dare refuse their orders, and
the goods ended up on sale in the Riyadh souq – the shop where
Arnold made this discovery being named, he noted, the 'Crown
Store'.
José Arnold later wrote a book about his experiences attempting to
manage the kitchens of King Sa'ud ibn Abdul Aziz, a vivid and
humorous little volume which must be the only work of comedy
inspired by the modern history of Sa'udi Arabia. The Swiss entitled it
Golden Swords and Pots and Pans, and King Sa'ud wanders through
its pages like a goodnatured King Lear, exploited by those he trusts,
bewildered by the problems into which he is constantly stumbling,
invariably gracious, occasionally angry, usually just wishing that life

337

could somehow be simpler and kinder to him – but lacking any clear idea of how to swing the game in his direction.

Sa'ud's economy drive certainly did not last very long. Once a new advance had been obtained from Aramco, construction started in Nasriyah on a $500,000 glassed-in veranda dining room modelled on a restaurant the king had admired in 1959 while taking the cure at Bad Nauheim.

Talal ibn Abdul Aziz had quarrelled with Sa'ud when he was Minister of Communications in 1954, and now as Finance Minister trying to stem the fresh tide of royal extravagance, Talal quarrelled with Sa'ud again, for it had rapidly become obvious that the king had no serious intention of implementing the changes and development programme that Talal held dear. After less than eight months in office, the prince was forced to resign from his brother's government, and then a few months later Sa'ud himself fell gravely ill. In the autumn of 1961 the sixty-year-old monarch started vomiting blood and losing weight. Sa'ud had to be flown to the Aramco hospital in Dhahran, where the doctors declared themselves unqualified to treat him properly, and his condition deteriorated so sharply that the oil company were faced at one stage with the alarming prospect of the king's passing away while in their care.

Sa'ud's massive and normally jovial bulk was deceptive. The Sa'udi king had a long history of eye trouble, stomach ulcers and digestive problems, and he also suffered from a recurrent liver complication which had defied medication for many years. When all these royal infirmities came together in November 1961, Aramco's physicians insisted that Sa'ud had to go abroad for the best available diagnosis and treatment. So Faisal returned to power again, less than a year after he had resigned the presidency of the Council of Ministers, agreeing, with some reluctance, to take over the Cabinet in which Tariki was becoming the predominant influence.

Faisal strode into the next Council meeting to occupy the president's chair, and ordered the clerk to play back the recording made of the previous meeting. Faisal wanted to bring himself up to date, and no one could tell what he was thinking as the angry voice of Abdullah Tariki came amplified through the loudspeaker into the silent room.

Tariki was denouncing an offshore oil concession that the Kingdom had sold some years previously to Japanese Petroleum Trading, a combine that included Mitsui and Mitsubishi. The Japanese had bid successfully in 1958 for drilling rights in the sea off the neutral zone

338

between Sa'udi Arabia and Kuwait, and Tariki himself had helped negotiate the concession on terms that were very favourable to the Arabs.

But there was something Tariki had not known when he was engaged in the negotiation, and it was this that was arousing his anger at the Council of Ministers meeting in 1961, for it had just been revealed by the secretary to Mr Taro Yamashita, chairman of Japanese Petroleum Trading, that the Japanese had been 'guaranteed' their Sa'udi offshore oil concession by His Excellency Sheikh Kamal Adham, the brother-in-law of Crown Prince Faisal.

Kamal Adham was the half-brother of Iffat, Faisal's wife. After Iffat's father, al Thunayan, had died, Iffat's mother had married a Turk of Albanian extraction, Ibrahim Adham, and Kamal was his son by this remarriage. Shrewd and personable, Kamal Adham had impressed his much older brother-in-law, Faisal, who treated him as another son, and Faisal had encouraged the young man's business aspirations – his involvement in the Japanese oil deal being one example of this.

Kamal Adham had acted openly as agent for the Japanese from the start of the negotiations. Tariki knew this. He had experienced some difficulty fitting in with Kamal Adham's idiosyncratic business schedule, which involved sleeping most of the day and working most of the night, and Faisal had insisted, it was known, that Adham's 2 per cent should come out of the Japanese, not the Sa'udi share of the oil income.

But the notion of the crown prince's brother-in-law 'guaranteeing' a contract to a foreign company made Tariki see red. The royal family had played with him, fixing the negotiations behind his back, and sullying the clear stream of public interest with sordid private profit. It was like the Onassis tanker deal over again – a positive national initiative marred and muddied by private greed – and at the Council meeting before King Sa'ud fell ill the Oil Minister had not spared his invective.

Now the crown prince listened impassively. 'Have you proof of this?' he asked shortly, and then moved the meeting on to other business. It was as though Faisal had not heard, or had not understood, the minister's attack.

But this was always the crown prince's style. He was not a direct man. Faisal never allowed his chiselled features to betray what he was really thinking, and he had already come to mistrust Abdullah Tariki.

He disliked the Oil Minister's high-profile campaign against the oil companies, the inflammatory interviews in newspapers, the tirades at international conferences; and the crown prince shared his family's unease that someone outside the clan should be speaking so loudly on behalf of Sa'udi Arabia.

Tariki had never hidden the fact that his radicalism extended beyond oil into politics. He criticized the Al Sa'ud openly and vigorously. His ideas and those of the 'Young Nejd' movement had a dangerous, Nasserite tinge, and when he first started causing Aramco trouble in the late 1940s a secret State Department report had noted this as 'a tendency on which Aramco dares hope he may "hang himself" '.

Tariki took rather more time and accomplished rather more of his ambitions than Aramco anticipated in the process of fulfilling their pious hope, but in the end the oil company's analysis proved correct. In March 1962 Faisal removed Abdullah Tariki from the Ministry of Petroleum and Mineral Resources, and in his place the crown prince appointed a more moderate and suave personality, the thirty-two-year-old Ahmad Zaki Yamani, a young Meccan lawyer whose subsequent career was to encompass the nationalization of Aramco and the elevation of Arab oil power to heights never dreamed of in 1962 – though without Tariki's passion and haste, and without treading upon the toes of the Al Sa'ud.

Faisal ibn Abdul Aziz represented much that was new and un-Arabian in the history of the Kingdom: working long, hard hours in his office like a Western executive, sticking rigorously inside the limits of predetermined budgets, and separating royal from public expenditure in the national accounts. But, when it came to family loyalties, Faisal was as fiercely traditional as his father Abdul Aziz. He fought like a tiger for the position, power and prosperity of his relatives, and, when Abdullah Tariki attacked these, the Oil Minister's public career was finished – though Tariki today, after nearly two decades of voluntary exile working as an oil consultant to other Arab governments, has returned to Riyadh, silver-haired and mellower, to set up his consultancy offices just a few hundred yards away from the Petroleum Ministry that he established.

1962 was the year of exiles. After resigning from the Ministry of Finance in 1961, Prince Talal ibn Abdul Aziz had gone to Europe,

340

and he was in Geneva in August 1962 when President Nasser marked the tenth anniversary of his Egyptian revolution by test launching the first Arab rocket missiles. Talal cabled Nasser his congratulations, which Nasser promptly broadcast on Cairo Radio with great fanfare.

But the news of Talal's gesture was not received with favour in Riyadh, for Nasser had of late been renewing his attacks upon the house of Sa'ud.

'To liberate all Jerusalem,' the Egyptian leader had proclaimed, 'the Arab peoples must first liberate Riyadh.'

Nasserite agents were known to be at work both in Yemen and in Sa'udi Arabia, and news of Talal's open praise for Nasser was taken in Riyadh as deliberate disloyalty. Crown Prince Faisal and those around him still resented the role Talal had played in the ousting of the Faisal government in 1960. Feelings had grown bitter. Talal was dubbed by many of his brothers with that most damning of Sa'udi titles, 'troublemaker', and his support for Nasser seemed to lend a sinister dimension to this. Police went into the outspoken prince's homes in Riyadh and Jeddah to search them for subversive material.

When Talal arrived in Beirut on 15 August 1962, he was told that his Sa'udi passport had been revoked. The Kingdom's Chargé d'Affaires in Lebanon arrived in the lobby of the St George's Hotel to take it from him – and the prince responded in kind. He convened an immediate press conference and launched an open attack upon his family the like of which had never been heard before, or since, from any member of the Al Sa'ud.

'In our country,' complained Talal, 'there is no law that upholds the freedom and rights of the citizen. . . . If a person like myself is treated with such harshness, what must be the position of the ordinary man?'

Talal appealed for the creation in Sa'udi Arabia of 'a constitutional democracy within a monarchical framework'; he appealed to the Koran, which 'forbids homes being entered, let alone occupied without their owner's permission'; he proclaimed himself 'a Fabian socialist', and then he flew off to Cairo, where he was embraced by President Nasser and where his proclaimed opinions shifted even further leftwards. The prince proposed state-owned industries for Sa'udi Arabia and the distribution of land to the poor, and he called for the establishment of co-operative farms. He renounced his princely title and broadcast vehement attacks on the Kingdom's existing government over Cairo Radio.

Talal's defection could have been shrugged off by his relatives as a gesture of personal pique, if the prince had not been joined in Cairo by his brothers Badr and Fawwaz ibn Abdul Aziz and by a cousin Sa'ad ibn Fahad, and if Abdul Mohsin ibn Abdul Aziz had not made clear in Riyadh his support for Talal's views.

King Sa'ud, back home after his illness, summoned the correspondent of the London *Daily Telegraph* to his palace for an *ad hominem* attack on Talal – 'he is a man of no weight,' declared the king dismissively – and Abdullah ibn Abdul Aziz travelled to Beirut to make a more philosophic response.

'Talal knows full well', said Abdullah, 'that Saudi Arabia has a constitution inspired by God and not drawn up by man. . . . True socialism is the Arab socialism laid down by the Koran.'

The worst had happened. Almost exactly a century after the family feuding that led to the break-up of the nineteenth-century Sa'udi state, the sons of Abdul Aziz were quarrelling, and amplifying their disagreements through the international media while the whole world looked on.

'I wish that Talal had never left,' said Abdullah, 'and now I wish he would return.'

In Cairo, Nasser gloated over the spectacle of the Al Sa'ud fighting among themselves, and his now daily prophecies of Riyadh's imminent collapse started to appear remarkably credible when, five weeks after the defection of Talal and his brothers, events in the Yemen took a dramatic turn. On 26 September 1962 revolutionaries in Sana'a ousted the Yemeni royal family, proclaiming Yemen a republic, and the Egyptian army arrived *en masse* within days to carry the revolution northwards across the border into Sa'udi Arabia.

Now it really did look as if Riyadh was in danger. Field-guns appeared outside the gates of the Nasriyah Palace, and when Western commentators heard that three Sa'udi aircrews had defected to Egypt they decided that the end was definitely in sight. *The Guardian* sampled opinion on the Middle East's trouble spots to conclude that 'the next coup is considered to be more likely in Saudi Arabia than elsewhere', while the *Financial Times* decided that, in a world where more regimes than ever before faced the prospect of violent overthrow, the Sa'udi monarchy must now be placed 'at the top of the list of prospective candidates for liquidation'.

37 Deposition

CROWN Prince Faisal ibn Abdul Aziz was in America when news of the Yemen coup reached the outside world. Ostensibly he was in the USA for the autumn opening of the United Nations, but the true purpose of Faisal's visit was to talk to President Kennedy.

The crown prince felt that the Al Sa'ud needed to re-establish credibility with the USA. The 'Eisenhower Doctrine' had proved another passing shower, scarcely dampening the furrowed track of Middle-Eastern history and leaving the ruts very much the same as before – except in Washington, where the doctrine's failure had quite discredited the notion of allying with the Sa'udi monarchy as a vehicle for moderation, change or almost any useful or coherent initiative in the Arab world. As friends or allies of any Western government the Al Sa'ud were becoming an embarrassment.

The comings-and-goings between Sa'ud and Faisal, the rhetoric of Tariki and now the squabblings between Talal and his brothers, all served to make Arabia one of those depressing no-win areas of the world which the State Department would dearly have loved to stuff down the back of a filing cabinet and forget about, had not American investment there made involvement unavoidable. Among Middle-Eastern leaders only Nasser seemed to have any clear idea of where he and the Arab world were heading; and the young and liberal President Kennedy felt inclined to back the Nasserite trend for good or ill. Britain, France and John Foster Dulles had all tried to beat the Egyptian leader, and all had failed in their different ways. Kennedy decided he was better off on Nasser's side, and by the early sixties American aid to Egypt totalled $198.7 million per year.

So Crown Prince Faisal met with a wary response in Washington in the autumn of 1962. His fiercely anti-communist feelings were treated as something of a joke by the men of the New Frontier.

'We'll book him six meetings with J. Edgar Hoover,' said one of the officials working on the crown prince's itinerary.

Faisal was treated less seriously than he might have been because it was known that he had been eclipsed yet again in Riyadh. King Sa'ud had returned from medical treatment in the spring of 1962 and had insisted on resuming his full regal powers, and the State Department did not see how Faisal, as Foreign Minister, could negotiate anything of much substance with Kennedy without first securing his elder brother's agreement.

But then came the news of the Yemen coup, followed a few days later by an urgent cable from Riyadh. Sa'ud had met with his uncles and brothers to discuss the threat posed by Egyptian arms along the Kingdom's southern borders, and the family had decided that Faisal must return to head an emergency war cabinet. The Foreign Minister became Prime Minister again overnight, and when Kennedy invited Faisal to the White House the president was more impressed than he had expected with the calibre of the man about to confront Nasser in open war.

Over lunch a State Department telegram arrived.

'The royalists have captured Sana'a!' reported Kennedy excitedly.

'That may be,' responded Faisal unastonished. 'We shall see what we shall see.' Two days later his scepticism was justified: the tribes loyal to the Yemeni imam had strong positions in the hills, but they had not captured the capital.

Faisal's calm and phlegm made an impact on the American president, who agreed to delay US recognition of the new Yemeni republic. Kennedy also agreed to arrange joint US–Sa'udi military exercises – implicit support for the war Sa'udi Arabia would have to wage along her southern border – and Faisal flew back to Riyadh leaving the American president a little less certain than he once had been that the future of Arabia lay in the hands of Gamal Abdul Nasser.

Faisal had promised Kennedy reforms, and at the beginning of November 1962 the crown prince duly announced a ten-point programme for the new government he was forming: a basic constitutional law would be drawn up from 'the Koran, the traditions of the Prophet and acts of the orthodox caliphs'; local government would be reorganized and a Ministry of Justice formed; 'innocent recreations' like television, a home-based entertainment, would be permitted (public cinemas remained taboo); expanded state welfare facilities were promised, along with the development of roads, water resources and industrial projects – and, in as casual a fashion as was possible in the circumstances, slavery was abolished at a stroke: 'It is known that the Moslem Sharia urges the manumission of slaves. It is also known that slavery in modern times lacks many of the stipulations imposed by Islam for the justification of slavery. . . . Now the government finds the time opportune for the total abolition of slavery.'

The government hurriedly purchased the freedom of the 4000 or so slaves in the kingdom for £1000 each, more than three times the going rate per head in the Buraymi market, and shrugged off questions as to why, at every UN debate on the subject up until the autumn of 1962, Sa'udi delegates had strenuously denied the existence of any slavery in their country.

The issue caused some commotion in the outside world, but inside Sa'udi Arabia most of the former slaves elected to stay on in their ex-owners' households, working as cooks, chauffeurs, nannies and companions as they had always done – and as they continue to do up to the present day.

As principal allies in his reform campaign, Faisal enlisted his uncle Musa'id ibn Abdul Rahman and his half-brothers Fahad and Sultan ibn Abdul Aziz, the two eldest sons of Hassa Sudairi (Abdul Aziz's twice-married wife, who was a close friend of Faisal's wife, Iffat).

Fahad, forty-one and Sultan, thirty-eight, were a tough and well-built couple whose ambition and organizing ability had already marked them out from their other brothers. Both men had served in Faisal's government from 1958 to 1960, and now in 1962 they took over the Ministries of the Interior and Defence, Fahad implementing Faisal's programme of reforms, Sultan organizing the war effort against the Egyptians in Yemen. Faisal gave command of the tribal National Guard to Abdullah ibn Abdul Aziz, who came between Fahad and Sultan in age, and the governorship of Riyadh was entrusted to one of Hassa Sudairi's younger sons, Salman.

So was formed in 1962 the partnership which continued after Faisal's death and which still governs Sa'udi Arabia today. Nearly two decades later, Fahad has become crown prince. But Sultan is still Defence Minister, Abdullah still commands the National Guard, while Salman is still Governor of Riyadh – and, though in the 1980s outside commentators like to speculate on the differences of opinion and ambition presumed to divide these four men, their twenty-year record of continuous collaboration suggests a certain penchant for togetherness. As a government team their longevity is exceeded internationally only by Mr Brezhnev's aged Politburo.

The brothers' first task was to defend their southern borders, against which Nasser had, by the beginning of 1963, amassed over 30,000 trained troops armed with the latest Russian weapons. This was far more formidable a force than anything Riyadh could muster, and President Nasser's generals looked forward to a smooth march northwards. The Yemeni republicans announced that they were claiming the Sa'udi province of Asir which, they said, the Al Sa'ud had stolen from Yemen in the 1920s, and Russian Ilyushins started flying missions into Sa'udi Arabia, dropping caches of rifles for the use of the local 'freedom fighters'.

But these heroes failed to materialize. Bedouin who came upon the parachuted arms tended to sell them to their friends, until the Governor of Asir started offering better prices, and inside the Yemen itself the Sa'udis found they could count on two invaluable allies: the loyalty of the Yemeni hill tribes to their deposed imam, and the mountainous terrain which had defeated the invading Sa'udi army thirty years earlier. Together these factors turned the Yemen war into a bitterly contested guerrilla conflict very different from the walkover that Gamal Abdul Nasser had anticipated, and his army soon found itself in trouble.

In January 1963 Egypt's two topmost commanders, Field-Marshal Abdul Hakim Amer and General Ali Amer, flew into Sana'a for a few days morale boosting, and found that they had to stay for two weeks of agonizing policy reappraisal. The royalists, who controlled the north of Yemen, were starting on a strong push forward. They were threatening republican positions, and the Egyptian answer to this threat was to carry the war into Sa'udi Arabia, for the guerrillas' supplies were clearly coming across the Sa'udi border. So in the spring of 1963 Egypt's Ilyushins started dropping bombs on the southern Sa'udi towns of Jizan, Khamis Mushayt and Abha, and since Sa'udi air defences were virtually nonexistent the Ilyushins reached their targets without difficulty. They inflicted considerable damage and loss of life, and on one raid thirty-six patients inside an Abha hospital were killed.

346

Crown Prince Faisal was eating lunch in Riyadh when news of the Abha raid reached him. Dr Rashad Pharaon received a call from the Defence Ministry with the casualty figures.

'What orders do you have for Prince Sultan?' Pharaon inquired anxiously, whispering into Faisal's ear, for the prince was lunching with the general public as he did every working day of the week.

'Sit down and eat your lunch,' responded Faisal tartly, and turned to resume his conversation about the likelihood of rain with a tribal chief who had come to the capital for a day or so. There were several dozen other guests around the table like the chief, townsmen and bedouin who had presented themselves for midday prayers at the palace, and after lunch Faisal led the assembled company into the *majlis* for coffee, tea, and then more coffee. It was nearly time for the afternoon prayer before Dr Pharaon was able to get the prince on his own and repeat his request. Faisal looked at him impassively.

'Tell my brother Sultan to let me know when the Egyptians reach the outskirts of Riyadh,' said the prince without emotion. 'Till then he should do nothing.'

Faisal knew that America would not tolerate Nasser's naked aggression, and that the Egyptian bombing was, in fact, precisely what he needed to build on the process, started the previous September, of weaning John F. Kennedy away from the Egyptian leader. Faisal already held a confidential promise from the American president guaranteeing 'full US support for the maintenance of Saudi Arabian integrity', and the Egyptian bombing pushed Kennedy into making the undertaking public. American jet fighters flew over Riyadh and Jeddah in displays of solidarity and deterrence, the Ilyushins did not venture north again, and America began to reassess her view of future trends in the Arab world.

Faisal held war rallies in Riyadh which he addressed with a vigour and eloquence no one had suspected. He was a natural and inspiring orator. He and the princes in his new government were not behaving like candidates for liquidation, while the sight of Egyptian planes, later in the Yemen war, dropping napalm and poison gas on defenceless villagers made the outside world think again about President Nasser's love for his fellow Arabs and also on the 'inevitability' of his revolution. By sticking his ground, Crown Prince Faisal rode out his most urgent foreign challenge.

* * *

It was the challenge from within that was harder to deal with, for King Sa'ud ibn Abdul Aziz simply could not reconcile himself to purely symbolic sovereignty. The king had now stood down in favour of his younger brother three times, and his *amour propre*, far from reconciling itself to the process, had grown more and more inflamed. Sa'ud's crumbling health spun out the confrontations, for he was abroad having medical treatment for long months in the early 1960s: Vienna, Lausanne, Boston, Mass., and Cannes all saw the Sa'udi king arrive in the course of these years with his entourage of black coffee servers and black-veiled ladies. They would take over and seal off the upper floors of some luxury hotel, and then drive the town wild with $100 tips and long limousines ferrying processions of whole roasted sheep and oriental delicacies in state from the nearest Lebanese restaurant.

But each time Sa'ud came home, the trouble started up again. Irked by the limitations on his action, the king would try to muscle in on finance or foreign policy, clash with Faisal, and then demand the restoration of his full powers.

Faisal's son Muhammad remembers one of the many meetings that king and crown prince held through these troubled years. It had been arranged in Taif by Muhammad ibn Abdul Aziz, next in seniority after Sa'ud and Faisal, and representing all his younger brothers in his attempts to restore harmony to the family. So Muhammad acted as arbiter when he brought Sa'ud to Faisal's palace.

All the servants were sent out of the room, and Faisal's son Muhammad found himself acting as coffee boy to his father and two uncles – and thus witnessing an extraordinary scene. Faisal refused adamantly to agree to the demands that Sa'ud was making of him. But he never raised his voice, he kept his eyes constantly downcast and he deferred with the most extreme subservience to the man with whom he had come to disagree so bitterly. Faisal sat throughout the interview on the floor below Sa'ud as he used to sit on the carpet in front of Abdul Aziz, and when the interview was over Faisal bowed to kiss Sa'ud's hand. Then he knelt to place the king's slippers on his feet.

Faisal was a proud man, and also an ambitious one. Events since the death of Abdul Aziz had clearly demonstrated that Faisal knew how to govern Arabia and that Sa'ud did not. By 1963 the crown prince had lost whatever willingness he had once possessed to compromise or to work in harness with his elder brother – and, if Sa'ud would not grant Faisal a free hand, then Faisal would turn on his heel and walk away, sheathing his sword like Achilles in his tent. He nursed grudges – as his younger brother Talal had discovered.

But Faisal was not prepared actively to disobey, flout or obstruct the wishes of his elder brother and king.

'If my brother Sa'ud ordered me to kill you,' said Faisal one day to his eldest son Abdullah, who was trying to enlist his father's help in a dispute he was having with the king, 'I would catch hold of you, take you to the steps of his palace, and sacrifice you there for him to see.'

Respect for age and seniority was etched into Faisal's brain, as into those of all his brothers. When the sons of Abdul Aziz gather today, you see them shuffle themselves instinctively into order of age, even though some are separated by only a few days. Deference to elders is one of the Al Sa'ud's inviolable ground rules, the best corset they know to discipline the outward thrust of so many assembled appetites. It is not perfect, and, as a mechanism for dealing with the waywardness of a senior like Sa'ud, Faisal was to find the system more and more of a straitjacket that frustrated him. But what was the alternative? Whenever the final confrontation came, the younger brother felt he lacked the basis ultimately to defy the elder, and Faisal would give way.

In September 1963 the family tried to restore some equilibrium. Sa'ud was in Vienna, convalescing after treatment for a duodenal ulcer which, it was said, had, with hotel bills, cost some $4 million to treat, when a delegation from Riyadh arrived at his hotel. It was a group of brothers trying to prevent yet another seesaw of government after Sa'ud returned home. Sa'ud, they said, must promise before he returned not to interfere in affairs of state, to live within his budget – and to sign a declaration that he would stick to. He must not pull rank over Faisal.

The king signed, but it did not make things any easier. Soon after Sa'ud was settled back in Riyadh, he refused to give his approval to the budget that Faisal presented to him, and when Faisal, using his powers as President of the Council of Ministers, approved the figures anyway, Sa'ud departed on a tour of the Kingdom to rally sentiment around him. It was November 1963, and the king's plan appears to have been to ride back to Riyadh on a wave of popular acclamation that would swamp his family's disapproval and would enable him to regain his absolute powers in defiance of their wishes.

This was the point at which King Sa'ud broke the family rules, and he started many of his relatives thinking that they might break the rules as well. Crown Prince Faisal, taciturn and severe, was not universally popular, and his rule had been far from faultless: his obsession with balancing the books had slowed down national development, while his inability to work with Sa'ud reflected his own touchiness as much as Sa'ud's incompetence; Faisal had an unhelpful tendency to sulk when he did not get his way.

'It is not my business, it is your business,' he had said to Talal and a group of the princes who came asking for his help in 1961 when their government was running into difficulties. 'If there are bad consequences, it's your problem, not mine.'

Just the same, Faisal had never set himself against his own. The crown prince had been careful only to move in response to his uncles and brothers, including Sa'ud himself – and for Sa'ud now to appeal outside the family for the popular support of the tribes, the merchants, Nasserite sympathizers, and even the religious sheikhs was unpardonable. It was an admission of how isolated the king had come to feel among his own relatives, and it breached the cardinal rule that the Al Sa'ud do not invite outsiders in on their disputes. So when Faisal ordered the local authorities in the Hijaz to scale down the receptions they were planning for Sa'ud in November 1963, he had the full backing of his brothers. The triumphal arches came down in Jeddah, Mecca and Medina.

Sa'ud was in Taif when he heard of the snub, and he called off his royal progress abruptly. Now it was his turn to feel that his brother had gone too far, for though the crown prince had intervened ostensibly on the grounds of economy at a time of national emergency, Faisal had hit directly as Sa'ud's personal prestige. If the King of Sa'udi Arabia was now to have his pomp and ceremony taken away as well as his executive powers, what then was left?

Sa'ud's misfortunes began to prey upon his mind. With his failing eyes, his vomiting of blood and his liver disease, he was a semi-permanent invalid, alternately self-pitying and furiously resentful at his afflictions. The king was barely sixty, but he walked like a man fifteen or twenty years older, slowly and stiffly, wearing thick black-lensed glasses through which he squinted like some subterranean creature suddenly dazzled by the daylight – and he no longer smiled. As Sa'ud ibn Abdul Aziz sensed the sentiment of his family turning against him, he responded with bitterness. In December 1963 Sa'ud retired inside the walls of the Nasriyah Palace, mobilized the 1500 red-bereted soldiers of the Royal Guard, and set them round his

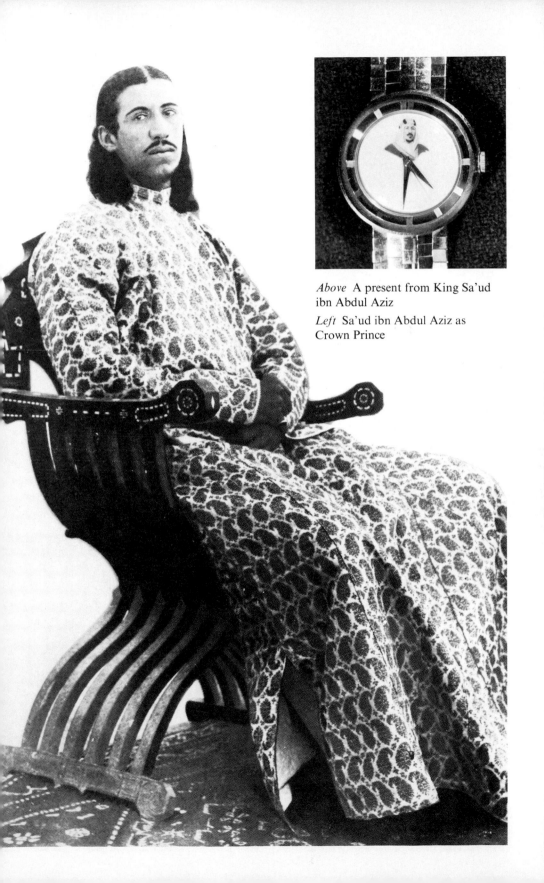

Above A present from King Sa'ud ibn Abdul Aziz

Left Sa'ud ibn Abdul Aziz as Crown Prince

Opposite
Top King Sa'ud dances the *ardha*
Below The tanker deal; King Sa'ud with
Aristotle Onassis, July 1955

This page
Top King Sa'ud on board SS *Constitution*,
travelling to America, January 1957
Above The Shah meets King Sa'ud, with
his crippled son Mashour ibn Sa'ud
Left Talal ibn Abdul Aziz gives a press
conference in Cairo, September 1962.

Top Ex-King Sa'ud arrives in London with his sons, October 1968
Above President Nasser welcomes ex-King Sa'ud to Cairo, January 1967

palace walls with loaded rifles. In response, Sultan ibn Abdul Aziz put the armed forces on red alert, and his elder brother Abdullah called out the National Guard.

Riyadh went very very quiet indeed. People who were in the town through those weeks of December 1963, when it seemed that civil war was about to erupt any minute, remember an eerie calm everywhere. The army mustered in their barracks; the bedouin of the National Guard gathered in the desert; King Sa'ud's guards bivouacked outside his palace, the smoke from their camp fires marking the blush-pink walls with black sooty trails. Everyone held their breath, as if the slightest sound would set off the shooting.

No one was quite sure what King Sa'ud wanted, or how he intended to achieve it. He gathered all his sons round him, and those who had been abroad came flying home and were seen sweeping in their limousines from the airport to their father's palace, their mouths closed grimly.

But few other members of the family paid visits to Nasriyah, and Faisal's strategy was to carry on work as normal. The crown prince's route to work took him past Nasriyah's walls every morning, and the soldiers stared at him balefully, cradling their loaded machine-guns as he drove past – until, one morning, the prince ordered his car to stop. Faisal got out, strode across the dust towards the soldiers, and the men leapt instantly to attention.

'Have you got enough to eat and drink?' asked the prince. 'You've been out here for some time now. I'll have more coffee sent round.'

It was not what he said, but the fact that he spoke to them at all which mattered, and thereafter the soldiers saluted the prince each morning as his car drove past Nasriyah.

Outsiders read the message in the Royal Guard's salutes. But the family knew that a more private corner had been turned, for when King Sa'ud had retired inside his palace walls he had sent a defiant note to Faisal.

'When my enemy has his hands around my neck, then I strike at him with all my strength.'

It was an ancient Nejdi challenge, a traditional declaration of war, and when Muhammad ibn Abdul Aziz saw it he exploded. Seizing the letter the prince drove at once to Nasriyah, ignored the guards at the gate, and stormed into King Sa'ud's presence.

'Did you send this letter to our brother?' he demanded.

351

Sa'ud peered dimly at the sheet of paper which Muhammad was waving at him, and said nothing.

'Never, never,' said Muhammad, 'do anything like this to us again,' and, flinging the crumpled paper back at its sender, the prince turned on his heel and left the room.

When this dramatic episode had passed into legend, an old friend of Muhammad's dared one day to ask the prince why he had favoured Faisal against Sa'ud at this crucial moment in the family's history.

'I did not favour Faisal,' replied the prince. 'If Faisal had sent Sa'ud such a challenge I would have thrown it back in his face also. Challenges are not the way we settle our differences inside the Al Sa'ud.

'And now,' added the prince, with his most intimidating frown, 'do not speak to me of this again, for these are family matters.'

It is a difficult task to piece together the events that made up the severest crisis to confront the Al Sa'ud in their more recent history, and this account cannot claim to be definitive.

'Why dig up old differences?' ask members of the family when questioned about the dark days of 1963–4, and they launch into long eulogies of Faisal or complicated explanations of why Sa'ud was not really such a bad chap after all.

The episode is their Watergate, a memory of mistakes on both sides, a certain amount of deliberate wrongdoing, and the long searing process of setting things to rights again. The Al Sa'ud could, if they wished, argue that their crisis, like Watergate, proved in the end the underlying strength of their established system, which faced up to the malignancy and managed to remove it with relatively little unheaval. But they prefer to forget the pain.

King Sa'ud came out of his stockade at the end of 1963 ready to talk to Faisal, and the crown prince was also ready to compromise. It was agreed that Faisal should remain in control of the government, but Sa'ud was worried at appearing to lose face after the tense confrontation which had been publicized all round the Middle East. There was an Arab summit conference coming up in Cairo early in 1964, and Faisal agreed that Sa'udi Arabia should be represented by its king. Sa'ud's presence would help suggest that the family retained its unity, and, since Sa'ud was not directly involved in the Yemeni campaign against Nasser, he might also be able to negotiate some sort of disengagement with the Egyptian leader.

It was a time for patching up old quarrels. All the rebel princes except Talal had already come back home from Cairo, and in February 1964 Talal himself returned to Riyadh. His assets in the Kingdom had been sequestered, so by the end of his exile he was driving round with all his family in one battered old Mercedes.

'I admit my wrong without equivocation,' the prince declared in a public statement. Talal had fallen out with Nasser when the Egyptian leader started bombing Sa'udi towns, and the Riyadh confrontation had given the entire family a nasty shock. Closing ranks was the order of the day.

But, not for the first time, King Sa'ud fell out of step. He enjoyed himself at the Arab summit, acting as a fully blown head of state and being treated as such, and he returned to Riyadh unwilling to lapse into impotence. A proposal had been made that Sa'ud might be pronounced 'Imam', leaving Faisal to rule as chief executive – as Abdul Aziz had once ruled in tandem with his father. But Sa'ud was not willing to be pushed upstairs, and on 13 March 1964 he wrote a letter to Faisal formally demanding the restoration of his full kingly powers.

This time Faisal did not give way, for during the crisis of the previous December the family had taken the momentous step of calling in the *ulema* to adjudicate on the quarrel between the brothers. The religious sheikhs had backed Faisal. Sa'ud had freely and openly delegated various powers to his crown prince, said the sheikhs, and they saw no immediate justification for revoking these.

Now the family wanted the *ulema* to go a stage further: to issue a *fetwa* (religious ruling) which would institutionalize Faisal's powers on a permanent basis and effectively turn Sa'ud into a constitutional head of state. The king would reign, but he would not rule, and once Sa'ud had accepted that position there would be nothing he could do to alter it. The crown prince could get on with governing without having to look backwards over his shoulder all the time.

It was Muhammad ibn Abdul Aziz who marshalled the family behind this proposal, and it was his uncles, Abdullah and Musa'id ibn Abdul Rahman, who then sold it to the *ulema*. The two family elders held a series of meetings with the religious leaders, and on 29 March 1964 the sheikhs issued their ruling:

May God be praised and bless His faithful Follower:
    In view of the current conflicts between His Majesty King Sa'ud and his brother, His Royal Highness Prince Faisal. . . .

In view of the fact that these divergencies have become more serious recently and that they have threatened to cause disorder and chaos in the country, with disastrous results which only God Almighty could foresee. . . .

And in view of the fact it is essential to find ways and means of permanently solving these unending divergencies and disputes . . . the undersigned have decided the following in the general interest:

(1) His Majesty King Sa'ud will remain the Sovereign of the country, with all the respect and reverence due to his position.

(2) His Royal Highness Prince Faisal, Heir to the Throne and Prime Minister, shall discharge all the internal and external affairs of the state, both during the presence and in the absence of the King, and without referring to him.

Next day seventy princes gathered at the home of Muhammad ibn Abdul Aziz, a large white palace on a little hillock near the Wadi Hanifah to the south-west of Riyadh. The princes' cars dropped them at the front porch, then waited for them in the shade of the fan palms that led down the avenue to the main gates. There were the sons of Abdul Aziz, their elder sons and cousins, and a number of the bin Jaluwis, headed by old Ibn Musa'id, the conqueror of Azaiyiz al Daweesh in the Ikhwan revolt, and still governor of Hail and the north. These seventy men, some of them old, but many of them – the grandsons of Abdul Aziz – still only in their twenties, represented all branches of the Al Sa'ud then present in the Kingdom, with the exception of the king's own sons and some descendants of the *araif* who supported Sa'ud, and they gave their gathering a formal title – 'Ahl al Hal wa al Aqd', which can loosely be translated as the 'Council of Those who Bind and Loose'.

Commentators at the time, and since, have described this 'council' as a permanent body, a sort of family parliament meeting regularly in secret and surfacing publicly on special occasions like the crisis of 1964 – the Supreme Council of the Kingdom.

But this overritualizes a much more informal process. The Al Sa'ud meet and talk together constantly. Every section of the family has its *majlis* whose make-up reflects the issue being discussed, and whose grievances and opinions filter to the circle of senior princes around the king and the crown prince. But no formal institution or 'council' exists, and the 'Council of Those who Bind and Loose' is not an especially Sa'udi entity. It derives from an ancient Islamic concept going back into the history of the early caliphs, a gathering that reflects high authority within the community and which, by virtue of its eminent membership, is entitled to make weighty decisions beyond the powers of the routine organs of government.

In the spring of 1964 the Al Sa'ud were evidently uncertain about what precise powers their emergency council might possess, for, although the initiative to downgrade the royal prerogative had come from the family itself, the princes were careful to delay their formal assembly until the day after the *ulema* had met. Abdullah and Musa'id ibn Abdul Rahman had found it quite difficult, in reality, to cajole all the religious sheikhs into disabling King Sa'ud on a permanent basis. But when the momentous decision was announced to the outside world on 30 March 1964, it was made to seem like a move which had stemmed from the religious leaders, and to which the assembled members of the royal family had subsequently given their assent. In 1964 the house of Sa'ud still felt it safest, in an emergency, to acknowledge the primacy of the *ulema*.

The Council of Ministers tacked its agreement on to the change, and that should have been the end of the matter. Tribesmen started flocking to Riyadh to swear their *bay'ah* to the new permanent powers that Faisal now possessed, and later that year it was the crown prince who represented Sa'udi Arabia at a meeting of Arab leaders held in Alexandria.

But King Sa'ud refused to accept his purely ceremonial eminence. He felt degraded and emasculated – 'I am not Queen Elizabeth!' he exclaimed with anger on one occasion – and, wounded vanity aside, the king had a valid point. It was not in the Arabian tradition for rulers to wear the appearance of power without its substance. Kings were kings, or nothing. How could Sa'ud feel self-respect, how could men respect him, if his dignity was just a façade?

Sa'ud told his brothers that he would not accept a position of permanent impotence, and he insisted that the *ulema* reconsider their ruling. Could there be such a thing in Arabia, he asked, as a king who reigned but did not rule?

It was Sa'ud's contention that such a hollow authority was unnatural and wrong, and in October 1964 his family and the religious sheikhs agreed with him.

But the king's final victory lost him the whole campaign, for in forcing his family and the *ulema* to reconsider their March decision Sa'ud forced them finally to face up to the question that everyone had been trying to avoid since the first stop-gap solution of 1958: if the King of Arabia could only be revered as king while he exercised total executive powers, was Sa'ud a man capable of exercising that authority with wisdom, prudence and enduring strength?

There was only one answer that the *ulema* and the Al Sa'ud could give when compelled to address the problem squarely, and, in forcing them to pronounce it, Sa'ud ibn Abdul Aziz effectively brought about his own deposition.

On 29 October 1964 a hundred senior princes of the Al Sa'ud and several dozen religious leaders converged upon the Sahari Palace Hotel beside Riyadh Airport. Today the Sahari stands at the corner of a vast suburb of villas, apartment blocks and offices. In 1964 it rose alone in the desert, a square, yellow-ochre box rather more impressive than the low terminal buildings across the road. The senior princes had already met at the home of Khalid ibn Abdul Aziz and had agreed that Sa'ud must be asked to abdicate. The leading members of the *ulema* had agreed that they would proclaim Faisal king instead of Sa'ud, and at the Sahari the two groups met.

They chose a mixed delegation to break the news to Faisal, who was at al Kharj, and, by the time this group of princes and sheikhs had motored the 50 miles from Riyadh, the evening prayer was being called.

'It is my right', said Faisal after the prayer was over, 'to ask how you propose to carry out this decision?'

'By proclaiming you king,' came the answer.

'And what about the reigning king?' asked Faisal. 'In the house of Abdul Aziz we do not depose the king except after all attempts at persuasion have failed. Have you exhausted all means of persuasion?'

It was another job for Muhammad ibn Abdul Aziz. For three days King Sa'ud held out in Nasriyah, obstinately refusing the requests of delegations from the *ulema* and from his brothers that he should step down with grace, and it looked as if some unseemly eviction might be called for. But then on 3 November 1964 Muhammad ibn Abdul Aziz came to call.

That same day King Sa'ud agreed to abdicate. His family gathered in strength at the airport to say their goodbyes, and the new king Faisal, at the end of the farewell line, kept his head bowed humbly to his elder brother as he had always done, and bent with respect to kiss Sa'ud's hand.

Sa'ud flew to Dhahran for a consultation with his doctors at the Aramco hospital, then he was loaded at dawn into a Sa'udi Boeing 720

– by a sergeant of the US Air Force driving a fork-lift truck. The ex-king was in a wheelchair.

No one would have guessed from the outward demeanour of the participants in the final ceremony at Riyadh Airport that Sa'ud ibn Abdul Aziz was not still King of Sa'udi Arabia, ruling over the Kingdom as his father had done, and receiving from his younger brothers all the homage that was his due. But when the ex-king had finally left Arabia, bound for Beirut, Cairo and the seaside hotel where he was to spend most of his remaining years in Athens, the order was given to tear down the 7-mile wall that had stood around the palace of Nasriyah. Today all that remains of it is one solitary squat pillared gate.

38 Reform

Like it or not, we must join the modern world and find an
honourable place in it. . . . Revolutions can come from thrones
as well as from conspirators' cellars.

King Faisal ibn Abdul Aziz soon after his accession in 1964

YOU could set your watch by King Faisal, his family and
friends used to say. His every waking hour had its own
function allocated to it, and every working day from 1964 to 1975
Faisal ploughed remorselessly through his timetable, its turning
points set by the five calls to prayer.

The king rose with the dawn prayer and strode across his palace
courtyard in the halflight to kneel among his servants and the bedouin
staying in the palace that night. Then he would go back to his
bedroom, a plain, austere little chamber with just a single bed.

It was not the bedroom in which the king was supposed to sleep.
When Faisal's wife and sons had fitted out his palace at al Ma'ather,
between Nasriyah and the road to Dar'iyah, they gave pride of place
to a plush master bedroom hung with mirrors and draperies in the
best Arabian tradition.

'Whose room is this?' asked Faisal, as his family proudly displayed its glories to him. 'It's too grand for me.' And he walked down
the corridor to select a little boxroom where he would feel more at
ease.

After breakfast the king would drive into town to the Riyassa
Palace beside the water tower, where he would receive visitors in his
majlis from 9 a.m. until 10 a.m. Faisal's office was near by, and at 10
o'clock he would adjourn to it for the rest of the morning, settling
behind his desk and working through his papers with the advisers who
sat in the half-dozen brocaded chairs around the room.

Dr Rashad Pharaon was always there, just across the desk from the
king. Nawwaf ibn Abdul Aziz, the younger brother of Talal, was often
present. A quieter character than Talal, Nawwaf had served briefly as
Finance Minister in the months after Talal's resignation in 1961. If an
urgent cable arrived, Faisal would take the temperature of the meeting, and then tell Rashad Pharaon what his decision was. The doctor

358

would draft out his understanding of the royal will, pass it across the desk to be checked, and then the response would go out.

The king would go home for the midday prayer and lunch, but not to his family. Before 1958 Faisal used to eat at midday with his wife and sons, but when he became head of government he started eating with the general public, and this continued to the end of his life. A long table at al Ma'ather was set for forty, and the king ate and talked with whoever turned up at the palace gates.

Faisal liked to finish his meal with an apple. His long, skinny fingers would reach out to the bowl, pick one, turn it over, examine it and put it back again. Then he would pick up a second apple, look at it and return it to its place, and likewise with a third and fourth fruit until eventually he would return to the one he had chosen to start with. This he would transfer definitively to his plate and he would then begin to peel it, slowly and deliberately dissecting, and finally eating the fruit segment by segment, before he turned to wash the stickiness from his hands.

Sheikh Yamani was fascinated by the process, and, like the technocrat he is, he decided to time Faisal's apple eating, from the second the king's fingers first reached out disdainfully to the pile of fruit, to the second they dipped into the water of the finger-bowl.

Seven minutes was the time the Oil Minister's watch always showed – never six-and-a-half, never seven-and-a-half, but always seven minutes precisely – and after a long series of timings Sheikh Yamani felt he had accumulated enough evidence to communicate his findings to the world.

'Do you know', he asked Dr Pharaon, 'how long it takes the king to eat an apple?'

'Precisely seven minutes,' replied the doctor.

After lunch Faisal would rest for half an hour, pray the afternoon prayer, and then go to his office again. But, as sunset approached, Faisal ibn Abdul Aziz evidently felt the same itch for the desert that his father used to, for every evening, wherever he was, in Riyadh, Taif or Jeddah, the king would be driven out of town at about 5 p.m.

This was one of the more relaxed moments of the royal day, for Faisal, who became king around the age of sixty, liked to meet up with such old childhood companions as Faisal and Fahad, the sons of Sa'ad ibn Abdul Rahman, who had grown up with him after their father's death – and also, almost always, with Muhammad ibn Abdul Aziz, the

brother who was closest to Faisal in age and who shared with him
most memories of the old days.

Together the old friends would squat on a rug thrown down upon
the sand, reminiscing fondly of Abdul Aziz and of their youth, sipping
the sweet tea brought out to them by the coffee servers in silver
vacuum flasks, and then, as the light began to fail, they would kneel
together side by side and prostrate themselves towards Mecca.

Muhammad was, by seniority, the brother who should have
become crown prince to Faisal. Fifty-four to Faisal's sixty in 1964, he
was two years older than the next in line, Khalid, his full brother, and
more than ten years older than Fahad – and he was feared and
respected throughout the family.

But 'Abu Sharrain', 'the Father of Twin Evils', had not mellowed
with age. He was still the fierce, abrasive character who had inspired
Abdul Aziz to coin that nickname, and he had ruffled many feathers
in the family arguments that led up to the deposition of Sa'ud.
Muhammad's private life was also a wild affair. He took off on long
forays to Beirut, and the prince himself freely confessed his unsuit-
ability for the job that would probably involve, in due course, much
more than simply being Faisal's deputy.

'I'd never make a king,' he once admitted to a friend. 'All those
ministers and advisers and secretaries telling me what to do. I'm a
simple man, and they'd just make a monkey of me.'

So Muhammad ibn Abdul Aziz stood aside from the succession in
the winter of 1964, and Faisal turned to his next brother in line,
Khalid, Abdul Aziz's second son by the beloved Jauhara.

But Khalid was no more enthusiastic than Muhammad had been.
'It's not the life for me,' said the prince. 'I like the desert, the bedouin,
my hawks. I am not a politician.'

Dr Rashad Pharaon was present at one of the several meetings in
which Khalid ibn Abdul Aziz refused the dignity that Faisal was
offering, and Prince Muhammad was there too, joining in the con-
certed campaign to pressurize the younger brother who normally
obeyed his every order.

It was the family which proved decisive. The Al Sa'ud had breathed
a sigh of relief at the news they would not have Abu Sharrain as their
monarch one day. They had lived dangerously long enough. But
Khalid was a different matter. Pious, quiet and moderate, he was a
natural peacemaker. He had been his father's choice to negotiate
reconciliation with the Yemen in 1935, and Faisal had wanted him as

his deputy from the start. Khalid had long been the king's favoured travelling companion on Faisal's missions abroad, and one of Marianne Alireza's first sights of the two brothers together had been of the pair of them in rowing boats at a San Francisco pleasure garden, splashing each other like children and bumping their boats around the lake, in between sessions of the United Nations' opening ceremonies in 1945.

In 1964 Faisal felt that Khalid – judicious rather than incisive, adaptable rather than forceful – was the emollient presence he needed to pull the family together again after the strains of the preceding years, and the family were of the same opinion. So in the spring of 1965 Khalid finally agreed to become crown prince and deputy Prime Minister at the age of fifty-three, though on the condition that he should have sufficient time from politics for the things he really enjoyed: his horses, his hawks, the desert. Khalid's role focused on the healing of family wounds. The new crown prince spent long hours in his *majlis* every day, listening to family grievances – and he might well be waiting to discuss these things with Faisal when the king returned from the desert after the sunset prayer.

Dinner for Faisal was a public affair, like lunch. His own close family, his wife and sons, ate on their own. Several nights a week the royal women would come to sit and talk before or after the evening prayer. But by 9 p.m. Faisal was down in town again, putting in another two hours at his office.

11.30 p.m. was the time the inner council began to gather. Musa'id ibn Abdul Rahman would come round to Faisal's home, and so would Fahad and Sultan ibn Abdul Aziz, the king's principal lieutenants getting their first chance to confer with him that day, unless there had been a Council of Ministers meeting or a state visit to disturb the routine. If the government was in Jeddah, Kamal Adham would certainly be there as well, for Faisal's brother-in-law was organizing Sa'udi intelligence in the Yemen, and in Kamal Adham's Jeddah home was the radio station that co-ordinated the Yemeni royalists' guerrilla campaign. Light relief was provided by the royal poet, Kana'an al Khateeb, whose job it was to make recitations at official functions.

For much of the time Faisal would fiddle with the radio tuning knob. The king knew the wavebands of the BBC, Cairo Radio, Voice of America and Radio Monte Carlo, and he would flip the dial rapidly to and fro to catch their Arabic news bulletins. As items caught his interest, the king would throw them out as subjects for debate, and then he would listen hard as the discussion flowed – though he himself seldom had much to say.

Faisal liked his sons to express themselves. His eldest, Abdullah, was in his mid-forties, physically a stouter version of his father, and older than both Fahad and Sultan ibn Abdul Aziz, with whom he had been brought up in the old king's household while his father ruled the Hijaz.

Faisal's other sons were just finishing their education: Muhammad, a BA from Menlo College, California; Khalid, at New College, Oxford; Sa'ud, an economics graduate from Princeton; Abdul Rahman, a Sandhurst cadet; Sa'ad, educated at Princeton and Cambridge; Bandar, soon to go to the RAF Flying College, Cranwell; and Turki, the youngest, still at college in America in the mid-1960s, but later to pursue postgraduate studies in Islamic law at London University.

Only a Sa'udi father could muster such a widespread consumer-test of the world's finer academies. But for each of these boys, when they were home on holidays, or when their foreign education was complete, their finishing school was listening to the debates in their father's midnight *majlis*.

How to respond to President Nasser's latest act of aggression or aggravation; how to deal with those Sa'udis who obviously still saw their country's future in terms of Nasser's prophecies; how to moderate the clashes between traditional religious values and the new *mores* brought by contact with the West: these were the issues debated by King Faisal's family and intimates every night.

Was America sincere in her aims for the Arab world? If she was sincere, was she well informed? And if she was indeed both sincere and well informed – which King Faisal was inclined to doubt – then had she, in any case, the capacity actually to accomplish what she promised?

Nor was discussion confined to matters of high policy. One July night in 1969, as the television showed the grey, flickering images of American astronauts setting foot on the moon, the conversation turned astronomical, for there was a serious belief among elderly Sa'udis, particularly the religious, that the whole stunt had been mocked up in an American television studio. Many more astonishing visual illusions, after all, were staged by that machine; and King Faisal himself thought the Western media capable of infinite deception.

In this case the king was prepared to give America the benefit of the doubt. He accepted America's conquest of the moon for the triumph that it was, but then a discussion developed about the nature of the moon itself, for Kana'an al Khateeb, the poet, maintained that the moon always kept the same face fixed towards the earth as it moved round the planet, so there was a dark side to the moon, facing eternally into outer space, that we could never see.

Nonsense, said King Faisal. The earth revolved upon its own axis, and so did the moon. Kana'an was as ignorant as Abdul Aziz bin Baz, the troublesome old member of the *ulema*, who had just issued a ruling that the earth was flat – and everyone had much fun at the poet's expense.

But next evening King Faisal had an announcement to make to his little group of friends. He had looked further into the subject of their discussion last night, he said, and he had discovered that Kana'an had been right. The moon did keep only one face fixed towards the earth all the time, and he apologized for laughing at the poet. King Faisal had had the curiosity and the energy to do some research of his own, and he had also had the good grace to admit that he was wrong.

Humility and honesty were two of the qualities marking King Faisal's eleven-year reign, which steered Sa'udi Arabia into the middle of the 1970s. Thrift and attention to detail were two others. When Faisal's intimates had finished their discussions some time around 1 o'clock in the morning, he would see them to the door, bidding each of them goodnight – and then the king would conclude his day by returning to the *majlis* and personally switching off all the lights.

In November 1964 Faisal ibn Abdul Aziz had disproved one generally accepted rule of Arab politics: that reactionary regimes can only be removed with bloodshed. Once confirmed in power, the sixty-year-old king proceeded rapidly to disprove another: that reform must be the prerogative of angry young army officers.

But reform in Sa'udi Arabia had never been a simple matter, and in the 1960s it was certainly not the universally longed-for process that Cairo Radio spoke of so blithely every night – as Faisal had had occasion to discover in September 1963 when he sent the National Guard to break up demonstrations in Buraydah. The citizens of that Qaseem town had had to be forcibly restrained from assaulting a building in which, they suspected, the ultimate wickedness was about to be committed, for Faisal ibn Abdul Aziz, they had heard, had laid plans there to educate women.

Starting schools for girls was the special concern of Faisal's wife, Iffat al Thunayan. King Sa'ud had begun the process. It was one of the several positive achievements overshadowed by the less happy aspects of his reign, and Iffat continued the work. She wished to broaden Sa'udi education as a whole to include more science, language and other Western subjects, and she had had the chance to put her ideas into practice in the early 1940s when she set up her 'Model School', the Madrasa al Numuthagiyyah, to educate her own sons in Taif.

Iffat and Faisal had decided that her ideas had to be introduced by stealth, and the 'Model School' was opened without fanfare. When questions were asked, it was described as a private academy for the sons of Faisal. The other pupils were carefully chosen from the Sudairis and certain prominent Hijazi families who thought as Faisal and his wife did, and the college's remote location in the Taif mountains was also intended to avoid trouble until Iffat's blend of modern and traditional had become accepted. Then the school was renamed, expanded and shifted to Jeddah.

Such circuitous manoeuvrings were not devised solely to sidestep the opposition of the religious sheikhs. Dragging Sa'udi Arabia into the twentieth century alarmed ordinary people as well, and even in the 1940s, when the Sa'udi government started sending a few bright schoolboys such as Abdullah Tariki abroad to complete their studies, women would come to Faisal's wife in tears, begging her to use her influence to make sure that their sons did *not* get scholarships. The foreign academies would corrupt their boys and alienate them from their families and roots, complained the mothers; and Abdul Aziz himself shared this suspicion. Sattam and Ahmad ibn Abdul Aziz, the first of the old king's sons to attend foreign universities, went abroad only after their father's death – and, when Faisal and Iffat started on their ambitious programme of Western higher education for their own boys in 1952, they sent their son Muhammad to America without telling the king, hoping that Abdul Aziz, failing in health and memory, would not inquire too hard about the whereabouts of one grandson among dozens.

If introducing Western subjects to the curriculum, and sending students for education outside Arabia, could stimulate such dragging of the feet, the proposition that the state – or anybody – should educate women provoked absolute resistance. The prospect of teen-age girls – nubile, marriageable women in Sa'udi eyes – travelling *en masse* through the public streets every day aroused horrified alarm in itself, so Faisal and Iffat felt that Jeddah's first female academy should be veiled with the same protective camouflage that had worked so well in Taif.

So 1956 saw the opening in Jeddah of a girls' 'institution' calling itself Dar al Hanan, the 'House of Affection', and claiming its inspiration from the Koranic commandment to care for orphaned children. The patron of the hospice, and deviser of its deliberately open-ended name, was Iffat al Thunayan, who provided the land and funds for the project and who personally helped to sew the costumes for the first young ladies expected – except that almost none presented themselves. Even the slaves and servants of the royal household were reluctant to let their young female relatives enter the House of Affection.

Institutional care for the deprived is not in the Sa'udi tradition. There is today at Taif a relatively humane and advanced hospital for the mentally ill. But, historically, the blind, crippled, orphaned and insane of Arabia have always been cared for within their own families. It would be a shame on a family to allow its less fortunate members, no matter how badly afflicted or distantly related, to be cared for by others, while the notion of sending away the elderly to die is anathema: the Western practice of calling old people's hostels 'homes' strikes Sa'udis as particularly hypocritical.

So the ingenious plan to start off Iffat's school as an orphanage misfired. For its first year the House of Affection contained just fifteen little girls. But slowly the idea of enrolling daughters in the classes there did come to appeal to some Jeddah families who knew what Faisal and Iffat were hoping for, and by 1957 Dar al Hanan had sufficient pupils to feel it should explain its objectives in the local press.

'The mother can be a school in herself if you prepare her well' was the title of an article which explained how the House of Affection aimed to produce better mothers and home-makers through Islamic instruction based on modern educational theories. Religion grows within the home, was Iffat's argument, so how better to improve the spiritual formation of future generations than by improving the spiritual formation of their mothers?

The authorities were cautiously on Iffat's side. King Sa'ud's

OIL

Minister of Education was Fahad ibn Abdul Aziz, who was heading a massive expansion of state schooling and had incorporated some of the Taif Model School's innovations into reforms of the national syllabus. King Sa'ud himself had developed a college for his daughters inside Nasriyah, he favoured Iffat's ideas, and in 1960 a national committee containing members of the *ulema* was established to oversee the introduction of female education throughout the Kingdom. Once they had started work, Iffat funded and opened a teacher-training school in Riyadh, the Kulliyyat al Banat, the Girls' College of Education. Female Sa'udi staff would be needed to teach in the new girls' schools.

Progress was not always smooth. The chairman of the religious committee in charge of girls' schools was a fierce old Wahhabi, Sheikh Nasr al Rashid, who insisted on replacing most of the hours that Iffat had blocked off for scientific instruction with Koranic repetition. Sheikh Nasr was a prickly character, who intimidated many men, but Iffat went to talk and argue with him and, though she did not get her way entirely, neither did he. When Iffat encountered special problems, she turned to her husband or to members of the family who felt like her, and in less than a decade she had managed to get over a quarter of a million women enrolled in Sa'udi schools and colleges.*

Iffat al Thunayan is described by those who have met her as short and handsome, fair-skinned with dark reddish hair. Because of the property bestowed upon her by her husband, she must figure prominently in the league table of the world's wealthiest women. But no photograph of her is publicly available, and when you ask her open, emancipated sons about her they fall silent, for, tuned to the same fine tension between ambition and caution as their parents, they still judge it imprudent in the Arabia of the 1980s to make too much fuss about the achievements of a woman.

Everyone *knows* about Iffat. People chuckle over the sleight of hand with which she infiltrated her ideas into the Kingdom. They tell stories of the battles she fought in the early years of her marriage to flush away Faisal's other wives and women. But public tribute there is

* Boys and girls enrolled in Sa'udi schools in 1974–5:

Level	Boys	Girls
Elementary	401,348	214,641
Intermediate	70,270	34,061
Secondary	19,892	7,616
Teacher training	9,585	4,561
Adult literacy	55,540	28,893

366

none: no newspaper interviews or profiles, no television documentaries, and those that are devoted to her husband seldom even mention her existence. It is as if the greatness of a great man would somehow be impugned if the strength and inspiration that he drew from his wife were to be acknowledged, so, though Iffat's efforts for one-half of Sa'udi society stand comparison with the achievement of any male member of her family now alive, she is, in her own way, if for different reasons, as much a non-person as her brother-in-law Sa'ud.

Iffat took her inspiration from a famous collection of verses from the Koran:

For Muslim men and for Muslim women . . .
For men who believe and for women who believe . . .
For men who speak the truth and for women who speak the truth . . .
For men who persevere in righteousness and for women who persevere in
    righteousness . . .
For men who are humble and for women who are humble . . .
For men who give charity and for women who give charity . . .
For men who fast and for women who fast . . .
For men who guard their modesty and for women who guard their
    modesty . . .
For men who praise God and for women who praise God . . .
For all of them,
God has prepared forgiveness and a vast reward.

In all these respects men and women are equal in God's eyes. The divisions in social function between male and female might call for different modes of behaviour in daily life, and long sections of the Koran are concerned with the duty of men to cherish and protect women – which sounds to cynical Western ears very much a recipe for subjection: men, for example, being awarded double shares in inheritance because of the women they must support.

But until the most recent years the legal rights guaranteed Muslim women by the Koran were far ahead of anything available to their Western sisters, and the point, as Iffat saw it, was that God set nothing between Himself and each of His believers, male or female. When it comes to the Day of Judgement, God will judge each woman, as He will judge each man, by what she has made of her life, and He will send her to Heaven or Hell accordingly.

Faisal agreed with his wife. No one could usurp a woman's responsibility for her own life, in his eyes, and it certainly was not for men to obstruct her attainment of her full potential.

367

'Is there anything in the Holy Koran which forbids the education of women?' the king asked the Buraydah protesters. 'Then we have no cause for argument. God enjoins learning on every Muslim, male or female.'

A bright young Jeddah girl, Fatina Amin Shakir, applied to the Ministry of Education for a grant to study abroad, and was refused.

'Why?' she asked.

'Because it is immoral to send single young women abroad,' came the reply.

So Fatina Amin Shakir petitioned King Faisal through her father, and the king told the Ministry to think again.

Today Fatina Amin Shakir is Dr Fatina Amin Shakir PhD (married, she has kept her own name, as many Sa'udi women always have), and for her thesis on the modernization of Third World countries she interviewed the king who had helped make her studies possible.

Tradition, Faisal told her, should be made the ally of development, not its victim. So, although the king sent the National Guard to keep the Buraydah girls' school open in 1963, no parents were forced to send their daughters there. Faisal denied the then modish assumption that if you want to modernize a country you must forcibly destroy its past. On the contrary, said King Faisal, the surest progress comes through tradition, for, though it might make change slower, it also makes it surer.

'We want to go forward on solid ground,' he liked to say, 'not find ourselves in a quicksand.'

Sa'udi tradition dictated, for example, that women's social activities outside the family should be segregated from those of men. But this did not prevent – rather, it encouraged – the formation of women's co-operative groups, and these women's collectives are today among the most active private associations in Sa'udi life.

Iffat's own Sa'udi Renaissance Movement, al Nahdha al Sa'udiyyah, provides free classes in Riyadh to combat adult female illiteracy, runs clinics and dispensaries with classes in hygiene and child care, and organizes courses in foreign languages and typing – all these activities being funded and run by the members of the collective themselves.

Government agencies provide all these services more or less efficiently, and al Nahdha works in co-operation with the Ministry of Labour and Social Affairs. But al Nahdha's ultimate importance, shared by the women's action groups that have sprung up in Riyadh and in other Sa'udi towns, lies in the alternative it offers to traditionally family centred relationships. Al Nahdha and its sister groups provide a context where Sa'udi women can look at themselves as more than just accessories in their husband's home. Working with other women, they can start to shape independent identities for themselves.

The Buraydah riots of 1963 showed the opposition that such social alterations had to face. Faisal had to install the headmistress in the girls' school there by force. The only pupil in the school throughout its first year of operation was the headmistress's daughter, and the trouble was not confined to education, for Faisal had included television among the 'innocent pleasures' that his reform programme of 1962 would encourage, and this did not please the *ulema*.

The older sheikhs could remember fighting wireless and the telephone in the 1920s. They conceded the value of a Riyadh radio station to combat the godless propaganda of Cairo Radio (from 1948 to 1965 Sa'udi Arabia's only radio station was the low-power transmitter of Radio Mecca, serving the Hijaz alone). But they continued to oppose an automatic telephone system, which would enable men and women lewdly to dial each other direct without going through the operator, and they could not see any good coming of television.

Faisal tried to cajole the sheikhs in the obvious way, programming an almost undiluted schedule of prayers, religious readings and theological discussions. He also described these broadcasts, which started in the summer of 1965, as 'test transmissions', so that when people complained to him at the starting of television he would reply that television had *not* started – it was just being 'tested' to evaluate its virtue and usefulness.

But the sheikhs' protests continued, and they found support inside the royal family. Khalid ibn Musa'id was the son of Musa'id ibn Abdul Aziz, a senior prince who kept out of the public eye. Musa'id, forty-two years old in 1965, was one of the sons that Abdul Aziz had fathered by the widow of his brother Sa'ad, and as a senior brother Musa'id could have played a prominent role in government if he had chosen to. But Musa'id was introverted – misanthropic even – and his son Khalid, who took up the cudgels against television in 1965, shared something of his father's temperament.

369

Khalid ibn Musa'id was, by later accounts, an unstable fellow who took to the vices of the West at an early age, travelling to Europe to spend his allowance on drink and drugs. But the prince was smitten by remorse one night in the course of a bizarre orgy upon a Paris rooftop, and when he came down from the roof his servants thought he had seen a vision. All their young master could say was *'Bismillah! Bismillah!'* – 'In the name of God!'

Back in Riyadh, Khalid ibn Musa'id began consorting with other young 'born again' Muslims. Historically his little group of zealots could be compared with the first Ikhwan activists, or the very earliest supporters of Muhammad ibn Abdul Wahhab: pious and fanatical social critics who looked out upon the society in which they lived, and found it rotten. Several were training for the religious life, pursuing further studies of the Koran under the supervision of a *qadi*; others, like Khalid ibn Musa'id, came from privileged, wealthy backgrounds against which they rebelled. They articulated their protests in religious terms; they cut their *thobes* short, let their beards grow, and shunned all foreign 'corruptions', externalizing their nonconformity in their dress and personal appearance as the Ikhwan had done before them.

In September 1965 Prince Khalid ibn Musa'id led his comrades to the television station that had opened a few months earlier on Riyadh's outskirts. At Koran readings and praying together, the little group of militants had worked themselves up to a holy fury, and now they planned to throw themselves upon the idolatrous foreign equipment.

Prince Khalid ibn Musa'id led the assault himself, confident that God would help him demolish the works of the devil. But the police intervened in force, and the demonstrators retreated to Khalid's palace, where the prince himself started firing upon their pursuers.

The chief of the security forces, General Muhammad ibn Hallal, went to tell King Faisal of the trouble. The police could storm the palace quite easily, the general told the king. But there was the risk of bloodshed, and he was not happy at opening fire on a prince.

King Faisal thought for a minute. He always used to say, when discussing all the problems of dragging Sa'udi Arabia into the second half of the twentieth century, that he would rather unlock doors than break them down. But there were clearly occasions when persuasion alone was not enough.

The King looked up again at Ibn Hallal. 'It does not matter who the man is,' he said. 'None of us is above the law. If the prince fires at you, then you must fire back.'

So Ibn Hallal returned to Prince Khalid ibn Musa'id's besieged palace, took charge of the police detachments surrounding it, and, when he saw Prince Khalid himself in the act of firing, the general picked up a rifle, took careful aim, and shot the king's nephew dead.

39 Two Faces of Faisal

The Severity of King Faisal

One day King Faisal heard of twelve soldiers accused of ambushing pilgrim buses after dark on the Medina road. Pilgrims had been robbed and women molested, but there were no witnesses. The police had found four jeeps with warm engines at the nearby army camp – and twelve fully clothed men lying in bed, pretending to be asleep beneath their blankets.

These twelve men maintained their innocence, refusing to confess, and, in the absence of conclusive first-hand testimony against them, the religious court sentenced them each to six months in prison.

King Faisal called for the papers of the case. Robbing and intimidating pilgrims was a capital offence, he said. Sa'udi Arabia was host to the Muslims of the world, and it must not be said that she allowed her people to rob her guests with impunity. The soldiers must be executed.

So, on the king's instructions, all twelve men were beheaded: four in Mecca, four in Medina and four in Jeddah.

The Frankness of King Faisal

King Faisal suffered from a malady that people often find embarrassing to discuss: piles. A specialist came from London, an operation was decided on, and out to Riyadh was flown a team of nurses and anaesthetists, for whom a purpose-built operating theatre was created in a room of Faisal's palace.

This made it all the easier for the king not to disclose to the outside world the true nature of what was afflicting him, but the night before the operation he called his friend the poet, Kana'an al Khateeb, to him.

372

'I want you to make sure tomorrow', said Faisal, 'that the people are told precisely what operation I am having. The Minister of Health will probably dress it up with long medical words, but I want the announcement to use the word that everyone understands – *bawassir*, piles.'

The poet looked surprised.

'I have suffered from piles for years,' said Faisal. 'Do you remember how, when we stayed in America, I would spend so much time in the bathroom? That was because I was washing my underwear and putting it to dry on the hotel radiators. I was too ashamed to see a doctor.

'But now I want the truth to be known because it may help other people who are suffering. If they see that their king is not too embarrassed to tell a doctor, they may follow my example and get relief.'

So next day, shortly before the announcement was made, Kana'an al Khateeb told Crown Prince Khalid what the king had said, and the crown prince called for the text of the Minister of Health's announcement. Sure enough, it was set out in vague and general medical terms from which even a doctor would have had difficulty working out the truth, and this was all changed to be replaced by the one word that everyone would understand.

The operation was a success. Everybody praised King Faisal for his candour. And within the next few days nearly a dozen princes got in touch with King Faisal's specialist while he was still in Riyadh and made appointments to be treated by him.

40 Challenges

The important thing about a regime is not what it is called, but
how it acts. There are corrupt republican regimes and sound monarchies,
and vice versa. . . . The quality of a regime should be judged by its
deeds and the integrity of its rulers, not by its name.

King Faisal ibn Abdul Aziz

W HEN Faisal ibn Abdul Aziz first proposed in 1956 that
Islam had a major role to play in world politics, few people
took him very seriously. It seemed a quaint and old-fashioned notion.
Arab revolution was on the crest of the wave. The growing numbers
of Third World countries in Africa and Asia looked for their future to
nationalism, socialism, technology, education – anything but religion.

Faisal himself, very much in his brother Sa'ud's shadow at that
time, did not seem a man of the future either. His holy musings in a
paper he prepared, around the time of Suez, on Islam's political
potential to combat the spread of materialism around the world,
sounded the wishful thinking of a man blinded by his own piety and by
the specially religious character of his own family history. Religion, it
seemed obvious to everyone except the Sa'udi crown prince, was in
retreat in the second half of the twentieth century.

But Faisal's whole life, from a comparatively wild and heedless
youth to pious old age, was a personal pilgrimage of ever-intensifying
devotional thought, and when the Al Sa'ud gave Faisal power in the
late 1950s he used his position to further his ideas. In 1962 Sa'udi
Arabia sponsored an International Islamic Conference in Mecca, the
first to be held there since the assembly which Abdul Aziz had called
after his conquest of the Hijaz, and this 1962 gathering led to the
creation of a Sa'udi-sponsored organization with permanent staff and
headquarters in Mecca: the World Muslim League.

Faisal believed it possible to transfer into the international arena
the domestic principles on which the Sa'udi state was based. Islam
provided stability, security, purpose and discipline at home – so why
not abroad as well? Through religion, Faisal believed he could strike
back hard at the threat which the radical ideas of Gamal Abdul
Nasser posed to the Kingdom.

374

'Those who distort Islam's call under the guise of nationalism', proclaimed the Mecca conference of 1962, 'are the most bitter enemies of the Arabs whose glories are entwined with the glories of Islam.'

The impetus of Arab radicalism in the 1950s and 1960s was to loosen the grip that Islam held over ordinary Muslims' minds and daily lives – a direct attack on the religious cornerstone of Sa'udi power. As a political realist, and also as a sincere Muslim fundamentalist, Faisal could not tolerate the state's overwhelming Islam to lock and chain it like the socialist societies with whom Nasser constantly flirted. The Sa'udi king called on his brother Muslims for a revival of godliness.

Nasser derided Faisal's attempt to raise Muslim consciousness as a device to obstruct the progress of his own great Arab revolution – which it certainly was – and the leaders of Syria and Iraq joined in, scoffing at Sa'udi Arabia's pan-Islamic project as a mutual insurance society for monarchs and reactionaries.

But Faisal ploughed doggedly ahead, and when he became king in 1964 he started on a series of foreign journeys to the 'monarchs and reactionaries' of the Islamic world, carrying out nine state visits in one nine-month period between December 1965 and September 1966.*

At each stop the king made the same call to his brother Muslims to join together in a pan-Islamic power bloc that could wield solid influence on the international scene, and his hosts heard him out politely. African and Asian leaders were intrigued by the possibilities of securing some share of Arabia's oil wealth. The monarchs of Jordan, Libya and Morocco were happy to consider anything that might neutralize the radical threats to their regimes, and there was a general resentment among the middle classes of several Arab countries that to be a good Arab it should be compulsory to embrace the socialism of Gamal Abdul Nasser.

Still, in 1966, ten years after he had composed his paper on Muslim unity, King Faisal had scarcely set his co-religionists afire with the notion of an Islamic revival. And in 1966 the king was too busy just surviving himself to push his campaign much further.

---

* The countries King Faisal visited between December 1965 and September 1966 were Iran, Jordan, Sudan, Pakistan, Turkey, Morocco, Guinea, Mali and Tunisia. He also visited Egypt in these months.

When Sa'ud ibn Abdul Aziz went into exile in November 1964, all fifty-two of his sons went with him. Loyal to their father, they felt bitter at the humiliation that deposition represented for him and them, and they did not accept the family verdict as final. They were determined to regain power by any means they could, and they wasted no time.

The trouble started within months of Sa'ud's departure, when, early in 1965, mysterious entrepreneurs started buying up old warplanes in the United States and flying them to Canada. But that was not the ultimate destination of the planes. They were flown north because official exportation licences were not required for Canada, and once beyond the Great Lakes the planes vanished, to reappear shortly afterwards in Portugal – an entrepôt much favoured by the world's undercover arms dealers in the 1960s. King Sa'ud was building himself a private air force.

These were the great days of the mercenary soldier – in the Congo and Katanga, in Biafra and also in the Yemen, where the Sa'udis had been employing small cadres of Europeans to lend expertise to the royalist war effort – and it had not proved difficult for ex-King Sa'ud's sons and middle-men to recruit themselves an exotic collection of guns-for-hire: a French aristocrat, a Canadian, an ex-RAF pilot, a freelance Australian who had done jobs for the CIA, and an adventurer from California. A film director could scarcely have assembled a more appropriate cast of tough guys to smuggle warplanes out of America for a dark-spectacled desert sheikh.

But the weak link in the plot was the sheikh himself, for even in adversity Sa'ud ibn Abdul Aziz was incapable of restraint. To finesse half a dozen planes to the Middle East and then mount a coup attempt in Riyadh might just have been a viable prospect. But endeavouring to marshal and fly across the Atlantic no less than twenty-three C47s, B26s and DC6s without anyone noticing or wondering who in the world could be financing such a massive armada, was too much to expect. The CIA soon got wind of the project, the plane smugglers were rounded up and charged with exportation violations, and Sa'ud's Hollywood scenario fizzled out. His twenty-three planes were confiscated by the Portuguese.

To hire foreign mercenaries to fight battles lost in the family *majlis* was the twentieth-century equivalent of inviting the Rasheeds to Riyadh. It broke the Al Sa'ud's ultimate rules of loyalty. But ex-King Sa'ud was now far outside the pale of family conventions, and there

376

was worse to come. In the autumn of 1966 the deposed monarch approached his one-time enemy, Gamal Abdul Nasser, to inquire if he could come on board the Egyptian revolution.

Nasser was looking for allies, for he had got himself into deep trouble in the Yemen. His troops could not win a decisive victory over the royalists, but neither could Egypt withdraw her armies without loss of face, and the already fragile Egyptian economy had had to suffer for five years the strain of keeping 65,000 soldiers involved in a totally non-productive war. So Nasser welcomed the discontented ex-king, and by the beginning of 1967 Sa'ud ibn Abdul Aziz was comfortably ensconced in socialist Egypt – on the seventh, eight and ninth floors of the Nile Hilton.

Sa'ud had spent most of his exile until 1967 in Athens, and from Greece he took delivery in Cairo of three huge fireproof safes flown to him by separate charter planes. Each safe, one of his sons was happy to tell an inquiring journalist, contained at least £15 million in cash, bullion and jewellery – and the ailing ex-monarch, sixty-five years old in 1967, intended devoting this treasure to the restoration of his fortunes.

Did Sa'ud really think he could regain his throne?, asked a reporter of the *New York Times*.

'That', replied the ex-king gnomically, 'is not impossible for God to decree.'

So in May 1967 the Kingdom was presented with the spectacle of its former ruler stumbling into the market-place in Sana'a, where President Nasser had flown him, to embrace as brothers the Yemeni republican leaders whom Sa'ud had, five years earlier, denounced as reptiles. Gaunt, frail, his eyes dimmer than ever, Sa'ud was led through Sana'a's streets in front of newsreel cameras to deride his own brother, Faisal, as an 'imperialist'; he declared President Nasser his 'dearest friend in all the world', and he presented a million dollars to the Yemeni republican cause. It was an astonishing and pitiful performance, and, when the myopic ex-monarch croaked into the microphones of Cairo Radio that he was still the rightful ruler of Arabia and that he called for a rising across the whole peninsula, even the Yemeni rent-a-crowd found it difficult to raise a cheer.

Ill and discredited, Sa'ud ibn Abdul Aziz could not, by May 1967, credibly threaten his brothers in Riyadh with anything much worse than embarrassment. But his troublemaking could have dragged itself out for some time, had it not been for Israel's spectacular victory

377

in the Six-Day War which, in June 1967, shattered so many Arab illusions, Sa'ud's among them. In the aftermath of defeat, President Nasser was compelled to mend his fences with conservative Arab leaders, and the price of reconciliation with Faisal was for Egypt to abandon Sa'ud and his pretensions.

So, less than six months after he had been welcomed to Cairo, the ex-king was on his travels once again with his fireproof safes. Nasser had shamefacedly to ask his guest to leave without commotion, and by the end of 1967 Sa'ud and his sons were back in Athens again, where the last few months of the former monarch's life were devoted to eking out such pleasures as his declining health permitted.

The last days of ex-King Sa'ud are still recalled with mingled horror and nostalgia by the hoteliers of the Athenian Riviera. The barefoot coffee servers and black-veiled women, the sealed-off upper-floor suites, the reek of incense, the chaffeur-driven takeaway banquets, all the exotic prodigality of the dark-glassed Sa'udi exile raised its usual storm: Sa'ud's sons' Ferraris turned car parks into combat zones, the royal milch camel devastated arbours of manicured privet, and guests at seaside terrace restaurants were diverted by the spectacle of fellow diners leaping fully clothed into the Saronic Gulf to claim the $1000 prizes Sa'ud offered to those taking on his dares.

In 1968 alone the dying ex-king managed to get through $10 million in living expenses – contributing, it was estimated, a full 1 per cent to Greece's total foreign currency earnings in that year.

But Sa'ud took his pleasures sadly. The lengths to which he had been prepared to go to wreak his vengeance on his brothers showed the anger that was consuming him, and the failure of the ex-king's attempts to dislodge Faisal only intensified his inner turmoil. Sa'ud brooded with increasing frustration, his thoughts became ever less coherent, and, as his spirits flickered more and more erratically, his physical disabilities piled on top of one another. Able to see virtually nothing, increasingly immobile as he lay wracked by liver and intestinal complications, ex-King Sa'ud ibn Abdul Aziz sank deeper and deeper into a blurred decrepitude from which death represented a welcome release when it came in February 1969.

Faisal sent a plane to bring his brother's body home for burial, and, trying to close in death the gap that had divided them both in life, he pillowed a Koran beneath the death's-head that was a travesty of the once jovial, fleshly features of Sa'udi Arabia's second king. Sa'ud was buried, near his father, in an unmarked grave in Riyadh's central cemetery, and for once the Wahhabi prohibition on graveside speeches suited the occasion precisely. What was there to say?

King Sa'ud's achievements had been greater than his sad end indicated: the first universities, the new roads and schools and hospitals, the first attempt at an oil embargo: Abdul Aziz's son and successor initiated many of the developments for which the credit later went to Faisal: his school for girls in Riyadh was operating several years before Iffat's Dar al Hanan; he had committees working on the abolition of slavery (under his brother Abdul Mohsin) and on the introduction of television before Faisal's 10-point reform programme forced the pace in September 1962.

But good intentions alone were not enough. King Sa'ud's own family weighed him in the balance and found him wanting. No man in history can ever have wasted quite so much money in so little time as Sau'd ibn Abdul Aziz, and while that in itself is some sort of distinction, it is easy to see why few modern Sau'dis glory in it. King Sa'ud lived beyond his means in every sense, and, like King Midas, he discovered the unique poverty and emptiness which can afflict a man whose riches are stacked high around him.

King Faisal was a severe man, and the challenges which he had to face from President Nasser and from his own brother Sa'ud did not soften his disposition. In the first months after his accession, Faisal sent his police out on sweeps of 'subversives' – labour organizers in the oilfields, outspoken young students, freethinkers, barrack-room lawyers, almost anyone who had spoken too warmly of President Nasser or had had one harsh word too many to say about greedy princes and their powers. Several hundred people were arrested.

King Faisal and the Television Technicians

Abdul Aziz made it a tradition for the King of Sa'udi Arabia to welcome the pilgrims to the Holy Places every year with a speech, and in 1966 King Faisal decided to use this speech as a vehicle for the ideas he was developing about international Islam and its potential to combat the godless socialism of Nasser and other Arab radicals.

Yet, when in 1966 Faisal made his first ever televised speech to the pilgrims, the television went dead after half an hour, just as the king was developing the main burden of his attack.

In the midnight *majlis* afterwards, Faisal's family and friends discussed the breakdown. King Faisal himself said nothing, but next day he took one of his sons aside.

'Dissenters derive their power', he said, 'from the noise that others make about them. So I said nothing last night about the Nasserites in the Information Ministry. But I know that they are there – at least thirty-five of them. They are under constant observation.'

'If you know that they are Nasserites, then surely you should have them arrested?' said his son.

'I cannot arrest everybody,' replied King Faisal. 'And, besides, you can remember how we ourselves used to look on Nasser a few years back. We thought he was our saviour, the leader of the Arabs.

'We know better now – and those thirty-five men will also come to know better themselves in time.'

Faisal's relatives tell this tale today to illustrate the king's coolness and nerve at a time of tension. But a ruler who felt the need to set spies on thirty-five civil servants in one ministry alone could scarcely be described as relaxed about challenges to his authority, and Faisal was not always so patient with his critics – as Abdul Aziz ibn Mu'ammar, his ambassador to Switzerland, discovered.

Ibn Mu'ammar came from an ancient Nejdi family, as eminent as the Al Sa'ud in their time, for the Mu'ammars were the traditional rulers of Uyainah, and had even controlled Riyadh at one period in the nineteenth century when the Al Sa'ud were in eclipse. Members of the family worked loyally for Abdul Aziz in the 1930s and 1940s. Their women were married to Al Sa'ud princes.

But Abdul Aziz ibn Mu'ammar was a radical. He spent some time in prison during King Sa'ud's crackdown on Nasserites, and he supported the 1960 putsch which had ousted Faisal in favour of the 'reforming' administration of Talal and Tariki. He was a friend of Tariki and, like the Oil Minister, Ibn Mu'ammar looked forward to the Republic of Arabia, in which the Al Sa'ud would be just one family among others. He was a leading member of 'Nejd al Fatah', the 'Young Nejd' reform movement.

But whereas other Young Nejd radicals – notably Faisal al Hegailan and Nasr al Mangour (in 1981, Sa'udi ambassadors to Washington and London respectively) – gratefully accepted the foreign assignments which were offered them and both kept their heads down, Ibn Mu'ammar remained a malcontent. He came back from Switzerland to Riyadh, where he criticized Faisal openly and continually, until Faisal lost patience.

'Either you stop stirring up trouble, or you go to prison,' the king eventually cried in exasperation.

Ibn Mu'ammar refused to be silenced and Faisal, edgy at Sa'ud's intrigues abroad, and out of humour with dissidence at home, had his critic locked up in prison, where Ibn Mu'ammar was to spend twelve years. By the time he was released in 1976, the ex-ambassador, whose eyesight had never been good, was half-blind.

The Nasserites in the Ministry of Information were wise not to have taken their dissent beyond the pulling of a plug in a television switchboard. When a network of small explosions spread across the country in the spring of 1967, seventeen Yemenis were arrested and publicly executed, and then in 1969 two more serious conspiracies were uncovered. Radicals in Jeddah planned to blow up buildings there and to proclaim a republic under the presidency of Yussuf al Taweel, a son of the Hijazi nationalist leader who had led resistance to the Al Sa'ud in 1925. At the same time, Lieutenant-Colonel Dawood Romegh, the Sa'udi commander of the Dhahran Air Academy, had fighter planes ready on standby to shoot down Faisal the next time he took off to fly anywhere – though this plot had no proven connection with the explosions and street demonstrations that were planned to usher in Yussuf al Taweel's Arabian republic.

Admiral John Wise, the retired British naval officer hired to organize the Technical Training College for military personnel at Dhahran, was just boarding a civilian airliner for Riyadh one bright autumn afternoon in 1969, when he saw his Sa'udi CO appear on the tarmac in a long white *thobe*. Dawood Romegh was attended by a military escort, as Admiral Wise would have expected, but something made the British officer hold back from greeting his superior. The uniformed officers were all kissing each other farewell in their normal fashion, but no one was kissing Romegh – and on the plane the Air Academy commander chain-smoked all the way to Riyadh.

It was the last time that John Wise saw Dawood Romegh, and when the admiral returned to Dhahran that night he found that all the non-royal pilots on the base had been 'transferred' to other assignments. The only operational pilots left on duty were princes.

Several hundred people disappeared in the course of the next few months, and later the story spread that they were all taken up handcuffed in transport planes over the Empty Quarter to be pushed out of the rear doors without parachutes.

This grisly myth is a major item in modern Sa'udi Arabia's underground folklore, particularly when liquor flows and the talk gets even more paranoid than usual at expatriate parties. It surfaced in 1980, like many other rumours, in the film *Death of a Princess*, and the Al Sa'ud deny it – not surprisingly.

But the facts appear to justify their protestations, for every single conspirator known to have been arrested in 1969 is today alive and living freely in modern Sa'udi Arabia.

Dr Salih Amba, the liberal-minded Dean of the Dhahran College of Petroleum and Minerals, who vanished in 1969, reappeared a few years later to be received as Faisal's guest of honour in Riyadh. Yussuf al Taweel, the ringleader of the conspiracy and would-be President of Arabia, came out of prison in the late 1970s to set up in business and garner spectacular profits representing foreign firms. He is now considerably wealthier than many members of the Al Sa'ud – as princes will frequently point out today with a wry smile. And the only name the author could not trace as this book neared completion late in 1980 was that of Lieutenant-Colonel Dawood Romegh, the air force plotter whom Admiral Wise last saw vanishing in handcuffs twelve years earlier.

It had to be concluded that Colonel Romegh's bones were bleaching somewhere in the Empty Quarter, the fate which he had, apparently, planned for King Faisal and certain members of the Al Sa'ud. But then in January 1981 Dawood Romegh turned out to be alive. He has little to say about the past, but he appears to be plump and well, selling Buicks in Jeddah – and he is very very proud of his six-year-old daughter.

41 The Russians and the Jews

THE June War of 1967 transformed the face of the Middle East. In the small hours of 4 June 1967 Israeli bombers struck at the airfields of Syria, Jordan and Egypt simultaneously, knocking out their air forces and preparing the way for a ground offensive which totally reversed the Arab–Israeli power balance as it had stood less than one week earlier. By the end of the Six-Day War, Israel had occupied Syria's Golan Heights, she had marched to the Jordan River to capture from Jordan all the West Bank and the rest of Jerusalem, and by driving her tanks and troop transports right to the Suez Canal she had conquered the entire Sinai Peninsula, capturing the Egyptian oilfields there and more than doubling the extent of her territories at a stroke.

For the Israelis it was a joyful, scarcely credible triumph. For the Arabs it was a calamitous blow which provoked revaluation everywhere – and nowhere more than in Egypt where Nasser felt impelled to admit his own responsibility for the catastrophe. He had shaken his fist once too often, threatening to close the Gulf of Aqaba to Israeli shipping and then being unable to make good his menaces. In tears the Egyptian leader offered his resignation to his people.

This uncharacteristically humble gesture generated a surge of sympathy in Cairo, and Nasser's resignation offer was rejected by mass rallies in the streets. But hastily arranged demonstrations could not get round the underlying realities of Egypt's many problems – and chief among them was Nasser's disastrous Yemen adventure. Egypt had bled, physically and metaphorically, for nearly five years to achieve virtually nothing in Yemen, and all in the name of a cause which came to seem positively frivolous and destructive when Israeli guns and soldiers were digging in along the Suez Canal.

What had 65,000 Egyptians been doing fighting their brother Arabs at the southern end of the Red Sea? Nasser used to refer ruefully to the Yemen adventure as 'my Vietnam', and it was exactly

383

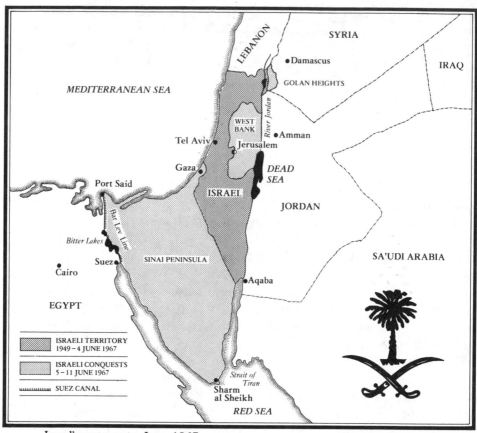

Israel's conquests, June 1967

that, a commitment which had seemed short-term and self-contained, but which had dragged him into a morass of pain, expense and frustration that divided the nation at home and humiliated it abroad. The South Arabian war, which had started in 1962 as an attempt to topple the house of Sa'ud, ended in 1967 by almost toppling its inspirer.

Nasser had no choice but to make his peace with Faisal. At the Khartoum Conference in 1967, the Egyptian leader dropped his patronage of ex-King Sa'ud. He agreed to withdraw his troops from Yemen, and Faisal responded by organizing aid for Egypt and the other war-damaged states of £135 million a year. President Nasser was finally enjoying the financial benefits of 'Arab oil' – though hardly on the terms that he had originally envisaged.

Egypt's double defeat in 1967 marked another decisive shift in the Arab centre of gravity from Cairo towards Riyadh. But it also marked a new and even more bitter development of the Arab–Israeli conflict, for the Jewish conquest of 1967 included the old quarter of Jerusalem.

Jews around the world rejoiced at their June 1967 retrieval of the Wailing Wall, the remains of the Second Temple of Jerusalem destroyed by the Romans in AD 70. But the Wailing Wall forms part of an enclosure surrounding two shrines no less holy to Muslims – the al Aqsa Mosque and the Dome of the Rock, the spot from which, one miraculous night, Muhammad was taken up by God to heaven – and, because of the associations that Jerusalem has with Jesus and so many of their other prophets, Muslims have come to regard the city as their third Holy Place after Mecca and Medina.

How to dispose fairly of a city so fiercely treasured by two of the world's greatest religions – and leaving aside the equally honoured Christian shrines in Jerusalem – must be one of the more complex dilemmas that humanity has ever set itself. Jews and Muslims revere the very same ground: the rock that Islam regards as Muhammad's is, for Jews, the sacrificial stone on which Abraham laid Isaac.

But King Faisal saw the problem in the simplest of terms. After 1967 his only great ambition, he used frequently to say, was to pray in the al Aqsa Mosque before he died, and he did not mean to do that by kind permission of the Jewish occupying forces.

King Faisal was bitterly grieved by the loss of old Jerusalem to the Jews. As guardian of Islam's Holy Places he felt a personal responsibility to recapture what had been lost, and his hatred of Israel went deeper than the antipathy and wounded pride common to all Arabs. Faisal genuinely believed that Zionism and communism were alternate faces of the same international conspiracy. Marx had been a Jew, so were Trotsky and many of the leaders of the Bolshevik Revolution, and when he was shown the tsarist forgery, *Protocols of the Learned Elders of Zion*,* Faisal accepted it at face value as proving all that his

* *Protocols of the Learned Elders of Zion* was a document, published at the beginning of this century, purporting to be an agenda for world domination devised in Basle, Switzerland, at the time of the first Zionist Congress in 1897. In the *Protocols*, Jews and Freemasons were presented as plotting together for the destruction of Christianity and of the civilized world-order through the promotion of liberalism and socialism, and, translated into many languages, the *Protocols* remained unchallenged staples of anti-Jewish propaganda for twenty years. Henry Ford, among others, would quote freely from them. Then in 1921 Philip Graves (later the biographer of Sir Percy Cox) demonstrated the extraordinary resemblance the *Protocols* bore to an obscure French satire of the nineteenth century, the resemblance being word for word in places. He suggested that the Zionist 'conversations' had been copied out from this old book, and the Russian historian Burtsev later produced evidence that the *Protocols* had been forged by the tsarist police to discredit Marxist and Jewish opponents of the tsar.

father had ever said about the perfidy of the Jewish race. Copies of the *Protocols* and other tracts linking Zionism with Marxism were given out in Faisal's reign as bedside reading to guests in Sa'udi hotels, and the ambassadors of foreign powers became used to being treated for the first half-hour of any meeting with the king to a fervent exposition of this theme.

'Zionism is the mother of Communism,' the king told *Newsweek* in 1970 in one of many interviews that he gave on the subject. 'It helped to spread Communism around the world.'

How did His Majesty reconcile this assertion with the fact that Israel and the USSR appeared to be on opposite sides in the Middle East, with the Russians providing weapons for Egypt and Syria to use against the Jews?

'It's all part of a great plot, a grand conspiracy,' King Faisal replied with confidence. 'Communism, as I told you, is a Zionist creation designed to fulfil the aims of Zionism. They are only pretending to work against each other.'

This firmly held conviction was the basis of Faisal's foreign policy throughout his reign. What had been the practical consequences of Zionism in the Middle East? he would ask. The radicalization of the Arab world. Arab countries, he liked to point out, had turned to the Soviet Union for help only because of the outside assistance that the Zionists had received. There were few Arab communists or socialists before Israel's creation. But the wound to Arab dignity that Israel represented had helped to generate revolutionary thinking in the Middle East, to the detriment of God-fearing countries like Sa'udi Arabia. Thanks to Zionism, Riyadh found itself threatened both by the Israelis and by the aggrieved Arab radicals with their irreligious policies – and Faisal had no hesitation in linking the two.

Arabians are conspiracy theorists, and not afraid to admit it. Just as they believe in an active power for good intervening daily in their lives, so they believe that evil and the powers of darkness are manifest here on earth. A Westerner takes the credit for his own successes and blames himself for his failures. An Arabian thanks God for the good things and blames the bad on evil influences beyond his control. It makes for a guilt-free existence.

It also makes for deep suspicions, and nowhere is this more obvious than in the Arab attitude towards the Jews. Examining their own recent past and the mysterious outside interventions that have affected it, from the Sykes–Picot Agreement and the Balfour Declaration to the unforeseen and massive role played by America in the creation and sustaining of Israel, Arabs have come to the conclusion that much of their history has been manipulated by alien forces hostile to Arab interests, and soon after the Israeli capture of old Jerusalem yet another incident occurred that King Faisal found hard to accept at face value. The al Aqsa Mosque was set ablaze by an arsonist, and the Jewish authorities said it was 'an accident'.

It was a deranged Australian (a Christian) who committed this sacrilege to Islam's holiest shrine in Jerusalem, and independent inquiry has since established that he acted for his own crazed reasons. The Israeli salvage workers, it is also agreed, acted with reasonable speed and efficiency in putting out the fire, and most of the mosque was saved from the blaze.

Still, Arabs and Muslims everywhere were outraged – and no one more than King Faisal. It bore out his worst suspicions. Having stolen one of Islam's Holy Places, the Jews were now intent upon destroying its great Islamic shrine and character, and Faisal called on Muslims everywhere to rise in jihad. Jerusalem must be freed from her impious captors. Within a month Faisal had pressured the entire Islamic world to confer in a summit conference at Rabat, Morocco – the first time in history that Muslim heads of state had gathered together in such numbers, and even President Nasser and the radical leaders of Algeria, Libya and the Sudan felt compelled to attend.

Rabat was a triumph for King Faisal. Only the Ba'athist* regimes of Syria and Iraq boycotted the conference, and their absence mattered little beside the attendance of twenty-five kings, presidents and prime ministers who combined to condemn the burning of the al Aqsa Mosque – and who, more significantly in the long term, unanimously called for the restoration of Jerusalem to Arab control, demanding the surrender by Israel of all her June 1967 conquests, and declaring their support for the aspirations of the Palestinians.

It was the first successful lobby of non-Arab opinion in support of the Arab cause, and it led to the first ever commitment to intergovernmental co-operation among Muslims: a permanent Islamic secretariat was formed to bring Muslim heads of state and Foreign Ministers together on a regular basis, and soon afterwards came the

---

* *Ba'ath* means 'resurrection' or 'renaissance', and was the name given by Michel Aflak, a Syrian Christian, to the progressive nationalist party he created in the 1940s. The aim of the Ba'ath is a secular state. It addresses its appeal to all Arabs, whether Muslim or not, so the Ba'ath were opposed to Faisal's stress on religious and exclusively Muslim unity.

foundation of an Islamic news agency, Islamic culture centres and various forms of economic co-operation between Muslim countries, including an Islamic Bank.

By the early 1970s King Faisal's pious pan-Islamic musings no longer seemed as fanciful as they had in 1956.

Aramco's oil town on the hill at Dhahran looks like a cover from the *Saturday Evening Post*. There are neat white weatherboard houses, gauzed porches and pitched red roofs, sprinklers play on the lawns, mowers chatter across the verges, and the yellow schoolbuses never fail to halt at the crossing signs. There are oleander hedges, barbecue pits, soda fountains and baseball bleachers. Visitors often comment that this leafy, ordered suburb could be Main Street, USA. All the picture lacks is a church spire poking up above the trees and some sort of bar or tavern – though new residents usually find themselves presented with a helpful little leaflet entitled *The Blue Flame*. Blue is the colour that a spirit lamp burns beneath a still, and, after a series of unfortunate lumber-room explosions, it has been considered prudent to instruct novices in the basics of the process.

You can very easily live inside Aramco's Dhahran township and never realize you are in the Kingdom. There is a cinema beside the hamburger bar, and women are allowed to drive cars inside the compound. America has really made herself at home up on the hill beside Well No. 7, and inside the sparkling headquarters' offices, where a glass case in the main hall displays the Tiffany-crafted trophies that are yours for thirty years' service, there are young men and women who were born, grew up and are now raising families of their own in the company town – second-generation Aramcons raising a third.

By January 1972, when Faisal ibn Abdul Aziz had been King of Sa'udi Arabia for eight years, it seemed as if it could go on for ever. When the writer Leonard Mosley went to Dhahran in that month to find out how the Aramcons viewed their future in a changing Middle East, they admitted to few anxieties.

Libya's new revolutionary leader, Mu'ammar Qadaffi, had just nationalized British Petroleum's installations in his country, and the Iraqi government was preparing to do the same to the northern territory operations of IPC. But the Aramcons were confident it could not happen in Sa'udi Arabia. 'It just isn't in the cards,' an official told Mosley with assurance.

In January 1972 Ahmad Zaki Yamani was pushing for Sa'udi 'participation' in Aramco, a 20 per cent share in operations, but the folks who lived on the hill declined to take the prospect seriously.

'Can you see our parent companies agreeing? Can you see Jersey [Exxon], Socal, Texaco or Mobil letting the Saudis in? . . . No matter how you slice it, it's still nationalization, and that's something we don't believe in. We're Americans, remember?'

The assumption in Dhahran appeared to be that, if the oil company did not agree to Sa'udi participation in its operations, then Sa'udi Arabia would have no choice but meekly to accept 'No' as an answer – and this was January 1972.

Throughout the 1960s oil had stuck at the price set by Monroe Rathbone in 1959, less than $2 a barrel, and there seemed very little that OPEC could do about it. The worldwide glut of oil continued: Russia went on dumping her surpluses, and the development of new fields in Nigeria, Libya and along the Gulf coast in Qatar, Dubai, Abu Dhabi and Oman made the situation worse, from the producers' point of view at least.

An attempt by the Arabs to impose an oil embargo at the time of the Six-Day War had proved a flop. It did not hurt the consumers, who found oil elsewhere, and the Arab producers' own economies could not stand the cutback in revenues.

'Won't Sa'udi Arabia be accused of sabotaging President Nasser?' King Faisal was asked when he decided to resume full pumpings shortly after the embargo started.

Sa'udi Arabia, replied the king, could hardly do anything worse to President Nasser than he had already done to himself.

OPEC tried to reduce the general glut by suggesting ceilings below which its members should keep their pumpings, but no one took these very seriously, least of all Sa'udi Arabia, who steadily expanded her production through the 1960s to exceed, by the early 1970s, the extraordinary level of 8 million barrels per day.

Faisal ibn Abdul Aziz's policy was basically to let Aramco pump and sell as much oil as it wanted. It meant more money for his development programme, and it met his side of the basic transaction on which Sa'udi security was based: oil in exchange for American military protection. Only Kennedy's fighter planes had deterred Nasser from ordering Egypt's armed forces into Sa'udi Arabia at the beginning of the Yemen war, and, in the face of Nasser's hostility, Faisal had little choice but to pursue a policy of compliance with American wishes. This was the reason why the inhabitants of Dhahran felt so secure in their little America, and it was the reason why radical Arabs denounced Faisal in the 1960s as an American stooge.

This particular insult never worried Faisal very much. Sa'udi Arabia had never been colonized by a Western power. It was an independent Arab country, created in its own style, by its own Arab efforts and often in defiance of the West. The inhabitants of the Kingdom felt no need to prove themselves: they were little moved by the sense of grievance animating countries which had, only recently, shaken off colonial tutelage. Faisal saw contact with the West as beneficial, on the whole, to Sa'udi Arabia, and he accorded more weight than he should have done to the United States' presentation of itself as a Christian state, 'one nation under God'. The Sa'udi king was happy to see his kingdom aligned with these 'people of the book' as a force for moderation and stability in the Middle East.

But the Six-Day War marked the beginning of a change, for Nasser's sudden weakness reduced the military threat he had previously posed, while the support the United States gave Israel in the aftermath of her victory made Faisal less and less happy with his role as America's best friend in the Arab world. After the Suez adventure of 1956, President Eisenhower had insisted that Israel abandon all her conquests to return inside her borders and, with a lot of grumbling, Israel had obeyed. But, after her victory in June 1967, Israel was no longer inclined to be so compliant, and nor was America, apparently, very much concerned to force her.

The presidential election of 1968 was marked by the now customary competition for the Jewish vote. On 9 September 1968 Richard Nixon told the Washington Convention of B'nai B'rith that if he were elected he would guarantee Israel 'a technological military margin to more than offset her hostile neighbours' immediate superiority', and one month later President Johnson, seeking support for Senator Hubert Humphrey, announced that he was authorizing negotiations to supply Israel with fifty Phantom F4s, supersonic fighter-bombers comfortably superior to any plane at the disposal of the Arab powers.

As president, Nixon and his Secretary of State, William Rogers, made polite noises about Israel's adhering to UN Resolution 242 which called on her to withdraw inside her pre-1967 boundaries, but

390

in practice the USA sustained the Israeli hold on Sinai, Golan and the West Bank: eighteen more Phantom F4s in September 1970, 180 M60 and M48 tanks in October 1970, eighteen Skyhawk fighters in November of that year, twelve more Phantoms in April 1971, forty-two Phantoms and ninety Skyhawks in February 1972. Nixon held regular meetings with Golda Meir which invariably resulted in increased loans and aid for Israel, and Mrs Meir's ambassador to Washington, with a direct access to the president enjoyed by no other ambassador accredited to the USA, was Yizhak Rabin, the former Israeli chief of staff and architect of the Six-Day War victory.

America justified her military assistance to Israel in terms of the substantial quantities of Soviet arms that Egypt and Syria were receiving, but Faisal's theory of Zionist conspiracy turned that rationale around: the more US aid Israel received, he argued, the more radical grew the feelings of the Arabs around her, and as proof of his claim he could point to the most menacing of all the many consequences of the Six-Day War: the emergence of the Palestinians.

780,000 Arabs had fled or been expelled from their homes by the creation of Israel in 1948, and the miserable existence that many of them had led in refugee camps stimulated the emergence in the late 1950s and early 1960s of the *fedayeen*, 'the men who sacrifice themselves' in Arab parlance – 'terrorists' in the eyes of many in the western world.

Still, Jordan's annexation of the West Bank and of old Jerusalem had meant that over a million Palestinians had been able to live under a Muslim, Arab government in peace and reasonable contentment for nearly twenty years and, so long as the West Bank remained Arab, the *fedayeen* were just a militant fringe, scarcely representative of mainstream Palestinian feeling. Then the Israelis invaded.

'Don't make war,' General de Gaulle had advised Israel's Foreign Minister, Abba Eban, early in 1967. 'You will create a Palestinian nationalism, and you will never be able to get rid of it.'

De Gaulle's warning proved correct. Between 1967 and 1970 the guerrilla activities of the *fedayeen* escalated from twelve per month to that many per day, and they culminated in September of that year with the spectacular triple hijacking of three Western airliners and their destruction in the desert near Amman.

The world was horrified, but King Faisal was more disturbed by the civil war in Jordan to which the Palestinians' defiant display of lawlessness led. 'Black September' 1970 saw King Hussein fighting to recapture his own kingdom from Yasser Arafat, and, though Hussein won, this was at the expense of the Lebanon, where Arafat and his guerrillas moved on, soon to provoke there the civil war which has brought ruin to that hitherto prosperous country.

In March 1973 Palestinian commandos attacked the Sa'udi embassy in Khartoum and murdered three diplomats; in September of that year terrorists assaulted the Sa'udi embassy in Paris. The world was horrified by bloodlettings like the massacre at Lod Airport and the death of thirteen Israeli Olympic athletes in the 1972 Munich shoot-out, but Faisal saw these as acts of war.

What worried him was the bitterness the Palestinians felt towards their brother Arabs. Desperate men with nothing to lose, the Palestinians had, within a matter of years, come to represent a major threat to any Arab regime which had not done enough, in their opinion, to help secure their rights. Placating them was more than a matter of morality; it was a question of survival.

The one bright spot in Faisal's increasingly gloomy view of the Arab world in the aftermath of the Six-Day War was the coming to power of Anwar Sadat, the vice-president who took over in Egypt after Nasser's surprise heart attack and death on 28 September 1970. Devoutly Muslim, more subtle and pragmatic than Nasser, and disavowing Nasser's expansionist ambitions in the Arab World, Sadat got on well with Faisal. The two men had known and liked each other since the 1950s; Sadat talked in simple practicalities, the language of the God-fearing Nile villager; he was no blinkered ideologue, and he privately acknowledged to Faisal the failure of the twin pillars of Nasserism – Arab socialism and dependence upon the Soviet Union.

This was Faisal's chance. The weak point of his criticisms of America's military aid to Israel had always been the Soviet arming of Egypt and Syria. Nixon and his National Security Adviser Henry Kissinger could hardly be blamed for reacting so strongly to the presence in Egypt alone of 16,000 or so Soviet military 'advisers' imported by Nasser – and nor could Faisal, of all people, welcome such a massive communist presence inside the Arab world. So in November 1970, within weeks of Sadat's confirmation as president, Faisal sent his brother-in-law Kamal Adham on a discreet visit to Cairo to broach the subject.

If America forced Israel into some sort of withdrawal, asked Adham, would Egypt respond by moving out the Russians?

Sadat said that he would. He agreed to let Faisal pass the message on to Washington, and so began the gradual loosening of Cairo's ties with Moscow that ended with Anwar Sadat's dramatic expulsion of his Russian advisers, all 16,000 of them, in July 1972.

Anwar Sadat spent much of his youth playing backgammon, a game where skill and concentration can minimize your losses, but where decisive victory comes with the throw of the dice; and his leadership of Egypt since 1970 has been marked by a succession of impulsive gambles, the most notable being his epoch-making journey to Jerusalem in November 1977.

His gamble of July 1972 did not work.

'Why has he done me this favour?' asked Henry Kissinger, astounded by the news of the Russian expulsion. 'Why didn't he demand all sorts of concessions first?'

Kissinger was engrossed by the wind-up of the Vietnam War, and it was election year again in Washington, no time for an administration to start forcing Israel to give up her positions along the Suez Canal. Messages were sent to Sadat that some initiative could be launched when the voting was over, but that was too late for the Egyptian leader. By November 1972 Egypt was buying arms from Russia again – and at a meeting of the Arab Defence Council in January 1973 King Faisal gave his support to this. He agreed that Sa'udi subsidies to Egypt could be directly spent on Communist weaponry.

Anwar Sadat had his own domestic political reasons for severing his military links with Moscow in July 1972, but King Faisal's role in encouraging the gesture has seldom been appreciated outside the Arab world. Kamal Adham had been a regular visitor to Sadat, shuttling across the Red Sea between Jeddah and Cairo. He distributed Sa'udi cash lavishly in Egypt to buy support for Faisal's anti-Russian push. Adham was in Cairo in the days leading up to the expulsion. So was Sultan ibn Abdul Aziz, the Sa'udi Defence Minister. He was travelling back from consultations in Washington, where Joseph Sisco, the Assistant Secretary of State, had enlisted his help to nudge Sadat towards peace talks.

Henry Kissinger has revealed in his memoirs that he knew nothing of this initiative until later. There was conflict between him and the State Department. America was not geared to make the grand response which Sadat's grand gesture demanded – and this failure brought King Faisal and Anwar Sadat together in shared disappointment.

In April 1972, Anwar Sadat gave an address in the mosque of the Imam Husayn in Cairo. It was the anniversary of the Prophet's

393

birthday, and Egypt's leader took as his theme the Arab struggle against Israel.

It was jihad, he said, a holy war. America and Israel had forgotten that the Arabs are bearers of Muhammad's message; they had forgotten that in the face of persecution Muhammad had never surrendered: 'He fought bravely, he stood fast and resisted until the message of truth, the message of faith, the message of Islam was realized'.

Today, declaimed Sadat, 'we are bearers of the same creed. . . . We believe that God, exalted be He, is with us, we believe that right is on our side'.

Times had changed indeed for Egypt's leader to be preaching the message of Islam – and no less remarkable was the transformation that was occurring in the perspectives of King Faisal in these same months. In the spring of 1972 he had brusquely informed Aramco's partners that the unacceptable bogey of 'participation' was not a matter for consideration or debate. It was something they had no choice but to implement immediately – and when the oil companies came to think about it, they decided that the king was right.

The 'conservatism' of Faisal ibn Abdul Aziz was not what it once had been. The Jewish occupation of old Jerusalem, the rising menace of the Palestinians, Faisal's shared Islamic convictions with Sadat, and his increasing mistrust of America as a 'partner' who took his own concerns at all seriously: all these factors were driving the sixty-eight-year-old Sa'udi king towards that momentous action whose repercussions are still being felt to this day.

Looking back to those years before the 1973 oil embargo, it is difficult to discover whether the West had any inkling of the changes that were about to occur, or whether the thoughts of King Faisal were reckoned of the slightest significance to our destiny. The index of the New York Times for 1968 shows twice as much reporting on Albania as on Sa'udi Arabia, five or six times as much on Malaysia in 1969, and four times as much on Burma in 1960. Time magazine managed only one article on the Kingdom in 1969, an obituary of ex-King Sa'ud, dwelling on his physical ailments and on the size of his harem. America's legislators had even less to say. The index to the record of the ninety-second Congress, for 1972, reveals twenty-three mentions of Mexico, fifty-seven mentions of Cuba, and 150 references to the State of Israel. But it carries not one single entry for the Kingdom of Sa'udi Arabia.

Part Five

Petropower

42 Two Weeks that Changed the World

We are not empty phrase-makers. What we will say we will do. If they look upon you lightly or disdainfully, answer them that God honours His Prophet and the citizens of this country. You are the sons of the heroes of old, you are the grandchildren of those who fought beside the Prophet. Be honey to those that seek your friendship, but deadly poison to those who are your enemies.

King Faisal ibn Abdul Aziz, 1973

AT five minutes past two in the afternoon of Saturday, 6 October 1973, 4000 Egyptian guns, rocket launchers and mortars opened up a barrage on the Israeli positions facing them across the Suez Canal. At twenty past, 8000 Egyptian soldiers in rubber boats took to the water, crossing the canal at five points under the cover of MiG fighters screaming in low overhead, and by three o'clock the first sandbagged positions along Israel's fortified Bar Lev line had been occupied.

Israel had prepared a secret weapon to repel attackers across the Suez Canal. Napalm would shoot blazing on to the face of the waters from concealed pipes. But on the night of 5 October Egyptian commandos had blocked the pipes with quick-drying cement – and now, as the Egyptian stormtroopers advanced into Sinai, 700 Syrian tanks along Israel's northern borders started rolling in parade-ground formation across the barbed wire of the cease-fire zone into the Golan Heights.

It was Yom Kippur, the Jewish feast of Atonement, and the Arab armies were taking their revenge for the humiliation of the Six-Day War.

Sheikh Ahmad Zaki Yamani was on his way to Vienna when he heard the news, and suddenly things fell into place. He had had to travel to a conference in San Francisco the previous month, an engagement accepted many months previously, but, when he had gone to King Faisal for permission to travel, the king had been curiously unwilling. Only when Yamani explained how the arrangement had been made long ago did Faisal agree that he could travel.

397

'Come back quickly,' said the king.

Then, on his return, Yamani had had to ask if he could travel again, for he had been chosen by the Gulf members of OPEC to negotiate a new round of price increases with the oil companies in Vienna from Monday, 8 October, for a week.

This time King Faisal was really unhappy. He wanted his Oil Minister beside him, he said, and not until Yamani had explained how crucial the meeting was, and how speculation would be created by his absence, did the king reluctantly agree to his going.

'Is something special going to happen then?' asked Yamani.

The king did not reply.

On the afternoon of Saturday, 6 October 1973, Sheikh Yamani suddenly understood the reason for King Faisal's strange anxieties.

Faisal ibn Abdul Aziz had decided he was ready to use the oil weapon soon after Sadat's expulsion of his Russian advisers in July 1972. After America's failure to respond to this, and during the autumn build-up of aid to Israel that had become one of the rituals of American presidential campaigns, Sadat had confided in Faisal that he now saw war as the only way to break the deadlock over Israel, and the Sa'udi king agreed.

Other Gulf sheikhs were contacted, and by early 1973 Faisal had gathered between $300 and $500 million for Egyptian arms purchases, $400–500 million in balance-of-payment support, plus the $250 million annual subsidy agreed at Khartoum. Sadat was able to pay for his Soviet arms with hard cash, and Faisal also pledged that when the battle started he would be willing to restrict oil supplies to anyone who came to Israel's help.

But King Faisal was a cautious man, and also an optimistic one. Even as he was bankrolling Anwar Sadat, he hoped that some initiative on America's part might remove the need for open hostilities, and early in April 1973 he gave instructions to Ahmad Zaki Yamani. The Oil Minister should go to Washington, said the king, and pass on a message to top officials there. In discussing the participation deal agreed with Aramco early in 1972 Sa'udi Arabia had spoken of expanding her production capacity to the phenomenal total of 20 million barrels per day by the early 1980s. But this level of production would generate far more revenue than the Kingdom could possibly handle – Faisal was having difficulty in 1973 spending the income generated by 8 million barrels a day – and he considered that he was doing the developed world a favour. Unless America took genuine steps to secure justice for Palestinian Arabs and to bring about the restoration to Muslims of Jerusalem's Holy Places, the increased production would stop. Friendship was a two-way thing.

In April 1973, Yamani went to pass the message on to William Rogers, Nixon's Secretary of State, George Schulz, US Secretary of the Treasury, and to Dr Henry Kissinger, National Security Adviser to the president.

Kissinger seemed quite disturbed by Yamani's message. 'This should not go further,' he said. 'I hope you have not mentioned this to anybody else.'

The Security Adviser was disconcerted to hear that he was the third recipient of King Faisal's message, and he repeated to Yamani his conviction that its contents should remain confidential.

Afterwards the Oil Minister wondered why Dr Kissinger should be so concerned to keep the threat of the Arab oil weapon a secret. The Security Adviser had talked in terms of the Arab image and of the importance of the Arabs not appearing threatening or extreme in American eyes.

But Yamani who, like many Arabians, feels that Dr Henry Kissinger's Jewishness hampers his impartiality in Middle Eastern matters, did not accept the Security Adviser's counsel at face value. Dr Kissinger, in the Oil Minister's opinion, could not care less about the Arabs' posture for the Arabs' sake: the security adviser was concerned to prevent the American public from reflecting too deeply on the price they might have to pay for supporting Israeli military conquests – so Yamani decided to release his warning to the press.

'We'll go out of our way to help you,' the Oil Minister told the *Washington Post*. 'We expect you to reciprocate.' America should be more even-handed in its dealings with Israel and the Arabs.

This was, noted the *Washington Post*, 'the first time that Saudi Arabia, the superpower of world petroleum, has publicly linked the flow of its oil to the United States with Washington's Middle East policy'.

But the paper declined to be panicked. 'It is to yield to hysteria to take such threats as Saudi Arabia's seriously,' declared the *Post*'s editorial writer next day, and the Nixon administration agreed.

'Yamani is getting above himself' was one of several off-the-record reactions, suggesting that the forty-year-old Oil Minister had strayed beyond the brief of his cautious master who, as everyone knew, was one Arab leader who could be relied on not to rock the boat.

The oilmen tended to feel the same, and when on 3 May 1973 the Aramco President Frank Jungers, a slow-speaking engineer who had worked in Arabia ever since graduating from Washington University, paid a routine courtesy call on the king he found Faisal warming to his customary theme. The Zionists and the communists, said Faisal, were working to get American concerns 'thrown out of the area', and only in Sa'udi Arabia could the USA feel that their interests were relatively safe.

But then the king developed his argument in a tone Jungers had never heard before. It was getting 'more and more difficult to hold off the tide of opinion,' said Faisal. There were extremists like Qaddafi; there was the bitterness of the Palestinians. The least the American government could do to help him was to issue some 'simple disavowal of Israeli policies and actions'.

Faisal was annoyed by the indifference with which Washington had shrugged off his well-meaning message via Yamani, which he had dictated word for word to his Oil Minister. The *Christian Science Monitor* and *Washington Post* were invited to Taif in July 1973 so that the king could make clear that the warning had come from him personally, and for the first time in his life he gave an interview to American TV. Faisal had not given a filmed interview to anyone since 1967.

'America's complete support of Zionism against the Arabs', he said, 'makes it extremely difficult for us to continue to supply US petroleum needs and even to maintain friendly relations with America.'

'He means what he says,' said Faisal's son Muhammad, who was his father's translator for the interviews, and the journalists nodded politely. But the media consensus was that the old king was bluffing, and inside the State Department Joseph Sisco, in charge of Middle-Eastern affairs, agreed. CIA informants had told him of the pressure that Anwar Sadat was putting on the Sa'udi king to back up the Egyptian campaign for restoration of its Sinai territories, but State Department analysts felt that Faisal's threats were intended to placate Egypt and would never be put into practice.

'There isn't the slightest possibility!' stated Israel's Foreign Minister, Abba Eban, when questioned in May 1973 about the likelihood of an Arab oil embargo. 'The Arab states have no alternative but to sell their oil because they have no other resources at all.'

Israeli intelligence knew that Faisal and Sadat had been stepping up the intensity of their contacts, but they misread the content of their activities. They had not realized that Sadat, while less vocally aggressive than Nasser, felt just as bitterly about the humiliation of the Six-Day War, nor that Faisal had committed himself to supporting an Egyptian counter-strike that autumn. The Sa'udi king believed that the basis of Israel's previous military successes had been foreign weaponry, and he reckoned that an oil embargo could cut off that reinforcement.

'Only make sure when you fight', Faisal told Sadat, 'that you keep on fighting.'

The king made this remark in the presence of Dr Rashad Pharaon and other advisers when he met Sadat in the early months of 1973 for general discussions on war and oil. Six months later, on a summer visit to Cairo, Faisal went into secret session with the Egyptian president, and the two men talked alone for nearly an hour.

'You have decided something,' said Rashad Pharaon afterwards to the king. 'I can tell it. You have decided something big!'

King Faisal said nothing. He did not even smile.

By the summer of 1973 the likelihood of some sort of trouble between Egypt and Israel was scarcely a secret. Israel had twice mobilized, convinced that Egypt was about to cross the Suez Canal, and in May 1973 Kamal Adham told Frank Jungers that Anwar Sadat would soon, in his opinion, have to 'embark on some sort of hostilities'. If he did so, said Adham, Sa'udi Arabia could not afford to stay aloof from the battle, and that could prove fatal to America's interests.

Jungers had no doubt the king's brother-in-law was passing on a message from Faisal himself.

'I knew he meant war,' Jungers later recalled. 'The King liked to give signals, first subtly, then explicitly. This was quite different from his earlier warnings.'

In retrospect, the number of signals Faisal gave out seems quite extraordinary. Late in May 1973, the four Middle East directors of Aramco's parent companies were meeting in Geneva as part of their negotiations with Yamani to implement participation, when the Oil Minister casually suggested they might pay a courtesy call on the king. Faisal had just arrived from Cairo where Sadat, confided Yamani, had been giving him 'a bad time'. The Egyptian president was pushing for more solid backers in his quarrel with Israel.

'Time is running out,' Faisal told the oilmen. He was not prepared, he said, to let Sa'udi Arabia become isolated as Arab anger with America mounted, and he talked in curt, abrupt terms which led the representatives of Aramco to believe that the whole basis of their oil concessions could be at risk. 'You may lose everything,' he warned.

Highly alarmed, all four men were in Washington within days trying to alert government officials to the risk as they saw it. But at the State Department Joseph Sisco had heard it all before. Henry Kissinger would not even give them an appointment. And finally, in the Pentagon, the acting Secretary of Defence Bill Clements, himself once an oilman, with his own drilling company, told the lobbyists they should not be so alarmed: the Arabs would never unite.

Henry Kissinger made policy projections around this time with his staff, and in a world where oil was still cheap they found it difficult to take the prospect of an energy crisis seriously; previous Arab oil embargoes had not worked; Egyptian talk of war seemed laughable, everyone knew the Arabs would get thrashed; while the warnings of Faisal and Yamani lacked the strength and credibility which hindsight attaches to them; in the summer of 1973 neither the Sa'udi king nor his Oil Minister possessed the global status they were soon to acquire.

'Disbelief' was the only word the oilmen could use when they cabled back to Dhahran Washington's reactions to their warnings. 'Some believe that His Majesty is calling wolf where no wolf exists except in his imagination.'

Ten bridges across the Suez Canal and 80,000 Egyptian troops dug into Sinai by midnight on Saturday, 6 October 1973, suggested otherwise. The Egyptians had used water cannon to squirt away the sand ramparts raised by the Israelis. 222 MiGs blasted over Sinai in a series of strikes which achieved 90 per cent of their targets with the loss of just five planes; and in the small hours of Sunday, 7 October, Israel's Sinai command ordered troops along the Bar Lev line to destroy their weapons, surrender, or retreat. At 08.10 hours that morning the Israeli tactical command announced it was surrounded.

'Israel had been boasting of the Six-Day War,' exulted Sadat later. 'Now we could boast of the Six-Hour War.'

Meanwhile in Vienna Sheikh Yamani was marshalling his negotiating team to talk prices at No. 10 Doktor Karl Lueger Ring, the unprepossessing headquarters of OPEC. The Sa'udi Oil Minister was representing the Gulf members of OPEC,* and Arab delegates were passing newspaper articles excitedly to each other and swapping radio reports of developments in Sinai and on the Golan Heights.

'The moment I heard of the war,' says Yamani today, 'I started turning over in my mind the measures we should take: cutbacks in production, embargoes on certain countries. This was quite separate from the question of price.'

But the size of the price increase that OPEC was demanding at Vienna in October 1973 was substantial. Yamani opened the bidding on Monday, 8 October, by asking for increases in the government tax levels which would almost double the posted price from $3 to well over $5 per barrel. George Piercy of Exxon, who headed the companies' team with André Bénard of Shell, responded with an increase of 70 cents per barrel.

All through the 1960s the price of oil had stuck below $2 per barrel. But, as the glut had started to ease towards the end of the decade, the militancy of Libya's Mu'ammar Qaddafi had revealed that by 1970 the surplus was actually turning into a shortage. Qaddafi succeeded with his nationalizations where Mossadeq had failed twenty years earlier because he was able to play off the companies against each other. The world badly needed Libyan oil in 1970 – any oil – and in 1971 at Teheran OPEC had squeezed out of the companies the first general price increase for a decade – the first outright increase, in fact, that OPEC had ever achieved.

The Vienna meeting of October 1973 was OPEC's attempt to bring the price up further. There had been massive devaluations of the dollar with inflation. World demand for oil had been increasing. Small independent companies were already happy to pay $5 per barrel for the oil that producer governments were getting through their participation agreements, so Yamani did not think his demand unreasonable. The company offer of less than $4 probably represented a fair adjustment for inflation and devaluation. But it did not reflect the fact that the great oil glut was now over.

That same Monday, 8 October, with the war still less than forty-eight hours old and Egypt continuing to make advances into Sinai against the unprepared Israelis, King Faisal received in Riyadh two special envoys sent by President Sadat to co-ordinate non-combatant Arab aid.

* The Gulf members of OPEC were Iran, Iraq, Kuwait, Qatar, the United Arab Emirates and Sa'udi Arabia.

'You have made us all proud,' Faisal told Dr Mustapha Khalil, Egypt's oil expert who was travelling with Sadat's assistant Sayed Marei. 'In the past we could not lift our heads up. Now we can.'

Faisal promised the Egyptians $200 million to buy more arms at once. 'What we are giving', he said, 'is not charity. What we offer in money is much less than anything you are offering in lives.' Faisal repeated his pledge to bring oil into play on Egypt's behalf.

Next day in Vienna the oil companies refused to budge on their offer of below $4 per barrel, and Yamani stood equally firm above $5. So Piercy and Bénard told him they needed to take further instructions from their head offices.

But, with Israel now bracing herself to make a counter-attack to retrieve her losses, it was becoming increasingly difficult to keep politics and pricing separate, and on Wednesday, 10 October, the Arab members of OPEC announced that they would be discussing the war and oil policy at a meeting to be held in Kuwait early the following week. This was the deadline that the companies must work to, and on Friday, 12 October, Exxon's Piercy had to tell Yamani that they could not make it. Oil at over $5 per barrel went far beyond existing understandings.

'They wanted someone else to take the blame' is the interpretation that Yamani today places on the reluctance of the companies to agree to OPEC's demand in October 1973. 'They were happy with the higher prices, because that meant higher profits for them, but they didn't want to be the ones to say yes.'

In 1981 Ahmad Zaki Yamani is never slow to point out how the Western oil companies have done very nicely out of the price explosion that followed on the events of 1973. As a direct consequence of dearer oil Exxon replaced General Motors in 1974 as the largest company in the world in gross sales revenue.

But in the first days of the crisis of October 1973 the oilmen's hesitation was understandable. In their opinion, the prospect of paying over $5 per barrel for oil that had cost less than $2 for more than a decade could not possibly be ratified on the nod. What no one quite realized as the negotiations in Vienna reached their climax was that the question of the companies' ratifying or not ratifying the OPEC price was about to become irrelevant.

George Piercy had been in touch with the Exxon headquarters in New York. He carried authority to consent to an increase of as much as $1 per barrel, if that would secure agreement, but he had to tell his principals he judged he would be lucky to settle at $2 more – and Exxon told him that a rise of such magnitude made government consultation 'mandatory'. This would take two weeks. So towards midnight on Friday, 12 October, Piercy and Bénard went to break the news to Yamani in his suite at the top of Vienna's Intercontinental Hotel.

Piercy explained how the companies had to talk to their governments before agreeing to a price increase that would have such an impact on living costs of every sort, and Yamani listened in silence. When the oilman stopped speaking, the minister said nothing. He continued to sit in a silence that seemed to stretch out for minutes, then he ordered Piercy a Coke, slowly took a knife to cut a lime and squeezed the lime into the drink.

Yamani had been on the phone to Riyadh, working out details of a partial embargo which would deter aid to Israel, and he wanted to tie up the price question and set it aside before he travelled home. He was not pleased to hear the company request for an adjournment, and he knew that his more radical fellow delegates would be still less happy.

'They won't like this,' he warned, picking up the phone to try and contact the other delegations in the hotel, eventually getting through to the Kuwaitis.

'They're mad at you,' he said, and soon afterwards one of the Kuwaiti delegation arrived in his pyjamas. Yamani started looking at airline timetables and the meeting broke up.

What was going to happen next? asked George Piercy, speaking on the phone to the Oil Minister next day.

'You can hear it on the radio,' came the reply.

It was the last time OPEC and the oil companies ever met with each other for mutual price negotiations.

Back in Riyadh Yamani discussed possible production cuts with Faisal. Israel was starting, after one week's fighting, to push the Syrians back towards Damascus. But Egypt seemed still to be making reasonable progress down in Sinai, and though there was evidence that American supplies were being flown directly to the Israeli front in Sinai, Faisal was hoping the US would stop short of major intervention.

'The king still wanted to give America a chance to stay out of the fighting,' Yamani now recalls. 'So we agreed to cut back production by just 5 per cent per month. A full embargo, we agreed, was something we would implement only if we felt that things were absolutely hopeless.'

On Tuesday, 16 October 1973, the OPEC delegates who had been in Vienna reassembled at the Sheraton Hotel in Kuwait to announce that they were unilaterally implementing the price increase which the companies had rejected the previous week: the price of oil would go up from \$3.01 to \$5.12 per barrel forthwith, and, in the heat of war, and without anyone fully realizing at the time, the concept that crude-oil prices were a matter for negotiation between producers and consumers via the companies had vanished into history. Henceforth oil prices would be set and announced by the producers as it suited them, and the world could like it or lump it.

'We have you – how you say it? –' remarked one of the delegates, 'over a barrel.'

The Iranian delegation then left for home, since the Shah wished to preserve a careful distinction between the general price rise, in which he shared, and any production cuts or embargoes, which were purely Arab matters – the Shah being a principal supplier of oil to Israel. The delegates got to work.

The radicals felt that their hour had come. Iraq's Oil Minister, Sadoon Hammadi, called for 'total nationalization' of all American oil interests in the Middle East, the withdrawal of all Arab funds invested in the United States, and the immediate severing of diplomatic relations with Washington. Libya's representative, Izz al Din al Mabruk, wanted to expropriate *all* foreign-owned oil companies, not just American ones. And the Kuwaiti cell of the Palestine Liberation Organization, hearing of the discussions, and furious that they had not been invited, leapt into a taxi and descended on the Sheraton to make sure that their demands were taken account of.

The news from the war was not encouraging. The Israelis had struck back in Sinai the previous day and had crossed the Bitter Lake. In the north the Syrians were losing all the ground they had gained on the Golan Heights, and Israeli air strikes were intensifying. It was a difficult moment for Yamani to maintain that the 5 per cent monthly production cuts he had worked out with King Faisal could really have a major impact on events.

406

But the Sa'udi king was still adhering to his original strategy.

'We discussed the philosophy of the embargo before I left Riyadh,' Yamani remembers today. 'Did we want to punish, or did we want to put on pressure? We were not interested in empty gestures.'

Threatening relatively gentle but progressive production cuts was, in Faisal's eyes, the best way to deter America from massive intervention on Israel's side – and it would also enable Sa'udi Arabia to maintain her sanctions over an extended period without crippling herself financially, for the failure of the embargoes of 1967 and of 1956 before that loomed large in his mind. In these first hurried hours after the price rise, no one had fully grasped how much easier it had suddenly become to sustain an embargo. The 70 per cent increase in prices now made it possible almost to halve production without any loss of revenue.

Algeria gave crucial support to Yamani as the delegates argued. King Faisal's schedule of phased reductions won the day, and at 9.30 that evening the journalists crowding the lobby of the Sheraton were presented with two sheets of lined writing paper hastily scribbled in Arabic. Several phrases had been lightly crossed out and others pencilled in, and, by the time the statement had been through the hotel copier, even those journalists who read Arabic found it difficult to work out exactly what the Oil Ministers were saying, for the document literally set out on paper the disagreements that had attended its making.

A sentence insisting on 'the legitimate rights of the Palestinian people' floated in one margin and was indicated by an arrow – presumably a last-minute inclusion at the insistence of the taxi-borne members of the PLO – while Ahmad Zaki Yamani, who had actually written the statement, was not available for elucidation, since he had set off for Riyadh in his private jet even before the statement was released.

Arab oil production would be cut back immediately by 10 per cent, with further reductions of 5 per cent for every month that the conflict was not settled to Arab satisfaction. But 'any friendly state which has extended or shall extend effective material assistance to the Arabs' would not have its supplies cut, and this went for 'any state which takes active and important measures against Israel'.

It was crude blackmail, routine power politics, or long-delayed justice, depending on your point of view, and the statement ended on a note of conciliation: 'The Arab Ministers confirm the Arab nations' sincere will for co-operation with all other peoples and our readiness to supply the world with its oil needs in spite of all sacrifices on our side, provided that the world sympathizes with us and condemns the aggression.'

The Iraqi Oil Minister, Sadoon Hammadi, had left the Sheraton before this final appeal for sympathy was agreed upon. He had walked out of the meeting furious that the Sa'udis should still be considering American feelings at the height of a great Arab war.

But Yamani was under the strictest orders from King Faisal. The old Sa'udi ruler was still hoping that he could keep America out of the conflict. The king had dispatched his Minister of State, Omar Saqqaf, to Washington with a personal letter to Richard Nixon, for Faisal knew that Russia had started airlifting supplies, particularly SAM 6 anti-aircraft missiles, to both Syria and Egypt on the previous Saturday. America was bound to insist on maintaining an equal balance of replenishment: 'we shall not', Richard Nixon had already announced with a flourish, 'let Israel go down the tubes.'

The oilmen had already put in their word. On 12 October, the day before the Russians started reinforcing Egypt and Syria, the four chairmen of Aramco's controlling companies signed a memorandum to the president pointing out that increased US military aid to Israel 'will have a critical and adverse effect on our relations with the moderate Arab countries'.

With the personal visit of Saqqaf, this letter from the chairmen of four of the USA's largest companies represented lobbying at a high level. But Nixon's chief of staff Alexander Haig did not reply to the oilmen's letter for three days after its delivery by special messenger, while Omar Saqqaf was also kept waiting, for the US President had other matters on his mind: on 10 October 1973 his vice-president, Spiro Agnew, pleaded guilty to tax-evasion charges and resigned; on 12 October the Court of Appeals directed the president to surrender his Watergate tapes; that same day Nixon nominated Gerald Ford as his new vice-president; on 20 October Attorney-General Elliott Richardson and Deputy Attorney General William B. Ruckelshaus resigned rather than obey Nixon's order to fire Watergate Special Prosecutor Archibald Cox – who was then fired in any case – and on 23 October the president agreed to surrender his tapes to Judge Sirica.

'This war', wrote Nixon later, 'could not have come at a more complicated domestic juncture'. Digging himself ever deeper into the

408

bunker of his own personal political fate, the US President left Henry Kissinger to manage the day-to-day details of the crisis in the Middle East.

The trouble was that Henry Kissinger had only moved one month previously from the National Security Council to the Secretaryship of State, and, as he was to say several times in the course of the next few weeks, Anwar Sadat had not given him the time even to open the Middle East file. So Kissinger was to interpret the Arab–Israeli conflict in these hurried early days primarily through the perspective he had developed in other areas – the US–Soviet rivalry – and, when the secretary of state started to receive reports of a Russian airlift of supplies to the Arab combatant countries, it made a deep impression on him.

Till that point Kissinger had been reflecting, with some subtlety, that the Egyptian successes in Sinai might provide an opportunity to open negotiations for some new settlement in the Middle East. He had deliberately obstructed Israeli reinforcement efforts, pleading the excuse of bureaucratic delays inside the Pentagon. His concern had been to safeguard Sadat's Sinai breakthrough. Kissinger wanted hostilities to end with the Israelis less arrogant and the Arabs less humiliated than had been the case after the Six-Day War, and he doubted that the Israelis needed all the supplies they were asking for. Promising Golda Meir full replenishment once the war was over, the Secretary of State restricted the flow of ammunition and missiles to Tel Aviv.

But news of the Soviet airlift changed all this. It has since become clear that many of the Russian transports screened by Western radar overflying Cyprus airspace towards Syria and Egypt were more than half-empty. Cyprus air traffic control records show no more than sixty flights on the peak night of Friday, 12 October, as compared to the magic 'hundred planes per day' figure which inflamed US popular opinion at the time – and which inspired Mayor Richard Daley of Chicago to proclaim: 'Go ahead, Israelites, be sure to remove every Arab from the soil of Israel!'

Even had the Russian planes been full, they were, in any case, too late to do much more than rally Arab disarray in face of Israeli counter-attack. By Tuesday, 16 October, the Israeli armies were well entrenched in an enclave on the Cairo side of the Suez Canal, while in the north they were approaching the suburbs of Damascus.

But after 13 October Henry Kissinger was no longer thinking in

409

terms of the realities on the ground. He saw himself locked once again in the battle of wills he had fought in other corners of the globe. The Russians must not be allowed to think that they could get away with it, and on 15 October 1973 the USAF planes which had been loading up for several days were given orders to take off for Tel Aviv.

Two days later Omar Saqqaf was finally granted his audience at the White House. The Sa'udi was angry from a remark made to him during a press conference the previous day.

The Sa'udis could drink their oil, said one reporter.

'All right,' replied Saqqaf bitterly, 'we will.'

Like the three Arab Foreign Ministers who accompanied him, from Algeria, Kuwait and Morocco, Saqqaf was not pleased to have been kept waiting while President Nixon argued with his people about a burglary.

Kissinger was at his most conciliatory: 'The President and I will be more active as soon as the war ends. We shall undertake a major diplomatic effort. . . . Any cease-fire that would now take place would have to take into account the efficiency and valour of Arab arms. . . . We recognize the new realities in the Middle East.'

And Nixon added, when the Foreign Ministers moved on into the Oval Office: 'We are not going to be constrained by domestic politics. We'll formulate our foreign policy on the basis of our national interests.'

Saqqaf was favourably impressed. President Nixon, he afterwards told the waiting press, had promised a settlement that was 'peaceful, just and honourable'. The president had succeeded in bringing peace to Vietnam and now he would bring peace to the Middle East as well. Saqqaf reported back positively to King Faisal, and it looked as if the Sa'udi policy of restrained warning had succeeded.

But Saqqaf and Faisal did not reckon with the effect that the continuing Russian airlift had upon the cold war anxieties of Henry Kissinger and Richard Nixon – while the Americans, for their part, had come to doubt that the old Sa'udi king would ever actually unleash his ultimate sanction as he threatened. On Thursday, 18 October 1973, the day after he had received King Faisal's personal emissary with such courtesies and promises of sympathetic action, Richard Nixon formally submitted to Congress a request for no less than $2.2 billion in emergency military aid to the State of Israel.

When the storm broke, State Department spokesmen maintained that no one should have been surprised. The president was merely seeking formal congressional approval for the airlift to Israel which, everybody knew, had been going on since the previous Monday to counterbalance Russia's reinforcements to the Arabs.

But $2.2 billion was an extraordinary sum of money. It was more than an adjustment to the power balance. It constituted a massive overweighting in Israel's favour, for the Israelis themselves had put in requests which the Pentagon reviewed and which were priced at only $850 million – and that had been the amount of US reinforcements agreed upon.

But then President Nixon had looked at the Russian airlift, and $850 million did not seem very much to him. 'If we're going to do it,' said the president, 'let's do it big.'

A really massive reinforcement would impress Israel, it would win over pro-Jewish opinion at a moment when the Watergate-beleaguered president desperately needed support, and it would hit the Russians right on the chin.

'I never believe in little plays when big issues are at stake,' Nixon proudly told Golda Meir two weeks later. The Arabs would get angry, whatever aid he sent.

It was the same instinct for overkill that would lead the American president, on 25 October, to put all US forces on a nuclear alert; in its sheer bravura it was, remarked one of Kissinger's aides, 'pure Nixon'. In his memoirs the deposed president was to boast that the 550 missions flown to Tel Aviv by American planes in October–November 1973 represented 'an operation bigger than the Berlin airlift of 1948–49' – though, as his next paragraph says, 'in fact, the Israelis had already begun to turn the tide of battle on their own'.

Henry Kissinger, at least, has had second thoughts. 'I made a mistake,' he was saying within weeks of the decision that he shared with Nixon.

'In retrospect,' he says today, 'it was not the best-considered decision that we made.'

It was a decision that was to cost America and the entire oil-consuming world dear. The president and secretary of state might have reflected that Omar Saqqaf, bearing Faisal's personal letter to Nixon, was considered by the Sa'udi king as an extension of himself, and that Faisal, battling against the extremism of his fellow oil producers, saw himself as holding the line for the USA. If Nixon or Kissinger had passed on their anxieties about the Russian reinforcements through Saqqaf, it might have mitigated the shock. But they

411

gave no warning, Saqqaf left the White House with the impression that the Americans respected the Sa'udi viewpoint, and Faisal took the news of the Israeli rescue package as a direct personal insult. Either Nixon had not bothered to consider the feelings of his Sa'udi allies, or, if he had, he did not care – and suddenly America's best friend in the Arab world became her fiercest enemy.

Friday is a day of rest in Riyadh, but on Friday, 19 October 1973, King Faisal was in his office when he received Richard Nixon's cable setting out his reasons, after the event, for his massive reinforcement to Israel. Faisal's uncle Abdullah ibn Abdul Rahman was with him. So was Rashad Pharaon. Ahmad Zaki Yamani was summoned by telephone and the Oil Minister arrived at the Riyassa Palace soon after eight in the evening.

'The TV News goes out at nine,' said Yamani. 'If you make a decision now, we can get it announced at once.'

'Write this down,' said King Faisal, and less than one hour later the world was told the news.

The Kingdom was declaring jihad, holy war, at King Faisal's express intruction and, as part of that holy war, all oil shipments to the United States were being halted at once. The anger of one old man was about to have undreamed-of consequences.

43 Burning Concern

KING Faisal's momentous oil embargo of 20 October 1973 did not achieve a single one of its stated objectives. The cease-fire which the USA and USSR together imposed two days later upon Israel, Syria and Egypt would have been imposed in any case; Israel ended the October war, thanks to US aid, better equipped militarily than she had ever been before, and Faisal's ambition to shrink Israel back inside her pre-1967 boundaries remains unfulfilled to this day.

Nor did the withholding of the 638,500 barrels of oil which Sa'udi Arabia had been selling to America every day for the first 10½ months of 1973 ever come close, in itself, to jeopardizing the power or diverting the policies of the United States, since it accounted for less than 4 per cent of America's daily 17 million barrel consumption. It was the interaction which Faisal's embargo had with other forces that made it so decisive.

Arab politics had an immediate multiplier effect. 'If Sa'udi Arabia moves from A to B,' remarked a Beirut oil consultant in 1974, 'then every other oil producer must move at least as far, if not to C.'

No one could let themselves be out-radicalized by the Sa'udis. Within days of 20 October every other Arab country but Libya and Iraq had joined in the total boycott of the USA – and also of the Netherlands, whose Foreign Minister had come out with some forth-right pro-Israeli statements – and by mid-November 1973 Middle-Eastern oil exports were down to 60 or 70 per cent of their normal levels. This hit hardest at Europe and Japan, dependent upon the Middle East for 75 per cent of their supplies, and the sudden shortage gave a vicious twist to the price increases that had marked the end of the sixties' glut.

Here was the 'sting'. Competing desperately for dwindling supplies, consumers showed themselves willing to pay unparalleled money for their oil – bids of $12–17 per barrel were made in an

413

auction the Iranian State Oil Company staged on 16 December 1973 – and, when OPEC's members met in Teheran a week later to survey the supply situation, they decided they could comfortably raise their posted price from $5 to $11.65 per barrel: a quadrupling of the price that had applied before Yamani's Vienna meeting ten weeks earlier.

Faisal himself, already worried by the effect that spiralling energy costs were having on the world economy, wanted a much smaller price rise, and was angry that Yamani had not been able to hold down the increase. But if any one man was responsible for the supply shortage it was Faisal, and, still committed to his embargo, he was powerless to undermine the price rise with extra Sa'udi production. $11.65 for a barrel of oil represented six times the level that had applied throughout the 1960s, and in his pursuit of his own political objectives Faisal ibn Abdul Aziz had sprung a trap that the developed world had been building round itself for more than a decade.

The trap was cheap energy. Since the end of the Second World War the Western oil companies had done a remarkable job in providing the West with a stable supply of petrol at a steady price. Governments had helped them from time to time, intervening, as in Iran in the early fifties, to preserve the cohesion of the system, and this had greatly aided economic progress and growth. All through the 1960s, Middle-Eastern oil had been marketed at the constant price of $1.80 per barrel, and, in a context of inflation, this meant that oil grew effectively cheaper every year. Even after OPEC managed to raise its prices above the $2 mark in 1971, the consuming countries were still paying less, in real terms, than they had in 1958.

Whole social patterns and ways of life were founded upon this happy phenomenon. Britain had never had it so good and enjoyed the binge of the 'swinging sixties'. All over the globe the surplus money in young people's pockets financed a new pop culture, a drug culture, assorted recipes for changing the world, and then a wave of youthful unrest when none of these fads delivered on their promises. In America the flight from the inner cities to the suburbs was based upon cheap petrol. The migration to the south-west Sun Belt cities like Phoenix, Arizona, was based on the cheap air-conditioning which made life tolerable there during the summer, and, in ways great and small, happiness in the developed world became bound up with a continuing supply of cut-price energy. In the decade up to 1973 the standard American car increased in weight by a third of a ton; colour television sets required 33 per cent more power than black and white

414

King Faisal at prayer, 1968

Top King Faisal dances the *ardha*
Above Yemen: peace agreed
between King Faisal and
President Nasser, Khartoum,
August 1967
Right Faisal as Foreign Minister
after a meeting with President
Eisenhower, March 1953

Opposite
Top King Faisal on pilgrimage,
Mecca, 1964
Below King Faisal, 1967

sets; frost-free refrigerators used 40 per cent more power than the conventional kind.

But the price of all this was ever-increasing dependence on oil. The massive domestic coal reserves of the USA became uneconomic to exploit in competition with cheap oil, and coal use fell from 51 per cent of fuel consumption in 1951 to 19 per cent in 1973.

America drank more and more heavily of her own oil reserves. In 1970, one of modern history's unsung turning points, US domestic oil production peaked, and from that day onwards American purchases of oil abroad increased remorselessly. Overall US oil imports expanded 52 per cent between 1969 and 1972, oil imports from the Middle East increased by 83 per cent, and, when energy prices exploded, the effect was catastrophic: in 1972 the foreign oil bill of the United States was $3.96 billion; by 1974 it was $24 billion.

The lights in Times Square were switched off; petrol stations started rationing sales; speed limits and weekend driving restrictions were introduced; Volkswagen sales expanded; the temperature set on the White House thermostat became a matter of national concern. All over America and the developed world ordinary people found that their lives became slower, darker and chillier as a result of King Faisal's oil embargo, and 'Arab' became a word of abuse – 'off the record', of course.

On the record, the politicians of the developed world suddenly discovered what burning concern they had always nourished for the political and social problems of the Middle East. The Foreign Ministers of the European Community met within two weeks of the embargo to call on Israel 'to end the territorial occupation which it has maintained since the conflict of 1967', and phrases that were to become the platitudes of post-1973 world politics – 'a just and lasting settlement', 'the legitimate rights of the Palestinians' – took flight for the first time.

Oil, and the panic which the possible deprivation of it had aroused, was not actually mentioned in the communiqué. That would scarcely have been dignified. But there was little dignity in the speed with which, after a brief attempt to act in concert, the consumers broke ranks to make deals of their own with the producing countries. By 11 December 1973 the Japanese Foreign Minister was in Riyadh for 'talks on improving bilateral relations'; Michel Joubert soon had a package signed guaranteeing France crude oil over a twenty-year period; and the Belgians, Germans, Italians, Swiss and Greeks all scurried along their own respective paths to the Middle East.

The British saved travelling expenses. Trade Secretary Peter Walker and Chancellor of the Exchequer Anthony Barber did homage in St Moritz on 24 January 1974, waiting for the shah to come off the ski slopes to promise them an extra 5 million tons of oil in the coming twelve months in return for £100 million of British goods.

In reality, Europe, America and Japan had more oil than they realized in the winter of 1973–4. The Shah took advantage of the Arab boycott to increase Iranian pumpings to the maximum, while Libya and Iraq, with that perverse logic particular to Arab radicals, actually increased their sales to the West in November and December 1973 in order to dissociate themselves from the 'reactionary' Sa'udis and sheikhs of the Gulf.

But the panic among the consumers was real enough. So was the new price of oil, and, as the cash to meet their energy bills drained out of the developed economies in the winter of 1973–4, people began to reflect on the grimmer, longer-term prospects that loomed beyond petrol station queues. Ever-expanding economic growth was not, it seemed, a fact of life. The progress that the developed world had made in the last quarter of a century could no longer be assumed to lie in the nature of existence, in Keynesian economics or even in the cleverness and industry of Western man. It owed much to very special circumstances that did not look like repeating themselves, and this betokened grim adjustments in the years to come. Governments must reconcile themselves to long-term balance-of-payments deficits; the reduced cash flow in national economies would mean higher rates of unemployment throughout the developed world; the temptation for governments to print more money, and thus fuel inflation, became even harder to resist; and it was difficult to see how all the waves of cash suddenly swamping the oil producers – the so-called petrodollars – could possibly be recycled for the benefit of the world economy.

With the prospect of international recession looming on a scale not seen since the 1930s, stock-exchange prices, capitalism's best indicator of its volatile hypochrondria, collapsed spectacularly. The American Dream itself seemed called into question, and the Secretary-General of the United Nations spoke gloomily to the General Assembly about the 'note of helplessness and fatalism creeping into world affairs'. As the *Financial Times* pronounced in a memorable headline in the winter of 1973, 'The Future will be Subject to Delay'.

All these consequences flowed from a combination of long-term economic and social forces that the world is still trying to unravel, but their coming together in the winter of 1973–4 was concentrated with rare impact by the anger of one Arab prince. So it was scarcely surprising that in a few short months Faisal ibn Abdul Aziz came to be credited with more international power and significance than any Arab ruler had possessed for centuries.

Henry Kissinger was perceptibly nervous as his plane banked over the desert approaching Riyadh.

'Only Wasps can disembark here,' he said, trying to joke with the journalists accompanying him. 'Aren't there any Wasps among you?'

Several hands went up.

'Good,' said the secretary, 'you can go first. . . . And *you* three,' pointing at three reporters he knew were Jewish, 'you three get off last.'

It was 8 November 1973, a month since Anwar Sadat's forward troops had stormed across the Suez Canal, two and a half weeks since the imposition of the Sa'udi oil embargo, and Dr Kissinger was embarking on the first visit of a US Secretary of State to the Kingdom for twenty years. Time was when no itinerary that included Cairo, Tel Aviv and Peking would have bothered with Riyadh on the way, but times had changed.

How did Dr Kissinger intend to get the embargo raised?, every journalist on the plane wanted to know.

'I'd like to enjoy a little night life with you fellows in Riyadh,' he replied, trying to parry the question. 'But I understand it starts at four in the afternoon and ends an hour later.'

When Kissinger had been talking to Anwar Sadat in Cairo the previous day, he had asked the Egyptian leader what to expect of 'the mightiest Arab of a millennium'.

'Well, Dr Henry,' Sadat replied, 'he'll probably preach to you about Communism and the Jews.'

So it proved, and Kissinger had framed his own approach to match.

'We were motivated', said the US Secretary of State, starting straight in with the $2.2 billion airlift that he knew was the heart of the matter, 'by a desire to prevent an increase of Communist

417

influence, and when the Soviets began to send in arms, we had to react.'

Faisal listened in silence, his never cheerful features frozen with even more distaste than usual, his long fingers plucking specks of lint from the blackness of his cloak. He was not impressed with the American excuses.

'The United States', declared the king in his thin voice, 'used to stand up against aggression – you did that in World War Two and in 1956 during the Suez War. If the United States had done the same after 1967, we would not have witnessed this deterioration. . . .

'Before the Jewish State was established, there existed nothing to harm good relations between Arabs and Jews. There were many Jews in Arab countries. When the Jews were persecuted in Spain, Arabs protected them. When the Romans drove the Jews out, Arabs protected them. At Yalta, it was Stalin who said there had to be a Jewish State.' With this, King Faisal soared into the litany that Sadat had predicted:

'Israel is advancing Communist objectives. . . . Among those of the Jewish faith there are those who embrace Zionism. . . . Most of the immigration to Israel is from the Soviet Union. . . . They want to establish a Communist base right in the Middle East. . . . And now, all over the world,' said the king, looking straight at Kissinger, 'the Jews are putting themselves into positions of authority.'

'Your Majesty,' responded the American, unabashed, 'our problem now is how to proceed from the present situation – which we know is intolerable – to genuine peace.'

'That's easy,' replied Faisal shortly. 'Make Israel withdraw.' It could have been Abdul Aziz advising Roosevelt to site the Jewish homeland in Germany.

Might not Faisal, asked Dr Kissinger, take steps to limit the application of his oil embargo?

The United States, repeated the king, should first order Israel to withdraw.

Might not His Majesty reflect on the psychological impact the embargo was having on American popular attitudes towards the Arab cause?

The Palestinians, said Faisal, should be restored to their rightful homeland.

The same blank simplicities met every effort the American made to inch forward his diplomacy. Edward Sheehan, one of the journalists

418

with whom Kissinger had joked on the plane, encountered equally stark responses when he later asked Faisal, in a private interview, about Jerusalem's Holy Places.

'Only Muslims and Christians have holy places and rights in Jerusalem,' said the king. 'The Jews have no shrines in Jerusalem.'

What about the Wailing Wall?

'The Jews have no rights in Jerusalem,' repeated Faisal, citing a League of Nations inquiry which showed, he said, that the Wailing Wall was part of the al Aqsa mosque. 'Another wall can be built for them and they can wail against that.'

Dr Kissinger flew out of Riyadh on 9 November 1973, with the Sa'udi oil embargo as firmly in place as it had been when he arrived.

On 22 February 1974 King Faisal convened his Islamic brethren to a summit conference in Pakistan, and all of them attended. It was indicative of the prestige, power and wealth that the Sa'udi king had acquired in a matter of months that even Iraq felt the time had come to put in an appearance at a pan-Islamic gathering, and eight other nations also attended for the first time.*

A significant ninth newcomer was the Palestine Liberation Organization, elevated from being a conference observer to full membership, and Yasser Arafat was welcomed and accorded all the dignity of a head of state. The oil boycott had made militancy respectable.

'The armies of Pakistan are the armies of Islam,' proclaimed Pakistan's Prime Minister, Zulfikar Ali Bhutto. 'We shall enter Jerusalem as brothers-in-arms!'

Islamic solidarity was the order of the day. Iraq suspended her border quarrel with Iran and resumed diplomatic relations she had broken off four years earlier. Libya's Mu'ammar Qaddafi sank his differences with both Anwar Sadat and Faisal. Sa'udi Arabia decided to normalize relations with the Marxist government of South Yemen that had taken over from the British in Aden, and even Pakistan managed a faint smile in the direction of Bangladesh, which had been East Pakistan until two years earlier.

Anwar Sadat had lost as much ground as he had gained in the war of October 1973, while Syria had sustained a serious defeat. But the impact of Faisal's boycott and the sight of the world's greatest nations

---

* As well as Iraq, the nations who joined the Islamic Conference for the first time in February 1974 were Bangladesh, Cameroon, Gabon, Guinea-Bissau, Uganda and Upper Volta.

grovelling for their oil had given Muslims in general, and Arabs in particular, a very warm feeling inside. Faisal's second Islamic summit overflowed with all the euphoria and self-confidence of a victory rally.

The conference resolutions satisfied every Arab ambition, short of actually accomplishing them, and from the summit emerged for the first time a coherent Muslim bloc which started to wield its power in other international forums: in 1974 the UN General Assembly invited the PLO to participate in its debates on Palestine, granted the PLO observer status and called for Palestinian self-determination; similar Islamic pressure got Israel barred from full membership of UNESCO and cut off all UNESCO aid; and in 1975 the United Nations condemned Zionism as a form of racial discrimination.

Israel's leaders learned in the years after 1973 to laugh off General Assembly resolutions as South Africa's rulers had been doing for a decade. Golda Meir and her successor Yitzhak Rabin rejected the victories of the Muslim bloc as 'bought votes', and Western analysts were soon pointing to the obvious link between Arab oil wealth and the rise of Islamic feeling and pressure after 1973.

But such criticism did not bother King Faisal, and whenever sceptical questioners suggested to him that oil wealth had, perhaps, played just as large a role as God in the 1970s renaissance of Islam, he would shrug his shoulders at the irrelevance of the distinction.

'Who', he would ask, 'do you think gave us the oil in the first place?'

Faisal saw the success of the second Islamic summit as vindicating everything he had worked for since he had written his first, unregarded paper on pan-Islamic unity nearly twenty years earlier, and buoyed up by it he agreed to the lifting of his oil embargo on 19 March 1974. He had not achieved the objectives he had set himself in his fury five months earlier, but the embargo had brought home to world opinion 'the importance of the Arab world for the welfare of the world economy', and, as the OPEC statement of 19 March continued, this had promoted 'the assumption of political stances which openly condemned Israel's expansionist policy.' It was a great improvement on 1967.

The resumption of supplies to America was only grudging. But in February 1974 America undertook to sell to the Kingdom modern tanks, naval vessels and fighter aircraft of a sophistication and power never previously released to Arab countries, and this, for King Faisal, was a real step forward. Dr Kissinger also promised that America

420

would launch a major initiative to transfer technology to Sa'udi Arabia, and this was equally significant, for the quadrupling of oil prices had created a serious and unusual problem for the Kingdom: what to do with all its money.

So that's a problem? King Faisal had discovered that it was.

Before the 1973 embargo Sa'udi Arabia had already been experiencing difficulty in disposing of an income of $8–9 billion a year. By the spring of 1974 revenues were running at an annual rate of over $34 billion, a quantum leap, and the country simply did not possess the population or the economy to absorb that sort of cash overnight. As Ahmad Zaki Yamani had explained in his unheeded warning of the previous spring, Sa'udi Arabia was actually doing herself damage by pumping up every barrel of oil that the developed world asked for, since she could earn more than enough to live comfortably on just 4 or 5 million barrels a day. All the Kingdom could do with its multiplying petrodollar surplus was to deposit it in Western banks and see its value eroded by inflation – and, with prices rising, oil was more valuable left in the ground.

But the more cash Sa'udi Arabia invested in the Western economies, the more dependent she became upon their help. So if she should refuse to supply the developed world with all the oil that it asked for, then her own investment in the West would be damaged by the resulting recession. The Kingdom lost money if it pumped more oil, and it lost money if it pumped less.

The only solution was development: dead money should be transformed into productive assets; industries and services should be created in the Kingdom; a framework of steel plants, cable factories, hotels, telephone exchanges, hospitals and refineries should be developed: the Stanford Research Institute was hired as economic advisers to the Kingdom, and so was hatched the hallowed 'infrastructure' to whose erection Sa'udi Arabia has been dedicated ever since.

It was to the creation of this infrastructure that Dr Kissinger pledged American support in the summer of 1974. Mountains of petrodollars would be lavished on industrial complexes that would rise in the desert, one at Yanbu on the west coast, one at Jubail on the east, as well as industrial estates outside Riyadh and Jeddah; there would be new roads, railways, airports and expensive new airliners to fly between them; more schools and universities would be born, the ministries would get new offices, there would be housing estates and

421

supermarket complexes for the foreign workers who would be needed to make possible the creation of the new utopia – the possibilities for expansion were legion.

King Faisal had launched Sa'udi Arabia's first Five-Year Plan in 1970, and through 1974 economists laboured to expand the goals for the second five years. The challenge was to soak up some of the extra revenues produced by the oil price explosion, and there was no shortage of helpful suggestions.

Suddenly the Kingdom found itself the destination for a new kind of pilgrim. He wore a collar and tie, he usually carried a briefcase, he was probably sleeping in a hotel corridor, and he could sell you *anything*: a cement-block factory, a string of emeralds, fitted carpets, the Koran on cassette, a ready-to-assemble port or an early-warning radar system – nothing was too bizarre or expensive to be offered to the Sa'udis as the petrodollars showered in.

'The sky over Riyadh is black,' wrote James Akins, US ambassador to the Kingdom, 'with vultures with new get-richer-quicker plans under their wings.'

In the early months of the post-embargo bonanza, sellers sold and buyers bought with a semi-hysteria that could be compared, and frequently was, with the Klondyke in the Gold Rush. During one month in 1974 property prices in Riyadh were doubling on a weekly basis. Fortunes were made overnight, and, if some made more money than others did, nobody actually lost out, for the boom took off and kept on soaring.

Car imports tripled in a year. Consumer goods congested the ports. To clear the ships queueing off Jeddah to service the Sa'udi construction boom, helicopters were flying in cement, twenty bags at a time. Inflation soared. You could not look around the towns of the Kingdom in 1974 and 1975 and fail to see someone making money hand over fist, and everybody was delighted – except the man who had made it all possible.

44 The Dreams of King Faisal

ALONE among the Kingdom's modern rulers, Faisal ibn Abdul Aziz was a direct descendant of the Teacher. He was the son of the *qadi*'s daughter, whom Abdul Aziz had married when he conquered Riyadh in 1902, and this meant that Faisal could trace his parentage straight back to Muhammad ibn Abdul Wahhab. Nor was the connection one of blood alone. Faisal's mother Tarfah died when he was still a baby, so his early childhood was spent in the strict Wahhabi household of his grandfather, Sheikh Abdullah ibn Abdul Lateef, and this imprinted Faisal's soul and fibre with asceticism of rare intensity.

The consequences of his 1973 oil embargo horrified the Sa'udi king. The flood of material goods into the Kingdom dismayed him. The spiritual dangers of easy affluence distressed him more. His single gesture of piety and honour seemed to have opened a Pandora's Box that threatened to turn his realm into a parody of all he held dear, for, with such wealth to play with, what need had his people to seek heavenly riches? If the national dynamic was now to be directed into steel mills and pipelines and gas-refining plants, would not life in the Kingdom come to be shaped less by the Koran than by the commandments of the Five-Year Plan?

This dilemma preyed on Faisal's mind. Had he betrayed his people? Which way should he lead them now? His great moment of success had proved sterile and empty for him, and in 1974 Faisal's closest family, his sons and intimates, suddenly found that he was growing away from them. The king went earlier to the office, stayed later, worked weekends, took no relaxation. Even when he was with his wife and children he seemed to be drifting in a different world, lost in an impenetrable melancholia. The unexpected problems that wealth had brought seemed to have overwhelmed him.

'The profligacy, the greed, he felt he could not stem it,' remembers his son Muhammad. 'He became so bound up in his work, there was almost nothing private of him left.'

'We used to feel the pain,' remembers his eldest son Abdullah, 'and we could do nothing.'

Abdullah resolved to try. He had a small villa at the creek north of Jeddah, and he invited his father to come there one Friday evening.

'There'll be nobody there but family,' he promised. 'We'll just sit out in the night air and talk.'

'Thank you,' said his father, 'but no.'

'Please,' said Abdullah, 'I want to change the atmosphere. I want you to relax.'

'Do you think I don't know why you're inviting me?' said his father. 'And do you think I do not love you for it? I yearn to come. But how could I feel free and happy? I would be thinking of work all the time. I cannot relax. I can no longer feel for life itself. I tell you, Abdullah, I can no longer tell the difference between what is cold and what is hot.'

It was soon after this that King Faisal confided to an aunt two recent dreams.

The First Dream of King Faisal

I was in an old mud house, like my grandfather's house where I lived when I was a boy growing up in Riyadh, and I was in the women's quarters. I opened a door, and there in a room I saw my grandmother, and the mother to my grandmother whom I can remember, and also Nura, my aunt who married Sa'ud al Kabeer, and, though I knew that they were all dead, it did not surprise me somehow to see them sitting together talking there.

But there was another woman sitting with them whom I did not recognize, and though she was talking to them as if she were a close friend, a member of the family even, I had no idea who she was.

So I stayed at the door, away from the stranger, until my grandmother caught sight of me and got up to draw me into the room.

'Why, Faisal,' she laughed, 'don't be shy. Come in! Come and greet Tarfah. Don't you recognize your own mother? It is time for you to meet her now.'

And suddenly I felt afraid.

424

The Second Dream of King Faisal

I was standing in the desert when a car came up to me, an old car, an open car, and sitting in it were my grandfather, the Imam Abdul Rahman, my father Abdul Aziz, my eldest brother Turki who died when I was thirteen, and my uncle Sa'ad who was killed in battle with the Ajman. They were all in the car together, and when they saw me they stopped and waved.

'Come in the car with us, Faisal,' said my father, and he got out to take my hand.

I was overjoyed to see my family who had been dead for so long, and I took a step towards them when I felt a terrible fear. I wanted to turn and run away, but my father gripped me by the hand.

I resisted, he pulled, I resisted more, and the others got out of the car to help him.

Together they dragged me into the car, the door slammed, and we drove away.

King Faisal confided these dreams to his aunt at the beginning of the Islamic year 1395, some time in January 1975, and he told her he could draw only one conclusion from them: that he was not destined to live out the year.

The king's twenty-six-year-old nephew, Faisal ibn Musa'id, must also, at around this time, have been deciding something similar. Faisal ibn Musa'id was the younger brother of Khalid ibn Musa'id, the prince who had been killed ten years earlier after the attack upon the Riyadh television station, and Faisal ibn Musa'id shared his brother's erratic moods. He had hopped from college to college in America, smoked pot at Berkeley, was picked up with LSD in Colorado, and got into at least one bar-room brawl with a girlfriend; the State Department had had to work hard to keep the prince out of the courts. When Faisal ibn Musa'id returned home, his uncle the king decreed he be detained inside the Kingdom for a while. He had disgraced the family with his escapades abroad, and some said that this travel ban was the reason for the young prince's anger. Others said the boy was moved to avenge the death of his brother Khalid.

On the night of 24 March 1975 Prince Faisal ibn Musa'id sat drinking whisky with another of his brothers, Bandar, and some friends. It was the typical bored evening with a bottle which passes for

425

nightlife among more inhabitants of the Kingdom than they care to acknowledge, and it was to go on for Bandar ibn Musa'id and his friends till 6 a.m. next day – television, whisky, cards, whisky, a bit of food, some more whisky, until soon after dawn everyone was stretched out asleep on sofas round the room. It was not so much a party, more a way of whiling away the night for people to whom the day had still less to offer.

But Faisal ibn Musa'id did have plans for the coming day, and he drank little. He went to his room before midnight, and next morning around 10 a.m. he was at the palace of his uncle the king, waiting in the anteroom outside the royal office. A delegation from Kuwait was there, come to discuss oil; and Ahmad Zaki Yamani went in ahead of them to brief the king before the meeting.

Ahmad Abdul Wahhab, King Faisal's chief of protocol, was puzzled by the arrival of the young prince, whom he did not recognize. Family meetings were usually held at Faisal's home, not in office hours, and Abdul Wahhab went in with Yamani to find out what the king wanted to do about his nephew.

Faisal ibn Musa'id, meanwhile, had discovered that he knew one of the Kuwaiti delegation, Abdul Mutalib al Qasimi, the young Oil Minister, whom he had met during his brief time in Colorado, and, when the door was thrown open to welcome in the Kuwaitis, the young prince went in with them.

Ahmad Zaki Yamani, Ahmad Abdul Wahhab and a television crew filming the king's reception of the oil delegation were horrified spectators of what happened next. As King Faisal reached forward to embrace and kiss his nephew, the young prince pulled a small pistol from the pocket of his *thobe* and shot three times at point-blank range. The first bullet went under the chin, the second through the ear, the third grazed the forehead. King Faisal was rushed to hospital still alive and was given massive blood transfusions while doctors massaged his heart. But the artery in his neck had been torn apart and within the hour the king was dead.

If every American knows where they were at the moment they heard the news of President Kennedy's killing, the same is true of Sa'udis and their King Faisal. An announcer, his voice choked with emotion, gave out the news on Riyadh Radio, then broke off sobbing. His wounded cry was broadcast all over the Middle East, and in Sa'udi cities the streets went silent. People could not believe what had happened and, numbed, they withdrew into their own homes.

426

'Riyadh gives out a sense of remoteness and austerity at the best of times,' wrote James Fox in the London *Sunday Times*. 'Since the assassination the city has closed down completely.'

At the news of the killing, armoured cars of the National Guard and army had moved out into the streets, and the assassin's brother Bandar and his friends were shaken rudely from their hangovers by police in pursuit of a conspiracy. But all they had to hide was contraband alcohol. The country stayed calm.

In the shock and sorrow, it was as if everyone had suffered a loss in their own family. In Jeddah women dressed in white, the Islamic colour of mourning. Heads of state flew from all the Arab countries. They knelt and prostrated themselves at Faisal's funeral, and over 100,000 grieving Sa'udis prayed with them at the open Eed mosque in the desert outside the city.

No one could make sense of the killing: a mixed-up assassin thrown off balance by the temptations of the West, an ancient impulse for blood revenge, the memory of the television station riots, the *majlis* tradition of open access to the ruler: the circumstances of Faisal's slaying were queerly strung with the same elements of old and new that the king had tried to weave together in his eleven-year reign. Sa'udis could only shrug their shoulders and sadly accept the will of God.

But God had wrought much through his servant Faisal. The solemn little boy who trudged through the rain at Victoria Station had watched the passing of the Ottoman, German, French and British power systems and had come himself to exercise a very special power of his own. He had inspired his brother Arabs with more solidly based self-respect than any leader had offered them for centuries, and with his wife's help he had done much to improve the lives of his sister Arabs too.

Austere, wrinkled, cautious, Faisal ibn Abdul Aziz had saved the Kingdom. When he took over power in 1962 the Al Sa'ud's days seemed numbered. The talk was all of Nasser and of republics. The family was tearing itself apart. But Faisal had unified his brothers and then, with a mixture of daring, discipline and extraordinary force of character, he had united the country as well.

Today the inhabitants of the Kingdom already look back to the reign of Faisal as to a golden age. Things were simpler then, it seemed. The Kingdom had a leader who made the whole world tremble, and who made his people tremble too; for no single member

427

of the Al Sa'ud will ever again be able to rule Arabia in such absolute fashion.

Of the three modern rulers consigned to the anonymous rubble of Riyadh's public cemetery, it was King Faisal who had most success preserving the traditional principles and values for which his family have always stood. Yet he achieved this by looking out on the twentieth century and finding a place in it for Sa'udi Arabia.

If Abdul Aziz united the Kingdom, it was Faisal who started to make of it a modern state.

45 Partnership: Khalid

MUHAMMAD ibn Abdul Aziz was camping in the desert outside Riyadh when he heard the news of Faisal's death, and he headed back to town immediately. Abu Sharrain, 'the Father of Two Evils', had renounced his place in the succession, but his voice would be decisive in what must happen next.

Muhammad had no doubts. Khalid should be proclaimed king as rapidly as possible and Fahad should be his crown prince. This meant bypassing the two brothers in their mid-fifties, Nasir and Sa'ad ibn Abdul Aziz, who came in order of seniority between Khalid, sixty-three, and Fahad, fifty-two, but this was no problem in Muhammad's eyes – nor to any other of the senior princes.

Within an hour of Faisal's death in hospital, Riyadh Radio announced that Khalid was the new king, and later that evening the sons and surviving brothers of Abdul Aziz gathered in the *majlis* of the palace just up the corridor from the office where Faisal had been murdered.

'I give my loyalty to you, oh Khalid,' declared Muhammad, 'in the name of God and in the name of His Prophet.'

He embraced his brother and kissed him, then turned without hesitating to Fahad, embraced him, and swore to him the same submission – the traditional *bay'ah* or oath of loyalty.

Muhammad's embrace and submission enunciated the succession, and one by one the other princes in the room, led by Nasir and Sa'ad ibn Abdul Aziz, walked forward to embrace and mutter their *bay'ah*. There were thirty or so princes at this gathering on the afternoon of 25 March 1975 – the sons of Abdul Aziz then in Riyadh, with their uncles – and, when they had finished, the doors were thrown open to the younger princes waiting outside. These trooped in to embrace and kiss their new leaders, and next morning the same ceremony was repeated in a public *majlis*, with tribal chiefs, cabinet ministers and heads of families joining in the swearing. Over the weeks to come, every *majlis* held by Khalid or Fahad was marked by extra mutterings and embracings as men swore their *bay'ah* to the new king and crown prince, and in remote areas like Tabuk, in the far north, local emirs opened books in which tribesmen had their names recorded.

The world decided that Khalid was a stop-gap monarch, chosen to mark time until the accession of the more forceful Fahad. But by the middle of 1981 Khalid had reigned for six full years, he had presided over more physical and social development than Arabia had known in six centuries, and it seemed to many that his unstudied and old-fashioned style had sidestepped much of the opposition which might have been provoked by a leadership whose façade was more obviously dedicated to change. The great limitation was Khalid's health.

Early in 1978 the world's leading aero-engineering companies, invited to tender for the engines to King Khalid's personal 747, were mystified that the specification should include the capacity to fly non-stop from Riyadh to Cleveland, Ohio.

'To Cleveland, Ohio?'

The choice of destination made sense later that year when King Khalid was admitted to the Cleveland Clinic. He had been through major heart surgery while he was Faisal's crown prince, and in 1978 he went to Cleveland for a bypass operation. Today Khalid's 747 – the only private Jumbo jet in the world – is equipped with an operating theatre and communications which link it directly to his specialists in Cleveland, and, wherever the king goes, several doctors carrying plasma and emergency resuscitation equipment unobtrusively dog his footsteps.

Now entering his seventies, King Khalid ibn Abdul Aziz gets tired towards the end of a hard day's ceremonial – state visits abroad are penances he tries to keep to a minimum – and there is no doubt where he is happiest: sitting in the desert with his falcons. So Western journalists visiting Riyadh send home the word that King Khalid is just a figurehead, that the real 'power behind the throne' is Crown Prince Fahad; and that is thought to explain everything.

But it is not as simple as that, for the house of Sa'ud has always operated by a consensus of its members. In the last troubled days of King Sa'ud, the experiment of having a king who reigned but did not rule was tested, and it did not work, for the man to whom other men give their loyalty in Arabia must be seen to have real power.

430

King Khalid has rather surprised his fellow countrymen by showing that he has that power, and also that he enjoys using it. If Khalid once proved a reluctant crown prince, he has not revealed himself a reluctant king, and a fortnight after his accession he proclaimed the release of the 150 or so political prisoners left in gaol from Faisal's reign, for Khalid had always thought his elder brother too severe.

'My brother Faisal, God rest his soul, had his own way of doing things,' he would say when people reminded him of what the dead king might have done in any particular situation, 'and I, God willing, will accomplish things in *my* own fashion.'

Khalid paid for Abdul Aziz ibn Mu'ammar, when he came out of prison, to go to America in the hopes that surgeons might be able to save something of his sight, and he welcomed back to Riyadh another object of Faisal's displeasure, the ex-Oil Minister Abdullah Tariki.

But no one could call the new king soft. Khalid would not countenance suggestions that Faisal's young assassin should be spared the death penalty. Faisal ibn Musa'id was kept alive for three months while his uncles cross-questioned him, trying to establish some sort of logic or motive behind his homicide, some evidence of a wider plot. When none was found, the prince was led out on the morning of 18 June 1975 into the main square in Riyadh and made to kneel in the gutter beside the mosque. There, where all other murderers are made to kneel, the young prince was beheaded, and paths were cleared through the crowd so that his cousins and uncles could witness his punishment.

Khalid ibn Abdul Aziz has proved on occasions the very opposite of what was expected of him. Soon after his accession he was taken to inspect a low-cost housing development, subsidized dwellings which ordinary Sa'udis could purchase at low rates. The king was shown round the compact little bungalows, ingeniously designed by space-efficient Western architects, and when, at the conclusion of the tour, the king was asked what he thought of it all, he was expected to nod genial praise in a polite sort of way. Instead, there came a long and regal silence.

'I am not happy', said His Majesty finally, 'to see my people living in matchboxes'; and that was the end of the low-cost housing programme, though its alternative – massive apartment blocks which tower impressively in Jeddah, Riyadh and Dammam – is not everyone's idea of an ideal home. The new blocks are awe-inspiring, and no expense has been spared to accommodate the Sa'udi way of life: each apartment has separate reception rooms for male and female entertaining and extra bedrooms so that children of different sexes may sleep apart; the Dammam towers alone represent the greatest transportation of ready-mixed concrete in human history (630,000 tons) and the largest elevator contract ever ($96 million). But towards the end of the project the Ministry of Housing started to wonder precisely how it was going to cajole bedouin and their goats up into a penthouse on the eighteenth floor, and it is still trying to work it out. The blocks stand empty to this day.

King Khalid spends a lot of time regulating the details of the Al Sa'ud's family life. All new-born princes and princesses are brought to him in his cream and gold Riyadh sitting room where there are wildlife videos beside the television and where a big black lump of ancient wood rests in a corner like a railway sleeper – a present from the King of Sweden.* Young bucks in need of direction are sent to the king to be dispatched towards the armed forces or government service. He approves the marriages and divorces of some members of the family, and he also supervises the distribution of land.

King Faisal's Ministry of Information made much of the ruthlessness with which Faisal disciplined the untrammelled payment of princely stipends in the early sixties. The payments were defined and regulated according to the recipient's closeness to Abdul Aziz, and it was not only the Al Sa'ud who benefited from them: stipends were paid to ex-ministers, to those who fought in the first Sa'udi armies and to their descendants, and also to families whose forefathers had been loyal to Abdul Aziz in the early days.

In 1981 this vast, consolidated welfare system, part Civil List, part Poppy Day Fund, pays out at the rate of some £1000 a month to ex-ministers and junior princes – perhaps ten times that to each of the thirty-one surviving sons of Abdul Aziz. It consumes less than 2 per cent of the Kingdom's revenues, and its share of the national wealth declines with every passing year, since stipends have not been increased since the early seventies. On its own the fund would scarcely make even Abdul Aziz's sons into millionaires.

It is land that has made the Al Sa'ud truly wealthy, and the basis for this wealth is the programme of land grants in the gift of King Faisal and of King Khalid after him. Until the 1960s the Al Sa'ud had never

*The wood is a beam from the fifteenth-century ship *Vasar*, raised from the floor of Stockholm harbour in the 1960s.

432

really capitalized on the vast block of real estate that their conquest represented, and distributing land seemed to King Faisal a painless way to cut the family in on the Kingdom's profits without trespassing obviously upon the government budget.

Every square inch of Arabia was owned, in theory, by someone, often by a chief of the bedouin in that area. But it was not difficult for the king or a senior prince to offer the chief more money than he ever thought his patch of desert could possibly be worth, and in this fashion the Al Sa'ud took control of the vast tracts of the Kingdom in the 1960s, passing it round among themselves in marriage settlements and business deals, and as a substitute for cash.

There were princes who complained at the time. Empty expanses of sand seemed a poor substitute for cash in hand, and King Faisal's wish to increase his family's physical stake in the Kingdom stemmed from reasons that were political rather than financial. Faisal was not a property speculator. Neither he nor anyone else foresaw, in the mid-1960s, the real-estate boom which was to follow the oil price explosion of 1973.

But when the boom came it yielded phenomenal dividends to Faisal's policy. A hectare of land which cost SR9–SR10 in the mid-1960s can sell today at over SR20,000, as the Sa'udi government discovers to its cost every time it seeks land for its roads, pipelines, airports and industrial cities; for princes seldom settle at less than the market rate when they sell the land that these developments require. The official budget of the Kingdom no longer bears the cost of princely stipends, but its real-estate purchases from the royal family help to keep the income of the Al Sa'ud topped up in other ways.

King Khalid is the ultimate controller of this lucrative source of patronage, and it is one way in which, standing aside from the day-to-day running of the Kingdom, he remains a very effective Chairman of the Board. He gives land to avoid potential friction in the family: Muhammad, Nasir and Sa'ad ibn Abdul Aziz have all been richly compensated for relinquishing their claims upon the succession. Ministers and generals who perform well are well rewarded – the basis of Ahmad Zaki Yamani's personal fortune is land given him by Faisal in the early seventies – and, at the humblest level, many of the petitioners in the royal *majlis* come in search of nothing more than real estate. Any Sa'udi is entitled to one free plot on which to build a dwelling, as of right; and, in a society where generosity matters, King

Khalid has built the reputation of being more open-handed than his brother Faisal.

Khalid ibn Abdul Aziz is an old-fashioned man, and he makes no secret of it. When January comes round, the inhabitants of the Kingdom know that all is well with their king, for that is when his men go out into the desert with their snaring nets, and when Khalid can escape for a week or two from the complications of being a twentieth-century head of state to concentrate on his falcons instead.

The king does not follow the Western practice of breeding birds of prey. Every winter his bedouin catch and train the saker falcons which migrate southwards across Arabia, and Khalid hunts with them for a month or so. He goes mainly after bustard – large, fast-running birds whose turkey-like flesh makes good eating – and then in April and May the falcons (which are traded for £10,000 each at the height of the season) are taken out for one last day of hunting, have their jesses removed, and are tossed up into the air to fly off free down the wind.

The royal hunting camp would scarcely be recognized by Abdul Aziz. Beside the tents are electrical generators, shiny air-conditioned trailers, radio transmitters with antennae, and a couple of desert-landing Hercules transport planes, one wood-panelled inside and fitted with sofas, the other equipped as a mobile operating theatre. But bedouin park their pickup trucks beside these modern gadgets unimpressed. They bump hundreds of miles across the sands to sit with their king during his desert sojourns, and Khalid, whose Arabic has a rough-hewn bedouin inflexion, sits talking to them for hours. These are his roots. Philby took a photograph of the Al Sa'ud in 1917 which showed Abdul Aziz's children huddled together in their ragged garments, a crowd of barefoot desert urchins staring at the first European they had ever seen.

'One of those is me,' says King Khalid, with evident delight, and his attachment to the bedouin way of life is more than easy sentiment. When British surgeons examined the king for a hip complaint in 1977 they were horrified to discover deep and ugly burn marks that had made recent scars upon his legs. Before coming to London, the king had resorted to the traditional desert remedy for his pains. He had had himself branded with hot irons.

King Khalid harks back frequently to his youth. He experienced women, fatherhood and battle before the age of twenty, he likes to say – and that is the best preparation for manhood that any boy could have. He supports his brother Sultan's oft-touted proposal that young Sa'udi males should be put through compulsory military service, and his favourite among his younger brothers is Muqrin, an ex-fighter pilot with a dozen children to his credit at the age of thirty-eight. Muqrin, a keen falconer, was one of the brothers whom Khalid picked to revitalize local government after the 1979 seizure of the Grand Mosque in Mecca, and the king sent him to Hail, one of the best spots to snap up the falcons as they fly south.

Young Sa'udi PhDs, trying to shoe-horn the inconvenient and often downright obstinate conservatism of their fellow countrymen into the requirements of the latest Five-Year Plan, might be expected to view their unsophisticated and apolitical elderly king as an outmoded figurehead, but the opposite seems the case. Just as wealth and Westernization have forced many Sa'udis back to the traditions of their religion and culture, so the old-fashioned simplicity of King Khalid seems to win favour as a talisman for stable and unthreatening change. Khalid is perceived as religious, traditional, honest, dutiful. People know they have Crown Prince Fahad to thank, or to blame, for the increased speed of Sa'udi development since 1975. They believe they can trust King Khalid to keep that development checked, or at least veiled, by the ancient virtues.

King Khalid did not on his accession adopt the gold-wired *aghal* worn by his predecessors as visible tokens of their authority. He dressed with plain black headropes like anyone else, and his style has been to diminish autocracy within the family and without. His Cabinet, appointed in the autumn of 1975, kept the key portfolios – Interior, Defence, Foreign Affairs and National Guard – safely in the hands of the Al Sa'ud, but fifteen of the twenty-five portfolios were entrusted to commoners, and all ministers were allowed considerably more latitude in the running of their departments than had been the case under Faisal.

King Khalid is a devout man. He keeps a little green leather-bound Koran in one pocket of his *thobe* and he refers to it quite frequently, mouthing the verses to himself. When Libya's Mu'ammar Qaddafi advised Muslims not to go on pilgrimage in the autumn of 1980, suggesting that the Kingdom's borrowed AWACS* planes would spy on them, and criticizing Sa'udi supervision of the pilgrimage in

---

*Airborne Warning and Control Systems. Four of these US aircraft were sent to Sa'udi Arabia in September 1980 to monitor possible escalation of the Iran–Iraq war.

general, he could not have hit upon a tactic better calculated to offend King Khalid.

'Qaddafi has become the spearhead of Communism and Zionism against Islam,' declared the king, severing relations with Libya in a statement which Riyadh Radio embellished on royal instructions. 'Qaddafi is a criminal with no conscience . . . a madman with a childish mind . . . an atheist. . . . He is facing his final days.'

King Khalid's reign has been marked by several such flare-ups that reveal the monarch to be more than just a figurehead. His anger over the British TV film *Death of a Princess* was an occasion when his intense personal feelings overruled the counsels of his brothers, and his insistence that law-breaking foreigners should suffer the same Islamic penalties as Sa'udis is another piece of policy that is very much his own. In the reign of Faisal, Westerners who were caught brewing or selling alcohol were quietly imprisoned and expelled from the country. In the reign of Khalid they have been caned publicly in the street.

The seizure of Mecca's Grand Mosque in November 1979 cast the king in yet another light, for the crisis induced real shock inside the Kingdom. National sentiment searched for a focus which was located in the king, and, when Khalid went to visit the several hundred Sa'udi soldiers injured in the siege, it was as a representative of the whole country.

He gave out jewelled watches, colour televisions, cassette radios, he had whole showrooms of cars bought up as presents for his soldiers: you could not find a new Toyota in Jeddah for two months after the siege. But as King Khalid moved from bed to bed, looking at the bandages, slings and plaster, and listening to the doctors' descriptions of the wounds scarring 461 of the Kingdom's finest young soldiers, he was obviously finding it difficult to come to terms with the wounds and injury on every side of him.

Sa'udi newsreels are not noted for the subtlety of their camerawork. Perhaps the fault lies in their editing – or the lack of it. So the TV camera focused long and lingeringly upon the face of Khalid ibn Abdul Aziz as he contemplated the total of pain and suffering spread out around him. Suddenly, in the unblinking electronic gaze, tears welled up into his eyes – and then, openly and unashamedly, in the sight of all his people, the king began to cry.

46 Partnership: Fahad

WHEN Mrs Margaret Thatcher visited Riyadh in April 1981, she came away from her first meeting with Crown Prince Fahad ibn Abdul Aziz distinctly unimpressed. 'You say that this man runs the country?' she asked her aides. 'He didn't have a word to say for himself.'

Next morning Mrs Thatcher found otherwise. The crown prince had so much to say that his hour-long discussion with the British Prime Minister ran into overtime. The difference between the two meetings was the company. At the first Prince Fahad had been in the presence of his elder brother, King Khalid, and he was careful not to speak unless he was spoken to. At the second, the crown prince was on his own in the office from which he has run the Kingdom since 1975.

Fahad ibn Abdul Aziz has spent all his adult life in the shadow of elder brothers. He made his reputation as an administrator by working for five years as Sa'ud's Minister of Education – the Kingdom's first. He rose to family pre-eminence through a long stint as Faisal's Interior Minister from 1962 to 1975. But throughout these years Fahad remained a submissive, rather shadowy figure. People found it positively unsettling to meet him in the presence of King Faisal, so nervous and subservient was his manner, and in 1981 the sixty-year-old crown prince whom foreign journalists call the 'strong man' of Arabia never fails to demonstrate similar respect and deference to King Khalid.

Still, no one doubts the reality of the situation.

'My brother Fahad', says King Khalid with a certain respect of his own, 'has a great appetite for administration.'

Crown Prince Fahad has an appetite for many things. Over 6 feet tall, broad, amply fleshed and incorporating both the loftiness of his father and the well-upholstered structure which is the other strand in

Al Sa'ud physique, Abdul Aziz's fifth surviving son is larger than life in many ways. He eats too much and smokes too much. His doctors tell him to cut down on both, but he pays them little heed. In years past Fahad earned the disapproval of his elders for his flamboyant indulgence in the good life. But after one especially dashing adventure in Monte Carlo he came home to a reception from King Faisal which bit deep into his soul; and since then the heir apparent has been a reformed character, say his friends. Fahad's considerable energies are channelled into his work, and the size and scope of the work facing him are immense.

More than any other member of his family, Crown Prince Fahad has grasped with relish the challenges which the post-1973 cornucopia has posed to the Al Sa'ud and to their Kingdom, and he was among the first to appreciate that the challenges to each are not necessarily the same. Oil wealth clearly means the end of the old Arabia. The face of the Kingdom is destined to be transformed in a momentous fashion before the twentieth century is complete – and the question for the Al Sa'ud is whether one of those alterations will be their removal from the scene, or whether they can remain on top.

Crown Prince Fahad believes that they can; and he has chosen to prove it by pushing forward his family to become the pre-eminent mechanism for change. Every May the government of Sa'udi Arabia announces its budget for the coming year, and to read the list of schools to be opened, kilometres of highway to be unrolled and gallons of free desalinated water to be brought on stream, one might imagine oneself in a socialist utopia. Less than a decade after the oil price explosion, Sa'udi Arabia already has one of the world's most modern and extensive free hospital systems per head of the population, and every other new social facility in the Kingdom enjoys, in technological terms, the very best that money can buy.

Budget time almost anywhere else in the world is tax time; the problem is how to raise the money. In Sa'udi Arabia the problem is how to spend it, for the Kingdom's revenues are not only immense; they are paid, by their nature, directly into the national exchequer, over $300 million hard cash every day. This gives the Sa'udi government, ideologically dedicated to free enterprise, the kind of dominance over the national economy which Kremlin commissars can but dream of. The only way for the cash to get into the economy is for the government to spend it, and this has provided Prince Fahad with massive economic resources that give a new twist to the paternalism with which Abdul Aziz established the political supremacy of his clan.

Sometime in the late 1960s Prince Fahad seems to have realized that he would one day be king. Faisal was old, Khalid ill, and Fahad, then in his mid-forties, set about preparing himself for his future responsibilities. He started taking private English lessons, though to this day he always talks through an interpreter, preferring to hear questions twice before he answers them. Audio-visual programmes to fill the gap left by his lack of formal schooling were ordered and solemnly ploughed through, and Fahad enlisted help on a crash course in great literature. Friends were asked to tape extracts from the books that had most impressed them, together with background on the book's author and history, and in this way the prince tasted the memoirs of Churchill and Eden and learnt of US politics under Eisenhower, Kennedy and Johnson.

Earnest self-improvement was scarcely Fahad's image in these years. The attention of his family centred on the long holidays he found time to take in the West with hedonistic friends like Adnan Khashoggi. But Fahad was also learning. He arranged himself briefings with bankers and economists, and those who met him in the late sixties were surprised by the sophisticated vision he was already working out of his country's future: infrastructure was just a beginning, it was a skeleton to be filled by ordinary Sa'udis creating their own trucking companies, small factories, take-away food chains or dry-cleaning shops – and more non-royal Sa'udi talent, he believed, should be enrolled into the government itself.

Seen from the outside, the government of Sa'udi Arabia is dominated to an extraordinary degree by one family. Viewed from the inside, by the inhabitants of the Kingdom whose fathers and forefathers were ruled exclusively by the Al Sa'ud, Al Rasheed and other sheikhly autocrats, what is remarkable about the government of King Khalid and Crown Prince Fahad is the responsibility delegated since 1975 to individuals outside the traditional élite.

Dr Ghazi al Qosaibi, the Industry Minister, Hisham Nazer, Minister of Planning, Muhammad Aba al Khail, Minister of Finance, Abdul Aziz al Quraishi, Governor of the Sa'udi-Arabian Monetary Agency: between them these youngish men handle a budget comparable to those administered by their equivalents in almost any country of the Western world.

'Fahad', says one of his associates, 'doesn't like men who blind him with science. But, if people do their job well, he leaves them alone to let them get on with it.'

The best monuments to Fahad's way of letting other people get on with it are probably the twin industrial cities of Jubail, on the Gulf Coast, and Yanbu on the Red Sea, both raised from the empty desert to recognizable identities in less than a decade, and both intended to harness the gas flared off for so many years as it came up from the earth with the oil. A 1201-kilometre pipeline carries this gas the width of the peninsula to Yanbu, together with a pipeline capable of conveying nearly 2 million barrels a day of crude oil – Fahad's attempt to reduce Sa'udi oil exports' vulnerability to disorder in the Gulf and to the blocking of the Hormuz Straits.

Linked across Arabia by their twin energy arteries of gas and oil, the Kingdom's new industrial cities are supervised by the Royal Commission for Yanbu and Jubail, a purpose-built agency devised by Fahad to avoid the red tape of existing bureaucracy. Employees of the Royal Commission are paid a 45 per cent premium on top of standard civil service salaries. Their priority is clear-cut – to build the new cities as rapidly and efficiently as possible – and similar agencies have been started for other specialized objectives, like the creation of the new airports of Jeddah, Riyadh and Dhahran. The new Jeddah International Airport, opened in April 1981, is half as large again as Kennedy, La Guardia, Newark, O'Hare and Los Angeles airports put together; the new Riyadh Airport will be larger than that; and Dhahran will be larger still.

These modern wonders of the world are not quite what they seem. Their size is a matter of the number of desert acres enclosed by their perimeter fences, not the mass of their plant and buildings, let alone their projected passenger traffic, and there is little doubt that they could have been built less expensively. But they remain achievements of which Crown Prince Fahad is justly proud. Each May the budgetary forecasts for the coming twelve months are preceded by the statistics of construction and development in the Kingdom in the previous year, and they are impressive even by the standards of the wealth available to fund them. It would be an arrogant man who claimed that he could have done much better.

The extraordinary thing is that the man who has actually sat at the centre of this unparalleled development since 1975 leads a personal life of extreme disorganization. If it was possible to set your watch by the activities of King Faisal, the very opposite is true of Crown Prince

440

Fahad. Briefcases of government documents are driven by Cadillac to his office every day to pile up in a corner while he pretends they are not there. Then suddenly one day, like a student cramming at the last moment for his exams, he will sit down and work late into the night to get them all sent away again.

When he is feeling energetic he is a workaholic, toiling all hours, firing off his instructions by telegram to different ministries. Then suddenly he collapses, vanishes to one of his palaces, and cannot be contacted by anyone. Ministers wait forlornly in the corridor outside his office, hoping to grab his robe for a hurried word as he goes by – and his private world is similarly disorganized.

Like his full brother Sultan, Crown Prince Fahad loves building new homes and extending old ones. But whereas Sultan's palaces are finished on time and run with almost military precision, as befits homes of the Defence Minister, somehow the workmen take much longer to pack up their tools and clear out of Fahad's compounds. Friends have the feeling when they walk down the corridors of his palaces that if they open the wrong door they would find disorder, a room that his servants had not bothered to organize, for Fahad is soft with his staff.

This is a little how Fahad runs the Kingdom. If he is not pleased with the performance of a particular minister, he does not sack him. In July 1981 almost all appointees of the 1975 Cabinet remain in place, undismissed. The crown prince deals with shortcomings by taking responsibilities away from those who cannot handle them and by giving them to those who can – transferring information policy to the Interior Ministry during the siege of the Grand Mosque, telling Defence and the National Guard to build their own hospitals and not rely upon the Ministry of Health.

Fahad has his father's tendency to shout and swipe at people when his temper cracks, but he is less irascible than Abdul Aziz and, in the eyes of his brothers, usually rather too forbearing. His eldest brother Muhammad, and his brother Abdullah who now stands next in seniority to Fahad, wanted the conspirators of 1969 to be executed. It was Fahad who insisted that most of them be kept in reasonably civilized confinement, ordering an apartment block and an old palace to be taken over so that each detainee had a room to himself. Nasserite attempts to subvert the Kingdom in the 1960s were not countered with the arbitrary bloodshed and torture to which so many, apparently more populist, Arab leaders have resorted to maintain their regimes – and Fahad's severest critics give him credit for this.

Like Abdul Aziz, Fahad revels in the company of beautiful women. He has two wives. He enjoys spoiling them with lavish jewellery, *haute couture* clothes and palatial homes, and, like his father, the crown prince dotes upon his children.

But if Fahad's critics are agreed upon one thing, it is that he is too indulgent towards his sons. It seems unlikely that his eldest, Faisal, would have secured his responsibility, the presidency of Youth Welfare, without his father's special favour; while criticism of the enormous commercial contracts secured by Fahad's sons Muhammad and Sa'ud has come to be a major grievance in the Sa'udi business community.

When the question of a new telephone and telecommunications system for the Kingdom arose in the mid-1970s, Fahad grasped the opportunity to break the Sa'udi dependence upon American technology. Like so many of the Kingdom's projects since 1973, the telephone contract was, and remains in 1981, the largest ever in its field: $4.5 billion on signature, $5.5 billion today after the escalation of expenses.

Fahad's bright, California-educated son Muhammad knew of his father's wish to place this vast undertaking somewhere outside the US orbit, and he put together a formidable consortium which combined, by any standards, technology and management that were among the world's best: switching equipment and machinery by N. V. Philips of Holland and L. M. Ericson of Sweden, with supervision by Bell Telephone of Canada. The young prince's company, al Bilad ('The Country'), boasted a number of able, hardworking young Sa'udis – it could be seen as a little private enterprise 'Royal Commission' in its own right, equipped with the native talent to meet tight deadlines and to get things done – and, after a twice-run bidding process whose details are still obscure, Prince Muhammad got the job.

But there was never any doubt that father had helped his son along, from the original idea to crack dependence upon America, to the signature of the final contract. The al Bilad package had been approved, the details were finalized, and the agreement was ready for signature, when the Americans played their final card – a personal letter to King Khalid from President Carter to be hand-delivered in Riyadh by Carter's Secretary of State, Cyrus Vance. In the event,

Carter's letter confined itself to general US–Sa'udi relations, avoiding any strong pitch for AT&T or ITT, America's two contenders for the contract. But Prince Muhammad ibn Fahad had taken no chances when he got to hear of Vance's mission and of the President's letter.

At 2.45 in the morning the Sa'udi Minister for Posts and Telecommunications was roused from his bed, and when Vance's plane touched down a few hours later, the already negotiated contract had been signed. $4.5 billion worth of business was safely in the hands of the Dutch, Swedes and Canadians – and of Prince Muhammad bin Fahad.

Since then the expansion of the Sa'udi telephone and telecommunications system has proceeded at a remarkable rate. On the basis of their performance in the Kingdom, the three component foreign companies have won most of the major contracts in their field elsewhere in the world. The bribery that was necessary six years ago to get a telephone or extra business lines has largely been eliminated, since there is nowadays more than enough equipment and capacity to go round, and your phone is installed quickly, works well and is serviced promptly. The wisdom of entrusting this mammoth project to Prince Muhammad bin Fahad seems amply vindicated. But the trouble with giving your own son multi-billion dollar contracts – or even just allowing him to bid for them – is that no one else, with the best will in the world, can believe that family feeling did not act to the disadvantage of his equally qualified competitors.

The importance that the Al Sa'ud place on blood ties is common to all the native inhabitants of the Kingdom. Sa'udi Arabia is a coalition of great families – merchant dynasties, sheikhly clans and humbler tribal groupings. Families of bedouin descent marry only with certain other tribal families, and never with Hijaz merchants, whom Nejdis describe as 'leftovers from the pilgrimage'; Hijaz families who have particular connections with the Grand Mosque or the pilgrimage, or who specialize in certain sorts of commerce, are fiercely proud of those traditions, and they marry and socialize within them as if they were royalty: so the preference that Crown Prince Fahad shows his sons, like Faisal's favour to his brother-in-law, Kamal Adham, is well understood by other Arabians. They would do exactly the same if they were in the same position – but that does not stop them complaining, and it is one reason why Fahad's brother Sultan has been careful to channel all his sons into the armed forces or government.

Once a week Crown Prince Fahad meets for dinner with all his full

443

brothers and sisters, the sons and daughters of Hassa Sudairi by her second marriage to King Abdul Aziz. Before Hassa died in 1969 the seven brothers used to go every day for lunch at Hassa's house. Their mother insisted upon it, and this special cohesion between Fahad and his brothers was one of the factors that helped them emerge, in the 1960s, as the predominant power group inside the Al Sa'ud. Misleadingly dubbed the 'Sudairi Seven' by foreign journalists, their support was crucial to Faisal in his arguments with Sa'ud, and they provided the backbone of the government as it rode out the challenges of the Nasserite years. Since then Turki bin Abdul Aziz, for many years vice-minister to his brother Sultan at Defence, has left the government, but the al Fahad remain at the very centre of power in the Kingdom.

Sultan, the Defence Minister, rather resembles Fahad in build and tastes. He plays hard and works hard, with the largest defence budget in the Western world outside America to spend in the cause of proving that the Kingdom does not need American bases to defend itself, and he has taken over King Faisal's mantle as the upholder of family militancy on Israel and the Palestinian cause: visitors to his office are cautioned to avoid the subject if they possibly can, for at the mention of the Middle East's central dilemma Prince Sultan ibn Abdul Aziz is quite capable of launching himself into a diatribe that can last half an hour.

Salman ibn Abdul Aziz, the governor of Riyadh, is Fahad's youngest brother but one. Tall and forthright, Salman can sometimes look uncannily like photographs of the young Abdul Aziz, and he spends his days receiving the chiefs of the great tribes in his office, built on the site of his father's original palace beside Riyadh's Great Mosque. He has also proved a businessman of some acumen: he is one of four Sa'udis sharing a 63 per cent stake in the Sa'udi Lebanese Bank, and he has millions invested in the visionary Sudanese attempt to turn the basins of the Blue and White Niles into the bread basket of the Middle East. When Sa'udis outside the royal family talk of whom they would like to see as a future king, it is Salman's name they always mention.

Sultan and Salman are Fahad's two most trusted henchmen. When King Khalid had his heart attack in February 1980 it was these two who, with Fahad, took rooms beside him and who ran the Kingdom for a month from the King Faisal Hospital.

Close to Fahad in another way are his brothers-in-law, Muhammad

444

and Khalid ibn Abdullah, the sons of Abdullah ibn Abdul Rahman. They are each married to a full sister of the crown prince, so they qualify, like the husbands of his other sisters, for the weekly al Fahad dinner party.

Muhammad bin Abdullah grew up with Fahad. He went through the same apprenticeship, learning the Koran and acquiring desert skills from the bedouin. A simple-seeming soul, Muhammad bin Abdullah is one of the few who would dare to tease the crown prince, to tickle him mentally, and the role that this prince seems to play as the technocrats come and go is to remind the man in whose hands lies such power for the happiness, or otherwise, of the late twentieth century, of the simple boyhood that they enjoyed together.

Naif bin Abdul Aziz and Ahmad, who is the youngest of Hassa's sons, run the Interior Ministry, and they control the Kingdom's internal security with a tight hand. They run yet another of the private armies which are the Al Sa'ud's device for balancing power inside the country – the Special Security Forces, Fahad's own creation when he was Interior Minister – and it was to these two brothers that Fahad entrusted the pacification of the Eastern Province and the framing of a constitution for the Kingdom in the shake-up that followed the seizure of the Grand Mosque in Mecca. Both men are hardworking, painstaking and austere, and Naif, who is older than Salman, is a senior figure in the Council of Ministers and a brother upon whom Fahad has come to place especial reliance.

All these powerful men, with their sisters, sons and brothers-in-law, usually gather for their weekly dinner in the home of one of the sisters. Work often makes it difficult for Fahad and his brothers to meet and talk easily, but at their weekly gathering together this family-within-a-family has the leisure and privacy to confer freely about the things that matter. If the curious outsider could choose any one wall in the Kingdom on which to be a fly there can be little doubt in which dining room it would be.

47 Riyal Politik

EVERY month or so Mr Yasser Arafat, leader of the Palestine Liberation Organization, occupies the first ten minutes of the Kingdom's 9 o'clock news. Airport welcoming ceremonies are the staple ingredient of Sa'udi television news bulletins. The leaders of America, the monarchs of Europe, Third World heads of state: all come to be serenaded by Riyadh's ceremonial brass and bagpipe band. Bedouin squatting round their portable televisions in the desert must imagine that their king has his palace at the airport.

The welcome extended to Yasser Arafat is as grand as any other. King Khalid, Crown Prince Fahad and their senior brothers embrace him warmly. He is photographed talking with them, drinking coffee in the marble and gilt splendour of the Guest Palace beside the Nasriyah Gate and then, in a day or so, he is filmed leaving the Kingdom to an equally warm and prestigious farewell. What is not televised is the several million dollars which the Palestinian leader takes home with him.

Sa'udi Arabia is Yasser Arafat's principal financial supporter. Increasing Sa'udi subsidies to the PLO since 1973 have given the organization currency reserves estimated at over a billion dollars – larger than those of many Third World countries – and most inhabitants of the Kingdom are proud that Sa'udi oil revenues should be supporting the cause of their Palestinian brothers.

But the idea that Sa'udi Arabia should lend such massive support to men usually seen in the West as 'terrorists' is deeply offensive to many people outside the Muslim world. This support to the Palestinians flatly contradicts in their eyes the word 'moderate' so often used by the Kingdom's Western friends to describe Sa'udi international strategy, and this contradiction has lain at the heart of the foreign policy pursued since 1975 by King Khalid, Crown Prince Fahad and their brothers.

446

Top Dancing the *ardha*: from left to right,
Khalid, Faisal, Fahad and Abdullah ibn
Abdul Aziz
Above left Muhammad ibn Abdul Aziz, elder
brother of King Khalid
Above Sa'ud al Faisal, Foreign Minister of the
Kingdom since 1975
Left Sultan ibn Abdul Aziz, Sa'udi Minister
of Defence and Aviation since 1962

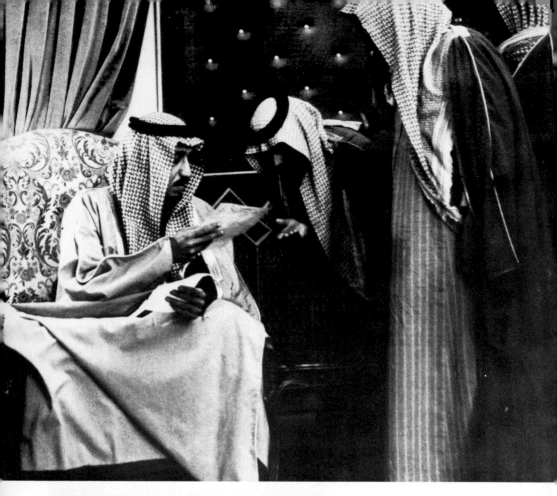

This page
Above Salman ibn Abdul Aziz,
Governor of Riyadh, receives
petitions in his *majlis*
Left Adnan Khashoggi in Arab and
Western dress

Opposite
Top Fahad (left) and Abdullah ibn
Abdul Aziz on pilgrimage
Middle A judicial caning
Below Mecca, November 1979; smoke
rising from the battle in the Grand
Mosque
Inset Juhayman, leader of the
Mecca revolt

King Khalid ibn Abdul Aziz and Crown Prince Fahad (left),
February 1977

'I often wish', said one young member of the house of Sa'ud to this author, 'that we could just slice ourselves off from the rest of the world and float out into the Indian Ocean where no one could trouble us. Life would be so much quieter.'

If that heartfelt escapism sometimes seems the best available explanation of the Kingdom's international posture, it is hardly surprising, for the wealth that the Sa'udis wish they could be left alone to enjoy in peace is linked to an area of the world which makes fierce demands on the loyalties of all who live there: as members of the Arab nation, the Sa'udis must support the cause of the Palestinians; as guardians of Islam's Holy Places, they must fight to regain Muslim control of old Jerusalem.

But the oil wealth on which the Sa'udis – and the Palestinians – depend is also linked to the US dollar in which it is traded; Arab financial surpluses cannot safely be invested anywhere but in the US-dominated Western economy; and the only outside power that can credibly defend Arabia's oilfields against the threat that Russian ambitions appear to pose is the United States – which is irrevocably committed to the support and maintenance of the State of Israel.

When Crown Prince Fahad ibn Abdul Aziz took over effective control of the Kingdom's foreign policy in 1975, he was itching to build on the pre-eminence in the Arab and Islamic world which King Faisal had created. Fahad had great confidence in the power of the cheque book – the ability of petrodollars to secure friends, neutralize enemies and settle quarrels – and his policy worked well to start with.

Britain was completing her withdrawal from her commitments east of Suez, and with the independence of the Trucial Coast, which became the United Arab Emirates in 1971, Fahad was able finally to settle the Buraymi dispute. Sheikh Zayid of Abu Dhabi kept Buraymi, but he surrendered to the Kingdom another portion of his deserts, and Sa'udi face was saved.

The settlement of the long-running dispute was hailed in Riyadh as a triumph for Arab fraternal feeling. It showed the great things the Arabs could accomplish together when foreign interference was removed, and this became the theme of Sa'udi foreign policy in the early years of King Khalid's reign. In the autumn of 1976 the protagonists in the Lebanese civil war were summoned to the Kingdom. Working through Kamal Adham, the Al Sa'ud had maintained

447

Faisal's links with Sadat, increasing their subsidies to Egypt. Yasser Arafat was also on their payroll, supported, despite his links with Moscow, as the most amenable of the wild men who headed the Palestinian cause, and since October 1973 Syria had also become a Sa'udi client. Abdul Aziz bought up the tribes. His sons buy up their neighbours.

In October 1976, the Al Sa'ud gently forced their friends to sit down together round the conference table. With a little arm-twisting, the promise of increased subsidies and liberal exhortations to mutual goodwill, a cease-fire was arranged which really did stop the fighting in Lebanon for more than a year. It was a significant step towards genuine and practical solidarity among Arabs who had seemed more intent on fighting each other than on uniting against the common foe. Khalid and Fahad could not claim the towering presence with which Faisal had come to dominate the Arab world, but they seemed able to secure practical results.

Arab unity was one problem, Russian encirclement of the Middle East was another. Britain's withdrawal from Aden had led to the effective occupation of Arabia's southern tip by communist forces. The port of Aden itself became a Russian naval base, complete with a Russian harbour-master. East German advisers flooded in, and, across the Red Sea, Cuban mercenaries made ominous advances to establish a communist presence in the Horn of Africa.

Still recovering from the trauma of Vietnam, America declined to do more than express concern. In Washington, Congress refused $50 million aid to help Zaïre's President Mobutu keep Soviet-backed Angolans at bay. So Sa'udi Arabia paid the bill instead, and then in 1977 the Kingdom financed the Moroccan troops that flew to put down a rising against the Congolese president.

Fahad spent liberally in Africa. $200 million in Sa'udi subsidies to Somalia helped speed the departure of the Russians from their Red Sea naval base at Berbera. Along the Eritrean coast, right opposite the Kingdom, the crown prince backed the local liberation front against the communist government of Ethiopia, and, in the Sudan, Sa'udi money helped President Numeiri to resist radicalism.

It was a formidable exercise in the purchase of loyalty, the Al Sa'ud's domestic forte deployed with panache in the international arena, and through America's uncertain post-Vietnam years Sa'udi Arabia stood alone, holding the pass for the West in the Horn of Africa. Western analysts started to write admiringly of the new

448

'regional superpower', and as Sa'udi Arabia used her production capacity to restrain OPEC from oil price rises from 1975 to 1978 the American news magazines raced each other to burble their praises.

'They have vaulted near the pinnacle of global power,' declared *Newsweek* in a special issue of March 1978, 'and turned their desert kingdom into nothing less than a financial superstate.'

In the spring of 1978 the Carter administration paid tribute to this estimate of expanding Sa'udi power when they pushed through Congress, in defiance of fierce Israeli protests, the sale to Sa'udi Arabia of sixty F15 fighter-bombers, the most sophisticated warplanes in the world, and President Carter welcomed Crown Prince Fahad to Washington in a state of emotion that appeared close to ecstasy.

'I don't think', enthused the president in a statement which raised eyebrows in London, Bonn and Teheran, not to mention Tel Aviv, 'that there is any other nation with whom we've had better friendship and a deeper sense of cooperation than we've found in Sa'udi Arabia!'

Carter was hopeful that he could sweep Sa'udi Arabia up into the peace process that followed on from Anwar Sadat's historic journey to Jerusalem of October 1977, but it was at this point that the regional superpower began to falter, for there are some problems that the fattest cheque book in the world cannot solve.

Anwar Sadat had been in Riyadh the week before he stunned the Arab world with his journey to Jerusalem. He had lunched with King Khalid to discuss the possibilities of a Sa'udi–Egyptian peace initiative, for ever since the October War Sa'udi Arabia and Egypt had regarded each other as principal allies. The Riyadh–Cairo axis was generally acknowledged as the main feature of Arab politics and diplomacy in the post-boycott years.

But in October 1977 Anwar Sadat gave no advance warning to King Khalid of the epoch-making gesture he was planning in a few days' time, and when the news of his Jerusalem initiative broke, the Sa'udis felt betrayed. They could not criticize Sadat openly without appearing slighted – simple bedouin who paid the clever Egyptian nearly $10 million a day and were not even consulted when he went to visit the Israelis. Nor could they defend their ally, for Sadat had gone to pray in the al Aqsa mosque in Jerusalem – the very thing King Faisal had sworn not to do until the Israeli occupation was ended.

'A cease-fire or peace, OK: he was in the front line and we were not. But why,' Sa'udis still ask today with pained bewilderment, 'why did he have to go and pray in the mosque as well?'

Praying by Israeli permission was something no Sa'udi leader, as guardian of the Holy Places, could possibly have done, and many outraged Muslims concluded that Sadat must have acted with the secret agreement of his Sa'udi paymasters. The Egyptian leader was preparing, it seemed, for a sell-out on Jerusalem that the Al Sa'ud were too scared to acknowledge themselves – and Riyadh became the object of as much Arab opprobrium as Cairo.

When faced with very complex problems, the Al Sa'ud have a tendency to do nothing and hope that the trouble will go away. It is the other side of rule by consensus. It took the family six years to face up to what they had to do about King Sa'ud. King Faisal would not have imposed his total embargo in 1973 unless caught off balance by Nixon's pro-Israeli overkill, and with the partnership between Fahad and Khalid swift and decisive action has proved still harder to obtain. Fahad is not so great a power that he can afford to ignore the throne. He has to take account of Prince Abdullah, head of the National Guard; there is old Prince Muhammad – and there are the influential younger brothers, Sultan and Salman, who also have views and power of their own.

So long as Fahad's cheque-book diplomacy had been working smoothly and unobtrusively, his brothers left him to make the decisions. Sa'udi Arabia kept a low profile and nuzzled cosily into the centre of the Arab consensus.

But Anwar Sadat's journey to Jerusalem called for exposure. The Egyptian leader had polarized the Arab world with his initiative. Sadat himself felt that he had won a victory in October 1973, and that he therefore possessed the 'face' to go and negotiate with the Jews. But the Syrians knew they had been defeated and felt humiliated by the very suggestion of negotiations; the Palestinians knew that their cause depended on marshalling every single Arab state behind their claims; countries like Iraq and Libya condemned Sadat with the easy outrage of arms-length belligerents who had not actually mourned thousands of their young men or seen their cities shelled and bombed three times in eighteen years; and Sa'udi Arabia, wanting to remain on good terms with all these touchy and dangerous brethren, while hoping at the same time to stay friendly with America and Sadat, found herself caught in the middle.

450

When Sadat, Carter and Menachem Begin emerged from Camp David with their draft peace agreement of September 1978, fence-sitting became still more difficult, for Arab feeling hardened further against the Egyptian president. 'When Sadat dies,' a Jeddah merchant told *Time* magazine, 'the Egyptians will dig up his bones and piss on them.'

The Arab consensus was that Sadat had sold out the general cause to get back his own land, for though Egypt regained Sinai at Camp David, Israel kept Jerusalem – within two years the Knesset was to incorporate the city as Israel's 'complete and united capital' – while all that the Palestinians were offered on the West Bank was a poor apology for a Bantustan, dotted with fortified Israeli settlements, which Begin was determined to expand. 'Carter is for self-determination in Rhodesia,' sneered Yasser Arafat, 'while he is against it for the Palestinians. A contradiction, yes?'

In November 1978 Iraq convened an Arab summit to frame sanctions against Sadat, and Fahad signed for Sa'udi Arabia. But the crown prince insisted that the sanctions should not be invoked until Sadat had finally signed the Camp David agreement as published. Perhaps Sadat could still squeeze out a deal which did more for Jerusalem and the Palestinians, and to give Egypt time, Fahad resisted the pressures of his brothers Khalid and Abdullah, who were by now arguing for a final break with Sadat. Fahad wanted the door left ajar. He felt that there was still some chance of peace with honour.

But as the details of Camp David became more solid through the winter of 1978–9 it became clear that the peace offered nothing that any Arab but an Egyptian could describe as honourable, while it was also radicalizing the Arab world, both governments and peoples, to a degree not seen since the October War. What incentive could there be for the Al Sa'ud to challenge such dangerously inflamed feelings? If the Sa'udis backed Camp David, they would gain Egypt's friendship, for which they were already paying $3 billion a year; they could swap bear-hugs with Mr Begin, which offered a devout Muslim leader all the attractions of cuddling up to Miss Piggy; and President Carter promised faithfully that Sa'udi backing for his peace process would earn the Al Sa'ud the unshakeable support of America against any repercussions that might ensue.

At this moment, the Shah fell.

Before January 1979 Sa'udi Arabia was already getting worried about Jimmy Carter. His Westernized definition of how 'human rights' should be defined seemed arrogant to people whose religion had always insisted upon the ethical content of politics, and it was also dangerous. America seemed to hope it could get out of fighting any more Vietnams by transforming the human race into a more moral category of animal, and in Iran this confused idealism had both encouraged opposition to the Shah, and fatally undermined the man whom America had installed and maintained for twenty-five years as her best non-Jewish friend in the Middle East.

It also undermined the wish of Fahad ibn Abdul Aziz to give the Camp David process some sort of life, for the crown prince had finally to agree with his brothers that an America that could not save the Shah could not save the Al Sa'ud either.

By inviting the Kingdom to join in the Camp David process, Carter was asking the Al Sa'ud to make their pre-eminence in the Islamic world hostage to Anwar Sadat, to Carter himself and to Menachem Begin. He was also requesting Sa'udi Arabia to antagonize the Palestinian guerrillas and several radical governments who would be more than happy to aggravate the opposition which support for Camp David would provoke among many ordinary people inside the Kingdom.

But what would happen if this opposition were aggravated and elevated, with outside help, into a serious threat to the Sa'udi government? President Carter was more likely to wring his hands and talk of human rights than to send in the marines – and the Al Sa'ud did not want the marines in any case. The family could look after itself, and the failure in the following year of the military attempt to rescue the US hostages held by student militants in Iran was fully to confirm the accuracy of this assessment: if that was the best the USA could manage for her hostages, what could she do for Arabia's oilfields – let alone for her 'friends' in the house of Sa'ud?

Crown Prince Fahad decided he must distance himself from Washington. In February 1979 he cancelled a trip he had scheduled to meet President Carter in the following month. 'A matter of health,' said the White House. Prince Fahad said nothing, but a few days later he seemed to be healthy enough as he was photographed showing Queen Elizabeth II the sights of Riyadh.

On 18 March 1979 the Sa'udi Council of Ministers met to ratify the agreement which Khalid, Fahad and their senior brothers had finally arrived at: that, if Sadat did actually sign the Camp David formula, then Sa'udi Arabia would instantly apply the general Arab counter-measures against him.

But Fahad had one last trick up his sleeve. The crux of Arab objections to Camp David was that it did not do enough for the Palestinians, nor for the Muslim shrines in Jerusalem, and, while Sadat had been cavalier in assuming a mandate to negotiate these issues unilaterally, they did represent an impossible responsibility for one man alone to fulfil.

Fahad's idea, once Israel and Egypt had finally agreed on a settlement between themselves, was that a delegation of Islamic Foreign Ministers should go to Washington to inspect the elements of the package that related to Palestine and Jerusalem and to test out the practicalities of these measures. This would broaden the peace talks from the base already established; it would undercut the criticisms of the hard-line 'rejectionist' Arabs; it would bring into play a number of countries on the Sa'udi payroll; and it would also preserve the Cairo–Riyadh axis.

Sadat was enthusiastic when the plan was put to him secretly in March 1979 – but President Carter was not. Carter had staked his presidential prestige on bringing home an agreement from a dramatic last-minute shuttle between Cairo and Jerusalem. He wanted to get off Air Force I waving his arms in triumph, not explaining how a crew of Third World diplomats with robes and worry beads were coming to stir the pot further.

Nor could the president in any case see how he could sell Fahad's idea to Menachem Begin. The Israeli premier had been drawn into the Camp David process by the prospect that concessions to Egypt would strengthen the Israeli position in Jerusalem and on the West Bank. Fahad clearly wished to prevent both these things, and his proposal, if carried through, would destroy all the advantage that the Camp David package held for Israel. The crown prince was informed that President Carter would neither approve his Islamic committee nor receive it if it came to Washington.

Fahad was mortified. He had been prepared to take a risk to expand the Camp David process, and he had thought he was offering Carter a helping hand. In disgust he told his brothers they could do their worst, and on 31 March 1979 Sa'udi Arabia announced that it was severing diplomatic ties with Egypt, cutting off all aid and joining the general Arab boycott of the Sadat regime. The Kingdom had lined up with the 'wild men' of the Arab world.

453

The Sa'udi ostracism of Camp David illustrated all the ambivalence of the US–Sa'udi 'special relationship'. Riyadh felt America had asked too much of her. But Washington felt equally betrayed. President Carter's National Security Adviser, Zbigniew Brzezinski, had conferred with Prince Fahad in Riyadh and come home with the firm impression that the Sa'udis would back US peacemaking efforts.

But Brzezinski had run into a problem which frequently off-balances negotiations between the West and the Arab world. Arabs do not like to offend their guests. Hospitality involves telling your guest what you think he wants to hear. Arabs do not, on the whole, enjoy direct face-to-face verbal confrontations with people they scarcely know – and this is especially the case with Fahad ibn Abdul Aziz.

In his conversations with Brzezinski the crown prince stressed his hopes for peace and his confidence in the long-standing 'special relationship' between America and the Kingdom. He did make clear the Sa'udi commitment to the Palestinians and to the recovery of Muslim Jerusalem. But Fahad did not probe the likely sources of disagreement on these two crucial issues, nor did he lay bare his full bitterness and distrust towards Israel. So Brzezinski left Riyadh in a glow of friendship. His hosts had not exposed to him the fears that would lead them to reject Camp David. Nor could the Carter administration appreciate, when the rejection came, that America's friends in the Arab world are generally safer, and more effective friends, if they are seen to maintain a certain distance from their Zionist-supporting ally.

The disgruntled State Department began leaking to the media tales of the disagreements that had occurred as Fahad and his brothers argued over policy. The Al Sa'ud, it was suddenly suggested, were no more reliable than the Shah had proved; and Middle East 'experts', caught out badly by what had happened in Iran, hastened to hedge their bets: Sa'udi Arabia had a new image in the news magazines: no longer a bulwark of the West, the Kingdom became the crumbling coping stone in a 'Crescent of Crisis' now perceived as stretching from the Horn of Africa to Pakistan, all of it about to fall victim to the marauding Russian bear in the north.

President Carter added insult to injury. No Arab leader he had ever met, he declared, actually wanted to see the creation of a truly independent Palestinian state – and, since the President had met with King Khalid and had discussed this very issue, the Sa'udi ruler felt personally defamed.

454

'He tells my people that I am a liar!' fumed the king.

In their meeting Carter and the Sa'udi leader had discussed the Palestinians' links with Moscow. The king expressed his displeasure at this and his fear of the growing communist influence inside the Arab world. But in criticizing the PLO's closeness to Russia, King Khalid did not deviate from his personal commitment to Arab rights in Palestine – starting with genuine elections in which the inhabitants of the West Bank could show freely what they feel about Israeli military occupation.

'Of course,' says one Sa'udi prince, 'if God granted us a wish, we would like the Palestinians to vanish off the face of the earth. We know they are only nice to us because they want our money. They are dangerous men with Marxist tendencies. But their disappearance would be a second wish. The first wish is the disappearance of Israel.'

President Sadat was withering in his scorn when the Kingdom finally rejected Camp David in the spring of 1979 – and with it, Egypt and all its works. 'They are not giants,' he sniffed. 'They are dwarfs standing on a pile of money.'

But the Egyptian leader had never been reluctant to accept that money, and he was saying no more than the Al Sa'ud already knew. Their Kingdom might be vast, but with a native population of perhaps one million adult male Sa'udis they had no delusions about their ability to get their way through force of arms.

Shah Reza Pahlavi always enjoyed the fantasy that Iran was a power that could stand comparison, militarily and economically, with Israel, Japan or any European country. But King Khalid, Crown Prince Fahad and their brothers have never nourished any such dreams. In the aftermath of Camp David, Crown Prince Fahad concluded agreements with General Zia of Pakistan whereby the Kingdom would finance two battalions of Pakistani commandos to be on permanent standby in case of trouble in the Gulf, for cheque-book diplomacy is the Kingdom's only option. They have to pay other people to do their fighting for them.

Arab military weakness was underscored in June 1981 when Israeli planes raided and destroyed Iraq's nuclear reactor near Baghdad, and the raid brought two alarming new developments into the open.

455

The first is that the future of the Middle East is clearly a nuclear one. Iraq's nuclear progress may be set back several years by the raid, but Pakistan will soon have the capacity to produce its own Islamic bomb, and Sa'udi Arabia announced in July 1981 that she would finance the rebuilding of the Iraqi reactor. The Israelis will not be able to hold off the evil day for ever, and well before the end of the century the Arabs will have a nuclear capacity to match that which Israel undoubtedly holds already.

The most fervent advocate of nuclear deterrence cannot view this development with much enthusiasm. Nuclear weapons in the hands of fanatical Arabs and fanatical Israelis will prove the ultimate test of the theory that nuclear stalemate ensures peace – and the Al Sa'ud have a more immediate worry. Israel clearly considers it her right to ignore international conventions in striking violently anywhere she feels her vital interests to be threatened, and if she had plans to knock out Iraq's nuclear reactor, she must also have worked out precisely how she could hit, if not take over, the Sa'udi oilfields. The Pentagon's contingency plans for doing this were leaked in 1974 in the course of an ill-tempered attempt at arm-twisting by the State Department, and at the time two reasons were advanced as to why the US government might one day wish to execute such a drastic step: a threat from Russia, or disorder inside the Kingdom itself.

These same reasons, not to mention some future Arab–Israeli war, might quite plausibly move Israel to direct her jets against Dhahran – and in that event the Sa'udis do not believe that America would discipline her Jewish ally any more seriously than she did after the raid on Iraq. The Kingdom will have to look after itself, and this is the reasoning behind Crown Prince Fahad and his brother Sultan's massive arms purchases in the West since 1975. Menachem Begin is quite correct in his frequent complaints that Sa'udi Arabia is arming herself as much against Israel as against the Russian threat.

Washington's remedy for this frightening scenario is the stationing in the Middle East of America's own Mobile Deployment Force. This could hold the ring and would forestall one very likely Israeli justification for moving in on the oilfields: that she should safeguard the energy resources of the West. But America's thirty-year support of Israel means that any Arab government offering the US some sort of base on its territory today risks incurring violent opposition from its own population, from its neighbours and from the Palestinians – and the Israeli raid on Baghdad has made things worse.

456

'Here come America's running dogs,' was the Syrian welcome to the Sa'udi negotiators trying to defuse the Lebanese missile crisis a few days after the nuclear reactor raid.

If anything epitomizes the dilemma which today bedevils the Middle East and the security of the entire world, it is the spread-eagled body of Sa'udi Arabia, her arms tied to the ground by Arab feeling and Islamic responsibilities, her legs pinned by her involvement with a superpower committed to the support of Israel. Her critics say the Kingdom wants the best of both worlds. The Al Sa'ud maintain that peace can never come until both sides get their due.

Unlike many of their fellow Arabs, the Sa'udis see their links with America as the best way of forcing Israel to compromise with the demands of the Muslim world and of the Palestinians. Unlike many Americans, they see their links with Yasser Arafat and the PLO as the best mechanism for getting a dispossessed and angry people involved in a peace process, whatever that might be.

Anwar Sadat chose his own visionary way. He believed he could outflank the deep and lethal rancours of Arab radical and Muslim fundamentalists. But in October 1981 it turned out that his Western admirers were as powerless to preserve him as they had been to save the Shah. The Sa'udi way forward is less obviously heroic, but its pragmatism does appear to offer the Al Sa'ud, and peace, rather better prospects of survival.

The unceasing litany of the Kingdom's foreign policy statements is that the priority in the Middle East is not rapid Deployment Forces, nor adjustments to the frontiers of Israel with Egypt (the Camp David process), but a settlement which satisfies the aspirations of the Palestinians and which restores Muslim rights in Jerusalem. This, say the Sa'udis, is the heart of the matter and, until such a settlement is reached, it will be impossible for America's friends in the Arab world to acknowledge their friendship effectively.

Such a settlement would be no panacea. If it were, somehow, miraculously arrived at, the Middle East would still be beset by many problems, not least the continuing Soviet pressure for oil to complement the dwindling capacity of the Russian fields. But the problem cannot wait much longer, for the Middle Eastern arms race is building up with inexorable momentum. There have been four Arab–Israeli wars since 1948 – and in 1981 neither side seems as worried as it should be at the prospect of a fifth.

48 Death of a Princess

ONE noon-time towards the end of July 1977, Princess Misha'il, granddaughter of Prince Muhammad ibn Abdul Aziz, was led out into a car park beside the Queen's Building in Jeddah and forced to kneel down in front of a pile of sand. She was then shot dead. Standing near by was her young lover, Khalid Muhalhal, nephew of General Ali al Shaer, special Sa'udi envoy to Lebanon, and, when the young man had seen the princess die, he also was executed – by beheading.

Nearly three years later, in the spring of 1980, a film dramatization of these executions and of one journalist's attempts to investigate them was broadcast by ATV in Britain, and this broadcast caused King Khalid such offence that he instructed Great Britain to withdraw her ambassador from the Kingdom. Four months later the ambassador was back in place again. Such were the bare essentials of the painful international melodrama that flourished for a season around *Death of a Princess*.

The outline of the princess's story was straightforward. Married off at an early age to an elder relative who took little interest in her, Princess Misha'il, the daughter of one of old Prince Muhammad's less distinguished sons, turned for consolation to young Khalid Muhalhal and enjoyed with him a romance whose flamboyance scandalized the rest of her family. The couple tried to elope, they were caught, and both suffered the death penalty prescribed for adultery in Sa'udi Arabia's code of Islamic law.

Love, drama, tragedy: the story was natural raw material for television; and it included details that made it the more appealing. To effect her elopement, the princess staged a drowning, leaving her clothes in a pile on the shore of the Red Sea. Then she tried to escape with her lover from Jeddah Airport, disguising herself as a man. Her grandfather Prince Muhammad had all the family feeling and ferocity

458

to be expected of a desert patriarch. And the milieu of the entire story
– mysterious palaces, bored princesses, the panoply of oil wealth, the
brutality of ancient justice – guaranteed the popular appeal of the film
to a Western audience.

Reasoning – correctly – that if he disclosed the true object of his
inquiries, he would not be granted an entry visa to the Kingdom,
Antony Thomas, a documentary film-maker of South African origin,
had visited Sa'udi Arabia in 1978 ostensibly to study the developing
role of women in Sa'udi Arabia; and under cover of these researches
he had succeeded in gathering together a body of contradictory
material. Everybody had a different story to tell about the princess,
and the rumours that Thomas heard in Beirut made the contradictions grow worse.

So, not surprisingly, these contradictions became the central theme
of the enterprise, and various actors, English and Arab, were hired to
reconstruct the interviews in which a succession of people had passed
on their own very personal glosses on the conflicting pieces of evidence they had heard: to a group of Palestinians, the princess was a
fellow Arab, trying to break out of her own sort of refugee camp; to a
lovesick German governess who had worked for the Al Sa'ud she was
a romantic heroine who had sacrificed herself for love; to a left-wing
progressive female teacher, the princess was a freedom fighter dying
at the hands of a reactionary and repressive regime imposed upon
Arabia by the capitalist world – and some of the stories hinted at what
her family say is the truth: that Princess Misha'il was a spoilt and
perverse child, happy to enjoy the privileges of her position but
heedless of the family reputation and conventions that are its price.

Thomas skilfully showed how different people, the majority of
them non-Sa'udis, had rearranged the facts they knew about Princess
Misha'il's life and death into patterns that had more regard for their
own preconceptions than for the complexity and reality of the truth.
But the mere reporting of such preconceptions was enough to prevent
many Sa'udis viewing the rest of the film dispassionately.

Death of a Princess might have caused less offence if it had not
aroused ambiguity in viewers' minds as to the kind of television
programme that it was. Antony Thomas made clear in the title
sequence that his film was a dramatization, and it was rounded off
with the credits of the actors who had taken part; but many of its
viewers undoubtedly believed that they were watching genuine
people being interviewed, not actors playing the parts of both re-

porter and interviewee; and the film itself seemed to maintain the illusion, with hundreds of Egyptians dressed up in *thobe*s and head-dresses to re-create the streets of Jeddah – though the authenticity was somewhat marred by the laundered cleanness of the *thobe*s and the startling appearance in one scene of a camel. People who have lived in the Kingdom for any length of time know that you no longer meet camels wandering through the main streets of Jeddah.

Thomas could scarcely be blamed for resorting to dramatization. The Sa'udi government would never have allowed him to make a genuine documentary about the death of Princess Misha'il. But in employing visual ventriloquism to create the texture of a documentary, he raised a serious issue: when an ordinary viewer sees a live interview he can make his own judgement of the speaker's veracity; but if he only hears the ventriloquist's dramatization how can he judge for himself?

Writing in the *Sunday Times*, Geoffrey Cannon compared *Death of a Princess* to two other recent works of television 'faction' where the director's presentation of controversial events had secured special emphasis over all others through the plausibilities of a quasi-documentary format.

There could be a danger, moreover, that in TV drama-documentary the truth might be overshadowed on occasions by the dramatized elements, and uncertainties as to whether this had happened with *Death of a Princess* were strengthened when Thomas's former collaborator, Penelope Mortimer, no special friend to Sa'udi Arabia, publicly criticized the film.

Ms Mortimer had helped Thomas with his research. She had accompanied him to Sa'udi Arabia, and she complained that many of the 'interviews' in the film were, in reality, 'amalgamations of many different interviews'. Thomas, replying publicly, explained that he had done this to protect his sources.

At the Edinburgh Festival, John Mortimer (ex-husband of Penelope) took Thomas's side. The Old Testament, the *Iliad* and the Icelandic sagas were all blends of fact and fiction, he pointed out – and so was Shakespeare. 'The critics who denounced *Death of a Princess*', said Mortimer, 'would have a field day with *Richard III*, which by mixing history and invention tastelessly displayed a physically handicapped member of a royal household in an unfavourable light, and no doubt caused needless offence to the Plantagenet family.'

The arguments were academic. Even if Thomas's film had been an unquestionable masterpiece, blessed with all the qualities of the Old Testament, the *Iliad* and the Icelandic sagas rolled into one, it would still have been unacceptable to the house of Sa'ud, for *Death of a Princess* breached a sacred taboo. Certain subjects that the modern West is happy to talk about openly, and which many Sa'udis themselves will talk about in private, are simply off-limits when it comes to public discussion, and, if that rule is ever breached, then the shame and anger provoked by the exposure can be intense.

A bright and impressionable writer called Linda Blandford had discovered this in 1975 when she came to the Kingdom in the early months of King Khalid's reign to chronicle the impact of the new oil wealth upon Arabia. Lively and attractive, with an unexpected limp that was distressing in such a pretty girl – 'she seemed so vulnerable,' Sa'udis say today – Linda Blandford was welcomed into private homes wherever she went: she saw a sex manual on the shelves of a minister's sitting room, she listened to a princess discussing the shape of her own breasts, she heard how one of King Sa'ud's sons got a boil on his bottom: and she wrote it all down in her book. The resulting furore was enormous, not helped by the fact that Ms Blandford had omitted to inform her hosts, until they read it in the foreword to her book, that she was Jewish.

It is difficult nowadays, when discussing Linda Blandford's book with inhabitants of the Kingdom, to get them to pin down what they actually claim to be untrue. She captured sharply the follies and pretensions of the Arab oil states in the first post-embargo boom months, and she painted a cruelly accurate picture of Jeddah's *nouveaux riches*.

But truth is not the issue. Linda Blandford made private things public. She printed gossip, and that, in Arabia, is an unacceptable contradiction in terms. Gossip in the Kingdom may be spoken, but it may not be written. Private things may not be unveiled to the public gaze, and, if they are, then that brings shame.

The shame that the worldwide screening of *Death of a Princess* provoked for Sa'udi Arabia in the spring of 1980 was twofold. A lesser shame was felt by younger, Westernized princes and by educated Sa'udis as a whole, who were embarrassed that the murderous anger of one powerful old man should be taken by outsiders as representative of the general flow of life in their country. The principle that the adulterer should die is an old-established concept in Islamic law, and Sa'udis, royal or otherwise, defended it vigorously in

461

the months after the screening of the film. 'What this proves', they would say, 'is that princesses must submit to Islamic law like everybody else.'

But this was not what they had said in the immediate aftermath of the executions in 1977. Then criticism was bitter and frank, particularly since a government order suddenly forbade women to travel unaccompanied by a male member of their family. Businessmen had to waste hours escorting their wives and daughters, or waiting in a prince's *majlis* for a signed exemption from the order.

The Al Sa'ud have always insisted that Princess Misha'il was properly tried and sentenced in a court of law according to the tenets of the Shariah. She confessed her adultery freely, they say, as did her lover, and it was on King Khalid's personal instruction that the judicial process took its course. But the king's brother Muhammad could have rescued his granddaughter before she went to court if he had wanted to, and for all the talk of Islamic justice, the law which truly did the princess to death was the unwritten and ancient law of the tribe, which places the purity of the woman, the heart of the family, at the heart of the family honour.

This was the source of the second, and greater, shame provoked by *Death of a Princess* – shame which incited King Khalid and his elder brother to such anger that there was wild talk at one stage in April 1980, of not only the ambassador but all 30,000 Britons working in Sa'udi Arabia being put on planes back to London. Prince Muhammad had let his granddaughter be executed precisely because he felt that her adultery dishonoured the Al Sa'ud in the eyes of others, and for a foreign film-maker to dig up that dishonour and re-expose her promiscuity revived the dishonour he thought he had purged.

Nor had *Death of a Princess* stopped at that, for the one passage in the film which Sa'udi representatives, after an advance screening in London, tried desperately, and at the highest level, to have removed before the programme was broadcast, did not feature Princess Misha'il. It was a sequence which showed other unspecified princesses parading a desert road in their limousines to look over and pick up men waiting in their cars; and this is the sequence which is still cited with most heat in Riyadh when the family discuss the film.

Thomas spoke to sources who satisfied him of their veracity. But this author has never witnessed such a spectacle. The Kingdom's chaotic car registration records and the absence of street names, numbers or addresses in the Western sense, scarcely facilitate the

462

number-plate tracing on which the game is supposed to be based – the Sa'udi police themselves cannot trace malefactors from registration plates – and though Thomas did not observe this bizarre and supposedly public ritual himself, his use of actors and hired cars had the effect of transforming his judgement of his sources into a striking visual 'fact' carrying the most offensive imputation: that the women of the Al Sa'ud habitually cruise the desert looking for sex.

It is difficult to imagine a worse insult, and it totally prevented the Al Sa'ud from seeing that *Death of a Princess* reflected the natural human shock felt by ordinary folk in the West that people should be executed for adultery anywhere in the world in the last quarter of the twentieth century. It irredeemably categorized the film in their eyes as a slur upon the honour of the clan's womenfolk.

When the normally placid King Khalid was shown a videotape, the sequence of the princesses cruising through the desert was translated and explained to him, and it stung him to a rare fury. He saw the film as a malicious smear upon his family honour, and since the political legitimacy of the Al Sa'ud is based upon its adherence to certain moral and religious norms, the affront was doubly barbed. Crown Prince Fahad, Sa'ud al Faisal and other princes knowledgeable of the West and its ways failed to restrain his fury, and from the royal outrage came the retaliation against Britain, and a worldwide campaign to try to stop the film being shown – which met with less than total success. When *Death of a Princess* was finally screened in New York on Channel 13 on 12 May 1980, it gathered 26.7 per cent of that night's TV audience. In Boston the figure was 49 per cent.

King Khalid's fury proved extravagantly counterproductive. All the fuss made by Sa'udi Arabia guaranteed that *Death of a Princess* was seen by millions of people the world over who would, otherwise, never have heard it. But tell the Al Sa'ud that they would have done better to shrug the film off, and they will tell you that there are some insults that a man of honour just cannot ignore.

49 Mr Khashoggi

JULY 1981, Cannes. Adnan Khashoggi is celebrating his birthday, and his yacht *Nabila* lies out in the bay, several hundred feet of polished grey steel with bronze reflective windows. On the fifth and topmost deck sits his helicopter on its pad beside the swimming pool, while in shark-like speedboats around the yacht, conservatively estimated to have cost $25 million, cruise watchful men with cropped hair, suntans and dark glasses. At the front of the vessel is a white communications pod linking Mr Khashoggi's telephone and telex lines, by satellite, to his other boats, planes, cars and bases around the world. James Bond never had it so good.

In the pile-carpeted staterooms of the *Nabila*, *Star Wars* seems a better comparison. There is a whole room of Space Invader machines. Doors slide by remote control, and some of them only function if you can tap out the right code on the calculator buttons set where the handle should be. Laser beams shoot into the sky from the projectors with which Mr Khashoggi is entertaining his 200 birthday guests. The yacht's command room is Star Ship Enterprise, and every illuminated panel in the marbled discothèque flashes with the smiling features of Mr Khashoggi himself. Here, floating off the South of France, is Arab oil wealth deployed with all the exuberance that visitors expect, but seldom find, on display in the Kingdom itself.

As the petrodollars poured into Sa'udi Arabia in the 1970s, the world got to know a new kind of Arab merchant, the multinational Arab tycoon, and Adnan Khashoggi has come to symbolize the type. In each of his private jets are two wardrobes, one containing three-piece suits and shirts and ties, the hand-stitched mohair combat kit of the modern Western businessman; in the other hang white cotton *thobe*s, headdresses and black ribbed headropes, the full traditional Arabian regalia – and as the Boeing hatch swings open, Mr

Khashoggi emerges to face the world costumed in the livery appropriate to his setting.

Adnan's father was a doctor. Dr Muhammad Khashoggi was the personal physician to Abdul Aziz, prosperous enough to send his boy to Victoria College, Alexandria – that exclusive English-run academy where Arabs paid for the privilege of having their sons caned if they were caught speaking Arabic – but Adnan's subsequent success was largely of his own making.

Few people have not surrendered when personally exposed to the charm of Adnan Khashoggi. 'You're going to have a problem when you meet the Chief,' says his chief of staff Robert Shaheen. 'You're going to like the guy.'

Adnan Khashoggi is a warm and engaging character. Kept spruce and groomed by his personal masseurs and by the barbers who travel with him round the world – the *Nabila* and all his homes feature old-fashioned barber chairs – he overflows with energy, and the role that his personality has played in his success is common to that of all the first generation of successful Sa'udi businessmen. Akram Ojjeh, Ghaith Pharaon (whose father was another physician to Abdul Aziz), Saleh Kamal, Suleiman Olayan, all are bluff, gregarious characters. Sa'udi business has not reached the stage where faceless men operate impersonal corporate strategies and make their money through the cold application of management techniques. It is very much a face-to-face affair, business relished as it was in America a hundred years ago, and the more zestful for the fact that the Kingdom levies no income tax.

Akram Ojjeh bought the liner *France* when the French Line could not run it any more, and sold it on very profitably as a cruise liner; Ghaith Pharaon bought shares in Bert Lance's Bank of Georgia to bail the financier out in his time of trouble, and has bought into other American banks since; Suleiman Olayan, today the largest private shareholder after David Rockefeller in the Chase Manhattan Bank, started his career as an employee of Aramco; Saleh Kamal, once a clerk in the Sa'udi Ministry of Finance, still spends his days plodding round humble Riyadh ministry offices, drinking cups of tea, and personally picking up tenders for the companies in his multi-million dollar construction and maintenance empire. Swashbuckling, sometimes eccentric, and rarely conforming to Western ideas of ethical business practice, the entrepreneurs of the Kingdom conjure up memories of the days of Vanderbilt and J. Pierpont Morgan.

This is a comparison which Adnan Khashoggi has always made. Early in his career he read and studied the biographies of the great tycoons of North America, analysing how they made their fortunes helping to put a great nation together, and he sensed immediately what the oil price rise of 1973 meant for Arab merchants like him. He was confident that petrodollars would enable the Arabs to become multinational businessmen every bit as successful as the Jews, whom he was eager to take on at their own game.

Like many of the Kingdom's richest men, Adnan Khashoggi laid the foundations of his fortune as an agent, that considerable figure on the Arabian commercial stage. Arabian merchants have been making money for over half a century in the agency business, transferring the products of the industrialized West to Arabia and collecting their commission on the deal – and Khashoggi became an agent almost by accident when he returned from college on the West Coast of America in the 1950s. A patient of his father's, Muhammad Bin-laden, a contractor who was building a business empire from the construction work that King Sa'ud's development programme stimulated, needed some trucks in a hurry – and young Adnan put Binladen in touch with an American truck manufacturer he had met while at college in California.

A few weeks after the $500,000 deal was completed, Adnan received a $25,000 cheque from America, his commission on the deal, and the boy sent it on to his father's friend. But a day or so later he got it back. Adnan should not be ashamed to take his commission, said Binladen, and since the trucks had turned out cheaper than he expected, he was adding in a second $25,000. Adnan Khashoggi was launched on his career as a middleman.

He got in on the ground floor of Sa'udi development. His Commercial Registration was No. 3, his Riyadh post office box, No. 6. He soon had the Sa'udi agencies for Rolls-Royce aero engines, Marconi, Fiat and Chrysler. He secured a maintenance contract for Dhahran airport after King Sa'ud expelled the Americans from their base in an access of pan-Arab feeling, and then one day in 1962 he was summoned to the office of Crown Prince Faisal ibn Abdul Aziz, to be handed a cheque for £1 million.

The money was to buy arms for the royalist guerrillas in the Yemen, said the crown prince. Faisal did not care where the arms came from, nor how they got there, just so long as the Sa'udi government's name was not linked to the deal.

After the royalists had received their rifles (British weapons supplied with the secret help of the British government) Khashoggi went to Prince Sultan, the Defence Minister, to hand back the change.

'What about your own expenses?' asked the prince. 'Are you not taking any profit?'

'I did this for my King,' replied young Adnan, who was not yet thirty. 'I do not want a profit.'

The commission Adnan Khashoggi waived was to be repaid him many times over. He became a friend of Prince Sultan, and also of Sultan's brother Fahad. As his agencies prospered, he entertained the brothers in the Kingdom and on their trips abroad, and in 1965 his progress received another boost from Faisal ibn Abdul Aziz, now king.

Eating dinner one night at the US Embassy in Jeddah, Khashoggi had been hurt to hear the ambassador make fun of the American military training programmes in the Kingdom: they were just devices to keep Sa'udi army officers out of mischief; no practical good would come of them.

Adnan Khashoggi went home, wrote down his recollections of the conversation, and took it to King Faisal.

'I have never seen a man tear a piece of paper like that,' he recalls today. 'The king was so angry I thought that my head was going to roll.'

But Faisal's anger was not directed at Adnan Khashoggi.

'These Americans will never understand us,' spat the king. 'They train us, then think we can only play in the sand dunes!'

The Kingdom was negotiating in 1965 for the purchase of fighter bombers. Adnan Khashoggi was representing Lockheed, who were putting up their F104 against the British Lightning, and Khashoggi concluded from King Faisal's anger that his own plane might have difficulty winning the battle. He had also caught wind, through his contacts with Rolls-Royce, of a secret US–British trade-off whereby, in exchange for deals in other areas, Washington was prepared to let the Lightning win the Sa'udi contract in a package that included certain US components.

Adnan Khashoggi nimbly secured himself representation for Raytheon, manufacturers of the Hawk missile, and he then helped put together the combination of British planes and US air defence which won the day: the Raytheon component of the deal was worth $136 million; Adnan took his percentage on the Rolls-Royce engines that powered the Lightnings, together with substantial maintenance contracts – and Lockheed were scarcely losers: their enterprising agent supplied the Sa'udi Defence Ministry with a fleet of desert-landing C130 Hercules transport planes ($2.5 million each, commission to Khashoggi $400,000 per plane), plus a flight of Tri-Stars (with Rolls-Royce engines) for the national airline, Saudia. If you want to succeed in business in the Kingdom, you must be quick on your feet.

By the mid-1970s Adnan Khashoggi's commissions from Lockheed alone totalled more than $100 million, and representing one arms company did not inhibit him from representing others; he secured business on behalf of Lockheed's rivals Northrop which netted him $54 million; the sale of $600 million of French armoured cars to the Sa'udi army brought him $45 million; and the sale of some Belgian firearms brought in $4.5 million – petty cash.

But Adnan Khashoggi wanted to be more than just an agent. He wanted to move outside the Kingdom to create the first multinational Arab conglomerate to stand comparison in wealth and expertise with the greatest in the world, and he hired McKinsey to reorganize his Triad group of companies to that end – though in practice Adnan was the company, and its headquarters were his private jet, a twentieth-century magic carpet shuttling him between his offices in London, New York, Geneva, Paris, Beirut and Riyadh.

Early in the 1970s Khashoggi bought himself two Californian banks. In Salt Lake City he organized and invested in a $450 million industrial park and foreign trade zone – the first Arab to develop land in the United States. In Arizona he bought into cattle ranching. In Brazil he helped finance a huge meat-packing plant. In Indonesia it was shipping, in the Pacific a chain of hotels, in Lebanon he made furniture, and in Paris he leaped into fashion and financed the Kenzo 'Jungle Jap' ready-to-wear company.

Assembling some fifty companies into his global conglomerate, Khashoggi demonstrated spectacularly what the private Arabian businessman could accomplish with the petrodollar, and his partners around the world waxed lyrical: 'My initial feeling is one of complete delight,' declared Scott H. Matheson, Governor of Utah in 1979. 'I had no idea that he could go out into that desert area of the Salt Lake Valley and turn it into such a delightful and productive place.'

Mr Khashoggi's concerns extended beyond making money for money's sake. He gave lavishly to charity. In the Sudan he master-minded the project intended to prove it was not only Israelis who could 'make the desert bloom', going to no less than twenty-five banks to raise $200 million, and he attempted, unsuccessfully, to persuade his friends Fahad ibn Abdul Aziz and Richard Nixon, whose presidential campaigns he assisted, to collaborate on 'Petro-stat', a scheme to recycle Arab oil wealth for the general benefit of the world economy.

But as Adnan Khashoggi soared higher and higher into the strato-sphere of international finance, he neglected one very important prin-ciple of Arabian business – the need to be discreet – and perhaps this was his father's fault.

'Look at these coins,' Khashoggi remembered his father once saying to him. 'Throw them on the carpet. You hear nothing. Throw them on a stone floor. They make a noise. My son, always put your money where it can be heard.'

Adnan certainly did that. By the mid-seventies every gossip column in the world carried stories of his private planes with their 40-foot, carpet-walled sitting rooms, video machines, telephones and double beds, his private yachts, his luxurious homes scattered around the globe. Khashoggi partied in Las Vegas, Paris, Cannes and Beverly Hills, and when his friend Harold Robbins published a best seller called *The Pirate*, in which the story of a high-flying Arab tycoon was spray-painted with all the glitter for which Mr Robbins is known and loved, nobody had any difficulty guessing who his model was.

Then came Watergate. As Archibald Cox's investigators looked into the extraordinary amounts of cash that some American businessmen had at their disposal to pay secretly into the coffers of politicians whom they favoured, they uncovered massive commission payments by these corporations all over the world. Records were subpoenaed showing that Lockheed and Northrop had paid millions to fixers like Prince Bernhard of the Netherlands, Japanese Premier Kakuei Tanaka, to prominent members of the Italian government – and to Adnan Khashoggi in Sa'udi Arabia.

Khashoggi was unashamed. He was proud of all the commissions he had taken from American companies, and if they thought he was passing it all on in bribes, then that showed how stupid they were.

'There is a very important distinction you must make,' he said. 'When I approach the Sa'udi government on your behalf, the money that you pay me is my commission. In Arabia it is honourable for you to give and for me to receive the money. It is only if I offer it to the government servant, and he accepts it, that it becomes a bribe.'

Like many Sa'udi businessmen, Adnan Khashoggi had complex personal and commercial relationships with the government officials with whom he did deals. He was their friend; he gave them presents; he let them use his private planes; he cut them in on his lucrative ventures in other fields.

But if Adnan Khashoggi *had* been paying bribes on a major scale, he could scarcely have become the wealthy man he was, and this became one bone of contention in the private litigation which followed the US Senate inquiries, for Khashoggi pocketed most of the fees his American partners paid him to pass on in sweeteners, and, in at least one documented instance, insisted they should pay extra, and through their own channels, to take care of a Sa'udi general who was asking for a cut.

A Pentagon official was once so insensitive as to ask Adnan Khashoggi how much money he had paid Prince Sultan in return for all the contracts he had secured from the Sa'udi Defence Ministry over the years. Mr Khashoggi was horrified.

'Prince Sultan does not need Adnan Khashoggi,' he replied. 'Adnan Khashoggi will never offer Prince Sultan money – that is like a beggar offering riches to a king.'

In his book *The Arms Bazaar* Anthony Sampson addresses himself to the extraordinary career of Adnan Khashoggi and concludes that he must be compared to 'the agents and quartermasters of the European courts in the sixteenth century' who made their fortunes catering for the palaces, armies and private pleasures of their princes. In this context, modern Western concepts of corruption were 'almost meaningless', and intruding upon the scene the executives of Lockheed and Northrop came from a different century – 'as if men in grey flannel suits walked into the middle of a Shakespeare play'.

Sa'udis' voices tend to rise when comparisons are made between their way of doing things today and Europe's habits in the Middle Ages. 'Feudal' is a term that causes special offence. But it is the only word to describe the extraordinary period in the late sixties and early seventies when so many Sa'udi arms purchases were channelled through one tried and trusted bailiff. Prince Sultan bought planes through Adnan Khashoggi as his father Abdul Aziz had told Abdullah al Qosaibi to deliver a motor car across the sands to Riyadh. Oil wealth apart, the essence of the transaction was the same.

Nowadays the Sa'udi Ministry of Defence does not buy weapons through Adnan Khashoggi, nor through any other Sa'udi middlemen.

Sa'udi agents were prohibited from acting in arms sales to the Defence Ministry by a decree which arose directly from the embarrassment which the Lockheed and Northrop hearings provoked – and the publicity stimulated by Adnan's private life did not help. Sa'udis were not impressed when his British wife Soraya launched a lurid divorce action against him, selling unsavoury 'confessions' about her wayward private life to popular newspapers. Adnan Khashoggi had represented the ambition that Arabian businessmen could take on the West and beat it at its own game. But somehow the West seemed to have got the better of him.

Adnan Khashoggi today is still fiercely proud to be a citizen of the Kingdom. He sees himself as one of its great champions and exemplars, building bridges between East and West – a merchant statesman..

His fellow merchants are not so sure. The private hangars and side runways of Sa'udi airports are awash with private jets sprinkled with their owners' initials from tailplane to packet matches. But the flamboyant Khashoggi style is not widely imitated in other respects.

If anything, the major commercial dynasties are more reclusive than they ever were, and Sa'udi businessmen get annoyed that when the West thinks of Sa'udi wealth, it thinks first of Mr Khashoggi.

'He is just one man who made wealth in his own style,' they say. 'He does not represent the Kingdom.'

They are being less than honest. Khashoggi's indulgence in the good things of this life, his willingness to cut corners, his ability to get favours from the Al Sa'ud and from non-royal ministers by doing *them* favours – these are not things unique to him. All Sa'udis know the 'I'll-scratch-your-back' basis on which business is conducted in the Kingdom, and Khashoggi is unrepresentative not because of what he did but because he let the world catch a glimpse of him doing it.

The *Nabila* is not the only Sa'udi yacht to cruise the Riviera every summer, and corners of Marbella, Cannes and Gstaad become totally Sa'udified each August as affluent Arabian visitors exchange *thobe*s for swimming trunks – though they prefer their fellow holidaymakers not to know who they are or where they come from.

These are the very Sa'udis who will tell you that Adnan Khashoggi is not representative of the Kingdom. But as they enjoy themselves like any other pack of millionaires on holiday, their women unveiled, their children in blue jeans, it is difficult to see what they mean – except, of course, that Adnan Khashoggi has had the nerve to admit to the rest of us that spending petrodollars can actually be fun.

50 $100,000,000,000

AUGUST 1979, Geneva. It is nearly midday and the foreign exchange managers of Switzerland's Union Bank are getting worried, for they have just started to pick up strange and massive movements in the international currency market. Has some government moved into the market, trying to shore up or reduce the price of its own currency? The size of the movements is big enough.

It could be a bank departing from its normal buying and selling policy – a really big bank. So the Swiss start putting out calls to their colleagues and competitors around Europe.

Yet they find that everyone else is just as mystified as they are, and it takes several days before the truth emerges. A money changer in the Riyadh *souq* has decided to put some of his spare cash into the international currency market, and he is playing it rather well. . . .

February 1980, Riyadh. A Texan billionaire with pebble glasses is squatting uncomfortably on his ample haunches making a brave attempt to dismember a sheep.

'What are those rings there on your head?' he asks, peering at the headdresses of the assembled princes, businessmen and bedouin picking at the array of dishes set out across the carpet.

The Texan has flown to Riyadh for the day because he is engaged upon an extraordinary adventure. He is trying to buy up so much of the world's silver that he can control the market and set the price himself. He is one of the richest men in America in his own right. But he has come to the Kingdom to raise real money and has found investors with $1 billion cash to spare. So together the Texan and the Sa'udis are going to take on the world.

Soon after the oil price explosion a new line of fiction began setting the fashion in the bookstalls. James Bond fell quite out of favour. The new style of thriller was set in the world of high finance. Its theme was the fragility of the international monetary system, the danger that it might be manipulated by a small group of fabulously wealthy and totally unscrupulous men – and those men were always Arabs.

The scenario was seductive. It appealed to the ancient Western fear of the Arab, and to the modern Western envy of the Arab's new-found wealth; and the real-life adventures of Suleiman al Rajhi,* the Riyadh moneychanger who started playing the currency market, and of Muhammad Hassan al Amoudi, leader of the Sa'udi syndicate which backed Nelson Bunker Hunt's daring silver coup, seemed to suggest that the truth can be just as extraordinary as fiction.

Some aspects of wealth in the Kingdom are extraordinary indeed. At the King Faisal Specialty Hospital in Riyadh all the patients eat their meals with gold-plated knives, forks and spoons. So did all the staff – until cutlery started vanishing from the expatriate canteen.

Several days a week a convoy of heavily protected armoured cars makes its way from the City of London to Heathrow Airport, where it unloads a couple of million pounds of banknotes into the strongroom of the British Airways jet to Jeddah. The notes have been purchased by the moneychangers for their tables in the Jeddah *souq*, and they are waiting for the plane in their open pickup trucks. When they get hold of the muslin sacks they dump them in the back of their trucks as if they were bags of fodder for their sheep, and then they bump off into town, the sacks swaying in the open vehicle behind them.

Bankers and moneychangers in the Kingdom can tell you how much any pile of notes is worth just by looking at it. A million riyals is a cube-shaped chunk of paper about one foot by one foot by one foot. You can see roomfuls of them in the vaults of the National Commercial Bank in Jeddah. Depositors bring them in like that, and then come back every so often to go down into the vaults to make sure that their money is still quite safe – though they seem to do so for reasons of anxiety rather than covetousness: many of them refuse to accept interest on their deposits for religious reasons.

*   *   *

* Suleiman al Rajhi is the most successful of Arabia's moneychangers. Their trade derives from the days when the peninsula did not have a currency of its own and when good livings could be made from trading foreign currencies like the rupee, Maria Theresa dollar and British sovereign against each other. The al Rajhi assets are not a matter of public record, but it is reliably estimated in Riyadh that they are comparable to those of the National Commercial Bank, the Kingdom's largest bank, and itself one of the two hundred largest banks in the world.

Sheikh Abdul Aziz Quraishi, Governor of the Sa'udi Arabian Monetary Agency, is responsible for the investment of roughly one hundred thousand million dollars per year – $100,000,000,000. Outsiders cannot be sure of the precise sum, but the declared foreign currency reserves of the Kingdom stood at $65 billion at the end of 1980, and the anticipated surplus of income over expenditure is budgeted to be in excess of $40 billion in 1981, so $100 billion would seem a fair enough guess.

This is the money which the Kingdom cannot find a way to spend, despite a government budget for 1981–82 of $93 billion, larger than the entire gross national product of Switzerland. It is also the money which, if capriciously or maliciously handled, could disrupt the international financial system, for Sa'udi Arabia's currency reserves, officially ranked third in April 1981 behind those of West Germany and France, are one of the largest single blocks of cash floating in the world money market.

Sheikh Abdul Aziz Quraishi is the man whose job it is to move the money. He is a short man, round and soft-spoken, who pronounces his r's as w's, and his office at the top of SAMA, the Sa'udi Arabian Monetary Agency, commands one of the best views of Riyadh – though Riyadh is not where SAMA keeps its money.

The $300 million a day which the Kingdom receives for its oil is paid on the nail, in dollars, in New York. SAMA's money managers phone round the New York banks to see who will give them the best rate of interest for a week, month or three-month deposit, and the money waits there in the hands of Chase Manhattan, Morgan Guaranty or any other of the big New York banks while SAMA decides what to do with it next.

That decision is usually taken in London, for most of the routine placements of the Kingdom's currency reserves are handled through the London money market. London operates in the same time zone, give or take a few hours, as Riyadh and it can handle all major currencies. So as the Sa'udi petrodollars come off deposit in New York they are transferred to portfolio managers in London.

'Like anyone else with money to invest, we hire investment managers,' says Sheikh Abdul Aziz Quraishi. 'But the zeros are different.'

Baring Brothers is one London merchant bank known to advise SAMA. Rothschilds and banks with Zionist connections do not get Sa'udi government money, but many private Sa'udi investors are rather proud of their Jewish banker in London.

SAMA does not invest in real estate. It is well aware of the sensitivities inflamed by the spectre of Arabs 'buying up' the West. But it does invest in equities on Western stock exchanges and in Japan through its investment managers. They decide what to buy and sell every day on their own initiative, without taking orders from Riyadh, though it is a standing guideline that SAMA investment should never reach 5 per cent of the voting stock of any company.

Sa'udi Arabia differs in this respect from Kuwait and from several of the other oil producers with surplus funds to invest, for Kuwait, which is little more, effectively, than a city, has lavished upon itself just about every development that that city could need. So it has deliberately set aside a proportion of its surplus every year to create a national 'pension fund', investing as a major shareholder in companies like Daimler-Benz against the day when the oil runs out and it may have to live, as a rentier, upon the income from its investments around the world.

Sa'udi Arabia, with territory the size of Western Europe to pull together, still has endless development projects on which to spend its money and, as leaders of the Islamic world, the Kingdom's rulers are not happy, in any case, at the idea of living on interest. They are sensitive enough about SAMA's day-to-day investments, which they defend with the Islamic concept of *darura* – necessity: if you are starving in the desert, then it is permissible to eat pork.

'We are turning a solid national asset, oil, into a wasting one, money,' says Quraishi. 'So we have to accept interest to try to maintain its value.' If a bag of rice costs 100 riyals this year, goes the argument, and you know it will cost 110 riyals next year, it is your duty to make sure you will still be able to purchase it then.

The Kingdom's financial surplus derives from its oil policy. In 1978 Sa'udi Arabia almost ran out of cash for a month or so. There was enough to keep the civil service and the infrastructure running, but all major contract payments stopped dead. A world oil glut had led to an unexpected million-barrel-a-day cut in Sa'udi oil production. Export revenues dropped accordingly, and SAMA found its vast financial surpluses embarrassingly tied up in deposit contracts. It took several months to restore liquidity and pay the bills, and nowadays Sa'udi investment managers, who have always placed a high proportion of their client's portfolio in short and medium term deposits, keep even more cash to hand. The Kingdom maintains its dominance of the world oil market by varying its oil production levels, and to do this

475

successfully it needs to draw on its money reserves rapidly if oil revenues drop.

The Kingdom lends money directly to governments. In the spring of 1981 Sa'udi Arabia lent $2 billion to West Germany. SAMA makes large purchases of American government bonds – though President Carter's freeze of Iranian assets means that the Kingdom will be yielding up fewer such financial hostages in the future.

SAMA also makes loans to private companies. In recent years both General Motors and IBM have borrowed millions of dollars from the Sa'udi government in private deals arranged through Salomon Brothers in New York, and the Sa'udis are anxious for investments like this. When you have one hundred billion dollars whose value you must maintain against inflation, there are not that many safe and profitable locations around – hence the problem of 're-cycling' which became the vogue economic issue of the late 1970s: how to put the oil producers' spare money to productive use.

After 1973 the private banks of the West found it possible to redistribute a large proportion of the new petrodollar surpluses to the less developed areas of the world. But the second, and in many ways more serious, major rise in the price of oil that followed the Iranian revolution in 1979 proved too much for the system, and there are now in practice little more than a dozen countries in the world to whom a commercial banker would consider it safe to make a loan. If you lend money to Brazil, Mexico, Taiwan or South Korea, you still have a sporting chance of getting your money back – and your interest as well. But rising energy prices have hit poor countries even harder than rich ones, and the great mass of the world's poor nations, seventy or eighty of them, have nil credibility in the commercial market place Funds can only be recycled to them through direct aid.

Between 1976 and 1980 Sa'udi Arabia gave 6 per cent of its national income to Third World countries, a total of $20 billion – 15 per cent of all the aid given by the industrialized West, making the Kingdom the largest per capita aid donor in the world. In addition, in May 1981, Sa'udi Arabia made $9.5 billion available to the International Monetary Fund for recycling purposes, the most substantial loan facility ever made in history.

'In the short term we are making a sacrifice,' says Sheikh Abdul Aziz Quraishi. 'We could obviously find more profitable outlets for $9.5 billion. But in the long term, it is no sacrifice at all.'

With its $9.5 billion loan facility in May 1981 the Kingdom joined the élite group of countries who dominate the IMF – the United States, Great Britain, West Germany, France and Japan. The 'Big Five' have become the 'Big Six', and they are the principal investors in the stability and health of the world economy.

Sa'udi Arabia has a large proportion of its surplus funds invested in dollars, many of them dollars purchased on the European market. It also has heavy investments in the Swiss franc, the yen, the Deutsche Mark, as well as smaller proportions in the French franc and the British pound. But SAMA's holdings in its basket of currencies are so vast that if it tried, say, to sell too many dollars, then the price of the dollar would fall; and if it then tried to move quickly into yen, then the price of the yen would move against it also. A small investor can shift his money between currencies and make profits if he is clever. If a big investor starts playing the market, then the market, by its nature, goes against him. So Sa'udi Arabia now has no choice but to take a long-term view and help to strengthen the system that it finds itself locked into, and this is why the Kingdom's vast financial surplus is not likely to be turned on the world in the way that the fiction writers imagine.

Individual Arab speculators get up to all sorts of games, as is the way with speculators. They win and lose fortunes, as is the nature of speculation: Suleiman al Rajhi, the moneychanger, has done well since he started playing the international currency market; Muhammad Hassan al Amoudi and the other Sa'udis who backed Bunker Hunt's silver heist did not do as well as they hoped: in July 1981 Mahmoud Fustok, one of the Sa'udi silver buyers, admitted to losses in excess of $80 million. Individual coups and follies have individual consequences, and the petrodollars that are more likely to shape our lives are those shifted by Sheikh Abdul Quraishi, who is not, frankly, the stuff of which pulp novels are made.

Does the sheikh never feel the urge to have a flutter, to give the world money market just a little nudge in the fashion that the paperbacks prophesy? SAMA's governor answers the question with a question.

'We have got to have stability in the world economy,' he says. 'How else can we sell our oil?'

51 The Mahdi

Mahdi. (Arabic, he who is guided aright.) The title of a coming Islamic messiah who will establish the reign of justice on earth.

New Twentieth-Century Encyclopaedia

EXPERIENCED pilgrims will tell you that the best time to visit the Grand Mosque in Mecca is in the small hours of the morning. The crowds are a little thinner then. You can perform your devotions in the cool of the night and, as the stars begin to fade, the worshippers can gather in rings close around the huge black Ka'aba to say the dawn prayer.

At 4.30 a.m. on Tuesday, 20 November 1979, there were more people than usual on their knees at dawn around Abraham's House to God – 50,000 or so. The pilgrimage had only recently ended, many pilgrims had lingered in the Holy City, and 20 November 1979 had a special significance in the Muslim calendar. It was the beginning of the Islamic year 1400.

Suddenly shots rang out. Men were firing rifles into the air, and a group of rough-bearded tribesmen were clustering around a young man, shaking his hand and offering him homage.

'The Mahdi! The Mahdi!' they were shouting. 'Behold the right-guided one!'

A wild-bearded figure with blazing eyes leaped up the steps to the public address office.

'The Mahdi will bring justice to the earth!' he cried, seizing the microphone with which the imam had just been leading the prayers. 'I am the Mahdi's brother. My name is Juhayman. Recognize my brother! Recognize the Mahdi who will cleanse this kingdom of its corruptions!'

From beneath their robes several dozen men produced rifles, joined in the shouts, and fanned out purposefully towards the mosque's thirty-nine double gateways. From among the worshippers a couple of hundred men leaped up as if this were the signal they had been waiting for. Policemen and a young assistant imam who tried to resist were shot dead. The gunmen reached the gates, the doors were

478

shut, and the shrine revered by Muslims all over the world as the holiest place on earth was sealed off. The House of God had been hijacked.

Belief in the future coming of a Mahdi, or Messiah, trickles back into the early years of Islamic history. The Koran itself makes no mention of a Mahdi, but during the leadership disputes that followed Muhammad's death, sayings with a messianic flavour began to be attributed to him.

'The princes will corrupt the earth,' Muhammad was said to have prophesied, 'so one of my people will be sent to bring back justice.'

Different *hadith*, or traditions, fleshed out this 'right-guided one' or Mahdi – though few Muslim theologians treated them as seriously as the more down-to-earth *hadith* on which Islamic law is based. The earth, it was prophesied, would swallow up the armies sent against the Mahdi. His coming would be marked by violence. He would come from among the blood descendants of the Prophet, his name would be Muhammad, he would appear at the dawn of a new century. One tradition even specified that the redeemer would bear certain facial characteristics – and these were seized on in the Sudan in the 1880s by Muhammad Ahmad, the most successful of the several 'Mahdis' who, at different times over the centuries and in different Muslim countries, appropriated the tradition of a coming Islamic Messiah to lend divinity to their ambitions.

The Sudanese Mahdi, who died shortly after his historic capture of Khartoum from General Gordon in 1885, cited as credentials his own first name, a mole on his cheek, a gap between his teeth and his emergence at the beginning of the fourteenth Islamic century.

In 1979, one hundred Islamic years later, the Mahdi in whose name the Grand Mosque in Mecca was captured and who sought, in God's name, to take control of the Kingdom of Sa'udi Arabia's twentieth-century destiny, laid claim to a slightly different set of stigmata: Muhammad Abdullah al Qahtani had the correct first name, his mother claimed descent from the Prophet, he manifested himself near the beginning of a new Islamic century – and his manifestation was marked by violence. As his followers took control of the Grand Mosque in the early hours of Tuesday, 20 November 1979, they shot dead the police and anyone who resisted them. The chatter of their machine-gun fire echoed round Mecca's rocky hills.

King Khalid was woken with the news in Riyadh before seven o'clock in the morning. A police car sent to investigate the trouble at the mosque had been fired on, and the mosque's imam, the white-bearded Sheikh Muhammad al Subayil, had managed to hide in his office and telephone out a description of the rebels, who appeared to be several hundred strong, well armed, well trained and utterly ruthless.

It was alarming news. The forcible capture of Islam's Holy of Holies, the most sacred spot in the entire world to Muslims, was shocking in itself. It represented an immediate disgrace upon the Al Sa'ud, who had deliberately linked their prestige to the protection of the Holy Places, and the speed, efficiency and strength of the terror-ists argued for a wider conspiracy. They must be expecting other uprisings, help from abroad even, and King Khalid ordered all tele-phone and telex links with the outside world to be severed com-pletely. The Kingdom went into international limbo and even Prince Fahad, away in Tunis heading the Sa'udi delegation to a meeting of Arab leaders, could not discover what was going on.

As reports of the trouble reached Jeddah, the embassies radioed home garbled stories of an armed uprising. When the Ayatollah Khomeini heard the news in Iran, he proclaimed that the Zionists and Americans had defiled Islam's most sacred shrine, and in Pakistan furious demonstrators attacked the American embassy, killing two Marines.

Inside the Kingdom road blocks were thrown up around every major city. The army and National Guard were put on red alert. The government braced itself, expecting a major challenge to its author-ity, and the brothers Sultan and Naif ibn Abdul Aziz, Ministers of Defence and the Interior, raced to Riyadh airport to fly to investigate the trouble on the spot.

Meanwhile at the Grand Mosque, the old Sheikh Muhammad al Subayil had escaped. The followers of the Mahdi had sorted out twenty-five to thirty hostages that they could guard properly, letting the rest of the dawn worshippers leave the mosque, and the imam had slipped out amongst them, jettisoning his cloak to avoid detection.

From the sheikh and other released worshippers, the police and soldiers now gathering around the Grand Mosque, sheltering from fierce fire directed downwards from the minarets, began to piece together some picture of what was going on inside. The armed men seemed mostly to be Sa'udis. Many were clearly proficient at using their weapons, Russian-made AK47s, pistols and .22 rifles. They were estimated to be 200 to 300 strong. They appeared to have

brought women and children with them. And though they were
hailing one particular young man as the 'Mahdi', the man in charge of
the whole operation was clearly the orator in his early thirties, with
the wild beard and blazing eyes, who had seized control of the public
address system to proclaim himself the Mahdi's brother – the man
who had called himself Juhayman.

Juhayman ibn Muhammad ibn Saif al Otaybi was indeed the ringleader and inspiration of the November 1979 coup which was to start
the entire world wondering whether the Al Sa'ud's grip upon the
Kingdom was as tight as it once had seemed. Juhayman came from
the Otayba tribe, which had risen fiercely during the Ikhwan Revolt
to cut off Abdul Aziz in Jeddah, and Ikhwan ideals reflected his own
beliefs. The Otayba traditionally grazed their camels on the plains
between Riyadh and the Taif escarpment, and Juhayman had volunteered while still a teenager in the mid-1960s for the Otayba section
of the National Guard.

As the Muslim world reacted in horror to the November 1979
seizure of the Grand Mosque, rumours were circulated about Juhayman which Sa'udi newspapers printed with glee – he was homosexual,
a drug addict, a drunkard, he had been discharged from the National
Guard in disgrace.

But as the Al Sa'ud struggled to get control of a situation which had
taken them totally by surprise, they discovered that accusations of
degeneracy against Juhayman were difficult to sustain. He had been
involved in cigarette smuggling and had dropped out of the National
Guard. But in the early seventies he had 'got religion', gravitating to
Medina where he used to attend the question-and-answer sessions
organized after the evening prayers in the Prophet's Mosque by
Abdul Aziz bin Baz, the blind religious sheikh who preached that the
earth was flat and who was a leading member of the *ulema*. Juhayman
had lived in one of the charitable hostels which offer free food and
accommodation to worshippers in the Holy Cities, and he had picked
up a certain following there among the religious drifters that he met.

Juhayman's movement can be compared to that of Prince Khalid
ibn Musa'id who was shot after the Riyadh television station riots.'
Juhayman found among the pilgrims and students of Medina certain
discontented souls who shared his mistrust of Westernization and the
way that Sa'udi society seemed to be heading. They were bewildered
and resentful of the new wealth and of the effect it was having upon
traditional religious values. They prayed and read the Koran

481

together. They derived inspiration from Ikhwan ideals, they external-
ized their alienation with long beards, clipped moustaches, *thobes* cut
short above the ankles – and, after the overthrow of the Shah in
January 1979, they drew lessons from the success in Iran of the
Ayatollah Khomeini.

In no way were Juhayman and his followers adherents of the
Ayatollah. Drawing their impetus from the fundamentalism of
Muhammad ibn Abdul Wahhab, they abominated the superstitions
of Iran's Shia Muslims. But Khomeini had demonstrated to the Shia
how preaching the word of God could bring down even a potentate
as mighty as the Shah – and this was what Juhayman had in mind.
His extraordinary gesture in the Grand Mosque on 20 November
1979 was intended to bring about the downfall of the house of
Sa'ud.

As Juhayman's demands were broadcast from the minarets of the
Grand Mosque into the surrounding streets, Ministry of Information
officials carefully filtered out his political grievances. When, after
twenty-four hours, the telephones were plugged in again and the
blanket embargo on news was lifted slightly, the outside world was
given to understand that a madman had seized Islam's holiest place
through anger at the spread of football, video machines and working
women in Sa'udi Arabia.

But these were incidentals. They were small examples which
Juhayman cited in his principal attack upon the house of Sa'ud and
upon the Western ways with which they were corrupting the Kingdom. Broadcasting his anger through the prayer microphones to most
of central Mecca, he denounced the drinking of alcohol by princes,
their frequent travel abroad to foreign fleshpots, their involvement in
big business, and the encouragement they gave to infidels to come in
and alter the traditional life of the Kingdom. Specific names and
business contacts were cited, and Juhayman singled out for special
condemnation Prince Fawwaz ibn Abdul Aziz, the Governor of
Mecca, whom he charged with love of gambling and of whisky.

Juhayman had been making such complaints for several years. He
had gone to Kuwait to get his fundamentalist fulminations printed in
pamphlets – and he had taken to preaching his message in Sa'udi
mosques. Any Muslim can address his fellow worshippers after the
prayers if he feels inclined – and if they will stay to listen – and in the
late 1970s Juhayman and his followers took to making such speeches,
denouncing the devilish corruptions afflicting the Kingdom, among

482

them the Ministry of Information, responsible for allowing women singers on TV.

These demonstrations landed some of Juhayman's companions in prison for a brief period when they appealed for funds to build mosques which did not exist, and among those imprisoned was Muhammad ibn Abdullah al Qahtani, an ex-student of Islamic law at Riyadh University. This was the young man whom Juhayman saw in a dream one night in the middle of 1979. God spoke to him, Juhayman later said, and told him to proclaim al Qahtani the future Mahdi, called to purify the earth of all iniquity.

Al Qahtani, who married Juhayman's sister shortly after this, appears to have been a likeable character of some suggestibility. After Juhayman described his dreams, his brother-in-law began to dream himself and to agree that, yes, God was indeed calling him to be 'the right-guided one'. He burned like Juhayman and his fellow zealots against the iniquities of the world around him – and a new century was coming up in a few months' time. The coincidences seemed divinely inspired.

Later Salman ibn Abdul Aziz, the Governor of Riyadh, was to point out that the fifteenth century could not begin until the year 1400 was over. The very first year in the calendar was numbered 1 from the beginning, so at the beginning of the year numbered 100 only ninety-nine years had been completed – and so on through the centuries. But such arithmetical niceties did not trouble the latter-day Ikhwan, intent on purifying the Kingdom and feeling that 1400 loomed auspiciously ahead of them as their date with destiny.

They were almost all young men, some of them members of the National Guard like Juhayman, and many of them members of the Otayba tribe. Affas bin Muhaya, the leader of a group of snipers, was the son of Ogab bin Muhaya, an Otayba chieftain killed during the Ikhwan Revolt. Many of the rebels were ex-theology students, who should, theoretically, have been cheerleaders for a religious-based regime like the Al Sa'ud, and a few of them were non-Sa'udis – Egyptians, Kuwaitis, Yemenis, who appear to have joined the conspiracy out of shared religious conviction.

In the earliest hours of their rising it was to seem frightening that 200 to 300 revolutionaries could synchronize such an ambitious rendezvous without the authorities knowing a thing. But, in fact, only a hard core around Juhayman were in on the planning of the coup which had started during the pilgrimage only twenty days earlier. All the rest, relatives and like-minded souls from the conspirators' prayer groups, women and children among them, turned up at dawn on the first day of 1400 in response to a *dawa* – an invitation to come to pray.

Juhayman and his aides had smuggled many of their arms into the mosque on biers beneath winding sheets. It was not unusual to see mourners bearing their dead into the Grand Mosque for a final prayer before consigning them to the cemetery – and Juhayman had his ammunition and supplies, mainly dates and water, the traditional Ikhwan fare, driven into the mosque's cellars the previous day in pickup trucks. Beneath the vast white marble pavement of the Grand Mosque's courtyard is an uncharted labyrinth of little storage rooms used by builders engaged on the year-round maintenance of the mosque, and Juhayman drove his supplies unchallenged through one of the service gates into this area. He had raised the money to pay for his provisions from tithes on his followers. The son of one rich Jeddah family contributed SR100,000. This helped buy AK47s, the Russian rifles that flooded the Yemen during the civil war and which had since spread all over the peninsula, and some of the arms and ammunition were stolen from National Guard depots.

The planning showed forethought, hard work and a considerable ability to reason. The fighting, when it started, showed discipline, training and a sound grasp of tactics – a tribute to the National Guard from which some of the conspirators came. But everything was dedicated to one grand irrational act, the proclamation of a Mahdi which, Juhayman genuinely believed and hoped, would inspire thousands of worshippers to join him and overwhelm any troops which the Al Sa'ud might send against him.

He was disappointed. Scarcely any of the thousands of men and women whom he attempted to corral inside the vast stadium of the Grand Mosque on the morning of 20 November 1979 wanted anything to do with his Mahdi. The Kingdom did not rise in response to his call – and with that failure, Juhayman's revolt was doomed. But 200 of the zealots whom Juhayman and his friends had invited to pray with them took up arms, and since the Grand Mosque is a natural fortress, they were strongly placed to hold off attackers for a considerable length of time.

The outside world speculated wildly as to what might be happening inside Mecca. It seemed impossible to Muslims of any persuasion that co-religionists could have sullied their Holy of Holies with gunfire and bloodshed, for the Koran carries the direst warnings against those who desecrate the House of God. No animal can be killed there, not even plants may be uprooted. In a country where every wild animal that moves is shot or snared, pigeons fly thick and free around the Grand Mosque, taking care never to fly more than ten yards away from it – and these taboos are strengthened in the first month of the Muslim year, Muharram, in which the taking of life is traditionally forbidden with particular emphasis.

All these prohibitions raised special problems for King Khalid, since he could not simply order the Sa'udi army to storm the Holy of Holies, guns blazing. Many would flatly disobey, and the king risked being accused of a sacrilege as great as that committed by the 'renegades' – as the English-speaking Sa'udi press soon learned to describe Juhayman and his followers.

So one of the first things that King Khalid did on Tuesday, 20 November, was to summon the *ulema* to his presence and ask for a ruling. Was it lawful for the forces of the government to shoot, to take life even, in the Grand Mosque so long as the present emergency lasted?

The religious sheikhs said yes, and Prince Sultan, who had made his headquarters in the Shubra Hotel near the mosque, was told he could open the attack. Anywhere else in the Kingdom Sultan could have called for mortars, bazookas, hand-held missiles even, to pummel the rebels into the ground. But the Al Sa'ud could not reduce God's House to rubble. They were already under sufficient criticism for letting the Grand Mosque fall prey to heretics. More conventional tactics were needed.

The infantry assault on the Grand Mosque was a long-drawn-out and bloody affair. The building had to be recaptured pillar by pillar, and some of the Sa'udi soldiers were unhappy at the prospect of fighting in God's house.

Prince Sultan spoke to a group of them. 'You can go home now if you want to,' he cried. 'You needn't fight. But what am I to do? Send for the Pakistanis?'

Pakistan, whose officers monitor the training of the Sa'udi army, had volunteered to send Muslim stormtroopers into Mecca. France had flown tear-gas shells and percussion grenades to Jeddah, together with instructors – to whom, later, the French press imaginatively gave the credit for recapturing the Mosque.

'This is our shame, and we must eradicate it ourselves,' cried Prince Sultan. 'This is God's House and you are His soldiers!'

The platoon to whom the prince spoke marched into the forest of pillars surrounding the great courtyard of the mosque – but two of the men who had refused to fight broke cover almost immediately. They rushed into the open firing wildly, to be shot down by the rebels before they had gone ten yards. As martyrs in defence of God's House, they had guaranteed themselves a place in heaven.

This was holy war. Every time the rebels saw one of the government forces fall, they cried out, *'Amr Allah!'* ('At the command of God!'). When one of their own comrades died, they shot off his face or tried to burn it in an attempt to mask his identity. This was a job they often gave to the women and children who were with them – and some of these took to mutilating fallen soldiers for good measure. After three or four days, said one lieutenant, the smell of the bodies around the courtyard in the November sun was nauseating.

Most of the Sa'udi assault troops had never seen action before. But here they were, actually stalking enemies a few miles from their homes with rifles loaded.

Creeping through the pillars around the courtyard, one officer heard the sound of a magazine being loaded only a few yards away from him. 'I knew it was not one of my men. I had checked every magazine before we started. They had all loaded up correctly. So I went round the pillar with my rifle ready.'

There the officer saw a rebel standing, a few yards away, with his back to him, loading his magazine.

'My first thought was to arrest him. But I remembered how others had pretended to surrender, then produced hidden guns, daggers, grenades even, and killed people.'

So the officer took point-blank aim at the rebel's head and blew it to pieces.

'I killed two, perhaps three men in those ten days. It made me sick. But they were killing so many. When they shot my radio operator right beside me I wept. After every sortie I lined up my men and called the roll, and every time there was at least one long silence.'

By the time the Grand Mosque was recaptured over 200 men had been killed, and many more than that seriously injured. The government announced their own casualty figures as 127 dead and 461 injured; 117 rebels were killed, and so were a dozen or more of the worshippers caught in the gunfire on the very first morning.

486

The last stages of the siege were fought out in the warren of cellars below the Grand Mosque's marble pavement. The Mahdi was shot and his dead body photographed after four days of fighting, proof that he was not the divinely promised one as he and his brother-in-law had claimed. But Juhayman and his followers fought on. They refused appeals to surrender, for they could not expect to live very long or very pleasantly if they did submit – and they withdrew to the basement, blackening their faces and holing up in the grubby little rooms with mattresses, their womenfolk, and what was left of their dates and water.

The government troops threw down tear-gas bombs, burning tyres, they flooded the cellars and they flung live mains cables into the water in an attempt to electrocute the last survivors. But it was a week before Juhayman and his followers came stumbling out, coughing and wide-eyed, into the daylight – and each of them was handcuffed. Every single one of the rebels had had to be overpowered and disarmed by gasmasked troops, and Juhayman was kicking and struggling even as his arms were pinned behind his back. Sa'udi Television covered the scene, and Juhayman stared defiantly at the cameras, thrusting forward his matted beard, his eyes fierce and piercing like a cornered beast of prey.

The government handled the conclusion of the siege with more aplomb than they had displayed at the outset. The cut-off of international links and the repeated assertions by the Ministry of Information through the first few days that 'all the renegades have been rounded up' had suggested more than a little panic. But towards the end the Interior Ministry took over the handling of information, actually admitting to a few mistakes, and concluding with a remarkable press conference in which Prince Naif, televised live, answered all comers.

'What shall we say about beards now?' asked one worried Sa'udi reporter, remarking on the wild long facial trimmings that all the rebels had sported, Ikhwan-style.

'These are but external matters,' replied the prince – but more than a few bedouin shaved down to a townsman's goatee in the weeks that followed.

Mecca was not quite all the story. In the last week of November 1979 there had been riots in the Eastern Province. Buses had been burned, the windows of shops, houses and a bank had been smashed – and at least eleven demonstrators had been killed by the National Guard. Several score more had been arrested, and the government did not report the trouble.

In one sense, the riots in the Eastern Province of November 1979 had nothing to do with the trouble in Mecca. They stemmed from the grievances of the 200,000 Shia Muslims who had lived in and around the town of Qateef for centuries, and there was no love lost between the Shia and Wahhabi fanatics like Juhayman, who felt that the Al Sa'ud were too tolerant of these Islamic deviants. But just as Juhayman had provided an uncomfortable reminder of the Ikhwan past that had helped to create the Kingdom – it was as if the ghosts of the Brethren had come back to haunt the sons of Abdul Aziz – so the riots in Qateef recalled that seventy years previously the eastern coast of Arabia had been independent of Nejd, and that regional feelings still burned strong.

If the Eastern Province had never been conquered by the Al Sa'ud, its massive oil wealth would have made it a prosperous state in its own right – richer than any other country around the Persian Gulf. But in 1981 none of the towns of eastern Arabia can stand comparison with the prestigious developments of Kuwait, Bahrain, or the ex-Trucial sheikhdoms. Dhahran, al Khobar and Dammam make up a cosy but scarcely glittering provincial conurbation, and the 200,000 Shia Muslims of Qateef and the Eastern Province live in poverty compared with the conditions enjoyed by Sa'udis anywhere else in the Kingdom.

The Shias actually carry out much of the manual work in the Sa'udi oilfields – they make up 40 per cent of Aramco's workforce – and their fate, producing the Kingdom's wealth but scarcely enjoying it, symbolizes the imbalance of which many easterners complain. During the disorders in November and December 1979 a daring cartoon showed a vast camel standing across Sa'udi Arabia: it was feeding in the east, it was being milked by a mercantile character in the west, and the milk was being handed to a slothful character sitting in the middle, just where Riyadh is. The brand-new palaces, ministries, highways and hospitals of the capital are built with money from the east, but the east itself has nothing so grand to boast of.

The problem is partly historical. Run since 1913 as an almost separate fiefdom by Abdullah bin Jaluwi and his sons, the Eastern Province was traditionally kept docile but underdeveloped. The bin

488

Jaluwis fiercely resisted King Sa'ud's attempts in the 1950s to bring the east under the Ministry of the Interior. Sa'ud bin Jaluwi, ruling the east as a prince in his own right through the 1950s, refused for years to have a numberplate on his car, only agreeing finally to 151, which, in Arabic, bore a rough resemblance to the brandmark on his camels. When the Five-Year Plans started in 1970, the bin Jaluwis were similarly unhelpful towards any initiatives which seemed likely to enhance the power of the central government over them. Local real-estate disputes held up the acquisition of land needed by Riyadh ministries for projects like highways, and, instead of using their authority to cut decisively through bureaucratic tangles, the bin Jaluwis seemed to make the tangles worse.

But the root of the eastern disturbances of November and December 1979 was religious – and here, once again, the baleful influence of the Ayatollah Khomeini was extended across the Gulf. Heartened by the revolution of the Iranian mullahs, their Shia brethren in Arabia felt inspired to fight for their own rights, and they came back from their pilgrimages to Shia shrines like Kerbela with cassettes, posters and pamphlets urging them to rise against the 'tyranny' oppressing them.

The 'tyranny' was more social than government inspired. The Al Sa'ud had, from the days of Abdul Aziz, defended the right of the Shia to worship in their own mosques and had allowed them to travel on the ritualistic pilgrimages to Shia tombs and shrines that Wahhabis found so offensive. But ordinary Wahhabis practised petty, day-to-day discriminations against the Shia minority that made the Shia feel like second-class citizens. They clustered together in the palm groves of Qateef, as in a ghetto, and when Aramco started recruiting for the oilfields, they were delighted to discover an employer for whom their religion was not a problem.

Their grievances came to a head every year in Muharram, the first month of the Islamic year, when Shia the world over traditionally march in processions to commemorate the death of the Prophet's grandson Hussein, publicly re-enacting his fatal last battle in powerful rituals reminiscent of the most melodramatic passion plays and beating themselves bloody in rites of public flagellation.

The Al Sa'ud have always banned the public observance of the festival as being likely to provoke local Wahhabi sensitivities. But in November 1979, the Shia of Qateef, urged on by Khomeini, and doubtless imagining that events in Mecca had weakened government

489

vigilance, came out on to the streets, lashing themselves with their ropes.

They miscalculated badly. The National Guard set on them with ferocity and Prince Ahmad ibn Abdul Aziz, Deputy Minister of the Interior, flew to Dhahran to coordinate a stringent programme of arrests and interrogations. By the end of December 1979, Qateef was ringed by National Guard road blocks, Hofuf gaol was full, and the Eastern Province was quiet again. All that remained for Riyadh, as it surveyed to east and west of it, was to work out what had gone wrong and how the trouble could be avoided in the future.

Juhayman and his followers were easily dealt with. Early in January 1980, little more than a month after they had staggered out of the cellars of the Grand Mosque, their eyes sore with tear gas, sixty-three of the Mahdi's adherents were split into groups of half a dozen or so each and dispatched to Mecca, Riyadh, Medina, Dammam, Buraydah, Hail, Abha and Tabuk. The dozen or so women who had helped them inside the Grand Mosque were sentenced to two years in prison, the children involved were consigned to a welfare centre, nineteen men who had supplied arms were sent to gaol, and thirty-eight men whose involvement could not be proved were set free. But for the sixty-three who were proved to have played an active role in fighting inside the Grand Mosque, there was no mercy.

'Kill those whose names are appended to this statement', ordered King Khalid in a letter to the Interior Ministry, 'in order to please Allah, to defend the sanctity of the Holy Ka'aba and of His worshippers, and to vent the anger of the Muslims.'

On the morning of 9 January 1980 the sixty-three rebels were led out into the squares of the towns to which they had been sent and were publicly beheaded. The Ministry of Endowments which regulates mosques dispatched instructions to all imams to denounce the rebels in their sermons the following Friday, and, trying to explain to Westerners what had happened, government spokesmen talked in terms of the Jim Jones cult and the mass suicides in Guyana – a freakish tragedy that could have happened almost anywhere.

But this was less than half the story. If Juhayman and his followers were aberrant and deluded cranks, totally unjustified in their rebellion and unrepresentative of any valid strand of feeling in the Kingdom, why did Prince Fawwaz ibn Abdul Aziz, the Governor of Mecca

490

singled out by Juhayman for special criticism, resign his post within weeks? Why did King Khalid replace existing governors in several areas of the Kingdom with his most energetic and able young half-brothers? And why did Fahad ibn Abdul Aziz promise the introduction into the government process of a Consultative Assembly, a Majlis al Shura?

In theory the Majlis al Shura of Mecca worthies who endorsed Abdul Aziz in 1924 had never been dissolved. Its members met ceremonially from time to time, and, among his promised reforms of 1962, Faisal ibn Abdul Aziz had included the transformation of the council into a national consultative body. The promise was revived in 1970 after the failure of the 1969 coup, both Khalid and Fahad had proclaimed their intention to implement the Majlis soon after their partnership started in 1975, and the seizure of the Grand Mosque prompted Prince Fahad to repeat the promise.

'New government concepts are needed,' said the crown prince in February 1980, and he set up a committee under his brother Naif to investigate the form that these new concepts might take.

Just over a year later Prince Naif announced the results of his deliberations. He proposed a new consultative council – 'men of wisdom, knowledge and high morals to advise the government in policy making'. The assumption was that this council would be a nominated body.

But more radical were the plans for the regions. Power in the Kingdom should be decentralized, proposed Prince Naif. Regional administrations should be reorganized – and some members of these new local governments should be elected.

52 Black Gold

I've never seen the public so mad. You take away gasoline
and you destroy the family – that's the way they feel.

Speaker Thomas 'Tip' O'Neill, during the post-Iranian
gasoline shortage, May 1979

I F you fly into Dhahran by night over the oilfields of the Kingdom,
the gas flares greet you, glowing orange and red. Some are no
more than bonfires. They look cosy and welcoming in the blackness.
Others are pillars of fire which roar high and fierce, shedding their
flickering light far out across the sands.

By day the oilfields are less romantic. The wells themselves are no
more than stopcocks in the sand. Banks of pipes run in straight lines
across the desert scrub to the horizon. There is barbed wire, rough
unfinished concrete, sun-blistered paint. The resource round which
the whole world turns should surely wear a more dramatic face.

You can take your choice of oilmen too. There are still the wildcat-
ters, out on the rigs of the Empty Quarter, suntanned, rough-living,
with tattooed arms, guzzling iced tea from quart-sized pickle jars. Or
there are the Aramcons in their hushed and antiseptic headquarters,
where Sa'udis wear suits and start their meetings on time, but where
office life seems oddly sterile without the viziers, coffee servers and
punctuations of tea and coffee that clog business everywhere else in
the Kingdom.

Aramco is now 100 per cent owned by Sa'udi Arabia. The takeover
was completed in March 1980, but the world did not find out about it
till six months later when the Governor of Petromin* let the news slip
out in the course of an interview.

'In Venezuela', said one much-travelled oilman in December
1980, 'they had the name changed and the bunting out next day. Here
you still can't tell the difference.'

In oil, as in other matters, the Kingdom moves in mysterious ways.
To outsiders its oil policy is synonymous with Sheikh Ahmad Zaki
Yamani. The West has made of him a media superstar. But inside the

*Petromin: The General Petroleum and Mineral Organization, the marketing arm of the Sa'udi
Petroleum Ministry.

492

Kingdom he appears only rarely on television. More prominent in the
Sa'udi newspapers is another Yamani, Dr Muhammad Abdo (no
relation), the Minister of Information – and no one imagines for a
moment that the really important decisions about the Kingdom's oil
are taken alone, or even principally, by Sheikh Ahmad Zaki himself.

'The trouble with Yamani', says one of his radical opponents in
OPEC, rather cruelly, 'is that, when it comes to the crunch, he always
has to make a phone call.'

The phone call, of course, is to Crown Prince Fahad, for it is the Al
Sa'ud who control the Kingdom's oil policy, and they have the last
word on the two questions that matter: who is going to get it, and how
much it is going to cost.

Parcelling out the supply is comparatively easy. Over half
Aramco's production still goes to the partners in the consortium, who
now have a management contract to run the corporation they
created. Socal, Texaco, Exxon and Mobil distribute their off-takings
around the world as they wish within the limits laid down from time to
time by the Sa'udi government – Israel and South Africa are permanently on the black list, certain quotas have to go, at fixed prices, to
the developing countries.

The rest of Sa'udi production, including Sa'udi oil from Percy
Cox's neutral zone shared with Kuwait, is distributed to different
countries under the terms of government-to-government agreements
which are straightforward horse-trading – guaranteed oil supplies in
return for good will and support for the Sa'udi position on issues like
Palestine – and these deals, a couple of dozen at the latest count, are
essentially concluded to the directions of Crown Prince Fahad.

Immensely more complicated is the question of price, and with it
the conundrum of production levels. How many barrels a day should
the Kingdom export?

'A good deal fewer than at present,' is the opinion of the average
educated Sa'udi in 1981. The success of King Faisal's embargo of
1973 derived from the simple market axiom that if you halve the
supply of a commodity you stand a good chance of doubling its price –
and many inhabitants of the Kingdom are mystified that Crown
Prince Fahad and Sheikh Yamani appear to conduct their oil policy in
flagrant contradiction of this principle. In 1975 Sa'udi oil production
stood at 6.8 million barrels per day. By 1981 daily exports were
running at 10.3 million barrels, and throughout this period the Kingdom consistently restrained its price below the market level. There

493

were months during the great price rise of 1979 when Sa'udi oil was $10 to $12 per barrel cheaper than oil on the European spot market and, though private entrepreneurs, Sa'udi and non-Sa'udi, made themselves fortunes out of the gap, the national exchequer did not benefit.

The price rise of 1979 was a direct consequence of the Iranian revolution. Iranian oil exports dropped from over 5 million barrels per day in early December 1978 to zero by the beginning of 1979 – and this dramatic shortfall produced a second energy crisis to round off the 1970s with effects which may prove as momentous as those that followed the embargo of 1973.

Oil doubled in price from $13 for Sa'udi marker crude in January 1979 to $28 per barrel in April of the following year. The Western economies were already in recession and, as companies saw increasing proportions of their budgets consumed by fuel costs, 'conservation' ceased to be a matter of ecological faddiness. Cutting fuel bills became an easier way to preserve profit margins than seeking non-existent new business. It was cheaper than making redundancy payments to laid-off workers, and the second energy crisis of the 1970s intensified the adjustments with which the developed world sought to combat the rising price of oil – though Sa'udi oil invariably lagged behind the general level of OPEC rises.

Until 1973 world oil consumption had been rising steadily at the rate of 7–8 per cent per year. After 1973 it had only risen annually by 1.5 per cent on average, and after 1979 consumption actually dropped – by 4.7 per cent worldwide, by 7 per cent in the US and by 14.7 per cent in the UK. 'What this shows', says Ahmad Zaki Yamani, 'is that price is the only effective mechanism for inducing conservation.'

In the short term simple recession probably played a greater role in the reduction than conservation. But in the long term the trend was set – an intensified search by the consumers for alternatives to oil, and an increased emphasis on fuel economies of every sort. The late Shah was at his most sanctimonious when preaching – usually from his chalet in St Moritz – that he sought oil price rises less for his own benefit than to educate consumers in the virtues of conservation. He wished, he would say, to 'save the world from itself'. The energy crisis which followed his fall helped make his wish come true.

The lesson which the oil producers finally drew from the second energy crisis was the importance of production levels in a tight market. As in the winter of 1973, the oil 'shortage' of 1979 was less a

494

shortage in real terms than the *fear* of a shortage, aggravated by temporary dislocations of supply. Iranian exports resumed in March 1979. But the shutdown illustrated the effects that the disappearance of a few million barrels from the world market could have – and it made the history of oil prices since the 1950s seem more than ever a simple reflection of supply and demand.

There were even studies that suggested that the role of OPEC as demand increased had been to hold prices down below their natural market level. How else to explain the emergence of the Rotterdam spot market in the 1970s, where large quantities of OPEC oil were sold onwards and found buyers at higher than OPEC prices?

Sa'udi Arabia's own production – almost half OPEC's 22 million barrels per day – proved a crucial element in the equation. When Iranian oil supplies started to drop, the Kingdom boosted its output from 8.5 to 9.5 million barrels per day. When the Iraq–Iranian war broke out in the autumn of 1980 Sa'udi exports were increased still further to 10.5 million – and by the end of 1980 it was clear that these extra barrels of Sa'udi oil on the world market had done much to restrain price rises. By the spring of 1981 there was even a world glut – and Sheikh Yamani was taking the credit for this. 'We engineered the glut', he said, 'and we want to see it to stabilize the price of oil.'

This statement was not well received in the Kingdom, where oil policy is one political topic on which everyone feels entitled to hold and to express his own opinion. Nudge a Sa'udi towards criticism of the royal family and he will usually ignore the bait. Ask him what he thinks of the Al Sa'ud's oil policy and he will say straight out that they are squandering the Kingdom's greatest asset. Even the press officers at Aramco and the Ministry of Information decline to defend the official line.

'You had better ask Sheikh Yamani about that,' they say, and fall silent in a meaningful fashion.

Crown Prince Fahad and his Oil Minister often explain their policy of exporting extra oil to restrain price rises as a 'favour' which the Kingdom does to the world's consumers, rich and poor. Many Sa'udis do not see why they should be so kind. 'What "favours" did the West do for us when we were drinking smelly water and eating sandy dates?' asks Abdullah Tariki. 'And what "favours" do they do for us now?'

Sheikh Yamani's Sa'udi critics like to use against him the argument which he has deployed so frequently in the West. Oil is more valuable

495

left in the ground than sold for paper money whose value gets eroded by inflation; so the Kingdom should only pump as much oil as she needs to meet the cost of her own development – and that, say these Young Turks, is very little: reduced production would lead to higher prices; national revenues would remain much the same as ever or might even increase.

It appears at first glance a compelling argument, and it is one reason why Crown Prince Fahad has launched his successive tests of the American 'special relationship' – his bids to purchase first the F.15 fighter, then auxiliary F.15 equipment, and at the end of 1980 the request for AWACS planes. Equivalent technology can be purchased or developed elsewhere with Sa'udi money and without open controversy. But the crown prince evidently feels a need to prove to his critics inside the Kingdom and in the Arab world generally that he can get solid political returns for the 'favour' that his oil policy has done the West.

Why a 1600 per cent rise in the cost of oil over the decade should be regarded as a 'favour' is, of course, not obvious to the average Western motorist filling his fuel tank. The idea that Crown Prince Fahad and Sheikh Yamani should be regarded as 'friends' of ours, helping to check the rise of our fuel bills, is a proposition greeted by most people outside OPEC with disbelief – if not with a response that is a good deal less polite – for increasing oil production is a good way to increase oil revenues. If the Al Sa'ud did not use their production capacity to restrain the price of oil, the resulting disruption of the developed economies would have a catastrophic effect upon the massive investments that the Kingdom has made in the West since 1973. It would also do severe damage to her own development plans. Sa'udi Arabia's 'moderate' oil policy suits her long-term interests more closely than she will always admit.

'Why do I caddy for you?' asks a Sa'udi sheikh in an Oliphant cartoon, carrying a bag of golf clubs for a scrawny little character who looks faintly like Jimmy Carter. 'Because I have great faith in you. Also I have a lot of bets on you.'

When analysts try to explain the policies of the oil-producing countries they tend to talk in political terms: Algeria is 'radical' and 'anti-Western', always pushing for price increases; Sa'udi Arabia is 'conservative' and 'pro-Western', always trying to keep the price rises in check. A glance at the oil inventories of each country suggests less rhetorical motivations.

496

Algeria has ten years' oil left – fifteen at the most. She needs to get as much money as she can now for a dwindling resource, and she has little real concern with the long-term effect of price rises upon the consumer. What if it drives him to alternative forms of energy? In twenty years it will not make any difference.

But Sa'udi Arabia has at least fifty years' oil in the ground, and probably a great deal more than that. It is in her interest to keep the world economy dependent upon oil. Although the glut of the 1950s and 1960s kept the price of oil low and denied revenue to the producers in the short term, it also got the world economy well and truly 'hooked' on oil, and the producers have reaped the dividend ever since. Sa'udi Arabia wants to keep things that way – and the dramatic drop in the world consumption that marked the end of the 1970s has given her cause to think.

The new global emphasis on conservation, the search for alternative energy sources and the return to conventional fuels like coal – none of this threatens to make oil redundant. Even if some revolutionary new energy alternative were discovered tomorrow it would take twenty or thirty years, if not longer, to phase out existing oil-burning technology – and massive capital investment. The oil age started in 1859, and 132 years later its successor is not in sight. 'Obsolescence' for oil remains a pipe dream.

But if the latest trends continue, the world as a whole will be a great deal less dependent upon Arab oil in the year 2001 than it is today – and twenty years is not nearly long enough for Sa'udi Arabia to kick *her* dependence on continuing lavish inflows of petrodollars.

'Oil in the ground' is like gold in the bank. It seems today the ideal hedge against inflation, but it is a commodity like any other. It *could* lose its value if existing fuel consumption patterns were attacked head on by production cuts and by price rises of the sort that the Kingdom's Young Turks advocate. So when Sheikh Ahmad Zaki Yamani leaves the room at OPEC meetings to make his phone call, he is only acknowledging the reality that, for all its wealth and power, the Kingdom is a one-crop economy.

Britons and Americans, with established and varied economies and oil inventories that are due to be exhausted in the foreseeable future, tend to look at the infrastructure that has been created with such rapidity in Sa'udi Arabia since 1973 and assume that it has all been

497

devised against the day 'when the oil runs out'. Many inhabitants of the Kingdom undoubtedly think the same.

They are wrong. The Kingdom's industrial infrastructure is being created on the assumption that the oil, and its associated gas, flared off in great quantities until recently, will continue well into the twenty-first century – if not till the end of it. Sa'udi Arabia is an oil state and has little choice but to remain one.

Oil reserves are measured in a variety of ways. There are technical factors – field size, well production rates, reservoir pressure. Oilfields are not great lakes below the ground waiting to be sucked out. They are layers of porous rock like Arab-D, thick Crunchie Bars, stone sponges whose pores run with the black gold – and a country's oil reserves are not a simple matter of how many cubic feet there are down below. It is a question of how much oil it is economically feasible to extract at the price of the day.

Socal's prospectors struck oil at their very first attempt in Sa'udi Arabia, but it was not until they had deepened Well No. 7 that they discovered oil in quantities that were commercially exploitable in the late 1930s. The successful extraction of oil from the North Sea and Alaska in the 1970s is related intimately to the increased price of oil which has made the heavy production costs in those difficult areas an economic prospect; and, as petroleum prices continue to rise, so hitherto marginal oil shale deposits all over the world become commercially viable.

It is for these reasons that Sa'udi Arabia's oil reserves almost invariably grow with every passing year, for even exporting oil at the rate of 10.5 million barrels per day, Sa'udi Arabia usually discovers more than that in her reserves to make up the gap. After two decades in which she has sold over 30 billion barrels of her oil to the world, the Kingdom actually has three times more oil to her name today than she had twenty years ago. In 1960 her reserves stood at 53 billion barrels. By the beginning of 1980 they had risen to 165 billion. To the rich shall be given. . . .

Sa'udi Arabia today owns forty-seven oilfields, and at present she is taking oil from only fifteen of them. The other thirty-two wait, capped off, against the future. One Sa'udi field alone, the Ghawar Field, the largest onshore field in the world, contains more oil than all the United States oilfields put together. The Kingdom's Safaniya Field that stretches out into the Gulf is the world's largest offshore field.

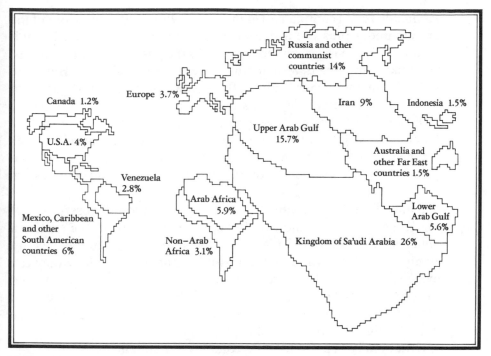

The world's oil. Countries have been sized according to their percentage share of the world's oil reserves at the beginning of 1980

The statistics are staggering. Whereas the average oil well, anywhere else on earth, produces less than 100 barrels per day, the average Sa'udi well produces 10,000. This is a function of the natural pressure of the oil and gas in the Sa'udi fields. The oil seldom needs to be pumped to the surface: it comes up of its own accord – and as a consequence Sa'udi oil is among the world's cheapest to produce. Less than 10,000 workers are needed to man the surface facilities* – and this means that 65 per cent of the Kingdom's gross national product, and 90 per cent of the government's revenue, are generated by less than 1 per cent of the national labour force. Since 1973 there have been massive investments, government and private, in non-oil sectors of the Sa'udi economy, but despite that, oil has actually increased in economic importance and now accounts for 98 per cent of the Kingdom's export earnings.

This will continue into the foreseeable future, and since 1975 the Kingdom has been gathering the 'associated gas' about whose flaring

* Aramco's work force currently stands at 35,000, but two-thirds are working on new projects not directly related to crude oil production, notably the new gas collection programmes.

499

Abdullah Tariki complained in the early 1950s. Oil coming out of the ground under pressure is like soda shooting from a syphon. There is liquid and there is gas, and until recently the gas was all flared. It was, as Tariki complained, a shameful waste of a natural asset. But there was not, in the 1950s and 1960s, any way to store the gas or to transport it economically to its market.

Today Sa'udi Arabia is the world's largest exporter of propane and butane. These gases are being gathered to provide the basic feedstock for the new industrial cities of Jubail and Yanbu, and associated gas is planned as the backbone of the Kingdom's long-term industrial development.

Some Western economists have cast doubt upon the usefulness of the Kingdom's great industrial complexes rising from the sands on either side of the peninsula. It will be some years before they are competitive in international terms; it is difficult to see how they can ever yield the astonishing revenues that the Kingdom has grown used to during the oil boom years; and, for all the talk of 'Sa'udi-ization' of the Kingdom's work force, they will create a long-term dependence upon foreign manpower and expertise.

Other analysts point to more complex dependencies: Yanbu's and Jubail's new industries will use the associated 'wet' gas which comes out of the ground with oil – so this would seem to make the prospect of another Sa'udi oil embargo less likely. The Kingdom will only be able to cut off her oil exports, it is argued, at the cost of halting the gas feedstock to her basic industries.

'That is not the case,' says Sheikh Ahmad Zaki Yamani. 'As well as the "wet" gas, the Kingdom also has some reserves of natural "dry" gas. We can pipe that in and burn it without pumping any oil – and the industries at Yanbu and Jubail are being designed to burn propane, butane, even naphtha. They can use almost any sort of gas. We intend to retain a high level of flexibility in our oil production.' The Oil Minister is clearly unwilling to surrender the embargo from his armoury.

Yamani is sitting in the study of his new, marble-clad home in Riyadh. He looks grey, dog-tired. It is eleven o'clock at night. He was in his office this morning before nine. He has been meeting delegations all day. On his desk are the red telexes he has still to read from his offices around the world, the latest data on prices, consumption rates, tanker patterns. Being one of the Kingdom's technocrats may be an exciting job. But it is also, clearly, very draining.

500

'I don't know what you'll get out of me that's any use tonight,' he says, flopping down into a sofa against which are propped large colour portraits of his children. He has not had time to direct where they should be hung.

He takes off his headrings, his red chequered headdress and the little white silk cap beneath. There is a small stiff spine-support on the sofa, and he picks it up to shove it round between his back and the cushions.

'One of the troubles with my job', he says, 'is that people never seem to listen very hard to what we say. We have to keep repeating it, and still they don't believe us.

'I remember in the summer of '73, before the embargo, King Faisal had just made his statement to American TV on the need for more even-handedness. He said that America should not count on Sa'udi oil if they went on supporting the country that is our enemy and is the root of the instability and radicalization of the Arab world.

'William Casey, who's head of the CIA now, was an under-secretary at the State Department then, and he made a comment on what the king had said.

' "This is not the policy of Sa'udi Arabia," he said.

'I remember I was in the king's office when that statement came over the radio. King Faisal was sitting there, turning the dial on the radio like he always did, and he turned to me and smiled.

' "Who else can state the policy of Sa'udi Arabia?" he asked. I can still remember him as he said it – that face, those eyes.'

Yamani was very much a protégé of Faisal's. He regarded the king almost as a father. He was devastated by Faisal's death, which he witnessed in the little office in the Riyassa Palace in March 1975. Soon after that Yamani himself was nearly assassinated. He was kidnapped in Vienna by the terrorist Carlos and held to ransom with other OPEC ministers in 1975. Carlos personally menaced Yamani with his pistol on the hijacked plane, taunting him as a stooge of the West, and promising him that he would be the first to die when the shooting started.

'I have a premonition', Yamani once said, 'that I will die violently. But that does not matter. I am just an instrument of my people and of God.'

Like many Sa'udis, Yamani studies the stars and believes in astrology. There is a lady astrologer in the outer suburbs of north London whom he frequently consults.

How has he kept going for so many years – assailed in the West as a 'blackmailer', scorned by the hawks of OPEC for his pricing moderation, and criticized by the Young Turks and almost everyone else inside the Kingdom for selling too much of the country's one and only diminishing asset?

'Some day I will write my book,' he says, smiling faintly. 'But there is still so much to do. I seem to spend half my time down here and half my time', gesturing towards the ceiling, 'up there travelling, travelling. . . .

'My great ambition', he said, 'is to help to bring about a new economic order for the world. Sa'udi Arabia seems rich today, but we are still just a developing country, and when I started work as a lawyer in the 1950s we knew all the poverty that the people of Africa and Asia still suffer from. We feel we are their brothers.'

The Oil Minister is in a contemplative mood. 'I never use the word weapon when I talk of oil,' he says. 'I prefer the word "instrument", political power, and I hope that we can use it for the good of all the world. We do not like the sudden jumps in oil prices every year or so. That is why we produce too much, to exercise some restraint. We have tried, and we shall go on trying to help the developed economies enjoy economic growth. It is in our interests as it is in yours. But we do ask two things in return.'

He gets up and moves out into the great marbled hall of his home. The floor is so shiny it looks liquid, and echoing off the walls are the splashing sounds of fountains filling a huge blue pool. He walks out into the soft warmth of a Riyadh night and looks up at the stars.

'Our corner of the world is torn apart', he says, 'by the tragedy of Palestine and Jerusalem. Until that is settled we can never know true peace and we expect the West to help us achieve it.'

He fingers his worry beads as he talks, speaking slowly, with the deliberation of someone who has grown used to his slightest word being seized on and turned into banner headlines.

'Then there are the poor of the world. Sometime soon there must be a real gesture towards them. We believe that unless we start solving the problems of the developing countries, they will fall into the hands of the communists. We do not want that and nor do you, but to avoid it we must start a real dialogue between rich and poor, north and south. We are all shareholders in the same world.'

There are robed figures all round the courtyard. A car is bringing more dispatch boxes and telexes. A relative has turned up from

Mecca and embraces the Minister, kissing him. They stand for a minute, holding hands. Then the Minister turns and goes back into the house. It is nearly midnight, and he has to take his wife out to dinner with some friends.

Riyadh's oldest rumour is that Yamani is leaving the Oil Ministry. He has done the job so long. He is known to have had his disagreements with Crown Prince Fahad. There are clearly times when the strains of eternal compromise grow too much for him, and after nearly twenty years the thrill of being one of the world's most powerful men must surely pall: everywhere he travels outside the Kingdom, he and his family are palisaded by bodyguards.

In any case, as he frequently points out, his power is not personal; it derives from the geology of Arabia and from the political ability of the Al Sa'ud to maintain their control over it. It is the new and wider challenges that Ahmad Zaki Yamani clearly finds compelling, the creation of the new world economic order, so easy to talk about, so hard to put into practice.

Like many Sa'udi technocrats, Yamani is a serious, rather heavy man to talk to: the ethics of development, the transfer of technology, the responsibilities of the Kingdom becoming one of the major economic components of the world. When he talks of Palestine and Jerusalem, his eyes flash with the fervour of any Arab – Crown Prince Fahad, Prince Sultan, Yasser Arafat. No one should underestimate the possibility that the Kingdom will again use the weapon which Yamani prefers to call an instrument to get its way over Jerusalem and the Palestinians.

But the drift of Sa'udi oil policy under Yamani has been to take account of the Kingdom's stake in the momentum and health of the planet earth, and Yamani's successor, when there is one, will have little choice but to follow the same path. Day by day and in many ways the Kingdom's own development and security are getting locked into those of the wider world – and the gas flares in the Sa'udi oilfields symbolize this. In a few years' time they will all be piped off for the gas-gathering programme with which the Kingdom hopes to create its own industrial base. Coming in to land at Dhahran airport will be a less vivid and romantic experience. But the world as a whole should be a more integrated place.

53 The Next Iran?

Schoolgirls at the Riyadh Model Institute have been suspended
for fighting with supporters of rival football teams. *Al Riyadh*
reported Sunday that the girls were sent home for a week after
arguments and blows with their fellow pupils. . . .
   'It is a sign of a wide, deep and dangerous trend,' the
newspaper said, 'that if not dealt with immediately could have
dangerous consequences. . . .
   'Nine months ago, during the last King's Cup final, a man
in Taif divorced his wife when she refused to stop cheering
on Ahli, which was in the process of beating his favoured
Ittihad 4–0. In front of the family television Abdul Rahman
al Otaybi, a father of four, pronounced her divorce. . . .
   'Mecca's Sunday Court ruled the divorce invalid, as
"the husband was not in full possession of his senses because
of anger." '
Arab News, 7 January 1980

King Khalid Monday received the *ulema*, religious sheikhs and
tribal leaders, as is customary every Monday.
Arab News, 8 January 1980

THE Shah's Iran, like Sa'udi Arabia, was an absolute monarchy
whose primary source of wealth was oil. Like Sa'udi Arabia it
was a developing country, desperately straining tradition to leap into
the twentieth century. Intense religious feelings were bound up in the
social and political life of both societies in ways that Westerners can
scarcely begin to understand. America and the West relied on the
Shah as a cornerstone of their influence in the Middle East, and he let
them down. Is Sa'udi Arabia going to let us down as well?
   The question has dimensions great and small. Sa'udi Arabia, like
the Shah's Iran, is a market place in which Western businessmen can
earn back some of the foreign exchange lost by the developed
economies since 1973. But investing in the Kingdom represents a
risk. Calculating their investments, businessmen must estimate their
future 'exposure' on a month to month basis, and they may find that
before they get their money back they will have to be 'exposed' in the
Kingdom to the tune of $40 to $50 million. Foreign companies lost
that much in Iran when the revolution came. They understandably
think twice before risking that much capital again – and the more
cosmic risks of Sa'udi Arabia's 10 million barrels of oil a day halving

504

or even ceasing as a result of some internal disorder scarcely bear thinking of.

When Juhayman and his zealots seized the Grand Mosque in the same year that the Shah had fallen, it seemed that the worst case scenario had come to pass: Sa'udi Arabia was degenerating into the same Islamic violence and chaos that had destroyed Iran. The American embassy put its nationals on standby to evacuate.

But the Mecca crisis of November and December 1979 did not bring down the house of Sa'ud. The Kingdom rode out its time of testing, and the way in which it did so indicated that the parallels between Iran and Sa'udi Arabia were not as close as they appeared at first sight to be.

Politics is not supposed to exist in the Kingdom. Reading the wall posters in Peking is child's play compared to charting the pressures and disagreements behind the Islamic consensus which the Al Sa'ud like to present to the world. Still, there *are* such things as Sa'udi dissidents. They organize meetings among Sa'udi students in American universities. They publish a magazine called *Sout al Taliah*, 'Voice of the Vanguard'. They complain at the very real restrictions upon freedom which exist inside the Kingdom. They denounce the undoubted corruption in Sa'udi government, the undeniable waste which many of the more prestigious development projects have incurred – and then they almost all go home again.

'We don't punish them,' says Dr Abdul Aziz al Zamil, Deputy Minister of Commerce and known to be a radical in his own days at university. 'Youth is youth.'

Sa'udi Arabia has its own mysterious mechanisms for dealing with dissent. It is pointless to pretend that it is a free and open society in the Western sense. All foreigners there, and particularly Western journalists, get a sense of oppressiveness, of caution among those to whom they talk, and when you win the trust of a radical Sa'udi then he will pour out his frustrations and complaints to you in a bitter torrent.

On the other hand, there exist few of the indicators by which political or personal oppression are conventionally measured, and which certainly existed in Iran. The Al Sa'ud do not murder their opponents or critics. They do not torture them. Amnesty International has no complaints to make in this respect. There are no political prisoners in Sa'udi Arabia: the ringleaders of the riots in Qateef were released early in 1981.

Censorship of foreign publications is severe. This book is banned from the Kingdom on the basis of eighty-two objections, from the reference on page 61 to the bedouin being 'fickle friends', to whole pages on Abdul Aziz's old age and the family quarrels in the reign of Sa'ud. *Time* and *Newsweek* magazines reach the Sa'udi shops with their whisky advertisements torn from them, and in photographs swim-suited, or even bare-shouldered, ladies have their modesty preserved by liberal application of black felt-tip. The local newspapers are rather like school magazines, complaining about lunches or library regulations, but not really questioning the basis of the system.

On the other hand, ordinary Sa'udis can, and do, voice the most direct and bitter criticisms to the king, princes and ministers to their faces – and here perhaps is a clue. You can say what you like in the Kingdom within the intimacy of the personal bond, face to face. That is acceptable; it is dignified; it is your right. But to make a public criticism is different: it implies disrespect; it invites shame.

Sa'udi Arabia is a society of deference. Sons defer to their fathers. Juniors defer to their elders. Children, no matter how old, do not smoke in front of their parents. Junior princes fall silent if a senior prince should enter the room. Everything has a sense of hierarchy built into it, a hierarchy which those lower down the ladder accept because they know that one day they will themselves be standing on the upper rungs – and also because, in a wider world which alarms them more than they care to admit, Sa'udis suspect that without their rigid, even tyrannical social discipline they might be lost.

In this sense of due order lies the reason why young Sa'udis go abroad, enjoy everything that American college life has to offer from pot to political demonstrations, and then come home, put on the *thobe* and headdress and go into the family business.

The family is the heart of the matter. When Sa'udis explain how their traditional Islamic way of life is going to safeguard them against all the hazards of affluence in the late twentieth century, a non-believing outsider can only nod his head and keep his counsel. But it is easy to see how the traditional extended Sa'udi family provides the Kingdom with a social cohesion that is rare in the world.

Many ordinary Sa'udis receive less money in their pocket at the end of every month than the average British civil servant. But each Sa'udi is conscious of belonging to a family, clan or tribe whose prestige and wealth he shares by virtue of his name. If his connections are tribal, he can, through the tribe's elders and chiefs, make direct contact with the king and tap the considerable government and personal subsidies which the Al Sa'ud devote to the bedouin. For every billionaire Juffali, al Rajhi or Alireza grown prosperous on government contracts, there are several dozen others who live in humble circumstances but who know that if an ageing mother falls ill, if a bright child needs educating abroad, or if a new Buick is needed for the Eed holidays, then the family will provide.

Put crudely, it is fairly easy for the government of the Kingdom to buy off its citizens through the mechanism of the extended family – and the Al Sa'ud do this consciously. When high-level American businessmen came to Riyadh in 1981 to discuss the opportunities offered them by the new Five-Year Plan, they were shown a list of established Sa'udi agents: Juffali, Alireza, Khashoggi, Binladen, Olayan – the big names were all there. 'These families have all done great things for the Kingdom,' said Prince Sultan ibn Abdul Aziz. 'But we would like you to look for new names.'

The prince is alleged at this point to have handed to his visitors a second list on which were set out the names of the new young tigers with whom the Americans might care to link – and who, it was suggested, would get preferential consideration from the government in the future. But who those new names are on the inside track, nobody is saying.

The Shah's Iran did not, by all accounts, operate in this fashion. The Shah's family took more than its fair share of business, just as the Al Sa'ud do in the Kingdom. But the connections between the ruling élite and the mass of the population were less diverse; they could not be otherwise. There are a multitude of ways in which the 4000-strong house of Sa'ud interrelates with the 4 or 5 million inhabitants of the Kingdom. The Shah's family and relatives numbered a few dozen at most, lost in a population of 35 million.

Iran's factory workers and wage earners made up a genuine proletariat. Pity the poor Marxist looking for such a phenomenon in Arabia. Shared out on a per capita basis the Shah's 5 million barrels of oil a day did not go very far – $5 per head per day at current prices. By the same rough calculation every Sa'udi man, woman and child gets $75. In 1981 they are still too busy enjoying that money to be significantly politicized, and when Prince Fahad's promised Majlis al Shura opens its doors, it is difficult to see what form its politics will take. Democracy in the Western sense requires a society where brother votes against brother, and where sons ignore their father's will – and this is not yet the Arabian way.

507

The Tale of Ajlan's Kidneys

When Abdullah bin Jaluwi pursued the Rasheed Governor Ajlan inside the Mismak on the morning that Abdul Aziz recaptured Riyadh, he did not just kill him. To revenge some special insults that Ajlan had done to his family, bin Jaluwi cut out the governor's kidneys and tossed them over a wall.

Now it happened that Abdul Aziz was entering the Mismak at that moment to see if his cousin bin Jaluwi needed help, and the kidneys fell in the sand at his feet.

'Bin Jaluwi is dead!' cried his slave in horror, looking down at the fat-covered organs.

'Nonsense,' replied Abdul Aziz. 'No prince of the house of Sa'ud could possibly have fatty kidneys like that.'

Eighty years on, this proud if grisly boast has an ironic ring. The well-padded forms who flop into the armchairs at the Riyadh camel races are scarcely the desert panthers who created the Kingdom. In all the 588 Sa'udis killed and injured recapturing the Grand Mosque in 1979, there was not a single prince of the house of Sa'ud – and, as is scarcely surprising in a clan 4000 strong, there are many lazy princes and many greedy ones.

It is very easy for a member of the Al Sa'ud to be a drone if his ambitions can stretch no further: he is given land for his palace, money to build it, his electricity and phone bills are paid, and he can live comfortably, if not extravagantly, upon his stipend and upon the stipends received by his children when they reach the age of three. If he bothers no one, no one will bother him – though the more dynamic members of the family stand no nonsense from idle relatives.

'I have several princes in my prison at this moment,' Prince Salman likes to tell visitors who inquire about princely privilege. Like Abdul Aziz outside the town of Layla seventy years ago, the Kingdom's modern rulers do not like to see family delinquents humiliated publicly; but if a prince breaks the law or creates a scandal, then the family discipline him firmly enough.

Lazy or criminal princes are not a major grievance in the Kingdom. Greedy ones are: a cut of this deal, advance knowledge of that – there are so many ways in which the Al Sa'ud can turn their position to their personal profit; and the system by which quotas of oil exports are channelled through marketing companies in which princes have an interest will cause increasing resentment in the future. If the house of Sa'ud does not restrain its appetites it will find itself in trouble if ever money gets tight – and 1981's glut in world oil supplies shows how money might get tighter sooner than anyone once imagined. When the boom stops the team spirit will get tested. The average Arabian is a pragmatic character, and if the day ever came when his government asked him to surrender any significant proportion of his income in taxes, the expense of maintaining 4000 pampered princes and princesses would be a luxury he could quite easily go without.

But there are certain strengths in numbers. The existence of a 4000-strong royal family in the final quarter of the twentieth century would appear to defy the laws of history, politics, logic and even gravity. But who would be the coup planner trying to dislodge them all? They fought to create the Kingdom and it does not seem likely that all 4000 of them will meekly get on jets for Egypt like the Shah.

In any case, few of their Arabian critics would advocate anything so drastic, for without the house of Sa'ud the Kingdom would probably disintegrate. Little but the family keeps east, west and central Arabia united in one state, for only the house of Sa'ud is capable of satisfying the conflicting aspirations of bedouin, merchants, technocrats, religious leaders, the military – and each group knows it.

King Khalid is no ordinary king. In a country created in the name and through the mechanism of religion, he is head of the religious community. In a society where the family matters so much, he is head of the largest family, and in controlling most of the peninsula divided for centuries between its component tribes, his is the tribe which has most recently and most successfully managed to establish its authority over all the others. Chief of chiefs, sheikh of sheikhs, his position is the nexus of a network of traditional relationships rooted in Arabian society as the Shah was never rooted in Iran.

As one watches King Khalid receiving his subjects before the noon prayer in the al Ma'ather Palace, it is difficult to see much parallel with the pretensions of the Peacock Throne. All human life is here, townsmen in their gold-trimmed robes, barefoot bedouin, the blind, the lame, an Egyptian in workman's overalls who looks as if, five minutes ago, he was digging in the hole in the street outside. They straggle across the *majlis*, eighty or ninety strong, and as they come up

509

to the king they shake him firmly by the hand. Some feel they may kiss his shoulder, others give him a hug or rise on tiptoe to kiss him on the nose – but when one falls on his knees to kiss the royal hand there is outrage.

'*Astaghfir Allah!*' shouts the king –'I ask pardon of God!' – and the offender is hauled to his feet in a commotion of tut-tuttings. He must learn to shake hands properly.

'*Towwil umrak*' is how most of the visitors address their king. 'May your life be long' is its literal translation – 'O long life', 'old fellow', 'old chap', it is difficult to find an English equivalent which conveys the same respect, but it is certainly not a majestic form of address. '*Towwil umrak*' is the term you might use to cajole one of Riyadh's elderly taxi drivers if he is trying to charge you too much, and some of the king's subjects call him simply '*Ya Khalid!*' –'O Khalid!' as they explain the crumpled pieces of paper that they are thrusting into his hand.

Most of these petitions are on lined pages torn out of exercise books, one has the appearance of a roll of wallpaper, all of them are scrawled in a fine tracery of Arabic, and as the king takes them he passes them to a chamberlain standing beside him, his hands a bulging in-tray of creased and crumpled missives.

'I have no money! I have no money!' an old man with an orange hennaed beard starts shouting.

'Why?' asks the king.

So the bedouin launches into a tale of hospital costs and ailing wives until his sovereign cuts him short.

'We have your paper and your name? I shall study it. Now go away.'

The usefulness of the Sa'udi *majlis* should not be overrated. It is a much needed antidote to the arrogance and inefficiency of the Kingdom's bureaucracy, but it is scarcely the 'Arabian democracy' which Information Ministry functionaries like to claim. Rather it demonstrates a closeness between ruler and ruled of remarkable casualness and trust – of affection even, and those qualities were never very evident in Iran.

King Khalid's al Ma'ather *majlis* is a large room, a grand room even, where some tasteful Western decorator has clearly been at work. There is one chandelier hanging in the centre, some palm fronds picked out in white on the blue pastel ceiling, and set round the walls four square, as if spun out against them by a centrifuge, are

510

identical blue velour conference-room chairs. The king picks one when he has finished shaking hands – for he has no throne here or anywhere else – and he settles down to read, taking a wad of papers from his chamberlain's crinkled bundle.

The room falls silent, save for the chink of the handleless little porcelain cups the coffee servers pass out, filling them swiftly with splashes of brown liquid as they walk around the chairs, and, as venturesome souls guess from the shape of the paper in the king's hand that their own moment has come, they steal across the carpet to whisper in his ear.

Suddenly there is another commotion. A man is shouting at King Khalid and King Khalid is shouting back. It appears the petitioner has brought the king a case that has already been through all the courts, and that he has lost every step up to and including the supreme court of appeal.

'Go away and stop wasting my time!' shouts the king. 'You're lucky I don't throw you in prison.' Taking grievances to the king after the legal system has finished with them is a gaolable offence, and King Khalid clearly means what he says.

It is a frequent misconception among Westerners that because an autocratic Islamic monarchy would be unacceptable to us, it must be unacceptable to everybody else in the world. But even the Al Sa'ud's native critics take perverse pride in the system which they criticize. It is, after all, their system. The Al Sa'ud have been heavy handed in the past; they appear no keener than any other autocrat to relinquish the power which they so much enjoy and from which they profit so handsomely; but they are a home-grown product. They were not, like the Shah, imposed upon the country with Western help; and though the editorials in *Sout al Taliah* ritually denounce the arrogance with which the Al Sa'ud have bestowed their own name upon Arabia, it is under this one family's firm hand that Arabia has developed from being the most barbarous and anarchic of Middle Eastern countries into a state whose comparative prosperity, stability and development are the all too obvious envy of its neighbours.

Islam is the vehicle through which Sa'udi chauvinism is most powerfully expressed – and it was Islam, of course, which brought down the Shah. But Islam in Iran and in Sa'udi Arabia play different roles. Arabia's Wahhabi imams taking tea with their king every Monday are not the Shia clergy of Iran with their separate hierarchy, privileges and traditions of independent power.

511

'That programme after the news last Thursday was disgraceful,' complains Sheikh Abdul Aziz bin Baz, who feels qualified to pass judgement on television programmes despite being blind. 'The women were clearly enticing.'

'I don't agree,' says King Khalid, and that is the end of that. The theology of the Sunni tradition which the Wahhabis follow teaches acceptance of the powers that be, save in exceptional circumstances. The Ikhwan revolt was led by tribal chieftains, not by imams. There were no imams fighting beside Juhayman in 1979.

This was partly because of Juhayman's great mistake, choosing to site his armed protest in Islam's Holy of Holies. 'If he had attacked my palace,' King Khalid said afterwards with remarkable candour to several foreign visitors, 'he might have met with more success.'

But while the seizure of the Grand Mosque clearly demonstrated the tension that exists between religious tradition and Western development in Sa'udi Arabia, it also demonstrated how little active support inflexible Ikhwan violence commands today. It is normal, if sixty-three men are led out into the streets of various towns around a country and have their heads cut off publicly one by one, for some-one, somewhere, to make a fuss. This did not prove the case when Juhayman and his companions were executed at the beginning of January 1980. Not even the radicals of *Sout al Taliah* mourned the Mahdi and his followers.

There are certain parallels between Iran's ayatollahs and the likes of Sheikh Abdul Aziz bin Baz. But considering themselves, and being treated by the government, as allies and not as adversaries, the Sa'udi *ulema* bring many strengths to the cohesion of the Kingdom. Their fierce independence of mind gives the legal system which they staff an impartiality and resistance to government pressure remarkable in the Arab world. And through feeling part of the government process, they are less of a practical obstacle to development than their pronouncements might sometimes lead one to expect.

The Committees for the Propagation of Virtue and the Prevention of Vice still patrol the streets of Riyadh with their canes as they did in the days when Amin Rihani was the only foreigner in town; but the times are changing. There is a singer on Sa'udi Television who remembers when he used to have to sing in secret. Veteran expatriates remember how, twenty years ago, it was not permissible to smoke in the street, and how cigarettes were purchased under the counter, in plain brown envelopes. In April 1981 a committee of

Islamic legal scholars ruled that a Sa'udi woman must be allowed to unveil in front of her prospective bridegroom: 'Any man forbidding his daughter or sister to meet her fiancé face to face will be judged as sinning,' the committee declared.

These seem small steps by Western standards, and they are easy to deride. The Shah used to. He had nothing but scorn for the caution and conservatism of King Faisal. But when we mock or deplore the ancient ways of Sa'udi Arabia we should remember that our late twentieth-century way of life has owed not a little to the stability and discipline that fifteenth-century values have imposed upon one very undisciplined corner of the world. We should also reflect on what could happen if that discipline were removed too rapidly.

54 As God Wills

Members of the Sa'udi royal family led prayers through the Kingdom Thursday, asking for God's help in bringing rain. . . .

In Mecca, Governor Prince Majid ibn Abdul Aziz performed the prayers with thousands of people at the Haram Mosque. In his rain-seeking prayers, the Imam Sheikh Abdullah al Khalifi also prayed to God to enhance the prestige of Islam and Muslims, and to defeat the enemies of Muslims.

In Buraydah, Qaseem Governor Prince Abdulilah prayed at al Eed al Kabeer Mosque. The Imam, Sheikh Saleh ibn Ahmad al Khreissi, the president of Qaseem's Shariah courts, prayed to God to shower His blessings on Muslims.

Simultaneously, heavy rains fell on Jeddah, Mecca and their outskirts . . .

Arab News, 8 November 1980

We live together in the same world. But you will have to meet us, the Arabs, half way. Perhaps if you do, we will all discover interesting things about one another and it will be a better world.

Ahmad Zaki Yamani, 29 November 1973

PRINCE Turki al Faisal, the youngest son of King Faisal ibn Abdul Aziz, is today the head of Sa'udi Foreign Intelligence. With an undisciplined, wispy beard and thick round glasses, he has an owlish look and he has a little trick that he likes to play on Western visitors.

'Arabia is rich today', he says, 'as it has never been before, and many simple people in this country believe that that is for one reason and for one reason only – because we have been good Muslims.'

He sits there urbane, intelligent, Westernized, a graduate of one American university and of one British one, and you have to smile with him at the notion that all the wealth and complexity of the Kingdom should be explained in terms of such primitive religious faith. But then you see that the prince is not smiling.

'Many simple people believe this', he says, 'and I believe it also. Everything comes from God, and the oil is no exception.'

Arabians have always been a proud people, arrogant even, and the extraordinary success story of the Kingdom, from Abdul Aziz's poverty-stricken exile to the present-day wealth of Sa'udi Arabia, has made them more so. Only thirty-five years ago most Sa'udis lived a life little different from that lived by ancient Britons at the time of

514

Boadicea, an existence of unspeakable physical hardship and material emptiness. There was no industry in Arabia, no agriculture beyond wandering camels and groves of date palms; the only permanent buildings were built from mud in Riyadh and from coral blocks hacked from the reef in Jeddah, and if the transformation that has occurred in the daily life of the Kingdom's inhabitants since 1945 should strike them as miraculous, then that is hardly surprising.

Since the end of the Second World War Arabia has crossed 2000 years of history to enjoy wealth, and potential wealth, the like of which the world has never known. The boy born in a goat-hair tent with a few shillingsworth of bowls and pots and bedding is now a cabinet minister with a Ph.D., enjoying the use of a private jet to take him anywhere in the world within hours. Pride at such achievement is understandable – and that pride is not diminished one jot by the fact that everything, every single material thing in the new life that the average Sa'udi enjoys so much, comes from the West.

It was Westerners who discovered and developed the Kingdom's fabulous treasure chest. Western economic theories and techniques are the basis of the Kingdom's ambitious development plans. Without the ongoing development of the Western economies there would be little market for the commodity on which the Kingdom's good life is based – and almost every detail of that good life depends upon imported foreign labour for its smooth running: in a Sa'udi hotel the receptionist is Moroccan, the waiters Filipinos, the room attendants Pakistanis, the cleaners Thais, the management Lebanese, European or American – and the Sa'udi guests feel superior to all of them. Does a duke feel inferior to his tailor because he cannot make a pair of trousers? Sa'udis *know* that God gave them all the wealth and power that they currently enjoy, and they feel neither lucky, nor surprised, nor grateful to anyone except themselves – and God.

The Westerner gets some glimpse into the origins of this extraordinary faith at pilgrimage time. Two million Muslims converge on the Kingdom for their once-in-a-lifetime experience, and for a week Sa'udi Arabia becomes, even more than usually, the centre of the entire Islamic world. Planes land every two minutes at Jeddah airport looking very heavy, and take off again, very light, to collect another cargo of the faithful. The streets go dead, the post office closes, shops and offices shut down, and television gives itself up to live coverage of the swirling, white-towelled multitudes as they circle the Ka'aba, stand on Arafat and stone the devils at Mina.

515

One sees heads of state among them, King Hussein, the Gulf sheikhs, the king and princes of the Al Sa'ud, white-towelled and bareheaded like any other pilgrim. Cameras peer down from helicopters at the white flood rippling round the long white buses from which the pilgrims fly their national flags. It is a pageant, a holiday, a celebration, a Silver Jubilee held every year. It is like Christmas – except that the newsreader ends the English bulletin on the Eed al Adha by saying, 'Many happy returns of the day.' Obviously the Sa'udis have no clearer idea of what it can all be compared to than we do.

For the pilgrims the *hajj* is an opportunity to take a new name. It washes them of all their sins. One prayer said in the Grand Mosque at pilgrimage time is worth 100,000 said elsewhere. For the Sa'udis the festival is a reminder that their forefathers were the very first Muslims, that Muhammad was one of them, and that God, having revealed some of His truth through the Jewish prophets, and more of it through Jesus, chose an Arabian as the vehicle for His ultimate revelation.

'Why don't you become a Muslim?' ask Sa'udi taxi drivers when they discover that you can speak a little Arabic. They cannot understand how anyone capable of reading the language in which God's truth is enshrined cannot accept that truth and embrace it totally.

'You are a good man, you are serious,' add your Sa'udi friends when they ask the same question. How can any intelligent and serious-minded man who has had the opportunity to see Islam in its highest manifestation fail to be convinced?

Islam is one way the Sa'udis can tell an envious world that there is more to them than just oil and money. Internally Islam acts as the Kingdom's national adhesive. The Al Sa'ud have always maintained that the Kingdom's constitution is the Koran, and the 'new government system' promised by Prince Fahad after Juhayman's revolt is described simply as a codification of that.

'Sa'udi Arabia is not a country,' says Muhammad, the eldest son of King Faisal by Iffat. 'It is an idea. It is a commitment to a pure and uncluttered vision of God.'

'In Islam', explains Professor Bernard Lewis, 'religion is not, as it is in Christendom, one sector or segment of life regulating some matters while others are excluded; it is concerned with the whole of life – not a limited but a total jurisdiction . . . a community, a loyalty, a way of life.'

As a personal religious faith Islam is both very arduous and very

516

easy to pursue. It makes severe demands on the believer – stopping everything to pray five times a day, fasting for a month during Ramadhan: no non-Muslim should underrate the physical and psychological effort of foregoing any refreshment during the hours of daylight, no sip of water, no cup of coffee, not even a puff on a cigarette. But when the ordeal is completed, the sense of achievement is tremendous. The poor Muslim has become a good Muslim, and he knows it.

Islam makes demands upon its adherents that are difficult, but they are not impossible. Muslims are not required to run Christianity's never-ending spiritual obstacle course. It is a faith of certainties, not doubt. There are good Muslims and bad Muslims, but there are no agnostic Muslims.

'Muslims do not have questions,' Sa'udis like to say, 'only answers.'

So Sa'udis do not find hypocrisy, the sin that the whole world lays at their door, a particularly troubling matter. They hire enticing young foreign girls as hostesses for their national airline; many of them keep whisky in their homes; when they are out of the Kingdom they indulge their appetites without inhibition, and they do not see why the West gets so upset about it.

'Do not assume that the faith is weak just because the flesh is,' says one prince. 'Hypocrisy is the homage that vice pays to virtue.'

Which is worse, ask Sa'udis, a bit of secret drinking behind closed doors, or widespread alcoholism? What would their fellow Muslims say if they came to Arabia on their *hajj* and discovered bars and cabarets in the Holy Land? Sa'udis read in Western papers of mugging, wife- and baby-battering, drug addicts, juvenile delinquents, wife-swapping, rape, housebreaking, gang warfare – and they consider that a little hypocrisy is a small price to pay for the moral regulations which have so far kept such evils out of their society.

Westerners assume that life in the Kingdom will, one day, be very much like life everywhere else. No Sa'udi will accept that assumption. We look at the opposing tendencies of Islamic tradition and Western development in Arabia and assume that sooner or later one will win out over the other. Sa'udi Arabia will become either Westernized and rich, or Islamic and poor, bedevilled by the sterile war on reality with which the ayatollahs have devastated Iran.

The inhabitants of the Kingdom do not see why they should not have the best of both worlds. When Europe lived in the Dark Ages, the Arabs enjoyed a way of life that was more affluent, cultured and sophisticated than any other in the Western world. They have no doubt that they are heading in that direction again, towards Islamic wealth and development which, in its spiritual essence, owes nothing to the infidel. This book has been the story of great deeds performed in the name of religion, and the Sa'udis are confident that there are more to come.

So, by Western standards, life in the Kingdom is a life of contradictions – and one can easily describe it in contradictions alone.

Capital punishment is practised publicly, but corporal punishment is banned in schools, and the idea of teachers caning pupils seems as barbaric to Sa'udis as judicial amputations seem to us.

The veil symbolizes to Westerners the subjection of Sa'udi women; but there are tens of thousands of women in the Kingdom who, thanks to the shares of inheritance specified by the Shariah, are millionaires in their own right; and there are just a few whose billions may even rival the fabled personal fortunes of Elizabeth II and of Queen Juliana of the Netherlands.

Sa'udi Arabia has the technological chutzpah to be planning the towing of kilometre-long icebergs, covered with insulating blankets, from the South Pole to the Red Sea as a source of fresh water. But video-taped imports of the *Muppet Show* are confiscated on the grounds that its heroine is a pig.

In February 1980 an international survey declared Jeddah the world's most expensive city: its cost of living index was 141, far outstripping Tokyo (106), Geneva (103), New York (84) and London (81). In the same month the Jeddah Municipality announced it had rounded up 4350 lost sheep and goats left to stray in the streets by the inhabitants. Life in the Kingdom is made up of so many opposing polarities, that the word the Westerner always takes down from the shelf is 'schizophrenia'.

As you come in by night over Riyadh or Jeddah, it could almost be Los Angeles. The lights of bungalows and highways stretch out an extraordinary distance into the soft darkness of the desert. What strikes you when you land is not the splendour but the disorder of it all – unmade roads, open rubbish dumps, painfully smashed-up cars, the unfleshed skeletons of prestressed concrete buildings, everything has a half-finished look. To live in the Kingdom is to pick your way round a never-ending building site – and there seems to be as much old rubbish about as there is new construction, for the influence of the West clearly has not eroded the belief of Sa'udi Arabia's garbage men

518

that Allah will provide: discarded tyres, scraps of skin and horn and bone, the Arabian scatters his debris round his new model cities as carelessly as he litters the endless wastes of the desert.

Wilfred Thesiger, the eulogist of simple desert existence in the 1940s, cannot bear to visit Sa'udi Arabia any more. The Arabs, he has written, 'are a race who produce their best only under conditions of extreme hardship', and he bemoans the tawdriness that soft living has produced.

Sa'udis do not see why they should be denied the right to pad their lives with the comfortable and convenient trivialities of the twentieth century like everybody else, and, while agreeing that the Western spirit has been eroded by materialism, they are not yet willing to accept that their ethic will go the same way.

'We can see the difference between money and riches,' says Prince Turki al Faisal. 'Sa'udi Arabia has a lot of money, but money does not bring true wealth. Oil does not enrich the essence of the person. We do not put faith in money, but in the conviction that the man who puts his faith in religion is a better man.'

What can one say? The inquiring Western interviewer points out to the prince that if religion survives in the Kingdom to the end of the twentieth century it will be the first time in human history that supernatural faith has resisted the advent of wealth on a universal scale. Will not Sa'udi Arabia go the way of every other society where the masses have become affluent, getting off their knees to sit in front of the television and polishing the car on God's day of rest?

'I don't think so,' says the prince calmly. 'If anything, I think that our children will be stricter Muslims than we are.'

There are two words of Arabic which every expatriate who comes to the Kingdom finds he cannot be without. One is '*alhamdulillah*', 'Praise be to God.'

'How are you?' you ask a Sa'udi.

'*Alhamdulillah*,' he replies.

The other word is '*insh'allah*'. It means 'As God wills', and it is the answer to almost every question you can ask about the future. Will it rain tomorrow? Will we see the king? Will the contract get signed? Will the payment cheque arrive? The answer is always the same.

It is twilight, and King Khalid is saying the sunset prayer. On either side of him are his people, come to pray with him as they pray every weekday evening in the homes of the king and in countless other palaces of the Al Sa'ud.

After the prayer King Khalid sits in his *majlis*, reading to himself from his little green leather Koran. It is a quieter occasion than the morning *majlis*: merchants, an ex-minister, several army officers, the king's brother Abdullah, head of the National Guard. Dr Rashad Pharaon is there, white-goateed, eyes twinkling, and as the little glass cups of tea come round on silver trays, Dr Pharaon injects sweetener into his from a dispenser like a fountain pen.

The king is talking of the old days. 'There are none left now, none of the men who rode with Abdul Aziz.' He is talking slowly, dreamily. 'They are all dead. . . . Most of the people who remember my father are dead now.'

The room goes quiet.

'It wasn't the adventure that mattered,' says Prince Abdullah, hesitating a little in his speech, but pushing forward his proudly manicured black beard. 'It was the religious inspiration. That was what mattered. People always talk about the adventure. What they should remember is the faith.'

We move in to dinner, fifty of us, to sit at a U of tables around the dining room. The plates are white, with a gold palm tree and crossed swords on each. To drink we are offered curdled camel milk from silver jugs – or mineral water from plastic bottles.

There is soup to start with, then macaroni, then *kapsa*, thick chunks of lamb, bones and ribs in dark brown rice, cooked Arabian style. Then there is lamb, roast and rolled European style, greyish and institutional with gravy, peas and carrots, followed by salad, fried doughnut cakes, and piles of fruit – apples, oranges and bananas on raised silver plates. The king eats just salad.

As people finish they get up and leave the room without ceremony, so that by the end of the meal the king is sitting at the head table talking with his brother Abdullah, with almost no one else in the room. As they get up themselves, coffee servers rush forward to serve them on the run, and the brothers walk out together to pray the evening prayer, two hours after sunset.

Will the ruler of Arabia still be regulating his life around the prayer calls from the minarets in the year 2001? Will that ruler be a member of the house of Sa'ud? Will there still be a state which embraces both the Holy Cities of Islam and the oilfields of the Gulf coast? Will those oilfields still be sustaining the economies of the West, or will the

Russians have moved southwards through Iran, in some way to secure those riches for themselves? Will Israel remain a grievance which makes it impossible for Arabs like the Sa'udis to acknowledge their Western sympathies? Or will some settlement over Jerusalem and the Palestinians have made the tension that today bedevils the Middle East just a bad dream in the past?

It is a peculiarly Western way of looking at the world to assume that every problem must have a solution. There are some uncertainties one must learn to live with, and if you ask a young Sa'udi Arabian cosmic questions about his own future and the future of his Kingdom, he will try to answer for a time, and then give up. After a moment of silence he may possibly suggest that you should read the Koran, for it is in the Koran that he finds his own strength and his own faith in the future. But reflecting, perhaps, that no infidel soul can reasonably be expected to grasp the profundity of the simplest faith of all, he may tell you this modern fable derived from the ever-changing roadworks and traffic diversions that characterize Riyadh, Jeddah and the other developing cities of the Kingdom:

The Tale of the Taxi

A man hailed a taxi one day, and as it drew to a halt the driver asked him where he wanted to go.

'Never you mind,' said the man as he got inside.

'Well, which route shall I follow?' asked the driver.

'Never you mind,' said the man. 'Just drive on and we shall see.'

So the taxi set off. When the man wanted to turn right, he told the driver. When he wanted to turn left, he told the driver. And then he told the driver to stop, paid the fare and got out.

He hadn't said where he was going, he hadn't said how he was going to get there, and nobody but he knew whether that was really the destination he had wanted in the first place. But he had arrived there just the same.

It is six o'clock on a Friday evening, the end of the Kingdom's day of worship and rest. The roads are packed with cars. The traffic jams heading to town are made up principally of foreigners, the expatriate work force returning to their quarters, red-faced and sticky after their

521

afternoon in the sun. The cars heading out of town contain the Sa'udis.

The men are driving, of course. The women sit in the back, so many black sacks, it would seem, in their veils. But they have their children bouncing on their knees, olive-skinned babies in bright dungarees and tee-shirts, and the women are leaning forward to talk and gesture with their menfolk in the front, for this is a family outing. There are grandfathers in the cars, grandmothers, uncles, aunts, who can tell? Each vehicle sways heavy and low on its suspension.

A mile or so out of town the traffic starts to thin. The road stretches straight ahead, a tarmac strip unrolled across the contours of the landscape. The houses get rarer – odd skeletons of breezeblock and prestressed concrete awaiting their marble cladding – and then there is just dusty red emptiness.

They go without warning, Mercedes, Cadillacs, Toyotas, suddenly veering sideways across the crusted lip of the tarmac, to bump across the laterite for several hundred yards, perhaps as much as half a mile, until each has found its own little patch of nothing.

A woven carpet is unrolled, some cushions are thrown down, little glass cups are set out on a silver tray, and from the vacuum flask is poured the tea – amber, clear and sweet. The men kick away their sandals and lift off their headdresses. If no other cars are near, the women remove their veils. The children grab 7-up from the cold box, or Pepsi.*

If you come in to land at Jeddah, Riyadh or Dhahran airports any Friday around sunset you will see the desert around the towns dotted with the little groups, many of them lit, as darkness falls, by the blue glow of a portable television on the corner of the rug.

The women lean back against the hubcaps of the cars, digging sweets and lollies for the children from their bags. The men lean with their elbows on the cushions, gossiping gently, listening to the soccer results, or just gazing across the desert.

This is where they have come from. The desert is the source of everything they hold dear – their religion, their code of honour, their ancestry, their black gold – and regularly the inhabitants of the Kingdom flee the modern pyramids their riches are creating to return to the bleak void that they find so consoling.

---

* Pepsi, not Coke. Coca-Cola's investments in Israel have resulted in the company's goods being banned in the Kingdom – along with Ford cars, Xerox machines, Alka Seltzer and several hundred other products on the Arab boycott list.

They talk a little, play cards, listen to cassettes, drink more tea, tease the children, but chiefly they just sit on their rugs, staring out across the sands and not saying very much at all.

Do they catch wind of some secrets, these Arabs, as the desert breeze blows? Do they find answers to their problems? What does this communion with emptiness tell the men and women of the Kingdom about themselves and about the world in which they live?

One of the older men shifts and looks at his watch. He points to the sun that is now sinking to touch the rim of the horizon. He rises to his feet, and the other men rise with him. They line up at the edge of the rug, facing in the same direction across the seared wastes, and then they all kneel together, a row of white bundles on the darkening sands.

'*Allahu akbar*,' mutters the old man, and the other men join in with him, intoning the phrase in a fashion that lends it meaning beyond its words.

'God is most great.'

Appendix A
The Ruling Line of the House of Sa'ud

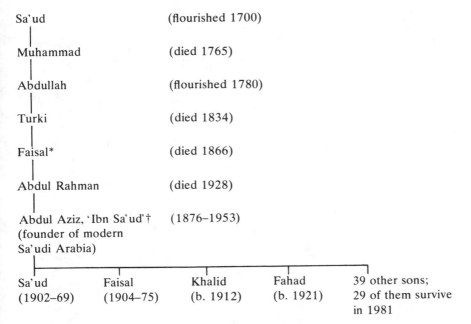

Sa'ud   (flourished 1700)

Muhammad   (died 1765)

Abdullah   (flourished 1780)

Turki   (died 1834)

Faisal*   (died 1866)

Abdul Rahman   (died 1928)

Abdul Aziz, 'Ibn Sa'ud'†   (1876–1953)
(founder of modern
Sa'udi Arabia)

| Sa'ud | Faisal | Khalid | Fahad | 39 other sons; |
| (1902–69) | (1904–75) | (b. 1912) | (b. 1921) | 29 of them survive in 1981 |

This family tree greatly simplifies the line of descent of the Al Sa'ud to the present day.

*For more details on the sons of Faisal ibn Turki see Appendix D.
†For more details on the sons of Abdul Aziz see Appendix B.

Appendix B
The Sons of Abdul Aziz

First name	Dates	Full brothers	Career
1 Turki	1900–19	2	Died in Riyadh Spanish 'Flu' epidemic
2 Sa'ud	1902–69	1	Born January 1902; proclaimed crown prince September 1932; Viceroy of Nejd 1932–53; proclaimed king 9 November 1953; deposed 3 November 1964; died 23 February 1969
3 Khalid	d. 1903		Died in infancy
4 Faisal	1904–75		Foreign Minister from 1919; Viceroy of Hijaz 1926–53; proclaimed crown prince 9 November 1953; proclaimed king 3 November 1964; assassinated 25 March 1975
5 Fahad	d. 1919		Born soon after Faisal
6 Muhammad	1910–	7	Commander of army which took the surrender of Medina 1925; renounced succession in 1965
7 Khalid	1912–	6	Proclaimed crown prince 1965; proclaimed king 25 March 1975
8 Sa'ad	1914–19	11, 18, 21, 25, 28, 31, 37	Son of Hassa bint Ahmad Sudairi by her first marriage to Abdul Aziz
9 Nasir	1920–		Governor of Riyadh until 1947; stood down from succession in March 1975

First name	Dates	Full brothers	Career
10 Sa'ad	1920–	15, 16	Son of Jauhara bint Sa'ad al Sudairi, widow of Abdul Aziz's brother Sa'ad; stood down from succession in March 1975
11 Fahad	1921–	8, 18, 21, 25, 28, 31, 37	First son of Hassa Sudairi after her remarriage to Abdul Aziz; Minister of Education, 1953–60; Interior Minister 1962–75; Second Deputy Premier 1968–75; proclaimed crown prince 25 March 1975
12 Mansour	1922–51	17, 19	Kingdom's first Minister of Defence, from 1944 till death
13 Abdullah	1923–		Commander of National Guard 1963 to present day; Second Deputy Premier March 1975
14 Bandar	1923–	29	Noted for especially strict religious observance; business interests
15 Musa'id	1923–	10, 16	Father of Khalid ibn Musa'id, who was shot during riots protesting against television in 1965; father of Faisal ibn Musa'id, the assassin of King Faisal, who was executed in June 1975
16 Abdul Mohsin	1925–	10, 15	Last child of Jauhara Sudairi, widow of Abdul Aziz's brother Sa'ad; Minister of the Interior 1961–2; supported the protests of Talal in 1962; today Governor of Medina; his son Sa'ud bin Abdul Mohsin is Deputy Governor of Mecca
17 Misha'al	1925–	12, 19	Minister of Defence 1951–5; one time Governor of Mecca

527

First name	Dates	Full brothers	Career
18 Sultan	1927–	8, 11, 21, 25, 28, 31, 37	Minister of Communications, 1954–60; Minister Defence and Aviation since 1962
19 Miteib	1928–	12, 17	Minister of Housing and Public Works since 1975; also in charge of Ministry of Municipalities since 1978
20 Talal	1930–1		Died in infancy
21 Abdul Rahman	1931–	8, 11, 18, 25, 28, 31, 37	Active in business
22 Badr	d. 1931		Died in infancy
23 Talal	1931–	27	Minister of Communications, 1953–4; Minister of Finance 1960–1; led protests of the 'Free Princes' in 1962; went into exile in Egypt 1962; returned home 1964; Special Envoy, UNESCO, since 1979
24 Mishari	1932–		Shot Cyril Ousman, British Consul in Jeddah, November 1951
25 Turki	1933–	8, 11, 18, 21, 28, 31, 37	Vice-Minister of Defence until 1978
26 Badr	1933–	34, 35	Minister of Communications 1961–2; joined Talal in exile 1962; Deputy Commander of the National Guard
27 Nawwaf	1933–	23	Special adviser on Gulf affairs to King Faisal
28 Naif	1934–	8, 11, 18, 21, 25, 31, 37	Former Governor of Riyadh; Interior Minister since 1975

First name	Dates	Full brothers	Career
29 Fawwaz	1934–	14	Joined Talal in exile in 1962; resigned as Governor of Mecca in December 1979
30 Majid	1934–6		Died in childhood
31 Salman	1936–	8, 11, 18, 21, 25, 28, 37	Governor of Riyadh since 1962
32 Majid	1936–	36	Minister of Municipalities 1975–8; Governor of Mecca 1980
33 Thamir	1937–58	38, 40	Died in the reign of King Sa'ud
34 Abdulillah	1938–	26, 35	Governor of Qaseem (Anayzah and Buraydāh) 1980
35 Abdul Majeed	1940–	26, 34	Governor of Tabuk
36 Sattam	1940–	32	Deputy Governor of Riyadh
37 Ahmad	1940–	8, 11, 18, 21, 25, 28, 31	Deputy Governor of Mecca 1975–8; Vice-Minister of Interior 1978
38 Mamduh	1941–	33, 40	Business interests
39 Hidhlul	1941–		Business interests
40 Mashhur	1942–	33, 38	Business interests
41 Abdul Salaam	1942–4		Died in childhood
42 Muqrin	1943–		Former Sa'udi Air Force pilot; Governor of Hail 1980
43 Hamoud	1947–		Business interests

Appendix C
Prominent Princes

The sons of Abdul Aziz dominate the Al Sa'ud, but not to the exclusion of other groups within the family. This is a partial guide to some prominent princes, but it is far from complete and is based upon the erratic researches of the author.

The sons of King Sa'ud

Abdul Aziz, Abdulillah, Abdul Kareem, Abdullah, Abdul Majeed, Abdul Malik, Abdul Mohsin, Abdul Rahman, Ahmad, Badr, Bandar, Fahad, Faisal, Fawwaz, Ghalib, Hadhul, Hamoud, Hassan, Hissam al Din, Is'al Din, Jaluwi, Khalid, Ma'atsam, Majid, Mamduh, Mansour, Mashhur, Mis'ab, Misha'al, Mishari, Mu'atiz, Mugrin, Muhammad, Musa'id, Nahar, Naif, Nasr, Nawwaf, Sa'ad, Saif al Daula, Saif al Din, Saif al Nasir, Saif al Salaam, Salman, Sultan, Sattam, Shuqran, Talal, Thamir, Turki, Waleed, Yazeed, Yussuf

A number of these sons held ministerial responsibilities during their father's reign, 1953–64. They returned to the Kingdom after their father's death in 1969, and some are active today in business.

The sons of King Faisal

Abdullah	b. 1921	Poet; Minister of Interior 1953–60
Muhammad	b. 1937	President, Islamic Bank
Khalid	b. 1941	Poet; Governor of Asir
Sa'ud	b. 1941	Foreign Minister 1975
Abdul Rahman	b. 1942	Armed Forces
Sa'ad	b. 1942	Formerly Deputy Governor, Petromin
Bandar	b. 1943	Formerly Royal Sa'udi Air Force, now in the Ministry of Defence, Riyadh
Turki	b. 1945	Director of Foreign Intelligence

The sons of King Khalid

Abdullah, Bandar and Faisal. Bandar bin Khalid is active in business.

The sons of Fahad ibn Abdul Aziz

Faisal	b. 1945	President of Youth Welfare
Khalid	b. 1947	

530

Sa'ud	b. 1950	Active in business: Chairman, Tihama Advertising
Sultan	b. 1951	Armed Forces
Muhammad		Active in business: Chairman, Al Bilad
Abdul Rahman		
Abdul Aziz		

The sons of Abdullah ibn Abdul Aziz

Khalid		Former Director of Administration, National Guard
Miteib	b. 1949	National Guard
Abdul Aziz		National Guard
Faisal		
Misha'al		
Turki		

The sons of Abdul Mohsin ibn Abdul Aziz

Sa'ud, Badr, Waleed. Sa'ud has been Deputy Governor of Mecca since 1976. Badr is a prominent poet and founder of the Sa'udi Arts Society.

The sons of Sultan ibn Abdul Aziz

Khalid	b. 1949	Army
Bandar	b. 1949	Air Force, Squadron Commander
Fahad	b. 1951	Deputy Minister and Director of Social Welfare, Ministry of Labour and Social Affairs
Faisal	b. 1951	

The sons of Turki ibn Abdul Aziz

Faisal, Fahad, Khalid, Sultan. Khalid is active in business.

The sons of Naif ibn Abdul Aziz

Sa'ud, Muhammad. Sa'ud is active in business.

The sons of Salman ibn Abdul Aziz

Fahad, Sultan, Ahmad, Abdul Aziz, Faisal. Ahmad is in the Army.

The sons of Abdullah ibn Abdul Rahman

The Emir Abdullah was a trusted adviser to his elder brother Abdul Aziz. He commanded the Sa'udi army which conquered the Hijaz, 1924–6, and he was a prominent commander in the suppression of the Ikhwan revolt in 1928.

531

Well-read and assertive, the Emir Abdullah was prominent in the circle around Abdul Aziz in the 1930s and 1940s, and after 1953 he assumed the role of 'elder statesman' to the nephews who were scarcely younger than he – Sa'ud, Faisal and Khalid. He played an important role in the negotiations which led to the deposition of King Sa'ud. He died in December 1976.

The Emir Abdullah had over twenty sons, among them:

Abdul Rahman		Business and property interests
Muhammad		
Khalid	b. 1937	Active in business
Sa'ud		In the Ministry of Foreign Affairs
Bandar	b. 1944	Assistant Deputy Minister for Provincial Affairs, Minister of the Interior
Turki		Consulting Engineer

The sons of Sa'ad ibn Abdul Rahman

Sa'ad was Abdul Rahman's second son by Sara Sudairi. He was Abdul Aziz's only full brother, and when he was killed in 1916 at the battle of Kinzan (see p. 123), Abdul Aziz married his widow, Jauhara bint Sudairi, and raised Sa'ad's sons as his own. These sons were Faisal (b. 1910), Fahad (b. 1912) and Sa'ud (b. 1914). By reason of their age they grew up closely with the future King Faisal and King Khalid, as well as with Muhammad ibn Abdul Aziz. Their sister Sara married Muhammad.

Sa'ud ibn Sa'ad married Abdul Aziz's daughter Anoud, and when he divorced her in 1935 she married his eldest brother Fahad.

The sons of Faisal ibn Sa'ad are Khalid, Sa'ad and Turki.

The sons of Fahad ibn Sa'ad are Sa'ad, Khalid, Faisal, Bandar, Badr, Abdullah and Abdul Rahman.

The sons of Sa'ud ibn Sa'ad are Sa'ad (died), Abdullah, Bandar, Mitab, Nawwaf and Sa'ad.

Muhammad ibn Sa'ud al Kabeer

Muhammad, the son of Sa'ud al Kabeer and Abdul Aziz's sister Nura, is one of the senior members of the Al Sa'ud in 1981. He is acknowledged by the family as an expert on tribal loyalties and rivalries. He is also an authority on Arabian horses and on the saluki, the bedouin hunting dog. He has invested, with his sons, in successful dairy farming projects around Riyadh. His sons are Abdullah, Faisal, Sultan, Turki, Bandar, Fahad, Sa'ud, Khalid, Salman, Sa'ad and Badr.

Warning   This list is *not* comprehensive. For more data on some of these princes, and on some others, see *Who's Who in Sa'udi Arabia* (London: Europa, 1978) and *A Handbook of the Al Sa'ud* by Brian Lees (London: Royal Genealogies, 1980).

Appendix D
The Relatives of Sa'ud al Kabeer

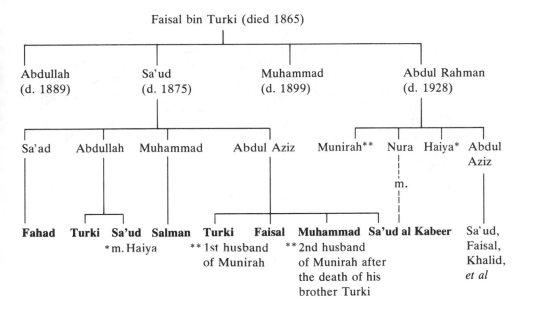

A simplified table to show the descent of the cousins who challenged Abdul Aziz in 1910, properly known as the branch of Sa'ud bin Faisal, but also known as the *araif*.

This table of the *araif* is presented to put on record a little previously unpublished material. But it is possible to fill a whole book with genealogical tables of the house of Sa'ud, and Brian Lees has done this in his *A Handbook of the Al Sa'ud* which translates and tabulates some important Arabian data about Abdul Aziz's line of the family.

For original data on this and other branches of the family, the bin Jaluwis and the al Thunayans, and for valuable first-hand research on the Sudairi family, see the works of Philby and of Dickson.

Appendix E
The Islamic Calendar

The Islamic calendar can be dated from sunset on the 15 July AD 622, the beginning of the *hijrah*, the migration of the Prophet Muhammad from Mecca to Medina. The Islamic year, twelve lunar months, usually contains 354 days, 8 hours, 4.8 minutes – irregular sightings of the moon may make it a day or so more or less (see note on p. 14). To be precise all Islamic years should be dated from sunset, but in this table they are dated from the day which begins at the midnight following that sunset.

The Islamic months are, in order: Muharram, Safar, Rabia Awwal, Rabia Thani, Jumada Awwal, Jumada Thani, Rajab, Sha'aban, Ramadhan, Shawwal, Dhul Qa'da, Dhul Hijja.

For complete conversion tables see G. S. P. Freeman-Grenville, *Muslim and Christian Calendars*, 2nd edn (London: Rex Collings, 1977).

534

AH	AD		AH	AD		AH	AD	
1	622	16 July	1322	1904	18 March	1372	1952	21 September
50	670	29 January	1323	1905	8 March	1373	1953	10 September
100	718	3 August	1324	1906	25 February	1374	1954	30 August
150	767	6 February	1325	1907	14 February	1375	1955	20 August
200	815	11 August	1326	1908	4 February	1376	1956	8 August
250	864	13 February	1327	1909	23 January	1377	1957	29 July
300	912	18 August	1328	1910	13 January	1378	1958	18 July
350	961	20 February	1329	1911	2 January	1379	1959	7 July
400	1009	25 August	1330	1911	22 December	1380	1960	26 June
450	1058	28 February	1331	1912	11 December	1381	1961	15 June
500	1106	2 September	1332	1913	30 November	1382	1962	4 June
550	1155	7 March	1333	1914	19 November	1383	1963	25 May
600	1203	10 September	1334	1915	9 November	1384	1964	13 May
650	1252	14 March	1335	1916	28 October	1385	1965	2 May
700	1300	16 September	1336	1917	17 October	1386	1966	22 April
750	1349	22 March	1337	1918	7 October	1387	1967	11 April
800	1397	24 September	1338	1919	26 September	1388	1968	31 March
850	1446	29 March	1339	1920	15 September	1389	1969	20 March
900	1494	2 October	1340	1921	4 September	1390	1970	9 March
950	1543	6 April	1341	1922	24 August	1391	1971	27 February
1000	1591	19 October	1342	1923	14 August	1392	1972	16 February
1050	1640	23 April	1343	1924	2 August	1393	1973	4 February
1100	1688	26 October	1344	1925	23 July	1394	1974	25 January
1150	1737	1 May	1345	1926	12 July	1395	1975	14 January
1200	1785	4 November	1346	1927	1 July	1396	1976	3 January
1250	1834	10 May	1347	1928	20 June	1397	1976	23 December
1298	1880	4 December	1348	1929	9 June	1398	1977	13 December
1299	1881	23 November	1349	1930	29 May	1399	1978	2 December
1300	1882	12 November	1350	1931	19 May	1400	1979	22 November
1301	1883	2 November	1351	1932	7 May	1401	1980	9 November
1302	1884	21 October	1352	1933	26 April	1402	1981	30 October
1303	1885	10 October	1353	1934	16 April	1403	1982	19 October
1304	1886	30 September	1354	1935	5 April	1404	1983	8 October
1305	1887	19 September	1355	1936	24 March	1405	1984	27 September
1306	1888	7 September	1356	1937	14 March	1406	1895	16 September
1307	1889	28 August	1357	1938	3 March	1407	1986	6 September
1308	1890	17 August	1358	1939	21 February	1408	1987	26 August
1309	1891	7 August	1359	1940	10 February	1409	1988	14 August
1310	1892	26 July	1360	1941	29 January	1410	1989	4 August
1311	1893	15 July	1361	1942	19 January	1411	1990	24 July
1312	1894	5 July	1362	1943	8 January	1412	1991	13 July
1313	1895	24 June	1363	1943	28 December	1413	1992	2 July
1314	1896	12 June	1364	1944	17 December	1414	1993	21 June
1315	1897	2 June	1365	1945	6 December	1415	1994	10 June
1316	1898	22 May	1366	1946	25 November	1416	1995	31 May
1317	1899	12 May	1367	1947	15 November	1417	1996	19 May
1318	1900	1 May	1368	1948	3 November	1418	1997	9 May
1319	1901	20 April	1369	1949	24 October	1419	1998	28 April
1320	1902	10 April	1370	1950	13 October	1420	1999	17 April
1321	1903	30 March	1371	1951	2 October	1421	2000	6 April

535

Appendix F
World Oil and Gas Statistics
(at the beginning of 1980)
Source: *Oil and Gas Journal* and Aramco

Top ten oil-exporting countries
(in thousands of barrels daily)

1	Sa'udi Arabia	9000
2	Iraq	3230
3	USSR	2800
4	Kuwait	2440
5	Iran	2350
6	Nigeria	2150
7	Venezuela	2050
8	Libya	1990
9	Abu Dhabi	1450
10	Indonesia	1275

Top ten oil-producing countries
(in thousands of barrels daily)

1	USSR	11,700
2	Sa'udi Arabia*	9530
3	USA	8596
4	Iraq	3450
5	Iran	3110
6	Kuwait*	2490
7	Venezuela	2356
8	Nigeria	2310
9	China	2120
10	Libya	2060

*Includes one half of the Partitioned Neutral Zone production.

536

Top ten oil-consuming countries
(in thousands of barrels daily)

1	USA	18,500
2	USSR	8900
3	Japan	5150
4	West Germany	2690
5	France	2120
6	China	1900
7	Canada	1770
8	United Kingdom	1700
9	Italy	1610
10	Brazil	1100

Top ten countries in proved oil reserves
(in millions of barrels)

1	Sa'udi Arabia*	166,480
2	Kuwait*	68,530
3	USSR	67,000
4	Iran	58,000
5	Mexico	31,250
6	Iraq	31,000
7	Abu Dhabi	28,000
8	USA	26,500
9	Libya	23,500
10	China	20,000

*Includes one half of the Partitioned Neutral Zone reserves.

Top ten countries in proved gas reserves
(in billions of cubic feet)

1	USSR	900,000
2	Iran	490,000
3	USA	194,000
4	Algeria	132,000
5	Sa'udi Arabia*	95,730
6	Canada	85,500
7	Qatar	60,000
8	The Netherlands	59,500
9	Mexico	59,000
10	Venezuela	42,800

*Includes one half of Partitioned Neutral Zone gas reserves, shared with Kuwait.

537

Appendix G
Note on Arabic Words

Rendering Arabic words and phrases into their precise English phonetic equivalents, complete with accents, gaps and symbols, is an exercise of great complexity – and not a little snobbery in a book for the general reader. The results are also confusing, for Q'run, badawin or Ramzan do not correspond to the spellings most people recognize.

Unless you are a devotee of a particular system, you can, in fact, spell Arabic words just the way they sound to you – Abdullah, Abdallah, Abd'Allah. T. E. Lawrence certainly did so in *Seven Pillars of Wisdom*, even changing spellings as he went along, writing Jeddah or Jiddah as the mood took him, and declining his publisher's attempts to impose uniformity. He was, in fact, quite restrained, for modern transliterations of that city's name have included Jaddah, Jedda, Jeddah, Jidda, Jiddah, Judda, Juddah, Jaddah, Jadda, Djiddah, Djuddah, Djouddah, Gedda, Dsjiddah, Djettah and Dscheddah – to name only some – and all are acceptable.

The general rule adopted is that Arabic words, common place names and personal names are rendered here whenever possible in the spellings which ordinary readers will most easily recognize – Koran, bedouin, Ramadhan. Other words, including less common personal names and place names, are transliterated according to the phonetic system below.

ا a	خ kh	ش sh	غ gh	ن n
ب b	د d	ص s	ف f	و w
ت t	ذ dh	ض d	ق g	ه h
ث th	ر r	ط t	ك k	ق aw, au
ج j	ز z	ظ dh	ل l	ي ee, y, i
ح h	س s	ع '	م m	ى ay, ai

Transliterations do not take account of the difference between 'sun' letters and 'moon' letters, so the definite article is invariably spelt 'al', whether or not it elides.

Bibliography

Interviews

Research for this book started in August 1977, and since then the author has undertaken several hundred interviews. Some were off the record and are not listed here. The following were on the record:

His Majesty King Khalid ibn Abdul Aziz. Audience in Riyadh, March 1980, and Jeddah, June 1980.

Their Royal Highnesses the Princes:

Musa'id ibn Abdul Rahman. Interview, Riyadh, November 1979, and written answers to previously submitted questions.
Abdullah ibn Abdul Aziz. Jeddah, June 1980.
Sultan ibn Abdul Aziz. Written answers to questions submitted through Sheikh Hassan Alalsheikh, December 1980.
Naif ibn Abdul Aziz. Interview, Taif, June 1979.
Salman ibn Abdul Aziz. Several meetings between January 1980 and May 1981.
Ahmad ibn Abdul Aziz. Interview, Taif, June 1979.
Sattam ibn Abdul Aziz. Interviews in Riyadh, February 1980 and May 1981.

Their Highnesses the Princes:

Muhammad bin Sa'ud al Kabeer. Written answers to questions, March 1980.
Sa'ud bin Sa'ad bin Abdul Rahman. Interview, Jeddah, April 1980.
Abdullah al Faisal. Interview, Jeddah, November 1980.
Muhammad al Faisal. Interview, Jeddah, November 1980.
Turki al Faisal. Several interviews between June 1980 and July 1981.
Muhammad bin Abdullah bin Abdul Rahman. Interview, Riyadh, December 1980.
Sa'ud bin Fahad bin Abdul Aziz. Interview, London, July 1981.

Numerous interviews and meetings between June 1978 and July 1981 with:

Bandar bin Abdullah bin Abdul Rahman.
Turki bin Abdullah bin Abdul Rahman.
Faisal bin Abdul Aziz bin Faisal al Sa'ud.
Faisal bin Abdullah bin Muhammad al Sa'ud.
Abdullah bin Faisal bin Turki al Abdullah.
Turki bin Muhammad bin Sa'ud al Kabeer.

BIBLIOGRAPHY

Outside the Al Sa'ud, the following were consulted:

James Akins. Interview, Riyadh, May 1981.
Marianne Alireza. Interview, Jeddah, December 1978.
Muhammad ibn Abdullah Alireza. Interview, Jeddah, July 1980.
Dr Midhat Sheikh al Ardh. Meetings in Riyadh, December 1980 and January 1981.
André Bénard. Correspondence, May 1981.
Waheeb Binzagr. Interview, Jeddah, July 1980.
Abdul Hamid al Derhally. Interview, Jeddah, July 1980.
Dame Violet Dickson. Correspondence, 1979–80.
Dr Fouad al Farsy. Several meetings since June 1978.
Col. Gerald de Gaury. Several meetings since September 1978 and correspondence.
General Sir John Glubb. Interview, Sussex, March 1979, and subsequent
    correspondence.
Raymond A. Hare. Correspondence, May 1981.
Faisal al Hegailan. Several meetings, London, 1978.
Jamal Bey Husaini. Interview, Riyadh, November 1980.
Sheikh Muhammad ibn Jubair. Interview, Riyadh, February 1980, and subsequent
    correspondence.
Abdullah ibn Khamees. Interview, Riyadh, January 1981.
Adnan Muhammad Khashoggi. Interview, Monte Carlo, July 1981.
Kana'an al Khateeb. Numerous meetings, Jeddah, 1980.
Dr Abdul Aziz Khuwaiter. Interviews, Riyadh, December 1978.
Dr Henry Kissinger. Interview, New York, July 1981.
Garnet Morgan Man. Correspondence, May 1981.
Muhammad al Mana. Interviews, al Khobar, June 1980.
Daan van der Meulen. Correspondence, June 1981.
Richard M. Nixon. Correspondence, May 1981.
David Parker. Interview, Jeddah, June 1980.
Sir (George) Clinton Pelham. Correspondence, June 1981.
Dr Rashad Pharaon. Numerous meetings in Jeddah and Riyadh between November
    1979 and May 1981.
George T. Piercy. Correspondence, May 1981.
John Pochna. Interviews in Jeddah and London, 1980–1.
Sir Shuldam Redfern. Interview, London, February 1979.
Sir George Rendel. Interview, London, January 1979.
Dr George Rentz. Meeting, Washington, February 1979, and correspondence.
Dr Fatina Amin Shakir. Meetings, London, February 1981.
Dr Abdul Aziz al Sowayeghr. Meetings, Riyadh, May 1981.
Abdul Aziz Suleiman. Interview, Jeddah, October 1979.
Abdullah ibn Hamoud al Tariki. Interviews in London and Riyadh between
    November 1980 and May 1981.
Dr Abdullah al Uthaimeen. Interview, Riyadh, November 1980.
Admiral John Wise. Interview, London, December 1980.
Ahmad Zaki Yamani. Several interviews between November 1980 and May 1981.
Dr Muhammad Abdo Yamani. Meetings in Riyadh, December 1978 and May 1981.
Muhammad Hussein Zaidan. Interview, Riyadh, January 1980.
Dr Abdul Rahman al Zamil. Interview, Riyadh, May 1981.

540

Manuscript collections

Official correspondence

Public Record Office, London:

Cabinet files, series 27 (Cabinet Committees).
Colonial Office files, series 727 (Arabia), 730 (Iraq).
Foreign Office files, series 371 (Turkey), (Arabia), (Hijaz and Nejd), (Sa'udi Arabia), series 406 (Confidential Print, Eastern Affairs), series 424 (Turkey, Asiatic prints), series 686 (Jeddah Archives), series 882 (Arab Bureau).

India Office Library and Records, London:

Home Correspondence, 1807–1911 (L/P&S/3).
Political and Secret Correspondence with India, 1875–1911 (L/P&S/7).
Department Papers Political and Secret Separate (or Subject) Files, 1902–31 (L/P&S/10).
Political External Files and Collections, 1931–50, Collection 6 (Arabia) (L/P&S/12).
Political and Secret Memoranda (L/P&S/18).
Political and Secret Department Library (L/P&S/20).
Records of the British Residency and Agencies in the Persian Gulf (R/15/5):
  1 (Bushire), 2 (Bahrein), 5 (Kuwait), 6 (Muscat).

Foreign and Commonwealth Office Library, London: *Arab Bulletin*, 1915–19.
National Archives and Records Service, Washington DC. General Records of the Department of State, Record Group (RG) 59. Decimal files, Sa'udi Arabia, Kingdom of (Hijaz and Nejd), 1930–49.
Department of State, Washington DC. Decimal files, Sa'udi Arabia, Kingdom of, 1950–63, released under the Freedom of Information Act.
Darat al Malik Abdul Aziz, Riyadh.
Petromin: Mineral Resources Library, Jeddah.
Aramco Headquarters Library, Dhahran.

Private correspondence

HRH Princess Alice, Countess of Athlone. Letters from Sa'udi Arabia, 1938.

St Antony's College, Oxford, Middle East Centre, Private Papers Collection:

the diary of Humphrey Bowman; the papers of Sir Reader Bullard; the papers of Dr W. L. Corkill; the diary of Charles R. Crane; the papers of H. R. P. Dickson; the papers of R. S. F. Hennessy; the diary of Lieutenant-Colonel G. E. Leachman; the papers of H. St J. Philby; the papers of Sir Thomas Rapp; the papers of Sir Andrew Ryan; the papers of J. W. A. Young.

Published documents

India Office Library and Records, London:

A Collection of Treaties, Engagements, and Sanads Relating to India and

Neighbouring Countries. Compiled by C. U. Aitchison. 5th Ed. Vol XI. Delhi: Manager of Publications, 1933.

Lorimer, J. G. *Gazetteer of the Persian Gulf, Oman, and Central Arabia.* 2 vols in 4. Calcutta: GPO, 1908–15.

Tuson, Penelope. *The Records of the British Residency and Agencies in the Persian Gulf (R/15/5).* (India Office Records, Guides to Archive Groups.) London: Foreign and Commonwealth Office, 1979.

Royal Institute of International Affairs, London:

United Kingdom Memorial: Arbitration Concerning Buraimi and the Common Frontier Between Abu Dhabi and Saudi Arabia. 3 vols. London, 1955.

Political and Diplomatic History of the Arab World, 1900–1967: A Chronological Study. Compiled by Menahem Mansour. 5 vols and Index 2 vols. Washington: NCR/Microcard Editions, 1972.

Department of State, Washington DC:

Foreign Relations of the United States (1933–1950). Washington: GPO, 1949–78.

United States Congress, Washington DC:

US Congress. 93rd, 2nd Session. Senate. Committee on Foreign Relations. Subcommittee on Multinational Corporations. *Multinational Oil Corporations and US Foreign Policy.* Washington: GPO, 1975.

US Congress. 94th, 1st Session. House of Representatives. Committee on International Relations. *United States Arms Sales to the Persian Gulf.* Washington: GPO, 1975.

US Congress. 95th, 1st Session, Senate. Committee on Energy and Natural Resources. *Access to Oil – The United States Relationships with Saudi Arabia and Iran.* Washington: GPO, 1977.

US Congress. 95th, 2nd Session. House of Representatives. Committee on International Relations. Subcommittee on Europe and the Middle East. *Review of Developments in the Middle East.* Washington: GPO, 1978.

US Congress, 95th, 2nd Session. Senate. Committee on Foreign Relations. Subcommittee on Near-Eastern and South Asian Affairs. *Middle East Peace Progress.* Washington: GPO, 1978.

US Congress, 96th, 1st Session. Committee on Foreign Relations. Subcommittee on International Economic Policy. *The Future of Saudi Arabian Oil Production.* Washington: GPO, 1979.

Department of Health, Education and Welfare, Washington DC:

Egbert, Robert, *et al. Education in Saudi Arabia: Findings, Recommendations and Proposed Projects.* (Report of Education Team's visit to Sa'udi Arabia, 8–27 November 1974.) Mimeo. Washington: Department of Health, Education and Welfare, 28 January 1975.

Sa'udi Arabia:

Memorial of the Government of Sa'udi Arabia. Arbitration for the Settlement of the Territorial Dispute Between Muscat and Abu Dhabi on One Side and Sa'udi Arabia on the Other. 3 vols. Cairo, 1955.

542

What a Muslim is Required to Know about his Religion. Ministry of Pilgrimage and Endowment in Sa'udi Arabia, 1386 AH.

Newspapers and magazines

Great Britain:

Daily Telegraph; *Sunday Telegraph*; *The Times*; *The Sunday Times*; *The Observer*; *The Economist*; *Financial Times*; *The Listener*; *Middle East International*; *Middle East and Economic Digest*; *The Middle East*; *8 Days*.

France:

Le Monde; *L'Express*; *Paris Match*; *L'Illustration*; *International Herald Tribune*.

Sa'udi Arabia:

Arab News; *The Sa'udi Gazette*; *Sa'udi Business*; *ARAMCO World*.

United States of America:

The New York Times; *The Washington Post*; *The Wall Street Journal*; *Newsweek*; *Time*; *Life*; *US News and World Report*; *Fortune*; *Town and Country*; *New Republic*; *Harper's*; *Leaders*.

Articles

Ahmad, Eqbal, and Caploe, David. 'The Logic of Military Intervention', *Race and Class*, XVII:3 (1976), 319–32.

Akins, James F. 'The Oil Crisis: this time the wolf is here', *Foreign Affairs* (April 1973).

Amiruddin, B. 'Woman's Status in Islam: A Moslem View', *Muslim World*, 28 (1938), 153–63.

Anon. 'My Friend the Sheikh', *Blackwood's Magazine*, 212 (July 1922), 34–48.

Anthony, John Duke. 'Foreign Policy: The View from Riyadh', *The Wilson Quarterly* (Winter 1979), 73–82.

Antoun, Richard T. 'On the Modesty of Women in Arab Muslim Villages', *American Anthropologist*, 70 (1968), 671–9.

—— 'On the Significance of Names in an Arab Village', *Ethnology*, 7 (1968), 158–70.

—— 'The Social Significance of Ramadan in an Arab Village', *Muslim World*, 58 (January and April 1968), 36–42, 95–104.

Arsenian, Seth. 'Wartime Propaganda in the Middle East', *Middle East Journal*, 2:4 (1948), 417–29.

Ashkenazi, Touvia. 'The Anazah Tribes', *Southwestern Journal of Anthropology*, 4 (1948), 222–39.

Azzi, Robert. 'Saudi Arabia: The Kingdom and its Power', *National Geographic*, 158:3 (September 1980), 286–332.

Barry, John O. 'Oil and Soviet Policy in the Middle East', *Middle East Journal*, 26:2 (1972), 149–60.

543

Bayyan, Hayyan ibn (pseud.). 'Poor Little Rich Nation', *The Nation*, 4 April 1981.

Borthwick, Bruce M. 'The Islamic Sermon as a Channel of Political Communication', *Middle East Journal*, 21:3 (1967), 229–313.

Boyd, Douglas A. 'Saudi Arabian Broadcasting: Radio and TV in a Wealthy State', *Middle East Review*, XII: 4 and XIII: 1 (Summer/Fall 1980), 20–7.

Bullard, Sir Reader. 'Portrait of Ibn Saud', *The Listener*, 4 February 1954.

Busch, Noel F. 'Ibn Saud: *Life* Visits Arabia', *Life*, 14:22 (31 May 1943), 69–88.

Candler, Edmund. 'Lawrence and the Hejaz', *Blackwood's Magazine*, 218 (December 1925), 738–61.

Carmichael, Joel. 'Prince of Arabs', *Foreign Affairs*, 20:4 (1942), 719–31.

Carruthers, Douglas. 'Captain Shakespear's Last Journey', *The Geographical Journal*, LIX: 5 and 6 (1922), 303–34 and 401–18.

Caskel, Werner. 'The Bedouinization of Arabia', *American Anthropologist*, Memoir 76 (1954), 36–46.

Chubin, Shahram. 'Soviet Policy Towards Iran and the Gulf', *Adelphi Papers* (International Institute for Strategic Studies), 157 (Spring 1980).

Clifford, R. L. 'The American Oil Company', *Asian Affairs* (Journal of the Royal Society for Asian Affairs), 63:2 (1976), 178–82.

Collins, John M., *et al.* 'Petroleum Imports from the Persian Gulf: Use of US Armed Force to Ensure Supplies', *Congressional Research Service* (Major Issues System). Washington: Library of Congress, reprint, 25 March 1980.

Cooley, John K. 'Iran, the Palestinians and the Gulf', *Foreign Affairs*, 57:5 (1979), 1017–34.

Crane, Charles R. 'Visit to the Red Sea Littoral and the Yaman', *Journal of the Royal Central Asian Society*, 15:1 (1928), 48–67.

Dame, Louis P. 'From Bahrain to Taif: A Missionary Journey Across Arabia', *Moslem World*, 28:2 (1933), 164–78.

Dame, Mrs L. P. 'A Woman's Trip to Central Arabia', *Missionary Review of the World*, 57 (November 1934), 517–26.

Dawisha, Adeed, I. 'Internal Values and External Threats: The Making of Saudi Foreign Policy', *Orbis*, 23:1 (1979), 129–43.

—— 'Saudi Arabia's Search for Security', *Adelphi Papers* (International Institute for Strategic Studies), 158 (Winter 1979–80).

Dawisha, Karen. 'Soviet Decision-Making in the Middle East: The 1973 October War and the 1980 Gulf War', *International Affairs*, 57:1 (Winter 1980–1), 43–59.

de Gaury, Gerald. 'The End of Arabian Isolation', *Foreign Affairs*, 25:1 (1946), 446–58.

—— 'Memories and Impressions of the Arabia of Ibn Saud', *Arabian Studies*, II (1975), 19–32.

Dowson, V. H. W. 'The Date and the Arab', *Journal of the Royal Central Asian Society*, 36:1 (1949), 34–41.

Duguid, Stephen. 'A Biographical Approach to the Study of Social Change in the Middle East: Abdullah Tariki as a New Man', *International Journal of Middle East Studies*, 1:3 (1970), 195–220.

Edens, David G. 'The Anatomy of the Saudi Revolution', *International Journal of Middle East Studies*, 5:1 (1974), 50–64.

Eilts, Hermann F. 'Survey of Social Development in Saudi Arabia', *Parameters*, 1 (Spring 1971), 4–18.

—— 'Social Revolution in Saudi Arabia', *Parameters*, 1 (Fall 1971), 22–33.

—— 'Saving Camp David (1): Improve the Framework', *Foreign Policy*, 41 (Winter 1980–1).

Field, Henry. 'Reconnaissance in Saudi Arabia', *Journal of the Royal Central Asian Society*, 38: 1, 2 (1951), 185–97.

George, Alan. 'Bedouin Settlement in Saudi Arabia', *Middle East International*, 51 (September 1975), 27–30.

Glubb, John B. 'The Bedouins of Northern Iraq', *Journal of the Royal Central Asian Society*, 22:1 (1935), 13–31.

Hamza, Sir Fuad. 'Najran', *Journal of the Royal Central Asian Society*, 22:4 (1935), 631–40.

Harrington, C. W. 'The Saudi Arabian Council of Ministers', *Middle East Journal*, 12:1 (1958), 1–19.

Harrison, P. W. 'The Situation in Arabia', *Atlantic Monthly* (December 1920), 849–55.

—— 'A Great Sheikh and his Great Lieutenant', *Asia*, 24 (September 1924), 711–34.

Helaissi, A. A. 'The Bedouins and Tribal Life in Saudi Arabia', *International Social Science Bulletin*, 11 (1959), 532–8.

Heller, Joseph. 'Roosevelt, Stalin and the Palestine Problem at Yalta', *Wiener Library Bulletin* 30:41–2 (1977), 25–35.

Hitti, Said, and Abed, George T. 'The Economy and Finances of Saudi Arabia', *International Monetary Fund Staff Papers*, 21:2 (1974), 247–306.

Hoya, Paul F. (ed.) 'The Haj', *ARAMCO World* (special issue), 25:6 (November–December 1974).

Hudson, Michael C. 'The Palestinians: Retrospect and Prospects', *Current History*, 78:453 (January 1980), 22–48.

Humphreys, R. S. 'Islam and Political Values in Saudi Arabia, Egypt and Syria', *Middle East Journal*, 31:1 (1979), 1–19

Ignatus, Miles (pseud.). 'Seizing Arab Oil', *Harper's Magazine* (March 1975).

Iseman, Peter A. 'The Arabian Ethos', *Harper's Magazine* (February 1978), 37–56.

Jong, G. E. de. 'Slavery in Arabia', *Moslem World*, 24 (1934), 126–44.

Karpel, Craig S. 'Ten Ways to Break Opec', *Harper's Magazine* (January 1979).

Kelidar, A. R. 'The Problem of Succession in Saudi Arabia', *Asian Affairs* (Journal of the Royal Society for Asian Affairs), 9:1 (1978), 23–30.

Kingston, A. E. 'The Vaginal Atresia of Arabia', *Journal of Obstetrics and Gynaecology of the British Empire*, 64 (December 1957), 836–9.

Klare, Michael. 'Gunboat Diplomacy, Lightning War and the Nixon Doctrine: US Military Strategy in the Arabian Gulf', *Race and Class*, 17:3 (1976), 303–18.

Knauerhase, R. 'Saudi Arabia's Economy at the Beginning of the 1970s', *Middle East Journal*, 28:2 (1974), 126–40.

—— 'Saudi Arabia: Our Conservative Muslim Ally', *Current History*, 78:453 (January 1980), 17–37.

Kohn, Hans. 'The Unification of Arabia', *Foreign Affairs*, 13:1 (1934), 91–103.

Kondrake, Morton. 'The Skittish Saudis', *New Republic* (17 March 1979).

—— 'The Saudi Oil Offensive', *New Republic* (4 and 11 August 1979), 21–3.
—— 'The New Republican Consensus: Henry's Revised History', *New Republic* (18 August 1979), 8–12.
Kumar, Ravinder. 'Abdul Aziz Al Saud and the Genesis of Saudi Arabia (1901–1907)', *Bengal Past and Present* (Journal of the Calcutta Historical Society), LXXIX–LXXX (January–June and July–December 1960), 60–6 and 83–9.
L. 'Downing Street and Arab Potentates', *Foreign Affairs*, 5:2 (1927), 231–40.
Lenczowski, George. 'Tradition and Reform in Saudi Arabia', *Current History*, 52 (1967), 98–104.
Lewis, Bernard. 'Communism and Islam', *International Affairs*, 30:1 (1954), 1–12.
Lewis, C. C. 'Ibn Saud and the Future of Arabia', *International Affairs*, 12:4 (1933), 518–34.
Long, David. E. 'The Board of Grievances in Saudi Arabia', *Middle East Journal*, 27:1 (1973), 71–5.
—— 'Saudi Arabia', *Washington Papers* (Center for Strategic and International Studies, Georgetown University), IV:39 (London and Beverly Hills: Sage, 1976).
—— 'Saudi Oil Policy', *The Wilson Quarterly* (Winter 1979), 83–91.
Lubin, Peter. 'The Second Pillar of Ignorance', *New Republic* (22 December 1979), 19–23.
Lustick, Ian S. 'Camp David (2): Kill the Autonomy Talks', *Foreign Policy*, 41 (Winter 1980–1), 21–43.
McHale, T. R. 'A Prospect of Saudi Arabia', *International Affairs*, 56:4 (1980), 622–47.
Mackie, J. B. 'Hasa: An Arabian Oasis', *Geographical Journal*, LXIII (1924), 189–206.
Maclennan, Norman M. 'General Health Conditions of Certain Bedouin Tribes in Transjordan', *Transactions of the Royal Society of Tropical Medicine and Hygiene*, 29:3 (1935), 227–48.
Malone, J. J. 'Saudi Arabia', *Muslim World*, 56: (1966), 290–5.
Mandaville, J. 'Al Hasa: An Outpost of Empire', *ARAMCO World*, 25:5 (September–October 1974).
—— 'America and the Arabian Peninsula: The First Hundred Years', *Middle East Journal*, 30:3 (1976), 406–24.
Mansur, Abdul Kasim (pseud.). 'The American Threat to Saudi Arabia', *Armed Forces Journal International* (September 1980), 47–60.
Melamid, Alexander. 'Boundaries and Petroleum Development in Saudi Arabia', *Geographical Review* (New York), XLVIII (1957), 589–91.
—— 'Political Boundaries and Nomadic Grazing', *Geographical Review* (New York), LV (1965), 287–90.
Merritt, Paul C. 'Karl S. Twitchell', *Mining Engineering* (Society of Mining Engineering) (September 1965), 78–83.
Mikesell, Raymond F. 'Monetary Problems of Saudi Arabia', *Middle East Journal*, 1:2 (1947), 169–79.
Monro, J. 'On Campus in Saudi Arabia'; *ARAMCO World*, 25:4 (July–August 1974).

546

Muksam, H. V. 'Fertility and Reproduction of the Bedouin', *Population Studies*, 4 (1951), 354–63.

Narayanan, R. 'A Review of Oil Contract Negotiations by Saudi Arabia with ARAMCO', *International Studies*, VII:4 (1966), 568–88.

Nickel, Herman. 'The US Gropes for a Mideast Strategy', *Fortune* (25 February 1980), 72–80.

Ovendale, Ritchie. 'The Palestine Policy of the British Labour Government 1945–1946', *International Affairs*, 55:3 (1979), 409–31.

——'The Palestine Policy of the British Labour Government 1947: The Decision to Withdraw', *International Affairs*, 56:1 (1980), 73–93.

Page, Stephen. 'Moscow and the Persian Gulf Countries 1967–1970', *Nizan* (incorporating *Central Asian Review*), 8:2 (1971), 72–84.

Philby, H. St J. B. 'A Survey of Wahhabi Arabia 1929', *Journal of the Royal Central Asian Society*, 16:4 (1929), 468–81.

—— 'The New Reign in Saudi Arabia', *Foreign Affairs*, 32:3 (1954), 446–56.

—— 'Saudi Arabia: The New Statute of the Council of Ministers', *Middle East Journal*, 12:3 (1958), 318–23.

Quandt, William B. 'The Middle East Crises in America and the World 1979', *Foreign Affairs*, 58:3 (1980), 541–62.

Rentz, George. 'Literature on the Kingdom of Saudi Arabia', *Middle East Journal*, 4:2 (1950), 244–56.

Roosevelt, Kermit. 'The Partition of Palestine: A Lesson in Pressure Politics', *Middle East Journal*, 2:1 (1948), 1–16.

Rubin, Barry. 'Anglo-American Relations in Saudi Arabia 1941–45', *Journal of Contemporary History*, 14 (1979), 253–67.

Rubinstein, Alvin Z. 'The Soviet Union and the Arabian Peninsula', *The World Today*, 35:11 (1979), 442–52.

Rugh, William A. 'Emergence of a New Middle Class in Saudi Arabia', *Middle East Journal*, 27:1 (1973), 7–20.

—— 'A Tale of Two Houses', *The Wilson Quarterly* (Winter 1979), 59–72.

Sanger, Richard H. 'Ibn Saud's Program for Arabia', *Middle East Journal*, 1:2 (1947), 180–90.

Sebai, Zohair A. 'Knowledge, Attitudes and Practice of Family Planning: Profile of a Bedouin Community in Saudi Arabia', *Journal of Biosocial Science*, 6:4 (1974), 453–61.

Shamma, S. 'Law and Lawyers in Saudi Arabia', *International and Comparative Law Quarterly*, 14 (1965), 1034–9.

Shouby, E. 'The Influence of the Arab Language on the Psychology of the Arabs', *Middle East Journal*, 5:3 (1951), 284–302.

Silverfarb, Daniel. 'The Philby Mission to Ibn Saud 1917–1918', *Journal of Contemporary History*, 14 (1979), 269–86.

—— 'The British Government and the Khurma Dispute 1918–1919', *Arabian Studies*, V (1979), 37–59.

—— 'The Anglo-Najd Treaty of December 1915', *Middle Eastern Studies*, 16:3 (1980), 167–77.

Smalley, W. F. 'The Wahhabis and Ibn Saud', *Moslem World*, 22:3 (1932), 227–46.

547

Solaim, Soliman A. 'Legal Review: Saudi Arabia's Judicial System', *Middle East Journal*, 25:3 (1971), 403–7.

Storrs, Sir Ronald. 'A Great Arab, A Great Man: A Tribute to His Late Majesty King Abd al-Aziz Ibn Sa'ud', *The Listener* (19 November 1953), 859.

Sweet, Louise. 'Camel Raiding of Arabian Bedouin: A Mechanism of Ecological Adaptation', *American Anthropologist*, 67 (1965), 1132–4.

—— 'The Women of Ain ad-Dayr', *Anthropological Quarterly*, 40 (1967), 167–83.

Thesiger, W. P. 'The Badu of Southern Arabia', *Journal of the Royal Central Asian Society*, 37:1 (1950), 53–61.

Tinnin, David B. 'The Saudis Awaken to their Vunerability', *Fortune* (10 March 1980), 48–56.

Toynbee, Arnold J. 'A Problem of Arabian Statesmanship', *Journal of the Royal Institute of International Affairs*, 8:4 (1929), 367–75.

Tucker, Robert W. 'Oil: The Issue of American Intervention', *Commentary*, 59:1 (1975), 21–31.

Turner, Louis, and Bedore, James. 'Saudi Arabia: The Power of the Purse Strings', *International Affairs*, 54:3 (1978).

Van Peursem, G. G. 'Guests of King Ibn Saud', *Moslem World*, 26:2 (1936), 112–18.

Vickery, C. E. 'A Journey in Arabia', *Blackwood's Magazine*, 211 (February 1922), 166–77.

Voll, John O. 'The Islamic Past and the Present Resurgence', *Current History*, 78:456 (April 1980), 145–81.

Wahba, Sheikh Hafiz. 'Wahhabism in Arabia, Past and Present', *Journal of the Royal Central Asian Society*, 16:4 (1929), 458–67.

Watt, D. C. 'The Foreign Policy of Ibn Saud 1930–39', *Journal of the Royal Central Asian Society*, 50:2 (April 1963), 152–60.

Wilton, Sir John. 'Arabs and Oil', *Asian Affairs* (Journal of the Royal Society for Asian Affairs), XI:2 (June 1980), 127–33.

Wise, Stephen S. 'In Reply to King Ibn Saud', *Life*, 14:25 (21 June 1943), 37–40.

Wolf, Eric R. 'The Social Organization of Mecca and the Origins of Islam', *Southwestern Journal of Anthropology*, 7:4 (1951), 329–53.

Wright, Claudia. 'Implications of the Iraq–Iran War', *Foreign Affairs*, 59:2 (Winter 1980–1), 275–303.

Yorke, Valerie. 'The Gulf in the 1980s', *Chatham House Papers* (Royal Institute of International Affairs), 6 (1980).

Books

The following books have been consulted. The chapter reference notes make clear where particular reliance has been placed on certain sources. I am grateful to those publishers and authors who have granted permission to quote brief extracts.

Abdalati, Hammudah. *Islam in Focus*. Damascus: International Islamic Federation of Student Organizations, 1977 (1397 AH).

Algosaibi, Ghazi A. *From the Orient and the Desert*. (Poems by Ghazi Algosaibi.) London: Oriel Press, 1977.

—— 'Saudi Development: A Unique Experiment'. Mimeo.

Ali, Abdullah Yusuf (text, translation and commentary). *The Holy Qu'ran*. London: Islamic Foundation, 1975.

Alireza, Marianne. *At the Drop of a Veil*. Boston, Mass.: Houghton Mifflin, 1971.

Almana, Mohammed. *Arabia Unified: A Portrait of Ibn Saud*. London: Hutchinson Benham, 1980.

Antonius, George. *The Arab Awakening*. London: Hamish Hamilton, 1938.

Armstrong, H. C. *Lord of Arabia: Ibn Saud, An Intimate Study of a King*. Beirut: Khayats, 1966.

Arnold, José. *Golden Swords and Pots and Pans*. London: Gollancz, 1964.

Asad, Muhammad. *The Road to Mecca*. London: Max Reinhardt, 1954.

Azzi, Robert, *An Arabian Portfolio*. Introduction by HE Sheikh Ahmad Zaki Yamani. Montrose, France: Draeger Editeur, 1976.

—— *Saudi Arabian Portfolio*. Introduction by HRH Prince Sa'ud al Faisal. Switzerland: First Azimuth, 1978.

Baker, Randall. *King Husain and the Kingdom of Hejaz*. Cambridge: Oleander Press, 1979.

Barber, Noel. *Lords of the Golden Horn*. London: Pan Books, 1976.

Basset, René-Marie-Joseph. *Mille et un contes, récits et légendes arabes*. Paris: Maisonneuve, 1924–6.

Belgrave, Charles. *Personal Column*. London: Hutchinson, 1960.

Belhaven and Stenton, R. A. B. H. *The Uneven Road*. London: John Murray, 1955.

Beling, Willard A. (ed.). *King Faisal and the Modernization of Sa'udi Arabia*. London: Croom Helm, 1980.

Bell, Lady (ed.). *The Letters of Gertrude Bell*. Vol. 2. London: Benn, 1927.

Ben-Gurion, David. *My Talks with Arab Leaders*. Jerusalem: Keter Books, 1972.

Benoist-Méchin, Jacques. *Arabian Destiny*. London: Elek Books, 1957.

—— *Le Roi Saud, ou l'Orient à l'heure des relèves*. Paris: Albin Michel, 1960.

Besson, Yves, *Ibn Saud: Roi Bedouin*. Lausanne: Éditions des Trois Continents, 1980.

Bidwell, Robin. *Travellers in Arabia*. London: Hamlyn, 1976.

Bindagji, Hussein Hamza. *Atlas of Saudi Arabia*. London: Oxford University Press, 1978.

Binzagr, Safeya. *Saudi Arabia: An Artist's View of the Past*. Lausanne: Éditions des Trois Continents, 1979.

Blandford, Linda. *Oil Sheikhs*. London: Weidenfeld & Nicolson, 1976.

Bowman, Humphrey. *Middle East Window*. London: Longmans, 1942.

Bray, N. N. E. *A Paladin of Arabia*. London: Unicorn Press, 1936.

Bullard, Sir Reader. *The Camels Must Go: An Autobiography*. London: Faber, 1951.

Bulliet, Richard W. *The Camel and the Wheel*. Cambridge, Mass.: Harvard University Press, 1975.

Burckhardt, J. L. *Arabic Proverbs, or the Manners and Customs of the Modern Egyptians*. Introduction by C. E. Bosworth. 3rd ed. London: Curzon Press, 1972.

Burton, R. F. *Personal Narrative of a Pilgrimage to Al-Madinah and Meccah*. 2 vols. New York: Dover Publications, 1964.

Busch, B. C. *Britain and the Persian Gulf, 1894–1914*. Berkeley and Los Angeles, Calif.: University of California Press, 1967.

549

—— *Britain, India and the Arabs 1914–1921*. Berkeley and Los Angeles, Calif.: University of California Press, 1971.

Buschow, Rosemarie. *The Prince and I*. London: Futura, 1979.

Calverley, Eleanor T. *My Arabian Days and Nights*. New York: Crowell, 1958.

Campbell, Charles G. *Tales from the Arab Tribes*. London: Drummond, 1949.

—— *Told in the Market Place: Forty Tales*. London: Benn, 1954.

Cantwell Smith, Wilfred. *Islam in Modern History*. Princeton, NJ: Princeton University Press, 1977.

Cattan, Henry (trans.). *The Garden of Joys: An Anthology of Oriental Anecdotes, Fables and Proverbs*. London: Namara, 1979.

Cheesman, R. E. *In Unknown Arabia*. London: Macmillan, 1926.

Cheney, M. S. *Big Oilman from Arabia*. London: Heinemann, 1958.

Childs, J. Rives, *Foreign Service Farewell: My Years in the Near East*. Charlottesville, Va: University Press of Virginia, 1969.

Clarke, J. I., and Fisher, W. B. *Populations of the Middle East and North Africa: A Geographical Approach*. London: University of London Press, 1972.

Clayton, Sir Gilbert F. *An Arabian Diary*. Ed. Robert O. Collins. Berkeley and Los Angeles, Calif.: University of California Press, 1969.

Clements, Frank A. *Saudi Arabia*. World Biographical Series. Oxford: Clio Press, 1979.

Cléron, Jean-Paul. *Saudi Arabia 2000*. London: Croom Helm, 1978.

Cobbold, Lady Evelyn. *Pilgrimage to Mecca*. London: John Murray, 1934.

Cole, Donald P. *Nomads of the Nomads: The Al Murrah Bedouin of the Empty Quarter*. Chicago, Ill.: Aldine, 1975.

Colyer Ross, Heather. *Bedouin Jewellery in Saudi Arabia*, London: Stacey International, 1978.

Coon, Carleton S. *Caravan: The Story of the Middle East*. Rev. ed. New York: Krieger, 1976.

Copeland, Miles. *The Game of Nations*. London: Weidenfeld & Nicolson, 1969.

Cornwallis, Sir Kinahan. *Asir Before World War I: A Handbook*. 1916. Introduction by R. L. Bidwell. Cambridge: Falcon/Oleander, reprint of 2nd (1917) ed., 1978.

Cottrell, Alvin J. 'The Political Military Balance in the Persian Gulf Region'. In Joseph Szyliowicz and Bard E. O'Neill (eds), *The Energy Crisis and US Foreign Policy*, pp. 125–38. New York: Praeger, 1975.

Courtellement, Gervais. *Mon Voyage à la Mecque*. Paris: Hachette, 1896.

Dawood, N. J. (trans.). *Tales from the Thousand and One Nights*. Harmondsworth: Penguin, 1973.

—— (trans. and notes) *The Koran*. Harmondsworth: Penguin, 1975.

de Gaury, Gerald, *Arabia Phoenix*. London: Harrap, 1946.

—— *Rulers of Mecca*. London: Harrap, 1951.

—— *Faisal: King of Saudi Arabia*. London: Arthur Barker, 1966.

—— and Winstone, H. V. F. *The Spirit of the East*. London: Quartet, 1979.

DeNovo, John A. *American Interests and Policies in the Middle East 1900–1939*. Minneapolis, Minn.: University of Minnesota Press, 1963.

Dickson, H. R. P. *Kuwait and Her Neighbours*. London: Allen & Unwin, 1956.

—— *The Arab of the Desert*. London: Allen & Unwin, 1972.

Dickson, Violet. *Forty Years in Kuwait*. London: Allen & Unwin, 1971.

Doughty, Charles M. *Travels in Arabia Deserta*. Introduction by T. E. Lawrence. 3rd ed. London: Cape/Medici Society, 1921.

Duncan, Andrew. *Moneyrush*. London: Hutchinson, 1979.

Eddy, William A. *FDR Meets Ibn Saud*. New York: American Friends of the Middle East, 1954.

Eden, Anthony. *Full Circle*. London: Cassell, 1960.

Encyclopedia of Islam. 4 vols and Supplement. Leiden: Brill, 1913–38.

Encyclopedia of Religion and Ethics. Ed. James Hastings. 13 vols. Edinburgh: T. T. Clark, 1908–28.

Evelyn, Wilbur Crane. *Ropes of Sand*. New York: Norton, 1980.

Fairlie, Henry. *The Seven Deadly Sins Today*. Washington, DC: New Republic Books, 1978.

Farsy, Fouad al. *Saudi Arabia: A Case Study in Development*. London: Stacey International, 1978.

Faruqi, Misbahul I. *Jewish Conspiracy and the Muslim World*. Jeddah: private publication, 1969.

Field, Michael. *A Hundred Million Dollars a Day*. London: Sidgwick, 1977.

Finnie, David H. *Desert Enterprise: the Middle East Oil Industry in its Local Environment*. Cambridge, Mass.: Harvard University Press, 1958.

Fisher, W. B. *The Middle East: A Physical, Social and Regional Geography*. London: Methuen, 1950.

The Forrestal Diaries. Ed. Walter Millis. New York: Viking, 1951.

Fraser, Nicholas, with Philip Jacobson, Mark Ottaway and Lewis Chester. *Aristotle Onassis*. Philadelphia, Pa, and New York: Lippincott, 1977.

Freeman-Grenville, G. S. P. *The Muslim and Christian Calendars*. 2nd ed. London: Rex Collings, 1977.

Galwash, Ahmad A. *The Religion of Islam: A Standard Book Companion and Introductory to the Koran*. 2 vols. Doha: Education and Culture Ministry, 1973.

George, Uwe. *In the Deserts of This Earth*. New York: Harcourt Brace Jovanovich, 1977.

Ghirshman, R. *Iran*. Harmondsworth: Penguin, 1978.

Gilbert, Martin. *The Arab–Jewish Conflict: Its History in Maps*. 3rd ed. London: Weidenfeld & Nicolson, 1979.

Glubb, John Bagot. *War in the Desert*. London: Hodder & Stoughton, 1960.

Goellner, William A. *Hofuf and the Jebel Al Qara Area of the Al Hasa Oasis*. Photostat. Dhahran: Aramco Library, 1972; rev. 1975.

Goldrup, Laurence P. *Saudi Arabia 1902–1932: The Development of a Wahhabi Society*. Published thesis. Los Angeles, Calif.: University of California, 1971.

Goldziher, I. 'The Arab Tribes and Islam'. In S. M. Stern (ed.) and C. R. Barber and S. M. Stern (trans.), *Muslim Studies*. Vol. 1. London: Allen & Unwin, 1967.

Gordon, Eugene. *Saudi Arabia in Pictures*. New York: Sterling, 1976.

Grafftey-Smith, Laurence. *Bright Levant*. London: John Murray, 1970.

Graves, Philip. *The Life of Sir Percy Cox*. London: Hutchinson, 1941.

Grey of Fallodon, Viscount. *Twenty-Five Years 1892–1916*. 2 vols. New York: Frederick A. Stokes, 1925.

Guillaume, Alfred. *Islam*. Harmondsworth: Penguin, 1977.

Habib, John S. *Ibn Sa'ud's Warriors of Islam: The Ikhwan of Najd and Their Role in the Creation of the Sa'udi Kingdom 1910–1930*. Social, Economic and Political Studies of the Middle East, XXVII. Leiden: Brill, 1978.

Halliday, Fred. *Arabia Without Sultans*. Harmondsworth: Penguin, 1975.

Hamui, Mamun al. *Diplomatic Terms: English/Arabic*. Beirut: Khayats, 1966.

Hansen, Thorkild. *Arabia Felix: The Danish Expedition of 1761–1767*. London: Collins, 1964.

Harrison, Paul W. *The Arab at Home*. London: Hutchinson, 1924.

Hawley, D. F. *Courtesies in the Trucial States*. Beirut: Khayats, 1965.

Heikal, M. *The·Road to Ramadan*. London: Collins, 1975.

—— *Sphinx and Commissar: The Rise and Fall of Soviet Influence in the Arab World*. London: Collins, 1978.

Helms, Christine Moss. *The Cohesion of Saudi Arabia*. London: Croom Helm, 1980.

Herzog, Chaim. *The War of Atonement*. London: Weidenfeld & Nicolson, 1975.

Hewins, Ralph. *A Golden Dream: The Miracle of Kuwait*. London: W. H. Allen, 1963.

Heyworth-Dunne, J. *Religious and Political Trends in Modern Egypt*. Washington, DC: published by the author, 1950.

Hindley, Geoffrey. *Saladin*. London: Constable, 1976.

Hirst, David. *The Gun and the Olive Branch*. London: Faber, 1977.

Hirszowicz, L. *The Third Reich and the Arab East*. London: Routledge, 1966.

Hobday, Peter. *Saudi Arabia Today*. London: Macmillan, 1978.

Hogarth, D. G. *The Penetration of Arabia*. New York: Frederick A. Stokes, 1904.

—— *Hejaz Before World War I (Handbook of Hejaz)*. Cambridge: Falcon/Oleander, reprint of 2nd ed. (1917), 1978.

Holden, David, *Farewell to Arabia*. London: Faber, 1966.

Hopwood, Derek (ed.). *The Arabian Peninsula: Society and Politics*. SOAS, Studies on Modern Asia and Africa, 8. London: Allen & Unwin, 1972.

Howard. H. N. *The Partition of Turkey: A Diplomatic History 1913–1923*. Norman, Okla.: University of Oklahoma Press, 1931.

—— *The King–Crane Commission*. Beirut: Khayats, 1963.

Howarth, David. *The Desert King: A Life of Ibn Saud*. London: Collins, 1964.

Howat, G. M. D., and Taylor, A. J. P. (eds). *Dictionary of World History*. London: Nelson, 1973.

Hull, Cordell. *Memoirs*. 2 vols. London: Hodder & Stoughton, 1948.

Hunt, Kenneth. 'The Middle East in the Global Strategic Context'. In Colin Legum (ed.), *Middle East Contemporary Survey (1976–1977)*. Vol. 1, 68–73. New York: Holmes & Meier, 1978.

Hurewitcz, J. C. (ed.). *Diplomacy in the Near and Middle East: A Documentary Record*. 2 vols. Princeton, NJ: 1956.

Hurgronje, C. Snouck. *Mekka in the Latter Part of the 19th Century*. Leiden: Brill, 1931.

Huxley, Julian. *From An Antique Land*. New York: Crown, 1954.

Ingrams, Doreen. *A Time in Arabia*. London: John Murray, 1970.

International Monetary Fund. *International Financial Statistics*, XXXIII: 12 (December 1980).

Igbal, S. M. *Emergence of Saudi Arabia: A Political Study of King Abd al-Aziz ibn Saud 1901–1953*. Kashmir: Saudiyah Publishers, 1977.

Islamic Council of Europe. *Jerusalem: The Key to World Peace*. London: 1980.
Istambuli, Mahmud Mahdi. *King Salahuddin Al Ayyubi*. Trans. M. Abdel El-Kalkili. Damascus: Islamic Civilization Society, n.d.
—— *Have You Asked about the Most Interesting Thing in the East?* Trans. M. Abdel El-Kalkili. Damascus: Islamic Civilization Society, n.d.
Jarvis, C. S. *Yesterday and Today in Sinai*. London: Blackwood, 1938.
Kalb, Marvin, and Kalb, Bernard. *Kissinger*. London: Hutchinson, 1974.
Katakura, Motoko. *Bedouin Village: A Study of Saudi Arabian People in Transition*. Tokyo: University of Tokyo Press, 1977.
Kedourie, E. *The Chatham House Version and Other Middle Eastern Studies*. London: Weidenfeld & Nicolson, 1970.
—— *In the Anglo-Arab Labyrinth: The McMahon–Husayn Correspondence and its Interpretations*. Cambridge: Cambridge University Press, 1976.
—— *Islam and the Modern World*. London: Mansell, 1980.
Kelly, J. B. *Eastern Arabian Frontiers*. London: Faber, 1964.
—— *Arabia, the Gulf and the West*. London: Weidenfeld & Nicolson, 1980.
Kerr, Malcolm H. *The Arab Cold War: Gamal Nasser and His Rivals 1958–1970*. London: Oxford University Press for the Royal Institute of International Affairs, 1971.
Khadduri, Majid. 'The Traditional (Idealistic) School: The Moderate King Faysal of Saudi Arabia'. In *Arab Contemporaries: The Role of Personalities in Politics*. Baltimore, Md, and London: Johns Hopkins University Press, 1973.
Kheirallah, George I. *Arabia Reborn*. Albuquerque, N. Mex.: University of New Mexico Press, 1952.
Killearn, M. L. *Diaries, 1934–1946: The Diplomatic and Personal Record*. Ed. T. E. Evan. London: Sidgwick, 1972.
Kim Linsu. *Motivation Survey in Saudi Arabia*. Seoul: Korea Development Institute, 1980.
Kirk, George. *The Middle East in the War*. Survey of International Affairs 1939–1946, Vol. 6. London: Oxford University Press for the Royal Institute of International Affairs, 1953.
Kissinger, Henry. *The White House Years*. London: Weidenfeld & Nicolson/Michael Joseph, 1978.
Knauerhase, Ramon. *The Saudi Arabian Economy*. New York: Praeger, 1977.
Knightley, Philip, and Simpson, Colin. *The Secret Lives of Lawrence of Arabia*. London: Panther, 1971.
Lackner, Helen. *A House Built on Sand: A Political Economy of Saudi Arabia*. London: Ithaca, 1978.
Laffin, John. *The Arab Mind*. London: Cassell, 1978.
Lawrence, T. E. *Seven Pillars of Wisdom*. London: Cape, 1935.
—— *Secret Despatches from Arabia*. London: Golden Cockerel Press, 1939.
Leatherdale, Clive. 'British Policy towards Saudi Arabia 1925–1939'. Unpublished thesis. University of Aberdeen, 1981.
Lebkicher, Roy, Rentz, George, and Steineke, Max. *The Arabia of Ibn Saud*. New York: Russell F. Moore, 1952.
Lees, Brian. *A Handbook of the Al Sa'ud Ruling Family of Sa'udi Arabia*. London: Royal Genealogies, 1980.

553

Legum, Colin (ed.). *Middle East Contemporary Survey (1976–1977)*. Vol. 1. New York: Holmes & Meier, 1978.

Lemu, B. Aisha, and Heeren, Fatima. *Woman in Islam*. Leicester: Islamic Foundation, Islamic Council of Europe, 1976 (1396 AH).

Levin, Z. I. 'Saudi Arabia'. In L. N. Vatolina and E. A. Beliaev (eds), *The Arabs in the Struggle for Independence*. Moscow: Academy of Sciences of the USSR, Politicheskoi Literatury, 1957.

Levy, Reuben. 'The Status of Women in Islam'. In *The Social Structure of Islam*, 91–134. Cambridge: Cambridge University Press, 1962.

Lewis, Bernard. *The Arabs in History*. London: Hutchinson, 1977.

Lilienthal, Alfred M. *The Zionist Connection: What Price Peace?* New York: Dodd, Mead, 1978.

Link, A. S. *Wilson: The Road to the White House*. Vol. 1. Princeton, NJ: Princeton University Press, 1947.

Lipsky, George A. *Saudi Arabia: Its People, its Society, its Culture*. New Haven, Conn.: Hraf Press, 1959.

Longrigg, S. H. *Oil in the Middle East: Its Discovery and Development*. London: Oxford University Press for the Royal Institute of International Affairs, 1968.

Luttwak, Edward. *Coup d'État: A Practical Handbook*. Rev. ed. London: Wildwood House, 1979.

McGregor, R. 'Saudi Arabia: Population and the Making of a Modern State'. In J. I. Clarke and W. B. Fisher (eds), *Populations of the Middle East and Near Africa: A Geographical Approach*. London: University of London Press, 1972.

Mandel, Neville, J. *The Arabs and Zionism Before World War I*. Berkeley, Calif.: University of California Press, 1976.

Mangold, Peter. *Superpower Intervention in the Middle East*. London: Croom Helm, 1978.

Mansfield, P. *The Ottoman Empire and its Successors*. London: Macmillan, 1973.

Masri, Abdullah H. *Saudi Arabian Antiquities*. Riyadh: Department of Antiquities and Museums, Ministry of Education, 1975.

Maududi, S. Abdula'la. *The Prophet of Islam*. Karachi: Islamic Research Academy, 1970.

—— *Purdah and the Status of Woman in Islam*. Lahore: Islamic Publications, 1972.

—— *Towards Understanding Islam*. 14th ed. Lahore: Islamic Publications, 1973.

Meulen, D. van der. *Faces in Shem*. London: John Murray, 1961.

Miller, Aaron D. *Search for Security: Saudi Arabian Oil and American Foreign Policy 1939–1949*. Chapel Hill, NC: University of North Carolina Press, 1980.

Monroe, Elizabeth. *Britain's Moment in the Middle East 1914–56*. London: Chatto, 1963.

—— *Philby of Arabia*. London: Faber, 1974.

Morison, David. 'The Soviet Bloc and the Middle East' and 'Inter-Arab Relations'. In Colin Legum (ed.), *Middle East Contemporary Survey (1976–1977)*. Vol. 1, 33–8, 158–60. New York: Holmes & Meier, 1978.

Morris, James. *The Hashemite Kings*. London: Faber, 1959.

Mosley, Leonard. *Power Play: Oil in the Middle East*. New York: Random House, 1973.

Mousa, S. *T. E. Lawrence: An Arab View*. London: Oxford University Press, 1966.

554

Musil, Alois. *Northern Nejd*. Oriental Exploration and Studies, No. 5. New York: American Geographical Society, 1927.
—— *Arabia Deserta*. Oriental Exploration and Studies, No. 2. New York: American Geographical Society, 1927.
Nadawi, Aliama Syed Sulaiman. *Heroic Deeds of Muslim Women*. Lahore: Sh. Muhammad Ashraf, 1976.
Nakhleh, Emile A. *The United States and Saudi Arabia: A Policy Analysis*. Foreign Affairs Studies, 26. Washington, DC: American Enterprise Institute for Public Policy Research, 1975.
Nelson, Cynthia (ed.). *The Desert and the Sown: Nomads in the Wider Society*. Institute of International Studies Research Series, 21. Berkeley, Calif: Institute of International Studies, University of California, 1973.
Niebuhr, M. *Travels Through Arabia and Other Countries in the East*. 2 vols. Beirut: Librairie du Liban, Repr. 1st ed., 1792.
Nieuwenhuijze, C. A. O. 'A Category Aside: Woman'. In *Sociology of the Middle East*. Leiden: Brill, 1971, pp. 649–57.
Nixon, Richard M. *The Memoirs of Richard Nixon*. London: Sidgwick & Jackson, 1978.
Nutting, Anthony. *The Arabs*. New York: Mentor Books, 1965.
—— *Nasser*. London: Constable, 1972.
Nyrop, Richard F., *et al. Area Handbook for Saudi Arabia*. 3rd ed. Washington, DC: GPO, 1977.
Palgrave, William G. *Personal Narrative of a Year's Journey through Central and Eastern Arabia 1862–1863*. London: Macmillan, 1868.
Patai, Raphael. *The Arab Mind*. New York: Scribner's, 1976.
Peck, Malcolm. 'Saudi Arabia in United States Foreign Policy to 1958: A Study in the Sources and Determinants of American Policy'. Unpublished dissertation, 1970.
Pederson, C. F. *The International Flag Book in Colour*: London: Blandford Press, 1971.
Pelly, Lewis. *Report on a Journey to Riyadh (1865)*. 1866. Introduction by R. L. Bidwell. Repr. Cambridge: Oleander/Falcon, 1978.
Pendleton, Madge, *et al. The Green Book: Guide for Living in Saudi Arabia*. 2nd ed. Washington, DC: Middle East Editorial Associates, 1978.
Philby, H. St J. B. *Report on the Najd Mission 1917–1918*. Baghdad: Government Press, 1918.
—— *The Heart of Arabia: A Record of Travel*. 2 vols. London: 1922.
—— *Arabia of the Wahhabis*. London: Constable, 1928.
—— *Arabian Days: An Autobiography*. London: Robert Hale, 1948.
—— *Arabian Jubilee*. London: Robert Hale, 1952.
—— *Sa'udi Arabia*. 1955. Repr. New York: Arno Press, 1972.
—— *Forty Years in the Wilderness*. London: Robert Hale, 1957.
—— *Arabian Oil Ventures*. Washington, DC: Middle East Institute, 1964.
Philby, Kim. *My Silent War*. London: MacGibbon & Kee, 1968.
Polk, William R. *The United States and the Arab World*. Cambridge, Mass: Harvard University Press, 1965.
Polk, William R., and Mares, William A. *Passing Brave*. New York: Knopf, 1973.

Raban, Jonathan. *Arabia Through the Looking Glass*. London: Collins, 1979.

Rashid, Ibrahim al (ed.). *Documents on the History of Saudi Arabia*. 3 vols.
   Vol. 1: *The Unification of Central Arabia Under Ibn Saud 1909–1925*.
   Vol. 2: *The Consolidation of Power in Central Arabia Under Ibn Saud 1925–1928*.
   Vol. 3: *Establishment of the Kingdom of Saudi Arabia Under Ibn Saud 1928–35*.
   Salisbury, NC: Documentary Publications, 1976.

—— *Saudi Arabia Enters the Modern World: Secret US Documents on the Emergence of the Kingdom of Saudi Arabia as a World Power 1936–1949*. 2 vols. Salisbury, NC: Documentary Publications, 1980.

Raswan, Carl S. *The Black Tents of Arabia*. London: Hutchinson, 1935.

Raunkiaer, Barclay. *Through Wahhabiland on Camelback*. Introduction by Gerald de Gaury. London: Routledge, 1969.

Rendel, Sir G. W. *The Sword and the Olive: Recollections of Foreign Diplomacy 1913–1954*. London: John Murray, 1957.

Rentz, George. 'Saudi Arabia'. In J. J. Thompson and R. C. Reischauer (eds), *Modernization of the Arab World*, 115–25. Princeton, NJ: Van Nostrand, 1966.

—— 'The Wahhabis'. In A. J. Arberry (ed.), *Religion in the Middle East: Three Religions in Concord and Conflict: Islam*. Vol. 2, 270–84. Cambridge: Cambridge University Press, 1969.

Rihani, A. *Ibn Sa'oud of Arabia*. London: Constable, 1928.

Rodinson, Maxime. *Islam and Capitalism*. Harmondsworth: Penguin, 1977.

—— *Mohammed*. Harmondsworth: Penguin, 1977.

Ronaldshay, Earl of. *The Life of Lord Curzon*, 3 vols. London: Benn, 1923.

Rubinstein, Alvin Z. *Red Star on the Nile*. Princeton, NJ: Princeton University Press, 1977.

Rugh, William A. *Riyadh: A History and Guide*. Published by the author, 1969.

Rutter, Eldon. *Holy Cities of Arabia*. 2 vols. London: Putnam, 1928.

Rutter, Owen. *Triumphant Pilgrimage*. London: Harrap, 1937.

Ryan, Andrew. *The Last of the Dragomans*. London: Bles, 1951.

Sadat, Anwar. *In Search of Identity: An Autobiography*. London: Fontana/Collins, 1978.

Sadleir, G. F. *Diary of a Journey Across Arabia (1819)*. 1866. Introduction by F. M. Edwards. Repr. Cambridge: Falcon/Oleander, 1977.

Sampson, Anthony, *The Seven Sisters*. New York: Viking, 1975.

—— *The Arms Bazaar*, London: Coronet/Hodder & Stoughton, 1978.

Sanger, Richard H. *The Arabian Peninsula*. New York: Books for Libraries, 1970.

Savory, R. M. (ed.). *Introduction to Islamic Civilization*. Cambridge: Cambridge University Press, 1976.

Schacht, Joseph, with Bosworth, C. E. *The Legacy of Islam*. 2nd ed. Oxford: Clarendon Press, 1974.

Schieffelin, Olivia (ed.). *Muslim Attitudes Towards Family Planning*. New York: Population Council, 1967.

Schmidt, Dana Adams. *Yemen: The Unknown War*. London: Bodley Head, 1968.

Seymour, Ian. *OPEC: Instrument of Change*. London: Macmillan, 1980.

Shadid, Irfan. 'Pre-Islamic Arabia'. In P. M. Holt, Ann K. S. Lambton and Bernard Lewis (eds), *The Cambridge History of Islam*. Vol. 1: *The Central Islamic Lands*, 3–29. Cambridge: Cambridge University Press, 1970.

556

Shahine, Dr Y. A. *The Arab Contribution to Medicine*. London: Longman, for the University of Essex, 1976.

Shaked, Haim, and Yegnes, Tamar. 'The Saudi Arabian Kingdom'. In Colin Legum (ed.), *Middle East Contemporary Survey (1976–1977)*. Vol. 1, 564–85. New York: Holmes & Meier, 1978.

Sheean, Vincent, *Faisal: The King and His Kingdom*. Tavistock: University Press of Arabia, 1975.

Sheehan, Edward R. F. *The Arabs, Israelis and Kissinger: A Secret History of American Diplomacy in the Middle East*. New York: Reader's Digest Press, 1976.

Sidiqui, Abdul Hameed. *The Life of Muhammad*. Lahore: 1969.

Simon, Lady Kathleen. *Slavery*. London: Hodder & Stoughton, 1929.

Smiley, David. *Arabian Assignment*. London: Lee Cooper, 1975.

Smith, Gary V. *Zionism: The Dream and the Reality: A Jewish Critique*. Newton Abbot: David & Charles, 1974.

Soulie, G. J. L., and Champenois, Lucien. *Le Royaume d'Arabie Séoudite face à l'Islam révolutionnaire 1953–1964*. Paris: Armand Colin, 1966.

Spitta Bey, Wilhelm. *Contes arabes modernes*. Leiden: Brill, 1883.

Stacey, T. C. G., *et al. The Kingdom of Saudi Arabia*. 3rd ed. London: Stacey International, 1978.

Stebbins, Richard P., and Adam, Elaine P. (eds). *American Foreign Relations 1974: A Documentary Record*. New York: New York University Press, 1977.

Stegner, Wallace. *Discovery: The Search for Arabian Oil*. Beirut: Middle East Export Press, 1971.

Stevens, J. H., and King, R. *A Bibliography of Saudi Arabia*. Occasional Papers Series, 3. Durham: University of Durham, Centre for Middle Eastern and Islamic Studies, 1973.

Storrs, Sir Ronald. *Orientations*. London: Readers Union, 1939.

Sunday Times Insight Team. *The Yom Kippur War*. London: Deutsch, 1975.

Szyliowicz, Joseph, and O'Neill, Bard E. *The Energy Crisis and US Foreign Policy*. New York: Praeger, 1975.

Tahtinen, Dale R. *National Security Challenges to Saudi Arabia*. Studies in Defense Policy. Washington: American Enterprise Institute for Public Policy Research, January 1979.

Thesiger, Wilfred. *Arabian Sands*. London: Readers Union/Longmans, 1960.

—— *The Marsh Arabs*. Harmondsworth: Penguin, 1978.

—— *Desert, Marsh and Mountain: The World of a Nomad*. London: Collins, 1979.

Thomas, Bertram. *Arabia Felix: Across the Empty Quarter of Arabia*. Foreword by T. E. Lawrence. London: Readers Union/Cape, 1938.

Toynbee, Arnold J. *The Islamic World Since the Peace Settlement*. Survey of International Affairs, 1925, Vol. 1. Oxford: Oxford University Press for the Royal Institute of International Affairs, 1927.

Tritton, A. S. *Islam: Belief and Practices*. London; Hutchinson University Library, 1951.

Troeller, Gary. *The Birth of Sa'udi Arabia: Britain and the Rise of the House of Sa'ud*. London: Frank Cass, 1976.

Truman, Harry S. *Memoirs: Years of Trial and Hope 1946–1953*. London: Hodder & Stoughton, 1956.

557

Twitchell, K. S. *Saudi Arabia: With An Account of the Development of Its Natural Resources*. 3rd ed. New York: Greenwood Press, 1958.

United Nations. *Statistical Year Book 1978*. New York: United Nations, 1979.

Vital, David. *The Origins of Zionism*. London: Oxford University Press, 1975.

Waddy, Charis. *Women in Muslim History*. London: Longman, 1980.

Wahba, Hafiz. *Arabian Days*. London: Arthur Barker, 1964.

Weir, Shelagh. *The Bedouin: Aspects of the Material Culture of the Bedouin of Jordan*. Museum of Mankind, Ethnography Department of the British Museum. London: World of Islam Festival, 1976.

Wenner, M. W. 'Saudi Arabia: Survival of Traditional Elites'. In Frank Tachau (ed.), *Political Elites and Political Development in the Middle East*, 157–92. Cambridge, Mass.: Schenkman, 1975.

Who's Who in Saudi Arabia 1978–1979. Foreword by HRH Prince Saud bin Fahad. London: Europa Publications, 1978.

Wightman, G. B. H., and Udhari, A. Y. (trans.). *Birds Through a Ceiling of Alabaster: Three Abbasid Poets*. Harmondsworth: Penguin, 1975.

Wilson, Lt-Col. Sir Arnold T. *Loyalities: Mesopotamia 1914–1917: A Personal and Historical Record*. Oxford: Oxford University Press, 1930.

—— *A Clash of Loyalties: Mesopotamia 1917–1920: A Personal and Historical Record*. Oxford: Oxford University Press, 1931.

—— *South West Persia: A Political Officer's Diary 1907–1914*. Oxford: Oxford University Press, 1941.

Winder, R. Bayly. *Saudi Arabia in the Nineteenth Century*. New York: St Martin's, 1965.

Winstone, H. V. F. *Captain Shakespear*. London: Quartet, 1978.

—— *Gertrude Bell*. London: Cape, 1979.

Winstone, H. V. F., and Freeth, Zahra. *Kuwait: Prospect and Reality*. London: Allen & Unwin, 1972.

Zahlan, R. S. *The Origins of the United Arab Emirates: A Political and Social History of the Trucial States*. London: Macmillan, 1978.

Zeine, M. Zeine. *Arab Turkish Relations and the Emergence of Arab Nationalism*. Beirut: Khayats, 1958.

Zirikly, Khair al Din. *Shibh al Jazirah fi Ahd al Malik Abdul Aziz. (Arabia Under Abdul Aziz.)* 4 vols. Beirut: Dar al Galum, 1970.

Zwemer, Samuel M. *Arabia: The Cradle of Islam*. Edinburgh: Oliphant Anderson & Ferrier, 1900.

—— *Childhood in the Moslem World*. New York: Fleming H. Revell, 1915.

Source Notes

Abbreviations used

FCO	Foreign and Commonwealth Office Library
FO	Foreign Office
FRUS	Foreign Relations of the United States
FSI	Secretary to the Government of India in the Foreign Department
GGI	Governor-General of India
GI	Government of India
IO	India Office
IOR	India Office Library and Records
PA	Political Agent
PR	Political Resident in the Persian Gulf
PRO	Public Record Office
SAC/MEC	St Antony's College, Oxford, Middle East Centre: Private Papers Collection
S of S	United States Secretary of State
SSC	Secretary of State for the Colonies
SSFA	Secretary of State for Foreign Affairs
SSI	Secretary of State for India
US/DS	United States of America, Department of State
US/NA	United States of America, National Archives and Records Service

The boyhood of Abdul Aziz and the early history of the Al Sa'ud

The basis for accounts of Abdul Aziz's earliest· years is largely reminiscence and anecdote. No detailed contemporary documentary evidence of his life before 1901 is known to exist, although reports on the exile and activities of the Al Sa'ud reached British representatives in the Persian Gulf in these years. These do not contradict the story as Abdul Aziz used to relate it.

H. St John Philby listed two primary chronicles on the early history of the Al Sa'ud:

1   *Iqd al Durur (String of Pearls)* by Ibrahim ibn Salih ibn Isa; this was the basis for a later work by Abdul Rahman ibn Nasir entitled *Unwan al Sa'ad Wa al Majd (Fortune and Glory)*; and Philby thought that Ibn Isa was also probably the source used by the chronicles of Sa'ud ibn Hidhlul al Thunayan al Sa'ud (on the early history of his family) and of Mutlaq ibn Salih, in his account *Shadha al Nadd (A Chip of Incense)*.

2   The other primary chronicle is *Al Nubdha Tarikhiya al Najd (A Historical Sketch of Nejd)*, which was written by the Emir Dhari ibn Rasheed and dated AD 1913.

These chronicles, plus other first-hand reminiscences, especially Yussuf Yassin's accounts of Abdul Aziz's own stories of his youth, form the basis of the encyclopedic four-volume *Shibh al Jazirah fi Ahd al Malik Abdul Aziz (Arabia Under Abdul Aziz)* by Khair al Din al Zirikly, published in 1970. This is the fullest work available on Abdul Aziz in any language, but Zirikly was a Sa'udi Foreign Office official, and he cannot be called critical.

My own Arabic is, unfortunately, far from capable of mastering the original version of this or other Arabic sources, and so I am grateful to Sheikh Muhammad Anwar Ahmad of Taif for his work in translating and interpreting this material for me.

Hafiz Wahba, a long-standing friend of Abdul Aziz and the first ambassador from Sa'udi Arabia to the Court of St James's, included much original material in his work in English, *Arabian Days*.

The most authoritative Western historian of these early years is undoubtedly Harry St John Philby. His Arabic enabled him to locate and consult the various local sources, and his close friendship with Abdul Aziz and residence in Sa'udi Arabia for over a quarter of a century from the mid-1920s enabled him to gather a collection of anecdotes and reminiscences that make his work unique – though his account of later events grew critical as he became disenchanted with the effect that money and Western influence had upon the Al Sa'ud.

I have consulted Philby's voluminous private papers at St Antony's College, Oxford, his various autobiographical memoirs, and especially his history books, *Arabian Jubilee*, an account of Abdul Aziz's reign published in 1952, and his subsequent *Sa'udi Arabia* (1955), in which he amended his earlier work in the light of researches by George Rentz and R. Bayly Winder, with whom he was in close contact.

These American scholars concentrated on the earlier years of the Sa'udi dynasty, and Bayly Winder's *Saudi Arabia in the Nineteenth Century* contains a good account of the relations between the Al Sa'ud and Ibn Rasheed in the 1880s, and the departure of Abdul Rahman and his family from Riyadh. Winder, like everyone else, had to rely on the family's own account of their past, but this did not prevent his presenting a fair and favourable picture of Ibn Rasheed.

Dr George Rentz's *Muhammad ibn Abd al-Wahhab (1703/4–1792) and the Beginnings of the Unitarian Empire in Arabia* (Berkeley, Calif.: University of California, 1948) is the definitive interpretation of the evidence on which Philby's more easily available work is based.

In June 1933 Captain H. C. Armstrong came to Jeddah, had a meeting with Abdul Aziz and then spent four two-hour sessions interviewing the king about his boyhood, youth and rise to power. This first-hand material formed the basis for his *Lord of Arabia*, a flamboyant work whose colourful style is far from the sober traditions of western historiography. Many Sa'udi Arabians, however, today regard it as the best book on Abdul Aziz written by a Westerner because of its interpretation of Islam and Arabian culture, and, where its facts can be checked, they coincide with all available evidence.

Western Arabists, however, do not view Armstrong with much favour. They prefer the anecdotes gathered by Lt-Col. H. R. P. Dickson, Political Agent in Kuwait (see Bibliography). His books are, indeed, bran tubs stuffed with good first-hand material, and hard burrowing can extract original insights into the early years.

560

Dickson was, after Philby, the first of a series of British representatives to use their meetings with Abdul Aziz as opportunities to record the king's reminiscences. Colonel (then Captain) Gerald de Gaury visited Abdul Aziz in 1934 and several times thereafter, and incorporated his own impressions and Abdul Aziz's stories into his books (see Bibliography). Sir John Glubb ('Glubb Pasha') met and talked with Abdul Aziz as early as 1928, and he also recorded some of the king's stories (see Bibliography).

Both these authorities were kind enough to talk to me at some length, and from these interviews came small amounts of previously unpublished material. I also interviewed Sir Shuldam Redfern, who came across from Sudan to meet Abdul Aziz in 1935, as well as Sir George Rendel, head of the Foreign Office Middle-Eastern Desk in the early 1930s, who visited Abdul Aziz in 1937.

HRH Princess Alice, Countess of Athlone, was kind enough to make available to me her private letters and diary of her visit with her husband to Sa'udi Arabia in 1938, in the course of which Abdul Aziz regaled the couple with tales of his youth.

Most usefully of all, I have been able to talk to a number of Abdul Aziz's sons who devoted long hours to retelling me the tales their father told them of his early years, and I hope this has added both detail and insight to my account.

I must, however, repeat the warning made in the text that almost all this material derives basically from the vivid memory of Abdul Aziz himself and from those close to him, and as such it was inevitably coloured by subsequent events, influences and motives. I have tried to correlate and cross-check these reminiscences as much as possible, but the reader should remember that we are dealing with a man who created, and became, a legend in his own lifetime, and that legends are not always too nice over mundane details. Nor should they be.

The birthdate of Abdul Aziz

November/December 1880 is the date commonly accepted for the birth of Abdul Aziz. But no record was kept at the time and this is only one estimate in a range of datings, varying from 1867 (Musil) to 1882 (Hamza).

This author favours 1876, and I am grateful to Dr Abdullah al Uthaimeen, Dean of the History Faculty in the College of Arts at Riyadh University, for drawing my attention to the inconsistencies which an 1880 birthdate creates when compared to the known facts of Abdul Aziz's life. A well-attested story, for example, describes the young Abdul Aziz accompanying a group of Sa'udi negotiators who met Ibn Rasheed in 1889. A nine-year-old boy would scarcely have accompanied such a party. A thirteen- or fourteen-year-old might have been taken along.

By this reckoning Abdul Aziz was fourteen or fifteen when he lived among the Murrah; twenty-five or twenty-six when he recaptured Riyadh; fifty-two, not forty-eight, when Glubb met him in 1928 and described him as 'the old king'; and aged seventy-seven or seventy-eight when he died in 1953.

Shortly before this book went to press, the author discussed this question with one of the sons of Abdul Aziz.

'My father always used to laugh at the official 1880 date,' he said. 'He used to say, "I swallowed four years of my age." '

For details of all books and articles cited, see Bibliography, p. 539.

Welcome to the Kingdom

p. 5   *on US Stock Exchanges . . . Tiffany's*: the total value of the three US Stock Markets at the end of 1980 was $1,448,654,619,740; the Stock Market capitalization of General Motors and Bankamerica was $13.295 billion and $3.895 billion respectively in February 1981; a price of $840 million for all the US football teams assumes an average asking price of $30 million per team; Avon Products Inc. was reported to have acquired Tiffany's for $104.2 million in 1979.

Chapter 1   Bedouin

The coffee ritual and certain other aspects of bedouin life described in this chapter are based on personal experience. So far as one can tell from accounts written in the last century (Burckhardt, Doughty, Palgrave, Pelly), the details have changed little in the last hundred years.

In April 1968 Donald Cole, a graduate anthropology student of the University of California at Berkeley, went to live among the Murrah for two years, and his account, *Nomads of the Nomads*, has been most helpful.

Lt-Col. H. R. P. Dickson, British agent in Kuwait 1929–36 and also in 1941, spent much time wandering among the bedouin of eastern Arabia and also listening to Abdul Aziz's reminiscences and tales of Murrah prowess. He gathered his data into his encyclopedic *The Arab of the Desert*, and there is also useful material in his private papers at St Antony's College, Oxford.

Colonel Gerald de Gaury, Dickson's successor in Kuwait, 1936–9, who was also a personal guest of Abdul Aziz on several occasions – noting, for example, his extensive use of Murrah phrases – was the first to describe to me the uncanny tracking skills of East Arabian bedouin. His *Arabia Phoenix* contains a detailed account of the coffee-making ritual in Nejd.

Lt-Gen. Sir John Glubb ('Glubb Pasha') recounted to me some of his personal experiences of being raided on the north-east frontiers of Arabia, and also of bedouin tracking techniques.

Dr Paul Harrison, an American missionary working on the Persian Gulf in the early years of this century, collected many valuable insights in his book *The Arab at Home*.

Hafiz Wahba, Abdul Aziz's long-standing Egyptian friend and envoy to the Court of St James's in London, compiled a collection of his master's stories in *Arabian Days*, which also illustrates nicely the mixture of admiration and disdain with which the sophisticated town-bred Arab views the bedouin.

Above all, the writings of T. E. Lawrence and Wilfred Thesiger itch with the texture of desert life as it appeals to the romantic Westerner, distilling the spirit and displaying all the detail of their months living among Arabs. Neither man lived with the bedouin in circumstances that could be really called typical, but their books are classics.

p. 25   *wisdom, his common sense*: Rodinson, *Mohammed*, p. 44.

bedouin to be hardened: de Gaury, personal interview, Brighton, September 1979.

studded with Murrah phraseology: ibid.

p. 27 *part of the game:* Glubb, personal interview, Mayfield, Sussex, March 1979.

p. 28 *unique beast, the camel:* Sweet, p. 1132.

They are its parasites: All the great travellers in Arabia, especially Lawrence and Thesiger, have addressed themselves to the extraordinary physiology – and psychology – of the camel. As a scientist of the desert, Uwe George presents an intriguing analysis of the camel as machine in his book *In the Deserts of This Earth.* Donald Cole actually worked as a camel herder among the Murrah preparing his *Nomads of the Nomads*, while another anthropologist, Louise E. Sweet, surveyed much of the published material and conducted her own interviews in preparing her 'Camel Raiding of North Arabian Bedouin: A Mechanism of Ecological Adaptation'. The analysis of the *ghazzu* given here draws heavily on this most original and thought-provoking article.

The definitive and elegant book-of-books on the beast is *The Camel and the Wheel* by Richard W. Bulliet, an Associate History Professor at Columbia University, whose fascination with the creature has extended to writing a murder mystery, *Kicked to Death by a Camel.*

it as a purgative: Dickson, *The Arab of the Desert*, p. 159.

dates and unleavened bread: Dowson, p. 33.

p. 29 *'it has no taste'*: Lawrence, *Seven Pillars*, p. 38.

Chapter 2 Exile

The few known facts about Abdul Aziz's life in Kuwait are contained in Zirikly, Wahba, Philby and Armstrong.

For Kuwait itself and Mubarak, the sources are much richer. Colonel Dickson's two books and his wife Violet's memoir *Forty Years in Kuwait* contain valuable first-hand material. However, Dickson's description of the town is based to a surprising extent on the *Gazetteer* which J. G. Lorimer compiled following his visit there in 1904. This was originally a secret briefing document prepared and published by the Government of India in 1908, and it provides the most comprehensive and accurate guide to the entire Gulf area at the beginning of the twentieth century.

Barclay Raunkiaer, a Danish geographer, was only twenty-three when he set off to Arabia in 1912 to smooth the way for an expedition which he hoped to lead into the Rub al Khali. Unfortunately he succumbed to tuberculosis, dying soon after his return to Copenhagen, but not before he had compiled a vivid description of all he saw and met – including Kuwait and its sheikh, Mubarak. Thanks to Gerald de Gaury we have a modern English edition of Raunkiaer's *Through Wahhabiland on Camelback*, and this little-known classic of travel literature is warmly recommended as a fresh and vivid first-hand account of Arabia seventy years ago.

My sources for the paragraphs on marriage and Islam were the Koran, which I consulted in the translations of N. J. Dawood and Abdullah Yussuf Ali, with the commentaries by Rodinson and Guillaume, and the careful comments on my manuscript of several Muslim friends.

Zwemer's and Harrison's works contain interesting first-hand material on Arab social practices in the first decades of this century, but one must bear in mind that they were written from the viewpoint of Christian missionaries struggling vainly in the Islamic world.

Richard T. Antoun's article 'On the Modesty of Women in Arab Muslim Villages' is an interesting piece of modern anthropological fieldwork.

p. 31 *Abdul Aziz and the Virgin Bride:* This was the first story about Abdul Aziz told to the author by any member of the Al Sa'ud, and it was repeated frequently with variations.

token of her chastity: Dickson, *The Arab of the Desert*, p. 205.

p. 32 *feet on her feet':* ibid., p. 163.

coitus is considered risqué': Cole. p. 79.

and how you will': Koran, II. 23.

or three or four': ibid., IV. 3.

then take only one': ibid.

p. 33 *is your ardent desire':* ibid., IV. 129.

once in any night: Philby, *Forty Years*, p. 190.

your right hands possess': Koran, IV. 3. See also Koran, IV. 24, on the annulment of captive women's marriage ties.

put up the cash: Armstrong, p. 16. Van der Meulen, p. 44, tells the same story without the merchant.

oil and human excreta: Lorimer, Vol. 2, p. 1051.

shore by rickety bridges: Raunkiaer, p. 43.

p. 34 *British Agency in 1904:* Violet Dickson, p. 17.

a patch of green': Dickson, *Kuwait*, p. 145.

near the Burqan hill': Lorimer, Vol. 2, p. 1066.

It sold kerosene oil: Harrison, p. 86.

a diminutive of that: Lorimer, Vol. 2, p. 1048.

p. 35 *sea by Allah's grace?':* Koran, XXXI, 31.

flying at the stern': Harrison, p. 71.

the captain's careful eye: ibid.

pearl merchants every summer: Lorimer, Vol. 2, p. 1053.

p. 36 *and high felt hats:* Raunkiaer, p. 46.

with mysterious sky signs: Lorimer, Vol. 2, p. 1051.

taste for fresh fish: de Gaury, personal interview, Brighton, October 1978.

Riyadh just like that: Armstrong, p. 18.

to the older man: IOR: R/15/5/25: draft letter, Shakespear to Political Residency, 9 March 1910. I am grateful to Victor Winstone for the information that Muburak and Abdul Aziz referred to each other as 'father' and 'son' (letter to author of 16 June 1980).

p. 37 *yet unquenched within him':* Lovat Fraser, cited in Winstone, *Shakespear*, p. 79.

I awoke, I knew': Asad, p. 171.

p. 38 *Abdul Aziz stayed at home:* Ahmad bin Abdul Aziz, personal interview, Taif, July 1979.

together somewhere more private: Jamal Bey Husaini, personal interview, Riyadh, November 1980.

Chapter 3 The Great Adventure

p. 39 *to relieve the monotony:* anon., 'My Friend the Sheikh', *Blackwood's Magazine*, 212 (July 1922), pp. 34–48. I am grateful to Jacqueline

Williams for discovering this original and personal account of the British intervention in Kuwait of 1901. The article was written by Admiral Sir Edmund Radcliffe Pears, KBE, RN (1862–1941), who was in command of HMS *Perseus* in September 1901. Admiral Pears retired in 1920 and became Nautical Assessor at the House of Lords.

was in the wind': ibid. This gathering is also described in IOR: R/15/1/474: Report by Captain G. M. Field, RN, 23 September 1901.

p. 40 *talk so much before':* 'My Friend the Sheikh'.

pictures from the Bible': ibid.

the messenger of God': IOR: R/15/5/27: *Bahrain News*, week ending 14 June 1913.

p. 41 *Gulf coast at Kuwait:* PRO: FO406/15: encl. in No. 48, 21 July 1900, Mr Lyle's visit to Kuwait.

Turkish authorities in Baghdad: IOR: R/15/1/474: Report by Captain G. M. Field, RN, 23 September 1901. Ibn Rasheed left Mubarak's territory on or around 28 September 1901.

in late September 1901: IOR: R15/1/474. This file from the archives of the Political Residency at Bushire contains interesting notes on the movements of Abdul Aziz in the months preceding his capture of Riyadh. These reports were compiled by the News Agent at Kuwait. He was a Persian in the pay of the Political Resident at Bushire in the years preceding the appointment of Major Knox as Political Agent in 1904.

p. 42 *derived from* jaluwa, *exile:* Winder, p. 52.

Majma'a north of Riyadh: IOR: R/15/1/474: News Agent, Kuwait, 19 October 1901.

p. 43 *back on the 15th:* IOR: R/15/1/474: News Agent, Kuwait, 11 November 1901.

p. 44 *took the safe option:* Armstrong, p. 27.

in November AD 1901: al Zirikly lists the names of sixty-seven men who rode with Abdul Aziz, but warns that some of the less detailed names may duplicate each other.

God willing, in Riyadh': ibid.

long periods without water: Bulliet, p. 31.

p. 46 *5 m.p.h. is really speedy:* Rihani, p. 122.

Eed al Fitr celebration: Philby, *Arabian Jubilee*, p. 10, and Armstrong, p. 30.

up on the plateau: Philby, ibid., p. 11.

of drama and gesticulation: Bullard, p. 208.

p. 47 *being of historical interest':* FRUS 1950 (Vol. V), p. 1147: 611.85A/3-2350, 'Memorandum of conversations, secret, Jidda, March 23 1950'. The ambassador was J. R. Childs.

to need repetition here': Philby, *Sa'udi Arabia*, p. 239.

could not follow properly: Bullard, p. 196.

p. 48 *felt like a change':* off-the-record interview. It is interesting that the records of the India Office contain a report from the Assistant Political Agent, Bahrain, received July 1902, which largely corroborates the traditional account of the Great Adventure as handed down over the years. See IOR L/P&S/20/C239; Précis of Kuwait Affairs, pp. 60, 61.

Riyadh in al Oud: also spelt al'Aud. Philby, op. cit., p. 11.

as a ladder: Armstrong, p. 30.

p. 49 *candle with one hand:* ibid., p. 32.

p. 51 *and then murder him:* Howarth, p. 22.

front of the house: Armstrong, p. 34.

back of his neck': Dickson, *Kuwait*, p. 139. Present author's punctuation and translation.

in the leg: Ahmad bin Abdul Aziz, personal interview, Taif, July 1979.

p. 52 *gate' and kill him:* Dickson, *Kuwait*, p. 139.

own lips in 1937: Bullard, p. 208.

Chapter 4 No god but God

Lt-Col. Lewis Pelly (1825–95) travelled from Riyadh on behalf of the Bombay Government, who were worried at the threat posed by the house of Sa'ud to Britain's allies in the Gulf, especially Bahrain and Oman.

p. 55 *of its recorded history:* The first European known to have visited Riyadh and/or Dar'iyah was John Lewis Reinaud, assistant to the British Resident at Basra, Mr Manesty. The Wahhabis had been attacking the Gulf coast and had cut off some of the caravans that the East India Company used to transport mail across Arabia, and Manesty sent Reinaud, probably in 1799, to talk to Abdul Aziz ibn Muhammad ibn Sa'ud, ruler of Dar'iyah (and son of the first Ibn Sa'ud). His report has not survived, but a letter briefly describing Dar'iyah was published in von Zach's *Monatliche Corresp.* (Gotha) for September 1805, p. 234, XXII, and is translated in Raunkiaer, p. 8.

The French engineer who accompanied Ibrahim Pasha to Dar'iyah in 1819 may be presumed to be the second European visitor to central Nejd, and there may have been other European mercenaries in the Turkish/Egyptian army. But no written European eye-witness accounts of this expedition are known to exist.

Captain G. Forster Sadlier (1789–1859) became the first European known to have crossed Arabia when, in 1819, he set out from the Gulf coast to negotiate with Ibrahim Pasha on behalf of the Bombay Government, only to arrive at Dar'iyah and find him gone. So Sadlier, whose name has been posthumously spelt 'Sadleir', pursued the Pasha to the Red Sea coast, describing Riyadh and Dar'iyah in the course of the diary he kept on his journey.

Some authorities would dispute William Gifford Palgrave's claim to be the fourth European visitor to the Wadi Hanifah. Philby convinced himself that Palgrave was a charlatan who never got beyond Hail (see his *Heart of Arabia*, Vol. 2, pp. 120–56), and Palgrave certainly had a penchant for exaggeration. The Al Sa'ud's palace, for example, cannot have been even two-thirds the size of the Tuileries, as he said it was. His concept of the truth was an Arabian one, a good tale for him being, as Hogarth wrote, 'a work of art not to be spoiled in the telling for lack of a little embroidery'.

The 1865 journal of Lt-Col. Lewis Pelly, the fifth known, and first visitor officially invited by the Al Sa'ud to Riyadh, confirms Palgrave's account at many points and even seems to allude to Palgrave's previous presence at one juncture (p. 47).

After Pelly no Europeans are known to have visited Riyadh for nearly half a century, Barclay Raunkiaer (March 1912) just beating Leachman (December 1912), Shakespear (1914) and Philby (1917).

strictly banned within them: Pelly, p. 45.

food, tobacco, soft clothes': Armstrong, p. 2.

prayer mats to kneel on: Palgrave, p. 208.

p. 56 *The Tale of the Teacher:* It is thought that Muhammad ibn Abdul Wahhab was particularly influenced by the teachings of the Syrian Hanbali, Taqi al Din ibn Taimiyah, in the thirteenth century AD (seventh century AH).

p. 57 *miles north of Riyadh:* Philby, *Sa'udi Arabia*, p. 39.

p. 59 *'co-founder' of Sa'udi Arabia:* Philby, *Sa'udi Arabia*, pp. 33–59.

p. 60 *The Tale of the Apple and the Carpet:* SAC/MEC: Dickson Papers, Box IIA, File 5: 'History of the House of Ibn Saud including the rise, decline and recent revival of Wahabism (Akhwan) in Arabia'. Report written by Dickson in February 1920.

p. 61 *attack the mud walls:* Sadleir, p. 79.

pair that he received: G. F. Sadleir, 'Account of a Journey from Qatif to Yamboo', *Transactions of the Literary Society of Bombay*, III (1823), pp. 449–98, cited in Winder, p. 18.

pierced through his heart: Winder, p. 20.

p. 62 *palm tree cut down:* Winder, p. 24.

Chapter 5 Fusillade

p. 65 *belong to Abdul Aziz:* I am grateful to Dr Fouad al Farsy for first emphasizing this point to me; to HRH Prince Musa'id ibn Abdul Rahman for his discussion of the mechanism of family government; and to Turki bin Muhammad bin Sa'ud al Kabeer and to Turki bin Faisal bin Abdul Aziz for their historical elucidations of the family traditions with regard to the sharing of authority between Abdul Aziz and his father.

refer to Abdul Rahman: Lorimer, *Gazetteer of the Persian Gulf*, refers to Abdul Rahman as 'Bin Saud' as late as 1905.

p. 66 *said. 'You keep it':* Musa'id ibn Abdul Rahman, personal interview, January 1980.

to reach the ground: van der Meulen, p. 55.

from an early date: I am grateful to Dr al Shaafi of the Faculty of Arts, Riyadh University, for telling me of these IOUs which he saw in the Darat al Malik Abdul Aziz.

p. 67 *of the Muslim community:* Turki bin Muhammad bin Sa'ud al Kabeer, personal interview, February 1980; and Turki bin Faisal bin Abdul Aziz, personal interview, July 1980.

p. 68 *is waiting round it':* Turki bin Muhammad bin Sa'ud al Kabeer, personal interview, February 1980.

p. 69 *of marksmen from Kuwait:* IOR: L/P&S/10/395: 3013/1902, Cartwright to Drury, 21 November 1902.

p. 70 *his decisive first encounter:* Philby, *Sa'udi Arabia*, p. 241.
   to fight by fusillade: Howarth, p. 34.

p. 71 *without a single pause':* Rihani, p. 197.

p. 72 *the help of God':* IOR: R/15/5/24: 'Koweit Confidential, O'Conor to Lansdowne, 11 May 1904, encl. Crow to O'Conor, 11 April 1904, and translation of letter from Abdul Aziz-bin-Abdul Rahman-es-Saud to Sheikh of Koweit, 10 Muharram, 1322'. Spelling has been modernized by this author. I am grateful to H. St John Armitage for his suggestion that Osheziye in the original document is a faulty transliteration of Uthaithiya.
   called for blood vengeance: Armstrong asserts that Ubayd had killed Abdul Aziz's uncle, Muhammad ibn Abdul Rahman, in one of the nineteenth-century battles for Riyadh. But all other sources agree that Muhammad died of natural causes in the 1890s.
   I kissed the sword': Rihani, p. 159.

Chapter 6   Britons and Turks

p. 73 *banished from the Kingdom:* Sa'udi Arabia broke off relations with Britain in 1956 over the Suez invasion. Largely because of the Buraymi dispute (which had provoked a previous downgrading of relations by the Sa'udis for a period in the winter of 1955/6) relations were not resumed until 30 January 1963, when a chargé d'affaires returned to Jeddah. An ambassador presented his credentials on 27 April 1963. In 1980 the British ambassador remained out of the Kingdom at the Sa'udis' request from April until August.
   Government must remain supreme': speech made by Curzon at Sharjah on board HMS *Argonaut*, 21 November 1903, cited in Lorimer, Vol. 1, Pt. 2, pp. 2638–9.
   along for the journey: an official account of Curzon's visit to the Gulf is found in Lorimer, Vol. 1, Pt 2, Appendix P. See also Ronaldshay, Vol. 2, p. 316.
   unselfish page in history': Curzon, cited in Lorimer (see above).

p. 74 *of a 'British lake':* IOR: R/15/1/475: Persia and Arabia Confidential, Lansdowne to Monson, 19 March 1902.
   in the Persian Gulf: Troeller, p. 3.
   King of the Gulf': Curzon MSS: Curzon to Hamilton, 12 August 1903, cited in Busch, *Britain and the Persian Gulf*, p. 258.
   intervention in the area: Winder, p. 37.
   became 'an absolute czar': Harrison, p. 179.
   and of incorruptible uprightness': ibid.

p. 75 *that it shall endure':* Lord Curzon, speech made at Sharjah.
   with the British government': IOR: L/P&S/7/146:948/02, Kemball to FSI,

22 May 1902, 'encl. copy of letter from Abdul Rahman bin Feysul el Saood' (this correspondence is also found in IOR: R/15/1/475); FSI to Kemball, 23 June 1902.

p. 77 *declared Lord Palmerston:* quoted in Leatherdale, p. 19. Lord Palmerston to Sir William Temple, 19 April 1833. *Cambridge History of British Foreign Policy*, Vol. 2, p. 162.

an 'Ayatollah' figure: I am grateful to Clive Leatherdale for this helpful modern comparison.

armies of Ibn Rasheed: PRO: FO406/21: Monahan to Townley, 24 February 1905.

forces in July 1904: IOR: R/15/5/24: Townley to Lansdowne, 8 November 1904, encl. Fakhri Pasha to Grand Vizier, 8 (21) November 1904.

with their field-guns: The details of the first battle of Bukairiyah are confused. Philby, *Sa'udi Arabia*, p. 246, describes the Sa'udi army being attacked; other sources agree roughly on the final outcome.

p. 78 *the Turkish field-guns:* IOR: R/15/5/24: Knox to Bushire, 17 October 1904. And see also PRO: FO406/21: Monahan to Townley, 18 February 1905 and 24 February 1905.

p. 79 *hitherto anti-Ottoman policy:* PRO: FO406/21: Monahan to Townley, 24 February 1905. And see also IOR: R/15/5/24: 'Notes of interview with Sheikh Moburak on the morning of the 28 February 1905, written by Knox'.

considered unnecessary and undesirable: PRO: FO406/20: IO to FO, 24 January 1905, encl. GI to Brodrick, 23 January 1905.

turn has come now': IOR: R/15/1/556: 'Translation of purport of a letter from Amer bin Shaban to the Chief of Abu Dhabi' (undated).

my father and grandfather': ibid.

look into certain affairs': IOR: R/15/1/556: 'Translation of the purport of a letter from Abdul Aziz bin Abdul Rahman bin Saud to the Chief of Debai', 22 August 1905.

p. 80 *as 'an ignorant savage':* IOR: R/15/1/556: Cox to FSI, 4 February 1906, encl. Knox to Cox, 19 January 1906.

somewhat out of line': Graves, p. 64.

his appetite for work: Wilson, *South West Persia*, p. 209.

if nothing had happened': Philby, *Arabian Days*, p. 139.

p. 81 *with the Trucial Chiefs':* IOR: R/15/1/556: 'Cox to Chiefs of Abu Dhabi, Debai, Shargah, Um-el-Kowein, Ajman and all the Trucial Chiefs', 22 April 1906.

p. 82 *presence in central Arabia:* IOR: R/15/5/24: Knox to Cox, 24 December 1906. Captain Knox was in camp near Kuwait and saw the withdrawing Turkish troops on 22 December 1906.

Chapter 7 The House of Hashim

p. 83 *grey, lustrous and cold':* Grafftey-Smith, p. 155.

p. 84 *lapsed readily into Turkish:* Storrs, p. 157.

secured him the emirate: Baker, p. 11.

p. 85 *his empire for dissent:* ibid, p. 12.
    and his favourite cat: Morris, p. 23.
    sad and mournful countryside': author's translation from Courtellemont,
        pp. 48–9. I am grateful to Conraad Noyon for drawing this book to my
        attention.
    was like a bath': Lawrence, *Seven Pillars*, pp. 65–6.
p. 87 *god of Mecca itself:* Rodinson, *Mohammed*, p. 16.
p. 88 *numbers at some 120,000: L'Illustration*, No. 3428, 7 November 1908, pp. 30
    ff.
    the Red Sea ferries: Sir Shuldam Redfern, interview, London, February 1978.
    forty-day desert trek: Charles Doughty set out for Arabia with the Syrian *hajj*
        caravan, which he describes in detail in the early chapters of *Arabia*
        Deserta.

Chapter 8 The Jewel

p. 90 *if they were separated:* Philby, *Arabia of the Wahhabis*, p. 68.
    took Jauhara from him: Asad, p. 163.
p. 91 *man that you see':* off-the-record interview.
    for her as well?': Sa'ud bin Abdullah bin Faisal, personal interview, Jeddah,
        July 1980.
    granted an extra ration': de Gaury, p. 55.
    sons did not know: off-the-record interview.
    year older than him: Philby, *Arabian Jubilee*, p. 259.
p. 92 *I had to do':* Asad, p. 163.

Chapter 9 Night Caravan

p. 93 *ibn Hamoud al Tariki:* details of this story were given to the author by
        Abdullah Tariki in a personal interview in London, October 1980.
    every night for safekeeping: Abdullah Tariki, personal interview, Riyadh,
        April 1981.
p. 95 *took up the cudgels:* see Dickson, *The Arab of the Desert*, p. 321, for a family
    tree of the Daweesh clan.
p. 97 *occasion for the rift:* I can discover no confirmation of the rumour recorded in
    the Kuwait Agency Diary, No. 6 (IOR: R/15/5/25), that two of the cousins
    prepared poisoned coffee for Abdul Aziz which their wives, sisters of
    Abdul Aziz, inadvertently drank – subsequently dying from. Were this
    story true, it is almost certain that the poisoning would have been alluded to
    in some other source, and Abdul Aziz would never have reconciled himself,
    as he later did, to men who had poisoned his sisters. Modern descendants of
    Sa'ud al Kabeer flatly deny the story, and the evidence is overwhelmingly
    on their side. In this section, and others, on the *araif*, I am most grateful for
    the help of Muhammad Sa'ud al Kabeer, the son of al Kabeer and Nura,
    and of Muhammad's son Turki.

his passion for Nura: Sa' ud al Kabeer' s son Muhammad today repudiates this
tale as servants' talk, but other modern descendants of the *araif* say they
believe it to be true. It squares, they feel, with al Kabeer' s sense of daring
and love for Nura.

p. 98　*amounting to some £4500:* IOR: L/P&S/7/245: 1906/1910, Shakespear to
Cox, 6 November 1910.

　　　were made under compulsion: ibid.

p. 99　*The Tale of the Shareef and the Historic Fart:* off-the-record interview.

Chapter 10　Captain Shakespear

p. 102　*He told his photographer:* IOR: R/15/5/25: Draft letter, Shakespear to
Political Residency, 9 March 1910. This correspondence is also found in
IOR: L/P&S/7/238: 621/1910, Shakespear to Trevor (who was in charge
of the Residency, August 1909–March 1910, in the absence of Major
Cox).

　　　Western table and menu': ibid.

　　　one documented instance: PRO: FO406/17: No. 42, Admiralty to FO, 22
April 1903, encl. Kemp to Drury, 14 March 1903.

p. 103　*an improvised desert darkroom:* I am grateful to Victor Winstone, author of
Captain Shakespear, for his help on this point and for his generous
assistance on many others.

　　　Arabia's New Solomon: Armstrong, p. 69.

p. 104　*personality of the commander':* FCO: *Arab Bulletin,* No. 38, 12 January
1917.

　　　further than most Arabs': IOR: R/15/5/25 (see above).

p. 105　*necessary grants and gifts':* Wahba, pp. 167–8.

　　　left him empty-handed: Rihani, p. 151.

　　　bore witness to it: IOR: L/P&S/7/248: 899/1911, Cox to McMahon, 20 April
1911, encl. Shakespear to PR, 8 April 1911.

　　　calm and intelligent reasoning': ibid.

　　　was no mad mullah: this phrase was coined by Lt.-Col. R. E. Hamilton,
Political Agent at Kuwait, who met Abdul Aziz at Riyadh in 1917. See
FCO: *Arab Bulletin,* No. 88, 7 May 1918, 'Situation at Kuwait', p. 150.

　　　of his own tent: Raunkiaer, p. 120.

　　　a bottle of Moselle: Winstone, p. 76.

p. 106　*the Koran were abominable:* IOR: L/P&S/7/248 (see above), para. 7.

　　　an intrigue against it': ibid., para. 4.

　　　touring in the desert': ibid., para. 2.

　　　their troops from Hasa': IOR/L/P&S/10/384: P2488/1913, Cox to FSI, 26
May 1913, encl. Shakespear to PR, 15 May 1913, para. 2.

p. 107　*of the British government':* ibid., para. 3.

　　　the late nineteenth century: the author has been unable to trace a precise
reference for al Hasa being offered to the Zionists, but several scholars
familar with the documents agree they have heard or read of such a
possibility being discussed in the course of negotiations which Theodor
Herzl conducted with the Ottoman authorities in the 1890s.

p. 108　*usually to English distilleries:* Zwemer, *Arabia*, p. 125.

owing allegiance to Riyadh: for details of the population and annual revenue of the districts in the Wahhabi territory of Nejd, see Pelly, Appendixes IX and X, pp. 85–6. Also cited in Winder, p. 212.

p. 109　*five hours of Hofuf:* IOR: L/P&S/10/384: P2488/1913, Cox to FSI, 26 May 1913, encl. Shakespear to PR, 20 May 1913, para. 3.

they would surrender immediately: ibid.

of rifles and ammunition: ibid.

Chapter 11 Jarrab

p. 110　*entire extent of Nejd:* IOR: L/P&S/10/384: P2182/1913, Viceroy to IO, 31 May 1913, forwarding message from Cox.

he has been charged': IOR: L/P&S/10/384: P2640/1913, IO to GGI, 11 July 1913, encl. FO to IO, 2 July 1913.

one point and 'nonsense': PRO: FO371/1820: 22076/29150, IO to FO, 24 June 1913, encl. Cox to FSI, 20 May 1913, and Shakespear to PR, 15 May 1913, with handwritten margin comments by A. P[arker].

p. 111　*Al Sa'ud did not qualify:* IOR: L/P&S/10/384: P2640/1913 (see above).

Islamic and Muhammadan Arabs': IOR: L/P&S/10/384: P3344/1913, Cox to FSI, 4 July 1913, encl. Abdul Aziz bin Abdul Rahman to HBM's Consul-General at Bushire, 13 June 1913.

loyalty that shone out': Harrison, p. 134.

p. 112　*The Big Toe and the Sack of Coffee:* I am most grateful to Abdullah bin Jaluwi's grandson, Faisal ibn Abdul Aziz ibn Abdullah bin Jaluwi, for first telling me this story.

stump into boiling fat': SAC/MEC: Dickson Papers, Box IIA, File 5: Dickson to Civil Commissioner Baghdad, 19 February 1920, encl. Diary, 29 January–20 February 1920, diary entry for 14 February 1920.

lying there, totally untouched: Rihani, p. 218.

p. 113　*over for the occasion:* IOR: L/P&S/10/385: P478/1914, Lorimer to FSI, 4 January 1914, encl. (No. T-805), Trevor to PR, 20 December 1913.

Britain in June 1913: IOR: L/P&S/10/384: P3344/1913, Abdul Aziz bin Abdul Rahman to HBM's Consul-General at Bushire, 13 June 1913.

to his own interests': PRO: FO371/1820: 22076/29667, IO to FO, 28 June 1913, encl. Cox to GI, 27 June 1913.

factor of British policy': PRO: FO371/1820:22076/29150, FO to IO, 2 July 1913. This correspondence is also found in IOR: L/P&S/10/384: P2640/1913, with a covering letter from the IO to GGI, 11 July 1913.

p. 114　*early part of 1914':* IOR: L/P&S/10/385: P4569/1916, handwritten minute dated 4 November 1916, with copy of translation of treaty between Ibn Sa'ud and the Turks, 15 May 1914. Modern Sa'udi Arabia has always refused to accept the authenticity of this 1914 treaty between Abdul Aziz and the Turks. Sa'udis maintain it is a forgery, either on Britain's part or by the Turks, and this is a matter of more than academic importance, since certain Middle East oil concessions were allocated after the First World War on the basis of where Ottoman frontiers had lain. If Abdul Aziz could have been shown to have accepted Ottoman authority in 1914 after the Anglo-Turkish Convention of 1913 which set the eastern boundary of le sandjak Ottoman de Nedjd' near the foot of the Qatar peninsula, then Sa'udi claims to the Buraymi oasis beyond would have been considerably weakened.

It is difficult to see why Britain would have gone to the trouble of forging a Sa'udi–Turkish agreement in 1916. It was no use to them then, and they made no use of it. Turkey had more reason for pretending she had secured the allegiance of Abdul Aziz, but, if she did forge the document, there is no evidence she ever sought to make use of it.

The most plausible explanation is that Abdul Aziz agreed to accept nominal Turkish suzerainty in 1914, as he had done through his father in the Safwan agreement of 1905, as a temporary expedient he did not intend to stick by. He repudiated it as soon as he could, negotiating a friendship treaty with Britain in 1915, and when the Buraymi dispute arose later, he simply denied having signed anything at all.

Sa'udi leader's English acquaintance: Winstone, pp. 193–4.

froze in the waterskins: Shakespear's letter to Gertrude Bell, January 1915, cited in Winstone, p. 205.

themselves up for battle: ibid., p. 202.

p. 115 *from the British Government':* IOR: L/P&S/10/387: P975/1915, Cox to FSI, 29 January 1915, encl. Shakespear to PR, 4 January 1915, para 6.

intervene on his behalf': ibid., para 7.

position with Great Britain': ibid., para. 8.

his present friendly attitude': Winstone, p. 206.

me to clear out': ibid.

p. 116 *Bin Saud's political adviser!':* ibid., p. 205.

said the captain: IOR: R/15/5/88: Cox to Grey, 19 June 1915. Statement of Khalid bin Bilal of Zubair, 20 May 1915.

to that as well: Winstone, p. 208.

closer, oblivious of danger: interview with Walayd bin Shawiyyah at the palace of Muhammad Sa'ud al Kabeer, Riyadh, March 1980.

ridge with his revolver: IOR: R/15/5/88: Cox to Grey, 19 June 1915. Statement of Ambush bin Ahman, butler and bodyservant to Captain Shakespear.

p. 117 *but its ganji vest:* ibid. Statement of Khalid bin Bilal.

involvement with the infidels: Sheikh Muhammad Zaidan told this author in an interview that the head of Captain Shakespear was cut off and exhibited on a spike outside the walls of Medina in 1915. But Britain's official inquiry into the captain's death came up with no indication that the captain's head was either severed or exhibited in this fashion. Colonel W. G. Grey, the Political Agent in Kuwait, rounded up all the eye-witnesses he could find, and Shakespear's cook, Khalid bin Bilal of Zubair, described to him how he had discovered the body of his master twenty days after the battle of Jarrab, marked by three bullets, one in the back of the head. (R/15/5/88.)

A report in the *Arab Bulletin*, No. 95, 2 July 1915, does not mention the grisly trophy either: 'The Shammar brought down to Madinah the flags captured by ibn Saud: but Sherif Ali interfered and prevented their display by the Turks in the market.' One would have expected the captain's head to be mentioned in such a context.

hesitation at all: 'Shakespear': Sir John Glubb, interview with the author at Mayfield, Sussex, March 1979.

Chapter 12 The Arab Revolt

p. 119   *of the Chancery safe':* Grafftey-Smith, pp. 20–1.

do that at once': Wingate Papers, School of Oriental Studies, Durham University, file 141/4: statement by Sir Henry McMahon, cited in E. Kedourie, *The Chatham House Version*, ch. 2.

Arabia and its inhabitants': McMahon to the Shareef Husain, 30 August 1915. HMSO correspondence between Sir Henry McMahon and the Shareef Husain of Mecca, Cmd 5957, 1939, cited in Baker, p. 73.

p. 120   '... *purely military business':* Wingate Papers, file 141/4 (see above).

p. 121   *he came they lost':* Sheikh Muhammad Zaidan, interview, Darat al Malik Abdul Aziz, Riyadh, February 1980.

Chapter 13 Sir Abdul Aziz bin Sa'ud

p. 122   *Abdul Aziz and the Leather Bucket:* Dickson, *The Arab of the Desert*, p. 335.

p. 123   *they would not forget:* IOR: R/15/5/25: Grey to PR, 25 November 1915.

to be defeated disastrously: IOR: R/15/2/32: Keyes to Cox, 12 July 1915, translation of letter from Ibn Sa'ud giving his account of Kinzan. See also Philby, *Arabian Jubilee*, p. 62.

a prisoner in Hofuf': IOR: L/P&S/10/387: P3508/1916, 'Memorandum on relations between Ibn Sa'ud and the Ajman and the recent history of the latter', Cox to Officer in Charge, Eastern Bureau, Cairo, 25 July 1916.

wrong horse' in Arabia: an official at the India Office commented on a minute paper that 'The F. O. not for the first time "put its money on the wrong horse!"' IOR: L/P&S/10/387: 975/1915, Minute Paper, 16 March 1915.

p. 124   *Anglo-Sa'udi friendship treaty:* a copy of this treaty, along with the British draft and Ibn Sa'ud's draft, is to be found in IOR: L/P&S/10/390: 5120/1918, printed with 'Memorandum on British Commitments to Bin Sa'ud', FO Political Intelligence Department, Special 7. See also Troeller, Appendix III, Pts 1 and 2, pp. 250–6.

rifles and 10,000 rupees: PRO: FO371/2479: 1385/150190, Cox to GI, 5 September 1915.

further £20,000 in cash: ibid., Viceroy to IO, 7 October 1915.

harassing the British flank: IOR: L/P&S/10/387: P4171/1916, minute by A. H[irtzel], 17 October 1916.

p. 125   *that it really mattered:* ibid., P4050/1916, minute by J. E. Shuckburgh, 3 October 1916.

protégés to a 'Great Durbar': IOR: L/P&S/10/387: P4877/1916, Cox to
FSI, 21 November 1916.
man as he was': Wilson, *Loyalties*, I, p. 160.
illustrates a historic type': PRO: FO395/133: 31380/1917, 'A Ruler of the
Desert'.

p. 126 *throughout the Middle East:* FCO: *Arab Bulletin*, No. 38, 12 January 1917.
shrill voice and gestures: Philby, *Arabian Jubilee*, p. 47.
service was most remarkable: Wilson, *Mesopotamia*, p. 192.

p. 127 *bereft of his reason':* SAC/MEC: Papers of J. W. A. Young: Chief
Political Officer in charge Iraq Section, Arab Bureau, to Director, Arab
Bureau Cairo, 12 Jan. 1917, with encl. No. 5, translation of letter from
Shareef Husain to Abdul Aziz ibn Sa'ud, 6 Zill Qaida 1334.
'struck the key-note': Graves, p. 214.

Chapter 14 Philby

p. 128 *is capable of amendment':* Wilson, *Loyalties*, I, p. 281.
a perfect fountain-pen': Philby, *Arabian Days*, p. 321.

p. 129 *'sharp-featured and bright eyed':* Monroe, *Philby*, p. 66.
giant of a man': Philby, *Arabian Days*, p. 146.

p. 130 *'God knows everything':* this section is based on the first chapter of Philby's
Arabia of the Wahhabis, pp. 1–67, an account of Philby's second stay in
Riyadh, in June 1918, six months after his first visit with the British
Mission.

p. 131 *sons of her own:* I am grateful to one of the little boys playing in the mud,
Prince Sa'ud bin Sa'ad bin Abdul Rahman, and to his son Miteib, for
explaining these family details.

p. 133 *on the new situation:* Monroe, ibid., p. 83.
reduced to 1000: PRO: FO882/9: IS/18/16, Cox to FSI and repeated to
Philby, 9 March 1918.
arms against the shareef: PRO: FO882/13: KH/18/6. *Arab Bulletin*,
Supplementary Papers, 2, Hogarth, 'Position and Prospects of King
Hussein', 1 March 1918, p. 5.
Ibn Saud and Shareef': PRO: FO371/3389: 2240/4279, Viceroy to IO, 5
January 1918.
'except very sparingly': ibid.
funds at his disposal: Monroe, pp. 82–92, and Silverfarb, 'The Philby
Mission to Ibn Sa'ud, 1917–1918', pp. 269–85, for the details.
their trust in you?': Monroe, p. 93.

Chapter 15 Britons and Arabs

p. 134 *our word than lose':* Lawrence, *Seven Pillars*, p. 24.
p. 135 *been an honourable adviser':* ibid., p. 283.
p. 136 *non-Jewish communities in Palestine':* the Balfour Declaration from *The
Times*, 9 November 1917; cited in Hurewitz, Vol. II, p. 26.

system after the war: Baker, p. 142.

92 per cent of the population: John Terraine, 'Exodus – The Cruellest of Words', *8 Days*, 9 July 1979.

inhabit that ancient land: Arthur Balfour, 11 August 1919: cited in Howard, *The King–Crane Commission*, p. 250.

p. 137 *co-ordinated action against us':* National Archives of India: Foreign Department Proceedings, Crewe to Hardinge, 12 November 1914; cited in Busch, *Britain, India and the Arabs*, p. 62, and in Troeller, p. 95.

they spin and spin': Rihani, p. 61.

have sufficient force, Inshallah': ibid., p. 68.

Chapter 16 Al Artawiya

p. 142 *he noted briefly:* This is the earliest contemporary reference to the Ikhwan that the author has been able to trace, and I am grateful to Victor Winstone for passing on this entry from Shakespear's diary for 16 February 1914, SSE of Hafar Wells.

The date 1330 AH/AD 1912 for the foundation of al Artawiya appears to have been set by the oral tradition of the inhabitants themselves. Raunkiaer visited the site early in 1912 and made no mention of any settlements, though he did describe the wells. Habib contains a lengthy discussion of al Artawiya's date of foundation, settling on 1330/1912 as the date of foundation after interviews with the modern inhabitants, including descendants of the founders. Habib is misleading when he discusses the evidence of contemporary Western travellers like Leachman, Raunkiaer and Shakespear, for he does not appear to have studied their own accounts at first hand. But since Raunkiaer's March 1912 report makes no reference to inhabitants, while Shakespear's diary entry two years later appears to refer to some sort of Ikhwan activity at the spot, there is no reason to disbelieve the folk tradition of 1330/1912.

Leachman in November–December 1912 got no closer to al Artawiya than Buraydah, 140 km to the west, so his failure to remark on any Ikhwan activity at that date does not really bear the significance which Philby placed upon it in his *Arabian Jubilee*, p. 39.

p. 144 *sign of his vocation:* I am grateful to Sultan Ghalib al Qaiti of Hadhramaut for making this point – as well as for his advice on many others.

ever in the deserts: Habib, p. 81.

p. 145 *'we kill everybody':* Pelly, p. 47.

dreadful to their adversaries': Burckhardt, *History of the Wahabys* (1831), p. 57.

on constant military alert: Habib, p. 54.

locations like Ghot Ghot: Turki bin Muhammad bin Sa'ud al Kabeer has studied Sa'udi family archives of this period and has discovered evidence of Abdul Aziz making land grants to the early Ikhwan. I am most grateful to him for passing this information on to me and also for his many discussions of the subject, especially with regard to the dates that should be set on the appearance of the Ikhwan and their subsequent emergence as a military force. Prince Turki believes that Philby, Habib and other writers set the rise of the Ikhwan too early, and I agree with him.

p. 146 *height of the movement:* for estimates of Ikhwan membership, see Habib, pp. 73–6.

from 3 miles away: Philby, *Arabia of the Wahhabis*, p. 352.

bottom of the matter': SAC/MEC: Dickson Papers, Box IIA, File 5: Dickson to Civil Commissioner Baghdad, 19 February 1920, encl. Notes on the 'Akhwan' Movement.

p. 147 *to become useful citizens':* SAC/MEC: Diary of Charles R. Crane written up by George Antonius (1931), pp. 3–4.

of Arabia', prophesied Feisal: FCO: *Arab Bulletin*, No. 32, 24 December 1917, p. 146.

to disperse the brethren: PRO: FO371/3390: 2240/177596, Husain to Acting British Agent Jedda, 18 September 1918.

of the Hashimite clan: Habib, p. 89.

Ikhwan preachers from Nejd: Baker, p. 196.

drove the holy man away: IOR: L/P&S/10/390: P 6995/1919, 'Some Notes on the Ownership of Khurmah', by Colonel C. E. Wilson, 8 August 1919.

p. 148 *two powers in Arabia':* PRO: FO371/3389: 2240/4423, GI to Wingate, 7 January 1918.

Arabia, including Ibn Sa'ud: see Silverfarb, 'The British Government and the Khurmah Dispute 1918–1919', in *Arabian Studies*, V (1979), pp. 37–60, for the best account of Britain's handling of the Khurmah dispute, and particularly for Cairo's 'Suzerainty Policy'. See also PRO: CAB27/23: MEC 23, Cornwallis to Ormsby Gore, 14 December 1917: PRO: FO882/3: AP/18/2, Wilson to Wingate, 1 May 1918.

it as 'entirely Utopian': IOR: L/P&S/10/390: P122/1919, Philby, 'Report on the Operations of the Najd Mission', 12 November 1918.

p. 149 *officers is so conflicting':* PRO: FO371/4144: 142/5815, 'Arabia: The Nejd–Hejaz Feud', Note by Political Department, India Office, 7 January 1919.

should support King Hussein': Silverfarb, 'Khurma', p. 46.

very striking or decisive': see above, 'The Nejd–Hejaz Feud', p. 4.

he [Husain] commits aggression': PRO: FO371/4147: 142/142443, 'Shaikh Sir Abdul Aziz bin Abdul Rahman Al Faisal as Sa'ud to Col. Bassett', undated, *c.* 16 June 1919.

and twenty machine-guns: IOR: L/P&S/10/390: P6995/1919, 'Note by Captain Garland on the Khurmah Dispute', 10 June 1919.

in a fortnight: Baker, p. 197.

Khurmah only,' he bragged: Rihani, *Najd*, p. 253; cited in Habib, pp. 92–3.

p. 150 *'I saw the blood':* ibid, p. 256; cited in Habib, p. 94.

Rasheed challenge from Hail: Rihani, *Arabia*, p. 19.

Chapter 17 Death of the Jewel

p. 151 *a traveller from Kuwait:* no one is certain precisely how the Spanish influenza epidemic reached Riyadh across the deserts which customarily insulated the town from outside infection, but Dr Rashad Pharaon believes that the infection came in a caravan from Kuwait: personal interview, February 1980.

'4 to a camel': IOR: R/15/2/34: Harrison to Mylrea, 18 January 1919.

affected by my loss': ibid., translation of a letter from Sheikh Sir Abdul Aziz to Lt-Col. Wilson, Official Civil Commissioner Mesopotamia, 27 February 1919.

p. 152 *of a lost love':* Asad, p. 163.

thousands to his presence: Rihani, p. 284.

account of one witness: Asad (see above).

the account of another: Wahba, p. 170.

Chapter 18 A Trip to London

Chapter 3 of Gerald de Gaury's biography of King Faisal contains an excellent description of the young prince's first visit to Europe. Elizabeth Monroe (pp. 103–4) describes those parts of the trip in which Philby participated, while the memoirs of Humphrey Bowman (pp. 232–9), N. N. E. Bray (pp. 296–8) and R. E. Cheesman (p. 168) describe their own experiences as escorts at first hand. The India Office archives (L/P&S/10/843. File 4006/1919, Part I) contain the Report of the Secretary, Government Hospitality Fund (P6775/1919, 28 October 1919), details of the Mission's expenses in Bombay (P1495/1919) and also the correspondence with King George V's private secretary, Lord Cromer (P6695/1919). The return journey via Bombay to Bahrain, ending in February 1920, is reported in IOR: R/15/2/35.

p. 153 *can produce in horseflesh!':* Bowman, p. 236.

'Tip, 5 rupees': IOR: L/P&S/10/843: P1495/1919, 'Nejed Mission from Bahrain – 1919: Charges incurred in Bombay'.

p. 154 *the red Dahna sands:* de Gaury, p. 28.

three years at least: Bray, p. 297.

building in the future: SAC/MEC: Bowman Diaries, Box III: Diary for 1919.

p. 155 *cutting and jabbing doggedly:* Bowman, p. 236.

'some scores of hotels': IOR: L/P&S/10/843: P6775/1919, Report of the Secretary, Government Hospitality Fund, on the Arab Missions, 28 October 1919.

p. 156 *as 'a government bungle':* de Gaury, p. 25.

lapse of government hospitality': 'Our Guests from Arabia', *The Times,* 17 October 1919.

his robes and fled: Cheesman, p. 168.

at the Foreign Office: Kheirallah, p. 269.

been treated 'like children': Bray, p. 296.

dismiss as 'nothing much': de Gaury, p. 29.

p. 157 *Thunayan told Major Bray:* Bray, p. 297.

ended at that point: ibid., p. 298.

negro slaves at home: Cheesman, p. 168.
bowl into his tea: Bowman, p. 239.
staircase at Piccadilly Circus': ibid.

Chapter 19 Sultan

p. 159   *of his own room:* the preceding paragraphs are based on Dickson's account
of his January 1920 journey as recorded in his diary: SAC/MEC:
Dickson Papers, Box IIA, File 5: Dickson to Civil Commissioner
Baghdad, 19 February 1920, encl. Diary 29 January–20 February 1920.
See also *Kuwait and Her Neighbours*, p. 249.

  Shareef's days are numbered': SAC/MEC: see above, diary entry for
13 February 1920.

p. 160   *I will consider arbitration!':* Grafftey-Smith, p. 157.

  Middle-Eastern affairs: Daily Express, 28 May 1920.

  authorities in the Middle East': Morris, p. 79.

p. 161   *the 'vacant lot':* Monroe, *Britain's Moment in the Middle East*, p. 68.

  crescent of Hashimite powers: PRO: CO730/2: 29463/1921, High
Commissioner to Sheikh Sir Abdul Aziz, 4 May 1921.

p. 162   *fools aping English wisdom':* PRO: CO730/4: 44326/1921, Intelligence
Report No. 18, 18 August 1921, encl. Abdul Aziz to Fahad Beg al
Hadhdhal, 29 April 1921.

  surrounded me with enemies': Rihani, p. 65.

  empire at a stroke: the April 1920 shooting of Sa'ud ibn Rasheed impelled
Sa'ud's successor, the young Abdullah ibn Mit'ab, to conclude a treaty of
protection with Riyadh. After the Cairo conference, Abdul Aziz decided
that this treaty did not give him sufficient control over Hail and he
launched his invasion in the summer of 1921. The description of his
conquest given here is based on a Confidential Note by Captain Gerald de
Gaury: IOR: L/P&S/12/2082: de Gaury to PR, 'Historical C – Events
prior to the end of Ibn Rasheed rule at Hail 1921' (C/164), 29 June 1937.
Rihani, pp. 165–73, also contains a good account of the fall of the
Rasheeds, based on his interviews in 1922 and 1923 when he stayed with
Abdul Aziz and met several survivors of the dynasty then living in
Riyadh.

p. 163   *The Tale of Abdul Aziz and the Captured Rasheeds:* Ahmad bin Abdul Aziz,
personal interview, July 1979.

Chapter 20 Boundaries in Men's Hearts

p. 164   *see an unusual sign:* Monroe, *Philby*, p. 123.

  two Beni Sakhr villages: ibid.

  line of their flight': Philby, *Arabian Days*, p. 221.

  ringleaders flung into prison: Habib, pp. 109–10.

p. 165   *be very like this':* Monroe, ibid., p. 198.

  as a friendship treaty: Besson, pp. 140–1.

control of Abdul Aziz: Asir's relations with Britain and the shareef in the First World War are described in Busch, *Britain, India and the Arabs*, chapter 5, pp. 215 ff. The text of the 1920 agreement is the Ryan papers: SAC/MEC: Ryan Papers, Box VI, File 7.

the Persian Gulf coast: the account of this dispute is based largely on Dickson, *Kuwait and Her Neighbours*, pp. 243 ff.

p. 166   *allegiance, leadership, human authority:* IOR: L/P&S/10/925: P6317/1920, Memo from PA Kuwait to Civil Commissioner Baghdad, 13 June 1920, citing Captain Shakespear's comments on 'unwritten desert law', C–62, 12 August 1912.

between Kuwait and Nejd: PRO: CO730/2: 35006/1921, PA Kuwait to High Commissioner Baghdad, 27 April 1921.

Abdul Aziz's warriors of Islam: IOR: L/P&S/10/937: P1214/1922, High Commissioner Iraq to SSC, 16 March 1922.

Chapter 21   False Start

p. 168   *Black Admiral of Qateef:* Dickson, *Kuwait*, p. 270.
p. 169   *Johnnie Walker whisky:* Rihani, p. 55.

wearing their dinner jackets: ibid., p. 56.

fomenting anti-British sentiments: in December 1920 *Atlantic Monthly* published an article by Dr Harrison. Two years later Sir Percy Cox found out about it and had Harrison banned from the Gulf, though he was allowed to return in 1924. During the First World War Harrison had made attempts to secure a commission in the British army and this suggested to Sir Percy Cox that the doctor's criticisms in his article had been 'injudicious' rather than malicious. In view of this, 'His Excellency did not feel justified in pressing for his permanent transfer to another sphere of labour.' See IOR: R/15/5/97.

p. 170   *£1000 a year:* IOR: R/15/2/109: Highcoma Baghdad to PA Bahrain, 24 May 1922.

tent at a distance: Rihani, p. 79.

p. 171   *fears losing his annuity':* Rihani, p. 78.

bags, boxes and guns: Dickson, *Kuwait*, p. 269.

Chapter 22   At Home with Abdul Aziz

This chapter is based principally upon Amin Rihani's account of Riyadh in 1922 in his book *Ibn Sa'oud of Arabia: His People and His Land*.

p. 173   *3000 gold-trimmed outer robes:* Rihani, p. 133.
p. 174   *house of her own':* ibid., p. 161.

covered with Valenciennes lace': ibid., p. 128.

The Tale of Abdul Aziz and Hassa: Ahmad bin Abdul Aziz, personal interview, Taif, July 1979.

p. 176   *little hand-cranked generator:* Rihani, p. 185.

'there is no distinction': ibid., p. 183.

like a prison cell: I am grateful to HH Prince Sa'ud, the son of Sa'ad ibn
  Abdul Rahman, for this description of the education of princes in Riyadh
  in the 1920s. Prince Sa'ud ibn Sa'ad was raised after his father's death in
  1916 by Abdul Aziz as a son (see p. 131).

p. 178 *the glory of man':* Rihani, p. 131.

not even of soul': ibid., p. 139.

to speak to us': ibid., p. 137.

p. 179 *Abdul Aziz would start sobbing:* Abdullah Faisal Turki al Abdullah al Sa'ud,
  personal interview, London, February 1981.

'he touches your heart': Rihani, p. 51.

p. 180 *the Kings of Arabia':* ibid., p. 41.

Chapter 23 Taif

p. 181 *was stuffing a turkey':* Grafftey-Smith, p. 158.

corners of his mouth': ibid.

a silence of death': Storrs, p. 175. According to Morris the shareef's
  telephone number was Mecca No. 1, and if you rang that he picked up the
  telephone himself.

do that in London': ibid.

p. 182 *have to go under':* IOR: L/P&S/10/390: P3827/1919, minute by J. E.
  Shuckburgh, 8 July 1919.

picture of King Husain': SAC/MEC: Bullard Papers, Box VI, File 5:
  Bullard to Ryan, 5 October 1923, encl. circular letter from Jeddah.

kept in darkness there: Grafftey-Smith, p. 155. See also PRO: FO686/27:
  Mecca Report to 29 January 1921.

skirt of your coat': IOR: L/P&S/10/390: P3896/1919, minute by A.
  H[irtzel], 9 July 1919.

p. 183 *his idea of 'conversation':* Baker, p. 181.

'the mask had fallen': PRO: FO686/27: Jeddah Report, 1–20 February
  1921.

word to the Arabs': S. Mousa, *T. E. Lawrence – An Arab View* (OUP,
  1966), p. 242. 'It is true to say', declared Sir Alec Kirkbride, whose
  dealings with Shareef Husain were far from happy, 'that he sacrificed his
  position for the sake of the Palestinians and got no gratitude whatsoever
  for it.' (1974: conversation with Randall Baker, cited in Baker, p. 232.)

p. 184 *down to their underdrawers:* Othman Jamjoom, Jeddah, May 1980.

a burial tax even: Baker, p. 176.

of transport were prohibited: ibid., p. 174.

for every good Muslim': PRO: FO686/27: Jeddah Report, 21 April 1921.

lizards could be purchased: Morris, p. 70.

the comity of kings': ibid., p. 72.

hostilized his neighbours': IOR: L/P&S/10/936: P2200/1923, High
  Commissioner for Iraq to SSC, 14 May 1922.

be a salutary measure': ibid.

did establish himself in Mecca': IOR L/P&S/10/936: P2377/1922, Minute
    by A. H[irtzel], 10 June 1922. This author's italics.

p. 185 *Hejaz inside a week':* SAC/MEC: Dickson Papers, Box IIA, File 5: Diary
    entry for 7 February 1920.

    stronger of the two': letter from Gertrude Bell to T. E. Lawrence, 10 July
    1920; cited in Winstone, *Gertrude Bell*, p. 225.

    stiff as a ramrod': Philby, *Arabian Days*, p. 232.

p. 186 *become the state religion':* PRO: FO686/29: Jeddah Report, 30 January–29
    February 1924.

    "Long live the Caliph Husain!": IOR: L/P&S/10/1115: P2062/1924,
    Bullard to Prime Minister, 29 March 1924.

    God for his effrontery: Baker, pp. 188–9.

p. 187 *of the Islamic World':* Toynbee, p. 297. Toynbee's studies of 'The Rise of
    Wahhabi Power' and 'The Delimitation of Frontiers' in the *Survey of
    International Affairs* (1925), Vol. I, are masterful analyses of the reports
    on Abdul Aziz's conquest of the Hijaz in contemporary English and
    Arabic newspapers and in *Oriente Moderno*. Some of Toynbee's
    conclusions, made as events unrolled and at a distance, have proved
    erroneous. But the facts stand.

    watchtowers constructed round it: Baker, p. 201.

    his small Charles I beard': Storrs, p. 178.

    without force of character': Hogarth, *Hijaz Before World War I*, p. 54.

p. 188 *from a police post:* Armstrong. p. 167.

    follow their natural course: PRO: CO727/8: 44525/1924, CO to FO, 23
    September 1924.

    to the Islamic shrines: PRO: CO727/8: 43017/1924, SSC to PR, 13
    September 1924.

p. 189 *assented to his abdication:* Baker, p. 206.

    £800,000 in gold sovereigns: Philby, *Forty Years*, p. 122.

    has floated off again': Bullard, p. 139.

Chapter 24 Mecca

p. 190 *to the empty air:* Armstrong, p. 171.

    encampment in the hills: Baker, p. 213.

p. 191 *Alone. Here am I':* Armstrong, p. 173.

    to shake hands only': Baker, p. 213.

    to caution at best: Besson, p. 175.

    of the Holy Places: Besson, p. 175.

    of the last Hashimite: ibid., p. 176.

p. 192 *of the Al Sa'ud:* Baker, p. 209.

p. 193 *red, white and blue':* ibid., p. 225.

    fly over enemy territory': PRO: FO686/29: Jeddah Report,
    20 November–11 December 1924.

p. 194 *and lack of rancour:* Baker, p. 213.

p. 195 *morale in the town:* Philby described the siege of Jeddah in grim terms in his
    Forty Years in Arabia, p. 113. He wrote of Jeddah's 25,000 inhabitants

crawling round pitifully on their hands and knees grouting undigested barley grains from the dung of horses. But no other eye-witness describes any such extremity of distress, and Philby was in the town for only a relatively short period of the siege. Soon after the bombardment started he was shipped out to Aden on 3 January 1925 after collapsing with dysentery and an abscess caused by injection with a dirty needle. He returned briefly the following October.

  not to send it: Philby, *Forty Years*, p. 122.

p. 196 *wadi on the way:* Clayton, p. 96.

  from the beleaguered Ali: IOR: L/P&S/10/1124: P4193/1924, SSC to High Commissioner for Palestine, 15 October 1924.

  attractively when he smiles': Clayton, p. 128.

p. 197 *policy of consistent obstruction':* ibid., p. 100.

p. 198 *at his table daily':* ibid., pp. 117–18.

  the inhabitants' resistance alive: Muhammad Zaidan, personal interview, Riyadh, March 1980.

  'to secure assistance' there: Baker, p. 226.

p. 199 *of modern Sa'udi Arabia:* Abdul Rahman Nasseef, personal interview, Jeddah, June 1980.

  mission has just begun': Muhammad bin Abdullah Alireza, personal interview, Jeddah, July 1980.

p. 200 *decide what they will':* Baker, p. 230.

Chapter 25 Sabillah

p. 201 *misdeeds which he committed':* Wahba, p. 133.

p. 202 *the streets of Mecca:* the Mahmal massacre occurred at the same time that delegates representing international Islam came to Mecca to discuss its new status. But, since Abdul Aziz prohibited the conference from discussing anything to do with local politics, the delegates confined themselves to well-meaning affirmations of Islamic unity, and the Sa'udi hold on the Holy Places was not affected. For details of this conference, see Wahba, pp. 151 ff., and also Besson, p. 179.

p. 204 *of the shepherd families':* Glubb, *War in the Desert*, p. 124.

p. 205 *king of all nomads':* Glubb, ibid., p. 209.

p. 206 *everyone else had done':* Glubb, personal interview, Mayfield, Sussex, March 1979.

  the beauty of women': Glubb, p. 218.

  than the other Powers': ibid.

  examination of the room': ibid.

p. 207 *Sir Gilbert Clayton's delegation:* this meeting occurred in the spring of 1928. Clayton came to Jeddah again in August 1928 for a second round of negotiations over the Iraqi frontier forts, but this meeting proved no more successful than the first.

p. 208 *were normally so serene':* Asad, p. 164.

p. 209 *Furious retaliation was expected:* Abdul Aziz claimed to the British that he had ordered the Ikhwan rebel leaders to resign their chieftainships if they would not come to Riyadh in November 1928, and that all three did this, sending him formal letters of resignation. But these letters have never been seen, the rebels denied they had resigned their chieftainships, and it seems likely that Abdul Aziz's claim was just propaganda. Throughout the Ikhwan rebellion he repeatedly claimed victories to the outside world which Yussuf Yassin, the editor of *Umm al Qura*, elaborated on – only for events to prove the claims false.

p. 210 *Abdul Aziz's men once more:* this account of the Riyadh Conference of November 1928 is largely based on Habib, ch. 10, pp. 121–35.

off with their beasts: Habib, p. 137.

an Ikhwan war party: Glubb, p. 281.

p. 211 *and our worldly concerns':* PRO: FO371/13736: E3457/2322/91, Faisal ibn Sultan al Daweesh to Amir Sa'ud [Sa'ud ibn Abdul Aziz]. This letter was sent to the British Agent in Jeddah by Fouad Hamza, 16 June 1929.

end of holy war: IOR: L/P&S/12/2082: 'The Future of Arabia', copy of report by Lt-Col. T. C. Fowle, Acting Political Resident, September 1931.

'*Pax Saudica':* IOR: L/P&S/12/2082: PZ4722/1938 (E2782/196/25), Bullard to Halifax, 25 April 1938 (amended copy), para. 6.

at home like women': Harrison, p. 133.

p. 212 *had completed his service:* al Mana, p. 103.

p. 213 *would fall on him':* Wahba, *Jazirat*, p. 304; cited in Habib, p. 139.

cooks and soft men: Habib, p. 140.

camel-bags without handles': al Mana, p. 103.

in half an hour: this account of the battle of Sabillah is largely based on that given by Muhammad al Mana (who was present) in his book, pp. 103 ff.; see also Habib, pp. 138–40.

that he must die: Besson, p. 251. Dr Midhat Sheikh al Ardh, personal interview, Riyadh, January 1981. Dr Midhat examined al Daweesh after Sabillah and did not think the rebel would die of his belly wound. So it seems that Abdul Aziz spared al Daweesh through a wish to be lenient to him, and also, perhaps, to tempt Ibn Bijad to give himself up, not because he thought the rebel was dying, as has often been said.

Chapter 26 The Kingdom

p. 216 *this as a threat:* al Mana, p. 121.

and also by Fahad: Dickson, *Kuwait*, pp. 304–5.

big Arab in Arabia': IOR: R/15/5/31: 437S/1928, Blockade of the Hasa Ports, PR to PA Bahrain and PA Kuwait, 6 December 1928, encl. PR to SSC, 6 December 1928 and PA Bahrain to PR, 25 November 1928.

were sent from India: al Mana, p. 126.

p. 218 *Umm Urdhumah, that decided him:* according to Muhammad al Mana, this information was false and Ibn Musa'id himself did not reach Umm Urdhumah until after the battle: al Mana, p. 127.

p. 219   *British government protect them:* ibid., p. 316.
          took, some 250 men: al Mana, p. 128.
          down in cold blood: Dickson, *Kuwait*, p. 357.
          No prisoners were taken: Muhammad al Mana describes (p. 133) how
              Muhammad bin Abdul Aziz persuaded his father to let him command this
              attack on Ibn Ashwan, and I am grateful to Sir John Glubb for his help in
              elucidating other aspects of the incident. 'It always surprised me that
              Abdul Aziz, who had such an amazingly genial, kind, patriarchal manner,
              should order everyone to be killed. But this was what happened.' Letter
              to the author, 10 June 1980.
p. 220   *in a fairy story':* Glubb, p. 322.
          nose in bedouin fashion: Dickson, *Kuwait*, p. 324.
          his throat that haemorrhaged: ibid, p. 327.

Chapter 27 A Man and a Horse

p. 225   *Mr Charles R. Crane:* I am grateful to Coleman S. Williams for his
              information on the Crane family; and to Gordon P. Williams for putting
              me in touch with Lawrence R. Houston and David H. McKillop who
              both provided me with their memories of Charles R. Crane, through
              my research assistant Jacqueline Williams.
          $1.5 billion: turnover of the Crane Company in 1979: Standard NYSE
              Stock Reports: Vol. 47/No. 167/Sec. 9: 680, 27 August 1980.
p. 228   *'A Man and a Horse':* Muhammad Alireza, personal interview, Jeddah, 2
              July 1980. Sheikh Muhammad, the son of Hajji Abdullah, was present in
              Cairo at the time of Charles Crane's meeting with Sheikh Fawzan al
              Sabik, and this account is based on that of Hajji Abdullah who was
              present in the *majlis* at which the horses and possibilities of mineral
              survey were discussed. Hajji Abdullah then travelled down the Red Sea
              to Jeddah with Charles Crane on the Khedeevial steamer in February
              1931.
          40,000 in 1931: Monroe, *Philby*, p. 173.
          £1 million per year: Hogarth, *Hijaz Before World War I*, p. 79.
p. 229   *days of the shareef:* Philby, *Arabian Days*, p. 290.
          optimism deserted him entirely: ibid.
          a million pounds now': ibid., p. 291.
          to Arabia to see: Muhammad Alireza, personal interview (see above).
p. 230   *his head turned downwards:* SAC/MEC: Crane Diary, p. 1.
          of fish and chips: Howarth, p. 181.
          his face is immobile': SAC/MEC: Crane Diary, p. 2.
          a leader of men': ibid., p. 7.
          offered in his honour: ibid., p. 6.
p. 231   *name in the middle:* Muhammad Alireza, personal interview (see above).
              Sheikh Muhammad was present when Sheikh Fawzan al Sabik received
              Crane's list of prospectors.
          artesian water around Jeddah: SAC/MEC: Crane Diary, p. 8.

something of a busybody': PRO: FO371/16021: E1896/412/25, FO
    Minute, 20 April 1932; cited in Leatherdale, p. 204.

in your country': for Twitchell's account of his interview with Abdul Aziz
    see Merritt, *Mining Engineering*, September 1965, p. 87.

p. 232   *structure on the mainland:* Philby, *Arabian Oil Ventures*, foreword by Fred
    A. Davis, p. xi. See also Stegner, p. 9.

count the strokes wrong: Stegner, p. 6.

of his Arab dress: Merritt, *Mining Engineering* (see above).

p. 233   *part I had played':* Philby, *Arabian Oil Ventures,* p. 76.

like to meet you': ibid., p. 77.

should have been Abdulqirsh: Monroe, *Philby*, p. 168.

p. 234   *one, Mariam, in 1931:* Monroe, p. 171.

on 11 July 1932: Philby, *Arabian Oil Ventures*, p. 78.

p. 235   *line rhymed with 'Ryan':* Philby, *Arabian Days*, p. 275.

p. 236   *keep the Americans out:* Philby, *Arabian Oil Ventures*, p. 106.

of £200 a month: ibid., p. 107.

be after the money': al Mana, p. 223.

was money for nothing: Muhammad Alireza, interview (see above). Sheikh
    Muhammad was told personally by Abdullah Suleiman and by Yussuf
    Yassin that on receipt of the very final bids Abdul Aziz still refused to give
    the concession to the Americans. It was only when the British minister,
    Andrew Ryan, had been consulted yet again and was reported to have
    given the answer that there was no oil and that Abdul Aziz should take
    the American money since it represented a free gift, that the king decided
    to let Socal have the concession. British documents, not surprisingly,
    contain no reference to Ryan giving any such advice. But they do show
    that the British had very little confidence in the existence of oil and that
    they were bidding essentially to keep the Americans out of the Middle
    East. The remark attributed to Ryan is in harmony with these.

£10,000: Philby, *Arabian Oil Ventures*, p. 119–20.

8 and 9 May 1933: ibid., p. 124.

p. 237   *trust in God and sign':* ibid.

Chapter 28 Well No. 7

p. 238   *to the sleeping quarters:* interview with Abdul Aziz Suleiman, Jeddah,
    October 1979.

p. 239   *money for my children':* PRO: FO371/16019: E1145/266/25, Biscoe to
    SSC, 5 February 1932, para 2.

him at other times: PRO, ibid.: E1119/266/25, Biscoe to SSC, 5 February
    1932, para. 8.

six months in arrears: Philby, *Forty Years*, p. 28.

p. 240   *headdress at all times:* IOR: L/P&S/12/2117: PZ1799/1932, Ryan to FO
    (copied to IO), 28 July 1932.

caught before his arrival: Sir George Rendel, personal interview, London,
    January 1979.

second category of importance': IOR: L/P&S/12/2117: PZ4292/1932
   (E2886/1494/25), Sir E. Ovey to Sir John Simon, 6 June 1932.
Comrades Kalinin and Molotov: ibid. Kalinin was President of the Central
   Executive Committee. Molotov, who was to become Minister for Foreign
   Affairs 1939–49 and again 1953–6, was Secretary of the All-Union
   Communist Party.

p. 241   *was delivered to Jeddah:* IOR (see above): PZ2941/1933 (E1488/1225/25),
   Ryan to Simon, 28 February 1933.
a three-year commitment: IOR (see above): PZ3468/1933
   (E2019/1225/25), Ryan to Simon, 23 March 1933.
left the Jeddah roads: Philby, *Arabian Jubilee*, pp. 171–2.
oil to Sa'udi Arabia: IOR (see above): Ryan to Simon, 23 March 1933.

p. 242   *tied up by his women:* IOR: L/P&S/12/2107: P2507/1928 (E2400/677/91),
   Stonehewer-Bird to Chamberlain, 20 April 1928, encl. 'List of Arab
   Personalities'.

p. 243   *can read and write:* Bandar bin Abdullah, personal interview, Riyadh,
   February 1980.
was round, not flat: Wahba, p. 49.
The Tale of Abdul Aziz and the Wireless: this story is one of the most
   common pieces of folklore making up the legend of Abdul Aziz.

p. 245   *in cold water:* Stegner, p. 68.

p. 246   *total dryness:* ibid., p. 79.

p. 247   *have no knowledge of':* cited in Howarth, pp. 192–4.

p. 248   *everlasting Muslim Arab brotherhood':* IOR: R/15/6/163: 1923/17/567,
   Ryan to Simon, 27 June 1934, encl. 1920/17/567, annotated summary of
   Sa'udi–Yemen Peace Treaty.

p. 249   *from the courtyard tiles:* IOR: L/P&S/12/2082: PZ3564/1935
   (E2302/7/25), Ryan to Simon, 22 March 1935.

p. 250   *proved that he did:* IOR: ibid.: PZ3783/1935 (E2574/7/25), *Umm al Kura*
   interview, cited in Ryan to Simon, 27 March 1935.
in London that June: Daily Telegraph, Thursday, 13 June 1935.

p. 251   *their outlooks a little:* IOR: ibid.: PZ4722/1938 (E2782/196/25), Bullard to
   Halifax, 25 April 1938 (amended copy).
to Riyadh from Syria: Dr Rashad Pharaon, personal interview, Riyadh, May
   1980.

p. 252   *far too mechanically:* Ryan, p. 273.
the shadows of archways': de Gaury, *Arabia Phoenix*, p. 65.
long-necked silver flasks: ibid., p. 100.

p. 253   *these three special joys:* ibid., p. 65.
Riyadh the following year: Bullard, p. 199.
than many educated Europeans': ibid., p. 197.
than as a statesman': ibid., p. 202.
king to drink from': ibid., p. 202.
publicly received a woman: Princess Alice was not the first Western woman
   Abdul Aziz had received in a private capacity. In 1937 he had met Lady
   Rendel, the wife of Sir George Rendel who, as head of the Middle East
   desk at the Foreign Office, had travelled across Arabia to prepare the way

for Princess Alice. It also seems likely that Abdul Aziz had met some of the wives of the oilmen who first came in 1932.

p. 254 *been disappointed after all':* letter 5 of 26 February 1938. I am grateful to HRH Princess Alice, Countess of Athlone, for lending me copies of her letters from Sa'udi Arabia and for answering my queries arising from them.

adores his small children: letter 6 of 2 March 1938.

'too absolutely romantic': ibid., sheet 10.

right around the walls': ibid.

any of the share': letter 7 of 20 March 1938.

p. 255 *21 March, 3372:* Stegner, p. 92.

Chapter 29 The Second World War

p. 256 *out of the air:* de Gaury, *Faisal,* p. 66.

unswerving and unflinching loyalty': Hansard, 27 February 1945: H. C. Deb., 5th series, Vol. 408, Col. 1289, cited in 'The Recession of the War, 1943–1945', *Survey of International Affairs,* Pt III, p. 352.

p. 257 *to the utmost limits':* Watt, 'The Foreign Policy of Ibn Sa'ud, 1930–1939', p. 158.

he 'hated the English': Hirszowicz, p. 52.

and the American diplomats: The Hon. Raymond Hare, letter to the author, 11 May 1981.

things to all men': Watt, p. 152.

p. 258 *the island in 1939:* Belhaven, p. 110.

destruction and eternal damnation': Dickson, *Kuwait,* p. 389.

p. 259 *presence of God Almighty':* ibid., p. 391.

who has helped it: ibid., pp. 389 and 391.

to the Persian Gulf: ibid., p. 391.

p. 260 *would be alive today':* Bullard, p. 205.

and not so dangerous': Dickson, *Kuwait,* p. 391.

for so many years: Sir George Rendel, personal interview, London, January 1979.

p. 261 *far afield for us':* FRUS, 1941 (Vol. III), p. 643: 890F.51/37, Roosevelt to Jones, 18 July 1941.

Arabia in his bailiwick: US/NA: 890F.6363, Standard Oil Co/118. Division Near-Eastern Affairs, Murray to Berle/Massersmith/Welles, 2 August 1939.

p. 262 *secretary to help him:* Miller, pp. 21–2.

from her own reserves: ibid., p. 55.

in the British mould: ibid., p. 49.

tables of the world': cited in Peck, p. 103.

p. 263 *the broad national interest':* US/NA: 890F.24/20, Alling to Berle/Acheson, 14 December 1942.

playing the rich uncle: Miller, p. 70.

post-war oil sales: it is difficult to arrive at precise figures for Sa'udi finances at this period. The estimates given here are based upon: US/NA: 890F.51/51 1/4, Department of State Financial Division Notes on Economic or Financial Assistance to Sa'udi Arabia, 3 April 1943, p. 1; also US/NA: 890F.51/52 1/2, Thornberg to Collado, 5 July 1943.

on less than two: a thorough American estimate of Sa'udi government income in 1930 set Abdul Aziz's revenue at $7.2 million per year, at a time when the pound exchanged for $4.80 (890F.01/28: State Department, Near East Division). See also 890F.51/19, Cairo, 8 March 1940, Fish to Murray, file no. 851/850.31. BF/RAH/ICG.

p. 264   *prepared to give them':* PRO: FO371/50379:E364/325/25, FO to Jordan, 16 February 1944, cited in Miller, p. 108.

His Majesty's Government's generosity': ibid. See also Charles Baxter, cited in Rubin, 'Anglo-American Relations in Sa'udi Arabia, 1941–45', p. 258.

is like date wood': IOR: R/15/5/123: (E1403/325/25), Jordan to FO, 2 March 1944.

p. 265   *of his Riyadh palace:* US/NA: 890F.00/71, Memorandum on Sa'udi Arabia, 31 October 1941.

'backward and very inefficient': US/NA: 890F.51/11–344, 'Some Observations on the Sa'udi Arabian Problem', 3 November 1944.

was a breezy Australian: Sir Maurice Peterson, Under-Secretary of State for Foreign Affairs, cited in Miller, p. 109.

water for a while: Nejib Salha was to bob up again soon enough and regained his position at Abdullah Suleiman's side in the Finance Ministry in the late 1940s.

Saudi Arabian oil reserves': Miller, p. 102.

p. 266   *patient with their mistakes':* ibid., p. 166.

drawn into this vortex': PRO: FO371/40266: E5672/128/25, Jordan to FO, 6 September 1944.

sniffed at America's 'squandermania': IOR: R/15/2/473: No. 569S/1946, Prior to Weightman, 7 May 1946.

p. 267   *to all his diplomats':* Eddy, p. 14. This biased American version of events does seem to be confirmed by British memoirs at the time. See, for example, Killearn, op. cit.

p. 268   *into the women's camp:* van der Meulen, p. 160.

father with interim authority: this paragraph and those following which describe Abdul Aziz's journey to Suez and his meeting with Roosevelt are based on William Eddy's monograph *F.D.R. meets Ibn Saud.*

p. 271   *from their religious duties':* ibid., p. 25

Germans who oppressed them': ibid., p. 34.

p. 272   *and England are misinformed':* ibid.

of a dozen letters': Congressional Record: 79th Congress, 1st Session, Vol. 91, Pt 2 (1945), p. 1622, cited in Peck, p. 180. See also *New York Times*, 2 March 1945.

enjoy seeing Mr Churchill': Eddy, p. 29.

p. 273   *the intervals between them':* cited in Howarth, p. 208.

589

   realistic compromise with Zionism': FRUS 1945 (Vol. VIII), p. 689:
    890F.001 Abdul Aziz/2-2245, Eddy to S of S, 22 February 1945.
p. 274 *for Feisal and Abdullah':* Grafftey-Smith, interview with Baker, cited in
    Baker, p. 172.
   valued at £3500: Killearn, *Diaries*, p. 331.
   £100 case of scent: ibid.
   car in the world': cited in Howarth, p. 208.
   Branch of this Government': FRUS 1945 (Vol. VIII), p. 698:
    867N.01/4-545, Roosevelt to Ibn Sa'ud, 5 April 1945.
p. 275 *the success of Zionism':* Eddy, p. 37.

Chapter 30 Riches

p. 276 *'The oil brings money':* G. Clinton Pelham, letter to the author, 25 May
   1981.
   upholsterers took no chances: IOR R/15/2/473: No. 569S/1946, Prior to
    Weightman, 7 May 1946.
   ex-works was £3281.17s: PRO: FO371/52817: E8620/757/25, note on the
    car by Inspector, Fighting Vehicles Design.
   of the royal bodyguard: Grafftey-Smith, p. 271.
p. 277 *Abdul Aziz in Riyadh:* I am grateful to David Parker for his personal account
   of this trip and of the reception of the king: personal interview, Jeddah,
   May 1980.
   him at the time: Bandar bin Abdullah, personal interview, Riyadh, 1980.
   King of Sa'udi Arabia: it is believed that Churchill's Rolls-Royce still
    reposes in a Riyadh garage, virtually unused, since Abdullah ibn Abdul
    Rahman disliked being driven in the car for the very same reason that
    Abdul Aziz off-loaded the vehicle on to him.
   alone totalled $10 million: figures taken from the Aramco Handbook, cited
    in Peck, p. 206.
   assistance than Sa'udi Arabia: Peck, p. 200.
p. 278 *The Tale of Abdul Aziz and the Gift Horse:* Grafftey-Smith, p. 273.
p. 279 *of only £13.2 million:* Philby, *Forty Years*, p. 197.
   got them building palaces: IOR: R/15/2/473: (see above).
p. 280 *could be more wonderful?':* off-the-record interview.
   ground in leather buckets: Grafftey-Smith, p. 265.
   wind through telephone wires': SAC/MEC: Hennessy Diary, p. 7.
p. 281 *wheels, screeching and gurgling:* Grafftey-Smith, p. 286.
   'a medieval walled city': Hennessy Diary, p 6.
   of his right hand': Thesiger, p. 242.
p. 282 *each night when undressing':* Alireza, p. 4.
p. 283 *you become a Muslim':* ibid.
   French counterpart with disdain: Childs, p. 140.
p. 284 *expression of individual personality':* US/NA: 890F.0011/7-1047,
    Development of Crown Prince Emir Sa'ud, Childs to S of S, 10 July 1947

attending him next day: US/SD: 786A.11/4-3050, Special Medical Mission for King Ibn Saud, 30 April 1950.

for their younger brothers: US/NA: 890F.0011/7-1047 (see above), 10 July 1947.

p. 285   *would have doomsday now!':* Philby, *Sa'udi Arabia*, p. 351.

lost weekends into one': US/NA: 890F.0011/7-1047, Childs to S of S, 10 July 1947.

Chapter 31 The Lion Dies

p. 287   *city of New York':* Grafftey-Smith, p. 273.

elections in that city: ibid.

p. 288   *the Zionists' Biltmore Program:* Peck, p. 178.

in our place today: PRO: FO371/61885: E10027/951/31, address to the United Nations given by Prince Faisal, 16 October 1947.

conflict he was right: Gilbert, p. 46.

p. 289   *with America at once:* Peck, p. 202, and also de Gaury, *Faisal*, p. 73.

America's Export–Import Bank: Miller, p. 201.

can and cannot do': Peck, p. 294.

a few million dollars': Niles Memorandum, 26 May 1946, OF204, Truman Papers; cited in Miller, p. 200.

p. 290   *little pretence at sorrow:* Philby first heard the news of Abdullah of Transjordan's murder from a BBC news bulletin and went to tell Sa'ud bin Abdul Aziz. 'It cannot be said that Sa'ud was anything but pleased and even exultant,' reported Philby, who found himself rewarded handsomely. Instead of a *bisht*, the traditional gift to good news bringers, Sa'ud gave the Englishman the Rolls-Royce he was just exchanging for a Cadillac. See *Forty Years*, p. 216–17.

on 14 October 1949: Kelly, *Eastern Arabian Frontiers*, p. 19.

p. 292   *who was colour-blind:* Sir George Rendel, personal interview, London, January 1979.

the Trucial Coast itself: Sa'udi Memorial quoted in Mosley, p. 242.

p. 293   *the plains of Picardy':* Memorial, I, p. 5.

for service in Riyadh: Thesiger, *Arabian Sands*, p. 284.

and armed policemen: Memorial, I, p. 444.

p. 294   *sovereignty of Sa'udi Arabia:* Memorial, II, Annexes 59–66, pp. 133–43. These declarations, sealed, thumbprinted and, in four cases, signed by over sixty bedouin described as sheikhs or emirs, were personal expressions of loyalty to Abdul Aziz, and in some cases, to Crown Prince Sa'ud as well. Yet not all the tribesmen swore allegiance to the crown prince, and it would seem from the declarations as translated that they were not acknowledgements of permanent Sa'udi sovereignty over Buraymi in the past, present and future; they were traditional bedouin protestations of loyalty which would expire with the death of the swearer, or on the death of Abdul Aziz, whichever came sooner. Aramco's scholars did not point this out.

anything you want . . .': Abdullah Tariki, personal interview, London, October 1980.

p. 295   *the precise dosage required:* Philby, *Forty Years*, p. 206.

present all his life: US/NA: 890F.001 Abdul Aziz/3–547, Childs to S of S, encl. report prepared by Dr E. A. White, 5 March 1947.

10 to 15 years': ibid., p. 3.

permanently to his wheelchair: US/SD: 786A.11/4–3050, 30 April 1950. This section of the report on the Special Medical Mission for King ibn Sa'ud, 30 April 1950, was deleted from the document when it was made available to the author in response to his application under the Freedom of Information Act. Fortunately the full report is printed for all to read, unexpurgated, in *Foreign Relations of the United States*, 1950 (Vol. V), on pp. 1169–73.

p. 296   *'Someone's going to sleep:* off-the-record interview.

of the country's finances': US/DS 786A.11/7–850, Childs to S of S, 8 July 1950.

gone out of it: van der Meulen, p. 228.

p. 297   *knew that long ago':* ibid., p. 229.

the end without chafing: this graceful phrase comes from Grafftey-Smith, p. 287.

Chapter 32   King Sa'ud

p. 299   *garden is 'little paradise':* van der Meulen, p. 232.

at least £4 million: ibid., p. 236.

p. 300   *is exactly the contrary':* the Sa'udi Minister of Information, Dr Muhammad Abdo Yamani, made these remarks in the course of a television commentary on the dedication of the new 180 kilogram gold doors presented to the Ka'aba at Mecca at a cost of some $6.75 million by King Khalid ibn Abdul Aziz. His remarks were repeated next day in *Al Nadwa* and in the English-language *Sa'udi Gazette* and *Arab News* on 15 October 1979.

p. 301   *the money from oil':* *Time*, 28 January 1957.

education and their health': Mosley, pp. 196–7.

a year plus expenses: *Time*, 28 January 1957.

p. 302   *charm as a conversationalist':* US/SD: 786A.11/4–2250, visit of the medical team to King Ibn Sa'ud, 22 April 1950.

behind his speeding car: Jamal Bey Husaini, personal interview, Riyadh, November 1980.

p. 303   *root of their monopoly:* Fraser, Jacobson, Ottoway and Chester, *Aristotle Onassis*, p. 142. Chapter 10 of this book contains a full and colourful description of the Sa'udi–Onassis tanker deal. R. Narayanan's article on oil negotiations (see p. 546) is a most accurate summary based on the documents. The account given here is based on these sources and also on personal interviews with Muhammad Alireza, John Pochna and Kana'an al Khateeb (both representatives at different times of Onassis in Jeddah

and elsewhere) and with a member of the Sa'udi delegation which
attended the launching of *Al Malik Sa'ud al Awwal* in Hamburg.

p. 304   *to read ordinary type:* Fraser, p. 140.
      irritation,' reported Wadsworth: ibid.
      gain in corresponding measure': ibid., p. 139.
      be in the world: Narayanan, p. 582.

p. 305   *sliding down the slipway:* off-the-record interview.
      to 'utilize every means': Fraser, p. 144.
      Kingdom would be 'disastrous': ibid.
      government and making money': off-the-record interview.
      not compete with you': ibid.

p. 306   *one shareholder among several:* ibid.
      'that's what you are!': Fraser, p. 147.

p. 307   *stir up local intrigue:* ibid.
      the oil company's favour: the final decision in Aramco's favour was handed
down on 28 August 1958 in Geneva. For the details, see Narayanan,
p. 585.
      who were still asleep': Fraser. p. 153.

p. 308   *expelled the Sa'udi garrison:* Bullard, p. 280. *The Economist*, 24 September
and 29 October 1955. Personal interview, Sir George Rendel, London,
January 1979. Holden, *Farewell*, p. 208.

p. 309   *gutters of the west':* Philby, *Sa'udi Arabia*, p. xvi.
      any alcohol to consume': ibid., p. 352.
      his entourage joined in: Jamal Bey Husaini, personal interview, Riyadh,
November 1980.
      towards Lebanon and exile: Monroe, p. 280.
      fall to his lot': Philby, *Forty Years*, p. 37.

Chapter 33   Colonel Nasser's New Way

p. 311   *by the carton full:* Marianne Alireza, personal interview, Jeddah, December
1978.

p. 312   *policies and growing instability':* US/NA: Department of State, R & A
Report No. 7144, 18 January 1956.

p. 314   *pandemonium broke loose:* Arnold, pp. 130–1.

p. 315   *heavily in debt: The Economist*, 16 March 1957, pp. 893–4.

p. 316   *put his guests in':* Arnold, p. 101: 'One of the coffee boys told me candidly
that President Eisenhower must be a poor man because he had such an old
place for his guests to stay in.'
      independent of Russian influence: Eisenhower, *Waging Peace*, pp. 117–20,
cited in Peck, p. 267.
      have our heads examined!': Congressional Record: 85th Congress, 1st
Session, Vol. 103, pt. 2, p. 1939, cited in Peck, p. 264.
      economic and military aid: Peck, p. 268.

p. 317   *one of Sa'ud's private secretaries:* de Gaury, *Faisal*, p. 90.

Chapter 34 Enter the Crown Prince

p. 320 *command the Private Guard:* Aramco Government Lists for 1954 and 1957, Headquarters Library, Dhahran.

p. 323 *a hundred dollars:* Dr Rashad Pharaon, personal interview, Riyadh, 9 May 1980.

Prince Faisal: ibid.

p. 324 *the New York banks:* US/NA: Department of State, R & A Report No. 8215, 28 January 1960. Intelligence Report on 'Faysal's Financial Reforms'. The account given here of the Sa'udi financial crisis of 1958 and Faisal's activities to set things straight is based upon personal interviews, contemporary newspaper accounts and this US Government Intelligence Report. All sources agree on the main lines of financial strategy adopted by Faisal and upon the main events that attended his assumption of power. But the figures do not agree precisely, and the first-hand financial data which could put definitive figures on the debts, loans and economies made remain today confidential to the Sa'udi Arabian Monetary Agency.

total of SR 1400 million: The Economist, 28 February 1959.

p. 326 *Prince Faisal and the Greedy Poet:* off-the-record interview.

Chapter 35 OPEC

p. 328 *cut by $30 million:* Sampson, *Seven Sisters,* pp. 156 ff.; Mosley, pp. 289 ff.

p. 329 *what he's talking about':* Abdullah Tariki, personal interview, London, October 1980.

p. 330 *a very long-range standpoint':* US/NA: 890F.00/8–2049, American Consulate Dhahran to S of S, informal summary, 20 August 1949.

tax to the IRS: Multinational Hearings, Vols 4 and 8, cited in Sampson, *Seven Sisters,* p. 110.

still struggling for survival: Sampson, *Seven Sisters,* p. 111.

p. 331 *the higher the price:* Field, p. 26.

p. 332 *to the Middle East:* Sampson, *Seven Sisters,* p. 158.

all sorts of problems: Abdullah Tariki, personal interview, Riyadh, 17 November 1980.

taken without our consent': Zuhayr Mikdashi: *The Community of Oil Exporting Countries,* London, 1972, p. 33: cited in Sampson, p. 160.

p. 333 *prevailing before the reductions:* Sampson, *Seven Sisters,* p. 161.

Arabia, not with outsiders': quoted by Sheikh Ahmad Zaki Yamani in an interview with Leonard Mosley, cited in *Power Play,* p. 293.

manner of different hats: Sampson, *Seven Sisters,* p. 163.

p. 334 *to the Arab producers:* Mosley, pp. 294–8.

Chapter 36 'Candidates for Liquidation'

p. 335 *slowed down economic growth:* US/NA: Department of State, R & A

Report No. 8215, 28 January 1960, 'Faysal's Financial Reforms', March 1958–January 1960.

p. 336   *Cabinet was thirty-nine:* The Economist, 18 March 1961, pp. 1074–6, 1079.

p. 337   *this spending by half':* Arnold, p. 223.

      supplies from now on': ibid.

      the 'Crown Store': ibid, p. 234.

p. 338   *cure at Bad Nauheim:* ibid.

      blood and losing weight: Jamal Bey Husaini, personal interview, Riyadh, November 1980.

p. 339   *Crown Prince Faisal:* Mosley, pp. 275–6. Mosley quotes from a photostat of this agreement between Japanese Petroleum Trading in the Research and Translation Office of the *Middle East Economic Survey*, then in Beirut, Lebanon.

p. 340   *he may "hang himself" ':* US/NA: 890F.00/8–2049, informal summary, 20 August 1949 (see p. 594, note to p. 330).

p. 341   *of the ordinary man?':* de Gaury, *Faisal*, p. 104.

      establishment of co-operative farms: The Economist, 25 August 1962, pp. 679–80.

p. 342   *declared the king dismissively:* Daily Telegraph, 24 August 1962.

      laid down by the Koran': de Gaury, *Faisal*, p. 106.

      wish he would return': ibid.

      Saudi Arabia than elsewhere': The Guardian, 13 March 1963.

      prospective candidates for liquidation': Financial Times, 5 December 1962. 'Will Reform Save the Royal Family?'

Chapter 37 Deposition

p. 343   *credibility with the USA:* Dr Rashad Pharaon, personal interview, Riyadh, November 1980.

      $198.7 million per year: World Affairs Handbook, Foreign Policy Association, March–April 1964, Vol. 6, No. 2, p. 52, cited in de Gaury, *Faisal*, p. 124.

p. 344   *not captured the capital:* Dr Rashad Pharaon, personal interview, Riyadh, November 1980.

p. 345   *abolished at a stroke:* de Gaury, *Faisal*, p. 113.

      total abolition of slavery': Holden, p. 134.

      in the Buraymi market: the precise number of slaves purchased and freed by the Sa'udi government in 1962 is not known, but nine months later it was announced that 1682 had been freed in the central area of Nejd alone (*Daily Telegraph*, 18 August 1963; cited in Holden, ibid.).

p. 346   *agonizing policy reappraisal:* The Economist, 9 February 1963, p. 488.

p. 347   *he should do nothing':* Dr Rashad Pharaon, personal interview, Riyadh, November 1980.

      of Saudi Arabian integrity': Dana Adams Schmidt, p. 186.

p. 349   *for him to see':* Abdullah al Faisal, personal interview, Riyadh, November 1980.

      arrived at his hotel: Time, 27 September 1963.

p. 350 *Jeddah, Mecca and Medina: Time*, 1 January 1964; *Newsweek*, 13 January 1964.

p. 351 *with all my strength':* Jamal Bey Husaini, personal interview, Riyadh, November 1980.

p. 352 *and left the room:* ibid. Also Kana'an al Khateeb, personal interview, Jeddah, November 1980.

these are family matters': ibid.

p. 354 *without referring to him:* Wahba, p. 176.

p. 355 *routine organs of government:* Turki al Faisal, personal interview, Jeddah, June 1980.

leaders held in Alexandria: de Gaury, *Faisal*, p. 102.

p. 356 *Sahari Palace Hotel beside Riyadh Airport:* ibid., p. 130.

all means of persuasion?': ibid.

Chapter 38 Reform

p. 358 *as from conspirators' cellars:* Gordon Gaskill, 'Sa'udi Arabia's Modern Monarch', *Reader's Digest*, January 1967, p. 118; cited by al Farsy in Beling, p. 59. Also de Gaury, *Faisal*, p. 138.

five calls to prayer: Muhammad al Faisal, personal interview, Jeddah, November 1980. Also Dr Rashad Pharaon, personal interview, Riyadh, November 1980.

feel more at ease: Muhammad al Faisal (see above).

p. 359 *response would go out:* Dr Rashad Pharaon (see above).

'Precisely seven minutes': Sheikh Ahmad Zaki Yamani, personal interview, Riyadh, January 1981.

p. 360 *never make a king':* Kana'an al Khateeb, personal interview, Jeddah, May 1980.

the life for me': Dr Rashad Pharaon (see above).

p. 363 *that he was wrong:* Kana'an al Khateeb (see above).

all the lights: Dr Rashad Pharaon (see above).

p. 364 *did* not *get scholarships:* Parssinen in Beling, p. 156.

one grandson among dozens: off-the-record interview.

p. 365 *of a girls' 'institution':* Parssinen (see above).

the 'House of Affection': Waddy, p. 184.

on modern educational theories: Abas, no. 2557, 23 September 1957; cited in Parssinen (see above).

formation of their mothers?: Turki al Faisal, personal interview, Riyadh, January 1981.

p. 366 *Sa'udi schools in 1974–5:* Central Planning Organization, *Five Year Plan 1979–1980*, pp. 300–34; cited in Parssinen, p. 160.

p. 367 *and a vast reward:* Koran, XXXIII, 35.

p. 368 *'every Muslim, male or female':* Dr Fatina Amin Shakir, personal interview, Jeddah, January 1981.

also makes it surer: Dr Fatina Amin Shakir, personal interview, Jeddah, January 1981.

ourselves in a quicksand': Waddy, p. 188.

p. 369   *independent identities for themselves:* Parssinen (see above). This article on the work of Iffat al Thunayan, based upon a personal interview with Queen Iffat, is the fullest account of her role in the development of girls' education in Sa'udi Arabia. See Beling, chapter 9.

p. 370   *the name of God!':* off-the-record interview.
In September 1965: Rugh, in Beling, p. 129.

Chapter 39   Two Faces of Faisal

p. 372   I am grateful to Sheikh Kana'an al Khateeb for telling me these two stories and many others. The story of the piles has been confirmed to me by 'several members of the family.

Chapter 40   Challenges

p. 374   *of the twentieth century:* Muhammad al Faisal, personal interview, Jeddah, November 1980.
the World Muslim League: for details of King Faisal's early attempts to build up an Islamic union, see Abdullah Sindi in Beling, pp. 184 ff.

p. 375   *the glories of Islam':* ibid., p. 186.
countries King Faisal visited: ibid., p. 188.

p. 376   *an adventurer from California: Daily Express*, 22 November 1965.

p. 377   *the Nile Hilton: Sunday Telegraph*, 1 January 1967.
cash, bullion and jewellery: ibid.
for God to decree': New York Times, 1 January 1967.

p. 378   *earnings in that year: Newsweek*, 10 March 1969.
came in February 1969: ex-King Sa'ud ibn Abdul Aziz died on 23 February 1969 of a heart attack at Kavouri near Athens: *The Times*, 24 February 1969.

p. 379   *King Faisal and the Television Technicians:* Abdullah al Faisal, personal interview, Jeddah, November 1980.

p. 382   *saw vanishing in handcuffs:* Rear-Admiral John Wise, personal interview, London, December 1980.

Chapter 41   The Russians and the Jews

p. 384   *£135 million a year: The Economist*, 9 September 1967, p. 858.

p. 385   Learned Elders of Zion: *Encyclopaedia Britannica, Micropaedia*, VIII, p. 253.

p. 386   *work against each other': Newsweek*, 21 September 1970, p. 11.

p. 387   *felt compelled to attend:* Abdullah Sindi, in Beling, p. 191.

p. 388   *including an Islamic Bank:* ibid.

p. 389   *isn't in the cards':* Mosley, p. 404.
We're Americans, remember?': ibid.
already done to himself: ibid., p. 344.

597

p. 390   *'one nation under God':* Long, cited in Beling, pp. 178–9.
　　　　 of the Arab powers: Sunday Times Insight Team, p. 21.
p. 391   *eighteen more Phantom F4s:* announcement made by the USA on 9
　　　　　September 1970: *Middle East Journal*, 25:1 (Winter 1971), p. 60.
　　　　 180 M60 and M48 tanks: announcement made by the USA on 23 October
　　　　　1970: *Middle East Journal*, 25:1 (Winter 1971), p. 62.
　　　　 eighteen Skyhawk fighters: announcement made by the USA on 12
　　　　　November 1970: *Middle East Journal*, 25:1 (Winter 1971), p. 63.
　　　　 twelve more Phantoms: announcement made by the USA on 19 April 1971:
　　　　　Middle East Journal, 25:3 (Summer 1971), p. 373.
　　　　 forty-two Phantoms and ninety Skyhawks: the *New York Times* reported
　　　　　'administration sources' on 5 February 1972: *Middle East Journal*, 26:2
　　　　　(Spring 1972), p. 164.
　　　　 Six-Day War victory: Sunday Times Insight Team, p. 266.
　　　　 get rid of it': Sheehan, p. 31.
p. 392   *since the 1950s:* Sadat, p. 185.
　　　　 to broach the subject: Heikal, *Road to Ramadhan*, p. 119.
p. 393   *all sorts of concessions first?':* Sheehan, p. 22.
　　　　 Sa'udi subsidies to Egypt: Rubinstein, *Red Star on the Nile*, pp. 235 and 242.
p. 394   *right is on our side':* cited in Kedourie, *Islam in the Modern World*, p. 58.
　　　　 the king was right: Mosley, p. 410.

Chapter 42 Two Weeks that Changed the World

I am grateful to Sheikh Ahmad Zaki Yamani, André Bénard, George T. Piercy and
to Jones McQuinn of Socal for their comments and corrections on this chapter,
together with the off-the-record comments of one American participant in the crisis.

p. 398   *king did not reply:* Ahmad Zaki Yamani, personal interview, Riyadh,
　　　　　January 1981.
　　　　 subsidy agreed at Khartoum: Rubinstein, *Red Star on the Nile*, p. 242.
p. 399   *warning to the press:* Ahmad Zaki Yamani (see above).
　　　　 you to reciprocate': The Washington Post, 19 April 1973.
　　　　 to yield to hysteria: ibid., 20 April 1973.
p. 400   *graduating from Washington University:* Sampson, *Seven Sisters*, p. 235.
　　　　 Israeli policies and actions': ibid., p. 245.
　　　　 dictated word for word: Sheikh Ahmad Zaki Yamani, personal interview,
　　　　　May 1981.
　　　　 friendly relations with America': cited in *Sunday Times* Insight Team,
　　　　　p. 355.
　　　　 means what he says': Muhammad al Faisal, personal interview, Jeddah,
　　　　　November 1980.
　　　　 no other resources at all': New York Times, 20 May 1973.
p. 401   *'keep on fighting':* Dr Rashad Pharaon, personal interview, Riyadh,
　　　　　November 1980.
　　　　 did not even smile: ibid.

some sort of hostilities': Sampson, *Seven Sisters*, p. 245.
from his earlier warnings': Jungers interview with Anthony Sampson,
    February 1975; cited in Sampson, *Seven Sisters*, p. 245.
p. 402 *could be at risk:* ibid.
policy projections: off-the-record interview.
except in his imagination': Multinational Hearings, Part 7, p. 509; cited in
    Sampson, *Seven Sisters*, p. 246.
the Six-Hour War': ibid.
p. 403 *the question of price':* Ahmad Zaki Yamani, personal interview, Riyadh,
    January 1981.
p. 404 *'You have made us all proud':* Heikal, *Ramadhan*, p. 271.
play on Egypt's behalf: ibid.
ones to say yes': Ahmad Zaki Yamani (see above).
p. 405 *'mandatory':* George Piercy, letter to author, 27 May 1981.
p. 406 *things were absolutely hopeless':* ibid.
'over a barrel': off-the-record interview.
were taken account of: Sunday Times Insight Team, p. 360.
p. 407 *important measures against Israel':* Financial Times, 18 October 1973. No
    official communiqué in English was issued by the Arab Oil Ministers on
    17 October 1973 in Kuwait. The *Financial Times* carried next day an
    unofficial translation.
p. 408 *and condemns the aggression':* ibid.
go down the tubes': Nixon, p. 924.
the moderate Arab countries': Sampson, *Seven Sisters*, p. 251.
more complicated domestic juncture': Nixon, p. 922.
p. 409 *full replenishment:* off-the-record interview.
the soil of Israel!': Sunday Times Insight Team, p. 278.
p. 410 *Saqqaf bitterly, 'we will':* Sampson, *Seven Sisters*, p. 252.
in the Middle East': Sheehan, p. 35.
of our national interests': ibid., p. 36.
Middle East as well: Sunday Times Insight Team, p. 362.
p. 411 *'let's do it big':* Sheehan, p. 70.
issues are at stake': Nixon, p. 943.
'pure Nixon': Sheehan, p. 70.
battle on their own': Nixon, pp. 927–8.

Chapter 43 Burning Concern

p. 413 *if not to C':* Sunday Times Insight Team, p. 363.
p. 414 *on 16 December 1973:* Sampson, *Seven Sisters*, p. 257.
p. 415 *it was $24 billion:* Sunday Times Insight Team, p. 349.
on improving bilateral relations': this visit was reported in the *Arab World*.
    See *Middle East Journal*, 28:2 (Spring, 1974), p. 168.
p. 416 *£100 million of British goods:* Kelly, *Arabia, The Gulf and the West*, p. 421.
creeping into world affairs': cited in Field, p. 14.

p. 417   *Subject to Delay':* ibid.
       three get off last': Kalb and Kalb, p. 514.
       ends an hour later': ibid.
       Arab of a millennium': Sheehan, p. 70.
       Communism and the Jews': ibid.
p. 418   *we had to react':* ibid.
       into positions of authority': ibid., p. 71. Kalb and Kalb, p. 516.
       'Make Israel withdraw': Sheehan, p. 71.
p. 419   *can wail against that':* ibid., p. 75.
       as brothers-in-arms!': Beling, p. 200.
       until two years earlier: ibid., p. 194,
p. 422   *'under their wings':* James F. Akins, 'The oil crisis: this time the wolf is here'.

Chapter 44   The Dreams of King Faisal

p. 424   *private of him left':* Muhammad al Faisal, personal interview, Jeddah, November 1980.
       we could do nothing': Abdullah al Faisal, personal interview, Jeddah, November 1980.
       and what is hot': ibid.
       The First Dream of King Faisal: Abdullah al Faisal, personal interview, Jeddah, November 1980.
p. 425   *The Second Dream of King Faisal:* ibid.
p. 426   *grazed the forehead:* James Fox, *The Sunday Times*, 30 March 1975.
p. 427   *has closed down completely':* ibid.

Chapter 45   Partnership: Khalid

p. 429   *younger princes waiting outside:* Turki al Faisal, personal interview, Jeddah, June 1980.
p. 431   *people living in matchboxes':* off-the-record interview.
p. 432   *($96 million):* Saudi Business, 16 November 1979.
       some £1000 a month: Abdullah Faisal Turki al Abdullah, personal interview, London, February 1981.
p. 434   *'One of those is me':* audience with King Khalid ibn Abdul Aziz, Riyadh, February 1980.
       branded with hot irons: off-the-record interview.
p. 436   *with a childish mind':* Arab News, 29 September 1980.

Chapter 46   Partnership: Fahad

p. 437   *Minister ran into overtime:* off-the-record interview.
p. 440   *get on with it':* off-the-record interview.
p. 443   *2.45 in the morning:* off-the-record interview.
p. 444   *a 63 per cent stake: Financial Times*, 5 May 1981, Supplement on Sa'udi Arabia, p. ix.

Chapter 47 Riyal Politik

p. 447 *just slice ourselves off:* off-the-record interview.
p. 449 *than a financial superstate':* *Newsweek,* 6 March 1979, p. 12.
found in Sa'udi Arabia!': *International Herald Tribune,* 23 December 1977.
p. 451 *'When Sadat dies':* *Time,* December 1978.
p. 453 *of Islamic Foreign Ministers:* Arnaud de Borchgrave, *Newsweek,* 23 April 1979.
p. 454 *his conversations with Brzezinski:* off-the-record interview.
p. 455 *I am a liar':* off-the-record interview.
granted us a wish: off-the-record interview.

Chapter 48 Death of a Princess

p. 460 *stray away from the truth: The Sunday Times,* 13 April 1980.
'amalgamations of many different interviews': *New Statesman,* 9 May 1980.
who denounced Death of a Princess': *Daily Telegraph,* 27 August 1980.
p. 461 *boil on his bottom: Oil Sheikhs,* p. 34.

Chapter 49 Mr Khashoggi

This chapter is largely based upon meetings with Adnan Khashoggi. I am grateful for the assistance of Robert Shaheen.

p. 467 *US–British trade-off:* the details of this trade-off are well described in Anthony Sampson's book, *The Arms Bazaar,* ch. 8.
p. 468 *C130 Hercules transport planes:* these, and other details of the commissions earned by Adnan Khashoggi from American companies, emerged in the Multinational Hearings of 1975, and are analysed by Anthony Sampson in *The Arms Bazaar,* ch. 11.
delightful and productive place': *Leaders,* June 1979, p. 63.
p. 470 *offering riches to a king':* Sampson, p. 197.

Chapter 50 $100,000,000,000

This chapter is based upon an interview and subsequent correspondence with Sheikh Abdul Aziz Quraishi, and upon off-the-record interviews.

p. 472 *August 1979, Geneva:* off-the-record interview.
February 1980, Riyadh: author's meeting with Bunker Hunt.
p. 474 *declared foreign currency reserves:* SAMA Annual Report 1400 (1980).
p. 477 *in excess of $80 million: International Herald Tribune,* 8 July 1981.

Chapter 51 The Mahdi

This account of the 1979 siege of the Grand Mosque is based upon off-the-record interviews with participants in the siege, with Muslims who were in Mecca at that time, and upon Sa'udi government statements at the time and subsequently, and particularly upon the press conference given by Prince Naif ibn Abdul Aziz.

p. 479   *the fourteenth Islamic century:* this exposition of the traditions concerning an Islamic messiah is based principally upon the article on the Mahdi by D. S. Margoliouth in the *Encyclopaedia of Islam*, and also upon the article on the subject by Sheikh Abdul Aziz ibn Abdullah bin Baz, Chairman of the Board of Religious Guidance, published in *al Jezirah* and in *al Riyadh* and translated in *Arab News*, 4 December 1979.

p. 486   *the very first morning:* On 9 January 1980 Prince Naif ibn Abdul Aziz announced that seventy-five rebels had died during the siege, that fifteen bodies were later found in the cellars, and that twenty-seven had subsequently died of their wounds. *Arab News*, 10 January 1980.

p. 490   *appended to this statement':* Arab News, 10/11 January 1980.

Chapter 52 Black Gold

This chapter is based upon interviews with Sheikh Ahmad Zaki Yamani and off-the-record interviews with a number of people involved in the oil business. I am grateful to the Institute of Petroleum for providing statistical information.

p. 494   *mechanism for inducing conservation':* Sheikh Yamani, personal interview, Riyadh, May 1981.

p. 495   *'We engineered the glut':* Petroleum Intelligence Weekly, 27 April 1981.
         were drinking smelly water: Abdullah Tariki, personal interview, Riyadh, May 1981.

p. 498   *forty-seven oilfields:* this and other statistics here on the Sa'udi economy come from the article by T. R. McHale in *International Affairs*. I am grateful to Tom McHale for his advice and help on this and other matters.

p. 502   *a new economic order:* I am grateful to Jules Arbose, Senior Editor of *International Management*, for showing me notes of his interview with Sheikh Yamani on this subject in May 1981.

Chapter 53 The Next Iran?

p. 505   *'Youth is youth':* Dr Abdul Aziz al Zamil, personal interview, Riyadh, May 1981.

p. 506   *of eighty-two objections:* letter from Dr Abdul Aziz H. Alsowayegh, received in London, 25 June 1981.

p. 507   *look for new names':* off-the-record interview.

p. 508   *The Tale of Ajlan's Kidneys:* Prince Faisal ibn Abdul Aziz Jaluwi, personal interview, Riyadh, February 1980.

p. 510 'Astaghfir Allah!': audience with King Khalid ibn Abdul Aziz, Riyadh, February 1980.

p. 512 'I don't agree': off-the-record interview.
had attacked my palace': off-the-record interview.

p. 513 'Any man forbidding his daughter': article by Peter Mansfield, *Financial Times*, 5 May 1981, supplement on Sa'udi Arabia, p. xx.

Chapter 54 As God Wills

p. 514 *have been good Muslims'*: Turki al Faisal, personal interview, Jeddah, June 1980.

p. 516 *'It is an idea'*: Muhammad al Faisal, personal interview, Jeddah, November 1980.
a way of life': Lewis, cited in Iseman.

p. 518 *an international survey:* the survey, compiled by the Union Bank of Switzerland, was cited in the *International Herald Tribune*, 13 February 1980.
lost sheep and goats: Arab News, 23 February 1980.

p. 519 *conditions of extreme hardship'*: Thesiger, *Desert, Marsh and Mountain*, pp. 297–8.
essence of the person': Turki al Faisal, personal interview, Riyadh, November 1980.

Acknowledgements

Far are the shades of Arabia,
Where the Princes ride at noon
'mid the verduous vales and thickets,
Under the ghost of the moon. . . .
They haunt me – her lutes and her forests;
No beauty on earth I see
But shadowed with that dream recalls
Her loveliness to me:
Still eyes look coldly upon me,
Cold voices whisper and say –
'He is crazed with the spell of far Arabia,
They have stolen his wits away.'

Walter de la Mare

This book was financed by my publishers in London and New York, and from the earnings of my last book, *Majesty*. My first thanks must therefore be to Messrs Hutchinson and to Harcourt Brace Jovanovich for staking such large sums on my researches in the Kingdom, and to my wife Sandi for agreeing to risk so much of our mutual savings on an enterprise whose outcome seemed at many times uncertain.

Almost every recent attempt to inquire and report on the Kingdom in a Western fashion has ended with the Sa'udis feeling pried upon, misrepresented and sometimes even betrayed. So I am particularly grateful to my friend Khalid Ahmad Yussuf Xenel Alireza for risking his good name on this book: he personally recommended me to His Majesty King Khalid ibn Abdul Aziz and vouched for me to secure a two year residence permit for myself and my family from HRH Prince Ahmad ibn Abdul Aziz, the Vice-Minister of the Interior, to whom I also express my thanks. I am sorry that, in the event, the Sa'udi Ministry of Information has requested changes to my manuscript which I feel unable to make: at the time of writing, it does not seem likely that this book will be permitted to enter the Kingdom. But I hope that the many friends that I made in Sa'udi Arabia will none the less feel that what I have written is worthy of the trust they placed in me.

On pp. 539–40 is a list of the many people who granted me interviews. I should like to thank all of them.

An author always draws heavily on the kindness of his friends and of the people he meets in the course of gathering material, writing, and checking the facts for a work of non-fiction. But this book has involved special demands, and I should like to express my gratitude to the people who have taught me Arabic; made available their telex machines and photocopiers; carried documents to and from the Kingdom; lent books, articles and photographs and, in some cases, unpublished theses and material; read and commented upon draft versions of the manuscript in whole, or in part; translated written material; interpreted at interviews; shared their secrets; arranged

604

meetings; and offered hospitality and support to myself and my family in the course of the many travellings and adventures that exploring the Kingdom has involved. I hope they will forgive me for simply listing their names:

Ahmad Ahmad; Muhammad Anwar Ahmad; Zahrah Ahmad; Jonathan Aitken MP; Dr Albert D. Akl; Madeleine Alatas; the late Seyyid Hussein Alatas and his sons Muhammad and Abdulillah; Ghada Alireza; Muhammad, Abdullah and Hisham Xenel Alireza; Sybel Alireza; Harry Alter; Mike Ameen; Abdul Rahman M. Anwar; Rupert and Venetia Armitage; H. St John B. Armitage; Muhammad Ashik; Azad Photo; Robert Azzi; Said Mubarak Baarmah; Ahmad Badeeb; Muhammad Badrawi; Muhammad Bahareth; Jan and Lady Sarah Baily; Dr Randall Baker; Tom Barger; Michael and Anstice Baring; George M. Baroody; Thomas Baroody; Roudi Baroudi; Seyyids Abdullah and Ahmad Baroum; Alan Barton; Faisal Bassam; Billy Beghani; André Bénard; Lord Patrick Beresford; Yves Besson; Sheikha Binladen; Eugene and Gerry Bird; Linda Blandford; Patrick Boddy; Paul and Becky Bodkin; David Bosch; Douglas Boyd; the Librarian of the British Library; Vivian and Jean Brown; Abdullah Bulayhid; Robin and Anne Burleigh; Angela Card; John Carter; Jim and Liz Chapman; Bridget and Trevor Clare; Frank Clifford; Ray and Marty Close; James Cochrane; Peter Collenette; Hugh and Delia Constant; Miles Copeland; Jeremy Cox; Sir James Craig; John Creighton; John Cushman; Rabea Sadik Dahlan; Ann and Ray Dent; Philip and Heather Dew; Kris Dahl; Dame Violet Dickson; Greg Dowling; Ben Dyall; John and Inocenta Ewart; Anton Felton; Michael Field; William Fifer; Doreen Fishwick; Paul and Gillian Friedman; Rommel Gammo; John and Patsy Gasperetti; Ibrahim Ghabieri; Said al Ghamdi; Martin Gilbert; Mary Goldie; Gerald Grant; John and Anthoula Grey; Gabe and Bay Gutman; Caroline Haffner; Adnan Hamoud; Raymond A. Hare; Morven Hay; Craig Herron; Tim Holloway; Dr Derek Hopwood; Chris and Sheila Housden; Doug and Angie Hulme; Khalid Jamal Husaini; Suha and Caroline Islam; Margaret Jones; Priscilla Jones; Joan Judge; Jalik and Sarah Kaulback; Robin Kealy; Geoffrey Keating; Ahmes and Munirah Khalifah; Omar H. Khalifati; Adnan Muhammad Khashoggi; Munir and Majda Khashoggi; Dr Geoffrey King; Tim and Adrienne King; Angela and Col. Murray de Klee; Andrew Knight; John Kobal; Gregorio Kohon; Joanna Layton; Clive Leatherdale; Clyde Leemaster; Howard and Margot Letty; Anthony and Eva Lewis; Allan Lockett; the Librarian of the London Library; Ahmad Lughod; Bill McDougall; André Maillard; Muhammad al Mana; Jim Mandaville; Garnet Morgan Mann; Dr Abdullah Masri; Daan van der Meulen; Hugh Millais; Christopher Moorsom; Sir Willy Morris; Muhammad Abdul Aziz Mu'ammar; Julian Muller; Bill Mulligan; Abdul Rahman al Mur; Fouad Nasr; Abdul Rahman Nasseef; Ismail Ibrahim Nawwab; Conraad Noyon; Ghalib Obaid; Michael O'Connor; John Oghli; Abdul Aziz Orayer; Lt-Col. Rex Osborn RE; Eamon O'Tuathail; Ethel Paley; David Parker; Leif Pedersen; G. Clinton Pelham; Brian Perman; Dr Guy Pharaon; Wabel Pharaon; Malcolm Peck; George T. Piercy; James Piscatori; John and Michael Pochna; John Pratt; Dr Robin and Layla Priscott; Abdullah Dabsan al Qahtani; Sultan Ghalib and Sultana al Qaiti of the Hadhramaut; Ahmad Abdul Qassim; Selina Rand; Stuart Ransom; Badr al Rasheed; Shawkat N. Raslan; John and Pip Reddaway; Dr George Rentz; John Roberts; Col. Bob Rogers; Peter Ryan; Issa Khalil Sabagh; John Sandoe; Jim Scott; Zeead Sha'ath; Said A. al

Shablan; Robert Shaheen; Mansour Shalhoub; David and Jennifer Sharp; Michael Shaw; David and Sue Sillar; Patrick and Ashkhain Skipwith; Ella Slingerland; John and Kerrie Smith; Alberto and Karin Solera; Tom Stacey; Charles and Christina Stagnetto; James Stevenson; Abdullah Sudairi; Muhammad Abdul Rahman Sudairi; Ian Sutherland Brown; Mamoun Tamer; Muhammad Tantawi; David Tatham; Antony Thomas; Ted Trainer; Jack and Jane Tressider; Dr Abdullah al Uthaimeen; Seyyid Ahmad Abdul Wahhab; Judy and Lt-Col. Tom Walcot; Brian and Audrey Walden; Peter Whitehead; John and Maureen Wilton; Tony Winlow; Victor Winstone; Admiral John and Peggy Wise; Karl Heinz Wittech; Valerie Yorke; Dorrit Zarach; Khalil Ziadeh; Henri and Genevieve Zipper.

I am grateful to the following who have given help to my research assistant, Jacqueline Williams:

Patrick Bannerman (Foreign and Commonwealth Office); Kitty Coleman; Gail Collis (The Institute of Petroleum); John Corson; the Librarian of The Economist; Hermann F. Eilts; Anna Girvan (Reference Library, Embassy of the United States of America, London); Gillian Grant (St Antony's College, Oxford, Middle East Centre); Andrew Griffin (India Office Library and Records); Timothy and Liza Harrison; Irene Hunter; the Librarian of the International Institute for Strategic Studies; the late Baroness Jackson of Lodsworth; Lois Khairallah (Middle East Institute, Washington DC); Bill and Jacqueline Keith; Nancy Keiser; James V. Knight; Joseph Malone; Katharine Murphy (Diplomatic Branch, National Archives and Records Service, Washington DC); the Librarian of the New York Public Library; Herman and Phyllis Nickel; C. Partridge (British Petroleum); The Population Council, New York; the Map Room of the Royal Geographical Society; the Librarian and Newspaper Librarian of the Royal Institute of International Affairs; The Royal Society for Asian Affairs; Sirgay Sanger; R. E. Swerczek (Diplomatic Branch, National Archives and Records Service, Washington DC); Eileen Tasca; Penelope Tuson (India Office Library and Records); Douglas and Priscilla Williams; Gordon and Carrie Williams; Conway Wilson-Young; Professor R. Bayly Winder; Dr and Mrs Raymond Zwemer.

Unpublished Crown-copyright material in the India Office and transcripts of Crown-copyright records in the Public Record Office appear in this book by permission of the Controller of Her Majesty's Stationery Office.

Certain sections of this book have been based upon documents secured by an application under the US Freedom of Information Act, and I should like to thank for their assistance Miss Carolyn Croak of the Information and Privacy Staff and Mrs Farrell, researcher at the Department of State, Washington DC.

I have some special debts of affection to acknowledge. This is the second book I have written with the help of Frances Ullman, who has typed and retyped endless drafts of the manuscript. Her patience, reliability and fondness have helped keep me going.

Jacqueline Williams has given me research assistance of exemplary thoroughness and energy, making new discoveries of real significance. She has also coped graciously with chores from air ticket reservations to chauffeuring. The wide range of photographs and accurate details of the reference section are principally to her credit, and, like Frances, she has done much to make the impossible possible.

My own parents have provided me with an unparalleled news cutting service and have checked the manuscript and proofs with their usual meticulous care; my wife's parents looked after our son Sasha for much of the time we were in Jeddah and provided an invaluable emotional base for us in London; my two children, Sasha and Scarlett, have coped with astonishing cheerfulness with the many dislocations that my work has brought into our lives: thank you all.

My greatest debt is to Sandi, my wife. She suffered uprooting and illness to accompany me to an environment in which few Western women would freely choose to live. She has been my most honest critic and my best friend. She made the good times better, and in the bad times it is her love and faith which have sustained me. This book is dedicated to her.

Robert Lacey
July 1981

Index
The House of Sa'ud

Members of the House of Sa'ud are listed under first names.

General Index

613

INDEX

Aflak, Michel, Ba'ath party, 387n
Africa, 375, 448; Nigerian pilgrims, 88, 89, 177
Aghal, the definition, 16
Agnew, Spiro, 408
Air force, Egyptian (Ilyushins), 1963 bomb attacks, 346, 347
Air force, Sa'udi Arabian, 381–2
Air force, US, 316, 317; *see also* Royal Air Force
Ajlan, Rasheed, Governor of Riyadh, 48, 49, 50–2
Ajman tribe, 31–2, 42, 94, 97–8, 101, 108, 209; and Riyadh expedition, 42; grazing grounds, 94; defection at Jarrab, 116, 118; and Arab Revolt, 118; leaders of tribal rebellion, 122–3; victory at Kinzan, 123; subdued by Abdul Aziz, 124; at battle of Sabillah, 212
Akins, James, US ambassador, 422
Al alSheikh, 63n
Alalsheikh, Abdullah ibn Hassam, chief *qadi* of the Hijaz, 243–5
Albania, 76n, 85
Alcohol, Islamic prohibition, 59, 245, 285, 286, 517
Alexandria, 355
Alfonzo, Perez, oil expert, 331, 332
Algeria, 331n, 333n, 387, 407; oil reserves, 497; gas reserves, 537
Ali ibn Husain, 187; and his father's abdication, 189; his constitutional Democratic Government, 192, 193; defence of Jeddah, 193; and annexation of Aqaba, 196; refuge with Feisal of Iraq, 188–9; leaves Jeddah in HMS *Cornflower*, 199
Alireza, business family, 239, 507
Alireza, Ali ibn Abdullah, 303 and n
Alireza, Hajji Abdullah, Governor of Jeddah, 188 and n, 199, 303
Alireza, Marianne (née Likowski), 282, 303n, 361; and Abdul Aziz, 283; *At the Drop of a Veil*, 282 and n
Alireza, Muhammad Ali Zainal, *Falah* schools, 188 and n
Alireza, Muhammad ibn Abdullah, Minister of Commerce, 303, 305
Alireza, Qasim Zainal, and Jeddah dissidents, 193–4
Alice, Princess, Countess of Athlone, meets Abdul Aziz, 253, 254
Amarat tribe, 217
Amba, Dr Salih, Dean of Dhahran College, 382
Amer, Abdul Hakim, Egyptian Field-Marshal, and Yemen war, 346
Amer, Ali, General, 346

American Arabian Mission, 34; in Bahrain, 169
Americans, oilmen, 172; diplomatic ignorance of Abdul Aziz's pro-Axis sentiments, 257; *see also* United States
Amman, 185, 311; Ikhwan raid, 164, 193
Amnesty International, 505
Amoudi, al, business family, 323
Amoudi, Muhammad Hassan al, 473, 477
Anayzah, 72, 212; Turkish–Rasheed forces, 77, 78; Turkish garrison, 81, 82; overrun by Sa'udi army, 96
Anazah tribe, 59, 164, 210
Anglo–French entente, 111
Anglo–Persian Oil Co., 170, 171; BP a descendant of, 170n; thwarted by Holmes, 172, 234; becomes IPC, 234
Anglo–Turkish Convention, 110; division of Middle East (Anglo–Ottoman), 110, 292
Anno Hegirae (AH), dating of Muslim history, 14
Antonius, George, 196, 197
Aqaba, 185, 189, 196; captured by Lawrence, 121; Gulf of, 383
Arab Defence Council, 393
Arab–Israeli War 1947/48, 288, 289
Arab–Israeli War 1967 (Six-Day War), 378–9, 401
Arab–Israeli War 1973, 402–4; US aid to Israel, 405, 406; Israeli counter-attack, 406, 410; Kissinger and, 409; Soviet airlift, 409; territorial results, 413
Arabia, geological features, 5, 26; poverty-stricken era, 11; role and status of Islam, 8; Sa'udi conquest, 13, 57–8; contending powers for control, 55, 83, 85; Kuwait–Medina caravan route, 72; Pirate or Trucial coast, 74; oasis–desert tension, relations between bedouin and *hadhar*, 94; Great Britain and, 106, 110–11, 119–20, 160, 161 (map), 172, 185, 216; Captain Shakespear's epic journey, 114; marriage customs, 131; Abdul Aziz's ambitions, 164; unification under Ragamah agreement, 199; agriculture, 226; treatment of children, 242; law and order due to Abdul Aziz, 253; as viewed by foreign visitors, 251–4; business ethics, 238, 279; United States and, 261, 343; influence of its ethos on oilmen, 291–2; areas of privacy, 306–7; anti-British demonstrations, 311; Sa'udi ban on Christian services, 315; land ownership, 432–3; kingly tradition, 355–6; treatment of sick and old, 365; debt to Al Sa'ud, 509, 511, 514–15; pre-oil, 514–15; Western

614

Balfour Declaration – *cont.*
Investigation, 225; aftermath, 260
Balkans, 76n, 85
Bangladesh, 419 and n
Barger, Tom, Casoc's field geologist, caving
with Ibn Khursan, 246–7; and Abdul Aziz,
247–8
Baroum, business family, 323
Basra, 79, 124, 126; capture by British troops
1916, 113, 133
Bay'ah, 52; definition, 16
Baz, Abdul Aziz bin, *ulema*, 512; rules the
earth is flat, 363; and Juhayman, 481
Bedouin, 4, 7, 16, 236, 313; desert dwellers,
23–4, 26–7, 29; hospitality, 24; education
of the young, 25, 28, 177; the *ghazzu*, 27,
28; bridal customs, 31–2; and defence of
Kuwait, 40; staple food when travelling,
45; tribal traditions, 66; raid *hajj* pilgrims
and caravans, 88, 93; prepare for battle,
114, 115, 229; Ikhwan call, 143–4; raiding
tradition, 145, 211, 272; interpretation of
boundaries, 166, 293; attack
sheep-herding tribes, 204; navigation of
the desert from Empty Quarter, 205;
Ikhwan massacre, 210; 1928 Riyadh
meeting, 209; use of royal doctors, 252; *see
also* Tribesmen; The House of Sa'ud index,
Abdul Aziz
Begin, Menachem, and Camp David
agreement, 451, 452, 453
Belhaven and Stenton, R. A. B. H., Lord,
British Agent in Bahrain, 258
Bell, Gertrude, 104, 116, 160; assessment of
Abdul Aziz, 125, 126, 129, 185
Bénard, André (of Shell), 403–4, 405
Beni Khalid tribe, 25, 42, 67, 319
Beni Sakhr, villages, 164
Berbera, USSR naval base, 448
Bhisht, definition, 16
Bhutto, Zulfikar Ali, Prime Minister of
Pakistan, 419
Bijad, Sultan ibn, 146, 210; and Ghot Ghot
settlement, 149; and Husain's claim to
caliphate, 186; and assault on Taif, 187;
enters Mecca in pilgrim guise, 190; absence
from 1928 Riyadh meeting, 209; rebels
against Abdul Aziz, 212–13, 215; defeat at
Sabillah, 213–14; religious fanaticism,
215
Bilkert, US missionary, killed by Ikhwan,
226
Bin ('ibn'), definition, 16
Bin Jaluwi, *see* The House of Sa'ud index
Binladen, business family, 323, 507
Binladen, Muhammad, 466
Bint, definition, 16
Binzagr, business family, 328

Biscoe, Col. H. V., Persian Gulf Resident,
240
Bismarck, Anne-Marie von, Princess, 304–5
Black races, Gulf traders, 36; members of
households, 177; children's playmates, 177
Blandford, Linda, 461
Bowman, Humphrey, Faisal's London escort,
154, 155, 156
Bray, Major N. N. E., Faisal's Paris escort,
156, 157
Brazil, oil consumption 1980, 537
Brewster, Owen, and US oil supplies, 262
British Mission to Riyadh 1917, 128 and n,
129, 133
British Petroleum (BP), 328; nationalized by
Qadaffi, 388
Brougham, Bob, President of Aramco, 333
Brzezinski, Zbigniew, 454
Bulgaria, 76n, 106
Bullard, Sir Reader, British Consul in Jeddah,
52, 195; on King Husain, 182; and his claim
to the caliphate, 185–6; visits Shareef Ali,
192, 253; and Princess Alice's visit, 253;
and BBC's first Arabic broadcast, 259–60;
and UK support for Zionism, 260; and
Buraymi arbitration tribunal, 308
Buraydah, 72, 212; girls' school, 368, 369;
Turkish garrison, 81, 82
Buraymi dispute, basis of Al Sa'ud claim, 290,
292; involvement of oil resources, 290,
292; slave market revenues, 293, 345;
Aramco involvement, 293–4, 307; flouting
of legal conventions, 307–8; occupation by
UK troops, 309, 311; settlement by Fahad,
447
Burckhardt, Jacob, on Sa'udi armies, 145

Cairo, 61, 120, 384; conferences, 160, 161,
273, 352, 353; Radio, 312, 314, 317, 341,
363, 369; Imam Husayn mosque, 393–4
California Arabian Standard Oil Co. (Casoc),
and Abdul Aziz's concessions, 245; Jubail
base, 245; oil production by Wells Nos.
1–6, 245–6; strikes oil with Well No. 7,
254–5, 256; payments, 256
Caliph, definition, 16
Caliphate, Islamic, 106; claimed by Husain,
185
Calverley, Mrs Elizabeth, at Kuwait in 1912,
34
Cameroon, 419n
Camp David peace agreement 1978, gains
and losses, 451; Arab resentment, 451–2;
the Al Sa'ud and, 452–5
Canada, 442; oil consumption 1980, 537;
natural gas reserves, 537
Cannon, Geoffrey, television critic, 460
Camel, the, 24, 281; identification by

Dhahran – *cont.*
440; oil inspection post, 291, 329; military training college, 381; Aramco hospital, 388; township, 388
Dickson, Col. H. R. P., British Agent in Bahrain, 51, 185, 245, 259; and bedouin, 28, 211; on Abdullah bin Jaluwi, 111, 112; and the Ikhwan, 146; meets Abdul Aziz, 158–9; witnesses camel migration, 158; visited by Holmes, 168; oil prospecting, 168; and al Daweesh plea for UK protection, 219
Dickson, Violet, 34n, 168
Dilam, al, 69; ibn Rasheed–Abdul Aziz confrontation, 69, 70–1, 75
Dishdasha (thobe), 51; definition, 16
Dodecanese Islands, 134
Dress, Arabian, 8, 16, 17, 18, 51
Dubai sheikhdoms, 74, 79; oilfields, 389
Dulles, John Foster, plan to foil Sa'udi bid to control its tanker fleet, 305; and Middle East 'non-alignment', 315

East Germany, 448
Eastern and General Syndicate, oil speculations, 170; Sa'udi oil concession, 172, 232
Eastern Province, 1979 riots, 487–8; Shia Muslim grievances, 488, 489; result of Al Sa'ud conquest, 488; underdevelopment, 488–9
Eban, Abba, 391; and an Arab oil embargo, 400
Ecuador, and OPEC, 333n
Eddy, Col. William, US Minister in Jeddah, 266, 267; and Abdul Aziz–Roosevelt meeting, 269, 270, 273
Education, traditional character, 176–7; today, 177, 243; the *Falah* schools, 188 and n; Abdul Aziz–Crane discussion, 230; of Faisal's sons and daughters, 242–3; for local Sa'udi employees, 292; Egyptian teachers in new schools, 311–12; of women and girls, role of Iffat, 364–9; Medina and Riyadh universities, 301n; *see also* The House of Sa'ud index, Iffat al Thunayan
Eed al Adha, pilgrimage feast, 17, 173, 186, 293, 516
Eed al Fitr, celebration of end of Ramadhan, 17, 43, 201
Egypt, 57; Turkish control, 62, 76n, 310; UK occupation, 74; intellectuals, 191, 201; acquisition of Gaza strip, 289; Sa'ud's abortive plot, 317; invasion of the Yemen, 342, 347; extent of US aid (1960s), 343; visited by Faisal', 375n; impact of Six-Day War, 383–4; Soviet military aid, 391, 392, 398, 408; and restoration of Sinai

territories, 400; attack on Israel's Suez Canal position, 397, 402, 403; Arab boycott of Sadat regime, 453; *see also* Nasser; Sadat; Suez Canal
Egyptians, Mecca pilgrimage, 57, 202; ceremony of the Mahmal, 202; impact on Sa'udi civil service, 311–12
Eisenhower, President Dwight D., and UK/French/Israeli evacuation of Suez, 315n, 390; and visit of King Sa'ud, 315–16
Eisenhower 'Doctrine', 315, 316, 343
Empty Quarter, the, *see* Rub al Khali
Esso, *see* Exxon
Ethiopia, 165, 448; GNP, 34n
Emir *(ameer)*, definition, 17, 29n
Europe, diversion of world's cash flow, 10; ignorance of Riyadh, 55; pre-war power politics, 75–6; dependence on Middle East oil, 413, 415–16
European Community, and 1973 Middle East crisis, 415
Euphrates, the, 77, 205
Exxon (Esso), 291 and n, 329, 493; and oil glut, 328; 1960 price cuts, 332; *see also* Standard Oil Company

Farouk, King of Egypt, 280
Feisal bin Husain, 120 and n, 187; entry into Damascus, 121, 148; and the Ikhwan, 147, 157; at Versailles Peace Conference, 156–7; and Churchill's Middle East conference, 160 and n; receives Iraq under UK tutelage, 161, 162; and his father's insanity and possible deposition, 184; UK support in Baghdad, 204–5; meeting with Abdul Aziz, 220
Firestone Rubber, Liberia, 291
First World War, European power politics, 7; Middle East warfare, 113–14, 119–20, 138; Arab Revolt, 118; British Expeditionary Force, 120; Western Front, 120, 156; Ottoman offensive 1917, 128; Versailles Peace Conference, 156–7; leaves Arabia in confusion, 160, 164; map, 161
Food, 28, 45, 64–5; Koranic prohibitions, 132; ceremonial occasions, 520; Arab boycott lists, 522n; Coca-Cola, or Pepsi, 522 and n
Ford, Gerald, US Vice-President, 408
France, 485; acquisitions from Sykes–Picot agreement, 134; Faisal ibn Abdul Aziz visits battlefields, 156; post-war Middle East acquisitions, 160, 225; boycotts US Commission on Middle East, 225; and Nasser, 343; and oil embargo, 415–16; oil consumption 1980, 537

Faisal, son of Abdul Aziz
1904-1975

MEDITERRANEAN SEA

E G Y P T

Tabuk

Hail

Buraydah
Anayzah

Yanbu

Medina

S U D A N

Jeddah
Mecca

Khurmah

Ghot Ghot

Taif

Turabah

al
Layl

Abha

Khamis Mushayt

Jizan

Najran

Eritrea

R E D   S E A

Y E M E N

R U B   A

Hodeidah

Sana'a

Iain Stuart

Aden

S O U T H

Hadhramaut

Y E

G U L F   O F   A D E N

Sa'ud, son of Abdul Aziz
1902-1969

Abd